Frozen in Ice

Frozen In Ice: The Story of Walt Disney Productions, 1966-1985

By Mark Arnold

Books by the same author:

The Best of The Harveyville Fun Times!

Created and Produced by Total TeleVision Productions: The Story of Underdog, Tennessee Tuxedo and the Rest (BearManor Media)

If You're Cracked, You're Happy: The History of Cracked Magazine, *Part Won* (BearManor Media)

If You're Cracked, You're Happy: The History of Cracked Magazine, *Part Too* (BearManor Media)

Mark Arnold Picks on The Beatles

Frozen In Ice:
The Story of Walt Disney Productions, 1966-1985

By Mark Arnold

BearManor Media

2013

Frozen In Ice: The Story of Walt Disney Productions, 1966-1985

All new material in this book is © 2013
Mark Arnold and Fun Ideas Productions.

All prominent characters mentioned in this book and the distinctive likenesses thereof are copyrighted trademarks and properties of The Walt Disney Company, except where indicated.

The images of the various theatrical movie posters included in this book are © The Walt Disney Company and are used as Fair Use to be illustrative for the text contained herein.

All additional material is their respective copyright holder. The material used in this book is used for historical purposes and literary criticism and review and is used by permission. It is not designed to plagiarize or in any other way infringe on the copyrights of any copyrighted materials contained herein.

All rights reserved.

For information, address:

BearManor Media
P.O. Box 750
Boalsburg, PA 16827

bearmanormedia.com

Cover design and artwork by Jeff Little; layout by Jerry Cornell

Permission is granted to other publications or media to excerpt the contents contained herein for review purposes provided that the correct credit and copyright information is included for any materials reproduced.

Typesetting and layout by John Teehan.

Published in the USA by BearManor Media.

Library of Congress Cataloging-in-Publication Data

Arnold, Mark.
Frozen In Ice: The Story of Walt Disney Productions, 1966-1985 / by Mark Arnold.
Includes index.
ISBN 978-1-59393-751-5

I. Arnold, Mark. II. Underdog (Television Program). III. Title.

DEDICATION:

Dedicated to the memory of Quinton Clem
(July 10, 1963 – August 11, 2012).
Although primarily a Harvey Comics fan, Quinton was always
instrumental in assisting me in my various projects in any
way he could, from 1990 until his untimely passing.

SPECIAL THANKS:

Christopher Barat, Jerry Beck, Greg Beda, Jerry Cornell,
Andrew Farago, David Lee Fisher, Lee Hester, William Kallay,
Jeff Little, Leonard Maltin, Tara Moore, Ben Ohmart, Patrick Owsley,
Lawrence D. Sander, Dave Smith, Joseph Torcivia and anyone else
I may have forgotten…

Table of Contents

Foreword by Bushrod Thomas 1
Introduction 7
The Feature Films 9

1967 11
    Charlie, the Lonesome Cougar 14

1968 19
    Blackbeard's Ghost 20
    The One and Only, Genuine, Original Family Band 26
    Never a Dull Moment 30
    The Horse in the Gray Flannel Suit 35
    The Love Bug 38

1969 45
    Smith! 46
    Rascal 50
    The Computer Wore Tennis Shoes 53

1970 61
    King of the Grizzlies 62
    The Boatniks 65
    The Aristocats 70
    The Wild Country 74

1971 79
    The Barefoot Executive 81
    Scandalous John 86
    The Million Dollar Duck 90
    Bedknobs and Broomsticks 96

1972 107
    The Biscuit Eater 109
    Napoleon and Samantha 113
    Now You See Him, Now You Don't 116
    Run, Cougar, Run 121
    Snowball Express 125

1973 131
    The World's Greatest Athlete 133
    Charley and the Angel 138
    One Little Indian 143
    Robin Hood 146
    Superdad 150

1974 157
    Herbie Rides Again 160
    The Bears and I 165
    The Castaway Cowboy 169
    The Island at the Top of the World 172

1975 177
    The Strongest Man in the World 179
    Escape to Witch Mountain 184
    The Apple Dumpling Gang 192
    One of Our Dinosaurs is Missing 198
    The Best of Walt Disney's True-Life Adventures 204
    Dr. Syn, Alias the Scarecrow 206
    Ride a Wild Pony 212

1976 217
    No Deposit, No Return 218
    Treasure of Matecumbe 223
    Gus 227

The Shaggy D.A. 230
Freaky Friday 237

1977 245
The Littlest Horse Thieves 247
The Many Adventures of Winnie the Pooh 252
The Rescuers 258
Herbie Goes to Monte Carlo 262
Pete's Dragon 268
Candleshoe 275

1978 281
Return from Witch Mountain 282
The Cat from Outer Space 289
Hot Lead and Cold Feet 294

1979 299
Take Down 300
The North Avenue Irregulars 305
The Apple Dumpling Gang Rides Again 310
Unidentified Flying Oddball 314
The Black Hole 318

1980 325
Midnight Madness 327
The Watcher in the Woods 333
Herbie Goes Bananas 340
The Last Flight of Noah's Ark 345
Popeye 349

1981 357
The Devil and Max Devlin 359
Amy 364

- Dragonslayer 369
- The Fox and the Hound 376
- Condorman 380

1982 387
- Night Crossing 389
- Tron 394
- Tex 408

1983 413
- Trenchcoat 417
- Ray Bradbury's Something Wicked This Way Comes 423
- Never Cry Wolf 430
- Running Brave 435

1984 443
- Splash 445
- Tiger Town 454
- Country 458

1985 465
- Baby... Secret of the Lost Legend 466
- Return to Oz 472
- The Black Cauldron 481
- My Science Project 488

The Rest of the Story 495
The Short Subjects 497
Disney on TV 501
Bibliography 529

Index 531
About the Author 591

Foreword
by Bushrod Thomas

What can one say to forward a book about the post-Walt Disney Company? My perception is that Walt's legacy came from his desire to create a wholesome family entertainment experience, an oasis in a dirty, unhappy world where people struggle and are bombarded with news of senseless tragedies. He created magical lands of adventure, of fantasy, of tomorrow... an ever-changing tomorrow that has to be re-imagined periodically as the future becomes today. Walt birthed the vision, but his death was not its demise.

Before hearing of this book, I hadn't considered the growing pains the company must have experienced with the loss of such a leader. It seemed to me that Disney was doing just fine as I grew up in this period, but survival and independence are never assured when you're always judged by your last work, pressed to successfully complete the current release, and struggling to conceive the next masterpiece.

Mark Arnold and I share the same birth year, 1966. However, being born in August I have the honor over Mark of having been alive (or at least out of the womb) while Walt Disney still lived. I met Mark, an amazing author and historian, not long ago through our mutual interest in Harvey comics and his Harvey fanzine, *The Harveyville Fun Times!* Upon hearing of my long-ago internship at Disney World, Mark asked me to share some recollections for this, his newest book. "Make it interesting," he said! Ha ha, well, even after all these years, I have a humble and respectful loyalty to the company that prevents me from sharing my juiciest stories, but I will nevertheless strive for entertaining relevance. Keep in mind that this is solely my own interpretation of a much, much bigger and more complex, living work... that of a truly extraordinary man, his gifts to the world of entertainment, his company, and of numerous people who worked and work for it, each with valued contributions in their own right. Thank you, Mark, for giving me this opportunity.

First, is it plausible that Walt Disney is in fact frozen somewhere? Absolutely! The company obviously has the resources. Is it likely? Well, just the fact that it is possible adds to the mythos. I like to think that my lost heroes could return. Hope and faith are different things, but as we romanticize and time passes, we will see where talk of second comings shakes out. Is Elvis Presley coming back? Steve Jobs? Walt Disney? The problem is that people tend to forget. Generations pass. What's left is an empire and conglomerate bigger than the man. Who remembers Walt Disney? People know Mickey Mouse, and whatever the latest princess or fairy movie is.

To me, the park in central Florida was the ultimate experience. Going to The Magic Kingdom with my grandparents, Ruth Anna and Clay Johnson, as a 4th grader meant absolutely everything to me. The nightly dreams I had before and after that first trip lasted for months. I took rolls and rolls of pictures, and it didn't get better than that. I asked a park employee how they were so lucky to work there, and was told to just keep my eyes open when I got to college.

Fast forward a dozen years, and voila! I saw an ad for the Disney College Program in Memphis State University's *Helmsman* newspaper, interviewed, and was offered a fall position for three credit hours to be earned by attending presentations covering corporate and operational units, but more importantly by working in the park! I made a glorious $4.25 an hour as an attractions Hos. More specifically, I was the skipper on the Jungle Cruise at Walt Disney World! That was 1987, the 16th anniversary of the park's opening. Mickey paraded daily in birthday celebration regalia, just like he probably did every other year, but it was special nonetheless. Disney Dollars were just coming to mint!

The call for College Program participants was wide, and people answered from all over the Eastern U.S., the Midwest, and beyond. We lived in trailers at the Snow White Village on Seven Dwarf Lane in Kissimmee, Florida. The grid of trailers, row after row on gravel roads, accommodated hundreds of co-ed college students. The trailers were double-wide or more, had wood paneling, and were arranged inside as a four-plex that slept two beds to a quarter unit with a bathroom between each pair and a shared kitchen in the middle. The facility had a pool, clubhouse, laundromat, and administrative office.

My trip from home to work consisted of walking from my trailer to a bus and riding that (or alternately driving) to the employee parking lot, riding another bus to the park/tunnel entrance, going through the gate, and stopping at wardrobe & lockers. Laundry service for costumes was fantastic... just tell them your size and you would get a fresh outfit for the day (not to leave the park). My uniform consisted of khaki, Indiana Jones-esque trousers, shirt, and hat with dark shoes. After dressing up I passed the cafeteria, which had normal, non-park-priced food. I then traversed the long tunnels, wide enough to drive in and lined with big pneumatic tubes that carried trash. Somewhere in the middle was a small store that opened once a week with a 75-90%-off damaged, unsellable merchandise sale just for us. Wow, a place where almost all the magic can be had for people who make $4.25 an hour. Yes, it was a mad, grabtastic dash for loot, and my extended family loved the stuff I got for them there!

I would emerge from the tunnels at one of the hidden points in Adventureland and walk to my attraction. Arriving at the Jungle Cruise before or after the park opened was a different experience. The ride literally teems with people at times... lines, lines, and more lines. Ah, the concrete, paint, plant-life, humidity, and distinctive odors... so many families, so many states and countries represented. There was a podium against one wall for the shift leader to keep figures, schedules, sign-ins, and watch. We would hang out there sometimes but usually we circulated, sweeping up debris, pushing away rain puddles with a big squeegee, re-arranging the line flow, greeting guests, helping them on and off the boats, and giving the tours.

Children bored from waiting in line sometimes needed to be reminded as they got to the front that the Jungle may be fraught with danger. Pony tails and pig tails make great guerrilla grips for gator bait! I had one unfortunate incident startling a young boy on the dock. He dropped his new toy figurine into the "river" and it quickly sank, never to be seen again. There was just no consoling him, and tantrum ensued. In my own youthful inexperience, I dismally failed to "wow him on recovery," and have often reflected on how I could and should have made it up to him, though it wasn't as simple as just buying him a replacement would make it seem.

Trips on the boat entailed a 10 minute spiel narrating various scenic wildlife sets as the boat traversed a submerged track. "Up there, we have a hibiscus! And down there, a lowbiscus!" There you have it... the one script joke I remember. Oh wait, after getting a surprise shower (the best part about operating the boat-- you control who gets wet!), "I bet you all thought that was water! Well, it'sssnot!" Remember the head shrinker? Any two of his heads for just one of yours?

On one of, if not the first, go-arounds that I took with my trainer, the skipper of a live boat behind us doing the show took notice of us past the waterfalls and actually fired his pistol at us. That was, as it turned out, against the rules! My trainer had to report him, and I wound up having to fill out a statement of what happened. I guess he was fired. The policy regarding prop weapons was strict (besides rules against going too far off-script). The guns only had blanks, but if a gun went missing we would have to close the whole park. Luckily, I didn't see that happen.

Every time or two around the river we got comparable time off, on dock. There was a great hangout upstairs where I read Piers Anthony and Philip

José Farmer novels and listened to hardcore punk and R.E.M. cassette tapes through headphones. At the end of every day, we cleaned the prop guns in the office with WD-40. Every so often a group of skippers would meet in the wee hours of the morning before the park opened, put on waders, and slog around with scrub brushes, cleaning hippos, etc.

    I can only imagine what it would be like to have my name on the gate at Disney, but I did have my name on a badge. I first went by the name Rod, which I was called growing up. My first name is actually Bushrod, so one day I thought I'd get a badge with Bushrod on it. The park manager refused to sign the form until I showed him my driver's license. He said he didn't believe it was my name. Some people had gotten in trouble for having badges made with joke names. Well, I guess Bushrod *does* sound "Jungle Cruise-ian."

    I shadowed that manager one day. We wore suits and walked around inspecting the park and rides. He was a great representative for the park and for management. He showed me how to deal with guests and conflict with benevolent authority. We also got to go right to the front of several lines and rides. Proper attire helped. I guess he had an office upstairs on Main Street; maybe the "command center" was there, but I don't remember it. I did ask him about future employment opportunities and he said they liked to hire people established in their careers, not fresh out of college.

    I wonder what surveillance and communication technology must be in use at Disney parks today. Though timing computers and sensors for the roller coaster attractions were sophisticated by necessity, Jungle Cruise technology seemed archaic. This was certainly before the proliferation of webcams and mobile phones, but perhaps it was just in keeping with the ride's theme that we only had a gunshot signaling system to alert of mechanical failure. One day there was a jam on the river as a boat a few minutes ahead had broken down. It seemed that an interminable time passed as we waited to proceed, and I tried in vain to entertain a boat full of guests off-script. You can only ask so many times, "Where's everybody from?" Beyond acting, the job presented a challenging opportunity to learn to engage and interact with strangers!

    By extension, maybe the challenge was the same for the business as a whole. Surely everyone was trying to do their best to entertain and live up to the legacy. Ultimately, a company is only as good as the talent it hires, retains, and replenishes. That's why they reached out with the College Program, beyond Orlando, to find fresh enthusiasm that would take word back home and perpetuate the cycle. Maybe not everything was great, but maybe just having grown through this period and beyond proves we did our part that we did enough. My experience working there was more than just a job. It was a taste of being part of the family's legacy. What a great memory!

    There was life outside of work. Orlando had a fun club called Faith in Physics where I went dancing whenever I could. John Dorosh, my friend and coworker on the Jungle Cruise and College Program, introduced me to Anthrax! When they came to Tampa with Celtic Frost and Exodus, I had to skip the College Program's graduation party to see the show. That was definitely a bummer decision to have to make. My chums from the program just couldn't skip, but the show that night was worth it to me.

As for my internship, it did get old by the end. To be a full-time, permanent, attractions host in the park, I shudder to think! There were some (somebody has to maintain continuity, after all), and they would move around among attractions to keep from burning out. There was an East side and a West side. Mostly employees didn't cross. I don't recall the precise boundary but you can count on the castle being somewhere in the middle.

On the other hand, Disney World is a place where can "chill out" and find a moment of happiness and spend time with family and friends. The young and the old, people from all nations, share in the "magic of the moment." Some sets may be static, but there is a willingness to change when the time comes, as was the case with female skippers. When I worked there, only men could be in that role. When I saw my first female skipper years later, I told her how surprised I was to see her running the boat since I had thought it was against Walt's wishes. He supposedly did not picture or want to cast women in the role. She was nonplussed. Times change and sometimes humanity triumphs.

The older animated Disney movies were a big part of my infancy, and the live action and animated hybrids enthralled my young mind-- *Song of the South* (Fantastic Soundtrack! Dollar a Minute!), *Bedknobs and Broomsticks* (OMG, Flying Bed! Move over, *Chitty!*), *Witch Mountain* (Can you say, *Escape*?). Today, watching them is my laughing place but I go there sparingly. Nostalgia, and anything written, drawn, or filmed is all about frozen time, but what's the point if not to impact the present by reconnecting us with feelings of yesterday? Disney, the story teller and memory maker, gifted us all. His movies and theme parks are time capsules and time machines left to connect us with previous generations and thoughts... progressive, emerging thoughts of decency and equality, of innocence, joy and triumph... in sharp contrast to so many of today's themes. The tragic demise of Bobby Driscoll, child star of 1946's *Song of the South* who reportedly died homeless in 1968, shows us that life is not always pleasant and does not always end well, but we can all have at least a moment of happiness. We can have a laughing place. It is up to each of us to find that. At Walt Disney World, we always smiled while above-ground. Downstairs was the real world. Nothing will scar you like seeing Snow White curse, frown, or smoke. I love to smile, and I wish people would smile more and be happy as a conscious choice if not by circumstance. It is my hope that when you read the plots in this book, watch the films, and visit the parks, that you will see the adventure and beauty of intent. The music, themes and production are art and history.

Disney's purchase of Marvel Comics was something I never saw coming. And now *Star Wars*!? When I was at Disney, I did not see the company sputtering. I felt some lingering fear of hostile takeover, though the proud heritage shone through and things were looking up. Perhaps an imperfect analogy is of a star in phases of life. Walt Disney was the birth, but his death was not its demise. It simmered for a long time before entering the next expansionary phase, absorbing neighboring bodies, and giving off more and more light as it grows. If the company is ever destined to supernova or collapse under its own weight, rest assured that we won't be here to see it, and thankfully so! I personally thank you, Walt and Company!!! BRAVO!!!!!

Now, go put on a collection of songs from Magic Kingdom attractions and read on: Electric Parade, Abraham Lincoln telling us that "Man was made for immortality," the grim, grinning ghosts coming out to socialize, "Yo ho, yo ho, a pirate's life for me," "Where the birds sing out, and the flowers bloom!" Whoa!

> – Bushrod Thomas,
> Walt Disney World college program alum
> Jungle Cruise skipper, Fall 1987

Introduction

December 15, 1966. The date holds two significant events in my life. One, it was the day that I was born at 2:13pm in the Good Samaritan Hospital in San Jose, California, but this event pales in comparison to the event that occurred some five hours earlier on the same day, at 9:35am. Walt Disney had died, prompting the inevitable question that would dog Walt Disney Productions for the next 18 years, "What would Walt do?"

Strangely enough, even though Walt was no longer here he had enough projects already in the planning that it seemed for a time that he hadn't really left us. Posthumous films such as *The Aristocats* (1970) and *Bedknobs and Broomsticks* (1971) owe their origins to Walt. Theme park attractions such as The Haunted Mansion (1969) and Space Mountain (1974) were planned by Walt. Heck, Walt Disney World (1971) and Epcot Center (1983) were conceived completely by Walt, albeit changed significantly in the latter form from what it was supposed to be, a city of the future, to what it became, a permanent World's Fair. In fact, Disney is still responsible for releases as recent at *Beauty and the Beast* (1991) and *Destino* (2003), so it is unlikely that his posthumous contributions will ever completely cease.

Yet, the years 1967-1985 are often the most overlooked or maligned years in the company's history. Most biographies ignore the period, favoring the follow-up period that was headed by Michael Eisner.

While I respect Eisner's work, especially in getting Disney back on track after a severe fall in fortunes, I truly believe that Eisner really didn't revive Disney as much as reinvent Disney into Paramount Pictures and ABC Television, companies he had previously headed up.

Robert Iger took over from Eisner in 2005 and seems to have steered The Walt Disney Company (as it is now named) back towards its roots, but with an Eisner twist. I don't think Disney as a company could ever completely go back, because too many changes have been made.

Gone are the days of the "dopey Disney comedy," a series of campy Disney films based on a simple premise or gimmick and using a regular cast of stock players and washed-up has-beens, filmed with the same crews and on the same back lot locations, with rear-screen projection used to excess. It's a procedure that finally stopped after movies like *Airplane!* (1980) poked tremendous fun at the outdated film technique.

After 1980 Disney started changing, culminating in the hiring of Michael Eisner and Frank Wells prior to stockholders taking over the company. As a result the changes Eisner made were absolutely necessary for the ultimate survival of The Walt Disney Company, but cherished memories I had as a child about all things Disney had to be sacrificed in order for the company to continue. Disney could no longer be an innocent bystander; it had to become a major player in the increasing dominance of others in entertainment.

This book takes us back to a simpler time when breaking even or small profits were the order of the day; a time when a few dollars could get you into a Disney theme park as opposed to now, where today a C-note can barely buy your way in; a time where Disney solely meant family entertainment; a time where Disney was quintessentially American with no offshore parks or cruise lines.

The inspiration for this book primarily comes from Leonard Maltin's *The Disney Films*. Maltin's book was first published in 1973, during the period discussed in this book. In the first edition of his book, little is mentioned after 1967 except as basically a footnote chapter describing "The Rest of the Story." Even in subsequent updates of his book and in other projects Maltin has participated in, such as the long-running Walt Disney Treasures DVD series (housed in tin containers and individually numbered!), scant mention or inclusion of films made post-1966 are even discussed, despite the fact that Oscar-winning shorts like *It's Tough to Be a Bird* (1969) and TV series like *The Mouse Factory* (1972-1973) deserved the same respect as the Walt Disney-produced material.

As a launching point I will cover each year separately, discussing each film, TV show, comic book, magazine, theme park attraction, parade, and lost project in detail and then go into greater detail about the theatrical film releases.

The Feature Films

1967

As 1966 wound down, despite the news reports the initial loss of Walt Disney was not completely evident. He still hosted *The Wonderful World of Color* and would continue to do so throughout the spring and summer of 1967 as Walt had filmed his final segments for that season of shows during recording sessions in October of 1966. Walt even recorded an audio Christmas card for the blind school featured in the upcoming three-part installment called *Atta Girl, Kelly*.

The news of Walt's death seemed somewhat unexpected as the Disney Studios said that Walt was in the hospital due to an old polo injury and not that he was being ravaged by cancer.

After his death, rumors started to run rampant that Walt was cryogenically frozen for thawing out at some future time when a cure for cancer would be found.

Although fanciful in idea and thought, and the jokey inspiration for the title of this book, Walt was instead cremated after he died. The rumors continued mainly because the funeral was a sparsely-attended, downplayed affair and it has been noted that Walt did do a little investigation into cryogenics at one point.

Yes, it seemed that Walt was not initially missed by the public, because it seemed that he was still with us. In Leonard Maltin's *The Disney Films*, Maltin discusses the 1967 releases in great detail beginning with *Monkeys, Go Home!*, released in February, and continuing with *The Adventures of Bullwhip Griffin*, released in March; *The Gnome-Mobile*, released in July; *The Jungle Book*, released in October; and *The Happiest Millionaire*, released in November of that year. *The Legend of the Boy and the Eagle* was a featurette released in the same year.

Work began on a follow-up animated feature to *The Jungle Book*, but although Walt himself had given his blessing for *The Aristocats* (1970), Charles Solomon's *The Disney That Never Was* reveals that *Hansel and Gretel* was revived in September, in an idea thrown about at Disney since the 1950s and as recently as 1961.

Hansel and Gretel was to have music by the Sherman Brothers, but they didn't seem to find much inspiration with the story that was toned down to remove some of its more graphically violent elements. There were also thoughts of starring Mickey and Minnie Mouse in the film, but everything was discarded and a Disney *Hansel and Gretel* has yet to appear.

Another project considered for animation by Walt was *Doctor Dolittle* (1967), but by the time they got around to considering it 20th Century Fox had released their live-action version. It was the biggest non-Disney children's film release at the time, but the film almost made 20th Century Fox go under due to its expense.

Snow White and the Seven Dwarfs (1937) and *The Shaggy Dog* (1959) were reissued this year.

On television, *The Wonderful World of Color* continued its 13th season and in the fall of that year began its 14th season, now sponsored by Gulf Oil. The new, made-for-TV episodes from the 14th season were the first in which no host was present. Completely new episodes premiering that season include *One Day on Beetle Rock* and *A Boy Called Nuthin'*.

Disneyland continued operations as usual and the next big event was another attraction that Walt had personally supervised, but did not live to see open, The Pirates of the Caribbean, opening on March 18.

Pirates was originally conceived as a walk-through, but as time went on it was modified and included more audio-animatronics figures than any other ride, save for It's a Small World, which premiered at Disneyland in 1966 after a successful run at the New York World's Fair in 1964 and 1965.

The attraction was and is one of the most popular ever conceived by the Disney folks and was not directly inspired by any specific Disney film, but based loosely on *Treasure Island* (1950) and *Swiss Family Robinson* (1960). Ultimately, this situation was rectified when a movie based on the attraction and starring Johnny Depp was released in 2003; it has to date spawned three theatrical sequels. The success of these films inspired the Disney team to modify the attraction to include an audio-animatronic model of Depp, along with other modifications.

The next and just as significant change to Disneyland arrived on July 2, with the total redux of Tomorrowland. Walt had noticed that his 1955 Tomorrowland had slowly become Todayland, despite the additions of the Monorail, the Matterhorn, and the submarines; all added in 1959. It was ultimately decided to overhaul the entire area, with attractions such as House of the Future and The Flying Saucers not making the final cut (although House of the Future did survive until December).

In their place were new attractions such as the PeopleMover, Adventure through Inner Space (opened August 5), The Carousel of Progress (another World's Fair transplant), and a revamped Flight to the Moon, Autopia, Circle-Vision 360, Rocket Ships and Tomorrowland Terrace.

This remodel remained essentially unchanged until 1996, but many minor changes were made to the area in the years after 1967.

Disneyland also opened Alpine Gardens and Club 33, a planned, private VIP lounge in New Orleans Square. After Walt's death, the VIP lounge idea was opened up to individuals willing to pay the high annual dues. Club 33 is the only place in Disneyland that serves alcohol and now has a waiting list for members.

Walt had planned to open a ski resort called Mineral King with land purchased in 1965. Plans seemed to be moving forward this year as the California Highway Commission had approved seven-year financing for road construction which would last until 1973.

Work also continued on the Disney World project in Florida. Roy Disney presented the EPCOT film to the Florida legislature on February 2. Bills were passed on April 17 and on May 12; Governor Claude Kirk signed the legislation required for the project to move forward, starting on May 30. Roy Disney renamed the area Walt Disney World in honor of his brother.

However, in Bob Thomas' book *Building a Company*, about the life of Roy O. Disney, Marty Sklar was quoted as saying that work on Walt Disney World stopped for about a year but finally began in earnest again in 1968.

Part of the reasons cited were that Roy instigated a leadership-by-committee policy and also the fact that he genuinely missed Walt and had to go through the grieving process.

Roy also muted his own successors and figuring that one person could not replace him and Walt, set it up so that upon his death the roles would revert to Donn Tatum and Card Walker, longtime employees of the company. The succession actually started taking place before Roy died, as Roy had planned to retire after opening Walt Disney World and CalArts in 1971.

Besides the typical soundtrack albums, there was *The Further Adventures of Jiminy Cricket*, which featured the final recordings of Cliff Edwards, the original voice of Jiminy. Also released were *Camarata Conducts Man of La Mancha* and *Walt Disney's Happiest Songs*, a Gulf Oil premium.

Carnival of the Animals, *A Happy Birthday Party for Winnie the Pooh*, and *The Jungle Book* soundtracks were all nominated for Best Recording for Children Grammys, but none won.

Comic books were a subject not touched upon in Leonard Maltin's book and also never really touched upon in any comprehensive history of Disney. Most biographies focus on the films or the animation or the theme parks, but rarely touch on anything else.

Disney's relationship with Western Publishing went back to the 1930s and the birth of the modern comic book. Western Publishing published their comics under the Dell Comics banner, but in 1962 they transferred to the Gold Key Comics moniker and also appeared simultaneously as Whitman Comics by the 1970s.

In any case, by 1967 Disney had continued to publish the long-running *Donald Duck*, *Mickey Mouse*, *Uncle Scrooge*, and *Walt Disney's Comics and Stories* titles as well as newer ongoing series such as *The Beagle Boys*; *Huey, Dewey and Louie Junior Woodchucks*; *Super Goof*; and *Zorro*.

Series debuting this year were *Chip 'n' Dale*, *Moby Duck*, and *Scamp*, as well as one-shots of *Snow White*, *Scrooge McDuck and Money*, *Lady and the Tramp*, and the *Best of Donald Duck and Uncle Scrooge*.

Longtime duck fans saw the end of the "good duck artist" Carl Barks on the *Junior Woodchucks* title before retiring. Barks didn't completely hang it up in retirement, as he began painting the ducks in portraits that today command high prices. Still later he wrote a couple of new stories before his death at age 99 in 2000.

Comic strips that started before the timeline of this book and continued after include *Mickey Mouse*, *Donald Duck*, *Scamp*, and the *Walt Disney Treasury of Classic Tales*. An *Uncle Remus* strip ended in 1972 and a *True-Life Adventure* strip ended in 1973, with a *Winnie the Pooh* strip beginning in 1978. There was also an ongoing annual Christmas strip series that ran each December.

In films, *Charlie, the Lonesome Cougar* was strangely absent from Leonard Maltin's *The Disney Films*, despite Walt's involvement as producer and despite the fact that it was released BEFORE *The Happiest Millionaire* and on the same bill as *The Jungle Book*.

As it eluded inclusion in Maltin's book, we begin here with the first of many theatrical film release entries, described in the same style and format as in Maltin's book...

Charlie, the Lonseome Cougar

RELEASED BY BUENA VISTA ON October 18, 1967, Technicolor. Producer: Walt Disney. Co-Producer: Winston Hibler. Production Manager: Erwin L. Verity. Production Co-Coordinator: Robert F. Metzler. Screenplay: Jack Speirs, Story: Jack Speirs, Winston Hibler. Sound: Robert O. Cook. Film Editor: Gregg McLaughlin. Music: Franklyn Marks. Orchestration: Wayne Robinson. Music Editor: Rusty Jones. Field Producers: Lloyd Beebe, Charles L. Draper, Ford Beebe. Photography: Lloyd Beebe, William W. Bacon III, Charles L. Draper. Animal Supervision: Marinho Correia, Dell Ray. Filmed by

Cangary Limited with the co-operation of Potlatch Forests, Inc., Weyerhaeuser Company. Running time: 74 minutes.

Song: "Talkin' About Charlie" by Jack Speirs and Franklyn Marks.

Cast: Ron Brown (Jess Bradley), Brian Russell (Potlatch), Linda Wallace (Jess's Fiancé), Jim Wilson (Farmer), Clifford Peterson (Mill Manager), Lewis Sample (Chief Engineer), Edward C. Moller (Mill Hand), Charlie (The Lonesome Cougar), Rex Allen (Narrator), Chainsaw (Fox Terrier).

Rex Allen narrates the story of the young cougar kitten discovered by Jess Bradley. Jess wonders why the cougar was out on his own and takes it into custody, although he knows that eventually he would have to release the cougar back into the wild.

Jess nurses the cougar back to health and names him Good-Time Charlie. Charlie accompanies Jess in everything he does, including fishing (where Charlie steals and eats the caught fish).

But Charlie does wander off on his own at times, encountering a black bear and playing with him before taking a nap together, until father bear comes by and takes his cub away.

The mill yard was Jess' home base. By this time in the story, Charlie got into battles with Potlatch's hound dog, Chainsaw. Charlie would regularly try to get extra grub from the local cook, Potlatch, and succeed much to Chainsaw's annoyance.

The battles regularly caused havoc throughout the cafeteria and Jess would have to take care of Charlie and Potlatch would have to take care of Chainsaw. At this point, Charlie was a fully-grown cougar and more difficult to manage.

Next, a drive of logs is sent down the river. The men are in a small boat to make sure there are no log jams. There is also a boat that has a few homes on it in order to feed the river crew.

Of course, Charlie and Chainsaw are along too and the battles and the mayhem begin anew, causing the cook to land in the water. His fear of the cougar causes him to leave and eventually he is stranded upstream.

The animals weren't the only problems, as the water could become rough as well. At one point Jess had to rescue Charlie who had floated down the river on a runaway log.

Jess needs help, but no one wants to help unless someone cooks a meal. Jess cooks, while the others help to get Charlie. The log drive continues.

More trouble happens with more rough water causing the kitchen to hit some rocks, overturning the stove and the causing the kitchen to catch on fire. Jess quickly tries to put out the fire.

Meanwhile, the others are dynamiting a log jam and the kitchen floats into the path. Jess is caught in the blast but is more-or-less unhurt, and Charlie licks his minor wounds.

There is some more fun as the men engage in a log-rolling contest. Of course, Charlie is interested and actually keeps up with the log-rolling man until Chainsaw distracts him and he falls in the water.

After the fun Charlie is locked inside a cougar crate, but when he hears another cougar's roar, he forces himself out of his cage to meet this other wild cat.

Soon it is winter and Charlie and his new female companion frolic in the snow. Charlie and his friend go hunting for a wild rabbit dinner, but his new playmate isn't willing to share and so Charlie abandons her and tries to find his way back to the camp.

Along the way, he comes upon a farm with a farmer milking a cow for some kittens. The farmer wasn't expecting a cougar, however, and is frightened out of his wits.

After the farmer runs to get his gun, Charlie scampers off to safety. Now lost and hungry, Charlie comes across a raccoon and a lynx and the battles begin again.

Soon hunger takes over and Charlie chases and eats a mouse. Winter eventually turns to summer and Charlie is still lost in the wilderness.

Charlie then is hunted by a man on horseback with his hunting dogs. He escapes just in time while riding a log down a flume. Success in getting to the river seems inevitable until Charlie is knocked off the log by a huge branch blocking his route.

Eventually, Charlie gets down to the river and the lumber mill, which amazingly is the one he had left all those months ago.

Charlie goes to see Potlatch but there is no answer, so he climbs in through an open window to find food for himself, licking the cold stove and various pots and pans.

There is plenty of food, but unfortunately it is all sealed up in cans. Charlie tries to eat cheese off a mousetrap and gets his nose snapped.

Charlie's frustration comes out in rage and he starts destroying the kitchen to get some food. He is now a dangerous cougar.

The next day, Potlatch and Chainsaw come to the restaurant to open up and receive a nasty surprise of an angry and aggressive Charlie.

Chainsaw is left outside but his incessant barking causes Potlatch to let him inside. Charlie is discovered and he lunges for Potlatch.

After a heated fight in the lumber yard, the men throw knives at Charlie and shoot at him. Jess discovers Charlie and tries to subdue him.

He does and plans to send Charlie to a wildlife refuge. Jess drives to the refuge with his fiancée and releases Charlie there. In time Charlie meets another female cougar, who could have been the same one as before, but it doesn't matter to Charlie.

A very simple and somewhat unexciting tale, and as such it did well at the box office only because it was shown on a double bill with the newly-animated *The Jungle Book* (1967), something that it would most assuredly not have done had it been released on its lonesome. It was on the Disney TV show in 1969 (also 1974 and 1979), but that didn't stop the Disney regime from doing more "Name, the Adjective Animal" movies. Disney's next animal-based film wouldn't be released until over a year later, and it would be more audience-friendly with the Dean Jones vehicle, *The Horse in the Gray Flannel Suit* (1968).

Though released prior to *The Happiest Millionaire* (1967) (except for the premiere and some pre-release engagements on the same day as *The Jungle Book*, Leonard Maltin chose not to cover this film in his book *The Disney Films* as one bearing the personal stamp of Walt Disney.

Thus begins a long-running series of semi-fictional Disney nature films, not dissimilar to the previous *Perri* (1957). These became a staple during the early post-Walt years on TV and in the theaters from 1967 to about 1975, when wiser minds finally prevailed and discovered that children didn't like THAT MANY nature films. Everything was capped off with *The Best of Walt Disney's True-Life Adventures* (1975).

Here's an interesting note found on IMDB about the film parody in the Farrelly Brothers comedy *Me, Myself and Irene* (2000): "In *Charlie, the Lonesome Cougar*, Rex Allen narrates. In *Me, Myself and Irene*, Rex Allen, Jr., who sounds the same, narrates similarly, both frequently referring to the main character, "Charlie."

1968

1968 began as another fine year on the Disney schedule, mainly because many more projects were in production that Walt had initiated, so it was still a feeling of "business as usual" at Disney. Even though their leader was still sorely missed, Donn Tatum assumed the role of Disney President this year succeeding Roy O. Disney, who retained his role as Chairman of the Board and CEO until his death in 1971. Those roles were in turn assumed by Tatum in 1971.

A popular film released this year that patterned itself strongly after Disney's *Mary Poppins* was *Chitty Chitty Bang Bang*, going so far as to hire Dick Van Dyke to star and featuring music written by the Sherman brothers. And as far as animated features go, the most successful was The Beatles' *Yellow Submarine*.

The Parent Trap (1961) was reissued this year.

According to Charles Solomon's *The Disney That Never Was*, *The Bremen Town Musicians* was an animated feature film idea toyed with from 1968 to 1970 and would probably or possibly be a follow-up to *The Aristocats* (1970), which was also still in production at this time. Nothing ever came of the project.

Progress on Mineral King continued. This year, the Department of the Interior approved the road routes with an opening date of winter 1973. Progress also continued on the construction of Walt Disney World.

For the anthology show, quite a number of all-new shows were produced, including *Way Down Cellar, Disneyland: From the Pirates of the Caribbean to the World of Tomorrow, Pablo and the Dancing Chihuahua, My Family is a Menagerie, The Young Loner, Wild Heart, The Ranger of Brownstone, The Mystery of Edward Sims, Nature's Charter Tours, Boomerang, Dog of Many Talents, Pacifically Peeking* (featuring Moby Duck, who was to become a major Disney comic book star), *Brimstone, the Amish Horse, The Treasure of San Bosco Reef, The Owl That Didn't Give a Hoot*, and *The Mickey Mouse Anniversary Show*.

Disney won yet another Academy Award this year, this time for the second Winnie the Pooh short, entitled *Winnie the Pooh and the Blustery Day*. Although this short was started long before Walt died, it took until now to release it according to Walt's plans to roll the Winnie the Pooh franchise out slowly in order to build US interest in the UK property.

Non-soundtrack record releases included *Walt Disney's Merriest Songs*, which was another Gulf Oil premium, an adaptation of *Heidi*, various Winnie the Pooh record readers, *The Enchanted Tiki Room*, *Disney Songs the Satchmo Way* featuring Louis Armstrong, *Mickey Mouse and his Friends* (celebrating Mickey's 40th birthday), *Acting Out the ABCs*, *It's a Small World*, and *More Jungle Book* featuring Phil Harris singing new songs.

Phil Harris also recorded a new version of the 1930s song "What, No Mickey Mouse?" for a Buena Vista single.

In the comic book world, Gold Key continued to publish *Donald Duck*, *Mickey Mouse*, *Uncle Scrooge*, *Walt Disney's Comics and Stories*, *The Beagle Boys*, *Huey, Dewey and Louie Junior Woodchucks*, *Super Goof*, *Chip 'n' Dale*, *Moby Duck*, *Scamp*, and a new one called *Walt Disney Comics Digest*, while *Zorro* ended its run.

One-shots included *Baloo and Little Britches*, *King Louie and Mowgli* both based on *The Jungle Book* and *Blackbeard's Ghost* and *The Love Bug* adaptations.

Richard Schickel released the first major biography on Walt Disney this year called *The Disney Version*, and *American Heritage* magazine saluted Walt in their April 1968 issue.

Blackbeard's Ghost

RELEASED BY BUENA VISTA ON February 8, 1968, Technicolor. Producer: Walt Disney. Co-Producer: Bill Walsh. Director: Robert Stevenson. Screenplay: Bill Walsh, Don DaGradi, based on the book by Ben Stahl. Director of Photography: Edward Colman, A.S.C. Art Directors: Carroll Clark, John B. Mansbridge. Film Editor: Robert Stafford, A.C.E. Set Decorators: Emile Kuri, Hal Gausman. Matte Artist: Pete Ellenshaw. Costume Designer: Bill Thomas. Sound Supervisor: Robert O. Cook. Sound Mixer: Dean Thomas. Costumers: Chuck Keehne, Neva Rames. Make-up: Gordon Hubbard. Hair Stylist: La Rue Matheron. Music Editor: Evelyn Kennedy. Second Unit Director: Arthur J. Vitarelli. Second Assistant Director: Robert Webb. Special Effects: Eustace Lycett, Robert A. Mattey. Unit Manager: Joseph L. McEveety. Assistant Director: Paul Cameron. Music: Robert F. Brunner. Orchestration: Cecil A. Crandall. Stunts: Dick Warlock. Camera and Electrical Equipment: Stan Reed. Running time: 107 minutes.

Songs: "Steady, Boy, Steady," "For He's a Jolly Good Fellow" sung by the cast.

Cast: Peter Ustinov (Captain Blackbeard), Dean Jones (Steve Walker), Suzanne Pleshette (Jo Anne Baker), Elsa Lanchester (Emily Stowecroft), Joby Baker (Silky Seymour), Elliott Reid (TV Commentator), Richard Deacon (Dean Wheaton), Hank Jones (Gudger Larkin), Norman Grabowski (Virgil), Michael Conrad (Pinetop Purvis), Herbie Faye (Croupier), George Murdock (Head Official), Kelly Thordsen (Motorcycle Officer), Ned Glass (Teller), Gil Lamb (Waiter), Alan Carney (Bartender), Ted Markland (Charles), Lou Nova (Leon), Charlie Brill (Edward), Herb Vigran (Danny Oly), William Fawcett (Mr. Ainsworth, Bank Official), Betty Bronson (Old Lady), Elsie Baker (Old Lady), Kathryn Minner (Old Lady), Sara Taft (Old Lady), Phil Arnold (Popcorn Vendor), Paul Bradley (Maître d), Richard Collier (Ticket Seller), Gertrude Flynn (Mrs. Starkey), Byron Foulger (Mr. Harrison, First Bidder), Paul Genge (Casino Manager), George Golden (Man at Auction), Harry Harvey (Mr. Finch, Third Bidder), Ralph Montgomery (Reporter), Ray Reese (Godolphin Member – Track and Javelin), Bing Russell (Second Track Meet Official).

Based on a novel by Ben Stahl, *Blackbeard's Ghost* tells the story of Edward Teach, the pirate better known as Blackbeard.

The movie begins with the following text: *In the early years of the eighteenth century lived the pirate, Edward Teach, known as Blackbeard.*

From the Spanish Main to the Carolinas, he wrought a bloody tale of destruction, unparalleled for its ferocity and terror.

Blackbeard was killed in seas battle off the American shore-. This was followed by widespread joy when it became known the dread pirate had gone at last—.

—or had he?

Thus begins the tale of *Blackbeard's Ghost*…

After a storm at sea, we find Steve Walker driving into town to become the new track coach at Godolphin College. The coach encounters one of his future students working at a local gas station.

Steve is driven to the Blackbeard Inn as a place to stay. A group of old ladies called The Daughters of the Buccaneers are trying to save the aging inn before it is taken over by Silky Seymour to be destroyed before becoming a gambling casino.

Dean Wheaton is introduced to Steve and the Dean reveals that replacing the track coach was not a favorable decision.

Later, Steve is introduced to Mr. Purvis, the football coach. Purvis laughs when he discovers that Steve is the track team's coach.

Steve still needs a room for the night and meets up with the eccentric Emily Stowecroft, who runs the inn but also has a side business of palm-reading and clairvoyance.

Still luckless in getting a room, he meets a woman at a kissing booth and plants one on her. It turns out that the kissee is not running the booth, but rather is Jo Anne Baker, an attractive woman who is helping the DOTB to auction off a number of items in order to raise money to save the inn from takeover.

Steve makes sure not to bid until he witnesses Silky Seymour's men convincing the participants that the items up for bid are fakes. Steve suspects foul play and decides to bid after all to keep the auctions going. Steve is told not to bid anymore, but does so anyway and wins an antique bed warmer for $200.

Later, Steve encounters Jo Anne again and she reveals that they still need $38,000 to pay off Silky after the auction's conclusion, and also tells the history of the island and why Silky wants to build the casino.

Finally Emily sets up a room for Steve; the one originally inhabited by Edward Teach, a.k.a. Blackbeard. Emily reveals that Blackbeard creates lots of noise as a ghost and says that a curse was placed on Blackbeard that caused him to be held in limbo between Earth and the afterlife. Steve dismisses her as an eccentric old coot.

Alone at last, Steve accidentally sits on his auction item and breaks it. He finds a secret message stuffed inside the item's handle that talks about the spell placed on Blackbeard, just as Emily had mentioned.

Steve reads the inscription on the paper, causing a thunderclap, and soon Blackbeard's ghost reveals itself. The ghost is thirsty and helps himself to some rum. It turns out that Steve is the only one who can see and hear the apparition.

Blackbeard turns out to be a pain in the neck, to say the least, and soon Steve leaves the room so he can get some well-needed sleep. He drives away thinking he's away from Blackbeard, but escape turns out to not be as easy as he had thought.

While Steve drives, Blackbeard reappears and takes over the wheel. The car spins out, grabbing the attention of a nearby motorcycle police officer.

The officer does not see or hear Blackbeard, but does see an open bottle of rum on the seat next to Steve. Soon Steve is hauled off to jail on a DUI, but not until after Blackbeard takes possession of the officer's motorcycle and chases the cop with it.

Steve finally gets his sleep in a local jail cell, but he is not rid of Blackbeard. Steve rereads the paper that brought Blackbeard to his attention and discovers that Blackbeard would be released from his limbo state if he proves that he's done something – anything – good! He has not.

Steve tells Blackbeard that he could give his treasure to the old ladies and save the inn, and in the process could also be released from the curse.

Meanwhile, back at the college there is a meeting discussing the decision of keeping Steve on staff as news of his DUI hits the newspapers. Ultimately they decide to give Steve a second chance, but the Dean tells Jo Anne to keep an eye on Steve.

Steve, now released, starts the track team in training and is soon harassed again by Blackbeard at the stadium. Blackbeard claims that he has a way to help his track team win. This claim will help Blackbeard help the old ladies and win his freedom from limbo but Steve rejects the idea, claiming that it's cheating.

Meanwhile, the Dean and Jo Anne witness Steve talking or yelling at himself and the subject of his dismissal is addressed again.

Jo Anne says that she is going to have dinner with Steve in order to find out some answers.

At dinner, Silky greets Steve and Jo Anne again. Silky owns the restaurant, which is the best one in town, so they have no choice in encountering him.

Steve reveals his problems with Blackbeard to Jo Anne. His claims are greeted with suspicion, but she claims to understand.

Blackbeard is in the vicinity and takes the large wad of bills located in Jo Anne's purse, then places a bet on the Godolphin track team. The betting parlor is coincidentally also run by Silky.

Blackbeard's bet wins big and he puts the receipt back in Jo Anne's purse after tripping the same waiter.

The next day, sports commentator Mel Willis of *Sports Spectacular* is hosting the track meet on TV. Steve gives his team a last-minute pep talk before they run.

Jo Anne stops by before the meet, accusing Steve of taking the $900 and producing the receipt. She leaves in a huff.

Steve re-encounters Blackbeard and he reveals the truth. Steve tells Blackbeard to stop helping him and keep his hands off the money and his team.

Broxton College is winning event after event until Blackbeard stubbornly helps Steve's team.

Jo Anne takes the Godolphin receipt to Silky to get the $900 back, which he refuses to do.

Steve sees Blackbeard is interfering with the events by sending the other team's runners backwards and helping the shot put, discus, and javelins go farther for Godolphin. He tries to stop Blackbeard but fails and Godolphin wins the meet, but not until Steve yells at Blackbeard for interfering.

Blackbeard quits before the final event and Godolphin starts losing. Steve has a change of heart and helps the team win in the end by replacing the batons with a bottle and a hot dog!

The delay is temporary as the other teams catch up and the Godolphin man poops out. Blackbeard picks him up and runs him over the finish line.

Everyone is excited, although Steve still feels guilty about cheating. The old ladies are setting up a mortgage burning party, but there is still a problem.

Steve tells Blackbeard that he has to leave and make a fresh start somewhere else. Jo Anne says he can't go and claimed that Silky welshed on the bet. Steve and Blackbeard go out to get the money back. Jo Anne doesn't see Blackbeard and thinks Steve is nuts, but follows him to help him out.

Silky still refuses to pay. He then agrees to give the original $900 back. Jo Anne rejects this, but Blackbeard convinces Steve to win the money again on the roulette wheel. Jo Anne is shocked.

Blackbeard makes sure that the money is won again by tampering with the wheel and the bets and the dealer. Jo Anne and Steve argue about how to do this. Steve wants to bet big and on one number because time is running out and Jo Anne wants to do things differently.

Eventually they do win but the dealer has his own tricks, such as an electrified wheel. Blackbeard affects this as well and the dealer gets an electric shock.

Jo Anne is now compulsively gambling but Steve stops her. They get the money again, but Silky steals it before they can leave the casino.

Steve "shoots" Silky's thugs with Blackbeard's help and the two finally leave with the money. Blackbeard ultimately finishes the bad guys off.

Jo Anne and Steve arrive just in time to pay off the mortgage for the old ladies, but just barely, and the mortgage burning proceeds.

Blackbeard shows up, and Steve gets Jo Anne and the old ladies to repeat the phrase from the crumpled piece of paper and now he's visible to all.

The old ladies are grateful to Blackbeard as he burns the mortgage. In the end, Blackbeard is free and goes on to his afterlife, no longer in limbo.

Again, Walt Disney is listed as Producer of this film, which was definitely in production during Walt Disney's lifetime as evidenced by the comments made by Walt's final filmed performance on October 27, 1966 where he mentions this fact.

Suzanne Pleshette remembers that Walt did visit the set in late 1966, but she knew it would be for the last time as he had a grey and yellow look that only cancer patients have.

Walt did have a lot of features prepared ahead of time. Leonard Maltin probably felt that it was better to end his Disney book on a classy note with *The Happiest Millionaire* (1967) rather than with this lightweight comedy.

That being said, this lightweight comedy is one of the best ones the studio ever produced.

The film was a huge hit, grossing over $21 million and prompting a theatrical rerelease in 1976. It did not appear on television until 1982.

Part of the film's success was due to the successful reteaming of Dean Jones and Suzanne Pleshette, who had previously acted together in 1966's *The Ugly Dachshund* and would team up again in 1976's *The Shaggy D.A.*

In this film, unlike the other two, they are not married but they still retain the same chemistry present in the other two films, which is the main reason Disney paired them up time and again.

Another reason for its success is due to its entertaining premise of a mischievous ghost creating havoc, frequently a winning idea for Disney, and high-quality special effects.

Peter Ustinov, not always an amusing actor, pulls off the role of Blackbeard effortlessly and humorously, inflecting the right amount of comedy and terror such a role commands.

Apparently, the flag flown in the film for Blackbeard is not authentic and was the flag flown by another pirate.

When asked for the book *Walt Disney and Recollections of the Disney Studios, 1955-1980*, Dean Jones had this to say about his continued success and acting style at Disney, "I think if I had a big flop that probably would have ended the string at Disney. The roles I play in Disney films really don't require me to act."

"What you saw on film WAS Dean Jones," according to Producer Jan Williams.

Jones said that Bill Walsh had a theory about the success of Disney pictures were that you could make the most outrageous plot believable if you play it straight.

Hank Jones made his first appearance in a Disney film playing one of the track runners named Gudger. It was on this film that he had a serious accident that fortunately wasn't fatal. He had to fly in a harness placed under his track suit that was literally cutting into his flesh. The wires then unraveled and he fell ten feet and landed on top of Peter Ustinov. Neither was seriously hurt.

A replica of the painting of Blackbeard used in this movie is now part of the décor of the Pirates of the Caribbean attraction.

The One and Only, Genuine, Original Family Band

RELEASED BY BUENA VISTA ON March 21, 1968, Technicolor. Producer: Bill Anderson. Director: Michael O'Herlihy. Screenplay: Lowell Hawley, based on the book *The Family Band: From the Missouri to the Black Hills, 1881-1900* by Laura Bower Van Nuys, published by University of Nebraska Press. Director of Photography: Frank Phillips, A.S.C. Art Directors: Carroll Clark, Herman Allen Blumenthal. Set Decorators: Emile Kuri, Hal Gausman. Matte Artist: Alan Maley. Costumes: Bill Thomas. Music and Lyrics: Richard M. Sherman, Robert B. Sherman. Music Supervision, Arrangement, Conductor: Jack Elliott. Choreography: Hugh Lambert. Film Editor: Cotton Warburton, A.C.E. Music Editor: Evelyn Kennedy. Sound Supervisor: Robert O. Cook. Sound Mixer: Harold Lewis. Costumers: Chuck Keehne, Emily Sundby. Make-up: Gordon Hubbard. Hair Stylist: La Rue Matheron. Unit Production Manager: Joseph L. McEveety. Assistant Director: Paul L. Cameron. Assistant to the Conductor: James MacDonald. Dance Foley: Jerry Trent. Running time: 110 minutes.

Cast: Walter Brennan (Grandpa Bower), Buddy Ebsen (Calvin Bower), Lesley Ann Warren (Alice Bower), John Davidson (Joe Carder), Janet Blair (Katie Bower), Kurt Russell (Sidney Bower), Bobby Riha (Mayo Bower), Jon Walmsley (Quinn Bower), Smitty Wordes (Nettie Bower), Heidi Rook (Rose Bower), Debbie Smith (Lulu Bower), Pamelyn Ferdin (Laura Bower), Wally Cox (Mr. Wampler), Richard Deacon (Charlie Wrenn), Steve Harmon (Ernie Stubbins), Goldie Jeanne Hawn (Giggly Girl), John Craig (Frank), Jonathan Kidd (Telegrapher), Larry J. Blake (First Outspoken Man), Ben Frommer (Burly Dakota Townsman), Hank Jones (Town Delivery Boy), Kenneth MacDonald (Dakota Townsman), Butch Patrick (Johnny), Pete Renaday (Dakota Townsman), Stephen Roberts (Second Outspoken Man), Andrea Sacino (Dakota Townswoman), Jerry Trent (Dancer), William Woodson (Henry White).

Songs: "Dakota," "The One and Only, Genuine, Original, Family Band," "Let's Put it Over with Grover," "Ten Feet Off the Ground," "'Bout Time," "The Happiest Girl Alive," "West o' the Wide Missouri," "Drummin' Drummin' Drummin,'" "Oh, Benjamin Harrison" by Richard M. Sherman, Robert B. Sherman.

In 1888, Grandpa Bower conducts his 11-member family with their own theme song ("The One and Only, Genuine, Original, Family Band") that they sing and play. The large family is literally that, a fully integrated band with trombone, banjo, tuba, drum, clarinet, trumpet, and more.

After their practice, the various family members drift off to do other things, disappointing Grandpa.

Grandpa is also upset with granddaughter Alice, who is corresponding with Joe Carder, an (ugh) Republican! Alice sings "The Happiest Girl Alive," to express her love for Joe.

Today, Joe is coming over to meet Alice for the very first time. Grandpa complains about Joe's newspaper columns. A man with a mustache arrives, but it is not Joe.

It turns out to be a man who wants to see Grandpa about the song he's written for the Democratic convention with his family performing.

Grandpa then conducts his family to sing and play "Let's Put it Over with Grover." After performing, Calvin admits that he is a Republican, which shocks everyone since he had sung the song with such gusto. Details aside, the family gets the job and is headed to St. Louis. They sing "Ten Feet off the Ground" to celebrate.

At this point Joe finally does show up, to the regret of Annie who didn't want to be seen while singing and dancing so heartily.

They make amends and Joe explains his fondness for Dakota to the family, a territory that is soon to become a state of the Union. Joe invites the family because he feels that they need more Republicans up in the territory, not knowing that he's talking to a predominantly Democratic family.

The family makes amends with Joe and goes to his meeting where he's trying to encourage people to move to Dakota. In fact, Joe sings "Dakota" to get his point across. In the end, Grandpa sits alone in disgust.

Calvin says that the family can't afford to go to Dakota this year, but eventually he changes his mind and off they go by horse and wagon.

Upon arrival Joe is already there, complaining about Dakota not yet having achieved statehood. Joe claims that the government is nervous because making Dakota a state would send four more Republican Senators to Washington. By now discussion has changed to make Dakota two states, North and South, in order to get four instead of two Senate seats.

Grandpa and the family arrive and reprise "Let's Put it Over with Grover," which does not go over with the Dakota citizens. After a debate with Joe, Grandpa bets that if Benjamin Harrison wins he'll give Joe a ride in a wheel barrow, but if Grover Cleveland wins, Joe will have to give Grandpa that ride. Joe agrees.

The next day, Joe stops by to see Alice and says that she has to prove her credentials as a teacher before she can teach. He asks if Grandpa can go to the school to tell the children to go home so that he and Alice can get this technicality taken care of. On the way, Joe and Alice sing "'Bout Time."

Sending Grandpa to send the kids home turns out to be a grave mistake. He initially does as he's told, but when one girl cries about getting dressed up for school and preparing a speech to recite only to discover that school has been canceled, he calls the children back and has school anyway. The little girl recites her speech and when she's done, a boy starts harassing Grandpa, asking about his qualifications to teach. Soon, Grandpa is spouting his doctrine and riling up the kids and sings "Drummin' Drummin' Drummin.'"

Later, Joe chews out Grandpa because his political views could put Alice's job in jeopardy. The arguments continue and Alice sends Joe home. Grandpa goes and tells Calvin of his excitement about Joe leaving, but Calvin is not happy about this and he and Grandpa have a little talk.

Calvin reluctantly tells Grandpa to stop causing trouble for Alice and Joe and makes him promise to stop arguing politics with Joe and to exercise a little self-control with his speaking. Grandpa does not accept this and packs and leaves, upsetting the children. Mayo threatens to leave with him, but Calvin stops him.

Meanwhile, Charlie Wrenn heads up a meeting about Grandpa's disruption of the school and Alice tries to defend his actions. She argues that both sides of any issue should be presented to the children.

Joe reveals that it was he who sent Grandpa to the schoolhouse. Grandpa then shows up. In the resulting turmoil, Alice decides to quit rather than have any more discussion about her being fired. As a result, the school is closed until further notice.

Grandpa stands up and says that the worst thing about this is that the school was closed just when it was reopening. He says that he will stop talking politics if Alice is rehired as the teacher.

Later, Calvin comes in to congratulate Grandpa on his speech, but Grandpa wants to move on anyway. Calvin convinces him to call Grandpa back to lead the family band, who has not been practicing.

On election night, The Family Band plays again at a dance and play and sing "West o' the Wide Missouri." Joe is at this dance and starts to dance with other girls in order to make Alice jealous. One of the girls he dances with is the giggly girl.

First reports come in that say Grover Cleveland is ahead in the results. After a quick reprise of "Let's Put it Over with Grover," Joe decides to sing a song about Benjamin Harrison with Calvin and Charlie. In the end Cleveland wins the popular vote, but Joe says that this doesn't end the fight for statehood. The wheelbarrow is rolled out and Joe wheels Grandpa around, but then word comes in that Harrison has won!

It turns out that the electoral vote went for Harrison and not Cleveland. This was not the first, nor the last, time that the electoral vote displaced the popular vote, as are the rules of our Constitution. A fight breaks out as a result and after the scuffle, the future of Dakota has also been settled. North Dakota and South Dakota become Republican states, but statehood is also granted to Montana and Washington, which are Democratic states.

Grandpa gives Joe a wheel barrow ride. Joe makes amends with Alice and sings "'Bout Time" in the wheelbarrow with her. During the credits everyone in town plays and sings a reprise of the title song.

This is an entertaining and underrated romp with some memorable songs by the Sherman Brothers. It's strongly reminiscent of *The Happiest Millionaire* (1967), mainly because of the presence of Lesley Ann Warren and John Davidson as the love interests.

Originally this film was conceived as a two-part TV movie called *The Family Band*, but as usual everything went better than expected and the film became a theatrical release.

The songs are very catchy, but the film falls flat for some as the subject matter of a Presidential election some 80 years prior wasn't as immediately accessible as, say, the subject matter in the more fantastic *Mary Poppins* (1964) or the upcoming *Bedknobs and Broomsticks* (1971).

This film, and not *Cactus Flower* (1969), is actually the film debut of Goldie Hawn but she doesn't really have much to do besides dance in her role as the giggly girl. The most significant event concerning her appearance in this film is that it is the first filmed appearance of Goldie and Kurt Russell together, though they shared precious little screen time and also did not hit it off with their long-term relationship for another decade.

This film also featured early appearances by Pamelyn Ferdin who went on to roles in the *Peanuts* specials and *The Odd Couple*, and Jon Walmsley, who went on to star in *The Waltons*.

The film did reasonably well, but not great, and it eventually appeared on the Disney anthology show in 1972 with the more streamlined title, *The Family Band*.

This was a return to form for Buddy Ebsen, as by this time he was no longer considered a dancer or singer after many years of starring as Jed Clampett on *The Beverly Hillbillies*.

According to Richard Sherman, this was originally designed to be a two-part TV show, but it came off so well that the decision was made to release it to the theaters instead. He also claimed that Walt Disney so loved *The Happiest Millionaire* that the decision was made to put out another large-scale musical in Walt's memory. He revealed in the DVD documentary that Walt did at least hear the title song for *The Family Band*, and that Walt died right before it was recorded.

John Davidson recalled that the filming of this picture was the first time he heard the phrase "What would Walt do?," as Walt had died just as film production was getting underway, but Walt did have his personal input on the picture despite its having been released well over a year after his death. Lesley Ann Warren mentioned on the DVD commentary that this was the last film Walt worked on.

Davidson also claims on the DVD commentary that this is the final Disney musical the Sherman Brothers did after *Mary Poppins* and *The Happiest Millionaire*. This is not correct, as the Sherman Brothers would be back for *Bedknobs and Broomsticks* and *The Tigger Movie* (2000). Disney would also return to the live-action musical format again with *Pete's Dragon* (1977) and *Newsies* (1992), among others.

Davidson was also impressed with the acting performance of the young boy who speaks up in the schoolroom, but did not know who he was. It turned out to be Butch Patrick (in an unbilled performance), who had portrayed Eddie Munster in the two years prior to this movie and went on to portray Mark in *Lidsville*.

Another notable unbilled performance was that of the man who comes to see to the family perform before bringing them to Dakota. It is William Woodson, who has done numerous voice-over appearances over the years including the opening narration on *The Odd Couple* TV show and the later narrator on *Superfriends*.

Bing Crosby was originally offered the Walter Brennan role, but he commanded too much money.

Brennan wasn't in the greatest of health at the time, as he was suffering from emphysema and had to have an oxygen tank nearby while reciting his lines.

Buddy Ebsen liked to nap between takes, so soundly in fact that the entire cast once posed for a photo surrounding the sleeping Ebsen.

Hank Jones believes he was cast in the film since he didn't sue after the accident he had in *Blackbeard's Ghost* (1968).

John Davidson's brother died during production but he wasn't allowed time off to attend the funeral, although Lesley Ann Warren did get time off to get married to Jon Peters.

Never a Dull Moment

RELEASED BY BUENA VISTA ON June 26, 1968, Technicolor. Producer: Ron Miller. Director: Jerry Paris. Screenplay: A.J. Carothers; based on the book by John Godey. Director of Photography: William Snyder, A.S.C. Art Directors: Carroll Clark, John B. Mansbridge. Film Editor: Marsh Hendry. Set

Decorators: Emile Kuri, Frank R. McKelvy. Matte Artist: Alan Maley. Special Effects: Eustace Lycett, Robert A. Mattey. Costume Designer: Bill Thomas. Assistant to the Producer: Tom Leetch. Sound Supervisor: Robert O. Cook. Sound Mixer: Dean Thomas. Costumers: Chuck Keehne, Neva Rames. Make-up: Gordon Hubbard. Hair Stylist: La Rue Matheron. Music Editor: Evelyn Kennedy. Assistant Director: John C. Chulay. Music: Robert F. Brunner. Orchestration: Cecil A. Crandall. Stunts: Richard Farnsworth, Max Kleven, Walt La Rue, George Robotham. Dialogue Coach: Bobby Hoffman. Running time: 100 minutes.

Cast: Dick Van Dyke (Jack Albany), Edward G. Robinson (Leo Joseph Smooth), Dorothy Provine (Sally Inwood), Henry Silva (Frank Boley), Joanna Moore (Melanie Smooth), Tony Bill (Florian), Slim Pickens (Cowboy Schaeffer), Jack Elam (Ace Williams), Ned Glass (Rinzy Tobreski), Richard Bakalyan (Bobby Macoon), Mickey Shaughnessy (Francis), Philip Coolidge (Fingers Felton), James Millhollin (Museum Director), Eleanor Audley (Matron), Anthony Caruso (Tony Preston), John Cliff (Museum Guard), Paul Condylis (Lenny), John Dennis (Second Museum Guard), Rex Dominick (Sam), Bob Homel (TV Actor), Ken Lynch (Police Lieutenant), Tyler McVey (Chief of Police Greyson), Jerry Paris (Police Photographer), Jackie Russell (Sexy Woman), Johnny Silver (Prop Man), Dick Winslow (Second TV Actor).

This film starts with a rather exciting car chase and shootout during the up-front credit roll. Jack Albany is hiding out but gets shot and falls out a high-story window.

It is revealed that this is a movie set and Jack is actually an actor playing a part in a gangster movie. He is lying in front of the open window mouthing the words of his co-stars.

"Cut!" is called and Jack goes back-stage to prepare for his next scene.

Later, Jack is walking home memorizing his lines for the next day's shoot. He realizes that he's being followed and so hightails it home. He ducks into an abandoned warehouse to be confronted by a gangster with a knife.

The gangster is named Florian and he believes Jack to be another gangster named Ace Williams and not an actor.

Jack tries to set him straight, but Florian is having none of it.

To save his own life, Jack goes along with the gag of impersonating Ace. Together, Florian and Jack get into a car. While riding, Jack tries to attract the attention of the people in another car, but the people in the other car think Jack is just making faces.

Florian brings Jack to the home of Leo Joseph Bloom, but first Francis and Frank Boley greet them. Finally Jack greets Leo, who goes by "Joe."

Joe discusses things with Sally Inwood, who claims to have met Joe before, but doesn't quite remember who or where. Sally is an art instructor helping Joe to make better paintings.

Joe makes Jack (Ace) feel at home with cigars and they discuss Jack's big run-in with the Federal boys. A discussion occurs as to the whereabouts of Jack's suitcase. Jack makes up a tale that in the previous scuffle, he had inadvertently left it behind. In actuality, he had no bag at all.

Joe goes back to his painting with Sally's help. The finished painting is just a bunch of nondescript smears and brushstrokes. (I wonder what happened to this painting.)

Jack goes outside and tries to make a phone call to get help but is intercepted by Joe's switchboard service, so he hangs up and goes back to Joe and Sally and tries to keep up his façade.

Joe explains that he wants to do something that will make him be remembered like Capone or Dillinger.

Soon afterward, Jack tries to tell Sally in private that he is not what he seems, but Sally is not buying it.

Then Jack goes in to meet the rest of Joe's gang and decides to get overenthusiastic and distract the others who are watching a TV show that just so happens to star Jack. His distractions were designed so that no one would realize that Jack is really an actor and not Ace. Eventually, they just switch off the TV.

Everything goes well until Jack meets Frank, who holds a grudge against Ace and slaps Jack's hand. Finally, Joe makes them shake and Frank gives a very strong grip that hurts Jack's hand, but he hides his pain.

After the formalities, Joe explains his plan, in which they are to break into the art museum and steal a painting called "Field of Sunflowers." Joe's gang is disappointed, but he explains that this is all part of his diabolical plan to gain the fame and fortune he desires.

To top it off, Joe doesn't allow anyone to leave the premises until the job is done, in order to keep any of the gang from leaking their plan.

Meanwhile, Sally has come back as her ride home has broken down. She happens to see the "Sunflowers" painting and Joe explains that his gang are really appreciators of fine art.

Jack offers to drive Sally home, but Joe rejects his offer because it is so late and instead invites Sally to spend the night as well, which she accepts.

With Sally safely taken away to her quarters, the gang resumes their plans. Joe asks Jack how he plans to kill someone if necessary, and somehow Jack passes the test with knowledge based on previous acting roles he's done.

Jack continues to sneak drinks, but is forbidden to drink as Joe knows Ace becomes very unruly when drunk.

Obviously Jack is not drunk, raising the suspicions of Joe's gang, so he has to act drunk in order to be accepted as Ace again. Jack finally retires for the night, but not before he makes another attempt to inform Sally of who he is.

Unfortunately, he goes into the wrong room and ends up in the room of Melanie Smooth, Joe's wife. Fortunately, Cowboy Schaeffer saves the day and takes Jack to his proper room.

In his room, Jack opens the window to try to escape, but he's very high up and there's a huge dog below. He walks out on the ledge to try to get over to the next room, but it turns out to be Melanie's room again so he keeps going, finally reaching Sally's room, and taps on her window to let him in. He explains that he's an actor, but doesn't convince her right away.

Jack almost falls off the ledge but Sally rescues him, but she can't let him into the room as Melanie goes to see Sally for something. Jack crawls back and as he passes by Melanie's room, she's back in her room and tries to bring Jack inside.

Joe sees Jack outside on the ledge and tells Melanie and Jack to stop fooling around and tells Jack to go to bed to sleep off his drunkenness.

After everything is settled, the real Ace Williams comes to the door, causing immediate suspicion. Joe wants to get everything straightened out so he invites Joe to meet Ace. Joe wonders who the imposter is. Now both have to prove who they are. Frank suggests putting the two into a room alone together and the real Ace will come out alive.

In the room, Jack tries to reason with Ace, so that he won't kill him, but the real Ace is not listening as they stumble around in the dark together.

It looks to be the end for Jack when Ace is struck upon the head by Sally, who happens to be in the room. She realizes who Jack is and helps him out. Before Jack goes out to become the victor, he and Sally discuss how they can escape, but for now he has to still be Ace.

The real Ace is locked in the cellar for later questioning and everyone goes back to sleep, except Jack who makes another attempt to escape with Sally. In the meantime Jack explains the plan to steal the painting, and ultimately they agree to continue the charade.

Jack does and the gang prepares their plot by posing as waiters and rehearsing their actions. Jack and Joe ride over together and discuss their respective destinies.

While the gang is over at the museum, Sally plans her escape. At one point she accidentally opens the cellar door housing Ace, but shuts it just in time. Next Sally tries to use the switch board, which just rings all the phones in the house. Sally then tries a diversion to distract Francis, who has stayed behind to watch the house.

Meanwhile, at the art gallery, the sunflower painting is revealed. Later, Joe is sitting alone and the Museum Director tells Joe that it's time to go. Joe explains that they are doing their cleanup, which they do and try to steal the painting.

During the heist, Jack tries to escape and blows his cover. He fights against the other guys as they run through the museum, passing other exhibits including a gigantic hot dog and a large panel comic strip featuring Pluto.

Frank is most intent on getting Jack, but all the guys are kicked over as Jack swings around on a gigantic orbiting mobile.

Jack then lights a lighter and sets off the museum's sprinkler and alarm system and is foiled by a forced-perspective painting, just in time for the rest of the gang to be hauled off by the police.

Joe meets up with Jack, who has been strolling the streets and Jack says that he has something better than the sunflower painting…the police!

Sally arrives and they go off together as Joe is taken off to jail.

Two films appeared with this title in 1943 and 1950, respectively. The first starred The Ritz Brothers; the second starred Fred MacMurray. Neither film has anything to do with this one, story-wise. The Ritz Brothers one does have gangsters as well, but that's where the similarity ends.

This was the only film Jerry Paris directed while at Disney. As such, it resembles Paris' other films of the same vintage such as *Don't Raise the Bridge, Lower the River*(1968), and *Viva Max!* (1969), meaning that it's a little bit more sophisticated than the typical Disney fare of the time but still has a superficial gloss to it. Paris appeared as an actor on Dick Van Dyke's eponymous show earlier in the decade, and appears here in a bit part as a police photographer.

Dick Van Dyke returns to Disney in his first post-Walt film, which is somewhat more substantial than the empty and unfunny *Lt. Robin Crusoe, U.S.N.* (1966). It would be his final film for Disney until 1990's *Dick Tracy*.

A continuity error mentioned on IMDB says: "When Sally is giving Smooth his art lesson, he says he will put more red on the canvas, but uses blue paint instead."

The film was re-released theatrically in 1977 with *The Three Caballeros* and didn't air on the Disney anthology show until 1979 and did reasonable box office business of $6,510,000.

The Horse In the Gray Flannel Suit

RELEASED BY BUENA VISTA ON December 20, 1968, Technicolor. Producer: Winston Hibler. Director: Norman Tokar. Screenplay: Louis Pelletier based on the book *The Year of the Horse* by Eric Hatch. Director of Photography: William Snyder, A.S.C. Art Directors: Carroll Clark, John B. Mansbridge. Set Decorators: Emile Kuri, Frank R. McKelvy. Film Editor: Robert Stafford, A.C.E. Matte Artist and Titles: Alan Maley. Special Effects: Tim Baar. Costume Designer: Bill Thomas. Sound Supervisor: Robert O. Cook. Sound Mixer: Dean Thomas. Second Unit Director: Larry Lansburgh. Costumers: Chuck Keehne, Emily Sundby. Make-up: Otis Malcolm. Hair Stylist: La Rue Matheron. Unit Production Manager: John Bloss. Assistant Director: Christopher Hibler. Music Editor: Evelyn Kennedy. Music: George Bruns. Orchestration: Walter Sheets. Assistant Director: William R. Poole. Gaffer: Otto Meyer. Running time: 113 minutes.

Cast: Dean Jones (Fredrick Bolton), Diane Baker (Suzie Clemens), Lloyd Bochner (Archer Madison), Fred Clark (Tom Dugan), Ellen Janov (Helen Bolton), Morey Amsterdam (Charlie Blake), Kurt Russell (Ronnie Gardner), Lurene Tuttle (Aunt Martha), Alan Hewitt (Harry Tomis), Federico Pinero (Lieutenant Mario Lorendo), Florence MacMichael (Catherine), Joan Marshall (Mimsey), Robin Eccles (Judy Gardner), Adam Williams (Sergeant Roberts), Norman Grabowski (Truck Driver), Bill Baldwin (Announcer), Introducing the Horse of the Year Aspercel, John Cliff (Horse Attendant), Jimmy Cross (Hank, Horse Trainer), Peter Paul Eastman (Spectator), John Indrisano (Masseur), Kenner G. Kemp (Horse Show Stands Extra / Horse Show Judge), Gil Lamb (Bit Comic), Tony Regan (Dugan Executive), Paul Smith (Eddie, the Policeman), Nydia Westman (Woman in Elevator).

Frederick Bolton arrives at Tomes Advertising to make an ad presentation. He is informed that Tom Dugan, the head of Allied Drug, is going to be at the staff meeting.

Before the meeting, Frederick's co-worker Charlie Blake shows off his three-dimensional prop to promote Aspercel, a new pill. It is a male torso with a spiraling transparent esophagus designed to show pills traveling through the body.

At the meeting Tom is not totally impressed with the campaign, claiming that the new campaign lacks imagination. Charlie demonstrates his torso prop again, but it backfires and smokes, so Fred is told that he has 24 hours to come up with a better campaign.

At the riding stable, the horses run around the practice ring with Fred's daughter, Helen, riding. Tom shows up and his allergies to horses set in.

Fred meets S.J. 'Suzie' Clemens, the owner of the stables. Suzie is annoyed that Fred's bills are seven months in arrears, but Tom said he will pay.

Fred and Helen go off together. Helen wants to ask her dad for something, but hesitates, knowing that it will cost a lot of money.

At home, Fred is frantically trying to come up with a new ad campaign that will please Tom.

Helen finally gets the courage to ask her dad for what she wants…a horse of her own. It will cost around $2,000. For Fred, this is out of the question and Helen runs off crying.

Fred and Aunt Martha then discuss Helen's other problems, with herself and with boys and Martha convinces Fred that a horse will build Helen's esteem.

By himself, Fred comes up with an idea that solves both problems… using a horse for the ads and for Helen. He tries to explain this to Tom the next day in the gym that the horse could be named Aspercel, giving out free publicity whenever the horse races.

Fred gets Allied Drug to buy Aspercel, a grey-coated horse who enjoys Fred's beer as he is taken out of the trailer. Helen is in love with the new horse, who turns out to be quite a jumper.

The next day, Judy and Ronnie Gardner are shown arriving at the stables at the same time as Fred, Helen, and Martha. Post time has been rescheduled to only three minutes away, so they hurry to get to the ring. Ronnie comes over to help Fred out and they finish just in time to qualify.

Helen does her jumps on Aspercel but not very well as she does not control the horse well, and she does not qualify for a prize.

Fred is very disappointed because he needs the horse to win for his ad campaign. Fred asks Suzie if she will help Helen with her riding every day so that Aspercel can win. She agrees.

They go through extensive training in order to raise Helen's confidence. The training works and Aspercel wins his first medal.

Tom investigates to see if the horse is working to make Aspercel sell. So far, he is disappointed. Unfortunately, Helen heard every word and is upset about what she has heard. Fortunately, Aspercel gives another flawless performance and wins the blue ribbon. Helen is still upset, however.

Later, Fred comes home early from a plane flight and discovers that he's home alone with Aspercel. He insults the horse but then apologizes, but the horse runs away anyway. Fred does get Aspercel back and tries to ride him to little avail, but eventually succeeds.

Meanwhile, Helen and Martha are upset because they can't find Aspercel anywhere, and they call the police.

When the police arrive, Aspercel runs off with Fred on board, jumping over everything. A police chase begins which ends up with Fred being thrown and some buildings being damaged.

Fred is thrown in jail, but Charlie uses this event to get some publicity and takes photos of Fred in jail. As no one identifies Fred, he spends the night in jail. Helen hears the news about the theft on the radio and dismisses it as another publicity stunt of her father's.

Ronnie shows up next, ready for a date with Helen, but she cancels the date because she is so upset with her dad.

Ronnie waits around and when Fred finally is driven home, he tells him a thing or two about how he's upsetting Helen and how his date was canceled.

Fred goes into speak with Helen and says that he won't force Helen to ride in any more horse shows, and tells her to go out on that date with Ronnie.

Suzie and Fred talk again and now she wants Aspercel to continue entering shows, since he jumped seven feet. Helen doesn't have to participate, so Suzie agrees to ride.

Archer Madison coaches Suzie, but Suzie is thrown during practice. She agrees to continue, but Archer informs her that she has been doing too much teaching and not enough riding, and she needs to do a lot of practice to win the Washington International Horse Show.

At the show everything seems to go well, with the other horse entries running at various skill levels, with some of them knocking off the poles and some of them throwing their riders.

Suzie is the final entry and rides Aspercel without any faults but this is just the preliminary round, with six more days to go. In the end, Aspercel and Rascala are tied for first and have to have a jump off.

Fred comes backstage to say something personal to Suzie, but is thwarted by all the intrusions from Aspercel's competitor Archer, riden by Lieutenant Mario Lorendo.

The final event comes in. On the first go-round, Aspercel does not miss. Lt. Mario goes next and he too has a perfect score, although there were a few touches. A second jump-off occurs.

Lt. Mario goes first this time on Rascala and knocks one brick off on the final wall. He does the course in 37.4 seconds.

Suzie goes next and Aspercel knocks off a pole, but ends up doing the course in 37.2 seconds.

The Allied Drug people are in attendance as Aspercel is declared the winner and gets the awards.

Fred goes down to congratulate Suzie, but sees Suzie and Archer kissing. Archer and Suzie used to be an item, so Fred is a little put off and he takes Aspercel back to the stable while everyone else poses for photographs.

Later Suzie comes backstage and says that she and Archer were kissing not for romance, but congratulations. In the end Fred and Suzie know they are meant for each other, but are still interrupted, although they do kiss in the final photo shoot.

This is a standard horse picture with the only redeeming value being the fine performances by Dean Jones and Kurt Russell and the excellent horse-jumping section in the latter part of the film. The movie aired on the Disney anthology show in 1971 and 1977, and was not a huge success. Jones would do better with his next film...

Note that the movie poster was the first to have the legend "Walt Disney Productions Presents" rather than the traditional "Walt Disney Presents."

The Love Bug

RELEASED BY BUENA VISTA ON December 24, 1968, Technicolor. Producer: Bill Walsh. Director: Robert Stevenson. Screenplay: Bill Walsh, Don DaGradi based on the story *Car-Boy-Girl* by Gordon Buford. Director of Photography: Edward Colman, A.S.C. Art Directors: Carroll Clark, John B. Mansbridge. Film Editor: Cotton Warburton, A.C.E. Set Directors: Emile Kuri, Hal Gausman. Costume Designer: Bill Thomas. Sound Supervisor: Robert O. Cook. Sound Mixer: Dean Thomas. Costumers: Chuck Keehne, Emily Sundby. Make-up: Otis Malcolm. Hair Stylist: La Rue Matheron. Unit Manager: Paul L. Cameron. Assistant Director: Christopher Hibler. Music Editor: Evelyn Kennedy. Special Photographic Effects: Eustace Lycett, Alan Maley, Peter Ellenshaw. Special Effects: Robert A. Mattey, Howard Jensen, Dan Lee. Music: George Bruns. Orchestration: Walter Sheets. Second Unit Director: Arthur J. Vitarelli. The Drivers: Dale Van Sickel, Regina Parton, Bob Drake, Hall Brock, Rex Ramsey, Lynn Grate, Richard Warlock, Everett Creach, Bill Couch, Robert Hoy, Jack Mahoney, Richard Brill, Rudy Doucette, Glenn Wilder, Robert James, Bob Harris, Richard Geary, Jack Perkins, Ronnie Rondell, Reg Parton, Tom Bamford, Marion J. Playan, Bill Hickman, Hal Grist, Larry Schmitz, Dana Derfus, Gerald Jann, Ted Duncan, Gene Roscoe, Charles Willis, Roy Butterfield, J.J. Wilson, Bud Ekins, Gene Curtis, John Timanus, Fred Krone, Jesse Wayne, Fred Stromsoe, Kim Brewer. Driving Sequence Supervisor: Carey Loftin. Second Assistant Director: Robert Webb. Sound Editor: Ben Hendricks, Bill Wylie. Stunts: Max Balchowsky, Steven Burnett, Carey Loftin. Stunt Coordinator: Bob Harris. Stunt Drivers: Carey

Loftin, Tom Steele. Key Grip: Stan Reed. Running time: 108 minutes.

Songs: "Tik-Tak-Polka op. 365," "Die Fledermaus" Written by Johann Strauss.

Cast: Dean Jones (Jim Douglas / Hippie at Carhop), Michele Lee (Carole Bennett), David Tomlinson (Peter Thorndyke), Buddy Hackett (Tennessee Steinmetz), Joe Flynn (Havershaw), Benson Fong (Mr. Wu), Andy Granatelli (Association President), Joe E. Ross (Detective), Ned Glass (Toll Booth Attendant), Gil Lamb (Policeman at Park), Nicole Jaffe (Girl in Dune Buggy), Russ Caldwell (Boy Driving Dune Buggy), P.L. Renoudet (Policeman), Alan Fordney, Gary Owens (Announcer), Iris Adrian (Carhop), Robert Foulk (Bice), Barry Kelley (Police Sergeant), Wally Boag (Annoyed Freeway Driver), Max Balchowsky, Brian Fong (Chinese Carrying Herbie), Stan Duke, Chick Hearn (Announcer), Pedro Gonzalez-Gonzalez (Mexican Driver), Herbie, The Love Bug (Herbie), Larry J. Blake (Race Track Timekeeper), John Cliff (Track Official), Harold Fong (Mr. Wu's Manager), Ben Frommer (Mexican Official), Allen Jung (Gas Station Attendant), Kathryn Minner (Flower Saleswoman), Bing Russell (Race Track Starter), Herb Vigran (Policeman on Bridge).

After a riveting title sequence featuring a smash-up derby, we find driver Jim Douglas crawling out from the wreckage of one of the cars.
Cut to San Francisco and Jim is told that he is too old to race cars anymore. He is driven home by Tennessee Steinmetz, his roommate and car mechanic.
Later, Jim goes to a car dealership to try to secure a car so that he can drive to Bakersfield to enter another car race. He sees the Thorndyke Special, a fantastic new racing car. He is shown the car by Carole Bennett.
Peter Thorndyke thinks Jim is a wealthy customer, but he is looking for something for about $75 when he spots a VW beetle that has mistakenly been left on the showroom floor. However, when they try to remove the car, they find it to be nearly impossible. Jim returns home on a cable car, only to be followed by the VW.
Soon, a man shows up to inform Jim that he's accused of grand theft auto. Jim goes back to the dealership to chew out Mr. Thorndyke, who reluc-

tantly sells the VW to Jim. The VW shows his annoyance with Mr. Thorndyke by squirting oil on his shoe.

Jim drives the car only to discover that the VW has a mind of its own. Carole helps Jim by driving the car with him. Since the car initially shows no apparent problems, Jim agrees that it was all in his mind and drives Carole back to the dealership. The fun begins when some hippies challenge the car to a drag race.

After everything settles, Carole tries to exit the car but cannot, prompting an amusing comment by another hippie (portrayed by Dean Jones).

It turns out the car is trying to match Jim and Carole up, and it takes them to a make-out point. They both get out of the car to walk and the car follows them. After an embarrassing encounter with a police officer, they decide to get back into the car and drive home.

Tennessee sees the car and since he's a spiritualist at heart, he feels that the machines will be taking over and will start to think for themselves. Jim thinks he's nuts and doesn't believe that there is anything unique about the car that can't be repaired.

Since Tennessee is convinced about the VW, he talks to the car and tells him to behave.

Tennessee and Jim take the car for a drive and it runs fine. The car is christened Herbie by Tennessee after his uncle.

Soon, Jim enters Herbie into the races and does remarkably well for a VW in comparison to the other, more powerful cars. Herbie now sports a number 53 on his body.

Thorndyke is in town to watch the race but is not impressed about Herbie until it wins, and then Thorndyke offers to purchase the car back.

Carol proposes to make a little wager at the next race in Riverside. If Herbie wins, Jim owns the car free and clear. If Herbie loses, then Thorndyke gets the car back.

Thorndyke also enters the race and takes a strong lead, with Herbie lagging behind until the final laps. As Herbie passes Thorndyke, he hurls a blob of oil into Thorndyke's face; after he wins, Herbie squirts more oil on Thorndyke's shoe.

Next is a montage of various races and of course Herbie and Jim win them all. Thorndyke also enters these races and loses.

One different type of race is held in Tijuana, where the competitors race through the desert, but he still wins.

Thorndyke still suspects foul play about the car. Meanwhile, Jim and Carole become an item and go on a date in Carol's sports car. Thorndyke uses this opportunity to check Herbie out. Tennessee offers Thorndyke his version of an Irish coffee, which is tremendously potent.

On the date, Jim reveals that he needs a better car that's more appropriate for his racing skills. He still doesn't believe that it's Herbie doing all the winning, and not his own driving skills.

Totally drunk, Thorndyke still manages to sabotage Herbie with the potent Irish coffee, which causes the car to lose the next race while Thorndyke is the victor.

Herbie gets the last laugh by spewing out globs of Irish coffee foam onto Thorndyke as he drives away.

The next day, Carole comes to visit the ailing Herbie at home and apologizes for Thorndyke's deception. She also says that she has resigned from Thorndyke Motors. While Tennessee and Carole discuss the car, Jim drives up in a brand-new Lamborghini. Tennessee is upset because Jim is also going to sell Herbie to Thorndyke to pay for the new car.

Jim and Carole get into a fight about Herbie and soon there is a lot of noise. Jim tells Tennessee to stop making so much noise, but Tennessee says that it's Herbie and not him. The noise does turn out to be Herbie, who has made short work of the Lamborghini, destroying it in the process.

Thorndyke comes by and offers $2000 for Herbie, raising Jim's suspicions about why Thorndyke wants the car so badly. Herbie has driven off during the conflict and Tennessee says that it's up to Jim to get Herbie back.

Jim finally finds Herbie being towed away, but he doesn't catch up to him in time. Herbie is towed to Thorndyke's garage, but soon escapes under cover of the Chinese New Year parade.

Eventually Herbie decides to end it all and Jim discovers the car trying to drive off the Golden Gate Bridge. Jim rescues the car barely in time. The police arrive to find Jim passed out on the hood of Herbie, looking like he was saved by the car and not the other way round.

Soon, a Mr. Wu cites Jim for damages incurred during the parade. Jim has no money to pay, so the car is impounded and will be sold to get the money for Mr. Wu.

Tennessee knows some Chinese and reasons with Mr. Wu, saying that the car that did the damage is the infamous Herbie racing car.

Mr. Wu says that he wants to keep the car now that he knows it is famous. Jim asks Tennessee to tell Mr. Wu that he can keep the car, but he wants to drive the car in the next race, on the condition that if the car wins, Jim gets the car back. Thorndyke approaches Mr. Wu the next day to try to purchase the car from him and to make a wager.

Thorndyke is in this race along with his accomplice, Havershaw. Meanwhile, Herbie is racing with Jim, Carole and Tennessee aboard. During the race, Herbie is back in fine form, tailing the leader Thorndyke by only a few lengths. Thorndyke tries to sabotage Herbie during the race with an oil slick, causing Herbie to spin out, but he skims over the lake water to safety, splashing Thorndyke with mud in his face.

Havershaw steps out of the car to help push Thorndyke's car out of the mud, but he doesn't get back to the car in time. Instead, a bear has replaced

Havershaw in the car.

When Thorndyke realizes that his new passenger is a bear, he loses control of the car again and faints. After he comes to, the car stops and both the bear and Thorndyke flee.

We cut to announcer Gary Owens, who is now monitoring the race on television. After all the chaos Herbie and crew are hopelessly lost, but Mr. Wu's staff helps carry Herbie back to safety and on track.

Since Mr. Wu owns Herbie and the service stations in the Chinese Camp area, the staff quickly gives Herbie a refill but take their sweet time with Thorndyke's car. On the next leg of the race, Herbie is far out in front.

Soon Thorndyke and Havershaw are up to more tricks, changing the arrows on a directional sign and causing all the cars to go into a mining tunnel. Thorndyke is back out in front and he and Havershaw celebrate with some champagne, but their celebration is short-lived as they witness Herbie back on track and out front again.

Their next plan is to bump Herbie, causing his front tire to fall off. Without a wheel, Herbie almost drives off a cliff. The passengers barely make it to safety. They try to put on the spare, but it has been sliced into sections.

The three manage to drive on three wheels for a while, but they eventually lose another wheel. Herbie comes in sporting a huge wagon wheel!

At night, during the leg rest, Jim tells Mr. Wu that the prospects of winning now look grim and Mr. Wu agrees. Soon, Thorndyke comes by to collect Herbie. Thorndyke is now the rightful owner, since they are forfeiting. Now Herbie is mad. He won't let Thorndyke take him and the Douglas team continues the next leg of the race.

The next day, Herbie tries to rush the Thorndyke car and almost gets disqualified. After this outburst things seem to be back to normal, but Thorndyke has more tricks up his sleeve. In the meantime, Herbie takes a number of shortcuts to get back into the lead but is soon bumped off the road by Thorndyke.

Eventually Herbie gets back in the race again and as Thorndyke tries another dirty trick, he manages to get thrown into Herbie's trunk. The glove box is opened and Thorndyke cries "Get me out of here!"

Herbie lets Thorndyke out and he screams for Havershaw. Announcer Owens states that Herbie is back in the lead, but they are not in the clear yet, as Herbie literally splits in two! With Herbie in two halves, Thorndyke is not allowed to pass but he eventually does as Herbie's back half passes Herbie's front half in the race. Herbie's back half goes past the finish line first, as Herbie takes both first and third place. Thorndyke comes in second.

Mr. Wu takes over Thorndyke's car dealership and Thorndyke and Havershaw are employed by Mr. Wu as car mechanics. In their annoyance, Thorndyke and Havershaw squirt oil on each other. Finally, Jim and Carole have gotten married and go off on their honeymoon together, leaving Tennessee and Mr. Wu to watch the store.

On the DVD commentary, Dean Jones claims that Walt Disney did give his personal seal of approval on this film after giving him a story about the first sports car brought to America, which is why this posthumous film seems so much in line with what Walt would do. Though Walt was long dead by the time of this film's general release in 1969, its outstanding success echoed the earlier times of *Mary Poppins* and it seemed for a time that Disney without Walt would seemingly do just fine. This was true during the 1960s and essentially true during the first half of the 1970s before trouble started to brew.

Incidentally, in the scene featuring Buddy Hackett speaking in Chinese with Benson Fong, they really were conversing in Chinese.

Yvette Mimieux was originally going to be cast as Carole and Herbie was originally going to be a red VW.

Herbie is a white, 1963 grey ragtop sunroof Sedan Volkswagen with added red, white, and blue racing stripes and a large number 53. According to Dean Jones, there were eight Herbies used in the film, including various stunt versions like the car that split in two and other bugs in various states of collision. One of the stunt versions is now owned by Dean Jones. Jimmy McDonald did Herbie's various car sounds. Herbie got his name from a gag in Buddy Hackett's comedy act. Los Angeles Dodger Don Drysdale's number was 53 and Disney used that number for Herbie in Don's honor (One wonders if Drysdale was ever aware of this dubious honor).

On March 23, 1969, Disneyland had a "Love Bug" Day, where park guests brought their VWs to decorate and show off in the parking lot. Silent film footage exists of this event. The entrants' cars paraded down Main Street inside Disneyland. Dean Jones was on hand to help judge the contestants. The winner of the best-dressed bug won their very own, full-sized Herbie VW.

Michele Lee reveals that both Martin Luther King, Jr. and Robert Kennedy were shot and killed during the shooting of this film; quite ironic considering the theme of the movie.

This turned out to be the top-grossing film of 1969. It was produced for $4.2 million and grossed $51.2 million in the first few months and was one of the top 10 highest-grossing films of all time for quite some time right behind *Gone with the Wind* (1939) according to Jones on the commentary. This is doubly strange, as it was a year where an X-rated film won Best Picture: *Midnight Cowboy* (1969).

It is also revealed on the commentary that Volkswagen put up $1.5 million in promotion. Working titles for this film included the original story title *Boy/Car/Girl*, *The Magic Volksy*, *Beetlebomb* and *Thunderbug* before settling on *The Love Bug*.

The Love Bug is quintessential Disney, and as such the movie spawned three theatrical sequels during the 1970s and 80s, a TV mini-series in 1981, a 1997 TV movie and yet another theatrical feature film in 2005. He even appeared in the 1973 edition of Disney on Parade. The original film first aired on TV in 1979 and again in 1981.

Though the property is somewhat dormant again, it is highly likely that it will be resurrected again for another movie or TV series. It's strange that Herbie has never spawned a theme park ride since its vehicle links would make it a natural, although the car did appear briefly as part of the Disney/MGM Studios Tour and as part of Walt Disney World's All-Star Movies Resort.

Wikipedia mentions two deleted scenes: "A scene shot, but not included in the final cut of the film, featured Jim calling at a used car lot prior to his visiting Thorndyke's auto showroom. This missing sequence has long since been lost, and all that remains is the script and a single black-and-white photograph of Jim talking with the salesman at the lot.

An unfilmed scene at the end of the story that was scripted and storyboarded was to have shown Herbie playing with children at a nearby playground prior to taking the newly-married Jim and Carole off on their honeymoon."

Also: "During one scene in the movie, Herbie has lost one of his wheels, and Tennessee is hanging out of the passenger side door to balance him. The door opens, and there is no "53" logo on the door. This image was used heavily to promote the film."

The opening scenes of the film featuring the smash-up derby are stock footage from the film *Fireball 500* (1966), starring Frankie Avalon and Annette Funicello.

Incidentally, Bing Russell is Kurt Russell's father.

1969

1969 was a bit slim on the Disney movie release schedule with only three new releases during the year, but what a year! *The Love Bug* turned out to be Disney's biggest movie hit to date, and the studio took home yet another Oscar for the animated short *It's Tough to Be a Bird*. *Hang Your Hat on the Wind* was a live-action short theatrical release.

Non-theatrical movies released this year include *Pancho, Fastest Paw in the West, The Secret of Boyne Castle, Nature's Better Built Homes, Ride a Northbound Horse, Wild Geese Calling, My Dog, the Thief, Varda, the Peregrine Falcon, The Secrets of the Pirates Inn,* and *Inky, the Crow*. The anthology show also had a title change from *The Wonderful World of Color* to *The Wonderful World of Disney*, reflecting the no-longer-necessary requirement of mentioning that the Disney show was in color, since by 1969 virtually all TV was in color.

This year continued the sponsorship of the show by Gulf Oil. This led to a six-issue magazine series also called *The Wonderful World of Disney Magazine*, which was given away to gasoline purchasers and featured new and reprinted articles from *Walt Disney's Magazine* from the 1950s.

The shorts *Donald's Diary, Donald's Dream Voice, How to Play Baseball, How to Swim, Pluto's Kid Brother, Sheep Dog, Tiger Trouble,* and features *Peter Pan* (1953), *The Incredible Journey* (1963), *Swiss Family Robinson* (1960), *101 Dalmatians* (1961) and *Fantasia* (1940) were reissued.

Work continued on *The Aristocats* (1970), but an idea called *Hootsie the Owl* was also worked on although nothing ever came of it even though it was worked on from time to time for over three decades, according to Charles Solomon's *The Disney That Never Was*.

At Disneyland, the Haunted Mansion finally opened on August 9 and the Walt Disney World project continued, with actual construction beginning in April.

Mineral King now hit a major snag as a conservationist group sought an injunction on the project that lasted for ten years. The results were that

Disney eventually abandoned the project and Mineral King became part of Sequoia National Park.

The big animated hit of the year was not a Disney cartoon, but rather *A Boy Named Charlie Brown*.

Non-soundtrack record releases included *Misty the Mischievous Mermaid*, *The Haunted Mansion*, a series of albums based on the *Oz* books by L. Frank Baum, and *Goldilocks*, a DePatie-Freleng animated TV special.

In the comic book world, Gold Key continued to publish *Donald Duck*, *Mickey Mouse*, *Uncle Scrooge*, *Walt Disney's Comics and Stories*, *The Beagle Boys*, *Huey, Dewey and Louie Junior Woodchucks*, *Super Goof*, *Chip 'n' Dale*, *Moby Duck*, *Scamp*, and *Walt Disney Comics Digest*, while *Zorro* ended its run.

One-shots included *Davy Crockett*, *Peter Pan*, and *Mickey Mouse Surprise Party*.

Al Taliaferro passed away this year. He had been drawing the *Donald Duck* comic strip since its debut in 1938. The strip continued with Frank Grundeen. Bob Karp continued the writing.

And, Disney on Parade debuted as a successful traveling stage show that pre-dated the latter-day success, Disney on Ice.

Smith!

RELEASED BY BUENA VISTA ON March 21, 1969, Technicolor. Producer: Bill Anderson. Director: Michael O'Herlihy. Screenplay: Louis Pelletier based on the book, *Breaking Smith's Quarter Horse* by Paul St. Pierre. Director of Photography: Robert C. Moreno. Art Directors: John B. Mansbridge, Robert E. Smith. Film Editor: Robert Stafford, A.C.E. Set Decorators: Emile Kuri, Hal Gausman. Associate Producer: Tom Leetch. Title Design: Alan Maley. Sound Supervisor: Robert O. Cook. Sound Mixer: Roger Parish. Costumers: Chuck Keehne, Emily Sundby. Make-up: Otis Malcolm. Hair Stylist: La Rue Matheron. Assistant Director: Russell Llewellyn. Music Editor: Evelyn Kennedy. Music: Robert F. Brunner. Orchestration: Walter Sheets. Running time: 102 minutes.

Song: "The Ballad of Smith and Gabriel Jimmyboy" Written and Sung by Bobby Russell.

Cast: Glenn Ford (Smith), Nancy Olson (Norah Smith), Dean Jagger (Judge James C. Brown), Keenan Wynn (Sheriff Vince Heber), Warren Oates (Walter Charlie), Chief Dan George (Ol' Antoine), Frank Ramirez (Gabriel Jimmyboy), John Randolph (Mr. Edwards), Christopher Shea (Alpie Smith), Roger Ewing (Donald Maxwell), Jay Silverheels (McDonald Lasheway), James Westerfield (Sheriff), Fred Aldrich (Restaurant Patron), William Bryant (Corporal / Court Bailiff), Eric Clavering (Native on Motorcycle), Ricky Cordell (Peterpaul), Melanie Griffith (Extra), Gregg Palmer (Sergeant / Court Bailiff).

Smith's son Alpie feeds his horse Tasha an apple and then tries to ride him, but is thrown. He then catches up with Smith, who has been gone for three days.

Charlie the dog chases the cows into the pen as Smith faces up to his wife Norah. She's not mad, but instead concerned about Gabriel Jimmyboy, who is a Native American suspected of murder and living on their land.

About this time, their good friend Antoine stops by and they all eat supper. Alpie asks Antoine if he's going to break his Appaloosa horse so that he can ride it.

Norah asks about the man who is living in an old shack near their property. She's concerned because of the murder and Antoine gets up and leaves. Norah is not ashamed because she is ultimately fed up with the Indians living in their town.

Soon, Alpie goes out to play with Peter Paul, an Indian friend of his.

Smith meanwhile says that he is the spokesman for the Indians, because they don't have a voice for themselves, and goes to check up on Gabriel.

Sheriff Vince is on the lookout for Gabriel and asks Smith if he's seen him. Smith sends them on the other way and Smith continues on to the cabin to check up on Gabriel.

Inside the cabin, a rifle is pulled on Smith as they don't trust him. Antoine is inside and he suggests Smith take Gabriel to Canada to hide. Smith says that to prove his innocence he has to go on trial, not run away.

Meanwhile, Norah tells Alpie to stay put as she looks for Smith, and she soon shows up at the cabin to bring him home.

Gabriel is worried because he cannot afford a lawyer. Smith explains that the Indian Bureau will get him a lawyer, but they don't trust the Bureau.

Norah continues to believe that Gabriel is guilty.

The next day, Alpie and Peter Paul are sneaking around the cabin to see what Gabriel is doing, and he pulls the rifle on them. He still claims his innocence of the murder. Alpie says that he will bring food to Gabriel and promises not to tell anyone where he is hiding.

Meanwhile, Walter Charlie rides up on his bike to visit Smith. Walter Charlie is a half-breed and will be the Court Interpreter for Gabriel's case. He offers Smith $150 to turn in Gabriel. Norah walks up and is upset at Smith for turning it down.

Soon, Sheriff Vince is back with some hound dogs to try to find Gabriel again and Smith sends them on their way to the old copper mine. It turns out that Gabriel really is at the old copper mine, as Alpie reveals, so Smith hightails it to the mine to warn Gabriel, but Vince gets there first. Gabriel is not there, however.

Instead he's at the Sheriff's office, as Antoine has turned Gabriel in and gets a $500 reward. It was all Gabriel's plan, in order to get Antoine some money.

Soon, Antoine is riding in a $500 used car with Walter Charlie driving, while Gabriel spends time in jail.

Vince says that he's going to take Gabriel down to Williamstown until the trial starts. Smith asks him why. He still believes Gabriel's innocence and wonders why Vince didn't stop the altercation that led to the murder in the first place. He suspects prejudice.

Smith catches up with Antoine and Walter and accuses Walter of being a chiseler. He then asks why Antoine can't drive and he says he doesn't want to. The car is in rough shape with lousy brakes and soon skids off the road into a lake. Smith catches up with them and helps rescue them out of the water.

Walter asks what to do with the car now and Smith suggests getting a paddle and turning it into a canoe.

Back at home, Smith is making a care package for Gabriel. Norah is trying to figure out how to make the farm they live on more profitable.

A group of Indians, headed up by one named McDonald, arrive in many cars to see Gabriel's trial. Smith is disappointed because they are supposed to be working on his crops.

Smith admits to Norah that he's a terrible rancher and that he spends too much time with the Indians. Norah says that he wants to go the trial. Smith wonders how she knows and Norah says that it's written all over his face. Ultimately, Norah lets him go. Before he goes he tries to get the trial on the radio, but fails.

Another Indian named Young Alexander rides up with news that Antoine is now in jail, because he went to the wrong court. Antoine sent Alexander to retrieve Smith.

Smith says he can't go, but he goes anyway. Norah says to go and will cut every single stalk of hay herself with a pair of scissors, and also gives Smith the $79 she was saving for a trip.

Smith takes Alpie and soon they are in Williamstown. On the way, Alpie asks why nobody likes Indians when some of their best friends are Indians.

Meanwhile, Gabriel's lawyer is trying to get some answers from him but he won't speak unless Antoine is there, who can't be since he is in jail.

Smith and Alpie inadvertently meet up with Walter, and they discuss the trial and Walter's interpretations.

Walter accidentally spills something on a fellow café patron, and a minor scuffle ensues. When Smith goes to intervene, the café owner thinks Smith is the one who is causing the commotion. After a slug in Smith's face, the fact that he and Walter are friends is revealed.

Soon the trial begins, but Gabriel's lawyer Maxwell says that he wants everything postponed until Gabriel speaks, who still won't talk until Antoine shows up. The other side is expecting the trial to continue regardless.

Antoine finally arrives with Smith and the trial can begin, but he needs an interpreter for his words and Gabriel does his interpretations. His lawyer needs to know exactly what happened on the night of the murder, but Antoine keeps talking about the lousy prison food.

Finally Walter shows up to interpret and to get Antoine to speak as a witness. The lawyer still wants Antoine to speak about the night of the murder, but Antoine insists upon speaking about anything but the murder and wants to tell an anecdote about Chief Joseph. This prompts laughter from the courtroom.

Smith stands up and gets angry about all the outbursts and is almost ejected from the courtroom. In the end he can stay, because Antoine wants Smith rather than Walter, to translate.

Antoine starts to explain what happened on the day of the murder, but still goes through his story of Chief Joseph in order to tell it.

After Antoine's interpretation, Sheriff Vince teases Smith about the Indians and he soon receives a right hook. Smith is fined $50 for contempt of court, but his flippant attitude towards the penalty throws him in jail for 33 days.

Unfortunately it is still haying time, so McDonald has to take Alpie home. McDonald assures Smith that they will take care of the hay.

Back at home, the Indians hold a vigil but they do take care of the hay.

The court has another problem now as Antoine is sitting on the steps of the courthouse until Smith is released. The judge tells him that it is illegal to do this. Antoine surprises the judge by speaking in English. The judge agrees to let Smith go early if Antoine speaks English in court from now on, and eventually Gabriel is set free.

Norah and Alpie keep working on the field. Smith has been released and comes home, but Norah still tries to work the fields by herself. The Indians finally come through to help them out to get the harvesting completed in time.

Antoine arrives and says that he will finally break Alpie's horse.

Smith! is a surprisingly realistic dramatic film in comparison to the fare usually released by Disney, but since it was not a success, Disney quickly reverted back to the formula comedic, animated, and animal films they were best known for. They would not do a film like this again for quite some time.

Chief Dan George and Glenn Ford both turn in excellent performances. Had the movie been made by another studio, it may have even been Oscar-worthy, but as it was Disney this aspect of the film was totally ignored.

Another reason this film stands out is that it was not made in the typical Disney way, with tons of syrupy music playing constantly in the background and punctuating every scene, so it looks like a contemporary film made by another movie studio. However, a negative complaint about the film is that everything is wrapped up a bit too swiftly and tidily, which is typical Disney. Strangely, it never aired on the Disney anthology show.

Rascal

RELEASED BY BUENA VISTA ON June 11, 1969, Technicolor. Producer: James Algar. Director: Norman Tokar. Screenplay: Harold Swanton based on the book by Sterling North. Director of Photography: William Snyder, A.S.C. Art Director; John B. Mansbridge. Film Editor: Norman R. Palmer, A.C.E. Set Decorators: Emile Kuri, Frank R. McKelvy. Animal Supervision: Henry L. Cowl, Gerry Lynn Washauer. Second Unit Director: Arthur J. Vitarelli. Matte Artist: Alan Maley. Special Effects: Eustace Lycett. Sound Supervisor: Robert O. Cook. Sound Mixer: Dean Thomas. Costumes: Rosemary O'Dell. Costumers: Chuck Keehne, Emily Sundby. Make-up: Otis Malcolm. Hair Stylist: La Rue Matheron. Unit Production Manager: John Bloss. Assistant Director: Christopher Hibler. Music Editor: Evelyn Kennedy. Music: Buddy Baker. Orchestration: Walter Sheets. Running time: 93 minutes.

Song: "Summer Sweet" by Bobby Russell.

Cast: Steve Forrest (Willard North), Bill Mumy (Sterling North), Pamela Toll (Theo North), Elsa Lanchester (Mrs. Satterfield), Henry Jones (Garth Shadwick), Bettye Ackerman (Miss Whalen), Jonathan Daly (Reverend Gabriel Thurman), John Fiedler (Cy Jenkins), Richard Erdman (Walt Dabbett), Herbert Anderson (Mr. Pringle), Robert Emhardt (Constable Stacy), Steve Carlson (Norman Bradshaw), Walter Pidgeon (The Voice of Sterling North), Maudie Prickett (Miss Prince-nez).

This story of a teenage boy named Sterling and his pet raccoon named Rascal begins on the last day of the school year. The students report on what they plan to do over the summer. When the teacher gets to Sterling, she discovers him drawing a picture of the canoe he plans to work on.

Soon, Sterling's father Willard shows up to take him home, but first he shows Sterling a lynx that he's found. Then they sit down and chat about life while grabbing a quick bite to eat.

They soon hear the lynx screech and come across a wild raccoon family that flees from them. After a bit, another one of the raccoons comes out by itself and Willard and Sterling decide to take him home.

Sterling names the raccoon Rascal. Sterling's sister, Theo, was home to help out during the school year.

We are introduced to neighbors Garth Chadwick and Cy Jenkins, who are not fond of Rascal and consider him a varmint and not a proper pet. It turns out that the other animals react positively to Rascal, so he is left alone.

Theo has a discussion with her father, who wishes that she would stay and not go back up North, but Theo has a boyfriend there that she's very fond of.

Soon snooty Mrs. Satterfield stops by to express her disgust with having a raccoon in the neighborhood, but Sterling's father lets him keep Rascal as long as he stays out of trouble.

Theo goes home and Willard goes on one of his regular trips, so Sterling is left to his own devices. Sterling and Theo exchange letters.

In the letters, Sterling discusses winning a pie-eating contest with Rascal, but Theo is concerned about Mrs. Satterfield. Sterling doesn't answer and only responds with comments about what Rascal is doing. Finally, Sterling responds that Mrs. Satterfield is fine.

Sterling claims that this is the best summer of his life. This is accentuated by a montage of various scenes of Sterling and Rascal hanging out.

Finally, Sterling gets around to building the canoe that he was dreaming about during the school year. With Sterling focusing his attentions elsewhere, Rascal starts getting into more and more mischief, and he gets into Cy's corn.

Sterling's problems were beginning just as his teacher Miss Whalen and Reverend Thurman come to visit.

Sterling explains that he has to train Rascal to act more human and less like a raccoon, and he shows how he's trained him so far. Miss Whalen explains that Rascal won't be so good when he gets older and will eventually leave.

Sterling's father comes home with the harvest and shares his good fortune of food with the guests. The reverend tries to explain that Sterling shouldn't be left alone, but Sterling's father ignores his suggestions.

During dinner, Rascal gets into Garth's eggs and things go from bad to worse. Mrs. Folger found Rascal in her jam jars, and Mrs. Kraus found Rascal in her molasses. Sterling tried to block the escape routes, but Rascal was able to escape again and again.

Finally, Mr. Stacy, the sheriff, puts his foot down about Rascal. In the meantime, an argument ensues about horses vs. motorcars among some of the local townspeople and Rascal escapes again and raids the local general store, creating general havoc.

The sheriff pulls out his violation book and later Sterling's father builds a reinforced cage made with chicken wire for Rascal to keep him under control. It is ultimately decided that Rascal should be set free in the woods to fend for himself.

Meanwhile, the big horse vs. motorcar race gets underway at Miller's Grove, with the horse ultimately the victor as the car ends up in the river thanks to Rascal's help.

Theo now comes home with her boyfriend Norman to meet her father. At one point, Norman steps into the bank. Theo meets up with Mrs. Satterfield, who claims to have not been over to the house during the entire summer. Upset, Theo takes the wheel and leaves Norman behind at the bank.

Theo gripes to Sterling about leaving Mrs. Satterfield in the lurch. Sterling responds by saying that Mrs. Satterfield is nothing like their deceased mother and he didn't want her around.

Father comes home and tells Theo to ignore the mess, but Theo starts cleaning anyway. She also reveals that she can't marry Norman because she wants to take charge of Sterling's life since father is never there for him.

At night, Willard and Norman can't sleep and they have a discussion about Theo and Sterling.

Meanwhile, Rascal sees a female raccoon through the window of Sterling's room and escapes to be with her. Sterling goes after Rascal, but Rascal bites him. Sterling's father mends the bite with some iodine and Sterling realizes that he will have to let Rascal go.

Sterling finally gets his canoe ready and takes Rascal back to where he belongs, where another female raccoon is waiting. Rascal runs off to her.

The same lynx from the beginning of the film returned to get Rascal, but this time Rascal was able to protect himself and his mate.

Sterling goes home on his canoe.

This film was Billy Mumy's first major acting assignment after completing three seasons on the popular *Lost in Space* TV series, which also starred another Disney alumnus, Guy Williams. Mumy's acting career went on a downward spiral after this and he eventually turned to music, becoming half of the popular novelty singing act Barnes and Barnes, whose biggest hit was "Heads."

Mumy remembers that he had to eat about 14 apple pies one day and that turned him off of eating apple pies for about 20 years.

He also said that on one take where he lifted up Rascal to say, "I'm going to call you…Rascal," the raccoon defecated on him. On that take, Mumy wound up saying "I'm going to call you…shit!"

One scene near the beginning of the film shows Sterling and Rascal eating out of the same pie tin. I don't know about you, but I don't think I would want to be eating off the same plate as a raccoon!

Herbert Anderson, who plays Mr. Pringle, is best known as Dennis the Menace's father on that popular sitcom. This was his final film role, but he continued to work in TV for a few more years before retiring in 1975. He died in 1994.

The film aired on TV in 1973. Apparently, this was the first film Gene Shalit reviewed professionally. He gave it a negative review. I don't find it that bad, but it's not that great, either.

The Computer Wore Tennis Shoes

RELEASED BY BUENA VISTA ON December 31, 1969, Technicolor. Producer: Bill Anderson. Director: Robert Butler. Writer: Joseph L. McEveety. Director of Photography: Frank Phillips, A.S.C. Art Director: John B. Mansbridge. Set Decorators: Emile Kuri, Hal Gausman. Second Unit Director: Arthur J. Vitarelli. Titles: Alan Maley. Sound Supervisor: Robert O. Cook. Sound Mixer: Dean Thomas. Costumes: Chuck Keehne, Emily Sundby. Make-up: Robert J. Schiffer. Hair Stylist: La Rue Matheron. Assistant Director: Christopher Hibler. Music Editor: Evelyn Kennedy. Associate Producer: Joseph L. McEveety. Film Editor: Cotton Warburton, A.C.E. Music: Robert F. Brunner. Orchestration: Walter Sheets. Digital Asset Manager Remastering: Diane Wright. Stunts: Dick Warlock. Running time: 90 minutes.

Song: "The Computer Wore Tennis Shoes" Robert F. Brunner, Bruce Belland.

Cast: Kurt Russell (Dexter Riley), Cesar Romero (A.J. Arno), Joe Flynn (Dean Higgins), William Schallert (Professor Quigley), Alan Hewitt (Dean Collingsgood), Richard Bakalyan (Chillie Walsh), Debbie Paine (Annie), Frank Webb (Pete Oatzel), Michael McGreevey (Richard Schuyler), Jon Provost (Bradley), Frank Welker (Henry Fathington), Alexander Clarke (Myles Mill-

er), Bing Russell (Angelo), Pat Harrington (Moderator), Fabian Dean (Little Mac), Fritz Feld (Sigmund Van Dyke), Pete Renoudet (Lieutenant Hannah), Hillyard Anderson (J. Reedy), Fred Aldrich (College of Knowledge Show Attendee), Ed Begley, Jr. (Student), Gail Bonney (Winifred, Dean's Secretary), Paul Bradley (Collingsgood Associate), David Canary (Mr. Walski), John Cliff (Police Turnkey), Howard Culver (Moderator), Peter Paul Eastman (Party Guest), William Fawcett (Dietes – College Regent), Robert Foulk (Police Desk Sergeant), Myron Healey (Police Detective), Jonathan Hole (Scientist), Kenner G. Kemp (Extra), Heather Menzies-Urich (Extra), Byron Morrow (Leonard – College Regent), Gregory Morton (Doctor Rufus Schmidt), George N. Neise (College of Knowledge Sponsor), Judson Pratt (Detective in Gambling Raid), Tony Regan (Party Guest), Bruce Rhodewalt (Man with Umbrella), Leoda Richards (Party Guest), Jeffrey Sayre (Man Seated in Control Room), Maid Severn (Party Guest), Olan Soule (TV Announcer), Hal Taggart (Waiter at Track), Arthur Tovey (Man in Suit Outside of Set).

We open with Dean Higgins complaining about the costs of a computer with Professor Quigley. Higgins argues that purchasing one is out of the question, due to the expense.

Dexter Riley and his friends are secretly listening in on the meeting on a walkie-talkie to hear what's being discussed.

Higgins looks out the window and wonders why Riley and his friends are always meeting at the same time when they are meeting.

The next item on Higgins' agenda is 'dead wood' and Higgins recommends certain students be placed on probation due to their lack of scholastic performance and achievement. Most of these students are the ones listening in on the proceedings.

Dexter radios in to the meeting about Schuyler, who was somehow missing on the probation list. Higgins adds Schuyler onto the list, blithely unaware that it is Dexter suggesting the name via walkie-talkie.

The gang decides to approach multi-millionaire A.J. Arno to hit him up for the computer to save the college expenses. Arno rejects the idea because of his many prior donations. Arno thinks again about it and decides privately that if he donates the computer, he could use the same computer to his advantage by feeding it information about gambling.

After the students leave, we see the inner workings of A.J. Arno's company; he's been using computers he owns for organizing and placing his gambling bets. He contributes the computer and withdraws his other monetary donations to the school.

Soon, Quigley is setting up the computer and Higgins is upset about the withdrawal of the cash contributions to the school.

Quigley starts teaching and sets about to prove how a computer can replace a human brain, by doing an experiment to feed a cat and deliver groceries while it's raining. The experiment goes off without a hitch, but some other experiments fail.

Higgins announces the upcoming University Intelligence Classification tests. Medfield came in 36th last year, but wants improvement this year.

The failed experiment on the computer turns out to be due to a faulty part. Dexter tells Quigley that he'll pick up the part even though the shop is 70 miles away. He studies while driving and arrives back at Medfield during a heavy rainstorm. Inside the classroom, he hooks up the missing part and accidentally electrocutes himself in the process. The result is not death, but a terrific shock that transfers the computer's database into Dexter's brain.

Dexter speaks in his sleep like a computer and the next day he quickly speeds through a test Quigley has handed out, finishing it in record time. With his spare time he decides to eat his lunch, which turns out to be especially crunchy and distracts all the other test-taking students with his loud crunching sounds. He even finds time to answer a few questions on Annie's paper.

Later, Higgins figures that Dexter has cheated, having finished the test in 4½ minutes without error. A doctor, Quigley, and Higgins look inside Dexter's brain with an x-ray and discover computer images, gambling images, and female images. Quigley feels that there was no cheating and recommends Dexter for the College Knowledge TV show for the brightest students. Prior to the show, a preliminary question and answer panel is held to test Dexter's knowledge. Dean Collingsgood from State is in attendance, much to Higgins' chagrin. Collingsgood brags about his college-building expansion. Higgins feels that he will try to recruit Dexter away from Medfield.

Dexter easily answers all the questions that are posed to him although he comes across as extremely cocky and self-assured, even with women, which annoys Dexter's girlfriend, the aforementioned Annie.

Dexter has now become a celebrity and is flown to meet other nations' delegates and is able to speak with all of them as he is now fluent with all languages. Dexter is now sent to various functions, including a diamond-cutting ceremony with Sigmund Van Dyke. Dexter warns Van Dyke about cutting the diamond incorrectly, but Van Dyke ignores Dexter's warnings and Van Dyke shatters the diamond.

Dexter is also on-hand at a rocket launch. He is now in great demand by Dean Collingsgood, who wants to recruit him to State and be on their team for the College Knowledge program. He's also in demand by A.J. Arno, who wants him to come work for him, and he's in demand by Dean Higgins, who has discovered that Dexter has not yet signed up for the next semester at Medfield.

Dexter shows up to the horseraces with Arno and Chillie, Arno's henchman, in tow. Arno uses Dexter to make betting predictions, which works great.

Meanwhile, Higgins and Collingsgood are still in competition to woo Dexter to their respective schools at a posh dinner party which unfortunately features illegal gambling and both Deans are thrown in prison, along with Dexter and Chillie. Dexter is soon freed as his friends come up with his bail.

Dexter is grateful and realizes what a jerk he has been in recent times. Back at the university, Dexter memorizes the encyclopedia. He has also agreed to re-enroll with Medfield.

Quigley comes by to remind him that he needs three other panelists for the College Knowledge show. Higgins recommends some smart students, but Dexter wants his friends. They go along with Dexter, in order to not ruffle Dexter's feathers.

Medfield wins easily over Patterson College, with Dexter answering virtually all of the questions.

The next time, Medfield is up against Franklin University and again sweeps, but a question at the end with the answer of 'applejack' causes Dexter to momentarily go into a strange computer tape loop.

Arno has been watching and he shuts down his Applejack gambling division as a precaution. He also sends Chillie (now free) to kidnap Dexter and see what makes him tick.

A detective is told of Dexter's disappearance, with Higgins suspecting Collingsgood of the kidnapping. Annie and Pete play back a tape with Applejack on it, trying to figure out why he was talking about Applejack. They figure it came from the computer when Dexter got that huge shock. They also figure that Applejack is code for A.J. as in A.J. Arno. They tell Schuyler to take the tapes to the detective, who feels that they do contain some useful information.

Meanwhile, Pete and Annie are scoping out Arno's office building and follow Chillie when he leaves in his car.

They find Dexter helping Chillie with the horse predictions, but decide not to do anything until they plan out their strategy and make sure they aren't caught.

When they come back, Dexter's friends are disguised as house painters. Chillie checks it out by calling the number, which goes to Schuyler back at the college. Schuyler is in on the gag and answers that everything's ok. They paint the house an atrocious orange and pea-green color. Bradley mixes this up, but it ultimately doesn't really matter.

Meanwhile, at the start of the College Knowledge show, Higgins and Quigley are frantically wondering where Dexter is.

Soon Arno shows up at the painted house and is wondering what the painters are up to. Chillie says he checked it out, but Arno checks again just in case. Without Schuyler there to intercept the call, Arno discovers that it's all a big joke and so the kids start to flee, but not before they get Dexter in a big trunk and shove him out the window.

Unfortunately, the fall from the upper floor has adverse effects on Dexter's brain, but this is not immediately apparent.

Chillie and Arno try to follow the kids, but they are out of gas. They follow in a cart␣that has been left behind and chase after the kids who have Dexter and are quickly taking them to the College Knowledge TV show.

To slow Arno down, they pour paint on the highway. This has a temporary effect, but eventually the kids resort to throwing everything onto the road. At the end, they spray paint into the face of Arno and onto the windshield and the bad guys crash, allowing the kids to get to the TV studio.

The game is underway and Medfield is failing without Dexter. Dexter arrives, but has difficulty walking after being trapped in the trunk so long. They finally get them in for the game.

Meanwhile, the detectives have used the kids' clues and discover Arno's criminal activities and go in for the arrest.

The game show continues, but Dexter is noticeably more stressed as he cannot answer the questions so easily, tying everything up with Springfield State. As time goes on it takes longer and longer for Dexter to reveal the answers until his computer brain finally gives out and he passes out. State answers the question and takes the lead.

There is one final question, but Dexter is done. He doesn't know the answer. Fortunately, the final question is one that Schuyler knows. He gives the answer and Medfield wins.

Arno and his gang finally show up to the TV studio, but Dexter and the gang leave just in time. Not so for Arno as they accidentally crash into Lt. Hannah's car and the arrests are made.

We end just as the film began, with Dean Higgins having a staff meeting bemoaning the fact that Medfield has no money for an electro-helio spectrograph, despite having won the money from the College Knowledge show. Annie asks Dexter what the electro-helio spectrograph is and he says he doesn't know, and they are happy about that.

This was the first of three Dexter Riley college comedies. The latter two were *Now You See Him, Now You Don't* (1972) and *The Strongest Man in the World* (1975). You could arguably say that this is a continuation of four previous college-related comedies from Disney: *The Absent-Minded Professor* (1961), *Son of Flubber* (1962), *The Misadventures of Merlin Jones* (1964), and *The Monkey's Uncle* (1965). In the latter two, the college is called Midvale and not Medfield as in the others.

The series may have continued beyond this point except for the untimely death of Joe Flynn in 1974. Kurt Russell was getting pretty long in the tooth by 1975 and was eager to move into more adult roles, which he did soon thereafter in his portrayal of Elvis as well as in the raunchy adult comedy, *Used Cars* (1980).

Some interesting casting choices for this film: Jon Provost appears in his first ostensibly grown-up role since vacating *Lassie*, and well-known voice artist Frank Welker, who was concurrently portraying Fred on the long-running *Scooby-Doo, Where Are You?* cartoon series for Hanna-Barbera, also appears as one of Dexter's friends.

Cesar Romero, looking for work post-*Batman*, makes his first of three appearances here as villain A.J. Arno. His work on this and subsequent Disney films is of the highest level. Strangely, in this film he closely resembles Walt Disney in his twilight years.

One uncredited role went to Ed Begley, Jr., who appears here as one of the Springfield State College Knowledge TV show panelists.

The Computer Wore Tennis Shoes was another in a long line of movies originally intended for television and the Disney anthology show, but as usual the results turned out far better than anticipated, so the film was released theatrically. This is one reason why many Disney films from the 1970s are 3x4 aspect ratio, as they were originally intended for the small screen.

The series represents some of my favorite Disney comedies of the 1970s, even though (particularly in this first one) the ideas are very dated, which is one reason why the film was remade for television in 1995. The original aired on TV in 1972, 1977, and 1980.

The film grossed $5.5 million domestically and was another decent hit.

Some errors as pointed out on IMDB: "When the doctor, Dean Higgins and Professor Quigley are looking into Dexter's eyes during the medical examination, they are using an otoscope (a device used to look into ears). The correct instrument should be an ophthalmoscope.

"The very last question in the $100,000 knowledge contest asked the name of the Midwest city that is in the area known as the "geographic center of the U.S." Medfield answered Lebanon, Kansas and won the contest. However, that answer is incorrect because of the way the question was phrased. Lebanon, Kansas is the geographic center of the 48 states, not the U.S. The official markers there are worded that way. The center of the U.S. is a site in South Dakota about 20 miles north of Belle Fourche. There is a USGS benchmark on the spot which moved from Lebanon, Kansas in 1959 after Alaska and Hawaii became states, 10 years before this movie came out.

"Although the character is known as Dexter "Riley," all onscreen spellings of his name in this film are 'Reilly.'"

Michael McGreevey reveals that he and Kurt Russell were actually roommates for about three years around this time. This was his first all-out comedy for Disney, having appeared previously in *Sammy, the Way-Out Seal* (1963).

This was stuntman Dick Warlock's first film standing in for Kurt Russell.

1970

More business as usual during this year: Walt Disney World was still under construction and it looked as if it would be a tremendous success. The Walt Disney World Preview Center opened in June at Lake Buena Vista in order to stir up more interest.

Work also continued on CalArts, with the college opening a temporary campus in September.

On the animation front *The Aristocats* would see release, being the final full-length animated feature to get a personal blessing from Walt. Walt even lured Maurice Chevalier out of retirement to sing the feature film's theme song.

On June 22nd of this year the Walt Disney Archives were established, with Dave Smith in charge.

New episodes for the anthology show included *Smoke, Menace on the Mountain, Disneyland Showtime* (a program about the opening of The Haunted Mansion), *Nature's Strangest Oddballs, Cristobalito, the Calypso Colt, The Boy Who Stole the Elephant* (working title: *The Boy and the Runaway Elephant*), *The Wacky Zoo of Morgan City*, and *Snow Bear*.

Dad, Can I Borrow the Car? was originally intended for the anthology show, but due to the success of the animation / live-action hybrid of *It's Tough to Be a Bird* in 1969, it was decided to release an edited version of *Car* to theaters in 1970 before finally airing it on TV in 1972.

Winnie the Pooh and the Honey Tree (1966) and *Winnie the Pooh and the Blustery Day* (1968) both made their TV debuts this year on separate occasions as half-hour specials sponsored by Sears, rather than as part of the anthology show. These shows ran annually for a number of years until the mid-70s.

In Search of the Castaways (1962) and *Sleeping Beauty* (1959) were reissued this year.

Non-soundtrack record releases included *Rubber Duckie and Other Songs from Sesame Street* and *The Orange Bird* featuring Anita Bryant.

The Aristocats soundtrack was nominated for a Best Recording for Children Grammy, but lost.

Non-Disney films of any significance released this year include *The Phantom Tollbooth*.

In the comic book world, Gold Key continued to publish *Donald Duck*, *Mickey Mouse*, *Uncle Scrooge*, *Walt Disney's Comics and Stories*, *The Beagle Boys*, *Huey, Dewey and Louie Junior Woodchucks*, *Super Goof*, *Chip 'n' Dale*, *Scamp*, and *Walt Disney Comics Digest*, while *Moby Duck* ended its run. It was replaced by *Walt Disney Showcase*, an umbrella title that mainly featured adaptations of current Disney movies. There was a one-shot of *The Aristocats* before this series began, which was reprinted as *Walt Disney Showcase* #16.

King of the Grizzlies

RELEASED BY BUENA VISTA ON February 11, 1970, Technicolor. Producer: Winston Hibler. Robert Lawrence Sequences Director: Ron Kelly. Screenplay: Jack Speirs. Adaptation: Rod Peterson, Norman Wright based on the book *The Biography of a Grizzly* by Ernest Thompson Seton. For Robert Lawrence Productions, Toronto, Ontario, Canada: Director of Photography: Reginald Morris. Set Decoration: Wilf Culley. Costumes: Roger Palmer. Make-up: William Morgan. Production Assistants: William Redlin, Don Hall. Wildlife and Grizzly Bear Sequences filmed by Cangary Limited. Field Producer: Lloyd Beebe. Assistance: William Bacon III, Terry Rowland, Marinho Correia, Bob Rowland, Al Niemela, Dell Ray with the cooperation of The Stoney Indian Nation. Associate Producers: Erwin L. Verity, Robert F. Metzler. Film Editor: Gregg McLaughlin. Matte Artist: Alan Maley. Titles: Jack Boyd. Sound: Robert O. Cook. Music Editor: Evelyn Kennedy. Music: Buddy Baker. Orchestration: Franklyn Marks. Running time: 93 minutes.

Song: "The Campfire is Home" Jack Speirs.

Cast: John Yesno (Moki), Chris Wiggins (The Colonel), Hugh Webster (Shorty), Jack Van Evera (Slim), Wahb (The Grizzly King), Winston Hibler (Narrator).

Winston Hibler starts his narration about the grizzlies similar to that of the old True-Life Nature Films. We see a grizzly bear and her two cubs fresh from winter hibernation. These would be the final cubs by the elder grizzly, as she was getting on in years. One of the two cubs, Wahb, would eventually become the grizzly king.

At this time, Mother Bear took her cubs to a new area to keep them out of danger. The twin cubs battle it out with Wahb's sister winning, and Wahb getting a drink from mother's nipple.

The bears lift heavy rocks in order to find grubs and beetles. Meanwhile, Mother Bear goes in for a bath in the river, but the cubs wanted no part of it and stayed along the shoreline.

Eventually, they do succumb and all three bears romp and play in the water. Mother Bear then pulls out a fish. The cubs go to eat it, but it's not quite dead, so they battle the flipping fish. The first one gets away, but mother retrieves a second one.

The bears continue to travel and eventually the seasons change and the bears hit snow and start playing again.

At one point, Wahb pushes a log over and it inadvertently becomes a sled; he slides all the way down the hill.

Soon it is spring and the bear cubs have shown growth, weighing in at about 40 pounds each.

We cut to Moki, a Cree Indian, who has returned to live with nature. He has the sign of a great bear tattooed on his hand and he soon witnesses the three bears. He works on his own ranch, raising and herding cattle.

The bears see the cows and the men and play it safe and stay hidden, but Wahb wants to go exploring.

Moki becomes Wahb's friend, but Colonel Pearson becomes Wahb's enemy. Mother Bear senses danger and keeps moving along, but Wahb is not with them so Mother Bear goes to look. Wahb meanwhile encounters a cow, but the cow runs away to a larger bull, which runs after Wahb and butts him.

Moki and the Colonel hear the commotion and come to the bull's rescue, with the Colonel firing shots at Wahb.

Moki is sad because of the Colonel's shooting, but the Colonel reminds Moki that his totem is for cattle and not for bears.

It turns out that Wahb is OK, and that the Colonel's shot only grazed him. Later, Moki searches around for any more stray cattle and again comes across Wahb, who is stuck in a tree. He decides to help Wahb out and rescues him. He then tries to capture Wahb, but Wahb fights back. Eventually, Moki captures the bear.

Moki sets him free and Wahb is now on his own. He keeps gaining weight and stands up for himself against a wild cougar.

After this encounter, he sees a black bear eating some honey from a hive. When the black bear leaves, Wahb moves in, but the black bear returns and chases Wahb up another tree.

Wahb escapes and grows still further. He can now truly fend for himself, weighing in at close to 400 pounds by winter. By the time snow falls again, Wahb is mighty sleepy. Strangely, by instinct, he returned to the same cave where he was born.

Wahb tried to sleep, but he was not alone as he shares company with a packrat. A pair of wolverines visits the cave, pestering the sleeping Wahb.

Spring arrives and Wahb wakes up, now weighing in at an astounding 800 pounds. He crosses the river and makes his own way around, looking for food, but he learns a lesson in traps when he spies some food hanging from a wire, designed to be a wolf trap. Unfortunately, the wolf trap soon becomes a bear trap. With the traps gone the wolves now eat the hanging meat, with Moki aiming and firing at them.

Later, some of the other cattle rustlers encounter Wahb and one of the rustlers named Shorty almost meets his fate until he plays dead. The Colonel informs Moki that he has to kill Wahb for the men's safety and that Moki cannot ally himself with the bear any longer.

Meanwhile, Wahb encounters a female bear in the river while fishing and he makes his romantic move. They frolic in the water. It is said that courtship and mating lasts about two weeks and then the bears go their separate ways, but their romance was to be cut short by Moki's bear traps.

Initially the traps stop them, but they defeat the traps and the couple battles over the exposed meat. The female bear runs off, but eventually Wahb follows her.

Four years pass, and the Colonel's ranch expands with mines and logging and, of course, more cattle. Moki is sitting by himself at a campfire when a stray bear comes along, startling him.

It turns out to be Wahb, who remembers Moki's kindness in the past and doesn't attack. By this time, Wahb weighs in at 1250 pounds.

Soon the big summer round-up is on its way, and Wahb interferes and messes around with the men's camp and chuck wagon while the men scamper up nearby trees.

The Colonel has had enough and is going to go out and get Wahb, telling Moki to stay behind. The Colonel battles Wahb and is about to be killed by the great bear until Moki shows up at the last minute and uses his powers to make Wahb go away, but the Colonel is not convinced and still wants to kill Wahb.

The Colonel aims at Wahb, but cannot fire as Moki has removed all of his bullets. Wahb is free and Moki and the Colonel go back home.

This film has much more in common with films like *Perri* (1957), which was a True-Life Fantasy, rather than the straight-forward True-Life Adventures.

In any case, for fans of the True-Life series it was a good return to form, but the film is very slow-moving, and the ending is pretty limp and unrealistic. It apparently took over two years to film due to changing color of the bear's coat. Big Ted the bear worked for marshmallows in order to get the scenes they wanted over that time period.

It first aired on TV on *The Wonderful World of Disney* in 1973, and again in 1977.

The Boatniks

RELEASED BY BUENA VISTA ON July 1, 1970, Technicolor. Producer: Ron Miller. Director: Norman Tokar. Screen Story and Screenplay: Arthur Julian based on a story by Marty Roth. Director of Photography: William Snyder, A.S.C. Art Director: Hilyard Brown. Film Editor: Cotton Warburton, A.C.E. Set Decorators: Emile Kuri, Frank R. McKelvy. Special Effects: Eustace Lycett, Robert A. Mattey. Matte Artist: Alan Maley. Sound Supervisor: Robert O. Cook. Sound Mixer: Dean Thomas. Costumes: Chuck Keehne, Emily Sundby. Make-up: Robert J. Schiffer. Hair Stylist: La Rue Matheron. Assistant Director: Christopher Hibler. Unit Manager: Irving Temener. Music Editor: Evelyn Kennedy. Music: Robert F. Brunner. Orchestration: Franklyn Marks. Associate Producer: Tom Leetch. Second Unit Director: Arthur J. Vitarelli. Hair Stylist: Joan Phillips. Assistant Directors: Michael J. Dmytryk, Robert Webb. Prop Master: Wilbur L. Russell. Boom Operator: Frank Regula. First Assistant Camera: Jim Luske. Assistant Camera: Jim L. Mathews. Still Photographer: Floyd McCarty. Gaffer: Otto Meyer. Key Grip: Stan Reed. Camera Operator: Roger Shearman. Script Supervisor: Eylia Jacobs. Running time: 100 minutes.

Song: "Boatniks" Bruce Belland, Robert F. Brunner.

Cast: Robert Morse (Ensign Garland), Stefanie Powers (Kate Fairchild), Phil Silvers (Harry Simmons), Norman Fell (Max),

Mickey Shaughnessy (Charlie), Wally Cox (Jason Bennett), Don Ameche (Commander Taylor), Joey Forman (Lieutenant Jordan), Vito Scotti (Pepe Galindo), Tom Lowell (Wagner), Bob Hastings (Chief Walsh), Sammy Jackson (Garlotti), Joe E. Ross (Nutty Sailor), Judy Jordan (Tina), Al Lewis (Bert), Midori (Chiyoko Kuni), Kelly Thordsen (Motorcycle Cop), Gil Lamb (Mr. Mitchell), Shaaron Claridge (Police Dispatcher).

A boat called the Burbank Temptress contacts the Coast Guard for help and it turns out their compass is going wacky because of a beer case nearby, ushering in the titles.

During the titles, a guy unloads a prop motor and accidentally sends his VW off the dock into the water.

The Coast Guard takes another call from a distressed sailor who answers "You mean under the boat or in the boat?" when asked about the depth of the water he's in.

Next, two speedboats collide and a guy lights his boat on fire when he puts lighter fluid on his barbecue grill.

Then, after putting the fire out, the Coast Guard rescues a heavily pregnant woman and get her safely to an ambulance.

Two U.S. Coast Guard men discuss their strange rescues, including being midwives. Lt. Jordan has put in for a transfer because of it and Commander Taylor has put in a replacement, Ensign Garland.

Unfortunately, Ensign Garland is running late due to having been pulled over by a traffic officer giving him a moving violation.

While the officer is writing Garland's ticket, a car containing Harry, Max, and Charlie pulls into a service station. The three are known jewel thieves. Charlie goes in to get an ice cream while the others fill up the tank. The ice cream machine doesn't work, so Charlie breaks into it to get his treat.

Meanwhile, Ensign Garland is on his way and so are the three men, but soon Garland rear ends their car. Harry forgives the crash and wants Garland to go on his way, causing passersby to give their comments about the accident.

Soon the same traffic cop from before rides up but Harry sends him on his way and they plan to go off, too, until they hear a police radio report about three jewel thieves heading off to Mexico. They decide to change their plans.

More silliness ensues when a nutty sailor tries to park his boat in the dock and crashes it instead.

Garland finally shows up and encounters Jason Bennett, who is a swinging, Hugh Hefner-type who is constantly partying on his yacht with many sexy, bikini-clad women.

Then Garland literally bumps into Kate, who dumps paint on herself.

Finally Garland gets in to see the Commander, and the departing Lt. Jordan shows him the ropes. As Garland observes the proceedings of who he is supposed to protect, he falls into the water and is chastised by the Commander for swimming while on duty.

Harry, Max, and Charlie are now holed up in a hotel room and Harry has a new plan saying that they should rent a sailboat. Max thinks a speedboat would be better, but Harry explains why he thinks a sailboat would be better.

Walsh tells Garland more about Jason, revealing that Jason parties on his boat constantly but never leaves the dock. In fact, Jason's boat doesn't even have a motor as he has taken it out.

Meanwhile, the three jewel thieves catch up to Kate and try to rent a sailboat from her. She agrees and then goes out sailing herself while supervising some small boys.

Garland's first rescue is of a landlocked boat with a bickering married couple named Bert and Tina.

Harry and the jewel thieves act like they've sailed before and don't need help, but while raising the sail Charlie is hoisted up with it and chaos ensues.

Garland has run aground due to a racing speedboat and the incompetence of the bickering couple. Kate sails by and offers her help to Garland.

The jewel thieves finally get organized and meet up with a Mexican man. They think they are in Mexico, but in reality they've landed at a local Mexican restaurant located at the dock.

Garland's rescue by Kate raises the ire of the Commander and he reprimands him before setting him back out to sea.

That night Garland bumps into Kate again at a local watering hole and he asks her to dine with him, but even though she rescued him, Kate is still mad at Garland for the paint dumping. The waitress advises that they do eat together to save time, but Kate says, "Separate checks."

At dinner it is revealed that Garland has a lot of work to do to live up to the reputation of his father, who was also a seaman. Kate reveals that she is part of a wealthy, well-known family, but has rebelled.

The next day, Garland is doing somewhat better and educates a group of children brought on board by Kate. Kate is impressed with Garland's sea knowledge.

Garland takes the kids out on a boat trip. It is somewhat foggy and their boat encounters Harry's and signals them for safety. Harry doesn't signal back and Garland smashes into the boat. Harry yells at Garland to send for the Coast Guard and Garland says he is the Coast Guard.

The crash lands Garland back in the Commander's office and another dressing down. The Commander says that if there is one more screw up, he will be discharged from the Coast Guard.

The next day, the jewel thieves head back out to sea trying to retrieve a picnic basket that went overboard in the previous day's crash. They try to look but only pull up an old guitar.

Garland is out on patrol again and first rescues a man stuck in the bathroom of his boat and then rescues a woman who's caught with her mini-skirt stuck to the boat, causing a sensation at sea. When Garland asks for volunteers to rescue her, they dive in before he finishes his sentence.

The jewel thieves still haven't brought up the picnic basket, but they have brought up quite a bit of other junk off the sea floor.

Harry, Max, and Charlie get into a fight and catch a strong fish that pulls their boat at high speeds. The speeding catches the eye of Garland, who tells them to slow down or get a citation.

The nutty sailor again tries to dock his boat and is still unsuccessful.

Next, Jason talks to Garland again and reveals that he is actually going to install a motor again and cruise the bay. Then Garland and Kate talk again and they are much more friendly and romantic than they were before, and they kiss.

The jewel thieves have now acquired a diving suit after being unsuccessful with the fishing lure. They send Charlie down in the water to find the submerged picnic basket.

While Charlie is still underwater, Harry and Max witness a shark swimming by, and of course, Charlie sees him soon and comes up for air and screams "Shark!"

Garland hears Charlie's screams and comes after it with a gun. Charlie is rescued and Harry decides to hire a professional pearl diver.

The repeated rescues and encounters with the jewel thieves raise Garland's suspicions, and he asks Kate about them.

Meanwhile, the nutty sailor is still trying to dock his boat and Garland spots a newspaper article about the jewel thieves. He goes to the hotel to investigate and bumps into the Commander, who is checking in with his wife because their house is being painted.

The jewel thieves go to the airport to retrieve their pearl diver, a beautiful Japanese lady named Midori. Midori barely speaks English, so Harry has to translate English into Japanese to speak with her.

Harry tells her to dive off the boat to retrieve the picnic basket. Garland and Kate are spying through binoculars on a nearby boat.

Harry's translating skills aren't that good and Midori brings up an octopus. Finally, after further discussion, she does find the picnic basket and brings it up. Garland and Kate are confused.

Back at the hotel, Midori reveals that she actually can speak English and wants a piece of the action. After some initial reluctance, Harry and the men agree.

Soon, Harry has a new plan. He calls Pepe Galindo to charter a seaplane in order for them to plan their escape.

By this point, Garland is suspect of Harry and he does everything he can to delay the jewel thieves departure, even inviting them to Jason's party.

Harry declines and he and Garland get into a scuffle, causing the contents of the picnic basket to fall on the dock. The Commander witnesses this and relieves Garland of his duties.

Harry collects the spilled food and leaves, but forgets a pickle. Kate picks it up and discovers that the pickle has been hollowed out and contains a priceless piece of jewelry.

Garland tells Kate to tell the Commander, who has already left the scene. Garland begins a high-speed boat chase trying to apprehend the three jewel thieves. The chase is a harrowing one as the two boats have to steer among many, many other boats already on the sea.

The jewel thieves are stopped by Jason's party boat, but the thieves escape by leaving their boat and joining the party. Jason thinks the jewel thieves are caterers, but of course they are not. They jump into a nearby yellow submarine to escape.

Garland goes after the submarine in a canoe. The Commander witnesses this and wonders what Garland thinks he's doing. Garland requests that they go after the thieves and against his better judgment, the Commander finally agrees.

The jewel thieves continue their getaway and for a time are traveling upside down. To fight their pursuers the submarine sends out a torpedo, which turns out to be a salami.

The pursuit continues, but the thieves get away to their chartered flight. Eventually they are caught by the Coast Guard and hauled away to jail. The Commander changes his mind about Garland, saying that he's as good as his father, and Kate is happy as well.

This was Walt Disney Productions' attempt to do something a little bit more sophisticated and adult with their comedies by adding a little sex and slightly mature themes into the mix. The problem is that it really isn't all that funny on that or any level. Despite all this the film did reasonably well, bringing in over $18.6 million at the box office.

Whoever did the casting must have been a fan of Nat Hiken's *Sgt. Bilko* and *Car 54, Where Are You?* as Phil Silvers, Joe E. Ross and Al Lewis are all featured.

Strangely, the DVD release includes outtakes, which is somewhat uncommon for a Disney release. There is nothing really remarkable about these, and they are unfortunately silent. It was re-released theatrically in 1972 and 1977 and then first aired on TV in 1978 and again in 1991.

The Aristocats

RELEASED BY BUENA VISTA ON December 11, 1970, Technicolor. Producer: Wolfgang Reitherman, Winston Hibler. Director: Wolfgang Reitherman. Story: Larry Clemmons, Vance Gerry, Ken Anderson, Frank Thomas, Eric Cleworth, Julius Svendsen, Ralph Wright based on a story by Tom McGowan and Tom Rowe. Directing Animators: Milt Kahl, Ollie Johnston, Frank Thomas, John Lounsbery. Production Design: Ken Anderson. Character Animation: Hal King, Eric Larson, Eric Cleworth, Julius Svendsen, Fred Hellmich, Walt Stanchfield, Dave Michener. Effects Animation: Dan MacManus, Dick Lucas. Music: George Bruns. Orchestration: Walter Sheets. Production Manager: Don Duckwall. Sound: Robert O. Cook. Film Editor: Tom Acosta. Assistant Directors: Ed Hansen, Dan Alguire. Music Editor: Evelyn Kennedy. Layout: Don Griffith, Basil Davidovich, Silvia Roemer. Background: Al Dempster, Bill Layne, Ralph Hulett. Layout Artist: John Emerson. Running time: 79 minutes.

Songs: "The Aristocats," sung by Maurice Chevalier, "Scales and Arpeggios," "She Never Felt Alone" by Richard M. Sherman and Robert B. Sherman. "Thomas O'Malley Cat," sung by Phil Harris, by Terry Gilkyson. "Ev'rybody Wants to Be a Cat" by Floyd Huddleston and Al Rinker. "Pourquoi?" sung by Hermoine Baddeley, by Richard M. Sherman and Robert B. Sherman.

Cast: Phil Harris (Thomas O'Malley), Eva Gabor (Duchess), Sterling Holloway (Roquefort), Scatman Crothers (Scat Cat), Paul Winchell (Chinese Cat), Lord Tim Hudson (English Cat), Vito Scotti (Italian Cat), Thurl Ravenscroft (Russian Cat), Dean Clark (Berlioz), Liz English (Marie), Gary Dubin (Toulouse), Nancy Kulp (Frou-Frou), Pat Buttram (Napoleon), George Lindsey (Lafayette), Monica Evans (Abigail), Carole Shelley (Amelia), Charles Lane (Lawyer George), Hermoine Baddeley (Madame), Roddy Maude-Roxby (Butler), Bill Thompson (Uncle Waldo), Robie Lester (Duchess singing voice), Ruth Buzzi (Frou-Frou singing voice), Pete Renaday (Milkman, Le Petit Café Cook).

Madame Adelaide takes her cats for a ride with Edgar the butler driving the horse named Frou-Frou.

After they get home, Edgar welcomes George to see Madame, her mother cat Duchess, and her three kittens. George romances Madame and they do a dance to music in her bedroom until one of the kittens, Berlioz, messes with the record player.

Madame calls upon George, who is also a lawyer, to help her create a will. Madame intended to will her fortune to her cats, with the estate reverting to Edgar upon the cats' deaths.

Edgar is eavesdropping and realizes that he cannot wait for the cats to go, so he makes plans to get rid of them in order to get the fortune sooner.

Duchess and her cats have their own discussion during their play. Duchess wants her kittens to be well-rounded with the arts so one of the kittens, Toulouse, shows his expertise with painting and paints a picture of Edgar.

Meanwhile, Edgar is creating a recipe for the cats with tons of sleeping powder.

Duchess sends Berlioz and Marie to practice their piano and singing, and together they sing "Scales and Arpeggios." Toulouse soon joins the singing and gets paint on the piano.

Edgar shows up with dinner for the cats, Crème de la Crème a la Edgar, a dish heavily tainted by sleeping powder.

Roquefort the mouse shows up and wants to know what the cats are eating. The cats are good friends with the mouse and he joins them in their meal. Soon, the cats and the mouse are becoming drowsy.

Once asleep, Edgar loads the cats into a covered basket and puts them onto his backfiring motor scooter, taking them out of town.

The racket attracts the attention of two dogs named Lafayette and Napoleon. Napoleon wants them to chase the scooter and when they do, they run Edgar into the river and the cats and the basket are thrown off.

Soon Edgar is too, and the dogs are driving the scooter. After more wild action, Edgar regains control and rides out of town, but not before destroying a windmill.

Duchess and the cats wake up not knowing where they are, and they very scared since they now have to brave the elements.

Meanwhile, Madame is upset to discover that the cats are all missing, so Roquefort goes out to find them.

The next day, Thomas O'Malley Cat shows up singing his eponymous theme song and charming Duchess and the kittens. After first declining to help them, O'Malley changes his mind and decides to assist. O'Malley leaps onto a passing milk truck and startles the driver. He then tells the cats to leap aboard the now-stopped truck. The truck starts moving again and heads back to Paris.

Roquefort and Frou-Frou are still distressed about not being able to find the cats. In fact, everyone is distressed except Edgar, who proudly shows off a headline claiming a mysterious catnapper has stolen Madame's cats.

Meanwhile, the cats partake in the cream aboard the truck and the driver sees this in his rearview mirror and chases them all off the truck.

They decide to follow the train tracks until a real train comes barreling down at them. They duck under the ties, but Marie slips and falls into the water below the railroad bridge. O'Malley dives in and rescues Marie, but gets caught up in the current himself.

Soon O'Malley comes across two geese named Abigail and Amelia, who help O'Malley to shore and back to Duchess and the other cats. The geese introduce themselves as being from England, on a walking tour of France.

O'Malley wants to leave the geese behind, but Duchess wants to join them on the way to Paris.

We cut to Le Petit Café just as the other geese and cats arrive, where we find another goose named Uncle Waldo who has been kicked out for being drunk,. The geese decide to put Uncle Waldo to bed so he can sleep it off, and they all leave the cats behind.

At night Edgar takes another ride on his motorcycle, this time with Roquefort in tow, but the mouse doesn't get very far. Edgar goes back to the scene of the crime in order to find his missing umbrella. When he gets there he discovers the basket, his umbrella, hat, and sidecar still in possession of Napoleon and Lafayette. Edgar tries to retrieve the items without disturbing the dogs, but he fails and wakes them up.

Edgar loses his shoes and Lafayette walks into them. Eventually, Edgar leaves with his items.

O'Malley leads the cats to his penthouse pad, only to discover that his place is currently being inhabited by some of O'Malley's swinging cat friends like Scat Cat, and Chinese, Italian, Russian, and English cats who are all fond of playing jazz. Soon, Scat and O'Malley start singing "Ev'rybody Wants to Be a Cat" with all the other cats. The jazz performance turns very psychedelic and colorful, until the cats get rough and destroy the house and their instruments.

The jazz quintet leaves and the rest of the cats go to sleep in an available bed. Meanwhile, Duchess and O'Malley start falling in love.

The next day, Duchess takes O'Malley to Madame's house. Roquefort sees the cats coming and decides to do something about Edgar before he discovers the returning cats, but it is too late. Edgar has spotted them.

Duchess has to say goodbye to O'Malley against her will while Roquefort is frantically trying to tell the cats to stay away, but Edgar quickly rounds the cats up into a sack. Madame feels that she has heard the cats, but Edgar fools Madame by acting like she's just seeing and hearing things.

Meanwhile, Roquefort goes after O'Malley to help rescue Duchess and the kittens. O'Malley tells Roquefort to round up Scat Cat and his pals for help, but they don't know Roquefort is a friend and not a meal. Roquefort is frightened and can't remember O'Malley's name. At the cats are about to eat Roquefort, he remembers and they decide to help.

Edgar has placed the Duchess and the kittens into a trunk to be shipped to Timbuktu, but just when he gets ready to ship the trunk the other cats arrive and foil the plans. While the cats attack Edgar, Roquefort opens the lock on the trunk and frees Duchess and the kittens. The cats get Edgar into the trunk and the delivery truck arrives just in time to take Edgar away.

In the end, Madame revises her will to exclude Edgar since he has left, and she has now adopted O'Malley and founded a home for all the alley cats of Paris. In the end there is a reprise of "Ev'rybody Wants to Be a Cat" with the cats, dogs, horse, and mouse all singing along.

This was the final animated feature to get the nod from Walt himself. It is believed that he even lured Maurice Chevalier out of retirement to sing the theme song, though Richard Sherman also makes this claim of luring Chevalier by recording a demo imitating Chevalier. Perhaps there are elements of truth to both stories.

The producers were less successful in getting Louis Armstrong to portray Scat Cat, so the job ultimately went to Scatman Crothers, who later voiced Hong Kong Phooey.

Eva Gabor and Pat Buttram were still working on *Green Acres* when they recorded their voices for this film.

Onscreen, the actual title is *The Aristocrats* for a moment and then it is amended to be *The AristoCats* with a capital "C," but no one ever writes it this way.

On the DVD, Richard Sherman talks about and sings a song that didn't make the final cut, called "She Never Felt Alone." They also feature a version sung by Hermione Baddeley and Robie Lester matched up with unused storyboards. Sherman says he doesn't know why this song was not used.

Interestingly, Phil Harris' song in this film, as with his song in *The Jungle Book*(1967), was not composed by the Sherman Brothers.

Ken Anderson once said that Roy Disney had planned to disband the animation department once *The Jungle Book* was completed. Anderson said that he wouldn't do anything unless an official memo was sent out. It never was which is good as this and all subsequent animation by Disney would never have been made.

Overall this is a very entertaining film, albeit somewhat slow-paced. I remember enjoying the "Ev'rybody Wants to Be a Cat" sequence the best when I first saw this in the theater in the early months of 1971.

The film was reissued to theaters in 1980 and 1987. It cost $4 million to make and grossed $10.1 million domestically and $16 million internationally upon its first release.

According to IMDB, this was originally going to be live-action for the anthology show.

There was to be a direct-to-video sequel released in 2007, but it was canceled and never made. A Blu-ray edition of the original was released in 2012.

The Wild Country

RELEASED BY BUENA VISTA ON December 15, 1970, Technicolor. Producer: Ron Miller. Director: Robert Totten. Screenplay by Calvin Clements, Jr., Paul Savage based on the book *Little Britches* by Ralph Moody. Director of Photography: Frank Phillips, A.S.C. Production Designer: Robert Clatworthy. Art Director: John B. Mansbridge. Film Editor: Robert Stafford, A.C.E. Set Decorators: Emile Kuri, Hal Gausman. Special Effects: Robert A. Mattey. Matte Artist: Alan Maley. Second Unit Director: Arthur J. Vitarelli. Sound Supervisor: Robert O. Cook. Sound Mixer: Jack F. Lilly. Costumes: Chuck Keehne, Emily Sundby. Make-up: Robert J. Schiffer. Hair Stylist: La Rue Matheron. Assistant Director: Paul Nichols. Unit Manager: Austen Jewell. Music Editor: Evelyn Kennedy. Music: Robert F. Brunner. Orchestration: Franklyn Marks. Hair Stylist: Jackie Bone. Makeup Artist: Paul Stanhope, Jr. Second Assistant Director: James Welch. Props: Terry Ballard, Jack Colconda. Plasterers: Charles Ceseri, Raymond Moss. Construction Coordinator: Bill David. Painter: Sam Eaquinta. Construction: Herman Lowers. Greensman: Phillip Michaels. Draughtsman: Bob Stahler. Radio Man: Les Gear. Boom Operator: William Hamilton. Cable Man: Bud Maffett. Sound Recordist: Jay Younger. Special Effects: George Lofgren. Stunts: George Orrison. Still Photographer: Bob Coburn, Jr. Lamp Operators: Dave Collier, James F. Cornick, Al Goelz, Fred Hernandez, Jack Holton, Richard Kamins, Bob E. Krattiger. Second Camera Assistant: Thomas Del Ruth. Camera Operator: Bill Johnson. Best Boy: Harry Kamins. Grips: Gene Kearney, Charles LaRocca, Peter Lomprakis, Pat Murphy. Gaffer: Bill King. Key Grip: Bill Masters. Second Grip: Mike Shaltz. Assistant Camera: Michael St. Hilaire. Wardrobe: Dorothy Barkley, Ron Dawson, Kent James. Driver Captain: Paul Stewart. Welfare Worker: Peggy Cobb. Wranglers: Don Crow, Edward Duarte, George Steele. Craft Service: Bill Degeneres, John Wagner. Wild Animal Trainer: Dan Haggerty. Representative, American Humane Association: Chick Hannon. Unit Publicist: Ben Hartigan. Dialogue Director: Rance Howard. Location Auditor: Nick Humphrey. Supervisor, Wild Animal Trainer: Frank Lamping. Script Supervisor: Lloyd Nelson. First Aid: Dan Novack. Script Supervisor, Second Unit: Lois Thurman. Running time: 100 minutes.

Cast: Steve Forrest (Jim Tanner), Vera Miles (Kate Tanner), Jack Elam (Thompson), Ronny Howard (Virgil Tanner), Frank DeKova (Two Dog), Morgan Woodward (Ab Cross), Clint Howard (Andrew Tanner), Dub Taylor (Phil), Woodrow Chambliss (Dakota), Karl Swenson (Jensen), Mills Watson (Feathers), Rance Howard (Cleve), Larry D. Mann (The Marshal), F. Ben Miller (Shelby).

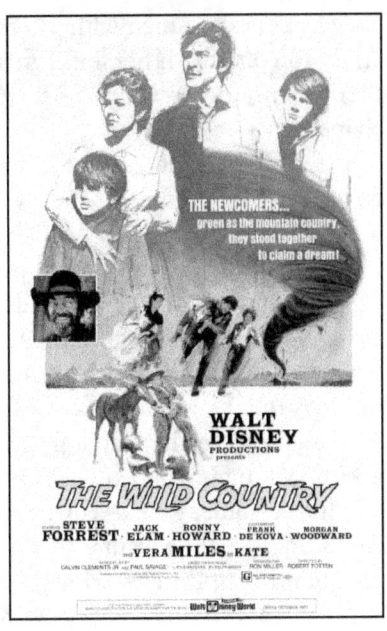

The film starts out with the Tanner family of Jim, his wife Kate, older son Virgil and young son Andrew traveling west in their covered wagon after having been uprooted from Pennsylvania. They arrive into town in the end by stagecoach. They are greeted by their cousin, who says that moving is the best thing that they could have done.

They soon meet Jensen, the man who runs the General Store. Brothers Virgil and Andy meet others like Hiram and Agatha.

The family gets back on their wagon and finally gets to their ranch home, which is somewhat dilapidated. Jim assures Kate that the house will be fine with a few repairs.

They soon encounter a man named Thompson and his pet wolf, who have been squatting in their house. They also meet Two Dog, an American Indian also living on the ranch.

Thompson warns Jim about Mr. Cross, who has been making demands about the property. Jim says that he will have to have a talk with Mr. Cross.

After Thompson leaves, Virgil questions his dad as to whether what Thompson was saying was true. Jim says he doesn't know, but to keep this information away from his mother.

The next day, after some repairs, Jim takes Virgil out hunting. They were going to shoot at an animal that turns out to be a wild horse. A shot rings out, but the horse is not injured. Eventually they get the horse under control and bring it back to the ranch. It turns out that the horse is a pregnant mare.

The horse is somewhat ill, so Virgil rides off in search of Thompson and Two Dog for help. Along the way he encounters a wild grizzly bear. Virgil scrambles up a tree, but Thompson comes to the rescue. Thompson wants to know why he wants Two Dog and Virgil explains everything about the wild mustang.

Back at the ranch with Thompson and Two Dog, Kate wants Virgil and Andy to come with her, but Jim says that witnessing a birth will help make them men. The newborn horse is cleaned off and both horses are in good shape.

Life goes on at the Tanner ranch as a herd of wandering bulls gets into Kate's garden. Thompson and Two Dog help to drive the cattle out.

The cattle belong to Ab Cross, so Jim and Virgil figure that it is finally time to talk to Mr. Cross about his bulls.

Ab says his bulls can wander anywhere they want to, but Jim says no. Ab says that there are no laws in this territory, so Jim would have problems trying to enforce them. In the end, Ab orders Jim off his land for trespassing. Jim says that he wants the same from him.

Jim goes to the General Store to mail out a letter to the Marshall and asks how long it will take. Jensen tells him it will take about a week.

Back home, Kate asks what type of man Mr. Cross is, and Jim says that Cross does what he wants.

Soon Virgil tries to ride the wild horse, succeeding briefly he's thrown. Virgil is not hurt and is very excited that he was able to ride her at all.

Jim checks in with Jensen about the letter and Mr. Cross is there and overhears the conversation. Cross wants to settle things with fists and a fight breaks out in the General Store.

Jim knocks Cross out and the family sets off to go home, but Cross wakes up and starts another fistfight outside which ends up with Jim and Cross wrestling in the water. Jim is victorious again, but just barely. Virgil helps Jim into the wagon and the family rides home.

Cross orders his men to shut off the dam in order to dry out the Tanners' farm, and it is Andy who discovers that they have no more water. Virgil wants to fight more, but Jim says that if the law won't come to him, he'll go to the law. As Jim gets ready, Virgil goes off to find Mr. Cross himself and settle things. He goes up to the dam first to remove the blockage. Jim chases after them.

Cross rides up and starts shooting at them. He gets up on them and aims to shoot them point blank, but is talked out of it at the last moment. Jim and Virgil run off and Cross orders the logs replaced in the dam.

Jim is injured and Thompson and Two Dog help him mend his wounds. The new hardships cause the family to bicker and argue with each other. Eventually they all get over their petty grievances and life gets better again.

Next there comes a new problem as a tornado hits the area. The family lets the animals free to fend for themselves and when the family tries to seek shelter, they discover that Andy is missing. Virgil discovers Andy and brings him to safety. Andy had been trying to save some of the animals, but Jim and Kate explain that the animals will be ok.

The Tanners leave their shelter after the tornado and discover that their ranch is in far worse shape than when they first arrived. Kate wants to go back to Pennsylvania as she's given up, but no one else wants to go back and Virgil takes the stand that he's not going back.

Soon the Marshall arrives and takes the side of the Tanner family, telling Ab Cross to back off and let them be. Cross does so reluctantly, and the dam is freed up.

Jim offers his hand in friendship, but Mr. Cross rejects him. After the Tanners and the Marshall leave, Cross throws the mandate in the water.

Later, the family celebrates as they were the ones to bring law and order to Jackson's Hole, but their celebration is short-lived as Andy discovers the barn is on fire.

When they go to put the fire out, Cross is nearby and fires shots at them. Jim runs to get his rifle, but is shot by Cross. Jim tells Kate to get his rifle and shoot, but she attacks Cross with a wood plank. Cross kicks her away and Virgil comes through with the rifle and shoots Cross dead. Jim will be all right, but the barn burns to the ground.

Cross' former cronies help out and rebuild the barn while Jim heals. Kate finally feels that this is their home. Andy's horse finally comes back, as well.

This is a pleasant little film with some interesting plot twists and turns and it is somewhat more adult in nature than many other Disney offerings.

Strangely, this story is very similar to the upcoming *Snowball Express* (1972), minus the humor and the setting, but the basic premise is the same: an uprooted family tries to make a go at a broken-down place, and against all odds they make it work.

This is an early, but not the first, time that the Howard brothers appeared in a film together. In later years Ron Howard became a respected film director and it became a regular occurrence for him to have Clint Howard appear in his films in featured roles, so much so that when Ron didn't cast Clint in *Backdraft* (1991), there was a little bit of upset for people looking for Clint.

At this point, however, Ron was happily making movies on the Disney lot between his significant roles in *The Andy Griffith Show* and *Happy Days*.

Note that the movie poster makes mention of Walt Disney World almost a year before its actual opening.

It aired on the anthology show in 1975 and 1981.

1971

Above and beyond anything else, the big news of the year was most definitely the opening of Walt Disney World. Test runs were handled throughout September and then Roy Disney was on hand to deliver the opening address on October 1, shortly before dropping dead in December of that year, his mission completed to see the opening of the new theme park, and to see it open under budget.

Most attractions were available on opening day, but a few held out for a couple months by choice and by design, such as Fort Wilderness Campground and Circle-Vision 360's *America the Beautiful*, both of which opened in November, and the first WDW professional golf tournament was held in December. Two unique attractions debuted at WDW: The Mickey Mouse Revue and the Country Bear Jamboree. The former moved to Tokyo Disneyland, while a duplicate attraction of the latter was built at Disneyland in 1972.

For the first time, the real "What would Walt do?" question could be asked in earnest as Roy's tenure from 1966-1971 could arguably have been a time of tying up loose ends of ideas and concepts introduced during the tail end of Walt's era.

By 1971, the last of these projects were completed with this opening and with the release of *Bedknobs and Broomsticks*, which was touted as an alternative to *Mary Poppins* (1964), should *Poppins* author P.L. Travers not give her blessing to the projects. Fortunately she did, and *Bedknobs* fell on the back burner like so many other projects, but now it was complete and the rest of the 1970s saw a complete regime change with no links to the very beginnings of the studio in 1923, but at least with links to the 1930s.

For the record, the new Chief Executive Officer of Walt Disney Productions after Roy O. Disney's death was Donn Tatum, who held the role until 1980. He would also be Chairman of the Board until 1980. Card Walker replaced Tatum as President.

It was unknown then, but this would soon be the time for an inordinate amount of sequels since fresh ideas were soon to dry up from the Disney folks. Tatum seemed to be one to really not rock the boat.

About the only things left from the Walt era were the Space Mountain ride, which opened in 1974 and EPCOT, which opened in 1982 as Epcot Center.

Back at Disneyland, they honored their 100-millionth guest with Valerie Suldo this year. The Indian War Canoes were renamed the Davy Crockett Explorer Canoes. The Indian Village was closed to make room for Bear Country, scheduled to open in 1972.

New films made for the anthology series include *Three Without Fear, Project Florida, Bayou Boy, Hamad and the Pirates, Charlie Crowfoot and the Coati Mundi, Hacksaw, The Strange Monster of Strawberry Cove, Lefty, the Dingaling Lynx*, and *Disney on Parade*. There was also *The Grand Opening of Walt Disney World*, an all-new 90-minute special.

Also, due to the overwhelming success of *The Aristocats*, Disney announced its next full-length feature, *Robin Hood*, which was not completed and released until 1973.

Lady and the Tramp (1955), *20,000 Leagues Under the Sea* (1954) and *Pinocchio* (1940) were reissued this year.

Among the films released by other studios that could have been released by Disney include *Willy Wonka and the Chocolate Factory*. Somewhat of a flop upon first release, the film has now achieved a tremendous cult following.

Disney also opened the California Institute of the Arts, also known as CalArts, in Valencia, California. The school was originally envisioned by Walt as a training ground for animators and illustrators.

Disney also formed The Walt Disney Distributing Company to create merchandise of its own design rather than relying on licensees. It ran through 1977.

There really wasn't much on the release schedule for Disney records as there were many cutbacks of staff, and so there were reissues, compilations, and soundtrack albums as new releases.

There were, however, four albums released based upon Walt Disney World attractions: *Country Bear Jamboree, The Hall of Presidents, Walt Disney World*, and *Mickey Mouse: This is My Life*, based upon the Mickey Mouse Revue attraction.

In the comic book world, Gold Key continued to publish *Donald Duck, Mickey Mouse, Uncle Scrooge, Walt Disney's Comics and Stories, The Beagle Boys, Huey, Dewey and Louie Junior Woodchucks, Super Goof, Chip 'n' Dale, Scamp, Walt Disney Comics Digest*, and *Walt Disney Showcase*.

The success of *The Aristocats* begat two spin-off comic books series: *The Aristokittens* and *O'Malley and the Alley Cats*. There was also a one-shot called *The Wonderful Adventures of Pinocchio*.

This was the year that comic book fans first got to know the name of the "good duck artist" Carl Barks in the book *Comix: A History of Comic Books in America* by Les Daniels, which was one of the first books to discuss comic books as an art form and also to discuss genres other than superhero comics.

And a strange related event occurred this year as a group of underground cartoonists who had produced a series of comic books stories called *Air Pirates Funnies* were sued by Disney, because the stories featured Mickey Mouse and company in unauthorized stories. It wasn't because the stories were necessarily offensive as much as they infringed upon copyright, because the stories were so close to the real deal without being parody that Disney lawyers took action. The ultimate result was that writer and artist Dan O'Neill is never allowed to reprint those stories.

The Barefoot Executive

RELEASED BY BUENA VISTA ON March 17, 1971, Technicolor. Producer: Bill Anderson. Director: Robert Butler. Screenplay: Joseph L. McEveety. Story: Lila Garrett, Bernie Kahn, Stewart C. Billett. Director of Photography: Charles F. Wheeler, A.S.C. Art Directors: John B. Mansbridge, Ed Graves. Set Decoration: Emile Kuri, Frank R. McKelvy. Optical Effects: Eustace Lycett. Matte Artist: Alan Maley. Sound Supervisor: Robert O. Cook. Sound Mixer: Dean Thomas. Costumes: Chuck Keehne, Emily Sundby. "Raffles" Wardrobe Designer: Shelby Anderson. "Raffles" Handler: Frank Lamping. Make-up: Robert J. Schiffer. Assistant Director: Ted Schilz. Music Editor: Evelyn Kennedy. Film produced with the co-operation of The National Academy of Television Arts and Sciences. Film Editor: Robert Stafford, A.C.E. Music: Robert F. Brunner. Orchestration: Franklyn Marks. Makeup Artist: Ray Steele. Hair Stylist: Vivian Thompson. Production Managers: John D. Bloss, Russ Walker. Leadman: John A. Kuri. Stand-by Painter: Leon Ocherman. Prop Master: Wilbur L. Russell. Sound Effects Editors: Leonard Davison, Ben Hendricks, Bill Wylie. Boom Man: Frank Regula. Head Special Effects: Robert A. Mattey. Stunts: Dick

Warlock. First Company Grip: Arthur Brooker. Second Assistant Camera: Gene Jackson. Still Photographer: Floyd McCarty. Camera Operator: Roger Shearman. Chief Set Electrician: Harry Sundby. First Assistant Camera: Ron Vargas. Wardrobe Woman: Lynne Albright. Wardrobe Man: Richard Butz. Unit Publicist: Gabe Essoe. Script Supervisor: Karen Hale Wookey. First Aid Man: Dan Novack. Running time: 96 minutes.

Song: "He's Gonna Make It" Bruce Belland, Robert F. Brunner.

Cast: Kurt Russell (Steven Post), Joe Flynn (Francis X. Wilbanks), Harry Morgan (E.J. Crampton), Wally Cox (Mertons), Heather North (Jennifer Scott), Alan Hewitt (Farnsworth), Hayden Rorke (Clifford), John Ritter (Roger), Jack Bender (Tom), Tom Alfinsen (Dr. Schmidt), George N. Neise (Network Executive), Ed Reimers (Announcer), Morgan Farley (Advertising Executive), Glenn Dixon (Sponsor), Robert Shayne (Sponsor), Tris Coffin (Sponsor), James B. Douglas (Network Executive), Ed Prentiss (Harry, Justice Department Man), Fabian Dean (Jackhammer Man), Iris Adrian (Woman Shopper), Jack Smith (Clathworthy), Eve Brent (Mrs. Crampton), Sandra Gould (Mrs. Wilbanks), James Flavin (Father O'Leary), Pete Renoudet (Policeman), Judson Pratt (Policeman), Vince Howard (Policeman), Hal Baylor (Policeman), Bill Daily (Navigator), Dave Willock (Doorman), Anthony Teague (TV Salesman), Edward Faulkner (Reporter), Raffles (Chimpanzee), Leon Alton (TV Executive), Beulah Bondi (Herself), Paul Bradley, Argentina Brunetti (Mrs. Bernaducci), Jeffrey Burbank (Homer J. Wilbanks), Cathy Crosby (Assistant at TV Awards), Howard Culver, Peter Paul Eastman (TV Executive), Ted Gehring (Motorcycle Cop), George Golden (TV Executive), John Harmon (Security Guard), Hank Jones (Stan), Tony Regan (TV Executive), Bruce Rhodewalt (Jason R. Wilbanks), Cosmo Sardo (TV Executive), Ernest Sarracino (Mr. Bernaducci), Jeffrey Sayre (TV Executive), Chet Stratton (Harry, TV Executive), Arthur Tovey (Man at Baseball Game), Herb Vigran (Fireman).

Steven Post dodges traffic as he rides his motorcycle at a fast clip in between cars to get to UBC, the television network he works for.

Steven's co-worker Roger is tired of waiting for him and argues with Steven's girlfriend Jennifer for being late to a party for the airing of a new show for the new TV season.

Farnsworth is the head of UBC's competing network and he calls in to sarcastically congratulate UBC head Francis Wilbanks about his new show. They all know that this new show is no good.

Roger is Wilbanks' nephew and soon gets E.J. Crampton, the head of the TV network on the phone, who is not pleased with the show and hopes that the ratings will be good in the morning.

The next day, Mertons, the driver, comes to pick up Wilbanks, who is cranky because he knows that the show will be a flop. As Mertons backs up, he accidentally runs over the paperboy's bike. Wilbanks agrees to help the boy deliver his papers from the limousine on the way to the TV station.

At the station, Steven tells Wilbanks about his new show idea called "Abraham Lincoln's Doctor's Dog," who feels that this new show will be a hit because of research of what people like. Wilbanks is not interested and wants Steven to get back to the mailroom and do his duties. Meanwhile, the ratings for the previous night's show are horrible.

Later, the Bernaduccis are sad because they have to move to San Francisco. Unable to take their pet chimp, Raffles, because of the weather, Jennifer takes him on.

Jennifer leaves Raffles alone with Steve. Together they watch TV until Steve changes the channel, causing Raffles to throw a fit. Raffles wants to watch "Mother Carey's Chickens."

Jennifer advises Steve to leave the TV alone when Raffles watches. Next up is "Star Journey," which Steve wants to watch, but Raffles doesn't. Raffles wants to watch "The Maxwell Family." Jennifer says to let Raffles watch want he wants for the night.

The next day, it turns out that "Mother Carey's Chickens" and "The Maxwell Family" were the two top rated shows of the night.

Later, at a TV appliance store, Raffles is watching the display TVs. As the appliance store man changes the TVs to an opera, Raffles changes the TVs back to a Western called "The Fastest Gun," one of TV's top-rated shows. At the end of the show, an announcer relays this fact and Steve gets an idea.

Steve pays strict attention to the shows Raffles is watching and takes notes. Raffles applauds when it is a show he likes and shakes his head when it is a show he hates. He tells Jennifer to order take-out from Chicken Licken instead of going out.

Steve's hunch works and he discovers that Raffles has picked all the previous night's top-rated shows. Steve's excitement about Raffles knows causes him to create some traffic disruption, and he gets pulled over by the police.

Steve brings Jennifer some flowers and wonders where Raffles is, and Jennifer says that Roger has taken Raffles for a walk. Steve goes after Roger and discovers that Raffles likes TV by watching a TV in a shop window, but Roger denies this.

Soon the store owner shuts off the TV in the window, causing Raffles to have a fit before he tosses a rock through the window and the TV. Raffles is arrested shortly thereafter.

At the jail, Steve bails out Raffles but he doesn't have enough to bail out Roger too, much to Roger's annoyance.

Jennifer says that she needs to return the chimp to the Bernaduccis because of the trouble he has caused and Steve panics, saying that he needs Raffles. She decides to give Raffles another chance.

Steve gives movie tickets to Jennifer and the now-released Roger to get them out of his hair, so he can test some of his new TV show ideas on Raffles without disruption.

Steve begs Wilbanks to let him prove to him that he has a fool-proof method for discovering hit TV shows. Wilbanks is not listening so he recruits Mertons to help him out.

The head of UBC, E.J. Crampton is in town and he's not happy to be in third place of three networks. Mertons hands over Steve's note and Crampton is willing to give Steve a chance where Wilbanks wasn't.

Steve wants to take the films of the new shows to view, but the films are not allowed to leave the studio, so Steve sneaks Raffles in by using the mail elevator.

Jennifer shows up to see Steve at the same time that Raffles is in the elevator so Steve has to send Raffles up and down the shaft to hide him, which makes Raffles kind of sick.

Finally Jennifer leaves and Steve and Raffles join Crampton and Wilbanks who are watching "The Happy Harringtons" in progress. Raffles hates it and he makes a raspberry noise which disrupts Crampton, so Steve takes Raffles to the projection room to get him out of the way.

"Devil Dan" is next up and though the network has no faith in it, Raffles loves it. Crampton is disgusted and feels that Steve doesn't know what he's talking about so they put "The Happy Harringtons" on the schedule.

Steve is so sure that "Devil Dan" will be a hit because of Raffles' reaction that he goes to the film library and switches the film reels so that "Devil Dan" airs.

At the TV show premiere party, Steve reveals his deception and is promptly fired by Wilbanks.

The next day the ratings come in and "Devil Dan" is found to be the highest-rated show of the week. Crampton calls in and wants Steve signed to a contract, but Wilbanks says that he's been fired. Crampton says to get Steve back and promoted to Program Director. Wilbanks is promoted to Vice President of Cultural Relations, a useless position.

Raffles is brought up again and again to the projection room and this time the hit and flop shows are consistently picked. Of course, Steve gets all the rewards and accolades, including TV's Man of the Year.

Even though Wilbanks and Crampton are happy, they suspect foul play and want to know how Steve does it, so they put Roger on the trail. Roger traces everything to Steve's place and discovers that it is someone else who's doing it, but he couldn't see anything specific. Wilbanks thinks that it is bananas that are causing Steve's abilities and he starts eating them.

Roger is hiding in the closet but he leaves in haste when he is discovered by Raffles, so he doesn't figure out who Steve was talking with. Back at the TV station, Jennifer overhears Roger's conversation with Wilbanks and knows that they were talking about Raffles. She zooms home to talk to Steve and he tells the truth about the TV shows and Raffles. Jennifer decides that Raffles can stay with Steve as long as she gets visitation rights.

That night, Roger, Wilbanks, and Mertons spy on Steve through a telescope and discover the truth and tell Crampton. Crampton orders them to get Raffles.

Wilbank and Mertons go on a window ledge to sneak in and kidnap Raffles. The high altitude makes Mertons wheeze.

Finally, they get to the correct room and take Raffles away back out on the ledge, but Raffles gets away and Wilbanks and Mertons almost fall to their deaths when they slip on the ledge. When they get back to the original room, they discover that the window is closed and locked so they have to go back to the monkey's room, but then Steve closes that window, too, so they are stuck on the ledge. Raffles is back, but instead of helping them, he closes the blinds on them. Soon, Mertons' wheezing changes into hiccups.

The police arrive and talk Wilbanks and Mertons down and not to commit suicide, but they keep slipping off the ledge before being brought back to safety. They are rescued by a hook and ladder truck, but first they are shown live on the UBC news. Crampton is watching and is livid.

Father O'Leary comes up to talk them out of suicide, but Wilbanks slips and falls. Fortunately, he is caught by the waiting net. Mertons is brought inside.

Mertons reveals to the police that the chimp is selecting the TV shows, but the papers say that this is utter nonsense and the other networks are crying foul, with Farnsworth and Clifford the most vocal. A meeting is held at the networld and they conclude that the chimp needs to be destroyed.

A Dr. Schmidt speaks up and says that rather than destroy Raffles, the best thing to do is to return the chimp to the jungle, but Steve and Jennifer don't want to give him up. Then Steve is offered $500,000 to give him up, then a million. Steve takes the money, but Jen leaves him over it. Raffles is taken away in chains.

Wilbanks and Crampton have to leave with the chimp to the jungle so that the other networks don't take him and put Mertons in charge. Steve shows up to offer the money back for Raffles, but they refuse.

On the flight to drop Raffles down into the jungle, Raffles panics and releases the door, blowing all of the network executives outside and they skydive with parachutes down into the jungle. The navigator comes back with Raffles and tries to explain everything.

With Mertons still in charge, Roger is now the chauffeur and Steve and Jen get back together with Raffles. Mertons puts Steve in charge of the network as he feels that he would do a better job than himself.

In the end, Steve, Jen, and Raffles take a motorcycle ride up the coast.

The UBC logo is a combination of the logos for ABC, CBS and NBC. The UBC building is actually the ABC building in Los Angeles.

Amusingly, many of the clips that are viewed on the television are from older Disney movies, including *Treasure Island* (1950), *Swiss Family Robinson* (1960), *Babes in Toyland* (1961), *20,000 Leagues Under the Sea* (1954) and *The Shaggy Dog* (1959).

The "Devil Dan" logo is probably one of the rarest pieces of Disney animation.

While not part of the Dexter Riley series, this film definitely fits into the same mold especially since both Kurt Russell and Joe Flynn star, and it is surprisingly very funny.

Haydon Rorke and Bill Daily come to this film straight off of wrapping up *I Dream of Jeannie* and John Ritter makes his screen debut here, while Wally Cox unfortunately wraps up his movie career here.

Bill Daily plays a navigator here, an occupation that he would continue to play on his next TV series, *The Bob Newhart Show*.

This popular movie was aired many times on the Disney anthology show including 1973, 1978, 1981, and 1989. It was remade for TV in 1995.

Hank Jones got a call to be in this film at the very last moment, replacing an actor who declined to show up.

Scandalous John

RELEASED BY BUENA VISTA ON June 22, 1971, Technicolor. Producer: Bill Walsh. Director: Robert Butler. Screenplay: Bill Walsh, Don DaGradi based on the book by Richard Gardner. Director of Photography: Frank Phillips, A.S.C. Filmed in Panavision. Art Director: John B. Mansbridge. Film Editor: Cotton Warburton, A.C.E. Set Decorators: Emile Kuri, Frank R. McKelvy. Matte Artist: Alan Maley. Associate Producer: Tom Leetch. Production Design: Robert Clatworthy. Sound Supervisor: Robert O. Cook. Sound Mixer: Dean Thomas. Costumes: Chuck Keehne, Emily Sundby. Make-up: Robert J. Schiffer. Hair Stylist: Vivienne Walker. Special Effects: Robert A. Mattey. Unit Manager: Paul L. Cameron. Assistant Director: Ted Schilz. Script Supervisor: Karen Wookey. Music Editor: Evelyn Kennedy. Vocal Advisor: Natividad Vacio. Original Music Score: Rod McKuen. Music Arranger: Arthur Greenslade. Second Assistant Director: Robert Webb. Special Effects: Hans Metz. Extras Casting: Frank Kennedy. Unit Publicist: Leonard Shannon. Craft Service: John Wagner. Running time: 114 minutes.

Song: "Pastures Green," "Iris and Fido," "Desert Lullaby," "Train to Quivara," "Touch and Go," "Scandalous John Suite," "Warbag," "McCanless Country," "Paco the Brave," "Amanda," "Mariposas D'Amora," "The Tribes," "Conquistador," "Quivira, The City of Gold," "Paco, the Great Engineer." Written and Performed by Rod McKuen.

Cast: Brian Keith (John McCanless), Alfonso Arau (Paco), Michele Carey (Amanda McCanless), Rick Lenz (Jimmy Whittaker), Harry Morgan (Sheriff Pippin), Simon Oakland (Barton Whittaker), Bill Williams (Sheriff Hart), Christopher Dark (Card Dealer), Fran Ryan (Farm Woman), Bruce Glover (Sludge), Richard Hale (Old Indian), James Lydon (Grotch), John Ritter (Wendell), Iris Adrian (Mavis), Larry D. Mann (Bartender), Jack Raine (Switchman), Edward Faulkner (Hillary), John Zaremba (Wales), Alex Tinne (Clerk), Paul Koslo (Pipes), Booth Colman (Governor Murray), Bill Zuckert (Abernathy), Robert Padilla (Paco's Cousin), Ben Baker (Doctor Kropak), William O'Connell (Men's Store Clerk), Sam Edwards (Bald Head), Lenore Stevens (Girl), Jose Nieto, Margarito Mendoza, Joseph Gutierrez, Freddie Hernandez (Mariachi Band), Donald Elson, Mark Stanoch.

Two Mexicans drive a truck in the desert and one named Paco is dropped off to meet Scandalous John McCanless, a salty old man who ropes and ties him down.
    His granddaughter Amanda McCanless stops him as John has made a mistake. He thought Paco was a man named Whittaker.
    Amanda convinces John to hire Paco to cook and do a few odd jobs, and to live on the farm, because she teaches at the college and doesn't have time to be out there all the time.
    John is always shooting his gun off for fear of interlopers and he destroys mirrors and other objects around the house. He also complains an awful lot.
    Amanda leaves and Paco tries to get John to eat, but he just throws a bottle at him. Soon Paco wins John over by showing his skills on the guitar, causing John to dance. John gives Paco the guitar as a gift.
    The next day, Amanda is trying to convince Jim Whittaker to deal with her grandfather and his land. Jim tells John he wants to turn it into a McCan-

less Museum, but reveals that he only has 40 days left to live on his land until it reverts to Whittaker due to bad debts. Jim gives his warning and drives off with John firing shots at his car.

Later, Paco is wandering around outside and John can't see him very well. John thinks he's a trespasser and fires shots at him. Eventually, Paco reveals himself. John and Paco fire shots together randomly. John shows Paco various items around the house, including a painting of his father.

John talks about Blackjack, which confuses Paco, but John doesn't reveal who he is. Then he talks about Quivera, the golden city and other things.

The next morning, John wakes Paco up bright and early with an out-of-tune bugle blast. John shows Paco all of his animals, such as mules and horses. Paco tries to ride one of the mules, but fails repeatedly.

John tries to rope his steer from his horse and falls flat on his face. He is witnessed by Jim, who offers money to help John out in exchange for helping him to get chummier with Amanda.

Later, John rides a horse and Paco finally rides his mule while being followed by a group of children looking for a coin handout.

John and Paco literally ride into a men's Western wear shop to buy Paco some new clothes. Then John sends Paco off to the general store with a list and Paco rides his mule into the store to retrieve the items. The proprietor of the store gets Sheriff Pippin, who plans to send Paco back across the border until John rides in to stop him. John and Paco leave the store rather than deal with the sheriff.

Back at the ranch, Jim is there again to see them arrive back home. Then he helps them leave again on their own in order to avoid the law.

Pippin and Amanda arrive shortly thereafter, but too late to do anything. Pippin was trying to support John until John stole the lights and sirens from Pippin's vehicle.

Amanda is mad at Jim for letting John and Paco leave. Meanwhile, John and Paco are doing fine, singing and playing by a campfire. John keeps thinking he hears a cougar and starts shooting his gun again.

The next day, they continue traveling while Amanda and Jim try to find them. They stop at the house of a farm woman who is kind until she discovers that he's a Whittaker and sics her dogs on them.

John and Paco happen across a wild bar filled with Indians and motorcyclists. John ropes them all and then starts shooting at them. Then he tries to communicate with the Indians in their native language, to which they respond, "I don't get it."

The bartender is upset with what has happened and John gives her a few bucks to shut her up. They continue to move on with Amanda and Jim continuing to follow.

At one point, John and Paco come across some billboards with beer and ice cream on them, but John insists that the signs are all mirages. Then they pass by a major city, but John insists that this is a mirage, too. Eventually, they find a river to bathe in and drink from.

Rod McKuen burbles out "Pastures Green" on the soundtrack as the two continue to travel. They come across some "Indians" in a "Wild West Town" designed for tourists and gamblers. John and Paco go into a bar and ask for whiskey, which is not normally served as this is a tourist attraction and not a real Western town.

John goes to gamble and he puts down a large amount of real money and also fires his gun when agitated. His bullets hit the train and he is ordered to be arrested by a man on the train who happens to be Barton Whittaker, but the arrest is temporarily interrupted by the arrival of Amanda and Jim.

Barton and Jim discuss that there's only one more plot of land in dispute and that soon they will have it. Jim reveals that the owner of the land is John, the one who shot at the train.

Amanda, meanwhile, puts John to bed in the jail. Barton comes to visit to somehow work out a deal to get John's land. John said that he's selling his cattle to raise the money for the debt. Barton says that John's cattle are tainted.

Jim is now against his own father and tells Amanda that that John is the only one who really can stop his father.

Paco looks out the jail cell window and realizes that the "Indians" in the town are actually a mariachi band. Amanda then springs her grandfather and Paco out of the jail by blowing up the cell wall. John and Paco ride off trying to catch a speeding train in order to hijack it. The mariachi band is playing on the train while John holds everyone else up. He wants his cattle back. Barton reminds John that the cattle are tainted, but John shoots a hole through the paper claim.

Meanwhile, at the next railroad crossing Jim and Amanda try to stop the train, but it does not stop and it continues to barrel down the tracks, not even stopping at the stations.

Paco joins the mariachi band. John asks who's driving the train and Paco says that the train drives by itself. What he doesn't know is that there is another train on the same set of tracks headed in the opposite direction, so the train has to go on a side track.

Then John boots everyone off the train, including the mariachi band -- everyone except Barton, who John now refers to as "Blackjack."

The two trains do collide but Paco, John, and Barton are safe. Barton has a gun and it looks as if he shoots John, but it is Wendell who has shot John. John is dying but Paco points out that they have made it to Quivera, the golden city. Amanda cries, hoping that John does not die, but it is too late.

At John's grave, Amanda says goodbye to Paco and stays with Jim on the ranch. Paco rides off back home. As he rides, he sees a ghostly image of John. Rod McKuen reprises "Pastures Green."

Disney must have had higher hopes for this movie than most as this is the first major release since Walt's death to be released in Panavision. It didn't help.

The film is touted as a comedy but is an overall bore, unless hearing Brian Keith grumbling around and acting crazy is your idea of humor. It was also a tremendous flop, grossing only about $1.5 million.

Although uncredited, the film is based upon Miguel de Cervantes y Saavedra's *Don Quixote*.

The Million Dollar Duck

RELEASED BY BUENA VISTA ON June 30, 1971, Technicolor. Producer: Bill Anderson. Director: Vincent McEveety. Screenplay: Roswell Rogers based on a story by Ted Key. Director of Photography: William Snyder, A.S.C. Art Directors: John B. Mansbridge, Al Roelofs. Film Editor: Lloyd L. Richardson, A.C.E. Set Decorators: Emile Kuri, Hal Gausman. Special Photographic Effects: Eustace Lycett. Titles: Ward Kimball, Ted Berman. Second Unit Director: Arthur J. Vitarelli. Sound Supervisor: Robert O. Cook. Sound Mixer: Dean Thomas. Costumes: Chuck Keehne, Emily Sundby. Make-up: Robert J. Schiffer. Hair Stylist: La Rue Matheron. Assistant Director: Christopher Hibler. The Million Dollar Duck handled by Henry Cowl. Music Editor: Evelyn Kennedy. Music: Buddy Baker. Orchestration: Walter Sheets. Production Manager: John D. Bloss. Second Assistant Director Trainee: Scott Adam. Second Assistant Directors: Ronald R. Grow, Dorothy Kieffer. Assistant Director Trainee: Nathan Haggard. Assistant Director: William R. Poole. Prop Master: Jack Calconda. Props: Bob McLing, Reggie Pierce. Assistant Property Master: Ralph Mikkelson. Cableman: Henry Maffett. Mikeman: Frank Regula. Set Effects Man: Greg Auer. Special Effects: Hans Metz. Stunts: Denny Arnold. Still Photographer: Bob Coburn. Camera Operators: Edward Colman, Bill Ion, Jack Willoughby. Assistant Camera: John C. Flinn III, Gene Jackson, Michael St. Hilaire. Best Boy: Bill Glascock. Gaffer: Otto Meyer. Key Grips: Bill Record, Stan Reed. Second Grip: Forrest Reed. Gaffer: Harry Sundby. Assistant Film Editor: James W. Swain. Transportation: Jack Snyder. Radios: Les Gear. Script Supervisor: Doris Grau. Unit Publicist: Ben Hartigan. Welfare Worker: Dorothy Masters. Script Supervisor: Lloyd Nelson. Location Manager: William T. Schneider. Running time: 93 minutes.

Cast: Dean Jones (Professor Albert Dooley), Sandy Duncan (Katie Dooley), Joe Flynn (Finley Hooper), Tony Roberts (Fred Hines), James Gregory (Rutledge), Lee Harcourt Montgomery (Jimmy Dooley), Jack Kruschen (Doctor Gottlieb), Jack Bender (Arvin Wadlow), Sammy Jackson (Frisby), Frank Wilcox (Bank Manager), Virginia Vincent (Eunice Hooper), Billy Bowles (Orlo Wadlow), Arthur Hunnicutt (Mr. Purdham), Bryan O'Byrne (Bank Teller), Ted Jordan (Mr. Forbes), Pete Renoudet (Mr. Beckert), George O'Hanlon (Parking Attendant), Hal Smith (Courthouse Guard), Bing Russell (Mr. Smith), Frank Cady (Assayer), Jonathan Daly (Purchasing Agent), Edward Andrews (Morgan),  Robert Shayne, Peter Camlin (Frenchman), Charlie (The Duck), Winnie Collins (Agitated Woman Driver), Howard Culver (Morgan's Assistant), Maurice Dallimore (Englishman), Bernard Fox (Car Salesman), John J. Fox (Agitated Driver #1), Jerry Fujikawa (Japanese), Stu Gilliam, Jonathan Hole (Refinery Agent), Hank Jones (Commencement Speaker), Jack Perkins (Agitated Driver #2), Tony Regan (Refinery Agent's Assistant), Edwin Reimers, Roy Roberts (The Judge), Fran Ryan (Mrs. Purdham), Maxine Semon (Woman Leaving Parking Garage), Vaughn Taylor (Bank President), Bruno VeSota (Russian).

Good duck animation by Ward Kimball and Ted Berman opens this comedy.

We find Albert Dooley trying to pay his bills, or actually reading the past-due notices on his bills. He reflects on his graduation ceremony in 1959 where he was voted most likely to succeed, only to be interrupted by his son, Jimmy, who wants a $50 dog. Albert says no and Jimmy runs off to his room.

Albert's wife Katie is cooking in the kitchen as a fan turns the pages in her cookbook, causing her to combine two unrelated recipes. Albert comes in to talk about economizing and Katie gives him a sample of the applesauce that she's preparing that has been made with curry powder and mustard. She proves her consistent dizziness again and Albert leaves her alone.

The next day, Katie packs Albert a lunch with the applesauce. Finley Hooper, an IRS agent, is Albert's next door neighbor and an irritable guy. Albert drives to work and picks up his friend, Fred, who's a lawyer and also struggling financially.

Albert gets to his psychology lab and says hi to his various animals and also discards Katie's inedible lunch, which is retrieved by a caged chimp that rejects it and gives it to a neighboring duck, which eats the applesauce with relish.

The duck is being used for intelligence experiments, but Dr. Gottlieb, Albert's boss, is not impressed and wants to stop using the duck for tests.

Gottlieb says to get rid of the duck, which escapes and wanders into the radiology department, with Albert trying to find out where she went. The duck is returned to Albert, but not before being hit with a small dose of radiation.

Since Gottlieb wants the duck out of the lab, Albert brings her home, where Jimmy befriends her and calls her "Charlie," not knowing she's a girl duck. Albert tells Katie to give the duck to Mr. Purdham, one of the local farmers.

Katie feels that Albert is causing a "generation gap" by not letting Jimmy have a dog or the duck. Meanwhile, the duck has flown over to Hooper's pool. Hooper tries to fish her out with a net, and he eventually falls in the pool.

After the duck is rescued, Charlie lays two eggs. It turns out that a dog bark causes Charlie to lay eggs; the same thing that happened at the lab when a recording of a dog bark caused the same thing. Katie says they could eat the eggs but Albert says no, because he knows the duck has been irradiated.

Later that evening as he goes to bury the eggs, he accidentally drops one and it cracks open to reveal that it has a solid gold yolk.

Fred wanders by and wants to know what Albert is doing. Albert claims that he is digging for night crawlers. Fred says that they lay awfully big eggs and calls Albert a nut.

The next day, Albert asks Gottlieb if radiation can make something organic into something inorganic. He says yes and proves it with a case from one of his textbooks. Albert asks if an egg can turn into something metal to which Gottlieb replies, "What do you want, gold eggs?"

They laugh and Albert leaves and goes to a testing lab. The assayer says that the egg shaped item has traces of pectin and garlic and various other strange impurities, but is basically pure gold.

Albert shows the report to Fred, and asks him for legal advice for the gold. When he gets home, he tells Katie that the duck lays gold eggs, but she says that she's given the duck to Mr. Purdham. Now, Albert scrambles to get Purdham's address and rescue the duck. Fred, Katie, and Jimmy go with him.

Albert offers Purdham five dollars to buy the duck back, but what they don't know is that there are hundreds of ducks to search through. Albert tells Fred to bark with him in order to find Charlie.

Jimmy is upset that they can't find Charlie and leaves the duck pen gate open and all the ducks escape. Charlie actually follows Jimmy and he cheers up.

Albert tests to see if it's the correct duck by barking. Katie suggests barking at different pitches and sure enough, Charlie lays another golden egg with a correctly pitched bark.

Later, Fred and Albert discuss how they can protect "their" fortune. Fred says that Albert will need a full-time lawyer and partner and suggests that no one tell anyone about this, especially Hooper.

The next day, Katie sends Jimmy off to school and then gets a call from the bank due to bad checks. She gets the idea of getting the money by turning in a couple of the golden eggs that Charlie has just laid.

Katie is taken out of line to see the bank's president, who tells her that they cannot accept the gold as payment. He advises that she take the gold to a refinery, which she does and gets a check and a new hat after depositing over $900.

Albert comes home and blows his top when he discovers what Katie has done. Fred comes over and says that what Katie has done was ok because they don't legally have the right to handle gold. Fred says that it's better to sell the eggs to the refineries, because they won't arrest her because they would feel that she's innocent.

Albert discovers that Fred has been purchasing some new things for himself including a new suit, and he glares at him for his extravagance.

Katie sells another egg to another refinery, but the man named Carter is more suspicious and puts a call in to the US Treasury Department.

Albert meanwhile is test-driving some new cars and says that he will be back once he gets enough money.

Soon, Rutledge and Morgan of the IRS conduct a meeting. They are tracking all the gold egg sales to the local refineries and wonder where the eggs are coming from, because the cost of nuclear bombardment to create gold is cost prohibitive. One of the men in this meeting is Albert's neighbor, Hooper.

During the meeting, Morgan starts receiving a number of phone calls from various nations wondering where the gold is coming from, because this will potentially affect the world's economy. They mention that the name of the person selling the eggs is named Dooley, and Hooper says that his neighbor is named Dooley.

Hooper starts snooping on Katie, and Hooper's wife thinks that he's just lusting after her, not investigating. Albert comes home and is worried that Hooper suspects something.

Fred drives up in his new car and Albert complains again about Fred's extravagance when they are not supposed to be spending. He also informs Fred that Hooper is snooping and that the duck could stop laying gold eggs due to the radiation's half-life.

Albert looks for Charlie, who is with Jimmy at the home of some teenage neighbors that drive recklessly when around Albert and Fred to annoy them. Charlie steps up on a car battery and starts to glow due to her radioactivity. The teenagers hook up a radio and a car horn to the duck and they work. Soon, Albert and Fred drive up and take Charlie and Jimmy home.

At home, Albert tests to see if Charlie can still lay the gold eggs, while Hooper spies on them. Hooper's wife calls him a masher, but he does see that the duck can lay golden eggs.

Later, Hooper sees Jimmy privately and wants to see if he can get Charlie to lay an egg, which she does, but Katie arrives just in time to pick up the egg.

Katie calls Albert to tell him that Hooper knows about Charlie and Albert tells Fred. Meanwhile, Hooper tells Rutledge about the duck, but he doesn't believe him. Agent Beckert says that he checked with Gottlieb and corroborates with Hooper's story.

Hooper and the other IRS agents arrive at Albert's house, but Fred says that he has no proof. Albert tells Fred that he won't bark in the correct pitch so that Charlie won't produce.

Jimmy, meanwhile, escapes with Charlie on his bike, prompting a major car chase with Albert and Fred and all the IRS agents in separate cars.

The agents stop and search a man's truck, thinking the duck is aboard, and the man thinks that he's on one of those *Candid Camera*-type shows.

Meanwhile, Jimmy climbs out of the dumpster he was hiding in with Charlie and escapes the other way. Everyone chases Jimmy again and all of the cars end up in a pile-up.

The teenagers drive by and pick up Jimmy and Charlie and speed away. Albert, Fred, and Katie follow on foot since their car is destroyed, but they eventually hijack a truck. Albert is on the back, holding on precariously to the truck's built-in ladder which swings from side to side and up and down.

The IRS men and two motorcycle cops are now chasing them through a tunnel and up a parking structure before another crash disables them.

Now, the teenagers, Jimmy, and Charlie are on foot, with Albert after them. The teenagers send Jimmy with Charlie on a ladder straddling two buildings to escape. Albert tries to rescue Jimmy, but Jimmy refuses because he feels that all his dad wants is the duck. Jimmy changes his mind when the ladder starts to crack and Albert rescues him and Charlie at the last moment.

By this time, the IRS agents have shown up and confiscate the duck and arrest Albert. With a police escort, Charlie and Albert arrive at the court house.

At the trial, Hooper claims that he has gotten Charlie to lay a golden egg and tries to repeat it in court. Albert says that Hooper is barking at the wrong pitch and gets Charlie to lay an egg. Fred advises against this, but Albert wants to get everything out in the open.

Albert gets Charlie to lay an egg, but this time it is just an ordinary egg. The case is dismissed due to lack of evidence and Albert hands Charlie to Jimmy.

The movie is based on a story by Ted Key, who also wrote *The Cat from Outer Space* (1978), but is probably best known for his comic panel from *The Saturday Evening Post* called *Hazel* that was later turned into a primetime TV sitcom.

Of course, Key's inspiration was from the classic Aesop's Fable.

Though the movie poster says *$1,000,000 Duck*, the actual title onscreen is *The Million Dollar Duck*.

Frank Cady is here straight off the set of the recently canceled *Green Acres* and *Petticoat Junction*, of which he was a star on both.

This was George O'Hanlon's first movie for Disney. He had a lengthy career doing theatrical shorts, but by this time O'Hanlon was best known as the voice of George Jetson.

Classic line in this movie, when Albert tries to grab one of the eggs from Fred: "I am the egg man." Goo goo goo joob.

This is another winning Disney comedy with a solid premise, much better than *Scandalous John* (1971) for that reason.

This was Vincent McEveety's directorial debut for Disney. He directed 12 more films for Disney over the years, including some of the studios' most popular.

The film was shot between August and October 1970.

The movie aired many times on the anthology show in 1974, 1979 and 1982.

Geez, nobody else likes Disney films. This apparently was one of three movies that film critic Gene Siskel walked out of in his lifetime. There are worse films than this, and even worse Disney films than this. I like this film. It's one of my favorites.

Towards the end of the movie, when Jimmy is chasing Charlie the duck, we see a VW Beetle with the license plate OFP 857, the same as Herbie's in *The Love Bug* (1969), which also starred Dean Jones.

Tony Roberts was in the middle of doing a stage play of *Promises, Promises* in San Francisco so he had to fly back and forth from LA to SF six times a week.

Pete Renaday, a.k.a. Renoudet, remembers that he had one of his largest parts in this film. Renaday was one of Disney's most consistent utility players during the late 1960s and the 1970s, appearing in many of their films in minor roles, and he also narrated many films and theme park attractions and film trailers, taking over eventually for long-time trailer narrator Dick Tufeld (best known as the voice of the robot on *Lost in Space*.)

Bedknobs and Broomsticks

RELEASED BY BUENA VISTA ON December 13, 1971 (October 7, 1971 in UK), Technicolor. Producer: Bill Walsh. Director: Robert Stevenson. Screenplay: Bill Walsh, Don DaGradi based on the book by Mary Norton. Director of Photography: Frank Phillips, A.S.C. Art Directors: John B. Mansbridge, Peter Ellenshaw. Film Editor: Cotton Warburton, A.C.E. Set Decorators: Emile Kuri, Hal Gausman. Costume Designer: Bill Thomas. Assistant to the Designer: Shelby Anderson. Title Design: David Jonas. Sound Supervisor: Robert O. Cook. Sound Mixer: Dean Thomas. Costumes: Chuck Keehne, Emily Sundby. Make-up: Robert J. Schiffer. Hair Stylist: La Rue Matheron. Assistant Director: Christopher Hibler. Scripts Supervisor: Lois Thurman. Music Editor: Evelyn Kennedy. Assistant to the Conductor: James MacDonald. Dance Accompanist: Albert Mello. Assistant Choreographer: Carolyn Dyer. Second Unit Director: Arthur J. Vitarelli. Technical Consultants: Manfred Lating, Milt Larsen, James McInnes, Bob Baker, Spunbuggy Works. Animation Director: Ward Kimball. Animation: Milt Kahl, Art Stevens, John Lounsbery, Julius Svendsen, Eric Larson, Hal King, Fred Hellmich, Jack Buckley, Jack Boyd. Animation Story: Ralph Wright, Ted Berman. Layout: Don Griffith, Joe Hale. Animation-Live Action Design: McLaren Stewart. Background: Al Dempster, Dick Kelsey, Bill Layne, Ralph Hulett. Animation Film Editor: James W. Swain. Music and Lyrics: Richard M. Sherman, Robert B. Sherman. Music Supervisor, Arranger and Conductor: Irwin Kostal. Choreography: Donald McKayle. Special Effects: Alan Maley, Eustace Lycett, Danny Lee. Original Music: Irwin Kostal. Hair Stylist: Sharleen Rassi. Makeup Artist: Lynn F. Reynolds. Production Manager: John D. Bloss. Second Assistant Director Apprentice: Dorothy Kieffer. Second Assistant Director: William R. Poole. First Assistant Director, Second Unit: Robert Webb. Prop Master: Jack Colconda. Assistant Set Decorator, Underwater Sequence: John Emerson. Props: Bob McLing. Assistant Property Master: Ralph Mikkelson. Assistant Art Director: Al Roelofs. Cablemen: Bud Maffett, Henry Maffett. Boom Operator: Frank Regula. Set Effects: Howard Jensen. Special Effects: Hans Metz. Still Photographers: Bob Coburn, John R.

Shannon. Gaffer: Bill King. Assistant Director: Jim Luske. Second Grip: Marvin Mayo. Best Boy: Otto Meyer. Key Grip: Stan Reed. Assistant Camera: Michael St. Hilaire. Camera Operator: Jack Whitman, Sr. On-Set Costumer, Women: Mary Dye. On-Set Costumers, Men: John George, Kent James. Orchestrator: Irwin Kostal. Publicist: Tom Clark. Rental of Barrows, Portobello Road Sequence: A. Keene. Assistant Choreographer: Bill Landrum. Running time: 139 minutes.

Songs: "The Old Home Guard," "A Step in the Right Direction," "The Age of Not Believing," "With a Flair," "Eglantine," "Portobello Road," "Portobello Street Dance," "The Beautiful Briny," "Substitutiary Locomotion," "Nobody's Problems." Music and Lyrics: Richard M. Sherman and Robert B. Sherman.

Cast: Angela Lansbury (Miss Eglantine Price), David Tomlinson (Professor Emelius Browne), Roddy McDowall (Mr. Jelk), Sam Jaffe (Bookman), John Ericson (Colonel Heller), Bruce Forsyth (Swinburne), Tessie O'Shea (Mrs. Hobday), Arthur E. Gould-Porter (Captain Greer), Ben Wrigley (Portobello Road Workman), Reginald Owen (General Teagler), Cyril Delevanti (Elderly Farmer), Rick Traeger (German Sergeant), Manfred Lating (German Sergeant), John Orchard (Vendor), Ian Weighill (Charlie Rawlins), Roy Snart (Paul Rawlins), Cindy O'Callaghan (Carrie Rawlins), Robert Holt (Voice of Mr. Codfish), Lennie Weinrib (Voice of Secretary Bird, Voice of King Leonidas), Dal McKennon (Voice of Bear), Leon Alton (Soldier at Portobello Road), Conrad Bachmann (German Soldier), Eric Brotherson, James Brugman (Soldier Playing Tenor Saxophone), Patrick Sullivan Burke (Soldier), Patrick Dennis-Leigh (Old Home Guardsman), Anthony Eustrel (Vendor), Morgan Farley (Old Piano Player), Ina Gould (Shopkeeper), Delos Jewkes (Old Home Guardsman), Sid Kane (Vendor), Milt Larsen (Spectator at Emelius' Failed Magical Performance), Arthur Malet (Mr. Widdenfield – Museum Guard), George Mann (Old Home Guardsman), Chris Marks (Minor Role), Barbara Morrison, Richard Peel (Vendor), Jack Raine (Old Home Guardsman), Maxine Semon (Portobello Dancer), Arthur Space (Old Home Guardsman), Hank Worden (Old Home Guardsman).

Additional credits for The 25th Anniversary Special Edition (1996): Film Editor: Tony Malanowski. Technical Supervisor: Paul Rutan, Jr. Restoration Coordinator: Ed Hobelman. Negative Cutting: Holly Austin. Color Timer: Romeo Fornoles. Laboratory Services: Four Media Company. Digital Color Sequence: Pacific Title Digital. Special Opticals: Pacific Title and Art Studio. Special Titles: Buena Vista Imaging. Original Backgrounds: Walt Disney Feature Animation Research Library. Music Reconstruction: Andy Belling. Sound Mixer: Dave Concors. Audio Research: Ron Moortgat. Music Research: John Armentrout. ADR Casting: Disney Character Voices. ADR Recording: Bill Komar, the Bakery. Sound Services: Buena Vista Sound. ADR Voice Artists: Jeff Bennett (Emelius Brown), Faye DeWitt (Mrs. Hobday), Gregory Grundt (Charlie Rawlins), Amanda MacQueen (Carrie Rawlins), Corey Burton (Bookman), Joe Baker (Captain Greer), Corey Burton (Mr. Widdenfield). Thanks: Harry Arends, John Baker, Fox Carney, John Chambers, Mark Dornfeld, Jim Everitt, Howard Green, Scott Kelly, Brian King, Angela Lansbury, Susie Lum, Leonard Maltin, Stephanie Mangano, Roddy McDowall, Ginger Navrides, Les Perkins, Kerrie Preston, Richard Sherman, Randy Thornton, Robert Tieman. Special Thanks: Tim Barbour. Restoration Supervisor: Scott MacQueen.

It is England in August of 1940, and World War II is underway. A British man paints out a road sign and children are evacuated out of town for protection against the Germans. Three children named Carrie, Charles and Paul Rawlins have been assigned to a woman named Miss Price.

In the meantime, the elder guards who fought back in World War I are marching and sing "The Old Home Guard."

Finally, Miss Price arrives to meet with Miss Hobday at the post office to pick up her parcel and the three children. Price's parcel includes a broom sent to her from Professor Emelius Brown.

Price is not fond of having children, but Hobday reminds her that she has to take the children by government order.

A local Reverend Jelk congratulates Miss Price for taking the children, but Price says that she won't be having the children for very long.

Hobday asks the Reverend Jelk if he will be joining the army, to which the Reverend Jelk replies with a cough that he can't because of his quinsy.

Miss Price arrives at her home with the children and they meet Cosmic Creepers, Price's cat. Price shows them their room and tells them to wash up for meals. The children are not fond of Miss Price because of her strictness.

The children reveal that they don't have any parents and they were living with their Aunt Betty, who died in an explosion.

Price asks the children what they like to eat and they list many fried foods. To their dismay, Price instead serves them cooked vegetables.

Later, with the children all tucked into bed, Miss Price sneaks into another room. Price locks the door and takes out her broom. With this broom, Miss Price can now call herself an apprentice witch.

Meanwhile, the children awaken in order to sneak out and back to London.

Price practices how to fly on her broom by saying the proper magic words, but on her first attempt lets the broom fly out of her hands and across the room. Eventually, she gets a grasp on it and flies around in the sky.

The children spy Miss Price, who initially flies well, but then drops out of the sky. The children take this opportunity to escape, but before they do they decide to stay and use her witch skills to their advantage.

Charles says that they will stay as long as they can get a sausage on the table, don't have to wash, and can get some money in exchange for not reporting that she's a witch.

Miss Price turns Charles into a rabbit, although she was really trying to turn him into a toad. Cosmic Creepers comes to attack Charles, but he turns back quickly and chases the cat away.

After this bit of magic, Price reveals that she is not a wicked witch and wants to use her magical skills to help the war effort. Price and Charles finally come to an agreement and work together. She shows the children her private work room and also gives the children a small traveling spell that they can use.

She needs some small items to make the spell work and Paul unloads various items from his pockets including a bed knob from the bed upstairs. Miss Price puts the spell on the knob and now the knob will make the bed travel anywhere they want to go, but only Paul can actually make it work.

There is a knock on the door and it is the Reverend Jelk from the village, who has a letter for Miss Price and also wants to chat. Price takes the letter, but shuts the door before the Reverend Jelk can get in.

It is a letter from Professor Browne who says that due to the war, the final witch lesson will not be sent. Miss Price now needs to go to London and asks Paul if she can use the knob to go to London.

Paul and Carrie agree to go, but Charles refuses to go which prompts Miss Price to sing "The Age of Not Believing." Paul follows the instructions to make the bed knob work, but at first it doesn't go because they didn't say where they wanted to go. A second try works like a charm.

At the last moment, Charles leaps on the bed to join them and they soon travel a very psychedelic route through the air and end up in London, near where the Professor resides.

It turns out that Browne is somewhat of a charlatan and uses simple magic tricks in a street show in order to get small change from passersby. He sings about his profession as a fraud and charlatan, "With a Flair." He's also not a very good magician in any case.

Miss Price, who has left the scene for a bit searching for Browne, is shocked to find that this man the children are talking to is Mr. Browne.

Price asks for the final lesson, but Browne insists upon no refunds and that he really doesn't have anything for her and tries to leave until she turns him into a rabbit.

Browne is shocked to discover that the spells that she has been using actually work. Price asks where he got them from and Browne says that he got the spells out of an old book that Browne keeps at his home.

Browne is invited to join the rest on the bed to go to Browne's home. He is surprised that the traveling spell works as well, and it does like a charm.

They arrive at a place that has been evicted for the war, but it is the place where Browne is illegally squatting. He invites everyone inside and offers them dinner from the abandoned foodstuffs left in the house.

After lunch, the children explore the house and discover quite a lot of toys, revealing that whoever used to live there had a number of children.

Price asks Browne for the spell of Substitutiary Locomotion, to which Browne shows off a poster where Price could become his personal onstage assistant and sings "Eglantine" to convince her to join him.

Meanwhile, Paul and Charles find a book called *The Island of Naboombu*. Charles feels that it is childish, but Paul likes it.

Eventually, Miss Price tires of Browne's singing and turns him into a rabbit again in order to get him to find the book she was looking for. He finally retrieves *The Spells of Astoroth* as a rabbit. Miss Price looks through the book and discovers that the Substitutiary Locomotion spell is missing.

Price demands to find out where the rest of the book is, and Browne says and sings "Portobello Road," an ode to a street sale that sells virtually everything from priceless collectibles to worthless junk, and everything in between.

They eventually get to the dealer of old books, who tries to push books other than the one Miss Price is looking for. When Price inquires about the book there are eavesdroppers and dancers, many of whom get in the way of Miss Price's book research.

Soon it is closing time, but no book has been found. The same eavesdropping stranger comes up, threatens Browne and Price with a knife, and leads them and the kids to the shop of one of the booksellers, bed and all.

The bookman has the second section of the book and has been seeking the first section of the book, which Price owns. Together they look at both sections of the book, but neither section tells the five magic words needed for the Substitutiary Locomotion spell.

The bookman says that the star that has the magic words on it would be available on the Island of Naboombu. Paul reveals his book and both the bookman and his accomplice pull knives, but before they can stab them and take Paul's book, Price, Browne, and the kids jump on the bed and travel to Naboombu.

At first the bed sinks to the bottom of the sea where they encounter an animated fish named Mr. Codfish. Price asks where Naboombu is, and Codfish says that's it up above.

They start singing "The Beautiful Briny" with various other animated sea creatures.

Price and Browne begin to dance and undersea ballet and win a large gold cup.

As soon as they win, a fish hook appears and a fisherman bear pulls up the bed with Price, Browne and the kids.

The bear is upset because there is a "No Peopling Allowed" sign, and he tries to throw them back. Price would rather see the king, so the bear reluctantly leads the way to his majesty's tent, where the king is apparently not in a good mood, as the secretary bird is thrown out as soon as they arrive to see the king.

Browne offers his talents as an entertainer to the secretary bird in order to cheer him up. The bird says that the reason for the king's rage is that the day's soccer game has been canceled.

Browne reveals that he is a good soccer player and offers to be the referee. The king, who is a lion, leaves the tent in a better mood since the game can begin. Price and the children see that the king has the star they are looking for hanging around his neck.

It's the yellow team vs. the blue team, with various animals taking turns kicking the ball, with Browne ending up the victim of much abuse due to being trampled repeatedly.

The soccer game is rather exciting, with both teams giving it their all until the ball hits the horn of a rhino and ball deflates while swirling around aimlessly. The king gets really angry and shouts, "Stop that ball!," causing a major hurricane.

After the dust settles, the king blows the now-deflated ball into the net and he wins the game.

After the game, Browne pulls a "gypsy switch" on the king and switches his whistle for the king's royal star with the magic words. Price, Browne, and the kids make a hasty retreat for the bed, but not before the king realizes what has happened, but Price is able to turn the king into a rabbit long enough for them to make their getaway.

They end up back in Miss Price's home, medallion and all, or so they thought. When Browne opens his handkerchief, there is nothing there but animated sparkles swirling away.

Browne takes the children to a local pub to grab some dinner and also to leave Price alone in her thoughts. Paul says he remembers what the medallion said, but no one is listening. In fact, Carrie takes Paul away.

Browne takes the kids to Mrs. Hobday for food and reveals his feeling for Miss Price. The Reverend Jelk overhears the conversation and wonders what it was all about.

Back at Miss Price's house, Paul is finally heard and he says that the magic words they are looking for were in his Naboombu book all along. Price tries out the words, but nothing happens.

Browne says that the words should be said with some rhythm and they start singing "Substitutiary Locomotion" and finally, some shoes start walking by themselves.

Soon all hell breaks loose as many items of clothing take a life of their own. Eventually Browne suggests his all-purpose stopping spell, but not before the snooping Reverend Jelk sees it at work.

Then, while they are all eating sausages and mash, Browne decides to juggle and drops one of the balls in his mash, which splashes in his face, prompting everyone including Miss Price to laugh.

Mrs. Hobday stops by and reveals that she has finally found a home for the children, but circumstances have changed and Miss Price doesn't want to let the children go, and neither does Mr. Browne.

Browne is not totally sure, however, and makes his escape back to London, and hopes that he can make it back to visit again after the war is over.

The children and Miss Price really don't want Browne to leave, especially Carrie, who is now in tears.

After he leaves, Price begins to sing "Nobody's Problems," but soon it's the Germans who are coming up the shore.

Later, Price puts out Cosmic Creepers for the night and when she opens the door, she is greeted by Germans.

Meanwhile, Browne will not be able to go home as no trains are running and he decides to spend the night sleeping on the bench at the train station.

Eventually he has a vision of Miss Price walking on the railroad tracks, and then actually witnesses some wires being cut by Germans. He knocks out one of the Germans and returns to Price's house, only to discover more Germans, so he discreetly climbs in through a window. Cosmic Creepers sees Browne and starts howling. The Germans check in and search for someone, but only find the cat.

The Germans hear more noises so Browne searches through Price's notes and casts the rabbit spell on himself by looking through a mirror and when the Germans bust in, Browne as a rabbit hops away.

Miss Price and the children are hauled away in handcuffs while Browne hops around observing everything. Paul tries to squeeze through the window bars of the cell they have been put in, but even he is too large.

Eventually a rabbit hops onto Miss Price's lap and then off and before turning back into Browne. The group makes plans to use magic to defeat the Germans.

Price says the magic words of Substitutiary Locomotion and soon she has an entire army consisting of suits of armor that are now moving on their own.

The Germans see this army of suits of armor and other clothing including bagpipers. Price, riding on her broom, leads the battle and the various suits of armor march into battle.

The Germans fire upon the suits, but since they are not truly alive, they do not fall and continue advancing. Meanwhile, the real British army reserves also join in the fight and start fighting back while the Germans are trying to understand who or what they are battling.

Eventually, the Germans retreat and head back out to sea, but not before one German has lobbed a hand grenade on Price's house and displaces Miss Price from her broomstick, causing her all the suits of armor to fall.

Browne and the children run to check on her, but she is alright. Meanwhile, the real army is firing shots to make sure the Germans stay away.

Price's magic spells are all destroyed, but she feels that she has done her duty and is now going to give up magic. Browne decides that the best thing for him to do is to join the army and defeat the Germans for good in the traditional way. He says that he will be back after the war.

The kids are sad again, but less so because Browne has promised to come back and they reprise the song, "The Old Home Guard."

Paul also reveals that there is still a bit of magic left in the bed knob, so who knows?

Walt himself had this film as a backup when he was making *Mary Poppins* (1964) in case he didn't get the go ahead from P.L. Travers. After *Mary Poppins* went into production, this project was shelved until many years later. Though compared consistently to *Mary Poppins*, it is quite a different film despite the presence of David Tomlinson and some live-action/animation footage and music by the Sherman Brothers.

The DVD version has scenes restored to it that fleshes out the story more. Amazingly for a studio that tended to keep EVERYTHING, the audio of these scenes no longer existed, so Angela Lansbury had to go in and re-record her voice while others like David Tomlinson's and the children's voices had to be fulfilled by impersonators as many actors had passed away or their voices had changed by the time of this restored release.

The DVD has a bonus feature about the Sherman Brothers' musical contributions to this film. Richard Sherman reveals that there was one meeting where Walt was falling asleep listening to the songs for *Bedknobs*, and shortly thereafter they got the green light for *Mary Poppins* and so everything was shelved until 1969.

The Shermans were originally assigned to complete their portion before their contract expired in 1968, but eventually were called in 1969 to start more work on the film.

Throughout 1970 and 1971, the Sherman Brothers worked on polishing the songs, even using one that wasn't used for *Mary Poppins* and revised for *Bedknobs*. It was originally called the "North Pole Polka," but eventually became "The Beautiful Briny."

"The Age of Not Believing" became Eglantine's theme song and Don DaGradi gave it the ok. It was also nominated for an Academy Award for Best Song.

Bedknobs did win the Academy Award for Best Visual Effects and was nominated for Best Art Direction / Set Decoration, Best Scoring, and Best

Costume Design. It was the last Academy Award that Disney would win until *The Little Mermaid* in 1989.

According to the Shermans, this was the first Disney film they worked on that had absolutely no Walt involvement once actual production was underway, because most of the songs were written after Walt's death.

In a 2009 documentary on the revised DVD, Les Perkins and Greg Kimble discussed the Sodium Screen Vapor Process that was developed by Ub Iwerks in the 1960s and used extensively and processed into the finished film. In my opinion, some of these "ancient" effects should be resurrected as they actually look more real at times than today's total reliance on green screen and CGI. A comparison is made between the effects in *Bedknobs* and the more recent Disney Channel TV series *Wizards of Waverly Place*.

The film originally was supposed to be 141 minutes, but 25 minutes were cut at the last minute before release. The largest cuts were to the "Portobello Road" dance sequence, which cut the scene from about 10 minutes down to less than four.

Apparently Radio City Music Hall had requirements that whatever film premiered there had to be less than two hours long, so the cuts were made but amazingly the footage wasn't saved in some cases.

"With a Flair" and "Eglantine" were cut down and "Nobody's Problems" and "Fundamental Elements" were cut entirely, as were many of Reverend Jelk's (Roddy McDowall's) scenes.

Scott MacQueen reveals that there was one song, "A Step in the Right Direction," that was the catalyst for restoring the film and after finding 20 minutes of footage, this song's footage was and is still missing. In fact, the song appears on the album soundtrack. A restoration utilizing still photographs is included on the DVD as a bonus feature.

Yet other songs like "Fundamental Elements," "Solid Citizen," and the children singing their version of "Nobody's Problems" didn't get recorded or filmed at all. Richard Sherman did record a demo of "Solid Citizen" that was released on the CD soundtrack as a bonus track.

There is footage from 1970 of David Tomlinson, sans mustache, singing "Portobello Road" in the studio.

The armor in the film was previously used in *El Cid* (1961) and *Camelot* (1967) before being rented by Disney.

The film was cut down to 117 minutes for its initial wide release in 1971 and then cut more to 98 minutes for the 1979 re-release (cutting all the songs, save two). It aired on the anthology show in 1987 and 1989.

Amazingly, the longest version works best and flows much better than any of the cut versions, but Disney in the wisdom of the time was only thinking of the kiddies and so the prevailing thought was to cut the singing and dancing and get to the cartoons and special effects as quickly as possible.

Animation-wise, *Bedknobs and Broomsticks* possibly has some of the best Disney animation done since the Xeroxography process was introduced a decade before, and certainly better than *The Aristocats* (1970) and *Robin Hood* (1973). The live-action/animation effects are significantly better here than in *Mary Poppins*.

Actresses Leslie Caron, Lynn Redgrave, Judy Carne, and Julie Andrews were all considered for the lead role until Angela Lansbury won out and Dave Tomlinson replaced Ron Moody and Peter Ustinov for his role.

The film took in $17.8 million upon its first release, which sounds like it was a major hit, but unfortunately it cost $20 million to make.

1972

Despite the box-office disappointment of *Bedknobs and Broomsticks*, this year was Disney's most successful yet, with profits of $27 million, more than twice as much as when Walt died. The major influx of cash was from the highly successful Walt Disney World.

The big news this year was to "Vote for Pooh in '72," sponsored by Sears. This was a much bigger deal than the similar campaign in 1968. I don't know if this was a subtle commentary on the political scene in 1972, but it seems appropriate in retrospect. Walt's old pal Richard Nixon was up for reelection and even Walt would probably be appalled at the actions Nixon took in order to get reelected, which ushered in the Watergate hearings and Nixon's eventual resignation, but for now, Nixon was still sitting on the top of the world, winning a landslide at the end of the year. Pooh indeed!

Another significant but now largely forgotten event was the debut of *The Mouse Factory*, an excellent little show featuring guest hosting by such Disney regulars as Kurt Russell, Wally Cox, and Annette Funicello, and footage from various Disney cartoons and feature films compiled in a central theme. Animator Ward Kimball was in charge of this series and it now would make an excellent "Walt Disney Treasures" release if Leonard Maltin cared about releasing anything from the vaults post-Walt. Apparently, Disney author and historian Maltin has incredible clout in this area, as this material could be released with or without his blessing.

Mouse Factory's other major significance is that this was the first regular non-anthology Disney TV series since *Zorro* and *Mickey Mouse Club*.

Making its debut in Disneyland on March 24 was a new land called Bear Country featuring a new attraction, the Country Bear Jamboree, which was already installed at Walt Disney World and originally planned for the now-aborted Mineral King.

Also debuting at Disneyland on June 17 was the long-running and highly popular Main Street Electrical Parade.

In Walt Disney World, If You Had Wings opened up on June 5 and writer and broadcaster Lowell Thomas celebrated his 80th birthday in the park.

Film-wise, Disney still held on, but other studios were making headway with such films as *Snoopy, Come Home*, again using the Sherman brothers for songs, and *Fritz the Cat*, proving that successful animation can have an R rating.

And, Disney on Parade continued as a successful traveling show that pre-dated the latter-day success Disney on Ice.

New films made for the anthology series include *Mountain Born, Justin Morgan Had a Horse, The City Fox, Chango, Guardian of the Mayan Treasure, Michael O'Hara the Fourth, The Nashville Coyote, The High Flying Spy, Nosey, the Sweetest Skunk in the West, Chandar, the Black Leopard of Ceylon, Salty, the Hijacked Harbor Seal*, and Julie Andrews did a one-hour salute to Disney on her *Julie Andrews Hour* show.

Three new short featurettes made it to the theaters in 1972, including *The Silver Fox and Sam Davenport*, a live action short originally released to TV in 1962, *The Magic of Walt Disney World*, a live action short promoting the new Florida theme park, and *Superstar Goofy*, a compilation cartoon of all those old Goofy "How To" films. In the 80s these were rechristened as *Sport Goofy*.

Dumbo (1941), *The Misadventures of Merlin Jones* (1964), *The Sword in the Stone* (1963) and *Swiss Family Robinson* (1960) were also reissued this year.

Disney finally chose this year to also reissue *Song of the South* (1946) coupled with a reissue of *The Boatniks* (1970)) after announcing in 1969 that it was to be shelved indefinitely. The film received no major uproar and in fact was reissued to theaters two more times before it was again shelved indefinitely.

This is a shame, as the film is not as controversial as legend would lead one to believe. The commonly available but not as notorious film *Band of Angels* (1957) is far more offensive in my opinion.

In *Song of the South* there aren't any slaves, as this is the Reconstruction period and Uncle Remus is the hero, while in *Band*, the action does take place during slavery times. The 1957 Warner Bros. release stars Clark Gable.

Strangely, the Sunday comic strip of the *Uncle Remus Sunday Color Page* which had been running since October 14, 1945 was canceled on December 31.

Non-soundtrack records released this year include *It's a Small World: Walt Disney's Greatest Hits* by the Mike Curb Congregation, which is still a best-seller on CD to this day.

In the comic book world, Gold Key continued to publish *Donald Duck, Mickey Mouse, Uncle Scrooge, Walt Disney's Comics and Stories, The Beagle Boys, Huey, Dewey and Louie Junior Woodchucks, Super Goof, Chip 'n' Dale, Scamp, Walt Disney Comics Digest, Walt Disney Showcase, The Aristokittens,* and *O'Malley and the Alley Cats* and a one-shot of *Lady and the Tramp*.

There was also the February 15th debut of a tabloid size *Disneyland* magazine that was initially published weekly and later every other week through 1974 by Fawcett Publications.

The first known attempt to create a Disneyana Collectors Club was formed this year by Stephen Horn.

The Biscuit Eater

RELEASED BY BUENA VISTA ON March 22, 1972, Technicolor. Producer: Bill Anderson. Director: Vincent McEveety. Screenplay: Lawrence Edward Watkin based on a story by James Street. Director of Photography: Richard A. Kelley, A.S.C. Art Directors: John B. Mansbridge, Al Roelofs. Film Editor: Ray de Leuw. Set Decorators: Emile Kuri, Hal Gausman. Titles: Alan Maley. Sound Supervisor: Robert O. Cook. Sound Mixer: Barry Thomas. Costumes: Chuck Keehne, Emily Sundby. Make-up: Robert J. Schiffer. Hair Stylist: La Rue Matheron. Moreover's Handler: Henry Cowl. Assistant Director: Dick Caffey. Music Editor: Evelyn Kennedy. Music: Robert F. Brunner. Orchestration: Walter Sheets. Stunts: Dick Warlock. Running time: 92 minutes.

Song: "Moreover and Me" Written and Sung by Shane Tatum.

Cast: Earl Holliman (Harve McNeil), Patricia Crowley (Mary Lee McNeil), Lew Ayres (Mr. Ames), Godfrey Cambridge (Willie Dorsey), Beah Richards (Charity Tomlin), Clifton James (Mr. Eben), Johnny Whitaker (Lonnie McNeil), George Spell (Text Tomlin), Mantan Moreland (Waiter), Rolph Von Wolfgang (Moreover), Pete Renoudet, Forrest Burns, Golden Eddie (Evans), Dorothy Hack, Paul Bradley, Sam Edwards (Gun Club Member), Jack Manning (Gun Club Member).

Lonnie McNeil is shown playing with his dog named Moreover. He teaches him some tricks until Moreover starts playing with another dog and then they wrestle in the grass.

He tells Moreover he's a bird dog and not a sheep dog. Lonnie's dad, Harve says that Moreover's nothing but a "suck egg biscuit eater" and they can't keep him because he's not a good hunting dog.

Harve goes to visit his friend, Willie, and offers him Moreover. Willie says he can't pay for it, but he'll trade. Harve says that he's not going to trade; he's giving him the dog. Willie is worried that the dog will eat his eggs, so Harve gives Willie three dollars to take the dog.

On the way back, Lonnie goes to visit his friend, Text, and tells him how he wants him to help him get the dog back by trading with Willie, but first they drop some eggs off to frame Moreover so that Willie will want to get rid of him.

Willie doesn't want to part with the dog, though, until he sees Moreover sucking the eggs Lonnie gave him, even though Willie thought they were his.

Willie trades the dog for a jack knife and also doing some work splitting and piling wood. Willie asks after the trade who is going to pay for the eggs and the kids reveal that they weren't his eggs.

A man named Eben rides by in a cart and says that Moreover killed one of his sheep, and threatens that if the dog ever sets foot on his property again, he will get shot.

Next, Eben rides over to Harve and complains about the dog and causes an argument. Harve's wife, Mary Lee tries to stop their argument, but then Eben makes threats about Lonnie and they both get angry.

Eben tells Mary Lee if Lonnie brings the dog back, he will have to be punished, because he got rid of the dog for a reason, and doesn't like the fact that Lonnie went behind his back.

After their work, Lonnie visits Text's mother, Charity, and shows her Moreover, who until this point doesn't have a name. They like the word Moreover when Charity reads a passage from *The Bible*. She says that's not a name, that's a word, but the name sticks.

By the time Lonnie gets home, his father has had a change of heart and does not punish Lonnie for getting Moreover back.

The next day, Lonnie and Text start teaching Moreover how to be a bird dog, by teaching him to retrieve.

Soon they are back at Willie's and he shows him a rifle they are interested in, but the cost in cash or trade is higher than they can afford. Willie lets them borrow the rifle if they bring him birds and mustard greens, but shells would be extra.

Harve inspects the gun and tells them that they need to keep it clean, and also tells them a few rules about handling a gun properly, like keeping the gun with the point facing up when it's not in use, so they don't accidentally shoot off their feet.

Harve also shows the boys how to hunt with a good hunting dog, but the boys prove that they have taught Moreover how to point and retrieve birds and hold them lightly in his teeth and not chomp down hard on them. Harve says that he will go with them back to Willie and help them get some shells.

The next day, Lonnie goes to see Text, but according to Charity he's in town. Lonnie's looking for Moreover, whose he's been sneaking around Eben's house. Lonnie discovers Moreover and points a gun at him.

Fortunately, Lonnie and Harve arrive just in time to take Moreover home without problems.

Text and Lonnie give Moreover a good wash and shampoo on the following day. Harve stops by to visit and Charity gives Harve some money to him for the entrance fee for the dog trials at the county seat. Harve doesn't want to take the money, because he feels that the dog won't win.

Charity wants him to take the money anyway so they can have fun and have the experience, but Harve still refuses and leaves.

Back home, Harve is upset at Lonnie for not telling him about the dog trials when Lonnie chose to tell Charity.

Later, Mary Lee is trying to figure out what Harve has against Moreover. If it's that he's really against Moreover, or if it's his pride or the possibility that Moreover might win over Silverbell, the dog that Harve is entering.

Eventually, Harve concedes to enter Moreover and also takes the money from Charity. They get to the show and enter Moreover into the competition.

The competition begins and all the participants go out into the forest with their dogs and go bird hunting. Moreover does exceptionally well.

One of the waiters at the lodge where they were staying says to another waiter that if Moreover wins, Harve will be fired out of spite. Text overhears this conversation and tells Lonnie.

After much elimination, it is now a competition between Silverbell and Moreover. Moreover does well again, but in the end, Lonnie calls Moreover a biscuit eater and calls him off because he and Text didn't want Harve to be fired.

Moreover doesn't want to eat, but then Text reveals that he's been feeding eggs to Moreover all along, so he's not been broken from his egg sucking habit.

Mr. Ames, who had been speaking with Harve during the competition, is now seeking out Text, Lonnie and Moreover to understand what happened to the dog and the competition.

Mr. Ames picks up Text and together they go see Lonnie. Ames reveals that the talk that Text overheard the waiter speak was a misunderstanding. Ames said it was a private joke that the waiter overheard and told it to the other waiter as a truth and not as a joke.

Ames says that Harve will have a job, as long as he has a job. Ames says he has to go to the city and takes Lonnie and Text with him. He says that he wants to see Moreover in competition again, but they need to rebuild Moreover's confidence. This time it is a lot tougher, because Moreover no longer trusts the boys since his morale had been broken.

At night, Text catches Moreover trying to break in to the chicken house to get some eggs. He follows Moreover to Eben's house and Eben is again ready to shoot, but instead he feeds Moreover poisoned eggs. Text runs and tells Harve and Lonnie, who go back to Eben's house.

Harve discovers Moreover in a weakened condition and places him in his truck. The dog has been poisoned and no one is sure if he'll be all right. Soon, the children fall asleep in front of the fireplace with Moreover asleep between them.

The next morning, Moreover seems to be back to his normal self and is alive and well. Willie stops by to check on the dog and offer something to kill the stomach poisoning. They offer Willie breakfast in exchange.

Text and Lonnie take a sniff at Willie's concoction and can barely stand it as the smell of it is so bad.

Harve goes back to Eben and ties up his Eben's dog. Eben doesn't admit guilt as he didn't feed Moreover the poisoned eggs. They were just there. Harve and Eben start a fistfight. After Eben admits defeat, Harve lets Eben's dog loose.

Lonnie is proud of his dad as Eben rides away. Text and Lonnie test Moreover with eggs to see if he'll eat them, but he does not.

Ames comes by to take everyone but Text, Lonnie, and Moreover to the competition. Ames says that he wouldn't be good in competition this year because of everything he went through, but maybe next year. Harve and Mary Lee go with Silverbell instead. Willie stops by Charity's house and offers to buy Moreover back if the kids won't train him anymore and pays the kids 50 dollars each. The kids refuse the money and decide to start training Moreover again.

It turns out that the money was actually Charity's and withdrawn from the bank temporarily for Willie to use in order for him to prove a point and get the kids back into training.

Mr. Ames comes back with Harve and Mary Lee and Willie tells them the good news. Ames gives Willie a box of cigars in exchange for more eggs. The good news in return is that Silverbell was the winner, and they predict that Moreover will be the winner next year.

Originally made in 1940, *The Biscuit Eater* is a fairly straightforward story. It flows pretty well as a movie, but a few scenes are a bit silly such as the one where the dog is able to become despondent after being called a biscuit eater in one scene, and then the kids are not able to break the dog out of his funk. It's not very effective or believable.

This and *Napoleon and Samantha* (1972) were made directly after Whitaker's tenure on *Family Affair*, as he was pretty much an in-demand child actor at this time. His hair is also probably at its wildest in this film.

This was comedian's Godfrey Cambridge's final film role as well. He looks rather slim here, having lost some weight since his mid-60s heyday as a stand-up comedian.

Another actor who makes his final film here was Mantan Moreland, who in earlier years played in many a film as a frightened black man with his eyes bugged out. Though his part is small, Mantan's role here is a little bit more respectable even though he is still portraying a waiter.

The movie aired on the anthology show in 1976 and also aired in syndication under the title *Tomorrow's Champions*.

Napoleon and Samantha

RELEASED BY BUENA VISTA ON July 5, 1972, Technicolor. Producer: Winston Hibler. Director: Bernard McEveety. Writer: Stewart Raffill. Director of Photography: Monroe P. Askins, A.S.C. Art Directors: John B. Mansbridge, Walter B. Simonds. Film Editor: Robert Stafford, A.C.E. Set Decorator: Emile Kuri. Titles: Jack and Jane Boyd. Associate Producers: Tom Leetch, Stewart Raffill. Sound Supervisor: Herb Taylor. Sound Mixer: Andrew Gilmore. Costumes: Chuck Keehne, Emily Sundby. Make-up: Robert J. Schiffer. Animals: Joseph and Stewart Raffill. Assistant Director: Ted Schilz. Music Editor: Evelyn Kennedy. Music: Buddy Baker. Orchestration: Walter Sheets. Property Master: Bob McLing. Gaffer: Jim Rose. Running time: 91 minutes.

Cast: Michael Douglas (Daniel Arlington Williams III), Will Geer (Grandpa), Arch Johnson (Chief of Police), Johnny Whitaker (Napoleon), Jodie Foster (Samantha), Henry Jones (Mr. Gutteridge), Major the Lion, Vito Scotti (The Clown), John Crawford (Desk Sergeant), Mary Wickes (Clerk), Ellen Corby (Gertrude), Rex Holman (Mark Pierson), Claude Johnson (Gary), John Lupton (Pete), Monty Margetts (Minor Role), John Ortega (Minor Role).

Napoleon and Samantha are crawling through the high grass pretending to be Indians. They attract Boots, a small dog who starts yapping at a local grocery store and its grocer.

After he goes inside, Napoleon grabs some empty bottles stored in the back that have already been redeemed. They bring the bottles into the store and redeem them again in order to get candy.

After they eat their candy, Napoleon and Samantha go see Charlie, a large horse in a stable and climb aboard his back without a saddle or bridle. They take Charlie to a stream and disembark.

Samantha goes home and is scolded by her grandmother Gertrude for being out so much with Napoleon. Napoleon goes home as well and talks to his Grandpa, who takes him on a walk.

On their walk, they come across Dmitri, the traveling clown with his lion called Major. They sit down together for a meal and Dmitri reveals that he has to retire, but he can't take the lion with him. All Major does is drink milk.

Napoleon says that his grandfather was a lion tamer, but Grandpa says that was a long time ago. Grandpa says that they don't have the space or the money to keep feeding the lion, but in the end, they take Major in.

The next day, Napoleon goes to school but Grandpa advises him not to discuss Major with his school friends. After school Samantha asks if Napoleon wants to play, but he says no. Then he reconsiders and tells Samantha about Major and shows him to her.

Grandpa takes Napoleon to the same store that Napoleon took the bottles from and buys a large quantity of milk. When Mr. Gutteridge asks why he's suddenly drinking so much milk, Grandpa replies that he's taking milk baths.

Later, Napoleon and Grandpa take Major for a walk and they relax atop a hill.

Grandpa exhibits the effects of aging and one day doesn't feel well and decides to spend the day in bed, so Napoleon prepares him breakfast, which isn't very good. Grandpa reveals that he is going to die soon and that Napoleon's uncle, Charlie Hammond, will be coming soon to take care of him.

The next day, Napoleon comes home with Samantha to discover that Grandpa has died. Napoleon is very sad.

Napoleon meets a man named Danny and he requests that Danny help him bury his grandfather. After Danny's initial shock, he agrees to bury him at the top of the hill, but he says that he will have to tell someone (although he never does). Samantha is in attendance at the funeral.

Danny is worried about leaving Napoleon alone with the lion, but Samantha says that she can take him in until Napoleon's uncle arrives.

Danny leaves but tells them how to get in touch with him if he needs to. Napoleon doesn't go with Samantha and continues to buy milk, acting as if Grandpa is still alive. Mr. Gutteridge wants to pay Grandpa a visit, but Napoleon lies and says that Grandpa is away for a few days.

The next day, Napoleon and Samantha decide to run away with Major to find Danny. On their way, they encounter a mountain lion that has chased a chicken up a tree. Major saves the kids and they continue on their way.

At one point they get to a stream of water and Major won't come, so Napoleon and Samantha pull him until he falls in the water.

They keep going and set up a temporary camp. After a good night's sleep, they continue on and travel up and over a very high mountain. Major doesn't want to go any further and Napoleon tries to force him and then slips off the side of the mountain. Samantha throws down a rope and Major finally moves and hoists Napoleon up.

In the meantime, the Chief of Police is checking around and asks Gertrude questions. They also discover Grandpa's grave.

Napoleon and Samantha encounter more troubles when they meet up with a wild bear, but Major fends for himself and after a battle, the bear runs off.

After more walking, Samantha sits down and starts to cry, something she said that she wouldn't do when they started their trek. Samantha is worried that they are lost. Napoleon says that they have nothing to worry about and that they could just live off the land like Indians if they had to.

At one point, Napoleon discovers a wild rabbit and chases him for food. The rabbit gets away, but Napoleon finally gets some food: snails.

Finally, they meet up with Danny and tell him of their adventures and that they are also starving. Danny is happy to see them, but upset that they lied to him. Danny says that living with him is out of the question.

In the meantime, the kids stay and Danny's friend Mark is put in charge of babysitting. Danny uses this as an excuse to go back to tell Gertrude everything. Before she opens the door, she calls the police. They arrive and arrest Danny and accuse him of murder and kidnapping.

While sitting in the police station, Danny sees a wanted poster with a photo of Mark on it. Danny says that they have to get up to the cabin and rescue the children and he escapes. He steals a motorcycle and drives on the sidewalk and heads home with police trailing him.

Danny gets back to the kids and the police take Mark away. Danny is cleared of any wrongdoing and the police take the kids back to Samantha's house. Major has to stay with Danny for a while until he can be brought back.

Napoleon leaves again with Major, but this time Danny stops him and says that people need to be with other people. He talks Danny out of running away again.

The film is ok, but rather preposterous. Serious and silly film ideas are interchanged and the entire picture rings as untrue and ultimately strange.

For instance, in the scene where Danny sees the wanted poster and flees the scene, he most surely would have been shot by the police with no questions asked. Also, to discover a retiring clown and take his lion seems weird, too.

This is touted as Jodie Foster's first film, which isn't entirely true. She had already starred in the 1970 Disney movie, *Menace on the Mountain*. Granted, that movie was made for TV, but was nonetheless still a movie. Foster had also appeared on other shows like *The Paul Lynde Show* and *The Partridge Family* by this time, so she was a little bit of a veteran. This is, however, Foster's first theatrical film and she would go on to make many more memorable films for Disney during the 1970s.

Major, the lion, was a veteran of a number of latter-day Tarzan movies as well as the TV series with Ron Ely.

This film also received an Academy Award nomination for Best Original Dramatic Score and aired on the anthology show in 1975 and 1981.

Kirk Douglas' son Michael makes his Disney debut here a couple months before he would begin work on the long-running TV series, *The Streets of San Francisco*. Kirk, of course was a Disney veteran from *20,000 Leagues Under the Sea* (1954).

Will Geer and Ellen Corby appear here a couple months before they would begin working together on the long-running TV series *The Waltons*.

According to Wikipedia, "Foster was mauled by a substitute lion used in the movie, named Zambo, on the set and still has scars on her back and stomach. 'I was walking ahead of him. He was on an invisible leash, some piano wire. He got sick of me being slow, picked me up and held me sideways and shook me like a doll. I was in shock and thought it was an earthquake. I turned around and saw the entire crew running off in the other direction. The trainer then said, 'Drop it' and he opened his mouth and dropped me.' The incident left her with a lifelong fear of cats."

On the *Freaky Friday* (1977) DVD documentary, Foster discusses being mauled by the lion and says that she still has the scars to prove it.

Now You See Him, Now You Don't

RELEASED BY BUENA VISTA ON July 7, 1972, Technicolor. Producer: Ron Miller. Director: Robert Butler. Screenplay: Joseph L. McEveety based on a story by Robert L. King. Director of Photography: Frank Phillips, A.S.C. Art Directors: John B. Mansbridge, Walter Tyler. Film Editor: Cotton Warburton, A.C.E. Set Decorators: Emile Kuri, Frank R. McKelvy. Special Effects: Eustace Lycett, Danny Lee. Sound Supervisor: Robert O. Cook. Sound Mixer: Dean Thomas. Costumes: Chuck Keehne, Emily Sundby. Make-up: Robert J. Schiffer. Hair Stylist: La Rue Matheron. Assistant Director: Christopher Hibler. Music Editor: Evelyn Kennedy. Music: Robert F. Brunner. Orchestration: Walter Sheets. Second Unit Director: Arthur J. Vitarelli. Associate

Producer: Joseph L. McEveety. Special Effects: Hans Metz. Stunts: Denny Arnold, Dick Warlock, Jesse Wayne. Gaffer: Carl Boles. Camera Operator: Ron Vargas. Running time: 88 minutes.

Cast: Kurt Russell (Dexter Riley), Cesar Romero (A.J. Arno), Joe Flynn (Dean Higgins), Jim Backus (Timothy Forsythe), William Windom (Professor Lufkin), Michael McGreevey (Richard Schuyler), Richard Bakalyan (Cookie), Joyce Menges (Debbie Dawson), Alan Hewitt (Dean Collingsgood), Kelly Thordsen (Sergeant Cassidy), Neil Russell (Alfred), George O'Hanlon (Ted), John Myhers (Golfer), Pat Delaney (Secretary Winifred), Robert Rothwell (Driver), Frank Aletter (TV Announcer), Dave Willock (Mr. Burns), Edward Andrews (Mr. Sampson). Jack Bender (Slither Roth), Frank Welker (Myles), Mike Evans (Henry Farthington), Ed Begley, Jr. (Druffle), Paul Smith (Road Block Officer), Billy Casper (Professional Golfer), Dave Hill (Professional Golfer), Paul Bradley (Man in Forsythe Entourage), Winnie Collins (Secretary), Edward Faulkner (Mike, the Bank Guard), Larry Gelman (Professor), Jack Griffin (Traffic Cop), Alvin Hammer (Elwood), Kenner G. Kemp (Reporter), Jack Manning (Man in Forsythe Entourage), Burt Mustin (Mr. Reed), Eddie Quillan (Charlie, the School Custodian), Benny Rubin (Golfer), Jeffrey Sayre (Budget Meeting Attendee), Arthur Tovey (Man in Forsythe Entourage).

Picking up from *The Computer Wore Tennis Shoes,* the previous entry in this film series, Dexter Riley and his college buddies are listening in again to another one of Dean Higgins' meetings via walkie-talkie. This time Higgins has one of his own spies, who alerts him that the kids have been listening in. Higgins searches his office after the meeting to try to find the bugging device, which has been hidden in a bouquet of flowers.

After the meeting, Schuyler goes in and distracts Higgins' secretary, so Dexter can go in and replace the bugged flowers with a fresh bouquet.

The secretary comes back in to change the flowers and Higgins yells, "Wait!" but it is too late. The switch has been done.

Professor Lufkin wants to enter the school in another science contest called the Forsythe Award because the winner would get $50,000. The most promising entrant seems to be Druffle, with his experiments involving bees.

Dexter Riley is working on an invisibility experiment which, according to Higgins, seems to not have any merit.

That night, another thunderstorm creates a strange scientific combination.

The next day, Dexter and the kids meet up with A.J. Arno and Cookie, whom they thought were in jail. It turns out that Arno has taken over the mortgage on the college and his being in jail was supposedly a mistake.

Dexter goes back to the lab to find his experiment burned out. He looks at the damage with his glasses and they accidentally drop off into the red liquid, but only half-way.

When he removes the glasses, they are only partially there. He tries to find the other half in the liquid and the tongs he uses turn partially invisible.

Dexter realizes that this red liquid causes things to turn invisible, and he experiments with a knife, a pencil and eventually dips in his hand.

Schuyler and Debbie enter the lab and Dexter reveals his half-missing hand to the shock of his friends. He encourages Schuyler to dip in his hand as well. He does, and his fingers turn invisible.

Schuyler asks how to get his fingers back and Dexter says that it should rub right off, which it doesn't.

Higgins walks in with Arno who is scouting around the college with blueprints.

After bidding farewell with left-handed handshakes, Higgins asks what's wrong with everyone's right hand. Debbie says that they got something on them and Higgins asks why they don't wash them. Dexter and Schuyler wash their hands and discover that simple water dissolves the solution.

Later that night, Debbie squirts Dexter and Schuyler with the solution and together they invisibly sneak into Arno's offices.

Schuyler happens to step his shoes into water and they are visible. A security guard sees the shoes and tries to lift them, but can't. Invisible Schuyler steals the guard's key and he and Schuyler go into Arno's office.

They get into a file about Medfield College and find a scale model of the college campus. It turns out that Arno wants to close the college and convert it into a gambling casino and a dog track called Arno's Golden Horseshoe Club.

Arno shows up unannounced and sees flashes in his office, which are Dexter taking flash photos of the model and the documents.

Dexter and Schuyler flee the scene with Arno suspicious. Dexter drives away still invisible, with Debbie visible in the passenger seat. Arno witnesses this strange scene from his office window.

Back to being visible, Dexter shows Higgins and Lufkin the photos he took. Higgins asks what to do and Lufkin mentions the Forsythe Award again and Higgins agrees to enter the school.

Higgins phones Mr. Forsythe, who is practicing his putting game in his office. Forsythe asks if Higgins plays golf and he says yes in order to bring Forsythe into his good graces so that Medfield can enter the competition. The truth is that Higgins has never played anything but miniature golf before.

Forsythe invites Higgins to play golf with him and Dean Collingsgood, Higgins' rival dean from State. Collingsgood and Forsythe are decent players.

Dexter and Debbie watch, and Schuyler caddies. It turns out that Higgins is worse than they thought when it comes to golf.

Dexter instructs Debbie to make him invisible again and Dexter helps Higgins to play a lot better, including getting a couple holes-in-one. In fact, Dexter interferes with Collingsgood's shots to make them worse.

Higgins' excellent playing catches the eye of the powers-that-be that run the golf club and they ask Higgins to become a member after he draws a tremendous crowd following his excellent performance. One of the people in this crowd is A.J. Arno.

Forsythe allows Medfield to enter into the Forsythe Award because of Higgins' excellent golf game.

After the game, Dexter goes into the shower to hose himself down and Arno happens to walk in and see an invisible Dexter become visible.

Higgins, meanwhile, is invited to participate in "Challenge Golf," a pro golf championship game to be televised in Oceanview.

Dexter hears this information from Druffle, but he is too late to get on the plane to help Higgins again with his golf game.

Professional golfers Billy Casper and Dave Hill get pointers from Dean Higgins before he takes his turn. Without Dexter's help, Higgins is awful and eventually the game is won by Casper and Hill, who have tied for first.

Dexter and the gang watch the disastrous game at the campus. Higgins takes multiple shots and he ends up being swallowed by a gigantic wave at the ocean.

The game is also watched by Arno and his crew, and they wonder how Higgins could be so great one week and so lousy the next.

Higgins comes back to Medfield in disgrace and Lufkin shows his progress with the bee experiment for the competition. Druffle comes in covered in bandages because it turns out that he is allergic to bee stings and is out of the competition.

Lufkin reminds Higgins of Dexter's invisibility experiment, which is not encouraging to Higgins.

Arno has asked Cookie to investigate Dexter and the gang and he comes back to report about the invisibility spray. Arno believes the report because of the strange stuff he has seen in recent weeks.

Dexter douses Schuyler again with invisibility spray to show Higgins and Forsythe how the invisibility formula works, but this time it doesn't work. Schuyler thinks he's invisible, but he is not.

At the end of the presentation, they douse Schuyler with water and tell him that the invisibility spray is just colored water and that the real spray has been stolen.

Some of Dexter's gang want to bug Arno's office, so in order to get the flowers into the office, the three pretend to be telegram singers. They sing "Happy Birthday" from Dean Higgins, even though it is not Arno's birthday.

After they leave, Arno reveals to Cookie his plan to use the invisibility spray to do a bank robbery.

Dexter's friends are bored in an ancient history class and slowly file out in order to stop Arno and his gang. Dexter tells bank president, Mr. Sampson of Arno's plans, but Sampson doesn't believe him because invisibility seems too improbable.

Soon, Arno and Cookie drive up. Their car is visible, but they aren't. The gang quickly rigs up a fire hose to a hydrant in order to spray Arno and Cookie as they leave, but they have trouble turning the valve on the hydrant. They do spray the hydrant, but it's too late to spray Arno and Cookie and they instead spray Mr. Sampson.

After Sampson composes himself, he telephones the police.

Dexter and the gang now try to set up a roadblock to stop Arno's car and Arno starts firing shots. Arno and Cookie decide to ram their way out and the chase begins. Arno and Cookie get way out in front and spray the car, to be totally undetectable.

The cops crash into the invisible car. Dexter and the gang still follow Arno who drives through a couple of men carrying a ladder and they crash through. They also crash through some other barriers.

The police try to set up a road block, which is difficult since they cannot see the car. To get away, Arno drives down a bridle trail and also along a bridge, disrupting some Boy Scouts.

Arno tells Cookie to go back to the office so they can wash up, become visible, and establish an alibi.

There's only one road that leads to Arno's office from where they are and the kids set up a blockade along Chester Avenue. The blockage causes Arno and Cookie to drive into a nearby yard and they end up visible after they drive into a swimming pool. The crooks are caught, but pool guests grab some of the now-visible money floating on the top of the water.

At the Forsythe Awards, Dexter shows up with the invisibility spray back in his hands and they perform their experiment again, this time spraying Dean Higgins by accident.

The spray takes a little longer to work since it has been diluted with water, but soon it does when Higgins' legs walk around by themselves at the Awards party. Higgins finally sees (or doesn't see) himself in a mirror and faints.

Dexter splashes water on Higgins, who becomes visible. Forsythe presents Higgins with the check for $50,000 that will pay off the school mortgage for this year, but what about next year?

This is the first sequel to *The Computer Wore Tennis Shoes* (1969). Missing from this film is William Schallert, who is effectively replaced here by William Windom.

Mike Evans appears here as one of Dexter's college buddies shortly before becoming a semi-regular on *All in the Family* and a regular on *The Jeffersons*. It is his movie debut.

This was the first of only two Jim Backus films for Disney (The other being *Pete's Dragon* (1977)). This was a shame as Backus had the Disney sensibility, but possibly his asking rate was too much, although he did also host *The Mouse Factory*.

Strangely, in this film Richard Bakalyan portrays Cookie, whereas in *The Computer Wore Tennis Shoes*, he portrays Chillie, despite it being the same character of A.J. Arno's henchman.

An interesting observation here is that Joe Flynn let his hair go gray in this film. It will be back to brown by the third and final film in the series, *The Strongest Man in the World* (1975).

According to Wikipedia, "The Green VW used by Schuyler was two Herbie cars from *The Love Bug* (1969). One was the vehicle carried by Tang Wu's Chinese Camp students, (this was a gutted car and a rubber truck tire tube was placed under the passenger door, and when inflated suddenly, it would tip the car over; this car was used in the scene where AJ Arno rams it). The other car was used in the scenes with Schuyler driving it on a flat tire. (The Art Dept. painted the car green, and dusted it to give a look of neglect. When the sunroof is open, the original Herbie pearl white paint job under the tarp sunroof can be seen where the green was not painted.)"

This is Michael McGreevey's favorite of the trilogy. He especially likes the scene where his character thinks he's invisible, but isn't.

This film was very popular on the Disney anthology show airing in 1975, 1978, and 1981.

Run, Cougar, Run

RELEASED BY BUENA VISTA ON October 18, 1972, Technicolor. Producer: James Algar. Director: Jerome Courtland. Screenplay: Louis Pelletier based on the book *The Mountain Lion* by Robert Murphy. Director of Photography: William Cronjager. Art Directors: John B. Mansbridge, Al Roelofs. Film Editor: Gordon Brenner. Sound Supervisor: Herb Taylor. Sound Mixer: Frank Regula. Costumes: Chuck Keehne. Make-up: Robert J. Schiffer. Assistant Director:

Michael Dmytryk. Animal Supervision: Cougars: Lloyd Beebe, Marinho Correia. Additional Animals: Hank Cowl. For Cangary Limited: Field Producer: Ron Brown. Principal Animal Photography: Hank Schloss, Ivan Craig, Herb Smith. Production Manager: Erwin L. Verity. With the assistance of Arches National Park, National Park Services, Dead Horse State Park, Division of Fish and Game, State of Utah, Game and Fish Department, State of Arizona. Music: Buddy Baker. Orchestrations: Walter Sheets. Running time: 85 minutes.

Song: "Let Her Alone" written by Terry Gilkyson and sung by Ian & Sylvia. Mexican Serenading Songs sung by Alfonso Arau.

Cast: Stuart Whitman (Hugh McRae), Frank Aletter (Sam Davis), Lonny Chapman (Harry Walker), Douglas V. Fowley (Joe Bickley), Harry Carey, Jr. (Barney), Alfonso Arau (Etio Alvarez), Seeta (The Mountain Lion), Ian Tyson (Narrator).

Seeta the mountain lion roams free as the song "Let Her Alone" plays in the background. The narrator explains that this type of cat can be referred to as a cougar or puma or various other names meaning the same thing.

She goes back to her kittens and cleans them. Her mate was a big Tom. The cats are playful and stay together until Tom goes out hunting. A Tom can be gone for days and often be miles away.

The cougar kittens are pretty much the same as any other kittens, but they aren't ready to go out on their own just yet.

Tom has a regular place that he likes to go to hunt. He encounters a beaver and goes to chase him off his dam, but Tom was of no use in the water.

Seeta, meanwhile, comes across a man named Etio, who is singing a song in Spanish and playing his guitar. Etio sees the lion, but he is not frightened and starts to serenade Seeta.

Etio, a sheepherder, also has other animal friends such as an owl, a deer, and a turtle. Seeta typically came and went about her business and didn't bother Etio.

Hugh McRae flies in via helicopter scouting for clues as to the mountain lion's whereabouts. He intends to capture the mountain lions. He spots Seeta at Devil's Arch and then flies back.

Tom, meanwhile, spots some deer and chases them, but he is unsuccessful as he is not as fast as the deer. Another deer scratches his antlers on a tree and this time Tom does a successful pounce and captures and kills the deer.

Etio keeps herding his sheep further across the land with his dog. Etio is friends with all the animals other than the poisonous Gila monster.

McRae shows up with his truck and ask Etio questions about mountain lions. Etio says that he has seen Seeta and that she's his friend. Etio asks if he's going to kill her. McRae says that he's only going to capture her.

Etio says that there won't be any more lions if he doesn't stop what he's doing. McRae drives on.

Tom retrieves Seeta to show her his kill, but when they get back, they are in for a surprise as a bear is eating the deer's carcass. Tom and the bear get into a fight. Seeta also joins in the fray and the bear runs off.

Joe Bickley drives into the area occasionally to bring in supplies. Etio asks him about McRae and he explains that McRae and his companions are from Denver, and that they want to capture and kill the mountain lions for sport. Joe leaves and tells Etio not to worry, but Etio knows better. He knows that this was not good news.

Etio is herding up his sheep again. This time one strays and Tom is in line to pounce on it, but Etio intervenes and takes the stray sheep back to the herd. Tom follows, but Etio is not afraid.

When Etio gets back, his dog chases after Tom and scares him off.

Joe and McRea talk about hunting the mountain lions. Joe says that it's kind of unfair, as the lions are outnumbered. McRea says that he's going to shoot the lion with a tranquilizer dart. Joe sends his colleague Barney out after him to hopefully discourage McRea's progress.

Etio plays and sings again, with Seeta and Tom overlooking everything, but this time the hounds are coming and McRae and Barney arrive riding on horses.

Seeta and Tom run away and eventually go in opposite directions, with Tom laying an open trail for the dogs to follow along the rocks. Tom gets trapped by the barking dogs below and McRea loads his rifle and shoots.

He hits Tom in the leg with the dart and Tom runs off. The dart falls out, but Tom has already been drugged by it. Before the tranquilizer can paralyze him, but he leaps a great ledge and falls to his death.

Seeta is now on her own and lonely, and she also has to become her family's provider and protector. She hunts whatever she can find.

The kittens are now getting larger and at times roam free while Seeta is out on the hunt. The kittens encounter a river toad. They taste him, but regret this as the toads have a bitter, awful taste.

Next, a hawk is in pursuit of the kittens. The kittens again don't know exactly how to react, but they're learning.

Etio starts pulling tarot cards, showing them to his animal friends and comically telling their fortunes. Seeta shows up and Etio tells her fortune. He pulls "The Tower" card and says that this is not good. Then he pulls "Justice" in reverse and this is also not good. He pulls the "Knight of Swords" and he feels that this is not good as well.

Etio pulls the other cards and then goes back to playing his guitar, saying that tomorrow will bring much trouble.

The next day, McRae drives out with a couple of other men to look at scenery, but Mr. Walker says that he's only interested in bagging mountain lions and not in looking at scenery.

Meanwhile, Etio has become friendly with Seeta's family, even going so far as to physically play with the kittens. Etio gives Seeta a warning that the hunters are coming and advises her to run away, far, far away.

After Seeta and her family leave, Etio goes to visit Joe for breakfast. Etio sees the cage in which McRae is planning to trap Seeta. The other men are currently playing horseshoes.

Joe tells the men that Etio is friendly with the animals. Etio tells the men that he has told Seeta to run away because the men are after her.

The men are indifferent and are actually glad to hear that there really is a mountain lion in the vicinity.

The hunt continues, with men on horses following after the hunting dogs who chase Seeta. The lion swims for it and in doing so, the dogs lose the scent. The men turn back and decide to try again later.

Back at the camp, McRae decides to use a trap laced with catnip. Etio warns McRae to stop doing this, because if he kills Seeta the kittens will be completely defenseless and they will die.

McRae doesn't care and goes out hunting again the next day. He finally succeeds in capturing Seeta with a combination of the trap and the tranquilizer gun.

Trapped and in the cage, Seeta is serenaded by Etio, who sits outside the fence. The cat responds with kindness and gentleness.

McRae's men see this and one of them has second thoughts about hunting and trapping mountain lions.

The next day, the men are up bright and early to hunt Seeta after turning her loose. Etio gives yet another warning to not do this and says that Seeta is essentially harmless.

Etio sets her free and tells her to go home and to be with her kittens. The other men take out their guns, but Etio stays with Seeta to save her from harm. He tells Seeta to run and then the dogs are released.

The men jump onto their horses, except Sam, who now reconsiders what they are doing and declines to participate any further.

Seeta outruns the dogs and the men. Seeta sets atop a high perch and the men shoot. Seeta starts running again and leaps across the same ravine that Tom had tried to leap earlier, but Seeta succeeds and gets away.

It would take five hours for the men to travel around to the other side, by which time Seeta would be long gone.

The men give up and Seeta and Etio remain friends with her kittens as "Let Her Alone" is reprised.

This is an ok animal film with lots of animal action. It is largely forgotten in the Disney canon, not even being mentioned in Leonard Maltin's *Disney Films* book. The film ended up on the anthology show very quickly, airing in 1973 and in 1977. As of this writing it has not been officially released to DVD.

Snowball Express

RELEASED BY BUENA VISTA ON December 20, 1972, Technicolor. Producer: Ron Miller. Director: Norman Tokar. Screenplay: Don Tait, Jim Parker, Arnold Margolin based on the book *Chateau Bon Vivant* by Frankie and John O'Rear. Director of Photography: Frank Phillips, A.S.C. Art Directors: John B. Mansbridge, Walter Tyler. Film Editor: Robert Stafford, A.C.E. Set Decoration: Emile Kuri, Frank R. McKelvy. Matte Artist: Alan Maley. Special Effects: Eustace Lycett, Art Cruickshank, A.S.C., Danny Lee. Sound Supervision: Herb Taylor. Costumes: Chuck Keehne, Emily Sundby. Make-up: Robert J. Schiffer. Hair Stylist: La Rue Matheron. Assistant Directors: Christopher Hibler, Ronald R. Grow. Animal Supervision: Hank Cowl. Technical Advisor: Joe Jay Jalbert. Music Editor: Evelyn Kennedy. Music: Robert F. Brunner. Orchestration: Franklyn Marks. Second Unit Director: Arthur J. Vitarelli. Second Unit Cameraman: John M. Stephens. Associate Producer: Tom Leetch. Film Location: Crested Butte, Colorado. Hair Dresser: Gae Clark Butler. Makeup Artists: Lynn F. Reynolds, Ray Steele. Assistant Director: Dorothy Kieffer. Assistant Directors, Second Unit: John M. Poer, R. Robert Rosenbaum. Second Propman: William Fannon. Leadman: Ralph Mikkelson. Prop Master: Wilbur L. Russell. Sound: Andrew Gilmore. Mikeman: Pat Mitchell. Sound Mixer: Frank Regula. Special Effects Foreman: Hal Bigger. Special Effects Foreman, Second Unit: Gene Grigg. Special Effects: Hans Metz. Stunts: Dick Warlock. Gaffer: Carl Boles. Best Boy: Ed Carlin. Still Photographer: Bob Coburn. Camera Operators: Bill Ion, Ron Vargas. Camera Operator, Second Unit: John Kiser. Camera Assistants: Jim Luske, Michael St. Hilaire, Ron Vargas. Camera Assistants, Second Unit: Mike O'Shea, Bob Simpson, Alex Touyarot. Second Grip: Forrest Reed. Key Grip: Stan Reed. Key Grip, Second Unit: Bob Rust: Second Grip, Second Unit: Ted Shinneman. Costumer, Women: Lynne Albright. Costumer, Men, Second Unit: John George. Costumer, Men: Jack Sandeen. Assistant Film Editor: Louis Terrusa. Transportation Captain: Art Goldberg. Location Auditor: Jeff Bush. Welfare Worker: Catherine Deeney. Assistant Location Manager: Charles W. Geiger. Timekeeper: Mike Goldberg. Script Supervisor: Doris Grau. Unit Publicist: Ben Hartigan. Location Manager: Howard 'Dutch' Horton. Script Supervisor, Second Unit: Lester Hoyle. First Aid: Dan Novack, Price Pinkley. Running time: 93 minutes.

Cast: Dean Jones (Johnny Baxter), Nancy Olson (Sue Baxter), Harry Morgan (Jesse McCord), Keenan Wynn (Martin Ridgeway), Johnny Whitaker (Richard Baxter), Michael McGreevey (Wally Perkins), George Lindsey (Double L. Dingman), Kathleen Cody (Chris Baxter), Mary Wickes (Miss Wigginton), David White (Mr. Fowler), Dick Van Patten (Mr. Carruthers), Alice Backes (Miss Ogelvie), Joanna Phillips (Naomi Voight), John Myhers (Mr. Manescue), George Kirkpatrick (Mr. Wainwright), Tony Regan (Insurance Office Worker), Jeffrey Sayre (Insurance Office Worker), Randy Whipple.

This film starts with Johnny Baxter working in an office but arriving late. His boss, Mr. Carruthers, catches him arriving late and sends him to his desk.

A man named Mr. Fowler is at Johnny's desk and he has some information that Jacob Nash Farnsworth, Johnny's great uncle, has died and that Johnny has inherited the Grand Imperial Hotel and some land in Silver Hills, Colorado, that has been taking in $14,000 a month.

There is also a letter from one Martin Ridgeway, who would be interested in purchasing if Johnny ever decides to sell.

With this newfound income and inheritance, Johnny makes a formal announcement about quitting his job and hands out some gifts on his way out, including his stapler, scissors, and staple remover. This outburst catches the attention of Mr. Carruthers and Johnny announces that he is leaving and jams his computer cards into the computer, effectively jamming the machine. Johnny then leaves to rousing cheers from his former co-workers.

At home, the response to Johnny's news is not so enthusiastic. His wife and daughter are not happy. His son is more excited, but is sent to his room so that Johnny and wife Sue can discuss things further.

Eventually, all agree to go with Johnny. When they get to Silver Hills, they stop at a service station for directions and the attendants are dumbstruck until Johnny mentions Jacob's name, at which point they remember where "Crazy Jake" lived and give them directions.

They finally get to the hotel and son Richard quizzically asks Johnny how badly he broke it off with his former employer. They are not impressed with the condition of the hotel, but try to make the best of it.

The door is unlocked, and there are cobwebs and dust all over the place. There are live animals inside as well, such as bats and raccoons. There is also no heat or electricity.

Johnny assures the family that they will be spending the night, as it is a hotel. Richard starts a fire while Sue and daughter Chris haul clothing into the hotel with their St. Bernard, Stoutheart. While in bed, Sue says at least they still have $1700. Johnny explains that they don't, as $135 went to repair the computer and $1000 went to the lawyer who gave them the deed to the hotel.

There hear more strange noises, so Johnny takes Stoutheart downstairs to investigate and discovers an old man named Jesse McCord who has been living in the hotel for the past 50 years. Johnny says he owns the hotel and makes Jesse pay $10 to spend the night until Jesse gives a sob story about being a 75-year-old man with nowhere else to go. Finally, Johnny agrees to let him stay as long as Jesse does his fair share of work.

They discover other problems, like fish in the drinking water, so Johnny decides to go into town and try to get a bank loan. He is immediately rejected for a loan by Martin Ridgeway, who happens to run the bank and most of the town. He was also the one who sent the letter asking Johnny to sell in the first place, and he again offers to buy the place.

Johnny discusses things with Sue, and they decide to stay and try to make things work. Wally, the kid who worked at the gas station when the Baxters first came to town, asks where Chris is. They get into a conversation and discover that there is an annual motor sled race and that Ridgeway has won the past three years. They also discover that they own far more land than they originally thought.

Johnny gets really excited and comes up with a plan to turn the hotel into a ski lodge. They decide to go to another bank outside the area to try to secure a loan. Mr. Wainright, the banker, asks Johnny to meet him at another ski lodge. Johnny has to pretend that he knows how to ski in order to secure the loan because he doesn't want to make the same mistake he did with Ridgeway.

Unfortunately, Johnny is not very good and after falling down a couple of times and feigning a knee injury, he ends up going down the hill only after sending everyone else's skis down the hill without their owners. He's also skiing backwards.

Eventually he rights himself, but also crashes into many people and finally a snow bank and then a tree, which knocks him out as the tree falls over.

Son Richard reads the paper the next day which describes all the wreckage that Johnny caused. Johnny also reveals that he didn't get the loan. Ridgeway knows about Johnny's exploits as well and comes to the hotel to make a new offer of a $3000 loan.

It isn't revealed initially, but the loan is a trick. Sue is skeptical. Meanwhile, Jesse and Wally try to fix the water heater, which eventually blows up and causes more damage than they already had at the hotel.

After repairing the damages with the loan money, they don't have enough money for a rope tow for the lodge. They do have a steam engine available, but the problem is that it's not near the lodge. Nobody wants to help them move it for fear of Ridgeway's retribution.

Richard insists upon telling his dad about the engine, but no one wants to listen. Finally, Richard gives his mom a written note asking why the engine can't hoist itself up the hill, which turns out to be a great idea.

After putting the engine in place, everyone is finally happy and feels that things are finally turning around. The next problem is that there are no guests. In fact, the skiers that are coming in by train are actually going to Crystal Highlands.

Luckily, on this day the train is stopped due to an avalanche. Since no one can get through, everyone is willing to give Johnny's ski lodge a try. They bring everyone in by sleigh and Johnny catches the eye of a sexy woman named Naomi.

With the hotel filled up, Johnny and Sue take a break outside. Sue brings up her jealousy by mentioning Naomi Tightpants. Their peace and quiet is disrupted by Stoutheart camping out in a woman's room. Meanwhile, Naomi makes her lustful intentions very well known. Johnny gets out of it by saying he has to relieve Jesse on the rope tow in a few minutes.

Wally is trying to teach a group of people how to ski. He tries to help one lady and ends up skiing off a cliff, grabbing a branch as he descends.

Jesse offers the rope tow to bring Wally up and they succeed in doing so with Johnny lowering himself slowly, but when Johnny slips, the tow rope tow catches on fire and it snaps.

Johnny does succeed in bringing Wally in safely, but the rope tow starts moving downhill and crashes through the main hall of the hotel, effectively stopping their resort business.

Johnny goes back to Ridgeway to discuss what to do next. Ridgeway offers to buy the hotel with his own money and not the bank's. Johnny says no and instead decides to enter into the Silver Hills Snowmobile Race; the top winner will receive $2500, but any prize would be good for Johnny. Sue objects again and says that she will leave Johnny if he goes ahead with the race. Johnny goes ahead with his plans anyway.

Of course, Martin Ridgeway is in the race and he plans to win for the fourth consecutive time. Ridgeway has Double L. Dingman as his racing partner, while Johnny recruits Jesse.

After a false start that knocks Jesse off the snowmobile, Johnny makes good time getting back into the race. After another misstep that dislodges Jesse again, they finally gain the lead only because the throttle gets stuck and they race recklessly through the snow, passing everyone in sight.

Ridgeway catches up and in the neck and neck battle, Ridgeway pushes Johnny away and they crash through a snowdrift and ride on an abandoned mine track. The damage to the snowmobile has broken the skis off, but they only have two miles to go. It looks as if Johnny will win, but the steering goes and they crash into another snow bank.

Johnny and Jesse decide to manually aim the body of the disabled snowmobile past the finish line, but without steering or skis the snowmobile veers way off course, never actually passing the finish line. Ridgeway is declared the winner.

Hours later, a horse drags the broken snowmobile across the finish line with Johnny as the sole passenger; Sue waits for him as he crosses and she jumps on the snowmobile. All has been forgiven.

The next day, Ridgeway has new forms for Johnny to sign over the hotel and land to him. Finally, Ridgeway's assistant Miss Wigginton has had enough and reveals to Johnny in Ridgeway's presence that Johnny owns another 3000 acres of Douglas fir trees which wasn't originally disclosed to him.

Jesse chimes in too, mentioning other items that have reverted in ownership to Johnny and the family due to the inheritance. Richard points out something which neither Johnny nor Ridgeway had realized: basically everything in Silver Hills is owned by Johnny.

Once this point is revealed, Johnny realizes that he actually owns everything in town, including Ridgeway's bank.

Another enjoyable Dean Jones vehicle and his last one until 1976, after making at least one film a year for Disney since 1965.

Nancy Olson is back again for her first Disney film since *Smith!* (1969). This will prove to be her final Disney film, as she retired from show business shortly thereafter.

This was Johnny Whitaker's third and final theatrical film for Disney. He made a TV movie for the anthology show called *The Mystery in Dracula's Castle* that aired in January 1973 and then he went on to star in the Saturday morning series *Sigmund and the Sea Monsters* with Mary Wickes shortly thereafter.

It's funny how they tried to make these Disney films "hip" in the early 70s, as in this film when Richard is sent to his room and he comments that he thinks that he's being sent away because his parents are going to talk about sex. In Dean Jones last film, terms like "bigot" and "generation gap" were sprinkled throughout.

David White appears here fresh off of his eight seasons as Darren's boss in *Bewitched* and George Lindsey appears after *Mayberry R.F.D.*, although he was already working for Disney doing voiceover work.

Kathleen Cody comes fresh off her long stint portraying Hallie and Carrie Stokes on the gothic soap opera *Dark Shadows*, signing a three picture deal with Disney.

Dick Van Patten makes his first appearance in a Disney movie, portraying his usual villainous role. When I met Dick a few years ago, he said that he loved the eight Disney features that he did, but was amazed that they always cast him as a villain. He felt that they probably did that because he didn't seem too threatening.

Michael McGreevey remembers that working on this film was not fun as it was exceedingly cold, which made it very difficult to act. He even got tremendously sick with the flu.

1973

Disney as a company was riding even higher this year, with profits of almost $329 million. This was due to the continuing success of the theme parks and the success of the modestly-budgeted feature films and successful film reissues.

1973 was a bit thin on the film release schedule, with the biggest news and hit of the year being the animated version of *Robin Hood*, the first such movie done completely without any involvement from Walt. Though the film has its many fans, it is a pale comparison to times past, especially in cases where footage from *Snow White* (1937) was traced and reused.

This was also a transitional year for Disney movies. After many years of films with Dean Jones, he was suddenly off the film roster. In fact, most actors who were making films when Walt was still alive were no longer making films at Disney and a new crop of film stars came in, including Tim Conway, James Garner, and Helen Hayes. The biggest star during this period continued to be Kurt Russell, who continued with the studio into 1975.

The biggest Disney promotion this year was "50 Happy Years," which celebrated the founding of Walt Disney Productions in 1923.

Disney saw animation competition with *Charlotte's Web*, which was Hanna-Barbera studios' first foray into an animated feature that used a book as its source, rather than using their tried-and-true TV characters in feature films as they had with The Flintstones and Yogi Bear in years past.

Once again, the Sherman brothers were recruited to write songs. The Sherman Brothers also scored this year when former Beatle Ringo Starr had a number-one hit with his cover version of "You're Sixteen."

A live-action film that had moderate success and was commonly assumed to be a Disney film this year was *Tom Sawyer*. Small wonder that the Disney comparison is there, as the film features *Napoleon and Samantha* (1972) stars Johnny Whitaker and Jodie Foster, plus the fact that Disneyland has Tom Sawyer Island.

In Walt Disney World, the Plaza Swan Boats, Pirates of the Caribbean, Tom Sawyer Island and The Walt Disney Story were added to the Magic Kingdom.

The 3rd Annual $150,000 Walt Disney World Golf Classic was held in November.

Meanwhile at Disneyland, Great Moments with Mr. Lincoln was closed, but reopened in 1975 due to popular demand and the Mule Pack was closed for good. The Carousel of Progress was closed and transplanted to Walt Disney World to soon be replaced in 1974 by America Sings.

Work was also completed or nearing completion on building a deluxe, 150-room Golf Resort Hotel, the Lake Buena Vista Village Townhouses and the Polynesian Village Luau Cove.

The Mouse Factory continued for its second and final season. The next regularly-produced TV series apart from the ongoing anthology show would be *The New Mickey Mouse Club* in 1977, following a brief reissue of the original *Mickey Mouse Club* in 1975.

New films produced for the anthology show included *The Mystery in Dracula's Castle, Fifty Happy Years, Chester, Yesterday's Horse, The Little Shepherd Dog of Catalina, The Boy and the Bronc Buster, Call it Courage, Fire on Kelly Mountain* (working title: *Firestorm*), *Mustang!,* and *The Proud Bird from Shanghai*. There was also a brand new 90-minute special that was not part of the anthology show, called *Walt Disney – A Golden Anniversary Salute*. Two unproduced shows were called *Tundra Summer* and *The Biggest Bongo of the World*, which may have been working titles for other shows.

A theatrical featurette was also produced called *Man, Monsters and Mysteries*. *Mary Poppins* (1964) and *Cinderella* (1950) were re-released to theaters.

Non-soundtrack records released this year include *The Sounds of Christmas* which was touted as a sequel of sorts to the classic Disney album *Chilling, Thrilling Sounds of the Haunted House*. It was not a best seller.

Other albums included *"Candy Man" and Other Sweet Songs, "The World is a Circle" from Lost Horizon, Little Gems from Big Shows, Silly Symphonies* (which is not a soundtrack from the old theatrical cartoon series, but rather a collection of songs from various Disney record readers), *New Zoo Revue* (based on the hit non-Disney TV show), *What a Wonderful Thing is Me!, Songs from the Electric Company TV Show* (featuring covers of songs from the hit PBS TV show), and *Bob McGrath Sings for All the Boys and Girls* featuring the *Sesame Street* star.

Songs from the Electric Company TV Show was nominated for a Best Recording for Children Grammy award, but lost.

In the comic book world, Gold Key continued to publish *Donald Duck, Mickey Mouse, Uncle Scrooge, Walt Disney's Comics and Stories, The Beagle*

Boys, Huey, Dewey and Louie Junior Woodchucks, Super Goof, Chip 'n' Dale, Scamp, Walt Disney Comics Digest, Walt Disney Showcase, The Aristokittens and O'Malley and the Alley Cats, and a one-shot of Junior Woodchucks Guide.

The *True-Life Adventure* comic strip which had been running since March 14, 1955, ended on April 14 of this year.

The tabloid-sized *Disneyland* magazine continued, but changed to an every-other week schedule beginning on June 12th. The other week was taken up by another tabloid called *Walt Disney's Fun to Know*. Both were published by Fawcett Publications.

Several important books were first issued this year, including *Magic Moments*, *The Disney Films* by Leonard Maltin, and *The Art of Walt Disney* by Christopher Finch. The latter two have been updated and reissued over the years and are considered essential reading for any Disney fan.

The World's Greatest Athlete

RELEASED BY BUENA VISTA ON February 1, 1973, Technicolor. Producer: Bill Walsh. Director: Robert Scheerer. Writers: Gerald Gardner, Dee Caruso. Director of Photography: Frank Phillips, A.S.C. Art Directors: John B. Mansbridge, Walter Tyler. Film Editor: Cotton Warburton, A.C.E. Set Decoration: Hal Gausman. Matte Artist: Alan Maley. Special Effects: Eustace Lycett, Art Cruikshank, A.S.C., Danny Lee. Sound: Herb Taylor. Costumes: Chuck Keehne, Emily Sundby. Make-up: Robert J. Schiffer. Hair Stylist: La Rue Matheron. Assistant Director: Michael Dmytryk. Music Editor: Evelyn Kennedy. Athletic Technical Advisor: World and Olympic Decathlon Champion Bill Toomey. Second Unit Director: Arthur J. Vitarelli. Animal Supervision: Gene and Bob Holter. Music: Marvin Hamlisch. Special Effects: Hans Metz. Stunts: Dick Warlock. Key Grip: Stan Reed. Unit Publicist: Leonard Shannon. Running time: 92 minutes.

Cast: Tim Conway (Milo Jackson), Jan-Michael Vincent (Nanu), John Amos (Coach Sam Archer), Roscoe Lee Browne (Godfather Baba Gazenga), Dayle Haddon (Jane Douglas), Billy De Wolfe (Dean Maxwell), Nancy Walker (Mrs. Peterson), Danny Goldman

(Leopold Maxwell), Don Pedro Colley (Morumba), Vito Scotti (Man in Stadium), Liam Dunn (Deaf Man, Dr. Winslow), Ivor Francis (Dean Bellamy), Leon Askin (Doctor Gottlieb), Howard Cosell, Frank Gifford, Jim McKay, Bud Palmer, Joe Kapp (Buzzer Kozak), Bill Toomey (The Announcers), Clarence Muse (Gazenga's Assistant), Virginia Capers (Native Woman), John Lupton (Race Starter), Russ Conway (Judge with Stopwatch), Dick Wilson (Drunk in Bar), Jack Griffin, Leigh Christian, Philip Ahn (Chin Yang), Sarah Selby (Woman on Safari), Al Checco (Doctor Checco), Dorothy Shay, David Manzy, Pete Carroll, Brian Sullivan (Football Player #31).

The film opens on a football game that features a losing team. After the game, Coach Archer gives a pep talk to try to reverse this trend. The team is revved up but they all run into the showers instead of onto the field.

Next up is baseball, and again this team is no better than the football team; the winning run slides far short of home plate and is tagged out. Archer gives a similar pep talk and the team runs out onto the field and slides over a bunch of bats.

The coaching continues to basketball and the results here are no better, so there's yet another pep talk from Archer. The team is riled up and goes onto the court and the coach reminds them that the game is over; he meant next week.

Over the credits are other sporting mishaps involving a boat race where the boat sinks, a high diver that loses his shorts, as well as mishaps involving tennis, cheerleaders, and a marching band.

At the next football game, Archer's luck has not changed. Archer's pal, Milo, tries to console him, but it is bad news when one of the backers of the athletic department and his son Leopold give Archer and Milo a severe dressing down. Archer is upset and rips up his contact...actually Milo's contract, but they both resign.

Next, Archer and Milo take a flight to Africa for a relaxing vacation. On safari, Archer and Milo are discussing their future when they spot Nanu, a Tarzan-like jungle man who can run faster than a cheetah and dodge through trees and throw items into baskets and pitch things and jump over things with great ease.

Archer gets ideas and wants to take Nanu back to America with him to play on his former teams and make him the world's greatest athlete. Nanu is not interested. The reason why Nanu is in the jungle is because his parents were missionaries and left him behind. Archer contemplates caging Nanu, but decides against it.

It is revealed to Archer that if a jungle man saves a man's life, he becomes his indentured servant for life, so Archer decides to set up a situation where he gets rescued by Nanu.

Archer starts drowning and is rescued by a heavyset African woman. Archer pretends like he was not rescued by her, but the woman reveals that the indentured servant rule doesn't apply to women, much to Archer's relief.

Milo hides Archer in a pit in order to be rescued by Nanu, but instead of Nanu, a tiger falls into the pit with Archer. Nanu gets the tiger out and then Archer. It turns out that the tiger is named Harry and is Nanu's friend.

Archer says that Nanu saved his life, but Nanu says that Harry is a house pet that his parents brought from India when he was young, so no rescue.

Archer feigns sickness and Milo gets Nanu to help. Nanu takes Archer to Godfather Gazenga, the witch doctor, for help.

At Gazenga's a potion is fed to the two men to see if they were faking illness. The two men drink and they both pass out. Gazenga points out to Archer that the one thing that he cannot stand is a faker.

He concocts a potion with various creepy ingredients and feeds it to Archer, who passes out. Milo gives the witch doctor an empty aspirin bottle and Gazenga decides that white man's medicine may be better for him and he sends Milo to retrieve more aspirin.

Archer gets better and Gazenga says that Nanu is now indebted to him because of tribal law. Archer pretends that he doesn't want Nanu, but then agrees to take him on a plane back home.

Gazenga speaks privately to his assistant that he knew of Archer's deception but really wants Nanu to go to see what civilization is all about.

Archer tells Milo that they have to enroll Nanu in Merrivale and get him a tutor and clothes. Milo says that Nanu cannot leave without his tiger, so when they get back home, they clothe the tiger to sneak him past Mrs. Peterson, the lady who runs the boarding house.

Mrs. Peterson actually says to the tiger that she doesn't allow pets in her house.

Later, Nanu shows Archer his voodoo doll from Gazenga. Archer says that the voodoo doll is all superstition, but as he explains things to Nanu and tosses the doll about, Milo is tossed about as well.

Archer introduces Milo to an attractive woman named Jane Douglas, who is going to be Nanu's tutor. While tutoring, Nanu and Jane eventually fall in love with each other.

Nanu is coached to practice high-jumping and football and the other sports and he turns out to be even better than Archer had expected.

After more practice, it is revealed that Jane actually has a boyfriend, and it is Leopold. There is the typically cheesy romantic running scene, but instead of Nanu running for Jane, he actually runs toward Harry. Leopold is now spying on their escapades since Nanu has stolen his girl, but his spying gets him in trouble with Harry.

Announcers Jim McKay and Bud Palmer cover the NCAA tournament and interview Coach Archer and Milo, too, as he continues to butt his head into the shot in order to be seen on TV. Archer discusses Nanu's qualifications.

Announcer Frank Gifford in Zambia speaks with Gazenga about Nanu, who now regrets his decision about letting Nanu come to America.

Nanu and Jane are getting closer and kiss, but Jane slows them down. The next day the headlines mention Nanu leaving for the NCAA tournament. As soon as they leave, Gazenga arrives to Merrivale to give a talk.

Leopold talks with Gazenga privately and deceptively states that Nanu is being abused by Coach Archer.

Next, Gazenga is requested to cure an old man's inability to walk when he's actually deaf. Milo then confronts Gazenga and takes the opposite stance of Leopold and says to leave Nanu alone. Gazenga reacts by shrinking Milo and dropping him in a filled drinking glass. Milo gets out and dries himself by standing next to a still smoldering cigarette in an ashtray.

Milo tries to get to a telephone, which is very far away. He tries to signal a woman, but his chipmunk-like voice is ignored by everyone. Milo ends up falling into the lady's purse, which is filled with large keys, cigarettes, a brush, bobby pins, and a spool of thread.

Gazenga now confronts Archer who wants to know where Nanu is. Gazenga misdirects Archer to stall for time as he doesn't want Nanu to be taken from him.

Milo finally gets out of the lady's purse and gets to the phone and with much difficulty dials Archer and warns him about Gazenga. Afterwards, Gazenga brings Milo back to his normal size to help him find Nanu.

It's now confession time for Archer and Nanu about what he really wants Nanu for. Nanu doesn't want to do it anymore because Archer lied to him.

The next day, Nanu forgives Archer and decides to go through with the NCAA Track and Field Championship, much to the chagrin of Gazenga and Leopold.

Announcer Howard Cosell and former Olympic Track Star Buzzer Kozack of Michigan State cover the event. Nanu is going to be the sole performer in every event. Buzzer tries to comment but Cosell interrupts at every turn. Jane and Harry (in disguise again) are in the stands cheering Nanu on.

The first event is the 100-yard dash. Nanu starts it from a standing position and still wins the race in eight seconds. Cosell comments that he has never seen anything like this in his career. The crowd goes wild.

The next event is the high hurdles and Nanu wins again despite helping an opponent out when he trips and falls. The crowd goes wild again and a man in the stands bumps Harry, causing him to roar.

Gazenga and Leopold are now in the stands as well, and Gazenga puts a voodoo curse on Nanu with a voodoo doll, causing him to fall back on his broad jump, the javelin to come back like a boomerang, and other failures.

Milo and Archer figure out that it's Gazenga that's messing with Nanu and they ask him what to do to stop him.

Cosell predicts defeat for Nanu as he needs to win every event from this point on to keep in the race. When Nanu is caught running in place at another track event, Archer has had it. Milo comes up with the voodoo doll out of his pocket and sticks in his lucky feather and shows Archer. Archer waves it away and it lands in a bucket of water, also causing Gazenga to be thrown from the stands. The spell is reversed and Nanu now races and gains the lead. Cosell is excited.

Archer tells Nanu that he needs to keep going in order to win everything, and he does, but it is a nail biter. Buzzer is so disgusted with Cosell by the end of the event that he dumps a basket of trash on his head.

Archer and Milo congratulate Nanu as Harry chases Leopold from the stands. Next up is the Olympics, but Nanu is still confused about the need for winning and getting his photo in the newspaper, and decides to go back to Africa.

Archer is upset again and he and Milo run out to get Nanu at the airport and stop him from leaving. Archer says that he can't leave because he's in love with Jane, but it turns out that Jane is leaving with him, so they let him go where he can be happy.

Archer tells Milo that he needs to get away again and this time they go to the Far East, where they meet Chin Yang, a fast Chinese runner, and so Archer and Milo go chasing after him.

Who knew that in five short years the jungle man's name would become Robin Williams' catchphrase on *Mork and Mindy*?

The TV jackets used by the announcers are the same ones used in *The Barefoot Executive* (1971).

For some reason, because of the similar titles or themes, this movie is often confused with *The Strongest Man in the World* (1975), despite the fact that neither film has the same cast or story.

The DVD features some 11 minutes of silent outtakes featuring various pool dives and Jan-Michael Vincent high-jumping, pitching baseball, and running track. There are also a marching band, cheerleaders, football playing, boat-racing, tennis, airplanes, and the tiger. Tim Conway appears in outtakes where he is stuck inside of an ice cube in a drink when he was shrunk.

The clap boards reveal various shooting dates of June and July 1972 on this film.

Tim Conway says that there was one scene in which the disguised Bengal tiger was getting upset and literally ripped the car seatbelt out when he and John Amos were driving him around.

This film features the classic Howard Cosell line, "I've never seen anything like this in my entire illustrious career." Illustrious, indeed! Also, "How can I tell my fans if I can't tell myself?" is another classic line.

Another illustrious figure is the person who composed the music for this picture, Marvin Hamlisch, who scored his only Disney picture before going onto more Oscar-winning compositions for *The Sting* and *The Way We Were* later in 1973, though he did come back to Disney during the Eisner years.

The film was highly popular, eventually grossing over $22.5 million. It aired on the anthology show in 1983.

This was actor Billy De Wolfe's final film. He died in 1974.

Charley and the Angel

RELEASED BY BUENA VISTA ON March 23, 1973, Technicolor. Producer: Bill Anderson. Director: Vincent McEveety. Screenplay: Roswell Rogers from the novel *The Golden Evenings of Summer* by Will Stanton. Director of Photography: Charles F. Wheeler, A.S.C. Art Director: John B. Mansbridge, Al Roelofs. Film Editor: Bob Bring, Ray de Leuw. Set Decoration: Frank R. McKelvy. Costume Designer: Shelby Tatum. Special Effects: Eustace Lycett, Art Cruikshank, A.S.C., Danny Lee. Titles: Jack Boyd, John Jensen. Second Unit Director: Christopher Hibler. Sound: Herb Taylor. Sound Mixer: George Ronconi. Costumes: Chuck Keehne, Emily Sundby. Make-up: Robert J. Schiffer. Hair Stylist: La Rue Matheron. Assistant Director: Ronald R. Grow. Music Editor: Evelyn Kennedy. Music: Buddy Baker. Orchestration: Walter Sheets. Special Effects: Hans Metz. Stunt Drivers: Craig R. Baxley, Bill Hickman. Stunt Performer: Jerry Brutsche. Stunts: Gary Combs. Stunt Coordinator: Bill Hickman. Running time: 95 minutes.

Song: "Livin' One Day at a Time" by Shane Tatum and Ed Scott.

Cast: Fred MacMurray (Charley Appelby), Cloris Leachman (Nettie Appleby), Harry Morgan (The Angel, Roy Zerney), Kurt Russell (Ray Ferris), Kathleen Cody (Leonora Appleby), Vincent Van Patten (Willie Appleby), Scott Kolden (Rupert Appleby), George Lindsey (Pete, the Handyman), Edward Andrews (Ernie, the Banker), Richard Bakalyan (Buggs) Barbara Nichols (Sadie), Kelly Thordsen (Policeman), Liam Dunn (Dr. Sprague), Larry D. Mann (Felix), George O'Hanlon (Harry, the Police Chief), Susan Tolsky (Miss Partridge), Mills Watson (Frankie Zuto), Ed Begley, Jr. (Derwood Moseby), Christina Anderson (Susie), Roy Engel (Driver), Pat Delany (Girl in Sadie's Place), Bob Hastings (News Reporter), Jack Griffin (Policeman #2), Harold Perry (Captain Bob, the Radio Announcer).

It is 1933 in Midwestern USA and Charley and Nettie Appleby are sitting on their porch. Charley is reading the paper and Nettie is sewing.

Business is slow at Appleby Hardware and Charley is concerned. Soon a shooting star streams by, which excites everyone in the family except Charley.

Nettie wishes upon the star and requests that the family could travel to the World's Fair. Charley wishes for the mosquitoes to leave him alone and says no to Nettie's request. Son Willie wishes for his mom's wish to come true.

Miss Partridge comes into the hardware store, which is having a one-cent sale. It's supposed to be "buy one, get one for one cent," but Miss Partridge just buys the one for one cent.

Willie and Rupert listen to a radio show teaching them how to build their own kite. Captain Bob speaks too quickly and Willie and Rupert end up with a mess instead of a kite. Nettie comes in and sees the mess and is shocked.

Rupert says that this wouldn't have happened if their dad had helped them to build the kite. Soon, the phone rings for daughter Leonora. It's Ray Ferris, who wants Leonora to go out with him and not Derwood Moseby, her boyfriend.

Later that day, Charley is driving his car and a huge truck causes him to bump into a wall, bending his fender. When he goes out and checks on the damage, a man in a white suit starts talking to Charley. It turns out that no one but Charley can see this man, who is an angel.

The angel is there to inform Charley that his time is up. Charley does not believe him, so the angel briefly appears with a white robe, wings, and a harp. Charley says that he can't die yet and that he needs more time.

Charley comes home with a bouquet of flowers for Nettie instead of going to his lodge meeting, which shocks Nettie because it's out of character for Charley. Later, at dinner, he asks the family if he could say grace, which is also new.

Charley then invites the family to go to the movies. Leonora says that she has dates with Ray and Derwood. Willie and Rupert have already committed to going to the movies with another family and Nettie says that she's scheduled to play bridge with Clara, leaving Charley and his dog completely alone with each other.

The next day, Charley asks Pete to fix his door and to paint his house. Leonora and Nettie witness this and are surprised that Charley is actually fixing up the house after all these years.

The angel shows up at this time and says that Charley is worth salvaging. Charley asks the angel what his name is, and after a moment the angel reveals that his mortal name was Roy Zurney. Charley asks him if he should take the family to the World's Fair, but the angel doesn't believe Charley will do it.

Charley goes to withdraw money but can't as there has been a run on the bank and it is closed. Charley goes to Ernie the banker's private entrance, but that doesn't get him his money.

Charley goes home and discovers that Nettie has given $100 to Pete for all the work he had been doing. Charley had wanted to stop Pete's work because of the bank freeze, but it's too late.

Derwood is at the door and he and Charley have a brief talk about what Derwood is doing for a living. Charley offers a job to Derwood, but he's happy working for his family's business. Derwood soon leaves with Leonora.

Charley sits down with the boys to talk to them about money and then the doorbell rings again. This time it's Ray. Charley asks him if Ray's working and he says no. Charley scoots him along.

Willie and Rupert want to talk to their dad again about money and jobs, but they are more interested in wishing a Happy Father's Day to their friend's dad Mr. Gossett than they are to their own.

Later that evening, Ray sneaks in after bringing Leonora home at 5am. Ray has a black eye after getting into a fight with Derwood. Ray and Leonora had gone out dancing all night.

Charley catches them sneaking in, but is still not excited about Ray and how he behaves. Charley has a shave and the angel appears in his mirror. The angel has no news about Charley's fate, but says that he is still rooting for him.

Nettie overhears Charley talking, apparently to himself. When confronted about this, Charley dismisses it and her.

Charley's talk apparently had some influence and Willie and Rupert get hired by a man named Felix to clean up a junk yard for 10 cents an hour. It turns out to be hard work and the kids are soon tired and take a rest in an old car. They turn the engine over and it starts.

Felix catches the kids goofing off, but soon Buggs comes by with a liquor shipment. Felix decides to use the kids to deliver the shipment to Sadie (a local bootlegger) instead of incriminating themselves, since Prohibition is still in effect. Felix lets the kids use the old car they were messing with. They aren't great drivers and almost run over a lady and her dogs.

Finally, they get to Sadie's place and tell her that they have their cooking oil. After double-checking with Felix, everything is cleared but the kids take forever to get back and Buggs feels that they took the money or lost it. They do come back and Felix pays five dollars to each boy.

They show the money to their parents, but Charley suspects something is amiss since it was such a large amount. After sending the boys off, Charley reveals that he's going to sell the shop in order to get enough money to take the family to the World's Fair.

Charley calls on Roy, the angel, to help him out and Nettie overhears Charley talking to himself again. Charley reveals that Roy is an angel, but Nettie doesn't believe him. When Charley wants to show her, Roy is gone.

Nettie sends Charley to Dr. Sprague to get things checked out, but physically everything is fine. Sprague asks Charley about Roy, and recommends Charley to see a psychiatrist.

Meanwhile, the kids are off to deliver their next load of "cooking oil." Buggs still doesn't like the plan, but Felix assures him that things will continue to be all right. While driving, the kids again almost run over the same woman with her dogs.

That night, Charley is looking for Leonora and Ray and ends up in Sadie's place, the same one that the boys are delivering the alcohol to. While waiting, Charley sits down and a woman named Susie comes up to chat, revealing that kids have been delivering the booze. The place is then raided and Charley is caught, going to jail and showing up in the newspaper article and photograph about the raid.

Back at home, Nettie asks Charley if Susie is the angel that he has been talking about. Charley says no and sends the boys up to get Leonora. All they find is a note saying that she's eloped.

Soon after, Leonora calls in and says that everything is ok. The angel is hobnobbing around in Charley's hardware store, waiting for him.

Charley shows up but he soon gets a phone call from Harry, a local policeman, who has questions about the two boys who are driving the liquor. Then Miss Partridge comes in and threatens to sue Charley for damages. She says that she was almost run over twice by the boys when they were driving the car.

Then Felix has more trouble as a gangster named Frankie shows up and knocks him out. The boys show up and Frankie and Buggs make them drive everyone away.

Charley shows up and finds Felix coming to and takes one of Felix's other cars to chase the gangsters and his boys. Frankie throws stuff out of the car to stall Charley, but with the angel's help, Charley gets through.

The angel finally has news for Charley, but the news isn't good and Charley slides on some ice and knocks himself out. The angel gets in to drive and it looks as if the car is driving without a driver.

A couple of cops shoot at the tires and the car swerves into a tree. The cops take Charley out of the car and throw him in jail because the car contains bootlegging equipment. The angel shows up at the jail and reveals that Charley's time is up at midnight that night.

Buggs, Frankie, and the kids are still on the lam. They need to hide out and the kids take them to their home. The boys go in first and act like nothing is wrong and rush Buggs and Frankie upstairs. Charley also comes home and he, too, acts like nothing is wrong.

Then Leonora and Ray stop by, and while they are all talking, Buggs and Frankie walk downstairs pointing guns before stealing Ray's car. Willie manages to escape. Nettie makes some food for the crooks and they want to take her hostage.

Charley lunges forth and Frankie fires, but Charley is not hurt. Pete comes by and narrowly misses getting shot. A scuffle breaks out between the family and the crooks. Rupert grabs the gun and Willie arrives with the police, who take the crooks away.

The family gets a reward of $5000 and Pete drops off the money he owes. Ernie the banker drops by with some hotel reservations and tickets to the World's Fair and says that the bank will be reopening tomorrow.

So, everything has come true except that Charley has to reveal that he has to go to the store. He says that he is no longer selling the store, but is giving it to Leonora and Ray. He insists that Nettie take the boys to the Fair, regardless if he goes or not.

Charley says good night to the boys, comes down and kisses Nettie and then leaves for the store. While driving, the angel shows up in the passenger's seat. Charley stops the car and asks when his death is going to happen.

The angel reveals that it happened when he was shot, but Charley didn't die and he doesn't know why. The angel reveals that he stopped the bullet and that he's going to live after all and die the way everyone else does, not knowing. The angel leaves because Charley is now a reformed man.

The next day, Charley, Nettie, and the boys drive to the World's Fair.

This enjoyable little film was a bit different for Disney at this time, mainly due to it being a period piece, which was rare for them to do, as well as having death as the subject matter.

This was Fred MacMurray's final film for Disney and his penultimate film overall. *The Swarm* (1978) has the dubious honor of being his final film. This film marked his return to Disney after 12 years doing *My Three Sons*.

A blooper in the film is where MacMurray calls Leonora "Leonore" about 20 minutes into the film.

The song "Hello, My Baby" is heard on the soundtrack virtually every time the angel shows up. This is the same song that Michigan J. Frog dances to in the Warner Bros. Looney Tune called *One Froggy Evening*.

Though nothing was said about it at the time, the age gap between MacMurray and Cloris Leachman was quite significant for a husband and wife.

For this film, Leachman was nominated for a Golden Globe in the category of Best Actress in a Musical / Comedy.

The movie aired on the anthology show in 1977.

One Little Indian

RELEASED BY BUENA VISTA ON June 20, 1973, Technicolor. Producer: Winston Hibler. Director: Bernard McEveety. Writer: Harry Spalding. Filmed in the State of Utah with the Cooperation of the U.S. Department of the Interior Bureau of Land Management. Director of Photography: Charles F. Wheeler, A.S.C. Art Directors: John B. Mansbridge, Leroy G. Deane. Film Editor: Robert Stafford, A.C.E. Set Decorator: Hal Gausman. Associate Producer: Tom Leetch. Sound Supervision: Herb Taylor. Sound Mixer: George Ronconi. Costumes: Chuck Keehne, Emily Sundby. Make-up: Robert J. Schiffer. Assistant Director: Ted Schilz. Animal Supervision: Gene Holter Enterprises. Stunt Coordinator: Bill Burton. Orchestration: Arthur Morton. Music Editor: Evelyn Kennedy. Music: Jerry Goldsmith. Production Manager: John D. Bloss. Stunts: Roydon Clark, Boyd 'Red' Morgan, Bobby Somers, Neil Summers. Stunt Double for Jay Silverheels: Norm Taylor. Unit Publicist: Gabe Essoe. Running time: 90 minutes.

Cast: James Garner (Clint Keyes), Vera Miles (Doris McIver), Pat Hingle (Captain Stewart), Morgan Woodward (Sergeant Raines), John Doucette (Sergeant Waller), Clay O'Brien (Mark), Robert Pine (Lieutenant Cummins), Bruce Glover (Schrader), Ken Swofford (Private Dixon), Jay Silverheels (Jimmy Wolf), Andrew Prine (Chaplain), Jodie Foster (Martha McIver), Walter Brooke (The Doctor), Rudy Diaz (The Apache), John Flinn (Cowboy), Lois Red Elk (Blue

Feather), Hal Baylor (Branigan), Terry Wilson (Stage Driver), Paul Sorensen (The Guard), Read Morgan (Reb), Richard Hale (Old Indian), Jim Davis (Trail Boss), Rosemary Forsythe.

Clint Keyes is being transported across the desert on a mutiny charge by Sergeant Raines. His hands are bound and a noose is thrown around his neck. Along the way, they encounter some other cavalry and the Sergeant asks for more help to keep Keyes in line. The request is turned down by Lieutenant Cummins, who is transporting a group of Indians to Captain Stewart's fort for medical examinations.

One of the child Indians makes a break, causing havoc with the horses and the other cavalry men, and he almost manages to escape the fort. As he is grabbed by the soldiers, the boy's pants are lowered somewhat and the men realize that the boy is white. The boy is kept captive until they figure out what to do with him.

While in custody, they give the boy the name of Mark, and they baptize him with water. Later that night, the soldiers are in church singing a hymn and later "Silent Night," as it is near Christmas and a donation collection is taken.

During the service, Mark tries to escape the fort again. This time he succeeds and the search is on for him again. An adult Indian receives him and gives him a large knife for protection. The boy goes out on his own, living off the land. Mark breaks his knife while cutting a cactus and in general wanders aimlessly in the desert.

He encounters Keyes, who has also escaped and riding a camel named Rosebud (Rosie). Keyes shoots at Mark and mistakenly grazes his arm to make him go away. Keyes then administers first aid to Mark after he injures him.

After bundling his pack, Mark pulls a gun on Keyes, but Keyes gets it back and asks him questions about who he is. Keyes explains that he's headed south to Mexico.

Keyes is also traveling has a smaller white camel, who has been nicknamed "Thirsty."

Mark and Keyes ride Rosebud together with Thirsty in tow. Meanwhile, the Sergeants that have had Keyes under arrest previously are now searching for him again.

Thirsty keeps trailing behind because he's so small, and Rosebud frequently and stubbornly stops. It is discovered that Rosie listens only to Mark's commands.

Later, Keyes decides to take a bath in a lake and asks Mark to bathe as well. Mark refuses, but finally agrees after pressure from Keyes.

Mark wants to leave, but Keyes said that if he leaves now, he will get caught for questioning and both of them will suffer. Mark agrees.

The Sergeants along with Jimmy Wolf, an Indian who wants Mark back, are still on the trail and eventually they do catch up to Mark and Keyes, but Keyes is ready and holds everyone hostage. He takes their guns and tosses them into the lake.

As they walk with their hostages back to their horses they encounter Shrader, one of the cavalrymen who scare the horses off so that Keyes cannot take them. Keyes then lets everyone go without guns and horses.

Keyes and Mark are hungry, so they try to steal some food from some cattle rustlers. As soon as Keyes gets close, Rosie enters the encampment and makes a huge mess, also dragging Keyes off through a field of cactus which Mark helps remove from Keyes' rear end.

Afterwards, Mark and Keyes continue on with their journey and stumble upon a house with a mother and daughter named Doris and Martha. Doris sees Thirsty in her yard and chases him to the barn. Keyes grabs her and asks for some food. Doris says that they can take whatever they want.

Keyes and Doris discuss their respective histories and Martha and Mark become fast friends and he shows her how to ride the camels.

Keyes tries to give Mark over to Doris, but she reveals that she can't keep Mark, either. Eventually, she reconsiders but Mark is upset as Keyes has left without him and he tries to leave with Thirsty.

He doesn't get very far, as Sergeant Raines shows up with new horses and more men and find Keyes.

Jimmy Wolf finds camel tracks, and off they go. Meanwhile, Mark finally does run off and Doris and Martha have to leave on the next stage. Martha is concerned because she knows that Mark has not gone far.

She is correct, but Mark does not follow and instead decides to press on by riding Thirsty to find Keyes and Rosie.

Keyes realizes that he is being followed, so he sends Rosie on her way and continues on by foot. Raines and Wolf continue on after Rosie and Keyes successfully escapes.

Mark finally catches up with Keyes and expresses his anger at Keyes leaving him. After some discussion, Raines finally catches up with Keyes, resulting in a wrestle and a fist fight. This time, Keyes and Mark are both captured and they are led back to the fort.

After a brief hearing about Keyes' charges, it's decided that Keyes is still guilty and will be hanged for his actions.

Prior to his hanging, Keyes speaks with the chaplain about Mark. The chaplain was the man who originally gave Mark his name and baptized him. Keyes requests that Mark be given to Doris McIver.

The hanging is about to take place when Mark drives a herd of cattle through the fort, disrupting the proceedings and knocking down the gallows.

Keyes escapes and jumps on Rosie, prompting a horse chase through the desert. Mark is captured. Eventually, Rosie poops out because she has been shot by one of the men.

In the end, Keyes is let go by Captain Stewart because he feels that Keyes has sufficiently paid his punishment and he won't hang a man twice. The chaplain goes out to find Keyes to bring him the good news, but Keyes is also drummed out of the service.

Keyes again asks about Mark and if he will be going with Doris and Martha. Mark reveals that he would rather be with Keyes and shows up soon thereafter.

By the Mark arrives, Rosie has died from the gunshot wounds and Mark sheds a tear. Because he is no longer a wanted man, Keyes decides to stay with Mark and go to Colorado instead of Mexico.

Not one of the best movies, mainly for its simple-minded story. Garner does an excellent job as usual, but the entire enterprise comes off as limp, and the box office reflected that.

This is the first of two Disney films to star James Garner. In his 2011 autobiography, he claims that he had taken a break in his film career to get some rest, which turned out to be a mistake as eventually the phone stopped ringing and Garner had to resort to this type of film. Disney was glad to have him, but his talents were under-utilized. Fortunately, after about a year at Disney, where he made this and *The Castaway Cowboy*, Garner returned to TV to star in the long-running and highly successful *The Rockford Files*.

This was also Jodie Foster's final Disney film before coming back to do *Freaky Friday* (1977) and *Candleshoe* (1978). By this point she had become a true star and after she left again, her stardom continued to grow. Foster worked with Garner again in the 1994 movie version of *Maverick*.

On the *Freaky Friday* DVD documentary, Foster says that she sprained her ankle right before filming and delayed shooting, and she thought she would be surely fired as a result.

It aired on the anthology show in 1976.

Robin Hood

RELEASED BY BUENA VISTA ON November 8, 1973, Technicolor. Producer: Wolfgang Reitherman. Director: Wolfgang Reitherman. Story: Larry Clemmons based on Character and Story Conceptions by Ken Anderson. Directing Animators: Milt Kahl, Frank Thomas, Ollie Johnston, John Lounsbery. Story Sequences: Ken Anderson, Frank Thomas, Julius Svendsen, Vance Gerry, Eric Cleworth, Dave Michener. Character Animation: Hal King, Art Stevens, Cliff

The Feature Films – 1973   147

Nordberg, Burny Mattinson, Eric Larson, Don Bluth, Dale Baer, Fred Hellmich. Effects Animation: Dan MacManus, Jack Buckley. Key Assistant Animators: Dale Oliver, Bob McCrea, Chuck Williams, Stan Green. Assistant Directors: Ed Hansen, Dan Alguire, Jeff Patch. Art Director: Don Griffith. Layout: Basil Davidovich, Sylvia Roemer, Joe Hale, Ed Templer, Jr. Color Styling: Al Dempster. Background Painting: Bill Layne, Ralph Hulett, Ann Guenther. Production Manager: Don Duckwall. Film Editors: Tom Acosta, Jim Melton. Sound: Herb Taylor. Music Editor: Evelyn Kennedy. Music: George Bruns. Orchestration: Walter Sheets. Sound Effects: James MacDonald. Assistant Animator: Floyd Norman. Running time: 83 minutes.

Songs: "Oo-de-lally," "Not in Nottingham," Whistle-Stop" Written and Sung by Roger Miller. "Love" Written by Floyd Huddleston and George Bruns, sung by Nancy Adams. "The Phony King of England" Written by Johnny Mercer, sung by Phil Harris. "Fight On," "On Wisconsin," "Happy Birthday," "Rock-a-Bye Baby."

Cast: Roger Miller (Allan-a-Dale), Peter Ustinov (Prince John, King Richard), Terry-Thomas (Sir Hiss), Brian Bedford (Robin Hood), Monica Evans (Maid Marian), Phil Harris (Little John), Andy Devine (Friar Tuck), Carole Shelley (Lady Kluck), Pat Buttram (Sheriff of Nottingham), George Lindsey (Trigger), Ken Curtis (Nutsy), Candy Candido (Captain of the Guards), John Fiedler (Father Sexton), Dana Laurita (Sis), Barbara Luddy (Mother Church Mouse, Mother Rabbit), J. Pat O'Malley (Otto), Billy Whitaker (Skippy), Dori Whitaker (Tagalong).

The story starts off with a book explaining the whereabouts of King John when a crooning rooster tells what really happened with Robin Hood. He sings "Whistle Stop" while walking along the pages of the *Robin Hood* book.

Allan-a-Dale, the rooster minstrel, tells the story of Robin Hood and Little John escaping from the Sheriff of Nottingham and his warriors by singing "Oo-de-lally."

Prince John is in charge while his brother King Richard is out fighting the Crusades. John is riding in a coach with Sir Hiss, who reveals that he hypnotized Richard and sent him off.

John also has a propensity to suck his thumb when their mother is mentioned.

Meanwhile, Robin and Little John dress up as fortune tellers in order to rob Prince John and his crew, which they do.

Robin proceeds to read John's fortune with a crystal ball filled with fireflies. Various mishaps occur, but Robin predicts that John's name will go down in history.

Little John takes the opportunity while Robin is doing his fortune telling to steal the gold hubcaps on the coach and gold from a treasure chest.

Prince John has had his clothing removed and is in his underwear as the guards go after Robin and Little John, but they get away.

Robin is now a wanted man, with a price of £1000 on his head. Everyone is poor, but the Sheriff doesn't care. He even collects taxes on Friar Tuck. The Sheriff stops by a rabbit family and takes the boy's birthday gift of a farthing.

Robin comes in disguised as a beggar and the Sheriff takes his begging money, too. After the Sheriff leaves, Robin reveals himself and gives the rabbit bag a small bag of coins.

The next day, three of the rabbits and Toby the turtle are running and playing with a bow and arrow that Robin had given him.

Skippy the rabbit shoots the arrow and it goes up and over the wall of Prince John's castle. At the castle, Maid Marian and Lady Kluck are playing a game of badminton. Skippy sneaks in to get his arrow back, but gets caught by Marian and Kluck, who say that there's nothing to worry about.

After getting his arrow back, Kluck and Skippy get into a fake duel, where she pretends to be Prince John and sucks her thumb and Skippy pretends to be Robin Hood.

After they have more fun, Marian reveals her love for Robin to Lady Kluck. At the same time, Robin reveals his love for Marian to Little John. Friar Tuck stops by and says that there will be a championship archery tournament put on by Prince John. The winner will receive a kiss from Marian.

Robin disguises himself as a stork and enters the tournament. The tournament begins and the participants shoot their arrows. The Sheriff gets closest to a bulls-eye and then the stork makes one bulls-eye and then another.

The competition is narrowed down to the Sheriff and the stork. The Sheriff tells his henchman Nutsy to move the target so that the Sheriff is guaranteed a bulls-eye. Stork shoots and is tripped up so that the arrow goes in the wrong direction; he quickly shoots another one to change the original arrow's direction and makes a bulls-eye that splits the Sheriff's arrow in two.

The stork wins, but Prince John has the final say and reveals the stork to be Robin Hood. Robin is captured and ordered to be executed. The execution is stopped because Little John is threatens Prince John, and Robin is set free.

The Sheriff knocks Little John away and Prince John again orders his guards to kill Robin. A battle occurs, but Robin escapes with Marian after he asks her to marry him. Eventually, after the scuffle, everyone else escapes too.

After everything is done, Sir Hiss reveals that the stork was really Robin Hood, prompting Prince John to tie him into a knot.

Robin and Marian walk through the forest together as the song "Love" plays over the soundtrack. This sentimentality is disrupted as all of Robin and Marian's friends congratulate them and party and sing "The Phony King of England."

This song is such a hit with the village that even the Sheriff comes into Prince John's quarters singing it. Prince John retaliates by raising taxes again, and if you couldn't pay your taxes, you were thrown in jail, including Alan-a-dale, who sings "Not in Nottingham."

About the only people that aren't in jail are Friar Tuck, Father Sexton, and his wife, Little Sister. The Sheriff comes by and takes money from the poor box and Friar Tuck is also thrown in jail.

Sir Hiss is trying to cheer up Prince John by reminding him that he has money and that everyone is in jail, but John is still upset, because he still doesn't have Robin Hood.

Robin Hood is back in his blind beggar costume and is told by the Sheriff that Friar Tuck is going to be hanged, so Robin's new plan is to release the Friar.

Robin disguises himself as Nutsy and tells the Sheriff to sleep and grabs the jail keys. Robin sneaks into the castle and sees Prince John and Sir Hiss fast asleep. He uses this as an opportunity to take multiple bags of gold from John's quarters.

The gold is given to the prisoners and Little John leads the prisoners out of the jail cell, each with their own bag of gold. Then Robin makes his escape after sending out the last bag of gold, but not before he is seen by Sir Hiss, Prince John, and the guards.

After some narrow escapes, everyone except Robin leaves with their money, leaving Robin to take everyone on by himself.

Robin and the Sheriff fight their final duel as the castle catches on fire. Robin is in a tight spot, but he dives into the moat. Arrows are shot at him, and it looks as if Robin is gone, but he escapes and Prince John is distressed again, taking it out on Sir Hiss as the castle burns.

Allan-a-Dale does a quick reprise of "Whistle Stop" as it's shown that Prince John, Sir Hiss, and the Sheriff are now in jail breaking rocks with a sledge hammer. Robin and Marian get married and go on their honeymoon, and King Richard comes back home and takes his rightful place back on the throne.

This was the first animated feature virtually completely selected by some of Disney's "nine old men", a select group of animators that were considered to be the top animators at Walt's studio. While the possibility of *Chanticleer* might have made for a more interesting project, they decided to play it safe and go with a tried-and-true story that had previously been done by Disney in 1952.

Initially this film was to be about Reynard the Fox, but Walt Disney objected to his unsuitability of Reynard as a hero, and the changes ultimately became this film.

The 2009 DVD reissue also contains an alternate ending that was storyboarded but never animated, and ultimately scrapped. It was released to Blu-ray in 2013 with a never before seen storyline called "Love Letters".

Strong criticism has been placed on this film due to its reuse of animation and concepts from *Snow White* (1937), *The Jungle Book* (1967), *The Aristocats*(1970) and *Bedknobs and Broomsticks* (1971). The last three are to be expected since they were the last three animated feature projects made by Disney prior to this film.

The film received an Academy Award nomination for Best Song for "Love." It lost to "The Way We Were" from the film of the same name. Marvin Hamlisch, who did the score earlier this year for *The World's Greatest Athlete* (1973), was the recipient of that award.

The film was in production from January 1971 through April 1972.

Tommy Steele and Monty Python's Terry Jones were both considered for the role of Robin Hood.

The film did a respectable $32 million at the time, but considering its $15 million budget, it was somewhat of a disappointment in comparison to earlier and later Disney animated features. It was reissued in 1982.

The film still has its many fans. I tend to like it but also agree with the assessment that it's a shame that Robin Hood is the most boring character in his own film.

Interestingly, in the Fall 1973 issue of *Disney News*, the film was touted as the 21st fully-animated Disney feature. Then, a few years later, *The Fox and the Hound* (1981) was touted as the 20th. Then still later, *The Black Cauldron* (1985) was touted as the 25th. Who's counting?

Disney would go on to make worse animated feature films. It aired on the anthology show in 1986.

Superdad

RELEASED BY BUENA VISTA ON December 14, 1973, Technicolor. Producer: Bill Anderson. Director: Vincent McEveety. Screenplay: Joseph L. McEveety based on a story by Harlan Ware. Director of Photography: Andrew Jackson, A.S.C. Art Directors: John B. Mansbridge, William J. Creber. Film Editor: Ray de Leuw. Set Decorator: John A. Kuri. Costume Designer:

Shelby Tatum. Special Photographic Effects: Eustace Lycett. Titles: Alan Maley. Associate Producer: Christopher Hibler. Sound Supervision: Herb Taylor. Costumes: Chuck Keehne, Emily Sundby. Make-up: Robert J. Schiffer. Hair Stylist: La Rue Matheron. First Assistant Director: Bud Grace. Second Assistant Director: Dorothy Kieffer. Music Editor: Evelyn Kennedy. Music: Buddy Baker. Orchestration: Walter Sheets. Special Effects: Hans Metz. Stunts: Dick Warlock. Musician – Guitar: Tommy Tedesco. Running time: 95 minutes.

Songs: "These Are the Best Times," "Los Angeles," "When I'm Near You" by Shane Tatum. "These Are the Best Times" Sung by Bobby Goldsboro.

Cast: Bob Crane (Charlie McCready), Barbara Rush (Sue McCready), Kurt Russell (Bart), Joe Flynn (Cyrus Hershberger), Kathleen Cody (Wendy McCready), Bruno Kirby (Stanley Schlimmer), Joby Baker (Klutch), Dick Van Patten (Ira Kershaw), Judith Lowry (Mother Barlow), Ivor Francis (Doctor Skinner on TV), Jonathan Daly (Reverend Griffith), Naomi Stevens (Mrs. Levin), Nicholas Hammond (Roger Rhinehurst), Jack Manning (Justice of the Peace), Jim Wakefield (House Manager), Ed McCready (Cab Driver), Larry Gelman (Mr. Schlimmer), Steve Dunne (TV Moderator), Allison McKay (Secretary), Leon Belasco (Limousine Driver), Sarah Fankboner (Scout Girl), With The Gang: Christina Anderson, Ed Begley, Jr., Richard Bushman, Don Carter, Joy Ellison, Ann Marshall, Mike Rupert, Peter Paul Eastman (Man in Restaurant), John Fiedler (Pharmacist in TV Commercial), Jack Griffin (Bailiff), Pitt Herbert (Grocer), Tony Regan (Father Getting Out of Limo), Jeffrey Sayre (Man at Wedding, First Row).

Beach footage is shown while the song "These Are the Best Times" plays in the background during the titles.

Charlie McCready dreams about his daughter Wendy at her childhood birthday party. Young Wendy is infatuated with Bart and loves hanging out with her friends. Charlie keeps dreaming as her daughter grows up.

Charlie wakes up and greets the present day Wendy and Bart, who are making out on his front door.

At work, Mr. Hershberger is complaining about Charlie's and Ira Kershaw's work performance, but Charlie is daydreaming. Hershberger blows his top, but Kershaw runs him out of the room.

Wendy and Bart and the gang are at the beach discussing their college plans. Wendy is worried that they will end up at different college campuses.

Wendy and Bart's friend, nerdy Stanley is worried that he will be caught goofing off and the gang leaves and sing "Los Angeles" as they drive home.

Hershberger is now golfing and Bart yells "Fore!" as the gang drives by, disrupting Hershberger's game.

Charlie discusses Wendy and her friends with wife, Sue. Then the gang stops by and Charlie asks Stanley what he's doing driving the ambulance to the beach when he's supposed to be on duty.

Stanley gets a call, so he has to get back on duty. They sweep the sand out of the back of the ambulance before he gets back to work.

Charlie questions Bart's future plans for school and work and Bart doesn't really have much to say.

Charlie sits down to relax before the television and catches a show about teenagers that suggests that parents involve themselves more in what their children do. His wheels are turning as he switches off the set during a Cure-all commercial.

Charlie decides to join Wendy and the gang at the beach the next time they go. At first, everything is really awkward between Charlie and the gang, but soon he joins in on a volleyball game and a football game, although he's not very good and he screams like a girl.

Charlie joins the gang in surfing and has to be carried back to the beach. Stanley shows up driving his new truck, as he is now working for an ice company.

Wendy is now trying to discourage her dad from participating in everything, but Charlie insists. The gang goes out on a speedboat and Bart water skis. Charlie insists on water skiing next which, as usual, he doesn't do very well as he crashes after going up a ski jump. Stanley gets all of the footage on Super 8 film and the gang watches the film later.

Charlie is in bed talking with Stanley's father. Charlie has a cold from the water. Stanley's father says that Charlie should stay away from all those wacky kids.

Sue reminds Charlie that Wendy is expecting to have another party on the beach for her birthday, but Charlie says no and wants the party to take place at home, so he can watch them. The kids dance to "When I'm Near You."

During the party, the music stops and Charlie wants to go downstairs to spy on the kids, which upsets Sue. He tries to be discreet, but takes a tumble down the stairs.

The next day, Charlie has a headache and nurses it with an ice pack while a neighbor, Mrs. Levin, comments on the wild party that took place.

The headlines scream "Dockworkers Claims Hershberger Unfair" on the local newspaper and Hershberger is upset. Kershaw tries to calm everything. Charlie is not listening; as usual as he's thinking about his family. Hershberger leaves in a huff and Charlie and Kershaw discuss everything. Kershaw shows pictures of his children, all happily married and with great careers.

Kershaw has a friend named Claude Archer who can give Wendy a scholarship to Hunnington. Charlie agrees to this so he can separate Wendy from Bart and the gang. Wendy is impressed but depressed as well with the news and turns down a glass of champagne and tells Bart her news.

Bart and Stanley are both really down about the news since now they would be separated.

Bart offers to take Wendy to Hunnington, but Charlie is upset since Wendy needs to talk to Claude Archer or she won't get in. Charlie calls up to Mother Barlow's Boarding House to speak with Wendy, but he doesn't get through so he takes a plane and taxi to Barlow's.

Barlow's is kind of a wild place, with boys chasing girls and even elderly Mother Barlow playing pool.

Charlie confronts Mother Barlow to see his daughter, but Barlow says that it's after visiting hours. Charlie tries to go up to visit anyway but is thrown out, so Charlie tries to use an outside trampoline and then a ladder to get up into her room.

A frightened woman in another room pushes the ladder away and Charlie flies off the ladder, bounces on the trampoline and ends up in the swimming pool. Wendy comes down to the jailhouse to bail out her father.

Afterwards, Wendy and Charlie have a little talk after sending Bart on his way. Charlie insists that Wendy talk to Claude Archer. Wendy thinks that it's really weird that Charlie came 400 miles to tell her this, but she says that she will talk with him and no one else.

Back at home, Mrs. Levin and her dog Napoleon are back again and she asks Charlie to pick up some dog food. At the store, Charlie bumps into Stanley, who is now working at the grocery store.

Stanley tells Charlie how impressed she is that Wendy is taking an art major. Charlie is upset about this move. Later, Wendy calls up and says that she's coming home for the weekend and will be driven by a new man that she's met. Wendy sees him as a ride, but Charlie sees him as a new potential mate.

On the day of Wendy's arrival, Bart shows up at the door and Charlie shoos him away. Soon Wendy shows up with Roger Rhinehurst, the man who drove her home. Roger is studying to become a lawyer and his father is a state Senator. Charlie is impressed.

Suddenly, the entire gang bursts in to everyone's surprise. Then Bart comes by and is upset with Charlie. Bart also says that Wendy's scholarship is phony, too. Wendy overhears this and is very upset at both Charlie and Bart.

Mrs. Levin shows up again and offers her advice about Wendy, but Wendy has turned her back on her dad. Charlie is concerned, but Kershaw says to stand his ground and not to worry.

Bart comes in and says that he's not been able to see or talk to Wendy for quite a while and is worried about her.

Hershberger is wild and is upset that he's on every station with protesters. Wendy is discovered to be one of the protesters. The striker's leader is a man name Klutch, who is an Abbie Hoffman-type protester.

Wendy keeps interfering in Klutch's protests and he pushes her on TV, causing Charlie to leave the office and go find Klutch. Even Sue wants to go get Wendy herself and forbids Charlie to go. She wants to settle this one herself. Bart shows up and offers his services, but Charlie says that this is a family problem and there would be nothing for him to do.

Sue decides to let Charlie talk to her after all at a lunch at San Francisco's Fisherman's Wharf. Sue briefs Charlie and says that Wendy has a slight problem. Charlie sits down and discovers that the problem is that Wendy is engaged to Klutch. Charlie blows his top.

Klutch gave Wendy one of his abstract paintings as an engagement gift. Charlie plans to return the painting, which is very large. Klutch lives on a house boat in Sausalito. Bart overhears Charlie talking to the cabby and follows to help.

The painting doesn't fit in the cab and Charlie holds onto it outside the window. After a gust of wind, Charlie lets go of the painting and a cable car runs over it, cutting the painting in two.

Charlie arrives at Klutch's place, which is a hippie landing. Bart follows close behind and tries to help Charlie, who says that he wants to handle this himself. At first he meets a hippie in a bathtub and then various other hippies, who all stare at the strange visitor wearing a suit and tie.

Charlie knocks on Klutch's door and is told to stay out. Charlie comes in anyway and sees a wide assortment of artistic projects. Klutch is in the process of painting a self-portrait.

Charlie gives back Klutch's painting, which is now in two pieces, and Klutch goes ballistic. He draws a gun and shoots paint on Charlie. Klutch tosses paint and other art objects at Charlie, which prompts him to scream.

Charlie knocks Klutch over with his own overhead mobile and when he is down, Charlie dumps a bucket of red paint on him.

Charlie exits, but it is not over. Klutch attacks again, and this time Bart fights him, knocking him out and onto a fishing boat.

Charlie congratulates Bart and then asks Bart how he knew about the fake scholarship. It turns out that Bart really had won a scholarship and turned it down to go to City College with Wendy.

In the final scene, Wendy appears in a wedding dress and she and Charlie ride in a limousine to the church. They are late and Charlie asks the driver to speed up. The driver crashes into a deli van, driven by Stanley on his new job.

Stanley offers to drive the van to the service. Charlie has to ride in back, since there is no room in front. Everyone shows up to this wedding including Mother Barlow, Hershberger, and Kershaw.

The deli van arrives a few minutes later, but after the next wedding's couple has already arrived.

The wedding is almost ready to begin, but the back of the van is stuck. Mother Barlow gives the van door a good whack and Charlie comes out smelling of garlic and meat. The wedding proceeds with a reprise of "These Are the Best Times."

This was another Disney attempt to be more adult, but is instead another interesting failure.

One interesting thing is that when Wendy gets the scholarship, the parents have no problem offering champagne to their underage kids.

This was the final film of Kathleen Cody's three-picture deal and she was the final female signed to a Disney contract.

Bob Crane hoped that this film would be a launching pad for a successful movie career post-*Hogan's Heroes*, but it was not to be.

Judith Lowry went on from this to play the hysterically funny Mother Dexter on Cloris Leachman's *Phyllis* sitcom, before her death in 1976.

Joby Baker, the actor portraying Klutch, is a long way from the disc jockey character he portrayed on the short-lived 1960s sitcom called *Good Morning World*.

Leonard Maltin rates this film a "Bomb" in his *Movie Guide*, but it is really no better or worse than other Disney comedies released during this vintage. Perhaps the most annoying aspects of this film are the irritating voice that Bruno Kirby uses throughout this film and Bob Crane's girly screaming.

What's funny is that while this film was considered a flop, 20 years later Gerard Depardieu made a similar film for Disney called *My Father, the Hero* (1994) (which itself was a remake of a French version also starring Depardieu). It was a surprisingly big hit. What a difference 20 years makes. *Hero* even has a water-skiing scene, and there's footage on YouTube of Maltin praising this *Hero*.

Apparently, *Superdad* sat on the shelf for a year before it was released.

Though not officially a Dexter Riley film, this seems like another entry due to the casting of Kurt Russell and a few of his young castmates, as well as Joe Flynn and Dick Van Patten thrown in for good measure.

It aired on the anthology show in 1976 and 1978.

1974

Disney continued to increase revenues, peaking out this year at $385 million in profits.

However, this was the year that the article entitled "Working for Mickey Mouse" appeared in issue #2 of *Inside Comics*, a great, but short-lived magazine about the comic book industry.

This appears to be the earliest appearance in print about the question of "How would Walt have done it?" as the erosion of Disney slowly continued despite higher profits, although the article originally appeared in a 1973 issue of *New York* magazine.

The article discussed in great detail how "the glitter of the Disney formula is tarnishing." David Marlow worked at Disney at the time as an East Coast film editor and expressed his dissatisfaction with the company. Marlow didn't retain his position as he resigned in frustration only after three months of coming up with film ideas suitable for the Disney image.

Marlow explained how he got hired by Disney in the first place, the process he went through, and how strange a company he felt Disney was, even initially.

He also explained how there had been five film editors in Disney's New York office in as many years, and it was because the New York office was, in effect, Disney's "whipping boy." Since Disney was a California-based company, they apparently treated the diminutive New York office with disrespect.

When hired, the Disney heads were concerned that Marlow had not watched any Disney films in a number of years, so that he wouldn't be familiar with how their films should look and feel. They directed him to watch 54 Disney films to catch up and understand the Disney formula.

In watching these films, Marlow noticed many recurring themes such as guns and hunting, gimmick comedies, women who seemed to remain in kitchens especially after marriage; heroes were nearly always bachelors or widowers, musicals, animation.

High hopes were riding on the film to be released at the tail end of the year, *The Island at the Top of the World*, going so far as to name a new area at Disneyland "Discovery Bay," complete with a full-size airship that resembled the one in the picture. Unfortunately, the movie fizzled and such plans were eventually scrapped.

The biggest film event of the year was the long-awaited sequel to *The Love Bug* (1969). Though the film was not as good as the first, it did do very well at the box office, despite the fact that none of the cast from the original film resumed their roles. It reconfirmed Disney's leadership at the box office for family films for another year, but this leadership was to continue to erode because of too many sequels and other lackluster product.

In fact, *Herbie Rides Again* was so big that Monty Python poked fun at its success with their trailer for their upcoming *Monty Python and the Holy Grail* film.

The other biggest film event was the release of the third Winnie the Pooh short called *Winnie the Pooh and Tigger, Too*. After *Winnie the Pooh and the Honey Tree* (1966), *Winnie the Pooh and the Blustery Day* (1968), the third and final installment of the Winnie the Pooh trilogy that comprised the majority of 1977's *The Many Adventures of Winnie the Pooh* feature was released. The film was nominated for an Academy Award and was the final time that the entire original cast was used.

Movies made for the anthology show include *The Whiz Kid and the Mystery at Riverton*, *Hog Wild*, *Carlo, the Sierra Coyote*, *Ringo, the Refugee Raccoon*, *Diamonds on Wheels*, *Shokee, the Everglades Panther*, *Return of the Big Cat* (working title: *The Year of the Big Cat*), *Two Against the Arctic*, *Adventure in Satan's Canyon*, *Runaway on the Rogue River*, and *Stub, the Best Cow Dog in the West* (working title: *Cow Dog*). Two other new shows were produced but aired outside of the anthology series: Sandy Duncan in *Sandy in Disneyland* and a salute to Herbie the VW in *Herbie Day at Disneyland*, to honor the theatrical release of the second film in the popular movie series.

Three unproduced shows were called *Harness Fever*, *Incident at Hawk's Hill* and *Ragwing*, which may have been working titles for other shows.

Alice in Wonderland (1951), *Old Yeller* (1957) and *Lt. Robin Crusoe, U.S.N.* (1966) were among the feature films re-released this year and a selected number of Mickey Mouse cartoon shorts were also reissued to theaters, including *Touchdown Mickey*, *Shanghaied*, and *Mickey's Mellerdrammer*.

Successful films this year that could have been made by Disney include *The Golden Voyage of Sinbad*.

Opening this year at Walt Disney World's Magic Kingdom was a new Circle-Vision 360 film entitled *Magic Carpet 'Round the World*, the Starjets, an expanded Goodyear Grand Prix Raceway, the transplanted Carousel of Progress, Pioneer Hall Dinner Theater, Discovery Island, and the Golf Resort Hotel. Work continued on Space Mountain.

Meanwhile at Disneyland, *America Sings*, a show saluting America's Bicentennial and its music, debuted in the Carousel of Progress Theater on June 24. Discovery Bay was a potential land with a ship model based on *The Island at the Top of the World*, but was shelved by the 80s as the movie was not a big hit and old news by that time.

CalArts finally opened its proper campus doors this year as the old-guard Disney animators were dead or dying and they needed new blood for work on *The Rescuers* (1977) and definitely for *The Fox and the Hound* (1981). Incidentally, work commenced on *The Rescuers* at this time.

It was not initially smooth sailing at CalArts as detailed in Bob Thomas' *Building a Company*, but eventually the kinks were worked out and CalArts is considered a quality art training school to this day.

Mineral King, which was to open as a mountain ski resort, was abandoned by this point and eventually the land became part of Sequoia National Park.

A surprising success this year that was not a Disney film, but eventually became a Disney property, was *Benji*, the tale of a small mixed-breed dog of the same name. Its success led to two non-Disney sequels and then a third called *Benji, the Hunted*, was released by Disney in 1987.

Non-soundtrack record releases this year included *America Sings* based on the new Disneyland attraction and a new pop version of *Mickey Mouse March*, anticipating the revival of the 1950s TV series the following year.

America Sings, the *Robin Hood* soundtrack, and the *Winnie the Pooh and Tigger, Too* soundtrack were all nominated for Best Recording for Children Grammy awards. *Winnie the Pooh* won.

In the comic book world, Gold Key continued to publish *Donald Duck, Mickey Mouse, Uncle Scrooge, Walt Disney's Comics and Stories, The Beagle Boys, Huey, Dewey and Louie Junior Woodchucks, Super Goof, Chip 'n' Dale, Scamp, Walt Disney Comics Digest, Walt Disney Showcase*, and *The Aristokittens*.

O'Malley and the Alley Cats ended its run as did the *Disneyland* tabloid magazine. There was a new series called *The New Adventures of Robin Hood*, based on the hit animated feature and *Daisy and Donald* and *The Best of Walt Disney Comics* were one-shot books reprinting classic comic book stories.

Interest in Disney comic books grew as new books like *The Comic-Book Book* by Don Thompson and Dick Lupott devoted an entire chapter on Carl Barks, the mystery "good duck artist" now revealed and another on Floyd Gottfredson's *Mickey Mouse* comic strip which was still being produced by Gottfredson.

The tabloid-size *Disneyland* magazine was canceled on July 30 after 99 issues. *Walt Disney's Fun to Know* was canceled after 16 issues on January 8. Both were published by Fawcett Publications.

Herbie Rides Again

RELEASED BY BUENA VISTA ON June 6, 1974 (February 15, 1974 in UK), Technicolor. Producer: Bill Walsh. Director: Robert Stevenson. Screenplay: Bill Walsh based on a story by Gordon Buford. Director of Photography: Frank Phillips, A.S.C. Art Directors: John S. Mansbridge, Walter Tyler. Film Editor: Cotton Warburton, A.C.E. Set Decorator: Hal Gausman. Sound Supervisor: Herb Taylor. Sound Mixer: Dean Thomas. Costumes: Chuck Keehne, Emily Sundby. Make-up: Robert J. Schiffer. Hair Stylist: La Rue Matheron. Unit Manager: Austen Jewell. First Assistant Director: Dorothy Kieffer. Music Editor: Evelyn Kennedy. Special Effects: Eustace Lycett, Art Cruickshank, A.S.C., Alan Maley, Danny Lee. Music: George Bruns. Orchestration: Walter Sheets. Second Unit Director: Arthur J. Vitarelli. Sound Editors: Ben Hendricks, Bill Wylie. Special Effects: Hans Metz. Special Effects Technician: Mike Reedy. Running time: 88 minutes.

Song: "Carnival of the Animals – The Swan"

Cast: Helen Hayes (Mrs. Steinmetz), Ken Berry (Willoughby Whitfield), Stefanie Powers (Nicole Harris), John McIntire (Mr. Judson), Keenan Wynn (Alonzo Hawk), Huntz Hall (Judge), Dan Tobin (Lawyer), Vito Scotti (Taxi Driver), Larry J. Blake (Police Officer), Richard X. Slattery (Traffic Commissioner), Elaine Devry (Secretary Millicent), Don Pedro Colley (Barnstorff), Iggie Wolfington (Lawyer), Raymond Bailey (Lawyer), Liam Dunn (Doctor), Chuck McCann (Mr. Loostgarten), Jack Manning (Lawyer), Ivor Barry (Chauffer), Herb Vigran (Window Washer), Edward Ashley (Announcer at Chicken Race), Hal Williams, Burt Mustin (Party Guest), Rod McCary (Red Knight), James Almanzar, Beverly Carter (Chicken Run Queen), Irwin Charone (Lawyer), Hal Baylor (Demolition Truck Driver), Candy Candido, Norman Grabowski (Security Guard #2), Gail Bonney (Rich Woman in Mansion), John Myhers (Announcer at San Francisco's Office of the President), John Stephenson (Lawyer), John Hubbard (Angry Chauffeur), Karl Lukas (Angry Construction Worker), Alan Carney (Judge with Cigar at Chicken Run),

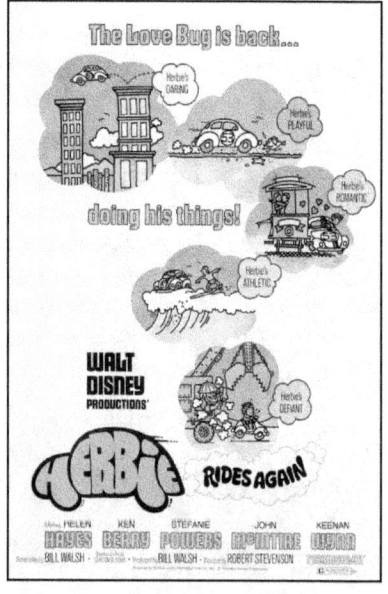

Maurice Marsac, Robert S. Carson (Lawyer), Fritz Feld (Waiter), Paul Micale (Fisherman's Wharf Worker), Hank Jones (Sir Lancelot, Surfer Dude), Arthur Space (Beach Caretaker), Alvy Moore (Angry Taxi Driver), John Zaremba (Lawyer), Ken Sansom (Lawyer), Martin Braddock, Frank Baker (Man at Party), Herbie (Herbie), Dorothy Konrad (Angry Woman in Crowd), David Mooney (Young Man Surfing), Joseph V. Perry (First Cab Driver), Lomax Study (Waiter with Cake), Arthur Tovey (Man at Party).

Alonzo Hawk delights in watching various buildings being demolished so he can replace them with his own skyscrapers. While in Italy, he tells his taxi driver how much he would love to tear down the Roman Coliseum in order to make a shopping center with a parking lot.

Soon, at a meeting, Hawk reveals his next skyscraper plans for Hawk Plaza, an H-shaped building in San Francisco. The problem is, Mrs. Steinmetz has refused to sell her home. Hawk sends his nephew Willoughby Whitfield, a lawyer, to convince Mrs. Steinmetz to sell.

Willoughby arrives, but cannot come inside as Herbie, the VW, rolls over Willoughby's foot. Steinmetz explains that Herbie is in retirement from racing at the moment. The eccentric Steinmetz also speaks with a music box and #22, a cable car that, like Herbie, are also 'alive.'

Steinmetz also explains the current whereabouts of her nephew, Tennessee, who has gone on a sabbatical to Tibet to see his guru and study Oriental philosophy. She also reveals the death of her husband, who was a famous firefighter.

Just then, Nicole shows up. She's an airline stewardess and a good friend and roommate of Mrs. Steinmetz. At lunch, Willoughby reveals his intentions about getting Steinmetz's property and Nicole slugs Willoughby in the face.

Willoughby and Nicole take a ride in Herbie. Willoughby explains that he feels that Herbie's personality is fictitious, but when he insults Herbie, he takes over the driving from both of them and races off to a Chicken Jousting Tournament, a fancy smash-up derby for cars where two cars race towards each other at high speeds.

When Nicole and Willoughby figure out what is happening, Nicole flees the car, but Herbie won't allow Willoughby to leave until Willoughby apologizes and believes in Herbie. Herbie wins the joust and the prize money. Nicole gets back in the car and they're back on their way.

At dinner, Nicole explains that she used to live across the street from Mrs. Steinmetz until Hawk tore her building down and moved in. Willoughby reveals that Hawk is his uncle and Nicole hits Willoughby with a lobster.

Herbie is shown asleep and he dreams of being a race car again, with stock footage from his previous races.

Willoughby decides to confront his uncle to say that he wants to leave Mrs. Steinmetz alone and not take part in his uncle's schemes.

Willoughby comes back to see Mrs. Steinmetz to tell her the good news and to let her know that he will be going back home to Missouri.

Meanwhile, Hawk gets a call from Barnstorff, the man in charge of demolition who is on the clock despite not being able to work until Steinmetz's house is secured.

When Hawk gets the news of Willoughby's departure, he blows his top and decides to take care of things by himself by repossessing Herbie.

Herbie is taken, but once Hawk insults him, Herbie takes things into his own hands and stops in the middle of the street, attracting the police. The police offer to help push Herbie who pushes back and crashes into multiple cars.

The police try to haul Herbie out of the way, but Herbie doesn't budge. Finally, Herbie does move and zips Hawk back to his office and dumps him out in front of his building.

At the airport, Nicole overhears a heavily disguised Willoughby calling his mother and explaining why he is leaving. He is disguised as he wants to leave discreetly.

Herbie is back home and drives Mrs. Steinmetz to the market. He is now being pursued by Hawk's men, but Herbie once again has the last laugh by driving on the wall and escaping in a circular parking garage before driving off the roof to another building.

The men eventually catch up to Herbie again and chase him on foot through a hotel restaurant and then up the huge cables on the Golden Gate Bridge. Mrs. Steinmetz is still seated calmly inside and wishes to get to the market. Finally she does and Herbie chases Hawk's cronies away.

Back at home, Nicole and Willoughby offer to do more shopping with Herbie. Willoughby has abandoned his plans to leave town and instead decides to stay behind and fight his uncle. Once they leave, Willoughby and Nicole are taken to the beach where they fall in love and Herbie frolics with the seagulls.

After the beach, the road has been blocked by an old fisherman who has been bribed to do so by Hawk's chauffer. Herbie takes things into his own hands and drives across the San Francisco Bay in order to get back. Soon, Nicole and Willoughby see that they are being followed by a shark.

Later, they are lost and ask a passing surfer for directions. The surfer points them in the right direction but falls off his board once he sees that it was a man in a car asking questions.

Meanwhile, Alonzo Hawk Van and Storage has stolen all of Mrs. Steinmetz's belongings. Nicole and Willoughby arrive back home and they all go to the storage facility to retrieve her things.

When they find them, the security guards stop them from taking their things back but they do eventually get them back. Herbie helps to push everything back home.

A passing drunk man hops aboard #22, thinking that it's a cable car in service, but really Herbie is pushing. The drunk reveals his name as Judson and starts to make the moves on Mrs. Steinmetz.

When Herbie arrives at the top of the hill, Willoughby gets out and restructures everything so that they won't go down the next hill dangerously. While stopped, they discover that Hawk is still in pursuit. Herbie speeds off, but #22 goes down the next hill anyway in a reckless run crashing through a garden party with the music box frantically playing tunes in a panic.

#22, with all of Mrs. Steinmetz's belongings as well as Mrs. Steinmetz and Judson, is headed right into the bay, so Herbie speeds up to try to stop the runaway cable car. Willoughby jumps aboard and stops #22 just before it falls into the water; Mrs. Steinmetz is as calm as ever, but she plans to go see Hawk in person and give him a piece of her mind.

Back at the Hawk building, Hawk meets his new lawyers, who advises not tearing down Steinmetz's home without authorization and they are summarily dismissed. Hawk's secretary gives him a massage to calm his mild whiplash from all of the recent activity.

After dismissing the lawyers, Hawk is disturbed by the regular window washers and the washer is summarily fired for his noisemaking.

The window cleaner gets to the bottom floor and leaves. Steinmetz asks which floor Hawk is on and takes the window cleaning cage up the building to the 28th floor. She has also taken the keys to get into his office. Willoughby has followed Steinmetz and grabs the cage and hangs perilously from the bottom and Steinmetz and Herbie ascends.

Steinmetz agrees to rescue Willoughby if he promises to let her talk to Hawk.

Hawk calls another demolition person and orders him to take the wrecking ball to Steinmetz's house.

Before she can, Herbie crashes into Hawk's office chases after Hawk, but Hawk still doesn't refuse to let up.

Steinmetz, Nicole and Willoughby get revenge in the end, by phoning demolition man Loostgarten and sending him and his wrecking ball over to destroy Hawk's home.

At home, Hawk is having trouble sleeping, but he finally drifts off after his doctor advises him to count sheep. Hawk does, but the sheep start appearing with #53 on their side and then they turn into man-eating Herbie cars. Herbie is then turned into Indians while Hawk is tied to a stake. Finally, Hawk dreams of being King Kong and swatting at a number of flying Herbie cars.

Hawk is awoken by Loostgarten, who confirms the address and tears down Hawk's house. Finally, Hawk gives up…or has he? Hawk reveals to his lawyers that he was lying, in order to catch Steinmetz off guard.

Nicole and Willoughby invite Steinmetz to dinner to celebrate, but she decides to have dinner on her own at home with Mr. Judson.

Soon, an earthquake turns out to be the wrecking crew travelling up to her house with Hawk leading the way.

Herbie goes for help and signals for Nicole and Willoughby to end their dinner prematurely and come back to help. Herbie also signals every VW bug in the city to help, even the ones in the wrecking yard.

Meanwhile, Steinmetz offers Judson her late husband's fire helmet as they use fire hoses to squirt away the demolition crew. This works until the hose runs out of water.

By this time, the onslaughts of VWs arrive to save the day. Hawk retreats again and tells the police that he's being followed by hundreds of VWs. Herbie backs off when Willoughby says that if he doesn't stop, he won't be invited to the wedding, which he does and he is.

Helen Hayes' part was to be played by Walter Brennan, but he passed away before shooting began. June 30, 1974 and July 11, 1974 was the second Herbie Day at Disneyland.

Hayes is probably the most celebrated actress to make films at Disney during this period, but apparently such a distinguished actress basically slumming it at Disney had no negative effect with Hayes as she went on to make *One of Our Dinosaurs is Missing* (1975) and *Candleshoe* (1978) in succeeding years.

Dean Jones was offered to reprise his role of Jim Douglas in this film, but declined as he felt the script was not up to par with the first movie. His part was re-written for Ken Berry.

There was a deleted sequence where Alonzo Hawk has a nightmare in which he is treated by VW Beetle doctors with mechanical arms and welding torches. The scene was deleted for being too scary for children.

This is a sequel of sorts to two other Disney movies, *The Absent-Minded Professor* (1961) and *Son of Flubber* (1963) as Keenan Wynn portrayed Alonzo Hawk in those two films as well.

Jan Williams said that he would be put on salary as a production assistant if he could come up with footage of various buildings being demolished. He delivered and the results appear during the opening scenes of this movie.

This film although not the huge success of the first film was still a great hit, grossing over $38 million and re-released to theaters in 1981. It aired on the anthology show in 1981 and 1986.

The Bears and I

RELEASED BY BUENA VISTA ON July 31, 1974, Technicolor. Producer: Winston Hibler. Director: Bernard McEveety. Screenplay: John Whedon based on the book by Robert Franklin Leslie. Narration Writer: Jack Speirs. Art Directors: John B. Mansbridge, LeRoy G. Deane. Film Editor: Gregg McLaughlin, A.C.E. Special Effects: Danny Lee. Location Manager: William Redlin. Sound Supervision: Herb Taylor. Costumes: Chuck Keehne. Make-up: Robert J. Schiffer. Unit Manager / Assistant Director: Don Torpin. Music Editor: Evelyn Kennedy. For Rio-Verde Productions, Ltd. Key Canadian Crew: David Anderson, Tom P. Holleywell, George Balogh, R. Martin Walters, David F. Clark. Photographers: John Koester, Pekka Kauppi, Herb Smith. Animal Supervision: Al Niemela, Dwayne Redlin, Bill Rowland. Field Producer: Ron Brown. Music: Buddy Baker. Orchestration: Walter Sheets. Director of Photography: Ted D. Landon. Sound Recordist: George Ronconi. Stunts: Charlie Picerni. Script Supervisor: Margaret Hanly. Running time: 90 minutes.

Song: "Sweet Surrender" Composed and Performed by John Denver.

Cast: Patrick Wayne (Bob Leslie / Narrator), Chief Dan George (Chief Peter A-Tas-Ka-Nay), Andrew Duggan (Commissioner Gaines), Michael Ansara (Oliver Red Fern), Robert Pine (John McCarten), Val de Vargas (Sam Eagle Speaker), Hal Baylor (Foreman).

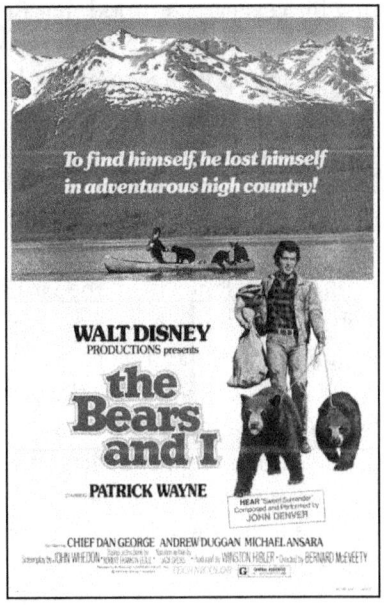

Bob Leslie explains that after leaving the service, he was supposed to come up to the forest with Larch A-Tas-Ka-Nay, but after Larch's death, he went to find Larch's father.

He comes upon Sam Eagle Speaker, Oliver Red Fern, and Chief Peter A-Tas-Ka-Nay and others at a local general store. Bob tells the Chief that he and Larch were friends and returns some of Larch's belongings. He also says that he plans to stay in the area.

Sam and Oliver sell Bob hunting and fishing licenses and some food.

Bob takes a canoe trip down the river spotting moose, wolf, elk, and other wild animals. He didn't have any plans except to stay in Oliver's cabin, which wasn't much to speak of and was home to raccoons and other assorted wild animals until Bob shooed them out.

A few days later, Bob first encounters a family of black bears. Bob learns that black and brown bears are the same, just going through different color phases. He also learns not to get between a mother bear and her cubs.

Bob is able to pan enough gold to pay his way without work. Soon, the Chief stops by with some of his son's belongings for Bob to use while staying at the cabin and Bob gives the Chief of photo of him and Larch.

Bob senses that the Chief wants to talk about his son, but refrains from doing so.

Later Bob tries to feed a small deer, who is soon scared off by hunters' gunshots. Bob goes to see if the bears were safe. He discovers that Sam and a couple others had killed the mother bear, so Bob goes in search of the cubs to check on their safety. Bob decides to take care of the cubs himself. It is initially hard to lure the bears into his cabin, but eventually he succeeds and names the bears Scratch, Patch, and Rusty.

The bears eventually become friendly with Bob and bonds form, with Patch forming the strongest bond. Bob shows the bears how to find food to eat, from berries to bugs, and he trains them how to survive on their own without their mom.

Bob treats the bears as if they were his own children, taking them fishing on his canoe and on other adventures. Everything was fine at first, but soon Bob had to protect the bears from creatures like wolverines.

Another problem Bob starts to have with the bears is that for every pound they gain, the more of an appetite they have. Soon the bears are getting into every bit of food that Bob had stored.

Bob has to go back to get more food from the store, but he didn't reckon on meeting up with Sam's dogs, who get into a fight with Bob's bears and chase them up a tree. Soon Bob and Sam get into a fist fight over shooting the bears.

The Chief disrupts the fight but doesn't understand why Bob keeps the bears tied up, saying that they are not dogs and they should be set free. Bob begs the Chief to reconsider, but he is adamant: the bears must be set free. Bob takes them back to his cabin and keeps them captive until they are older.

A plane lands from the Parks and Recreation Department and Commissioner Gaines gets out. He explains that they are having trouble meeting up with the Indians and that every time he shows up, they hide.

Gaines explains that the land will become a National Park and that it is not a Reservation. His buddy, John, adds that they would like Bob to explain to the Indians that they have to be transplanted to the nearest Reservation and leave this government land. Bob needs to go back into town and this time he hides the bear cubs in an abandoned root cellar so that he could go alone this time.

Trouble happens when Bob turns in some gold and he is paid money and the photo that he had given the Chief. The Chief returned the photo since Bob was conversing with the government men and the Indians felt betrayed.

Winter arrives and Bob plays with the cubs in the snow. The bears accidentally push Bob's sled down the mountainside with Patch aboard. Bob skis down the hill to rescue Patch. After Patch's rescue, the bears were soon ready for hibernation and Bob decided that the old root cellar would be the best place for the bears to hibernate.

While the bears hibernated, Oliver made a surprise visit to Bob's cabin. Oliver explains that the Indians are not set against a National Park, but just not there. Oliver also strongly suggests that Bob get rid of the bears once the hibernation season is over.

Finally spring arrives, and the bears emerge from the root cellar. The cubs were now big enough to be on their own, so it was easier for Bob to let them go. This time the bears encounter a wild cougar, a much tougher adversary. The bears fend for themselves and no longer need Bob, but they do return on occasion, with Patch still being the friendliest.

The Chief and Oliver pay a visit at this time, but the Chief is still upset that the bears are still hanging around. Bob explains that the bears are free to come and go as they please. Oliver gives Bob the written mandate to vacate the area and the Chief blames it on the bears. Bob explains that it is not the bears, it's them. They have to leave.

Soon, as expected, trucks arrive to tear down the Indian village. John gets out, giving official notice to vacate the area, but the Chief tears up the notice and Sam holds up a rifle, but John and the wrecking crew proceeds anyway and tears down the homes.

John offers to bring the Indians and their possessions to the nearest Reservation, but the Indians refuse and try to sabotage the efforts of the government. Bob is caught in the middle.

Because of all the problems, John radios for more protection so that the men can continue on with their work. Bob offers to talk to the Chief about the situation. The Indians still plan to keep their land and will continue to battle the government until the bitter end. Sam sees Bob talking with the Chief and threatens to scalp him. Oliver restrains him and says to leave Bob alone.

Bob gives up on being a peacemaker and decides to check on the bears, who are soon shot at by Sam. Another fistfight ensues between Sam and Bob. Sam flees and Bob checks on the shot bear. Patch was alive, but with an injured paw. Going back to his cabin, Bob discovers that Sam has set fire to it. He tries to put the fire out, but makes the decision to save Patch instead and lets the cabin burn to the ground, which in turn starts a major forest fire.

Both Indians and workers initially flee, but then they join forces to put out the fire. Oliver meanwhile decides to help Bob with Patch. Bob asks the Chief for help after exhausting all of Oliver's medication and the Chief doesn't want to do anything, claiming that it is the will of the spirits. Finally the Chief reconsiders and offers to help Bob and Patch if Bob promises to have nothing more to do with the bears.

After helping Patch, the Chief reveals that Patch wants to die. Bob doesn't believe this and keeps trying to heal the bear, who does get better.

Gaines finally arrives to talk with the Indians and still insists that the Indians have to leave. The Chief disagrees with their plans and all of them decide to fast until they die rather than go to the other Reservation.

Bob asks why the Indians can't be made Rangers in order for them to continue to live on the land. Bob goes to talk once more with the Chief and the Chief says that they will not change where they live. Bob goes back to John and informs that he will contact the newspapers if the workers don't reconsider.

Meanwhile, Patch has gotten better and Bob takes the bear back to be with Scratch and Rusty. The fire had scared them off, and Bob almost gives up looking for them when they suddenly reappear. Bob sends Patch off with Scratch and Rusty and keeps the Chief's promise to leave the bears alone from this point on.

Chief and Oliver show up, with Chief saying that he had a vision that they would not leave, and he shows off his Ranger badge. Bob's idea was agreed upon and houses are now to be rebuilt for the tribe.

Chief still believes that good things have now happened now that the bears have been freed. Soon, however, Patch shows up and the Chief and Oliver are certain that they will have more trouble. Bob shoos Patch away, but the bear tries to board the boat. Bob hits Patch with a rope and Patch finally leaves.

Bob concludes that he would like to stay in the area and become part of the forestry service.

This film was shot in British Columbia over a two-year period since the bears had to be shown growing up. During the first summer, Patrick Wayne's father, John, visited the set.

Since they were 130 miles from the nearest town, a small village was constructed for the purposes of shooting and for housing more than 100 cast and crew members.

John Denver's hit song "Sweet Surrender" was originally from this movie though few actually know this fact, as this film wasn't a success.

It aired on the anthology show in 1976 and was a surprise hit for Disney.

The Castaway Cowboy

RELEASED BY BUENA VISTA ON August 7, 1974, Technicolor. Producer: Ron Miller, Winston Hibler. Director: Vincent McEveety. Screenplay: Don Tait. Story: Don Tait, Richard Bluel, Hugh Benson. Production Design: Robert Clatworthy. Art Director: John B. Mansbridge. Film Editor: Cotton Warburton, A.C.E. Set Decorator: John A Kuri. Matte Artist: P.S. Ellenshaw. Associate Producer and Second Unit Director: Christopher Hibler. Unit Manager and Assistant Director: Dick Caffey. Second Assistant Director: Gary Daigler. Sound Supervisor: Herb Taylor. Sound Mixer: Frank Regula. Costumes: Chuck Keehne, Emily Sundby. Make-up: La Rue Matheron. Music Editor: Evelyn Kennedy. Music: Robert F. Brunner. Orchestration: Franklyn Marks. Director of Photography: Andrew Jackson, A.S.C. Special Effects: Hans Metz. Stunts: Roydon Clark, Branscombe Richmond. Stunt Coordinator: Kim Kahana. Running time: 91 minutes.

Cast: James Garner (Lincoln Costain), Vera Miles (Henrietta MacAvoy), Robert Culp (Calvin Bryson), Eric Shea (Booton MacAvoy), Elizabeth Smith (Liliha), Manu Tupou (Kimo), Gregory Sierra (Marrujo), Shug Fisher (Captain Cary), Nephi Hannemann (Malakoma), Lito Capina (Leleo), Ralph Hanalei (Hopu), Kim Kahana (Oka), Lee Woodd (Palani), Luis Delgado (The Hatman), Buddy Joe Hooker (Boatman), Patrick Sullivan Burke (Sea Captain), Jerry Velasco (Hawaiian Cowboy).

In the Sandwich Islands, a missionary's son named Booton MacAvoy discovers a man in the surf and calls his friend Kimo for help and then rushes to tell his mother Henrietta.

Henrietta instructs her maid Liliha to take the man into the guest room and to retrieve hot water and swabs. The man eventually wakes up and reveals himself as Costain and starts asking a lot of questions about where he is and if he could have a shave.

He also reveals that he had been thrown off of his ship. Liliha then comes in to offer some strange Hawaiian food.

Suddenly, a stray cow that is native to the island appears and starts eating up the vegetable garden. Henrietta goes outside to shoo the large beast away.

Soon Costain is nursed back to health and asks Henrietta to send for a ship when she goes into town. Booton is upset because he knows his mother is really going into town to see Bryson. Bryson is interested in marrying Henrietta and he tries to convince her to become his wife.

Booton reveals that his mother owns 10,000 acres of land. Costain says that he would like to get back to Texas. Their conversations are cut short when an alarm is sounded for the Hawaiians to battle the invading cattle. Booton and Costain join in to drive them away.

Costain eventually wrestles down the last bull and then sends him on his way. Booton and Henrietta are very impressed with his cattle wrangling skills. Costain says that they could get $20 a head for the cattle if they shipped them to California.

The next day, Henrietta has a meeting and says that they can make more money selling the cattle than they can selling potatoes, so Costain is put in charge of teaching the Hawaiians how to wrangle a cow and also how to ride a horse.

One by one the Hawaiians try out mounting and riding a horse. Costain also shows them the fine art of the lasso. He also complains about the lack of equipment and horses necessary for rustling cattle.

Soon, more equipment arrives and Costain continues with his training. Everything is fine until Malakoma throws a spear at Costain in order to challenge him as he doesn't like him. Soon, they are battling each other with Malakoma ultimately taking a slug in the face from Costain.

The new horses arrive shortly afterward and Costain teaches the men how to put a saddle on a horse and how to rope cattle while on horseback.

Henrietta shows Bryson the progress Costain has been making with the men and then introduces Bryson to Costain. They are not impressed with each other.

It is break time and the Hawaiians decide to ride the waterfalls and dive into the river. Costain doesn't watch where he's going and he soon finds himself sliding down into the river. Costain is upset because he doesn't feel that the men deserve to have play time when they aren't making progress as quickly as he feels is necessary.

Costain gives up and wants to leave. He asks for his wages from Henrietta so that he can go on to Texas as he originally planned. Booton looks for Costain and Henrietta reveals that Costain has left. Before Costain leaves for good, he gambles for some more money with Bryson as a witness.

After winning a few hands Costain tries to leave, but he is greeted by the Hawaiians on horses. They promise not to goof off anymore and buckle down on learning, but Costain is adamant about leaving and hops aboard a rowboat, which takes him out to a waiting ship.

Costain is eventually convinced to return by Booton and the natives and comes back to the island rather than leaving on the ship. He starts more training. Everything seems fine until Kimo is thrown from his horse.

The natives trust the witch doctor Malakoma and they feel that Kimo is going to die in a couple of days due to a condition called "death by sorcery". Costain does not believe this and tells Henrietta and Liliha that it is all nonsense.

Costain goes into Malakoma's cave in order to get him to lift the curse placed on Kimo. He finally finds Malakoma and they battle each other again.

Costain is victorious and he brings Malakoma out to lift the curse placed on Kimo, which he does. Afterwards, Costain gets everyone back to working. Henrietta says that they'll do anything for him now. Costain is doubtful.

Finally, the men are ready and they head out to round up some cattle. Now successful, Costain celebrates by singing the old standard, "Ky-I Yippie Yippie Yay."

Rounding up the cattle in theory turns out to be much easier than in actual practice and at one point the men have to retrieve the cattle after they drift into the water. Costain uses his superior roping skills in order to help them out.

Eventually they succeed and they take the cattle to sell. Henrietta drives a hard bargain and insists upon $20 a head for each cow and not a penny less. She finally gets what she wants.

Later, after everything seems calm and settled, there is a stampede of cattle that tears everything down.

Bryson claims that Henrietta owes him money for damages and Costain says that isn't fair since the cattle stampede wasn't caused by them, and he and Bryson get into a fist fight. Costain wins again and again they retrieve all the cattle. Costain ultimately decides to stay instead of going back home to Texas.

This was James Garner's second and final Disney film as he was soon to have a major career resurrection with the starring role of Jim Rockford in *The Rockford Files*. It's a pleasant, but unremarkable, and ultimately forgettable film in the Disney canon.

Shooting for the film took place in Kauai in the Hawaiian Islands beginning September 5, 1973.

62 craftsmen and 25 actors, along with 150 local residents, helped make this film a reality.

The original working title for this film was *Paniolo*. It was good that they changed it, but it didn't help the box office. It aired on the anthology show in 1977 and 1981.

The Island At the Top Of the World

RELEASED BY BUENA VISTA ON December 20, 1974 (December 16, 1974 in UK), Technicolor. Producer: Winston Hibler. Director: Robert Stevenson. Screenplay: John Whedon based on *The Lost Ones* by Ian Cameron. Production Designer: Peter Ellenshaw. Art Directors: John B. Mansbridge, Walter Tyler, Al Roelofs. Film Editor: Robert Stafford, A.C.E. Set Decorator: Hal Gausman. Costume Designer: Bill Thomas. Second Unit Director: Arthur J. Vitarelli. Special Effects: Peter Ellenshaw, Art Cruickshank, A.S.C., Danny Lee. Matte Artist: Alan Maley. Sound Supervisor: Herb Taylor. Sound Mixer: Dean Thomas. Costumes: Chuck Keehne, Emily Sundby. Make-up: Robert J. Schiffer. Hair Stylist: La Rue Matheron. Unit Manager: Austen Jewell. Assistant Director: Ronald R. Grow. Second Assistant Director: Dorothy Kieffer. Music Editor: Evelyn Kennedy. Music Composed and Conducted by Maurice Jarre. Director of Photography: Frank Phillips, A.S.C. Special Effects: Chuck Gaspar, Hans Metz. Special Effects Technician: Mike Reedy. Miniatures: Terence Saunders. Gaffer: Carl Boles. Assistant Camera: Robert D. McBride. Running time: 94 minutes.

Cast: David Hartman (Professor Ivarsson), Donald Sinden (Sir Anthony Ross), Jacques Marin (Captain Brieux), Mako (Oomiak), David Gwillim (Donald Ross), Agneta Eckemyr (Freyja), Gunnar Ohlund (The Godi), Lasse Kolstad (Erik), Erik Silju (Torvald), Rolf Soder (The Lawspeaker), Torsten Wahlund (Sven), Sverre Ousdal (Gunnar), Niels Hinrichsen (Sigurd), Denny Miller (Town Guard), Brendan Dillon (The Factor), James Almanzar (French Engineer), Ivor Barry (The Butler), Lee Paul (Chief of Boat Archers), Ian Abercrombie (Train Conductor), Jackson Bostwick (Pilot), Herman Poppe (Sentry).

It is 1907 in London and Sir Anthony Ross has sent for Professor Ivarsson. Ross brings Ivarsson on an Arctic expedition to find his son, Donald who has gone missing on a whaling ship.

Ross has received a crumpled letter explaining what had happened. There is an island up in the Arctic called 'the place where the whales go to die' or 'the graveyard of whales.' Whoever finds this graveyard would theoretically be rich from all of the whale bone.

Ivarsson rejects Ross' proposal to help find Donald, but with a whale bone map indicator he does help Ross find where the island supposedly is.

Ivarsson says that the place to which it points is not an island and claims that everyone agrees that it is just a bunch of ice. He is ready to leave, but due to the deception of Ross, Ivarsson discovers that they are already underway to the Arctic.

While riding in a car, Ivarsson asks how they are going to travel north. Ross brings Ivarsson to a floating, motorized airship called the Hyperion, piloted by Captain Brieux. Brieux has planned to fly the ship elsewhere, but Ross convinces him to take the ship to the Arctic.

The next day, Brieux, Ross and Ivarsson, Marcel (Brieux's mechanic), and Brieux's pet poodle are on their way, sent off by a couple of farmers and small children.

Everything is uneventful until they have traveled about 150 miles, when Brieux slows the engines due to inclement weather. Ross insists upon full speed and despite the rain he pushes the gears as far forward as they will go.

The high speed soon damages the propeller and it breaks. Brieux wants to go back, but Ross does not let him. Ivarsson suggests putting the spare propeller on in mid-flight. Brieux does this, but he falls. Fortunately, he has been secured by a rope. He is hauled up to try again, and he succeeds. They are soon on their way once more.

They fly across the beautiful Arctic scenery and soon descend between large ice floes with their ship. Soon they land the ship near a small Eskimo village, startling all.

Fortunately, Ivarsson speaks fluent Eskimo and instructs them to pull on the lines to help the Hyperion land.

There is one man that does speak English and they discuss what has happened. They find that one Eskimo, Oomiak, was with Ross' son when he disappeared.

Oomiak explains that there were evil spirits and he and Donald Ross ran away during a great blizzard. Ivarsson suggests that Oomiak can show them where he last saw Donald, but everyone feels that Oomiak will not want to go, so they fool him by giving him a tour aboard the airship. While taking the tour, they leave Marcel behind due to the extra weight and lift off with Oomiak aboard.

Since there is no mechanic aboard, Ross volunteers to do Marcel's duties and helps Brieux steer the ship.

While they travel again, Ivarsson and Ross witness a number of various species of whales swimming north, in the same direction they are traveling.

Oomiak is asked if they are traveling in the correct direction and Oomiak says they are not, which leads them to believe that they actually are traveling in the correct direction.

Soon the ship is slows down and Brieux explains that he did it because it is harder to navigate when it is more difficult to see.

Ivarsson says that they can go the rest of the way on foot and he suggests that he, Ross, and Oomiak disembark after they find a good place to land. Unfortunately, the weather kicks up again and they have to travel through thunder and lightning before they find a good place.

The load is too heavy to navigate and soon they toss overboard everything that isn't nailed down. They narrowly dodge a cliff and eventually the three, minus Brieux, are thrown from the ship. Brieux drifts off to parts unknown.

The three travel on foot and eventually do come upon a settlement with people and possibly Donald. Their excitement at the prospect is short-lived when a spear is thrown at them and they are captured.

The captors speak with each other, but Ivarsson reasons that they are speaking ancient Norse. Ivarsson tries to communicate even though he has never spoken Old Norse. Somehow he succeeds in telling them that they are searching for Donald.

Oomiak pulls a knife at this point, but he is quickly subdued. Ivarsson and Ross are freed, but Oomiak is kept under close observation with his hands bound. The Norsemen reveal that Donald is safe and sound in their settlement.

The settlement is very lush and green, and the three are led to Donald. They meet up with a beautiful woman named Freyja who explains in English that Donald is away at battle but will now be held prisoner because of the three showing up. They feel that the three are there to cause trouble, but they realize their mistake and lead them to Donald.

Oomiak makes another escape attempt and he is thrown over a bridge into the water. The other two are led inside a city hidden behind a great fortress wall. Once behind the wall they are led to a temple, where a tribunal is being held to determine what to do with the invaders. It is here that they bring out the other prisoner, who turns out to be Donald.

At the trial, the Norse leaders say that Donald was originally allowed to run free until the others arrived. The Hyperion was misinterpreted as a bad spirit. Ross tries to tell the leaders that they have come in peace that he just wants to get his son back.

The chief Norseman Godi speaks against them and says not to listen to their lies, claiming that they should be put to death without a hearing. He argues if they are spared, others will come and pillage their land.

The three are sentenced to death in an old Viking funeral, where they are to be burned at the stake. Freyja helps them to get free and the three swim for their lives, escaping certain death. After getting ashore, they come upon Oomiak, who hasn't died after all.

The four weary travelers hide in a cave and Donald and his father have a very frank discussion about why they are in the predicament they are in.

Donald explains that he wasn't escaping his father, but rather that he was seeking adventure. He says he now wants to come back home and share in his father's work. Freyja catches up with the rest and the five decide to escape together.

Soon they are escaping over the mountain and they see that their captors have stopped chasing them, until Ross accidentally sets off a minor avalanche which attracts their attention.

The five keep running and come across a sulfur pit and volcanoes. The volcano erupts and the five run for their lives to escape the approaching lava. They jump out to safety just in the nick of time.

They discuss which way to go next. They are still being chased by the Norsemen, who roll a huge boulder towards them. The boulder breaks a beautiful icicle sculpture and causes major flooding. Once again, the five flee for their lives before they drown.

They succeed again and this time they hop aboard an ice floe and row it like a boat. Now they encounter some killer whales that attack and try to knock them from the flow.

Soon, gunshots are heard. It is Captain Brieux, still aboard the Hyperion. They discuss how to leave and Brieux says that they have to release the motors and everything else, leaving a free balloon that should float all of them to safety.

Donald wants Freyja to come back with him to England and she agrees, but she is sad because she knows that in doing so she will never see her father again.

Brieux then tells the group that they may not make it back because the wind has changed and since they are a free-floating balloon, they could theoretically travel anywhere.

The Norsemen see the Hyperion and flee in terror. Godi fires a flaming arrow at the Hyperion, causing the ship to burst into flames. The ship descends on Godi, killing him instantly.

Everyone is taken back to the trial and it is ruled that everyone can go free except for one hostage, Donald. It turns out to work out satisfactorily when Ivarsson volunteers to take Donald's place. The rest are free to go back to England and Oomiak is allowed to go back to his people. Freyja goes with Donald.

The DVD reveals that this movie was in the planning as far back as 1968 and production drawings are shown in a bonus feature dating from that time, narrated by Winston Hibler.

The original 1968 documentary was revised and expanded for a 1974 promotional release, explaining the history of Viking ships in the Arctic and the possibility of such a ship surviving there.

It is explained that 1907 was chosen to predate Robert Peary and it is also revealed that at the time, the only way one could travel to the Arctic was by air. Of course, some creative license was taken with the design of the Hyperion.

Maurice Jarre was brought in to do the music, which was very different for a Disney film, and as such these film themes are much sought after by soundtrack collectors.

There are also some special-effects camera dailies included to show how the film was made. Effects filming were shown as taking place as far back as July 1972 and as late as January 1974, according to the slates.

A lot of money and promotion were riding on this film, but like 1979's upcoming *The Black Hole*, the final results and box office success were more than discouraging, grossing only $10 million domestically. Productions like this were what eventually killed Walt Disney Productions in its then-current incarnation.

Fortunately, in 1974 films like this weren't that far off the mark from what other studios were doing and so the film's failure wasn't too traumatic. By 1979, making films like this was a totally different story, as we will see with the 1977 release of a film that should have been a Disney film, *Star Wars*. No longer could studios get away with the simpler special effects in *Island* as *Star Wars* set the bar higher.

There was a sequel planned for this film. It was to be called *The Lost Ones*, but it was abandoned when *Island* was not a box-office success.

It's not that bad of a film, really. It gets a little cheesy at times, but the film does move and there are a few plot twists along the way. It was originally released with the short *Winnie the Pooh and Tigger, Too!*, proudly proclaiming in the trailer that it was "In the Walt Disney-Jules Verne tradition."

It was nominated for an Academy Award for Art Direction and Set Decoration.

This was the first film on which Jan Williams was officially added to the payroll as a Production Assistant.

1975

Disney continued to increase revenues, peaking out this year at $520 million in profits.

1975 was a much more ambitious year, film-wise, for Disney and it showed in their releases, which are some of the most memorable and successful of the 1966-1985 period.

Work continued on *The Rescuers* (1977) for another two years and Disney continued its reign as the most successful animation studio during the 1970s, with all of its competition driven to television by this point.

Films reissued this year include the shorts *Crazy with the Heat, Pluto's Christmas Tree*, and *Pluto's Housewarming*. A new live-action short released this year was called *Fantasy on Skis*.

The Disney anthology show experimented with showing two-hour movies rather than their typical way of breaking the shows up into two or sometimes three segments lasting as many weeks. New movies produced for the show included *The Sky's the Limit, The Footloose Goose* (working title: *The Footloose Goose from Saskatchewan*), *Deacon, the High Noon Dog, The Boy Who Talked to Badgers* (working title: *The Boy Who Talked to Animals*), *The Outlaw Cats of Colossal Cave, The Secret of the Pond* (working title: *The Pond*. This film was originally scheduled to be released theatrically), *Seems There Was This Moose,* and a show called *Welcome to the "World"* about the opening of Space Mountain.

1974's *Winnie the Pooh and Tigger Too* followed the pattern of the previous Winnie the Pooh shorts by airing on TV in its own half-hour special, annually sponsored by Sears.

Another significant television event this year was the return of the original *Mickey Mouse Club*, running in daily syndication beginning on January 20 in edited, half-hour shows. *The Club* hadn't aired since 1965.

There were also books published this year about the original TV club, called *The Mickey Mouse Club Scrapbook* and *Of Mice and Mickey*.

Snow White and the Seven Dwarfs (1937), Swiss Family Robinson (1960), Bambi (1942) and Treasure Island (1950) were reissued to theaters this year. With Treasure Island, Disney was not yet prepared to release a movie with a PG rating in order to retain a G rating, they cut a scene where a pirate is graphically shot in the head. The ratings board had not existed in 1950, when Treasure Island was originally released.

At the theme parks, a Bicentennial-themed America on Parade took place over the next two years, debuting on June 14 (Flag Day) and replacing The Main Street Electrical Parade. The Flight to the Moon is revamped to become the timelier Mission to Mars attraction and Great Moments with Mr. Lincoln returned after a two-year hiatus.

But the biggest event for the theme parks was the long awaited opening of Space Mountain at Walt Disney World on January 15. The thrill ride was originally planned for Disneyland as far back as 1965, but various logistics prevented it from opening until now. The transplanted Carousel of Progress and the revamped Mission to Mars re-opened on January 15 as well, and Gerald Ford was added to The Hall of Presidents. The America the Beautiful film was also updated.

Since Mineral King was definitely a dead issue by this point, many of the plans were transferred over to the revamp of the originally headache-inducing EPCOT project, making it more into a World's Fair instead of a true city of tomorrow.

In the meantime, Lake Buena Vista Village Marketplace opened on March 22.

Non-soundtrack records released this year included Dickens' Christmas Carol Featuring the Walt Disney Players. The significance of this album was felt a few years later as it was the first time that Alan Young was cast as the voice of Uncle Scrooge.

Young went on to portray Scrooge in the 1983 animated featurette Mickey's Christmas Carol, and the subsequent DuckTales animated TV series in 1987.

Other records included read-along books and records for various classic Golden Books, such as The Poky Little Puppy and The Saggy Baggy Elephant.

In the comic book world, Gold Key continued to publish Donald Duck, Mickey Mouse, Uncle Scrooge, Walt Disney's Comics and Stories, The Beagle Boys, Huey, Dewey and Louie Junior Woodchucks, Super Goof, Chip 'n' Dale, Scamp, Walt Disney Comics Digest, Walt Disney Showcase, and Daisy and Donald.

The Aristokittens and The New Adventures of Robin Hood ended their runs and there was a new book line called The Walt Disney Paint Book Series.

Floyd Gottfredson retired from the Mickey Mouse comic strip after 45 years and was replaced by Roman Arambula. Bill Walsh, who was also Disney's line producer on the anthology show and wrote many of their films, was the writer on the strip until he passed away this year. Walsh's death may have hastened Gottfredson's retirement.

The *Air Pirates Funnies* copyright infringement case tried to get artist Dan O'Neill to settle with Disney out of court, but he refused.

The Strongest Man In the World

RELEASED BY BUENA VISTA ON February 6, 1975, Technicolor. Producer: Bill Anderson. Director: Vincent McEveety. Writers: James McEveety, Herman Groves. Art Directors: John B. Mansbridge, Jack Senter. Set Decorator: Bill Calvert. Special Effects: Art Cruickshank, A.S.C., Danny Lee. Titles: Art Stevens, Guy Deel. Sound Supervisor: Herb Taylor. Sound Mixer: George Ronconi. Unit Manager-Assistant Director: Dick Caffey. Second Assistant Director: Pat Kehoe. Costumes: Chuck Keehne, Emily Sundby. Make-up: Robert J. Schiffer. Hair Stylist: La Rue Matheron. Music Editor: Evelyn Kennedy. Second Unit Director: Arthur J. Vitarelli. Film Editor: Cotton Warburton, A.C.E. Music: Robert F. Brunner. Orchestration: Walter Sheets. Director of Photography: Andrew Jackson, A.S.C. Special Effects: Hans Metz. Stunts: Denny Arnold, John Ashby, Dick Warlock. Stunt Coordinator: Buddy Joe Hooker. Running time: 92 minutes.

Cast: Kurt Russell (Dexter Riley), Joe Flynn (Dean Higgins), Eve Arden (Aunt Harriet Crumply), Cesar Romero (A.J. Arno), Phil Silvers (Kirwood Krinkle), Dick Van Patten (Harry Crumply), Harold Gould (Regent Dietz), Michael McGreevey (Richard Schuyler), Dick Bakalyan (Cookie), William Schallert (Professor Quigley), Benson Fong (Ah Fong the Acupuncturist), James Gregory (Chief Blair), Ann Marshall (Debbie), Don Carter (Gilbert), Christina Anderson (Cris), Paul Linke (Peter 'Porky' Peterson), Jack David Walker (Slither Roth), Melissa Caffey (Melissa), John Debney (John), Derrel Maury (Hector), Matthew Conway Dunn (Matthew), Pat Fitzpatrick (Pat), David Richard Ellis (David), Larry Franco (Larry), Roy Roberts (Mr. Roberts), Fritz Feld (Frederick), Ronnie Schell (Referee), Raymond Bai-

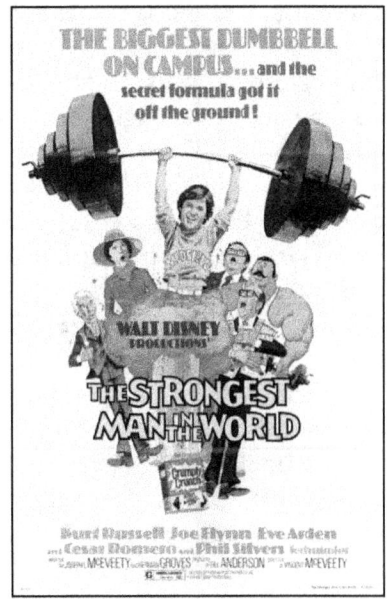

ley (Regent Burns), John Myhers (Mr. Roscoe), James E. Brodhead (Edward), Dick Patterson (Mr. Secretary), Irwin Charone (Irwin), Roger Price (Roger), Jack Bailey (Jack), Larry Gelman (Larry), Eric Brotherson (Eric), Jonathan Daly (TV Announcer), Kathleen Freeman (Officer Hurley), Iggie Wolfington (Mr. Becker), Ned Wertimer (Mr. Parsons), Milton Frome (Mr. Lufkin), Laurie Main (Mr. Reedy), Mary Treen (Mercedes), Eddie Quillan (Mr. Willoughby), Jeff DeBenning (Mr. Rogers), Henry Slate (Mr. Slate), Byron Webster (Mr. Webster), Burt Mustin (Regent Appleby), Arthur Space (Regent Shaw), Bill Zuckert (Policeman), Larry J. Blake (Pete), William Bakewell (Professor), Art Metrano (TV Color Man), Pete Renoudet (Reporter), Lennie Weinrib (State Coach), Danny Wells (Drummer), James Beach (TV Man), Francis De Sales (Regent), Barry Greenberg (Elmer), Jack Griffin (Driving Cop), Harry Holcombe (Regent), John Holland (Regent), Jack Manning (Krinkle Krunch Executive), Tyler McVey (Regent), Tony Regan (Crumply Crunch Executive), Cosmo Sardo (Crumply Crunch Executive), Jeffrey Sayre (Crumply Crunch Executive).

The opening credits of this movie are highlighted by great animation featuring Atlas, King Kong and a number of strongmen.

Dean Higgins drives up in his refurbished antique car and stops in his designated parking place at Medfield College, sporting a cast on his left foot for a painful corn. He loves this car and constantly wipes it down because of birds and bugs.

Regent Dietz is in his office to tell Higgins the news that he is to be replaced because he's been unsuccessful in the years he has had to get the college back on its financial feet. Higgins suggests he fires Professor Quigley, but Dietz disagrees and says change has to happen from the tippy-top.

Higgins asks for a 30-day extension. Dietz agrees and reports back to the Board of Regents. Walking Dietz out, Higgins spies the college students walking in a cow. Higgins delays his exit until the cow is out of view of Dietz.

The cow has been brought in by Dexter Riley and Richard Schuyler to come up with a new cow food. Higgins comes in to tell everyone including Professor Quigley a special announcement, but Quigley is not in. While Higgins waits, he asks Schuyler what he's doing. Schuyler says he's grinding up vitamins for Ruthie Belle the cow and says that everything they are doing in the lab is being done for the cow.

Quigley finally shows up and Higgins fires him after Quigley discovers that the college is spending $15 a day on cow rental. The cow steps on Higgins' foot, causing Higgins to go into a rage and slam the door. The slam causes all of Schuyler's chemicals to mix together and cause a chain-reaction that inadvertently creates a strength formula that falls into a large bowl of cereal set out for Ruthie Belle.

Ruthie Belle eats the cereal and later Dexter is woken up in the middle of the night by the farmer who rented the cow to the college. The farmer reveals that the cow has already produced 80 gallons of milk.

The next morning, Dexter eats a bowl of Crumply Crunch, the same cereal that was fed to Ruthie Belle, and he experiences a strange reaction that causes smoke to come out of his nose.

Dexter doesn't finish the cereal and tells Schuyler to give the rest of the cereal to Brutus, the dog, because he'll eat anything. Brutus eats the cereal, gaining strength and chasing after a huge bully Doberman that has been tormenting him.

Strange things are now happening with Dexter, too. First he breaks a shoelace, and then he rips off a door knob. Leaning against a lamppost, he bends it over.

On the way to school, he decides to shoot some hoops. He jumps higher than the basket and tears it off its mounting. Dexter and the gang race over to Higgins to tell him the good news.

Quigley is there to pick up his severance check, which Higgins refuses to give him. The kids bring Quigley in to Higgins' office to show off the strength formula. Unlike the invisibility formula of *Now You See Him, Now You Don't*, the strength formula works, so Quigley gets to keep his job.

After succeeding with the formula, Dexter and Schuyler are quickly excused. Higgins pulls Quigley aside and tells him that a formula like this will save the college. Higgins asks his secretary to put him in touch with the people who make the Crumply Crunch cereal, in order to give a demonstration.

At the Crumply cereal company, Harry tries to start the meeting before his Aunt Harriet arrives. She is the true owner of the company, and when she finally arrives, she says that everyone including Harry can be fired.

Finally, Higgins sits down to eat a huge bowl of cereal to show the effects of the strength formula. As the bowl is so huge, a large amount of cereal pops and crackles all over the table and floor.

Higgins lets out a Tarzan call and demonstrates his weight-lifting and karate skills, lifting heavy weights and slicing the meeting table in two. He also lifts up Aunt Harriet and swings from the trapeze-like lighting fixtures hanging from the ceiling.

Though Harriet is not happy with the split table and is especially chagrined when Higgins tries to knock over some support pillars in the meeting room, she is impressed with the formula. She calls her competitor in the cereal business, Kirwood Krinkle, and asks Krinkle Krunch to sponsor a Medfield vs. State weightlifting competition; with her cereal supporting Medfield and Kirwood's supporting State.

After the phone call, Uncle Frederick Crumple expresses concerns about Krinkle Krunch's industrial spies learning about the secret formula. It turns out that there is a spy amongst them: Aunt Harriet's nephew, Harry.

Later, Harry privately calls Kirwood and tells him to withdraw from the competition because Krinkle Krunch is going to lose. Kirwood offers a large sum of over $150,000 to get the formula and A.J. Arno and his partner Cookie are released from prison to be the men to do the job. Harry is there to pick them up and to tell them all about the caper.

Cookie is disinterested, saying that every time they get involved with the Medfield kids, they end up in jail. Arno decides to leave it up to Cookie to handle this job, and Cookie ultimately decides to do it.

Cookie tells Arno to help him go up some scaffolding to get into the college science lab. Of course, Cookie's plan is not without its hitches and he and Arno almost fall to their deaths.

Finally they do lower the window-washing scaffolding down to the correct floor. They sneak inside the science lab, but none of the equipment is set up. They hear snoring and it turns out to be a sleeping security guard. They sneak out, but they fall to the ground and the break-in story makes the newspapers.

The next day, Harry tells the two crooks to be more careful as they don't want to draw attention to the break-in and the competition.

Arno takes over and decides that an acupuncturist might be the answer. Arno feels that by placing Schuyler under hypnosis, he may reveal the formula's ingredients, so they kidnap Schuyler and the acupuncturist hypnotizes him.

At first they threaten Schuyler, but eventually they try to ease out the answers with the aid of a couple acupuncture needles. They do get some information, but not the critical pieces they need for the formula, as Schuyler doesn't have that information.

Arno is concerned that Schuyler will talk about this interrogation once he comes to. The acupuncturist tells Schuyler that once he wakes up, he will not remember anything that was done to him and to go home to his dog, Brutus. In his hypnosis he is told to take the first means of transportation he sees, which turns out to be a police car. The police were in town for a testimonial dinner at the same time Schuyler was under the trance.

Schuyler drives the police car back to the college and quietly gets out as dozens of other police cars and motorcycles chase after him and tackle him to the ground. Schuyler is soon bailed out of jail for $100 by Higgins and Quigley. Quigley asks what happened, but Schuyler doesn't remember anything.

Meanwhile, Krinkle is having another meeting and decides to try his cereal. He hits his meeting table in the same manner as Higgins at Aunt Harriet's meeting, but almost breaks his hand in karate-chopping the table.

Harry pays Arno and Cookie $50,000, but takes it back when Krinkle calls and says that the formula doesn't work. Harry reasons that if the formula doesn't work for Krinkle, it won't work for Harriet Crumply.

The weight-lifting championship begins with the heaviest of heavyweights eating Krinkle Krunch and the lightweight Medfield team eating Aunt Harriet's new vitamin-enriched cereal called Super Formula X.

The referee blows his whistle and soon the teams are eating, but Dexter notices right away that the Super Formula X doesn't have an acidic taste and that smoke isn't blowing out of his nose.

There is a two-minute warm-up before the weight-lifting and Dexter tells Quigley that the formula is not going to work because there is no more acidic taste and, and that Dexter's formula, and not Schuyler's, worked.

Dexter needs to get back home to get the formula and he borrows the keys to Dean Higgins' antique car.

The competition has begun and the first Krinkle weightlifter lifts 250 pounds with ease. Then it's Crumply's turn and Porky goes out to lift but ends up stretching his arms out about two feet instead of actually lifting the weight. Soon his arms retract back to normal, but the Medfield team scores no points.

State continues with a 275-pound weightlift. Medfield is ready to forfeit, but Quigley encourages them to not give up. Meanwhile, Dexter is driving well below the speed limit as Higgins' car can't go any faster.

Slither Roth, a gangly Medfield student, tries to lift 100 pounds and succeeds. The problem is that he can't put the weight down after he clears it, and he falls flat on his back with the weight extended above him. The score is now 850-100.

Dexter finally gets home to the college lab and gets the test tube with the formula, but leaving will not be as easy as Arno and Cookie have followed him to the lab to get the formula.

Dexter downs the formula and with his super strength throws off Arno and the henchmen who have piled on top of him. Dexter leaves, but comes across Harry and literally bowls him to knock out all the rest of Arno's men. Exiting the building, he gets back into Higgins' car.

The score is now 1560-450 and it doesn't look promising for Medfield. There is only one contestant left (Dexter) and he will have to lift over 1100 pounds to win the tournament.

Dexter pours more of the strength formula into Higgins' car and gets back to the competition in record time, as he only has five minutes left before the team will have to forfeit. While speeding back, parts of Higgins' car including the roof and the fenders fly off as a result of the dizzying speed. There is a red light and Dexter smashes through the floor boards to stop the car.

At the light, the radio announcement says that he only has two more minutes and he leaves the police car that has stopped him in the dust.

At the last moment, Dexter crashes through the wall with Higgins' car a total wreck. Dexter goes to lift the 1150 pound weight, but can't. He excuses himself for a short moment and drinks the remainder of the formula, then lifts the weight with ease and only two seconds left on the clock. The final score is Medfield 1651-1650 and Dexter is declared the strongest man in the world as he drops the tremendous weight.

As Dexter is congratulated by everyone, Krinkle sneaks into the back to eat a bowl of Crumply's Super Formula X and tries to karate chop the table again…and again fails.

This is the third and final of the Dexter Riley Medfield College comedies following *The Computer Wore Tennis Shoes* (1969) and *Now You See Him, Now You Don't* (1972), which could have possibly continued if it weren't for the premature death of actor Joe Flynn on July 19, 1974. Flynn was an integral part of these types of films and also of Walt Disney Productions.

Kurt Russell by this time was itching to do some more adult roles, and he let his contract with Disney lapse after 10 years (although he did do a voice for 1981's *The Fox and the Hound* before leaving). He was to return much later in films like *Captain Ron* (1992) and *Sky High* (2005).

This was Raymond Bailey's final film; he passed away until 1980 from a heart attack.

Michael McGreevey feels that it was a mistake to do this film as they were all far too old to still be in college and he felt that it wasn't as funny as the other two in the trilogy.

I disagree. This is my FAVORITE live-action Disney film and I have watched it over 100 times. I just love the cereal concept, and I love that it has Phil Silvers and Eve Arden, and I love the Medfield College series in general. I'm sad that they didn't get to do more, but happy that the series ended on such a high note.

Incidentally, the name Medfield is not made up. Walt Disney was very fond of Medfield, Massachusetts, and many of his friends lived there. There is even a plaque honoring Disney at Medfield Middle School. There is no actual Medfield College, and the scenes in all three movies were shot on the Disney back lot.

It aired on the anthology show in 1977, 1979 and 1982.

Escape To Witch Mountain

RELEASED BY BUENA VISTA ON March 21, 1975, Technicolor. Producer: Jerome Courtland. Executive Producer: Ron Miller. Director: John Hough. Screenplay: Robert Malcolm Young based on the book by Alexander Key. Art Directors: John B. Mansbridge, Al Roelofs. Film Editor: Robert Stafford, A.C.E. Set Decorator: Hal Gausman. Special Effects: Art Cruickshank, A.S.C., Danny Lee. Sound Supervisor: Herb Taylor. Sound Mixer: Frank Regula.

Unit Manager-Assistant Director: Fred Brost. Second Assistant Director: Jerry Ballew. Costumes: Chuck Keehne, Emily Sundby. Make-up: Robert J. Schiffer. Hair Stylist: La Rue Matheron. Music Editor: Evelyn Kennedy. Music: Johnny Mandel. Director of Photography: Frank Phillips, A.S.C. Makeup Artist: Lynn F. Reynolds. Production Manager: John D. Bloss. Assistant Director: William R. Poole. Illustrator: George Jenson. Assistant Prop Man: Joseph Kuri. Property Masters: Bob McLing, Al Williams. Mikeman: Ronald R. Cooper. Sound Mixer: Lee Strosnider. Special Effects: Hal Bigger, David Domeyer, Hans Metz. Matte Artist: Alan Maley. Stunts: Jerry Brutsche. Gaffer: Carl Boles. Best Boy: Jack Holton. Key Grip: Lloyd Isbell. Second Assistant Camera: Cecil Luske. First Assistant Camera: Jim Luske. Second Grip: Essil Massinburg. Still Photographer: Sterling Smith. Camera Operator: Ron Vargas. Grip: Dennis Young. Costumers: Lynne Albright, Kent James. Assistant Editor: Louis Terrusa. Transportation Captain: Gerald R. Molen. Script Supervisor: Edle Bakke. Animal Handler: Henry Cowl. Craft Service: Bill Degeneres. Location Manager: Howard 'Dutch' Horton. First Aid Man: Dan Novack. Unit Publicist: Leonard Shannon. Utility Man: Jay Younger. Running time: 97 minutes.

Cast: Eddie Albert (Jason O'Day), Ray Milland (Aristotle Bolt), Donald Pleasence (Lucas Deranian), Kim Richards (Tia Malone), Ike Eisenmann (Tony Malone), Walter Barnes (Sheriff Purdy), Reta Shaw (Mrs. Grindley), Denver Pyle (Uncle Bene), Alfred Ryder (Astrologer), Lawrence Montaigne (Ubermann), Terry Wilson (Biff Jenkins), George Chandler (Grocer), Dermott Downs (Truck), Shepherd Sanders (Guru), Don Brodie (Gasoline Attendant), Paul Sorensen (Sergeant Foss), Alfred Rossi (Police Officer No. 3), Tiger Joe Marsh (Lorko), Harry Holcombe (Captain Malone), Sam Edwards (Mate), Dan Seymour (Psychic), Eugene Daniels (Cort), Al Dunlap (Deputy), Rex Holman (Hunter No. 1), Tony Giorgio (Hunter No. 2), Mervin W. Frates (Bolt's Butler), Lance Kerwin (Boy in Green-Striped Shirt), Kyle Richards (Young Tia), Alfred Rossi (Highway Patrol Officer).

Animated dogs chase silhouetted children during the opening credits. We meet Tony and Tia, who have just arrived at Pine Woods Child Welfare Department where they will now be living. Pine Woods is somewhat of a ramshackle place, but there are many children in residence.

Upon walking in, Mrs. Grindley comments positively on the pretty star-decorated case Tia carries.

Soon, Tony and Tia are being assimilated into school and they meet a curly, red-haired, mischief-making boy named Truck.

Mrs. Grindley comes in to speak with the children when Tia suddenly has some visions. When asked about what is happening, Tia dismisses it as nothing.

The kids are playing baseball when the first strange occurrence happens, where Tony jumps much higher than normal to catch a fly ball.

Tia reveals that she can speak with Tony through E.S.P. Truck is annoyed with Tony and calls him a cheater. Tony responds by mashing his baseball glove into Truck's face and hitting him with a baseball bat, but the difference is that the glove and bat do it by themselves as if the items have a life of their own.

Tia is upset with Tony's behavior and tells him about it telepathically.

The next day, Truck steals Tia's star case and Tony threatens to beat him up again. Instead, he sends her cat Winky to attack and Truck drops the case.

The kids file onto the school bus for a field trip when Tia has a vision about a man getting into trouble if he gets into his car. Tia warns the man and he decides to walk instead. As soon as he walks away, a speeding tow truck crashes into the empty vehicle. The man turns out to be Mr. Deranian, an accomplice of Aristotle Bolt, who is a wealthy businessman in search of someone with powers similar to what the children possess.

Deranian is sent back to Pine Woods to talk to the kids and capture them. He does it subtly, by thanking them for saving his life.

That night, privately, Tony plays his harmonica and lifts a pen telepathically to draw a picture across the room. Tia comes in to say that her star case has been damaged, but it reveals a hidden map inside mentioning Misty Valley and Stony Creek.

Tony mentions that he was drawing a map of a place where dogs bark. Tia is shocked because the map is of a place they have never been before.

Bolt has said that Deranian should pretend to be Tia and Tony's uncle so that he can take possession of the children, and they forge the proper paperwork in order to get them.

Deranian takes the kids to Xanthus mansion. A steel gate is opened by the security guard who is allergic to Tia's cat that she had been holding. Xanthus turns out to be the same place that Tony was drawing, and is the mansion owned by Bolt. Deranian says that he lives there.

Tia and Tony are led to their rooms, which have all the latest toys and even a soda shop and a carousel, gymnasium, tennis court, and riding stable. There's even a room for Winky the cat.

Tia and Tony ask if there are any other children and Deranian and Bolt say that there aren't any. Tia is excited to take riding lessons and speaks telepathically to a horse named Thunderhead, who hasn't been trained. Tia calms him and is able to ride him. The trainer goes to rescue her, but she's fine.

Later, at another private moment, Tony uses his harmonica to make some marionettes dance by themselves. Tia dances and laughs along with the puppets. Unbeknownst to the kids, there are hidden cameras watching them.

Tia wakes up in tears as she senses that Bolt and Deranian are not what they seem.

Bolt confronts the children about their powers and he says he wants to use their powers for good and not evil. The children send them away and discuss their powers privately, but they don't even know how or why they have their powers.

The kids decide to make a break for it because of their suspicions and they are chased by a pack of dogs. They get to the gate and telepathically turn the dogs on the men who are in pursuit behind the dogs. Tia telepathically calls Thunderhead, who comes to the rescue and helps the kids escape with the help of Winky, who appears in the security guard's office, causing him to sneeze and allowing the children to escape on the horse with their cat.

Bolt makes a stern phone call to get the kids back, but the kids get away on the horse and then eventually travel on foot. A man named Jason O'Day is loading up his RV to travel the world and get away from it all. As he is packing up, Deranian drives up and asks if he's seen the kids. O'Dayhe says he has not, but the kids are actually stowaways in his RV.

Jason drives to the ocean to get some fresh air and meets up with Winky. He gets back inside to find some tuna for the cat and discovers Tia and Tony. Jason boots them out of his RV, as he doesn't want any part of runaway kids. He does reconsider long enough to feed them breakfast.

By this time, the police too are on the lookout for the kids and the RV.

Tony asks if Jason knows a place called Stony Creek. Jason says that there is good fishing there, but is upset to discover that the kids have taken Jason's keys in order to get him to drive them there. They start the engine telepathically and Jason finally relents and takes them where they want to go.

Before they depart, Jason fills up the RV with gas but he feels that the gas station attendant suspects something.

They drive on, but then a motorcycle cop pulls the RV over. Tony decides to take matters into his own hands and plays his harmonica, causing the motorcycle to turn back on, get into gear, and drive off the sea cliff. Jason drives away, leaving the cop looking over the cliff at his crashed motorcycle.

Tia is still having visions about being in the ocean after being thrown off a boat. The visions are becoming clearer as time goes on. Jason reminds them that everyone is going to be on the lookout for their RV.

Later, Tia and Tony show Jason the map inside the star case. Jason reveals that he never had kids and never married, but the kids say otherwise, revealing that Jason was indeed married, but his wife died and he took an oath that he would never give his love to anyone again. This revelation upsets Jason.

Deranian is still on the hunt for Jason and the kids, but the kids are now aware of Deranian's intentions. Winky causes Deranian and his henchman to drop their gun and the kids telepathically hold the gun on them.

Jason decides to drop the kids off at his brother Hiram's house in Longview and Jason will continue on, hoping that the police and Deranian will keep chasing him and not the kids, who will now be safe.

Unfortunately, the children are seen by a local police officer and he captures them before they can even get inside Hiram's house. The kids are taken to the police station and locked in the jail cell.

Tia's visions are getting even more clear, revealing that they were on a small boat out at sea and that at times in their past they spoke a different language and even no language.

Afterwards, Tony uses his powers to unlock the cell door and he and Tia escape by distracting the police officer by animating his hat and coat. The officer is literally attacked by his own hat and coat, wielding a broom.

Tia and Tony escape, getting their star case back in the process. They free a caged bear and take it along to protect them.

The next day, the police officer calls the townspeople and claims that they have to get those kids and destroy them because they are witches. Deranian drives up and witnesses the hunters going out after them. He also orders them to get Jason.

Later, the kids decide that taking the bear might not be such a good idea as the bear might get shot or hurt, so they leave it and continue on foot. They go back to Hiram's house and discover that Jason has gone back there.

Deranian discovers that Jason has a brother named Hiram and gets his address and decides to go there to see if the kids or Jason are there.

Tia and Tony are still trying to discover why they gave the name "Castaway" when they were asked their names at the police station. In their discussions, Jason concludes that one of the places the kids are talking about is Witch Mountain, and that they have probably come from there, which would explain why they didn't originally know English.

The three discover that Deranian has driven up, so Tia telepathically calls the bear back to stop Deranian's progress. As he steps out of the car to knock on the door, the bear gets inside the car so that Deranian can't get back in.

Eventually Deranian gets back in his car and resumes his chase, while Bolt chases from a helicopter above. Jason takes the kids to Misty Valley Cooperative in Stony Creek.

Tony makes a phone call to a Mr. Castaway. The voice on the other end reveals that the children have been sought for years. Castaway says to get back into the RV and go to Witch Mountain. He also says that now they are in contact, they will be protected from Deranian and Bolt.

Deranian has secured some of the hunters and raised the reward for the return of the children, giving the hunters their own vehicle in order to chase Tony and Tia.

Tony plays his harmonica again and douses the chasing cars with flour, causing most of them to crash.

Castaway now speaks to the children telepathically and tells them that they want Deranian and Bolt to see with their own eyes why they won't be messing with the children any longer. In the meantime, the chase is still on with limo and helicopter getting nearer and nearer to the speeding RV.

Eventually Deranian takes another road and sets up a road block, but the RV is lifted high above the blockage and they go flying away. One of the other remaining cars chasing them flies off into the water below.

Jason is astounded at the kids' powers, but they reveal that they are not making the RV float. They float up to the level of the helicopter and wave to Bolt. The RV appears to be upside down to Bolt, but it isn't the RV that's upside down, it's the helicopter.

With Bolt and Deranian out of the way, the RV lands in a vacant field in the middle of nowhere. The kids tell Jason they have to leave, and give Winky to him.

Suddenly, a man with white hair appears out of the bushes. He turns out to be the kids' uncle, Bene. Deranian and Bolt are still in pursuit, with Bolt landing the helicopter upside down. Bene and the kids leave in spectacular fashion in a flying saucer. Jason and Winky wave goodbye and the villains are left frustrated.

Director John Hough was brought in to Disney at this point to beef up their film releases. Many of Disney's films were really lightweight prior to this, especially following Walt's death. Hough's pedigree includes films such as *Twins of Evil* (1971), *The Legend of Hell House* (1973) and *Dirty Mary, Crazy Larry* (1974), and 1960s TV series such as *The Saint* and *The Avengers*.

In the film, Jason complains about the prices of gas, even though it's laughable now to know that it cost only $10 to fill up the tank on the RV in 1975.

Kim Richards reveals in a DVD documentary that there were a lot of UFO sightings that inspired the film. Iake Eissinmann (who has changed his name to this spelling since the original film) and Dermott Downs agree that this was going to be one of Disney's great adventure films.

Director John Hough discusses his supernatural directorial past and says that that was why he was chosen to head this picture.

Eissinmann says that the children were older in the book than in the movie, but of course they did the sequel, so they were more the age of what they should have been according to Alexander Key's book.

Hough says that action situations in the movie were enhanced in comparison to the book, but otherwise everything else was pretty faithful, although in the book, Jason was a priest.

The kids liked Hough as a director as he was stern, but also fair and patient. Hough says that he has a natural affinity for children. He also says that Richards and Eissinmann were perfect for their roles and had a natural chemistry together.

Hough reveals that Ray Milland was very professional, but also a bit aloof according to the kids. He says that this probably had to do with the fact that he was the bad guy and wanted to stay in character.

Hough says that Eddie Albert was a tremendous character actor and the kids felt that he was a great father figure.

Hough says that Donald Pleasence was great and that he had always wanted to work with him. He goes on to say that he truly admired him, as did the kids, despite his playing a villain.

Hough reveals that Jodie Foster was one of the hopefuls for the picture, but she went on to another film so the part was given for Kim Richards.

Eissinmann says that he learned the harmonica, but it was for naught as the harmonica sounds were dubbed in. He also said that the star case still exists in the Disney archives.

Both Eissinmann and Downs say that Richards was, and is, really pretty and that everyone asks about her all the time.

Richards says that she always liked to do pajama scenes in movies and TV shows. She also says that she loved working with the animals in the picture.

Hough says that all the animals used were in conjunction with a handler close at hand.

Hough says he did things that Disney didn't do at the time, such as a lot of location shooting. Eissinmann says that the orphanage was shot in Palo Alto, CA, and other scenes, such as the mansion, were shot in Carmel, CA.

The orphanage apparently was a real one, and all the kids other than the lead roles were portrayed by real orphans living there at the time.

Hough says that at the time, Disney had the edge over everyone else in special effects, which is rather amazing looking back on it today since the special effects now seem so primitive. But remember, we are still two years away from *Star Wars* (1977), the film that would change everything.

Special Effects Artist Danny Lee talks about how everything was done with physical objects and with opticals.

Eissinmann reveals that one of the hardest tricks was jumping high in the air while catching a ball on the fly, but it was done in one take.

Eissinmann and Downs says that when he hit the flying baseball bat, it actually hit Eissinmann in the eye, causing a black eye and the stoppage of shooting for the day. This take is in the final film.

Of course, the flying saucer was a miniature and the set was cardboard and plywood. The scene where Tony is playing the harmonica and drawing an image was done with wires and magnets.

Hough says that some of the effects look so good that you would think they are computer-generated. I feel that Hough is being overly generous, but the effects aren't appallingly bad, and are indeed very acceptable even by today's standards. The effects were tested months in advance of the primary shooting.

Special Effects Artist Harrison Ellenshaw discusses in another documentary the special effects that he and his father, Peter, had created for the studios, with earlier films utilizing a lot of matte paintings. The process was used until *Dick Tracy* (1990), after which CGI completely took over.

Lead Digital Artist Michael W. Curtis comments as well about later films done this new way where you can correct virtually anything now in post.

Hough says that the film's success took everyone at Disney by surprise. He says in a separate documentary that he had always wanted to work for Disney, because he wanted to make films for children.

He claims that in 1974, Walt Disney Productions still ran the way that Walt Disney ran it. It was the Disney as it used to be. The people wore suits and everything was still done in-house. There was no improvisation and everything had to be written out to the final detail.

Hough explains that he used different camera angles and flashback sequences that were not common in the Disney pictures of the time, and that this was a tremendous departure. He really liked to experiment and improvise as much as he could.

He also said how much he enjoyed working with American actors like Eddie Albert, because they emote differently than British actors. Incidentally, this was Albert's first film for Disney since 1963's *Miracle of the White Stallions*.

Eissinmann gets really touched by the fact that this film touched the lives of so many children and almost sheds tears of joy.

Downs says that people get so excited when they discover that he was in this movie and many people reveal to him that this was their favorite film as a kid. He still works in film, behind the scenes.

A movie script for this film is shown that is dated April 9, 1974.

Apparently, the 1940 short cartoon called *Pluto's Dream House* was re-released to coincide with the original release of this movie and is included on the DVD.

Richards ends with the tempting prospect of another Witch Mountain film after 2003, which happened in 2009 and was called *Race to Witch Mountain*. It starred Dwayne Johnson. Richards and Eissinmann have cameos in the film.

As the original film was highly successful, earning $20 million, many sequels were made, including *Return from Witch Mountain* (1978), the TV movie *Beyond Witch Mountain* (1982) (which was a pilot for a proposed TV series), the TV movie remake of *Escape from Witch Mountain* (1995), and the aforementioned *Race*.

Escape to Witch Mountain aired on the anthology show in 1980 and 1981. It was originally planned as a two-part TV episode for the 1975-76 season.

The Apple Dumpling Gang

RELEASED BY BUENA VISTA ON July 4, 1975, Technicolor. Producer: Bill Anderson. Director: Norman Tokar. Screenplay: Don Tait based on the book by Jack M. Bickham. Art Directors: John B. Mansbridge, Walter Tyler. Set Decorator: John Kuri. Costume Designer: Shelby Anderson. Special Effects: Art Cruickshank, A.S.C., Danny Lee. Portions of this motion picture were filmed in the Los Padres and Deschutes National Forests. Second Unit Director: Arthur J. Vitarelli. Film Editor: Ray de Leuw, A.C.E. Sound Supervision: Herb Taylor. Sound Mixer: Frank Regula. Unit Manager / Assistant Director: Ronald R. Grow. Second Assistant Director: Pat Kehoe. Costumes: Chuck Keehne, Emily Sundby. Make-up: Robert J. Schiffer. Hair Stylist: La Rue Matheron. Music Editor: Evelyn Kennedy. Music: Buddy Baker. Orchestration: Walter Sheets. Director of Photography: Frank Phillips, A.S.C. Special Effects: Hans Metz. Stunts: Donna Hall, Kim Kahana, Walter Robles. Running time: 100 minutes.

Song: "The Apple Dumpling Gang" by Shane Tatum; sung by Randy Sparks and The Back Porch Majority.

Cast: Bill Bixby (Russel Donavan), Susan Clark (Magnolia Dusty Clydesdale), Don Knotts (Theodore Ogelvie), Tim Conway (Amos), David Wayne (Colonel J.R. Clydesdale), Slim Pickens (Frank Stillwell), Harry Morgan (Homer McCoy), John McGiver (Leonard Sharpe), Don Knight (John Wintle), Clay O'Brien (Bobby Bradley), Brad Savage (Clovis Bradley), Stacy Manning (Celia Bradley), Dennis Fimple (Rudy Hooks), Pepe Callahan (Clemons), Iris Adrian (Poker Polly), Fran Ryan (Mrs. Stockley), Bing Russell (Herm Dally), James E. Brodhead (The Mouthpiece), Jim Boles (Easy Archie), Olan Soule (Rube Cluck), Tom Waters (Rowdy Joe Dover), Dawn Little Sky (Big Foot), Joshua Shelley (Broadway Phil), Richard Lee-Sung (Oh So), Arthur Wong (No So), Dick Winslow (Slippery Sid), Bill Dunbar (Fast Eddie), Wally Berns (Cheating Charley), Jimmie Booth (Barfly), Jackson Bostwick (Additional Voices), Owen Bush (Sleeping Fireman), Richard Farnsworth (Mover), Bruce Kimmel

(Bank Teller), Hank Robinson (Barfly), Larry Vincent (Townsman), Charles Wagenheim (Old Prospector).

Amos and Theodore come out to rob a man riding by on his horse. It looks to be a serious robbery, but when the barrel of Theodore's gun falls out and it's shown that Amos has poor roping skills, it is realized that they are no threat.

In the meantime, there is a poker game going on in a nearby saloon with Homer McCoy, Russel Donavan, and Leonard Sharpe. While playing the game, John Wintle comes in to say that he's leaving Quake City for San Francisco and there are some valuables that he needs to have picked up. Donavan agrees to do it when Wintle offers him five dollars, which he promptly uses as a bet in the game.

The next day a stagecoach comes through, driven by Dusty and carrying three children, the smallest of which, constantly has to stop to go to the bathroom.

Finally the stage comes into town and Donavan is there to pick up his "cargo," which turns out to be three small children named Celia, Clovis and Bobby. Donavan refuses to sign for them, but Colonel Clydesdale and Homer say he has to live up to his word. Donavan reluctantly signs for the children and takes them, with Celia having to go to the bathroom yet again.

Later, Donavan and Homer have a discussion about the children's welfare and Homer convinces Donavan that he needs to keep up his part of the bargain and that there is no orphanage for the kids to go to. He also advises Donavan not to leave, as a hangman's noose may be waiting for him.

Donavan learns his new children's quirks. Celia always has to go to the bathroom and if Clovis is touched, it results in a swift kick in the shin.

Later, Donavan's house is leaking and everyone puts out pots and pans to capture the water. Celia can't seem to move herself out of the rain and the dinner of salt pork is ruined while trying to move her. Clovis suggests making apple dumplings instead.

Dusty checks on the "family" and brings dinner in order to help out. Donavan tries to palm the kids off to Dusty, but he isn't having it so Donavan tries to palm off the children on others, but as he tries to negotiate, Celia and Clovis tend to get into trouble.

While trying, a runaway stage coach is on fire and being chased by a fire engine that almost hits Celia. Donavan rescues her just in time and Homer witnesses this, commenting on how much work it is to be a family man.

At one point Donavan goes in for a poker game while the children are left to their own devices, and they start a self-performing band machine called a melodeon. They are soon scooted away, afterward encountering a Chinese laundry, which they are shooed away from. Next, the children find an abandoned mine high atop a hill.

Meanwhile, Donavan continues to win at poker, all the while being watched by Amos and Theodore, who plan to rob him once he leaves the saloon.

The children climb into a minecart, which rolls down the tracks and then derails at high speed and rolls down the hill, crashing through the Chinese laundry, knocking over the water tower, crashing through a mirror, and destroying the melodeon.

Donavan leaves the saloon much richer, but with so many people coming to collect for damages caused by the children, he leaves penniless and has to pawn off a small piece of jewelry to raise some money in a hurry.

The kids recommend getting the gold out of the Commodore Mine, but Donavan says that there is no gold in the mine, because someone would have found it years ago.

That night, Amos and Theodore plan their attack on Donavan, but their scheme fails as Amos falls off the roof instead of pouncing on Donavan.

Donovan bumps into Dusty and she reveals that Theodore and Amos worked with the Stillwell Gang until Amos accidentally shot Stillwell in the leg. They are now the Hash Knife Outfit and pretty harmless now.

The next day, the kids beg Donavan to take them to get the gold in the mine, but Donavan tells them to go dig it up themselves. Leonard Sharpe is shown to have Donavan's piece of pawned jewelry, which he won in last night's poker game.

Amos and Theodore try again to rob Donavan, this time with rifles. The kids meet up with them and ask where the Commodore Mine is. They point the correct way and then argue with each other for having their secret hideout discovered by children.

The kids go inside the mine and look for a good place to dig. Incidentally, the mine is the home to various forms of wildlife. While digging, there is a large earthquake and the children try to flee the mine, but they are temporarily trapped. The earthquake has done good as it reveals a huge gold nugget, which the kids carry back to the bank and place in the safe. It is not revealed how they escape from the mine.

Amos and Theodore decide to rob the bank and get that huge gold nugget. They plan to take a ladder and go in through the skylight.

Meanwhile, Donavan has taken the children to a nice dinner where they can have all the apple dumplings they want. Celia reveals that Donavan has purchased her a nice dress.

Homer asks what the plans are now, since with money Donavan plans to leave for New Orleans. Of course, now that the children are rich, everyone wants them, but Homer says that the court has to decide what to do with them.

Homer suggests Dusty be the kids' guardian, and also suggests that Donavan and Dusty get married. The kids are for it but Donavan is not, although he eventually he gives in after they get a good night's rest.

That night Theodore and Amos are up to their antics again, trying to steal the gold from the bank. They first go into the fire station to steal a ladder from the fire truck while trying not to wake a sleeping fireman. In their incompetence, they pull the scaling ladder out all the way.

They do eventually get the ladder out and extend it to traverse the gap between two buildings. They barely make it and almost fall to their deaths. Eventually they do fall, but only a short distance, after destroying the ladder.

Meanwhile, Donavan is trying to convince Dusty to get married, but Dusty is still not interested. She is really worried that Donavan wants sex, but he assures her that he doesn't, so Dusty agrees to marriage, but only for the kids.

Amos and Theodore are still trying to get into the bank and enlist the services of their stubborn mule. Meanwhile, the kids are awake and looking for Donavan. They see Theodore with a rope around him, slowly being hoisted up off the ground and ask him why. Theodore shoos them away and is soon hoisted to the roof by Amos and the mule.

The next morning, Amos and Theodore are found trapped by their own devices, hanging from their own rope and suspended in mid-air in the middle of the bank.

Homer arrives and sentences them to be hanged and to bring their own rope. Then, Home and Leonard free Amos and Theodore from their entrapment. Homer is really not that serious about hanging them; he really hopes that Amos and Theodore leave town.

Soon there's a new problem, as Frank Stillwell and his gang come back into town once they hear about the gold that was found in the mine.

Homer presides over the marriage Dusty and Donavan, with the children in attendance. There isn't a ring, so Homer gets one from a nearby bottle of shaving lotion.

After the ceremony Dusty takes the children to the general store, where a nice bed catches her eye. The store owner reveals that Donavan had purchased the bed that morning, sending Dusty into a powerful rage and she finds him in the saloon and throws everything at him, because she suspects that he wants sex after all.

Donavan finally gets to speak and says that the bed was purchased for the kids, and not them.

After the fight Homer has had enough, so he holds a trial to determine once and for all who gets the children. He gives the children to Dusty and Donavan.

At that moment, John Wintle comes back into town with a lawyer and a legal document, saying that the children are his. Homer looks at the document and all is awarded to Wintle.

Afterwards, Donavan and Dusty have a discussion about their marriage and actually fall in love with each other even though they still decide to part ways, with Donavan heading off to New Orleans.

As Theodore and Amos discuss their fates, the kids arrive from Wintle's and say that they are giving them the gold so that they can get away from Wintle and back with Donavan and Dusty.

The five decide to rechristen themselves The Apple Dumpling Gang and make a plan to get the gold.

Stillwell, disguised as a priest, is also trying to get the gold. He holds a gun on Leonard and gets in after hours to rob the bank. The kids arrive and witness the robbery and are soon captured by Stillwell's gang.

Amos and Theodore finally show up, but it's too late and they are also captured by Stillwell. Stillwell removes their masks and remembers that they used to be in his gang.

Soon after, Dusty and Donavan arrive and a full-blown gun fight erupts. Finally Stillwell escapes with the children and leaves the gold with Amos and Theodore.

Now a chase ensues, with Dusty and Donavan chasing after Stillwell and his men. They chase them into a river, where Donavan and Stillwell wrestle. The children are now safe with Dusty.

After Stillwell nearly drowns, Donavan brings him to safety. Dusty greets Donavan and they fall into the river, kissing romantically.

Homer arrives with the other horses and orders the men to lock up Stillwell and his gang.

Back in town, a huge explosion blows up the bank. The residents of the town go to see what has happened, only to find that the gold nugget has been blown up with the bank, leaving pieces for everyone to find in the rubbish.

Leonard bemoans the loss of his bank, but Homer says he can run the bank out of his courthouse until it is rebuilt. Wintle says he'll sue for damages to the gold, claiming that it is his and Amos and Theodore emerge unscathed from the bank vault.

Donavan gets paid by the bank for the gold and is given the deed to his home as the gold was the property of the kids and he is now their legal guardian. Dusty emerges wearing a dress and looking more feminine, and she, Donavan, and the Colonel go to the homestead with the children.

Donavan says he'll be playing poker and Dusty says he won't. As Donavan and Dusty find their way home they encounter Amos and Theodore and give them a ride and a place to stay as well. Everyone is happy, but Celia still needs to go.

This is a fun, entertaining film that is also one of my favorites.

This was John McGiver's final film role, as he died shortly after this film's release on September 9, 1975.

This was also the first film to team up Don Knotts and Tim Conway. They went on to make other non-Disney movies such as *The Prize Fighter* (1979) and *The Private Eyes* (1980) after making the sequel to this movie.

This was Bill Bixby's only role with Disney, which is a shame since he seems to fit the Disney image quite well. I don't know for sure, but it is possible that his part may have been designed for James Garner, who by this point had left the studio.

Also, Clay O'Brien (whose last name is really Cooper; O'Brien is his middle name.), who plays eldest son Bobby Bradley, is virtually unrecognizable as the same kid who played Mark in *One Little Indian* (1973). *The Apple Dumpling Gang* was his fourth Disney film.

There is a documentary on the DVD, with comments by Susan Clark, Tim Conway, Stacy Manning and Clay Cooper, Don Knotts and Brad Savage. Conway, Clark, Knotts, and Savage also do an audio commentary. No real insights are made except how much fun they had, how good a director Norman Tokar was, and how nice Bill Bixby and Harry Morgan were.

Susan Clark says that she did not use a double in the fight scene, but that it was also extremely choreographed with breakaway and rubber furniture.

Brad Savage reveals that the outfit he wore was worn by Kevin Corcoran about a decade earlier and that his name was still printed inside the cap.

Don Knotts says that he always used a stunt man, whereas Tim Conway says he liked to do his own stunts. The crew had to stifle laughter in order to not laugh at their antics while shooting.

There is another documentary on the DVD about the Disney back lot, with comments by Susan Clark, Tim Conway, Stacy Manning, and Clay Cooper. Kim Richards and Kevin Corcoran, as well as Disney Archives Director Dave Smith, give comments as well.

Smith reveals that the back lot was first used for *The Three Caballeros* in 1944, when they created a beach. The next major use was for the *Zorro* TV series. The set was used for many later films like *Monkeys, Go Home!* (1967) and *Bedknobs and Broomsticks* (1971), before it was torn down in the late 1980s.

Fortunately, I did have a chance to walk on this back lot in 1988, shortly before it was destroyed to make room for parking lots and office buildings.

Comments are also made by set decorator John A. Kuri and senior VP of corporate operations and real estate, Harry S. Grossman. Kuri reveals that continuity from Walt continued at this point meaning that the studio hadn't really changed much since Walt's death. He also said that the entire bank was brought in and then removed and destroyed and replaced to resemble the time after the bomb went off.

Yet another documentary features an exclusive interview with Tim Conway, who discusses his many features at Disney including *The World's Greatest Athlete* (1973), *Gus*(1976) and *The Shaggy D.A.* (1976). He says that when you work for Disney, you go to wardrobe and then you meet your animal.

Incidentally, *The Apple Dumpling Gang* is actually the name applied originally to the three children, not Amos and Theodore, but similar to *The Pink Panther* (1964) and *The Thin Man* (1934), the name stuck to the incorrect set of characters for the sequels.

The Apple Dumpling Gang did very well upon release and warranted a theatrical sequel in 1979, a made-for-TV movie called *Tales of the Apple Dumpling Gang* in 1982, and a short-lived TV series called *Gun Shy* in 1983. Things were continuing to ride high for Disney during 1975. This was their biggest success of the year at almost $37 million in receipts. In fact, this film was the Disney's biggest success in the 1970s.

The movie aired on the anthology show in 1976, 1980, 1986, and 1989.

One Of Our Dinosaurs Is Missing

RELEASED BY BUENA VISTA ON July 9, 1975, Technicolor. Producer: Bill Walsh. Director: Robert Stevenson. Screenplay: Bill Walsh based on the novel *The Great Dinosaur Robbery* by David Forrest, filmed at Pinewood and E.M.I. Studios, London, England. Director of Photography: Paul Beeson, B.S.C. Art Director: Michael Stringer. Assistant Art Director: George Richardson. Editor: Peter Boita. Sound Editor: Peter Best. Costume Designer: Anthony Mendleson. Set Dresser: Hugh Scaife. Second Unit Director: Anthony Squire. Second Unit Photography: H.A.R. Thomson, B.S.C. Special Effects Processes: Cliff Culley. Special Effects: John Stears. Production Manager: Eric Rattray. Assistant Director: Terry Clegg, Dickie Bamber. Continuity: Tilly Day, Georgina Hamilton. Camera Operators: Godfrey Godar, Walter Byatt. Location Manager: John Southwood. Make-up: Freddy Williamson. Hairdressing: Betty Glasow. Casting: Maude Spector. Construction Manager: Gus Walker. Stunt Arranger: Bob Anderson. Sound Recordists: Danny Daniel, Ken Barker. Music Composer and Conductor: Ron Goodwin recorded at Anvil Studios. Associate Producer: Hugh Attwooll. Second Assistant Director: Andy Armstrong. Sound Re-Recording Mixers: Graham V. Hartstone, Otto Snel. Production Runner: Christopher Newman. Running time: 94 minutes.

Cast: Peter Ustinov (Hnup Wan), Helen Hayes (Hettie), Clive Refill (Quoin), Derek Nimmo (Lord Southmere), Joan Sims (Emily), Bernard Bresslaw (Fan Choy), Natasha Pyne (Susan), Roy Kinnear (Superintendent Grubbs), Joss Ackland (B.J. Spence), Deryck Guyler (Harris), Richard Pearson (Sir Geoffrey Wilkins), Jon Pertwee (Colonel), Amanda Barrie (Mrs. B.J. Spence), John Laurie (Jock), Max Wall (Juggler), Hugh Burden (Haines), Arthur Howard (Thumley), Joan Hickson (Mrs. Gibbons), Wensley Pithey (Bromley), Anthony Sharp (Home Secretary), Frank Williams (Dr. Freemo), Michael Elwyn (Haycock), Percy Herbert (Mr. Gibbons), Angus Lennie (Hamish), Jane Lapotaire (Miss Prescott), Peter Madden (Sanders), Kathleen Byron (Colonel's Wife), Aimee Delamain (Millicent), Lucy Griffiths (Amelia), Leonard Trolley (Inspector Eppers), Erik Chitty (Museum Guard), Molly Weir (Scots Nanny), John Bardon (Bookmaker), Andrew Dove (Lord Castleberry), Max Harris (Truscott), Joe Ritchie (Cabbie), Monique Kaufman (Little Girl), Arthur Hewlett (Older Man), Frederick Jaeger (Man), Patsy Smart (Older Woman), Robert Stevenson.

Lord Southmere recounts the time when ruthless warlords reigned in China. He tells how he got the rare Lotus X, a special secret formula out of China by disguising himself in a small town outside of Tibet. He is soon thrown out of Tibet by an abominable snowman.

Southmere returns to London and is taken home, but his driver turns out to be a spy. Southmere realizes he is literally being taken for a ride when he doesn't recognize the route.

Southmere leaps out of the car when the driver slams on his brakes to avoid hitting a nanny pushing a baby carriage.

The following car stops as well. and everyone runs into the Natural History Museum. Southmere tries to shake the men off his trail by stealing a pram from another nanny inside the museum in order to make a faster getaway.

The Chinese men chasing him follow in short order, but don't succeed in getting another pram, and instead incur the wrath of the nannies, who hit them with their umbrellas and purses.

The museum guard orders everyone to stop the disturbance and rings the alarm.

Meanwhile, Southmere escapes and the Chinese men are thrown out of the museum and retreat to Hnup Wan's car. Hettie and Emily search for their missing pram.

The Chinese men then perform some feats of acrobatics in order to distract the guard and other passersby so that Hnup Wan and his henchman Quoin can enter the museum undisturbed.

The young boy named Lord Castleberry is asked by another nanny to see what has happened to his nanny because she doesn't want to look after his baby sister any longer. He really doesn't want to look for his nanny, but finally agrees.

Southmere, weaing a baby bonnet, finally exits his pram and sees his potential captors still chasing him. He runs down the hall and eludes everyone by climbing into a large dinosaur skeleton that is currently under cover for repairs. Before he leaves, he hides the Lotus X inside one of the dinosaur bones.

Hettie and Emily finally catch up with Southmere and he recognizes Hettie as his childhood nanny. He passes out after recognizing her, as he had recently received a bump on the head by Hnup Wan and his gang.

Before going unconscious, he tells Hettie about the Lotus X that he has hidden in the dinosaur bone and to protect it and find it before the others do.

Just then Hnup Wan and Quoin rush by saying they are looking for something, so the nannies realize how important this is to Southmere.

Since the nannies do not know exactly in which bone he hid the Lotus X, they take their time examining each individual bone while discussing how Southmere has grown up into a fine secret agent. Hettie says that when they find the Lotus X, she will take it to the king.

Meanwhile, Castleberry arrives with the museum guard and they discover the nannies searching for the Lotus X. The nannies agree to leave and will resume searching the dinosaur again at a later time.

Later, Hnup Wan and his men regroup at a Chinese restaurant called The Reluctant Dragon. They have captured the unconscious Southmere and are now keeping him in a holding cell in the restaurant's basement. Hnup Wan wants to know what Southmere knows about the Lotus X microfilm, but Southmere won't talk.

Hnup Wan realizes that he must have passed the information to the nanny in the museum. Southmere can't help because he only knows her as "nanny."

Quoin is now following various nannies and trying to find the right one. Hettie, the nanny in question, is at the zoo with Emily. She sends Castleberry on his way so that she and Emily can discuss plans.

Quoin finally tracks Hettie down, but he is delayed by a large bear in a cage. Eventually Quoin hides in an ice cream cart and freezes himself trying to eavesdrop on the nannies' conversation.

Hnup Wan rescues him and tries to get information, but Quoin is frozen solid. Hettie gets many of the nannies together and mentions a time when they will all meet again in the museum, which Hnup Wan overhears.

The nannies meet inside the artificial whale exhibit and when closing time is called, the nannies start to emerge from the whale's body. Before they do, they see a wealthy Texas businessman who wants to purchase something from the museum, but the museum is not selling anything.

The nannies file out and Hettie tells each nanny to take a different section of the dinosaur and inspect its bones. None of them finds anything and the nannies all have to leave to tend to their children.

Hettie sends them all home and everyone leaves except Emily and Susan. The three continue to look and are captured by Hnup Wan and his men. Hnup Wan asks them about Lotus X. Hettie wants to see Southmere and Fan Choy is ordered to take them to the holding cell.

They reencounter Southmere and are upset with the deplorable conditions he's been kept in. They themselves are incarcerated, but convince Fan Choy and others to use their karate skills to bust them out of the cell.

Back at home, Hettie and Emily discuss their next move while Castleberry eavesdrops. When they start their next attempt with Susan, Castleberry and his pal are now following them.

Hnup Wan and all his men leave The Reluctant Dragon for an outing, so the nannies go in to rescue Southmere. Hettie goes to rescue him and Susan wants to come along, but Hettie says no.

Castleberry follows Hettie in and they are somewhat afraid of the dark. They discover some masks and decide to scare Hettie with them, but it doesn't work.

Emily, meanwhile, has followed the Chinese and they are planning to go back into the museum again.

Hettie finally gets to Southmere, who now remembers exactly which bone he hid the Lotus X in and sends her off to find it. Then Castleberry comes up and tries to get the same information from Southmere, but he won't talk. They leave after Southmere hits his head again out of shock after meeting Castleberry's pet snake. For reasons unknown, he is left imprisoned.

On the way to the museum, Quoin asks Hnup Wan why they have taken along so much soy sauce. Hnup Wan says that it is impolite to take a dinosaur without leaving something in return.

Meanwhile, the three nannies are hot on the trail as they rush to the museum to try to beat the Chinese and find the film, running over people in the process.

Hnup Wan gets to the loading dock of the museum and the security guard refuses to let them in and goes to his superior to discuss it.

The superior comes out and then goes back in to call the ambassador to check things out, finally giving the ok for them to go in. Hnup Wan tells

Quoin to take the dinosaur. The superior overhears this and wonders why they're taking the dinosaur and refuses to let them take it, but Quoin and his men lift it out just the same.

Once they get the dinosaur outside and take the security guard hostage, the nannies intervene and drive the truck carrying the stolen dinosaur away, beginning a huge chase.

The museum theft is reported to Scotland Yard, who at first do nothing.

Two Scottish drunks see the dinosaur drive by and they shout out "Nessie!" Another man sees the dinosaur drive by and hauls out his elephant gun to take a shot at it.

Eventually the nannies get away as Hnup Wan and Fan Choy crash into each other, while the nannies take the truck onto a moving train.

Meanwhile, the curator of the museum, Sir Geoffrey Wilkins, is visited by news reporter Mr. Haycock about a missing dinosaur. Geoffrey assures Haycock that the dinosaur is not his, but it turns out that it is his and Scotland Yard is called in, with Superintendent Grubbs in charge.

Grubbs discovers that a group of nannies and Chinese men are all chasing after a dinosaur skeleton.

Hnup Wan goes to Southmere again to uncover why the nannies would have taken the dinosaur and Southmere claims ignorance. Castleberry stops by and wonders where the nannies have gone, and Southmere tells them.

Castleberry says that there are many dinosaurs at the museum and Hnup Wan may have gotten the incorrect one.

The nannies are now with the stolen dinosaur and Hettie says that she has to get back to London while the other nannies watch the bones.

Hnup Wan searches the dinosaur that's still in the museum and he finds the Lotus X film. Castleberry and Truscott come back home and reveal to Hettie that he had been in the museum with Hnup Wan and that the nannies had the wrong dinosaur.

Hettie tells Emily and Susan over the phone and that they have to bring back the stolen dinosaur and save Southmere. Since Hnup Wan has the Lotus X, Southmere is no longer needed.

Hnup Wan is going to look at the Lotus X, but Quoin comes in and sabotages his plans and takes the Lotus X from him, claiming that he is now in charge.

The nannies are back in town and Castleberry insists on joining them. Hettie says to stay home, but Castleberry says that he'll tell the press about the spies and the stolen dinosaur if he isn't allowed to come along, so she lets him.

Hettie gets to Hnup Wan's location and takes Southmere away. A fight breaks out, and Scotland Yard is still on the trail.

While the fighting progresses, Hnup Wan and Southmere are sitting on the sidelines watching the proceedings and calmly having a drink, while Hnup Wan's henchmen do all the work.

Emily and Susan are still driving the stolen dinosaur back. Scotland Yard intervenes and declares the case of the stolen dinosaur closed.

Finally, after everything is settled and the nannies stop fighting, the Lotus X film is returned to Southmere as the rightful owner and he shows Hnup Wan and the nannies that the Lotus X is just a recipe for won ton soup, but nobody listened.

Southmere reveals that he is not a spy and actually works for a soup company and was traveling the world for new soup recipes. Hnup Wan is very disappointed.

All is not lost, as in a recap Southmere reveals that he has kept Hnup Wan in his employ as the on-air ad spokesman for the won ton soup.

This is a pretty silly film even by Disney standards. Despite the fact that Helen Hayes and Peter Ustinov were both Disney veterans by this time, the movie has a different look and feel than some other Disney movies made around the same time, mainly because the film was shot in England, with a primarily British cast and crew.

It is unknown why this film is not available as a Region 1 DVD. Perhaps it has to do with the Asian stereotypes portrayed by Caucasian British actors. The fact that there are predominantly British actors and British situations is probably the reason why it is available as a Region 2, but I never understand why a DVD would ever be released in another country before it is released to its country of origin. However, I have a copy and I can play it, so I don't really care.

Peter Ustinov basically portrays his Chinese character with a series of weird grunts and groans, surely now offending those with 21st century sensibilities.

The Reluctant Dragon restaurant is a droll nod to the Walt Disney cartoon of the same name produced back in 1941.

Many of the actors in this film including Joan Sims, Jon Pertwee, Amanda Barrie, Joan Hickson, and Bernard Bresslaw were from the very popular British film series called *Carry On*, so this has an element of the same silliness that marks those films.

In fact, this film did much better in Europe than it did in the US.

Leonard Maltin gives this film a "bomb" rating in his annual *Movie Guide*, but again I see it no better or worse than any other film Disney was making at this time.

The Best Of Walt Disney's True-Life Adventures

RELEASED BY BUENA VISTA ON October 8, 1975, Technicolor. Producer: Ben Sharpsteen, James Algar. Director: James Algar. Narration Writers: James Algar, Winston Hibler, Ted Sears. Narrator: Winston Hibler. Music: Paul Smith, Oliver Wallace, Buddy Baker. Orchestration: Joseph Dubin, Edward Plumb, Clifford Vaughn. Photographed by Alfred G. Milotte, Elma Milotte, N. Paul Kenworthy, Jr., Robert H. Crandall, Hugh A. Wilmar, James R. Simon, Herb Crisler, Lois Crisler, Tom McHugh, Jack C. Cooper. Additional Photography: John H. Storer, Stuart V. Jewell, Bert Harwell, Dick Borden, Alfred M. Bailey, Karl H. Maslowski, Lloyd Beebe, William Carrick, Cleveland P. Grant, Murl Deusing, Olin Sewall Pettingill, Jr. Production Manager: Erwin L. Verity. Film Editors: Norman Palmer, A.C.E., Anthony Gerard, Lloyd L. Richardson, Gregg McLaughlin, Gordon Brenner. Music Editor: Evelyn Kennedy. Sound: C.O. Slyfield, Harold J. Steck, Robert O. Cook, Herb Taylor. With the co-operation of The Royal National Parks of Kenya, The Serengeti National Park of Tanzania, Queen Elizabeth National Park of Uganda, Kruger National Park of South Africa, Hluhuwe Game Reserve of Zululand, The Game Departments of Kenya, Uganda and Tanzania, Canadian Wildlife Service, National Park Service of Canada, Province of Alberta Department of Lands and Forests, Province of Manitoba Game Branch, Hudson's Bay Company, McKinley National Park, The United States Department of the Interior, National Park Service, Wind Cave National Park, Yellowstone National Park, Fish and Wildlife Service, Bureau of Indian Affairs and the Crow Indian Tribe, National Audubon Society, Denver Museum of Natural History, Government of Brazil, Smithsonian Institution, Montana Fish and Game Department, Minnesota Division of Game and Fish, Everglades National Park, Arizona Game and Fish Department. Running time: 89 minutes.

After a brief introduction showing Walt Disney from various episodes of the anthology show and various animated clips featuring Mickey Mouse and Donald Duck and feature length animation like *Snow White* (1937), *Dumbo* (1941) and *Bambi* (1942), the narration continues on with the introduction of clips from the various True-Life Adventures films; the first one being *Seal Island*.

The narration explains how *Beaver Valley* (1950), *The Living Desert* (1953), *Bear Country* (1953), *The Vanishing Prairie* (1954), *White Wilderness* (1958), and many more of the Academy Award-winning films came to be.

Clips are shown from virtually all of the True-Life Adventures produced, with a look at *The Vanishing Prairie* buffalos first.

Next, we cut to footage of the bighorn rams crashing their heads to the "Anvil Chorus."

Then the music of the strutting sage grouse is shown, along with the mystery migration of the wild geese and other birds.

The Living Desert tells the story of many strange species that live in the desert, including a tarantula wasp being attacked by a number of ants and various desert flora such as cactus. Finally, the wasp encounters the tarantula and together they fight.

Next is the classic square dance of the scorpions that Walt found so amusing, but it is one of the scenes that most naturists found too contrived.

We follow the adventures of a petite ground squirrel and his activities, and then a Gila monster comes along to ruin their fun.

In the desert, an antelope is being chased by a bobcat. The antelope gets away, so the bobcat turns his attentions to a wild peccary which winds up chasing the bobcat up a cactus.

A red-tailed hawk pounces on top of a rattlesnake and together they wrestle to see who will be victorious.

The classic slow-motion flowers follow, and then the narration leaves the desert and travels to the African plain and *The African Lion* (1955).

The lions are mostly shown napping until food wanders by, which in this case is a herd of impala antelope.

Next the elephants are featured, showing them eating leaves off high trees with their trunks and drinking and wading through water. After a bit, the camera turns its attentions to the hippopotamus and the biggest mouth in all of the animal kingdom.

The movie turns its attentions to *Jungle Cat* (1959), with a black panther and a jaguar trying to get a crocodile, eventually succeeding in drowning it.

From the crocodile scene we transition to a talk about the alligator. Night falls and a discussion begins about various nocturnal creatures such as frogs, toads, and crickets, with many bullfrogs being featured.

Back to daytime, there is a focus on the back-scratching bears of *Bear Country*.

Winter comes in with an avalanche of snow, as in *Winter Wilderness*. Otters are shown romping and playing and sliding in the snow. There are also polar bears shown romping and playing in the snow.

A discussion of the wolf says that they are not the villains as often portrayed in stories, and we go on to follow the weasel.

The film continues with the notorious expose on the lemmings that take their suicidal leaps off the cliff.

A few more birds are shown flying in various formations, and then the film is wrapped up.

The lemming scene has since been revealed to have been faked, with the lemmings literally being thrown by the filmmakers over the side of the steep cliff and into the water down below.

Strangely, this film is only currently available as a streaming video through Amazon. All of the individual True-Life Adventures were compiled into four DVD sets, thus rendering this compilation film practically unnecessary.

I honestly don't remember this film coming out, yet it was promoted in *Disney News*. I think that these nature films were considered very passé by the time this compilation reached the theaters and this was many years before the resurgence of things like *March of the Penguins* (2005), but since it was all recycled footage, it couldn't have cost too much for Disney to produce.

Dr. Syn, Alias the Scarecrow

RELEASED BY BUENA VISTA ON November 21, 1975 (December 6, 1963 in UK), Technicolor. Producer: Walt Disney. Co-Producer: Bill Anderson. Director: James Neilson. Screenplay: Robert Weston based on *Christopher Syn* by Russell Thorndike and William Buchanan filmed at Pinewood Studios, London, England. Director of Photography: Paul Beeson, B.S.C. Additional Photography: Ray Sturgess. Art Director: Michael Stringer. Costume Design: Anthony Mendleson. Associate Producer: Hugh Attwooll. Editor: Peter Boita. Production Manager: Peter Manley. Assistant Director: John Peverall. Camera Operator: David Harcourt. Set Dresser: Peter James. Make-up: Harry Frampton. Hairdressing: Henry Montsash. Continuity: Pamela Mann. Casting: Maude Spector. Sound Editor: Les Wiggins. Sound Recordists: C.F. Le Mesurier. Music Composed and Conducted by Gerard Schurmann. Running time: 98 minutes.

Song: "The Scarecrow Song" by Terry Gilkyson.

Cast: Patrick McGoohan (Doctor Christopher Syn / The Scarecrow of Romney Marsh), George Cole (Mr. Sexton Mipps / Hellspite), Tony Britton (Simon Bates), Michael Hordern (Squire Thomas Banks), Geoffrey Keen (General Pugh), Kay Walsh (Mrs. Waggett), Eric Pohlmann (King George III), Patrick Wymark (Joseph Ransley), Alan Dobie (Mr. Frank Fragg, Prosecutor), Sean Scully (John Banks / The Curlew), Eric Flynn (Lieutenant Philip Brackenbury), David Buck (Harry Banks), Percy Herbert (Dover Castle Jailer), Robert Brown (Sam Farley), Jill Curzon (Katharine "Kate" Banks), Mark Dignam (The Bishop), Gordon Gostelow (Ben), Bruce Seton (Beadle), Allan McClelland (Second Jailer), Richard O'Sullivan (George Ransley), Simon Lack (Dragoon Corporal), Elsie Wagstaff (Mrs. Ransley).

A man disguised as a scarecrow rides his horse and creates fear across the land in his perverse quest to preserve order. He pays off a smuggler who has just arrived on shore. He is spotted by lawmen and a chase ensues along the beaches.

The Scarecrow and his men escape inside a small cottage and elude the lawmen. They search the cottage but don't find anything. Once everything is clear, The Scarecrow and his men remove their costumes and abandon the cottage. They are wanted men, with a huge reward for their capture.

Other men who have protected The Scarecrow discuss their loyalties and realize it is still best to protect The Scarecrow, as he helps them with their taxes.

There are spies everywhere, even amongst the British aristocracy. One spy is discovered and he leaps out of a moving carriage, and another chase ensues. This man escapes into the swamps and then to the tavern of the old lady that takes these men into hiding.

The old lady refers the man to Dr. Syn, the man who is The Scarecrow while in disguise. He can give the man proper sanctuary.

Dr. Syn is asked why he does what he does, when he sees no monetary advantage for himself. Dr. Syn says that he does it for the common good, in a Robin Hood sort of way.

The man makes it to Dr. Syn and says that his name is Simon Biggs. He tells Syn that he needs to give to The Scarecrow. Syn says that he will not be able to find him easily, but he takes the message anyway.

Dr. Syn goes on an aristocratic visit and complains about The Scarecrow running rampant as a dodge, since he is really referring to himself. The aristocracy swears that the military men will get The Scarecrow.

The hunt is on, with men searching every trail and highway. The following Sunday, Dr. Syn leads a church service as a vicar and a man dressed as an owl bursts in and throws a dagger at the pulpit, but misses, hitting a nearby wall. Dr. Syn pulls it out. It contains a message from The Scarecrow, ordering the men to leave town or they will all be captured.

The man looking for The Scarecrow says that he will not leave until he gets his man or information leading him. He offers this to all the women. Sir Thomas is appalled but Dr. Syn says to the man go, but he does want the man followed.

The man barges his way around town with his men demanding drinks from Mrs. Wade, the owner of a local pub. Meanwhile, a young man named Joe Hadley runs in to warn Mrs. Wade and the men beat Joe and tie him up, taking him hostage until he talks.

The news travels back to Dr. Syn, but he decides to take it slow and not react quickly.

The men are still trying to capture The Scarecrow and at night, The Scarecrow does come out with his group. He captures the men and orders them to be captured and blindfolded.

The Scarecrow demands a hostage exchange. At first this idea is dismissed, but then they decide to go ahead with the exchange.

They head out to the beach to make the exchange, but in an act of sabotage, the men surround The Scarecrow and his men and try to capture them outright. After a short battle, The Scarecrow and his men escape.

The military men go to get their hostages, but The Scarecrow has tricked them by offering up nothing of value. The Scarecrow rides off, laughing his evil laugh.

Dr. Syn pays a visit to Mrs. Ransley to talk about her husband George. George shows up and they discuss The Scarecrow and his liquor smuggling. Their discussion is brief, as George doesn't want to talk. After he leaves, Dr. Syn eavesdrops through the door and hears of George's next plan to sell brandy before The Scarecrow finds out.

The Scarecrow and his men prepare for the next smuggling attempt, as does the military. George plans his sabotage, but The Scarecrow and his men are ready and the military is tipped off and they capture George.

After the capture, a court case begins, with George being accused as an arch smuggler. Dr. Syn suggests that the kegs be examined before any judgment is made. It turns out that the kegs are filled with seawater and Dr. Syn recommends that the case be dismissed.

Later, a celebration occurs at the pub as George has been set free, but the celebration is short-lived as there is still more work to be done.

George is still under suspicion and a visit is made by the prosecutor, who says that George did not know that the kegs were filled with water and that he was set up by The Scarecrow. The prosecutor makes a deal that if he turns in the names of The Scarecrow and others he will still be free, but George does not talk. The prosecutor bribes George to get him to talk and vows to make him safe from General Pugh and the rest who are out to capture The Scarecrow. George is finally swayed and agrees to help.

The prosecutor is now prosecuted as The Scarecrow and his men attack him in order to save George. The Scarecrow captures both George and the prosecutor and conducts his own trial.

George is accused of treason against The Scarecrow and his men. Prosecutor Fragg is also accused of bribery.

George says that he's been acquitted and The Scarecrow reminds him of the treason he mentioned in court, saying that he would do anything to get rid of The Scarecrow.

The Scarecrow's court finds George guilty and orders him to be hanged. Fragg runs away in fear and the men are ordered to get more gold.

After they leave, George is lowered to the ground. He is still alive, but is ordered to run for his life as he's now considered dead. If he doesn't run he actually will be killed, so he runs off. A phony funeral is held for George.

The military is still after The Scarecrow and Dr. Syn is told to save a plot for him in the cemetery.

Dr. Syn brings Harry Banks' son, John, to him and tells him of George's hanging. Meanwhile, General Pugh is still trying to get the smugglers. *Kate Banks'* fiancé, Mr. Brackenbury, asks her father, Sir Thomas, for Kate's hand in marriage. Thomas turns him down. Kate is Harry's sister.

After turning him down, Thomas goes into the prison and discovers his son Harry, thin and scarred, but not beaten. Thomas then leaves with John and is seen by Brackenbury. Thomas is now worried that he is under suspicion.

Meanwhile, Dr. Syn and Harry Banks make their next plans. Harry is introduced to Simon Bates as another member of the underground group, but Harry and Simon are soon captured after the plans are made. Everyone recognizes Harry as Sir Thomas' son as they are taken to Dover castle.

Dr. Syn and John go to the dungeons to talk to Harry and Simon, but are first stopped by Brackenbury and Pugh. After getting clearance, Dr. Syn feels that he has his new scapegoat.

While in the cell, Syn observes six prisoners being taken away for other duties. He vows to set everyone free, and resorts to biblical verse when observed.

Syn and John leave and John asks Syn if he can really free everyone. Syn says he doesn't know. However, he does have a key and makes a copy of it using a wax mold.

Syn becomes The Scarecrow again and tells of his new plan to blackmail Syn and to rescue all of the prisoners and capture General Pugh and his men.

After a short battle, Syn uses his pass key to get into the prison cell with Brackenbury and his men. The prisoners are rounded up and escorted out to make it look like a prison transfer. General Pugh stops Brackenbury to question what is going on and it looks as if Syn and John are going to be captured, but they are let go.

Meanwhile, some of Scarecrow's men capture Kate and Sir Thomas. Syn and John are brought to safety and then let Harry Banks and Simon Bates and the others go free.

Syn reappears as The Scarecrow and gives Harry and Simon and the others over to Thomas and Kate. They are all sent to Holland and then America to escape.

Brackenbury is grilled by Pugh about what had happened and Brackenbury claims ignorance about how the transfer was handled. He also says that reports were sent to the king and Brackenbury is summarily dismissed.

Dr. Syn sits with John and Sir Thomas and explains what went on. Brackenbury resigns his commission in order to wed Kate with Thomas' approval.

The Scarecrow's identity remains a mystery.

Many films that were produced for Disney television were later released as feature films to theaters, usually in countries outside the U.S.

Examples within the U.S. include the Davy Crockett movies based on the anthology show mini-series and *The Sign of Zorro* (1960), a compilation of various episodes from the *Zorro* TV series.

Usually, these theatrical versions hit the theaters within a year or two of their original TV airing. With *Dr. Syn*, it was based on the 1964 made-for-TV anthology series called *The Scarecrow of Romney Marsh*, which also ran in theaters overseas in 1963 as *Dr. Syn*.

Both versions did make it temporarily onto DVD with the Walt Disney Treasures DVD series, and it is a highly sought-after collectible. In fact, Leonard Maltin makes reference to this fact. Why Disney doesn't keep this in regular release is puzzling since the demand is obviously there and the film commonly trades upwards of and well over $100.

On the DVD there is a documentary with comments by Disney historian Brian Sibley, who claims this to be "powerful stuff," writer Rick Lai who discusses the "Dr. Syn" books, and author Russell Thorndike (or Thorndyke), with additional comments by comic book artist Bret Blevins, Disney archivist Dave Smith, and Disney historian Paula Sigman, who compares the character to Robin Hood. Syn is also compared to Jekyll and Hyde.

The original story ends with Dr. Syn's death, so subsequent books dealt with Dr. Syn's life as a series of prequels. The commentators discuss the other differences between the book and the film; mainly that Syn comes across as more moral in the Disney film than he does in the books.

The documentary also discusses other film versions, including the 1937 film starring George Arliss and the Hammer film released in 1962. They released their own version of the Dr. Syn story called *Night Creatures*, with Peter Cushing in the title role. This film is also known as *Captain Clegg*, which they claimed was a remake of the 1937 film. They renamed Dr. Syn as Dr. Bliss. It's unlike Disney's version, which was based on the *Christopher Syn* book.

Disney star Patrick McGoohan gives one of his last interviews commenting on this film, as he passed away on January 13, 2009. He didn't know that the film was to be shown theatrically in some parts of the world and on television in America.

Comments were also made about on location shooting in Romney Marsh, the fine British actors used, and the director and the music used.

George Patterson was the singer of the Scarecrow's theme song and he comments on it. The writer of the song, Terry Gilkyson, is also credited with "The Bear Necessities" from *The Jungle Book* (1967).

There is another documentary on the DVD with many of the same commentators discussing Walt Disney's consistent use of Britain as a place to film and get story ideas.

For this book I reviewed the longer VHS version of this film, which essentially was the 1975 theatrical version with extra footage from the TV version to help round out the story. Theatrical versions ran 98 minutes, while this version is 139.

Equally puzzling is why this was released to theaters in 1975, but the comedy *Carry On Dick* (which follows the same basic plot) was released in the UK in 1974.

Disney wasn't particularly hurting for product this year and also had tremendous success with the new films that they did release, yet they felt obliged at this time to release this to theaters as well as to release *The Best of Walt Disney's True-Life Adventures* compilation film this year.

Dr. Syn was issued with either a re-release of *Snow White* (1937) or *Treasure Island* (1950).

Disney would not see another successful film year like this for at least another decade.

Interestingly, *The Scarecrow of Romney Marsh* originally aired on NBC on February 9, 1964, opposite of *The Ed Sullivan Show* episode on CBS that featured the US TV debut of The Beatles, though *Scarecrow* started a half-hour earlier. It aired again on the anthology show in 1970 and 1978.

Ride a Wild Pony

RELEASED BY BUENA VISTA ON December 25, 1975 (November 2, 1975 in Australia), Technicolor. Producer: Jerome Courtland. Executive Producer: Ron Miller. Director: Don Chaffey. Screenplay: Rosemary Anne Sisson from the novel *The Sporting Proposition* by James Aldridge filmed on location in Australia. Director of Photography: Jack Cardiff. Art Director: Robert Hilditch. Costumes: Judith Dorsman. Supervising Editor: Peter Boita. Editor: Mike Campbell. Unit Manager: Sue Milliken. Assistant Director: Mark Egerton. Continuity: Gilda Baracchi. Make-up: Monica Dawkins. Hairdressing: Ricquette Hofstein. Production Accountant: Fred Harding. Sound Editor: Peter Best. Sound Recordists: John Heath, Ken Barker. Music composed by John Addison conducted by Marcus Dods recorded at Anvil Studios. Sound Re-Recording Mixer: Graham V. Hartstone. Running time: 91 minutes.

Songs: "Alexander's Ragtime Band," "In the Good Old Summertime."

Cast: Michael Craig (James Ellison), John Meillon (Charles E. Quayle), Robert Bettles (Scotty Pirie), Eva Griffith (Josie Ellison), Graham Rouse (Bluey Waters), Alfred Bell (Angus Pirie), John Meillon, Jr. (Kit Quayle), Roy Haddrick (J.C. Strapp), Peter Gwynne (Sergeant Collins), Melissa Jaffer (Mrs. Pirie), Lorraine Bayly (Mrs. Ellison), Wendy Playfair, Elizabeth Alexander, Kate Clarkson (Jeannie Quayle), Phillip Ross, Jessica Noad, Neva Carr-Glyn, Martin Vaughan, Gerry Duggan, Harry Lawrence, Les Foxcroft, John Fegan, Kevin Manser.

A poor boy named Scotty Pirie decides to ride one of a rancher's wild ponies, causing him to chase after them. He rides to a river and is thrown off and escapes. The rancher yells at the boy for his mischief.

Sergeant Collins arrives at Mrs. Pirie's house with a summons saying that Scotty has been skipping school and should stay away from the horses.

The next day, Angus Pirie goes to Charles Quayle, a lawyer, to discuss Scotty's absences. Mr. Pirie says that Scotty would have to walk seven miles each way if he was to go to school.

Charles goes to Mr. Strap to argue for Mr. Pirie and to tell him that Sergeant Collins must dismiss the summons until a solution is discovered. The solution is to give Scotty a Welsh pony so that he can ride the seven miles to school.

Mr. Pirie pays the small fee for the pony and Scotty takes to the horse.

Soon Scotty gets a bit reckless with his pony, riding him in front of speeding trains.

Eventually Scotty rides the pony to school, impressing the other school children. He is asked the pony's name, and names it Taff.

While in class, the wild pony kicks himself out of the stable as he is not trained to be caged up. Scotty jumps aboard Taff in order to control him and rides home.

Josie Ellison, a handicapped girl sitting in a wheelchair, is visiting her horses. She is sad because she cannot ride due to her polio.

Meanwhile, Scotty is once again daring the trains on his pony. This time he doesn't make it in front of the train and instead rides Taff into the river.

Scotty also helps out his lawyer with his gardening while riding Taff. The next day, Taff is missing and Scotty says that he will look for Taff rather than go to school.

Josie says that she wants to ride again and says that she can without stirrups. Her family says no.

Scotty gives up looking for Taff and shows up at school, upset. The other children are concerned, but offer no advice. Later, he stops by an auction house to discover that Taff may have been put up for sale.

Josie, meanwhile, has disobeyed her parents and tries to ride a pony but fails due to her paralysis. She argues again with her parents about the situation.

Scotty is still getting in trouble for not attending school and Quayle informs his son, Kit, to also stay in school rather than help Scotty.

Josie is cheered up by being shown some new ponies that she can train from her wheelchair. She is especially fond of a pony she names Beau.

Scotty is still tracking down Taff and comes across a man sitting by a campfire and asks if he's seen a pony. The man says yes and shows him his bicycle. Scotty is disappointed.

Josie keeps training Beau to make him a better pony. Beau is now trained to wear a bridle and to haul a small wagon, but there is still much more work to be done as Beau is still quite wild.

Eventually Josie's persistence pays off, as Beau is now quite tame. She now takes the reins and rides in the wagon pulled by Beau.

Scotty finally arrives home only to be greeted by a whipping from his father for running away so long. The next day he arrives back at school and gets reprimanded by his teacher for his absences. He starts getting into more mischief again because he still misses Taff.

Soon, there is a small carnival in town and both Scotty and Josie attend. Scotty sees Beau from the merry-go-round. Realizing Beau as Taff, he tries to take the pony away. Scotty is arrested and taken from the fairgrounds and dropped off at home.

Kit asks his dad who the pony really belongs to and he says that "Possession is 9/10ths of the law." So Scotty goes and steals the pony from Josie.

Josie's father pays a visit to the Pirie household to discuss the matter with Scotty's parents and to get the pony back, but there is no pony there, nor is Scotty anywhere to be found. Josie is now despondent about her missing pony.

Scotty shows up at school the next day on foot and everyone asks where his pony is and Scotty doesn't want to discuss it. George advises Scotty to stop hiding the pony and to bring him back.

Scotty decides to obey the law and let the courts decide who the pony really belongs to. It is determined that Mr. Crisp, the original owner of the pony, would know who he belongs to. Most people want Josie to get the pony because she's rich and Scotty is a poor bush boy.

Scotty is still determined to get the pony back and he even sleeps outside the stable at the police pound. Josie is also allowed to see the pony as long as she doesn't take it away. Scotty is allowed to feed the pony while a decision is being made.

Bluey Waters is a local townsman, who gets into a minor scuffle in a nearby pub discussing the rightful owner of the pony. Mr. Ellison stops by and says the pony should be fed oats, and both Scotty and Josie disagree.

The trial gets underway with everyone attending the case of Ellison vs. Pirie. Bluey and Josie take the stand and explain why they know that the pony is theirs including using subterfuge about the horse biting in order to win the case.

Scotty feels that he is going to lose the case because of this. He takes the stand next, but all he can say is that the pony is his because he says so.

George says that the burden of proof can only be made if Josie and Scotty go see the pony and let the pony make the decision.

As soon as this proposition is made, bets are being made at the school and at the pub as to whose horse it is.

Fights break out among those who are betting against Scotty, and Josie threatens to never set foot in town again if she doesn't win.

The next day the challenge is on. Scotty brings a bridle, as Taff always responded to the bridle. The judges say that that is not fair and don't allow him to use it.

The pony is released and both Josie and Scotty try to call the pony to them using their respective names of Beau and Taff.

There is a struggle and the horse almost comes to Josie, but ends up coming to Scotty. The judge awards the pony to Scotty, but afterwards the pony goes to Josie for a brief moment. Scotty then takes the bridle and goes for a ride on Taff.

The next day, Kit and Scotty discuss the outcome, but Scotty is tempted to ride off when a truck comes by again with Josie and Mr. Ellison aboard. Kit advises Scotty not to leave. Josie shows up and apologizes for accidentally taking his pony. Scotty forgives her.

The pony is fond of both of them and it is decided that Josie can still see the pony from time to time, either by Scotty visiting her or Josie visiting him. They become best of friends.

A charming film that views much better than it seems on paper, probably due to the fact that it was filmed on location in Australia and doesn't look like a typical Disney film of this vintage. The story is very simple, but effective.

Incidentally, the working title for this film was *The Sporting Proposition* and was filmed in October and November 1974.

Disney had hoped that this film would earn an Academy Award or at least be nominated for something, but it was completely ignored. It aired on the anthology show in 1979.

1976

As 1976 came in, it was not initially evident that this was the year that Disney was really starting to lose ground. The films produced this year were unremarkable, the biggest being the sequel to 1959's *The Shaggy Dog*, featuring the return of Dean Jones to the Disney fold.

America on Parade continued through the country's bicentennial at Disneyland and Walt Disney World, and a book was issued saluting the event. Walt Disney World also welcomed its 50 millionth visitor with Susan Brummer. River Country opened there this year and Winnie the Pooh ran for President again.

Disneyland opened The Disneyana Shop on Main Street, which was Disney's first attempt to publicly sell collectible Disney merchandise.

On the TV front, the anthology series continued for yet another year with these new shows: *Twister, Bull from the Sky* (working title: *A Bull from the Sky*), *The Whiz Kid and the Carnival Caper*, *The Survival of Sam the Pelican*, *The Flight of the Grey Wolf*, *The Secret of Old Glory Mine*, and *Disney's Greatest Dog Stars*. There were also two other new specials which were not part of the anthology series: *Monsanto Night Presents Walt Disney's America on Parade* and *Christmas in Disneyland*.

The popularity of the resurrected *Mickey Mouse Club* returned for a second but not nearly as popular season. It would soon be replaced by *The New Mickey Mouse Club*, scheduled to debut in January 1977.

It was during this era that most of Disney's problems started to occur, with the rejection of one film destined to frustrate Disney and its fortunes for years to come: *Star Wars* (1977). There were also management changes as Donn Tatum became Chairman of the Board and Card Walker succeeded him as CEO.

Dumbo (1941) and *Peter Pan* (1953) were reissued to theaters.

Another successful film made this year that could have been made by Disney, but they would have cast it differently and deleted the swear words was *The Bad News Bears*. The film was so popular that two sequels

(*...in Breaking Training* (1977); *...Go to Japan* (1978)) and a remake were made.

Also, longtime producer and writer Bill Walsh died in 1975 and his untimely demise also had a detrimental effect on the future of Disney films, his last being *One of Our Dinosaurs is Missing* (1975). Although he would go on to live until 1986, Robert Stevenson, one of Disney's most prolific directors, retired after directing *The Shaggy D.A.*

Many more Disney crew regulars were to begin retiring during the next few years in both the animation and live-action areas, leaving Disney with a complete line of novices not affiliated in any way with Walt's initial vision.

Non-soundtrack record releases this year included *Winnie the Pooh for President*. Sebastian Cabot was replaced as narrator as he was possibly in ill health at this time, since he passed away in 1977, but Sterling Holloway and John Fiedler were on board as Pooh and Piglet, respectively.

The record also features the singing debut of Larry Groce at Disney. He scored a major hit in 1975 with his *Junk Food Junkie* novelty hit and made a home at Disney for many years performing multiple children's songs.

Dickens' Christmas Carol, the *Snow White and the Seven Dwarfs* complete soundtrack and *Winnie the Pooh for President* were all nominated for Best Recording for Children Grammys. None won.

In the comic book world, Gold Key continued to publish *Donald Duck, Mickey Mouse, Uncle Scrooge, Walt Disney's Comics and Stories, The Beagle Boys, Huey, Dewey and Louie Junior Woodchucks, Super Goof, Chip 'n' Dale, Scamp, Walt Disney Showcase,* and *Daisy and Donald. Moby Duck* resumed publication, while *Walt Disney Comics Digest* ended its run.

There was also *Mickey Mouse Mini-Comic* and the *Uncle Scrooge Mini-Comic* one-shots and another major biography on Disney called *Walt Disney, An American Original* by Bob Thomas was issued.

No Deposit, No Return

RELEASED BY BUENA VISTA ON February 5, 1976, Technicolor. Producer: Ron Miller. Co-Producer: Joe McEveety. Director: Norman Tokar. Screenplay: Arthur Alsberg, Don Nelson. Story: Joe McEveety. Art Directors: John B. Mansbridge, Jack Senter. Set Decorator: Frank R. McKelvy. Matte Artist: Peter S. Ellenshaw. Special Effects: Eustace Lycett, Art Cruickshank, A.S.C., Danny Lee. Titles: Art Stevens, Terry Walsh. Second Unit Director: Arthur J. Vitarelli. Film Editor: Cotton Warburton, A.C.E. Assistant to the Producer: Jan Williams. Sound Supervision: Herb Taylor. Sound Mixer: Frank Regula. Unit Production Manager: Christopher Seiter. Second Assistant Director: William

St. John. Costumes: Chuck Keehne, Emily Sundby. Make-up: Robert J. Schiffer, La Rue Matheron. Music Editor: Evelyn Kennedy. Music: Buddy Baker. Orchestration: Walter Sheets. Director of Photography: Frank Phillips, A.S.C. Set Dresser: Kurt V. Hulett. Sound Editor: George Fredrick. Special Effects: Hans Metz. Stunt Double: Jerry Brutsche. Stunts: Dale Van Sickel. Gaffer: Carl Boles. Electrician: Dan Delgado. Assistant Camera: Robert D. McBride. Assistant Editor: Barney Cabral. Running time: 111 minutes.

Cast: David Niven (J.W. Osborne), Darren McGavin (Duke), Don Knotts (Bert), Herschel Bernardi (Sergeant Turner), Barbara Feldon (Carolyn), Kim Richards (Tracy), Brad Savage (Jay), John Williams (Jameson), Charlie Martin Smith (Longnecker), Vic Tayback (Big Joe), Bob Hastings (Peter), Louis Guss (Freddie), Richard O'Brien (Captain Boland), Barney Phillips (Sergeant Benson), Ruth Manning (Miss Murdock), Olive Dunbar (Mrs. Hadley), James Hong (Ming Lo), Jean Gillespie (Reporter), Jack Wells (Reporter), Stu Gilliam (Policeman), Jack Griffin (Policeman), Milt Kogan (Policeman), Hank Jones (Banana Cop), Iris Adrian (Housewife), Henry Slate (Truck Driver), Larry Moran (Michael).

Cool animation featuring a skunk starts off the titles, and then it's off to the Marion Hadley School where Tracy is off on Easter vacation. Her brother Jay is hanging off of a flagpole looking for Duster, his pet skunk.

Soon, Miss Murdock shows up pick up Jay and Tracy. She is hesitant about having the skunk in the car, but relents.

Tracy gives Mrs. Hadley a present before leaving – a frog.

Miss Murdock reveals to Jay and Tracy that their mother is in Hong Kong, and that she will be going on to Bermuda. However, the kids are to be sent to grandfather's in L.A. for the week. The kids are not thrilled about this and neither is their grandfather, J.W. Osborne.

Meanwhile, Duke and Bert are two clumsy crooks driving around trying to find their next crime. They break into a building to rob a safe.

Osborne arrives at the airport to pick up the grandchildren and sends his butler Jameson in. Jameson he asks which flight is number 801 but shouldn't have bothered, as soon everyone on the flight with the children flees when they discover that a skunk was on board with them.

Meanwhile, Duke and Bert try to make their robbery in the treasurer's office but leave when spotted by a cleaning woman and dash into and then back out of the airport.

The children run out of the airport and get into the same cab as Duke and Bert. Tracy and Jay tell them that they are running away.

Sergeant Turner and his assistant Longnecker are on the case to try to find Duke and Bert, despite the fact that they didn't steal anything.

The cab stops and all four get out. Tracy and Jay want to stay with Duke and Bert, but they don't want them to, so Tracy feigns an asthma attack to play on their sympathies and Duke and Bert take them back.

All the while they have been followed by Osborne, Jameson, and their chauffer, and Osborne concludes that it would be good for the children to stay with these crooks for a time to learn a lesson.

Duke and Bert open their home to discover Big Joe sitting in their living room, waiting for them. He's waiting for his dough and Duke shows that he doesn't have any money. Duke asks Big Joe for some more time to pay off his debt of $9000. Big Joe gives them 72 hours, then leaves.

Tracy overhears what went on and devises a plan that will get them the money. She creates a ransom note and sends it to her grandfather, claiming that Duke and Bert kidnapped them.

Duke is shocked because of the penalties for kidnapping, but Tracy convinces him that this would be better than upsetting Big Joe.

The next day, Osborne gets his mail and reads the ransom note, but realizes what Tracy is doing and doesn't do anything. Duke and Bert sit and wait.

Duke asks Bert where the kids are and Bert says that they are both fine, but Jay is actually climbing outside the window ledge trying once again to retrieve Duster. Bert goes after them.

The chase leads them to the roof and aboard a huge crane being used in the construction of a nearby building and then across the girders of that same building. Jay finally gets Duster back and Bert almost falls to his death getting down.

Osborne finally responds to the ransom note saying that it may take over a week to get the money together. This, of course, would make it after Easter vacation and Tracy and Jay will be sent home.

Tracy and Jay fake a call to the police saying that Duke and Bert are torturing them. Afterwards, Tracy says it's time to do a second ransom note.

Duke says no until Big Joe comes by to remind them that they only have 48 hours left to come up with the new amount of $11,000.

Turner and Longnecker are taken off the safe break-in case and transferred to the kidnapping case. They show up to question Osborne about the kids and request that Osborne do absolutely nothing, which is what Osborne was planning to do.

Duke and Bert watch TV and see Turner discussing their kidnapping case. They have the latest ransom note ready and send it out.

Jay is bored and practices judo on Bert while Duke is out mailing the letter. Duke comes back and finds out that Jay was sent for some liniment.

A police officer picks up Duke and Bert and they think it is for the kidnapping, but it is for having the skunk without a license. Duke pays the fine, but while they are filling out the forms, Turner comes in trying to figure out the kidnapping case. Duke and Bert hide their faces.

The four of them make it back to their apartment and Duke sends out another ransom for yet another lower amount. Originally it was a ransom for $100,000, but now it has been lowered to $30,000.

Even though Duke and Bert really want to get rid of the kids at this point, Tracy turns out to be a pretty good cook around the house.

Turner and Longnecker get the latest ransom note and Osborne continues to do nothing, but Longnecker proposes the idea that the safecracker may be their kidnapper. Turner says that this is preposterous.

Tracy makes some plane reservations to Honolulu for her and Jay under phony names in order to not expose their true identities since they were under ransom.

Big Joe pays another visit and now the debt is up to $13,000.

The children's mother, Carolyn, finally gets the news about the kidnapping and pays an angry visit to Osborne, wondering why he hasn't done anything. Osborne says that he was only doing what the police told him to do.

Big Joe also reads about the kidnapping which has made the papers and decides to take matters into his own hands as he feels that he can get more than $100,000 out of the wealthy Osbornes.

Meanwhile, Turner plans to disguise himself as Osborne with a rubber mask. Duke and Bert also disguise themselves as a clown and the big bad wolf. Together, they meet up at the prescribed time and place to make the ransom exchange.

While the exchange is taking place, the real Osborne drives up with Carolyn. Duke and Bert flee the scene when they discover that it's a trap. A high speed police chase ensues after Carolyn manages to climb aboard Duke and Bert's car.

Carolyn says she'll pay the money and give the kidnappers what they want. Duke says that they are "sort of" the kidnappers and they argue about how the children should be treated with Carolyn globetrotting all over the world.

During the chase, Turner and Longnecker tear off the top of their police car. With the open top and the fact that the chase is near the boat docks, a huge amount of fish are eventually dumped into their car.

At the end of the chase, Turner and Longnecker are teetering off the end of the pier and try to sit still so that they don't end up in the water, but when part of their tail pipe breaks off, in they go.

Big Joe, meanwhile, instructs the children to write a new ransom note for half a million dollars. Big Joe wants to take the kids elsewhere, but Jay says that they can't go because they are waiting for Duke and Bert and flips Big Joe judo-style. Jay also kicks him in the shin (like in *The Apple Dumpling Gang* (1975)) for good measure and then strings them up with some rope traps that he has set.

After Joe and his henchman are taken care of, Tracy and Jay spy grandfather coming up with his chauffeur. When the adults arrive, the kids are gone and the two are strung up like Big Joe with more rope traps.

Jay looks for Duster again, finding him inside Ming Lo's Chinese Market, and then the kids hitch a ride with a cement truck.

Turner and Longnecker's car is hauled out of the water. They finally arrive at Duke and Bert's hideout and Longnecker, too, is strung upside down with a rope trap.

The kids arrive in grandfather's house and break into his safe in order to get enough money to buy the tickets to fly to Hong Kong to meet their mother. They don't know that mother is in L.A. with them and they soon get locked in the safe.

Duke, Bert, and Carolyn arrive at Osborne's place with Sergeant Turner close behind. Turner recognizes Duke and Bert, but doesn't know where from.

Soon, grandfather's bulldog runs downstairs smelling of skunk and everyone runs upstairs to discover that the children are inside. Duke uses his safecracking skills in order to open the safe as Osborne is the only one who knows the combination.

Turner is amazed that Duke knows so much about safes and he claims that he used to work for a safe company. Turner puts two and two together and figures out that Duke is the safecracker and also the would-be kidnapper.

Duke is successful at opening the safe after a few tense moments with the children locked inside the airtight safe, since he cannot hear the tumblers very well and his stethoscope failed him.

The children burst free and are happy to see their mother. Turner knows that Duke and the safecracker he's been searching for are one in the same, but he lets him go on the condition that he retires from his safecracking.

The other crooks and Osborne are freed. The children and grandfather are now getting along better and it is agreed that he should help Duke and Bert out in some way by letting them stay with Osborne as surrogate parents, and Carolyn decides to stick around more, too.

This was the first of two Disney films to star David Niven. His appearance in this and *Candleshoe* made me a lifelong fan of Niven's dignified coolness. It is sad that he was dead less than a decade later, as he seems so robust in these films.

Niven always wanted to star in a Disney film when Walt was still around, but either other film commitments or the wrong script kept him away until now.

Staff composer Buddy Baker must have had *The Pink Panther* (1964) in mind when composing, as the music has a definitive Henry Mancini feel to it. This was probably due to Niven's appearance and the fact that newer Pink Panther films were being made around this time.

Great line: "I can't see, I can't breathe and there's no room for my nose!" –Herschel Bernardi, as Sergeant Turner trying to disguise himself as Osborne.

Charles Martin Smith also begins a lengthy run at Disney, beginning with this film.

The working title for this film was *Double Trouble*. It aired on the anthology show in 1982.

Treasure Of Matecumbe

RELEASED BY BUENA VISTA ON July 1, 1976, Technicolor. Executive Producer: Ron Miller. Producer: Bill Anderson. Director: Vincent McEveety. Screenplay: Don Tait based on the book, *A Journey to Matecumbe* by Robert Lewis Taylor. Production Designer: Robert Clatworthy. Art Director: John B. Mansbridge. Assistant to the Producer: Kevin Corcoran. Set Decorator: Frank R. McKelvy. Costumes: Shelby Anderson. Choreographer: Burch Mann. Special Effects: Eustace Lycett, Art Cruickshank, A.S.C., Danny Lee. Sound Supervisor: Herb Taylor. Sound Mixer: Frank C. Regula. Unit Production Manager / Assistant Director: Paul "Tiny" Nichols. Second Assistant Director: Bud Grace. Costumes: Chuck Keehne, Emily Sundby. Make-up: Robert J. Schiffer. Hair Stylist: Judy Alexander. Music Editor: Evelyn Kennedy. Sound Editor: Raymond Craddock. Editor: Cotton Warburton, A.C.E. Music: Buddy Baker. Orchestration: Walter Sheets. Director of Photography: Frank Phillips, A.S.C. Sound Editor: George Fredrick. Special Effects: Hans Metz. Stunts: Denny Arnold, John Ashby. Stunt

Coordinator: Buddy Joe Hooker. Gaffer: Carl Boles. Grip: Dennis Young. Running time: 107 minutes.

Song: "Matecumbe" Richard McKinley, Shane Tatum performed by Bahler, Olsson, Murray and Haas.

Cast: Robert Foxworth (Jim Burnie), Joan Hackett (Lauriette), Peter Ustinov (Dr. Ewing T. Snodgrass), Vic Morrow (Spangler), Johnny Doran (Davie Burnie), Billy Attmore (Thad), Jane Wyatt (Aunt Effie), Virginia Vincent (Aunt Lou), Robert DoQui (Ben), Don Knight (Skaggs), Mills Watson (Catrell), Dub Taylor (Sheriff Forbes), Val DeVargas (Charlie), Dick Van Patten (The Gambler), George Lindsey (Coahoma Sheriff), Logan Ramsey (Coley), Jonathan Daly (Paxton Farrow), John Myhers (Captain Boomer), Warde Donovan (Sheriff Coffey), James E. Brodhead (The Groom), John Steadman (Guide), Rex Holman (Informant), Clint Ritchie (Flatboat Leader), Ken Renard (Customer), Brion James (Roustabout), John Hayes (Mule Driver), John Flinn, Louie Elias, Richard Wright, Dave Cass (Spangler's Men).

In post-Civil War Kentucky, Davie Burnie becomes the unexpected heir to the family secret: a map leading to buried treasure on the Florida isle of Matecumbe.

Davie is friends with former slaves Ben and Thad. Ben tells Davie about the treasure. Ben says that he needs to take Jim Burnie in order to get there because he has a ship that can sail there. He also says that he needs to get there soon as others, including a man named Spangler, are now questioning him about the treasure.

When Spangler arrives unexpectedly, the family protects Ben and hides him. Ben then jumps out the window and is shot. Davie and Thad go after him to rescue him, but run off and jump on a horse before they are hurt, too.

The chase is on but the boys escape and continue on foot and then by boat. Spangler and his men are back on the trail, but they are too late to get them as the boys continue down the river.

Later on down the river, the boys encounter a huge steamboat and buy two passages aboard. With nowhere else to sleep, the boys hide out in the steamboat's livestock area. The boys discover a woman stowaway named Lauriette, who is dressed in a wedding dress and trying to escape her pending marriage.

After a quick search, Lauriette is not discovered by Spangler and his men, as the boys have hidden her quite well, and the steamboat continues down the Mississippi River to New Orleans.

Later, Lauriette comes out of hiding and decides to gamble in order to earn more money for herself. She bets $500 which she refuses to show, because she doesn't really have it. The gambler makes sure to win at Three Card Monte by hiding the card with a picture of a baby on it.

Lauriette tricks the gambler by lifting the other two cards and by simple logic if the other cards do not have the baby, then the remaining one does. The gambler refuses to show the remaining card and agrees to pay the $500 with a ring.

Later, while the boys sleep, Davie had his pocket picked and loses his money and the map. Lauriette tries to stop the thief and is thrown overboard. Davie and Thad leap in the water to rescue Lauriette and all three almost get sucked up by the waterwheel. They do not get back aboard.

Now on shore, Lauriette asks why Davie and Thad are traveling. They don't want to tell her, but did say that she will be rewarded if she helps them get to where they are going.

A man riding a mule rides by and Lauriette trades the ring she won for the mule and cart.

They take the cart into town and Lauriette drops the boys off with the Coahoma sheriff, who locks them in the jail cell. While in the cell the boys start moaning. When the sheriff and Lauriette come to check on them the boys turn the tide, locking Lauriette and the sheriff in the cell and making their escape.

Traveling by foot, they encounter a medicine show salesman named Dr. Snodgrass. They ask if Snodgrass will take them further south to their goal. Snodgrass offers to have them become his apprentices, which they agree to do.

Lauriette discovers where the boys have gone and she tells Sheriff Coffey of their whereabouts. Coffey has been interested in getting Snodgrass and agrees to go after them. Snodgrass uses Coffey as a test subject to prove that his elixirs are genuine. He does this with trickery.

Thad calls Snodgrass to help Davie, who is pretending to be injured, and he drinks one of Snodgrass' elixirs. He comes to and sees Spangler among the crowd of onlookers, and then pretends to pass back out. Lauriette is another onlooker and reveals who Davie is.

Davie springs to action and runs away from Spangler, who chases him on a horse and finally catches him. Spangler asks for the map, but Lauriette pulls a gun on Spangler and forces them to jump off the cliff into the water below.

The boys, Lauriette and Snodgrass are now traveling together on the river and then on foot where they discover a lynching by the KKK. It turns out the Klan is hanging Davie's uncle, Jim.

To stop the hanging, Snodgrass and Thad light some of Snodgrass' remedies on fire and hurl them at the Klansmen, scaring the Klansmen away.

The five continue on down the river as Davie discusses the treasure and where to find it. Snodgrass warns that even if they find the treasure, Spangler will come in and kill them for it, but they decide to press on anyway.

At one point they pull into a port but the reception is not friendly, so only Jim goes ashore. Snodgrass decides that music will soothe the savage beast and he starts playing the banjo and Thad starts dancing. The atmosphere changes completely as Jim comes back aboard with some new supplies and everyone is singing and dancing. Lauriette dances with all the men and they make a getaway as everyone is making merry, but just barely.

All is quiet as they travel downstream, but soon Spangler and his men are chasing after them on Spangler's boat. Spangler opens fire as everyone jumps on shore and runs for their lives.

Spangler also goes ashore and he and his men chase them on foot. Then Snodgrass and everyone except Jim rushes back to the boats and they leave the dock, but not before Snodgrass set a trap in Spangler's boat.

Spangler shoots at Jim as he runs towards the boat to catch up. Spangler and his men then they go to shore to shoot at everyone escaping on the boat. Then Spangler and his men board their boat which explodes as they board, allowing everyone except Jim to get away.

Now, finally in New Orleans, everyone gets some new clothes and dines out. They conclude that Jim is dead, but decide to continue looking for the treasure.

Spangler is still following them and has also arrived in New Orleans. He discovers that they are now going to travel by train down to Tampa, but that's a smokescreen to throw Spangler off their trail, and they travel by canoe down the Everglades instead.

During their canoe trip, the group encounters some Native American Seminoles and various exotic birds and animals and alligators.

The canoe man, Mr. Skaggs, says that they need to stop to get the last fresh water until they reach their destination. It turns out to be a trap and the four are led right to Spangler and his men.

Spangler asks for the map, but Davie says that he's lost it. Spangler doesn't believe him and draws a gun. At the critical moment, Snodgrass pulls out his version of the map which has been sewn into a handkerchief and Spangler takes it and leaves with his men in the canoe.

The four decide to accept their fate and are soon attacked by a swarm of insects which get into their mouths and noses. They are saved at the last moment by a sudden rainstorm and also by another canoe paddled by Jim, who is not dead after all, and a Seminole Indian named Charlie.

Jim gets everyone aboard and they try to see if they can beat Spangler to the treasure. As they continue down river, they encounter many scary tribal masks along the river bed. They also paddle into a wild storm and eventually have to stop.

The storm knocks trees over in their paths and one hits Charlie. They arrive at a flat, open spot and start digging, eventually digging up the treasure only to be whisked away by a flash flood. Snodgrass is hauled out to sea.

They can't save him because the storm is too violent, so the rest of them haul the treasure out of the way. Davie wants to rescue Snodgrass anyway and gets separated from everyone else, eventually falling into a hidden trap in the ground.

Jim and everyone else come to Davie's rescue, but in doing so they may become enslaved by the Indians. The storm subsides and they look at the treasure. As they haul it away, Spangler and his men arrive and shoot at them, demanding the gold.

Jim says that the gold is Spangler's as long as they get safe passage out. Spangler says yes, but it's a time-delaying trick to catch everyone off guard. They pick up the treasure chest and run off before Spangler can fire his guns again.

Later Spangler discovers that they have left the treasure behind. As he and his men rifle through it, they crush many of the Indian artifacts which cause the Indians to shoot arrows at them.

Spangler goes to lift the treasure chest himself and as he does so, the Indians shoot him and also surround and hold up Spangler's men, who drop their weapons and are taken away.

With Spangler and his men out of his way, Jim, Davie, Charlie, Thad, and Lauriette bring the treasure to their canoe when Snodgrass appears along the shore and they all leave on the canoe.

Billy Attmore went on to appear as "Pop" in *The New Mickey Mouse Club*.

This film wasn't particularly successful, grossing only $4 million, and was soon on the anthology show about a year later in 1977. A lot of the reason has to do with the overall superficial look of the film and the fact that this adventure is somewhat boring and a bit long, although it is not every day that you see a G-rated Disney film with cross burning, lynching, and the KKK.

Is it just me or is Robert Foxworth Robert Reed's doppelganger?

Gus

RELEASED BY BUENA VISTA ON July 7, 1976, Technicolor. Producer: Ron Miller. Director: Vincent McEveety. Screenplay: Arthur Alsberg, Don Nelson based on a story by Ted Key. Art Directors: John B. Mansbridge, Al Roelofs. Film Editor: Robert Stafford, A.C.E. Set Decorator: Frank R. McKelvy. Matte Artist: Peter S. Ellenshaw. Special Effects: Eustace Lycett, Art Cruickshank, A.S.C., Danny Lee. "Gus" Trained by Robert Davenport. Stunt Coordinator: Buddy Joe Hooker. Sound Supervisor: Herb Taylor. Sound Mixer: Frank Regula. Unit Production Manager / Assistant Director: Ronald R. Grow. Second

Assistant Directors: Pat Kehoe, Bud Grace. Technical Advisor: Les Josephson. Costumes: Chuck Keehne, Emily Sundby. Make-up: Robert J. Schiffer. Hair Stylist: La Rue Matheron. Music Editor: Evelyn Kennedy. A special acknowledgement to the National Football League for their assistance in the football sequences. Associate Producer: Christopher Hibler. Second Unit Director: Arthur J. Vitarelli. Music: Robert F. Brunner. Orchestration: Walter Sheets. Director of Photography: Frank Phillips, A.S.C. Sound Editor: George Fredrick. Special Effects: Hans Metz. Stunts: Denny Arnold, May Boss, Ken Del Conte, Allan Graf. Gaffer: Carl Boles. Running time: 97 minutes.

Cast: Edward Asner (Hank Cooper), Don Knotts (Coach Venner), Gary Grimes (Andy Petrovic), Tim Conway (Crankcase), Liberty Williams (Debbie Kovac), Dick Van Patten (Cal Wilson), Ronnie Schell (Joe Barnsdale), Bob Crane (Pepper), Johnny Unitas (Himself), Dick Butkus (Rob Cargil), Harold Gould (Charles Gwynn), Tom Bosley (Spinner), Titos Vandis (Papa Petrovic), Hanna Hertelendy (Mama Petrovic), Liam Dunn (Doctor Morgan), Virginia O'Brien (Reporter), Kenneth Tobey (Assistant Warden), Irwin Charone (Hotel Clerk), Timothy Brown (Calvin Barnes), Jackson Bostwick (Stjepan Petrovic), John Orchard (Pemberton Captain), Richard Kiel (Tall Man), Henry Slate (Fan at L.A.X.), Larry McCormick (New York Broadcaster), Larry Burrell (Locker Room Announcer), Danny Wells (Referee), James Almanzar (Coach Garcia), Milton Frome (Lukom), Iris Adrian (Fan's Wife), Bryan O'Byrne (Grocery Store Manager), Jack Manning (Mayor), James Brown (Mammoth Coach), Warde Donovan (Butcher), Jeanne Bates (Nurse), Dick Enberg (Atoms Announcer), George Putnam (TV Interviewer), Stu Nahan (Los Angeles Sportscaster), Ken Del Conte (Field Goal Kick O'Brien), Fred Dryer (Atoms Player), Peter Paul Eastman (Man in Airport), Bowman Upchurch (Binocular Man in Press box).

In Yugoslavia, Andy Petrovic is continually put down by his father, who favors the skills of his soccer-playing brother. Andy's mother is more sympathetic and encourages her son to find a comparable talent. Enter Gus, the family mule, who happens to have the ability to kick a soccer ball the length of a football field.

Meanwhile, the California Atoms, a low-ranking professional football team owned by Hank Cooper and coached by

Coach Venner, are having another disastrous season. Upon finding out about the talented mule, Cooper tries to boost his club's spirits by offering to fly Andy and his mule out to California to be the team's half-time entertainment.

Debbie Kovac is assigned to be Andy's escort in order to help him adjust to his new surroundings and help take care of Gus, much to the chagrin of Debbie's boyfriend Rob Cargil, who eventually breaks up with her. The team's losing streak continues and Charles Gwynn informs Hank that this may be his last season with the Atoms unless they start winning games.

Hank tests Gus during a game and decides to make a bet with Charles. If the Atoms win seven games during the season, he gets to keep his job and the team. Charles decides to up the ante and counters that the Atoms have to win the Super Bowl in order for Hank to keep the team.

At the next game Hank pulls out his secret weapon, Gus. After a question as to whether a mule can legally play in the NFL, Gus is allowed, as there is no such rule against it. The losing team now has added new fuel to the fire to the commentary of regular booth sportscasters Johnny Unitas and Pepper.

Meanwhile, convicts Spinner and Crankcase have been released from prison and vow to cease their criminal ways. That is, until Cal Wilson hires them to aid Charles in capturing Gus so that the Atoms cannot possibly win the Super Bowl.

Spinner and Crankcase bumble around in a supermarket trying to capture Gus, but do not succeed. Meanwhile, Andy's parents have come to California to cheer on their son, but Andy's dad is still not convinced. He feels that anyone can hold the football and that Gus really has the talent. This fact is proven in one game when Andy is unavailable and Debbie holds the ball.

All of these issues really affect Andy and he's ready to pack it in and go home. Ultimately, he is convinced to stay on and is told that he is talented after all, just in time for the Super Bowl.

In the big final game, the rain and mud impede the progress of the Atoms, especially affecting Gus. It looks like they will be sure losers, but Andy saves the day by making a lengthy and slippery run through the mud to achieve the game-winning touchdown. Andy wins the approval of his family, and gets the girl in the end.

Gus is an enjoyable film, but it is definitely in the typical "cookie-cutter" style of the mid-70s Disney comedies.

Cartoonist Ted Key (*Hazel*) came up with the gimmick concept for this field goal-kicking mule in between two other gimmicky comedies – 1971's *Million Dollar Duck* and 1978's *The Cat from Outer Space*. (By the way, Key's earlier work makes a cameo; *Million Dollar Duck* is the film playing during the scene at the drive-in theater.)

The film is competently directed by Vincent McEveety, who was one of Disney's go-to comedy directors once veteran director Robert Stevenson slowed down on his way to retirement. McEveety would surely have been at home here, having found himself in the director's chair for similar fare such as *The Strongest Man in the World* (1975) and later, *Herbie Goes to Monte Carlo* (1977) and *The Apple Dumpling Gang Rides Again* (1979).

The film was made with the cooperation of the National Football League and, as such, gridiron action featuring the likes of the Green Bay Packers and other real football teams is utilized in stock and newly-created footage. Some of this material was shot at the Los Angeles Memorial Coliseum and its neighboring Sports Arena. Other scenes were staged on a portable field covering part of the parking lot at the Disney Studios in Burbank. Real ex-football players and commentators like Johnny Unitas, Dick Enberg, Stu Nahan, Dick Butkus, and George Putnam appear throughout. Even producer Ron Miller was once a Los Angeles Ram, giving added appeal for football fans.

A note of sadness: this was Bob Crane's (*Hogan's Heroes*) last feature film appearance before he was murdered in 1978. Crane also appeared in Disney's *Superdad* in 1973.

Tim Conway says that when you make a film like *Gus*, you don't have to rent a tuxedo on Academy Awards night as you won't be nominated.

This was Conway's second film with Don Knotts, but this time they weren't together as a team, with Conway doing his crook business with Tom Bosley. The movie aired on the anthology in 1977, 1979 and 1982 and did well at the box office taking in almost $22 million.

The Shaggy D.A.

RELEASED BY BUENA VISTA ON December 17, 1976, Technicolor. Executive Producer: Ron Miller. Producer: Bill Anderson. Director: Robert Stevenson. Screenplay: Don Tait suggested by *The Hound of Florence* by Felix Salten. Art Director: John B. Mansbridge, Perry Ferguson. Editors: Bob Bring, A.C.E., Norman Palmer, A.C.E. Second Unit Director: Arthur J. Vitarelli. Assistant to the Producer: Jan Williams. Set Decorator: Robert Benton. Special Effects: Eustace Lycett, Art Cruickshank, A.S.C., Danny Lee. Matte Artist: Peter S. Ellenshaw. Titles: Guy Deel, Stan Green, Ed Garbert. Sound Supervision: Herb Taylor. Sound Mixer: Frank Regula. Unit Manager / Assistant Director: Christopher Seiter. Second Assistant Director: Dorothy Kieffer. Costumes: Chuck Keehne, Emily Sundby. Make-up: Robert J. Schiffer. Hair Stylist: La Rue Matheron. Sound Editor: Raymond Craddock. Music Editor: Evelyn Kennedy. Music: Buddy Baker. Orchestration: Walter Sheets. Director of Photography: Frank Phillips, A.S.C. Production Manager: John D. Bloss. Assistant Director: Gary LaPoten. Second Assistant Director: John

M. Poer. Sound Editor: George Fredrick. Special Effects: Hans Metz. Stunts: May Boss, Jerry Brutsche, Steven Burnett, Bobby Porter. Assistant Camera: Louis Niemeyer. Assistant Editor: Barney Cabral. Animal Trainers: Henry Cowl, Don Spinney. Production Assistant: Bill Hutchinson. Running time: 92 minutes.

Song: "The Shaggy D.A." sung by Dean Jones, written by Shane Tatum and Richard McKinley.

Cast: Dean Jones (Wilby Daniels), Tim Conway (Tim), Suzanne Pleshette (Betty Daniels), Keenan Wynn (John Slade), Jo Anne Worley (Katrinka Muggelberg), Dick Van Patten (Raymond), Shane Sinutko (Brian Daniels), Vic Tayback (Eddie Roschak), John Myhers (Admiral Brenner), Dick Bakalyan (Freddie), Warren Berlinger (Dip), Ronnie Schell (TV Director), Jonathan Daly (TV Interviewer), John Fiedler (Howie Clemmings), Hans Conried (Professor Whatley), Michael McGreevey (Sheldon), Richard O'Brien (Desk Sergeant), Dick Lane (Roller Rink Announcer), Benny Rubin (Waiter), Ruth Gillette (Song Chairman), Hank Jones (Policeman), Iris Adrian (Manageress), Pat McCormick (Bartender), Henry Slate (Taxi Driver), Milton Frome (Auctioneer), Walt Davis (TV Cameraman), Albert Able (TV Technician), Mary Ann Gibson (Daisyette), Helene Winston (Daisyette), Joan Crosby (Daisyette), Sarah Fankboner (Shopper), Danny Wells (Police Official), Herb Vigran (Bar Patron), Olan Soule (Bar Patron), Vern Rowe (Dawson), Karl Lukas (Painter), John Hayes (Stranger), Christina Anderson (Lonnie), George Kirby (Pound Canine Character Voices), Peter Renaday (Roller Derby Ticket Taker), Paul Sorensen (Policeman in Squad Car).

After a rousing opening sung by Dean Jones over some clever animation, this sequel to *The Shaggy Dog* (1959) gets underway.

Two workers named Freddie and Dip are loading up a moving van with furniture and drive away. Meanwhile, Wilby Daniels and his wife Betty and son Daniel drive home and discover that the movers were crooks and that their house has been robbed.

The next door neighbor, called the Admiral, has mistakenly helped the movers to load up their stuff and even gives them a beer.

Wilby is angry and wants to replace Honest John Slade as District Attorney. He wants to clean up the crime in the area and help the police be more aggressive and assertive.

Wilby backs down until he's robbed a second time in two days and launches his campaign. He stands in front of a grocery store and hands out flyers. He is told by Betty to kiss the babies, even the messy ones.

Slade sees the headlines and is confident that he will remain in office. Gangster Eddie Roschak is not so sure, but Raymond laughs in the background, agreeing that Wilby is not a threat.

At the local museum, a guided tour is being held by Professor Whatley, who tells the legend of the Borgias and their ring, which is supposed to change its owner into a dog. Freddie and Dip are in attendance and are fascinated by the ring because of its high value. They steal it for Eddie, who is in cahoots with the would-be movers.

Tim works for Dolly Dixon's ice cream and names off the 44 flavors for Brian Daniels, Wilby's son, who ends up taking vanilla. After getting his ice cream, Brian comes home to discover Medfield TV's UBC network setting up for an interview with Wilby with an interviewer and a director.

A news item that Eddie is listening to on his headphones mentions the stolen Borgia ring, which causes Wilby to break out into a sweat before his broadcast. He tells Betty of the legend of the ring and how he became a dog.

Freddie meets up with Tim at his ice cream truck and offers him the ring for a small fee. Tim decides to buy it for his girlfriend Katrinka, who works in pies for Dolly Dixon's and is also a roller derby champion.

The TV interview begins, first with an interview with Betty, who puts flowers in a vase in order to calm her nerves while on TV. The director cuts her interview short due to her nervousness.

Next, Wilby rehearses his speech. Wilby becomes Tim's shaggy dog named Elwood when Tim reads the inscription on the ring. By the time the cameras are ready, Wilby is missing and Brian is sitting with Elwood in Wilby's place.

To pad time until Wilby comes back, Brian gets Elwood to perform some tricks. Meanwhile Tim walks the streets looking for his now missing dog as Elwood has disappeared from Tim's side and has reappeared next to Brian as Elwood and Wilby have become one. Tim finds Elwood in the Daniels' house and chases after him, crashing into the Admiral in the process and ruining his flowers.

Tim gets Elwood back in the truck and Elwood tells him to let him go. Tim gets the idea to go into show business because Elwood is a talking dog. Elwood escapes before anything else happens and takes refuge in the dog house of a vicious dog named Brutus.

By the time Elwood gets out of the dog house, the spell is broken and Wilby as a human again races back home with Brutus chasing after him. The real Elwood dog reappears on the seat of Tim's ice cream truck.

Slade, Eddie, and Raymond are all watching the broadcast. Slade is not worried, but decides to look for some dirt on Daniels to be on the safe side.

Tim takes Elwood to a local bar and makes a bet with Harry the bartender that Elwood can talk, which of course he can't while the spell is in remission.

Wilby is worried that the dog transmutation spell will ruin his chances of becoming D.A. if this continues, so they have to find the ring.

The Admiral comes to the door to take Wilby and Betty to the Daisies, a group of women who have invited Wilby to speak about his campaign.

Katrinka helps Tim reload the ice cream truck and he tells her that he has gotten her a ring and gives it to her. Katrinka reads the inscription once she receives it and Wilby turns into Elwood once again. Betty cuts Wilby's speech short as he turns into a dog and disrupts the Daisy ladies.

Raymond is in attendance and discovers Wilby's weakness, reporting back to Slade. Elwood jumps into a cab and Tim searches for him again and chases the cab down the street on foot. At a stoplight he catches up with the cab, leashing Elwood and bringing him back to the ice cream truck.

Elwood asks for his freedom and Tim says that he will free him if he talks for Harry. Harry is not interested, but Tim bets $40 that the dog can talk.

While negotiating the deal, Elwood turns back into Wilby and Wilby leaves before Tim comes back. Tim brings Elwood in to the bar again and again no talking occurs.

The next day, Wilby goes to Dolly Dixon's headquarters and offers to pay $2000 to get the ring back, but Katrinka has lost it in a mixing vat for an order that went to a local hotel. All of the cooks including Katrinka and Tim rush to the hotel in order to be the first to get the $2000 reward.

At the hotel, hundreds of pies have been set out on tables and a huge pie fight ensues with everyone trying to find the ring which has been concealed in one of the pies.

In the same hotel, Slade is having a campaign fundraiser with Freddie and Dip in attendance. The pie with the ring is thrown out the window just as Freddie and Dip are passing by and they decide to take it and sell it again.

Slade and Raymond see what is going on and everyone is smashed with pies. In the end, Betty is the only one that remains pie-free.

Freddie tries to sell the ring, but mistakenly offers it to an undercover policeman who shows his badge and takes Freddie in.

Wilby is alerted about the ring and he and his family rushes to the police department to retrieve it, but the ring is given back to Professor Whatley and he reads the inscription to the police officer before returning back to the museum.

Raymond overhears this conversation and somehow gets the ring from the Professor and drops it off at Slade's office. Slade realizes that he now possesses Wilby's Achilles heel.

Slade calls Wilby to his office and tells Wilby to drop out of the race. When Wilby refuses, Slade reads the inscription and Wilby changes into Elwood once again.

Slade orders Raymond to lock up Elwood, but Elwood slugs Raymond and runs out being seen by the Department of Animal Regulation truck, who now chase after him as a stray dog.

The police are also involved as Elwood runs for his life. Slade continues to read the ring inscription to make sure that Wilby remains Elwood.

Elwood runs into Katrinka's roller derby game with Slade and Raymond chasing after him with a huge net. Elwood disguises himself as a roller derby skater and then escapes with Tim in his truck.

Slade and Raymond chase after him but smash their car in the chase. Animal Regulation says that they have caught Elwood in a tree and Slade and Raymond arrive to witness them shoot Elwood with a tranquilizer gun. Slade gives Elwood one more chance to drop out of the race, but he refuses.

The Animal Regulation guys shoot the gun, but in their incompetence shoot Slade instead of Elwood, who promptly falls asleep. Elwood is taken to the dog pound.

Tim has been arrested for crashing his ice cream truck earlier and Katrinka bails him out. Tim blames Elwood for his predicament.

At the dog pound, the dogs start digging to escape and they all leave the pound and jump into the Animal Regulation truck with Elwood at the wheel.

Slade wakes up and wonders if Howie and Sheldon have gotten rid of Elwood, and they explain that all of the dogs have escaped.

Elwood gets home and knocks on the window. Betty and Brian let him in briefly. As the cops arrive, Elwood leaves wearing a hat and trench coat.

Elwood goes back to Tim to help him capture Slade. He tells Tim that he needs him to testify in court what Slade has been doing and sets Tim on the handlebars of a bicycle while Elwood pedals and steers.

Tim shows up at Slade's door and gives Slade a cryptic message that he's going to be off of Eddie's gravy train.

Next it's off to Slade's warehouse and Brian catches up with them to help. The three discover their stolen merchandise, but hide when they see Eddie. Tim accidentally turns on a tape recorder full blast, but turns it off before Eddie suspects anything.

Elwood takes the tape recorder into Eddie's office and hopes to get incriminating evidence on the tape about Slade and his criminal involvements.

Slade and Raymond are on their way to the warehouse, and Raymond warns Slade about reading the inscription too many times, which Slade dismisses as rubbish.

Slade and Eddie meet in the office and Elwood turns on the tape recorder to get some evidence on tape, but Elwood is discovered after making his recording. Slade drops the ring when all the escaped dogs come back to help Elwood and the dogs return the ring to Elwood who transforms back into Wilby.

Slade and Eddie get up and start firing shots at Wilby who jumps aboard a stolen jeep that gets coated in orange paint and feathers as they try to escape.

Slade jumps into the car driven by Raymond, and they are pulled over by a police officer for speeding. Raymond says that he's driving D.A. Slade in his car, but the only thing the police see is a cigar-chomping bulldog as Slade has turned into this bulldog.

Wilby drives home and Betty greets him, Tim and Brian covered with paint and feathers. Wilby gives the ring and the tape recorder to the police as evidence.

Soon, everyone is cleaned up and Tim is back with Katrinka and Elwood and the other stray dogs, which they now own. They are also engaged to be married.

Newly-elected D.A. Wilby Daniels and his family are off to start his new job.

Though this is a sequel, none of the actors who appeared in 1959's *The Shaggy Dog* appeared in this film, although it would have been fun if someone appeared from the previous cast.

This was Dean Jones and Suzanne Pleshette's third teaming together after *The Ugly Dachshund* (1965) and *Blackbeard's Ghost* (1968). Pleshette had been away from Disney since that time as she concentrated more on her TV work on *The Bob Newhart Show* (1972-1978), but the chemistry between her and Jones is always evident.

This was Jones' first major film role since 1972 and *Snowball Express*. Jones became a born-again Christian in 1973 and took a break from heavy acting for a time, but came back to Disney for this and the upcoming *Herbie Goes to Monte Carlo* (1977).

This was the final film directed by Robert Stevenson, who retired after completing the movie. Dick Van Patten says that he was an easy director to work with.

This was also the final film with actor Liam Dunn, who passed away hours after completing his scenes. John Fiedler was hired to do some additional scenes that were originally intended for Dunn.

It is also the final film Michael McGreevey acted on, as he hung it up in favor of writing and producing.

Tim Conway says that he had one incident on this film where he and Stevenson clashed, in which Conway sitting on the handlebars of a bike was driven by the dog (actually a midget in a costume). Stevenson said that it wouldn't be logical for Conway to pet him, at which Conway says that sitting on the handlebars in the middle of the night being driven by a midget in a dog suit is?

Conway says that the pie fight scene was difficult as you had to have pie on you for three weeks. He also was annoyed when a real cherry pie was thrown at him during a rehearsal and not an actual live take. The pies used were real pies, not fake shaving cream pies with cherry juice and decaying whip cream going down your shirt all day for four days.

He says he also had to suffer going through a paint factory and crash into pillow feathers for this film and he finally wonders if he's in the wrong business.

Dick Van Patten discusses how he played a villain in all seven Disney movies he did, including in this film. Shooting usually started at 7am, with make-up starting about 4:30am. He says that there were no rehearsals, they just did it.

Van Patten and Conway only have kind words for both Jones and Pleshette and also Jo Anne Worley and Hans Conried. They both admitted that on shooting breaks, Van Patten and Conway went to the racetrack together and lost a lot of dough.

In a DVD documentary, make-up artist Robert Schiffer discusses the elaborate make-ups used in transforming Dean Jones into the dog, including five or six various tongues. The hair was all laid by hand using hair from an Icelandic bear. Sometimes it took four to five hours to make the transition. Schiffer also worked for other directors and studios in his 60+ years.

The DVD also features a commentary by Tim Conway, Dick Van Patten, and Jo Anne Worley talking about how much fun it was to make this film.

Worley mentions that her first film for Disney was actually *Moon Pilot*(1962), in which she played a beatnik.

Conway said that when you work on films like this, you devote your full time to it and don't think about your personal problems. You leave that stuff at home. He also said that he did a little ad-libbing here and there throughout the picture.

Van Patten reveals that Keenan Wynn portrayed his father on an old radio show. He also said that Hans Conried spoke with an affected accent and that should be the way that actors should speak. He also said that Conried was a very intellectual person.

The UBC truck was the same one used in *The Barefoot Executive*(1971), and the film takes place in Medfield, the same location as the two "Flubber" films and the "Dexter Riley" trilogy.

The Richard O'Brien in this film that portrayed the Desk Sergeant is the same person who created *The Rocky Horror Picture Show* (1975).

Iris Adrian appeared in many other Disney films, but in her younger days also in a lot of James Cagney films.

Benny Rubin used to appear on *The Jack Benny Program* and is in the great pie fight, as is Adrian.

Van Patten reveals that Liam Dunn died on April 11, 1976, the day after doing his scene in the roller derby. He is best known for his small parts in such films as *Blazing Saddles* (1974), *Young Frankenstein*(1974) and *What's Up, Doc?* (1972).

According to Conway, the roller derby scenes were filmed at a real roller derby at Olympic Stadium.

Suzanne Pleshette worked with John Fiedler here and also on *The Bob Newhart Show*.

Pete Renaday shot a scene that was ultimately cut, in which he played a roller derby ticket taker with Tim Conway.

This movie aired on the anthology show in 1978, 1980 and 1987. It was followed up with a 1987 made-for-TV sequel *The Return of the Shaggy Dog* and another theatrical film called *The Shaggy Dog* (2006) starring Tim Allen.

Freaky Friday

RELEASED BY BUENA VISTA ON December 17, 1976, Technicolor. Producer: Ron Miller. Associate Producer: Tom Leetch. Director: Gary Nelson. Screenplay: Mary Rodgers based on the book by Mary Rodgers. Art Directors: John B. Mansbridge, Jack Senter. Editor: Cotton Warburton, A.C.E. Set Decorator: Robert Benton. Special Effects: Eustace Lycett, Art Cruickshank, A.S.C., Danny Lee. Titles: John Jensen, Art Stevens. Sound Supervision: Herb Taylor. Sound Mixer: Ron Ronconi. Unit Production Manager: Tom McCrory. First Assistant Director: Ronald R. Grow. Second Assistant Director: Cheryl Downey. Technical Advisor: Larry Meddock. Costumes: Chuck Keehne, Emily Sundby. Make-up: Robert J. Schiffer. Hair Stylist: Gloria Montemayor. Sound Editor: Raymond Craddock. Music Editor: Evelyn Kennedy. Music: Johnny Mandel. Director of Photography: Charles F. Wheeler, A.S.C. Set Dresser: Kurt V. Hulett. Sound Editors: Barney Cabral, George Fredrick. Special Effects: David Domeyer, Hans Metz. Stunts: Richard E. Butler, Paula Dell, Kevin N. Johnston, Randy L. Shelly, Dick Warlock. Second Assistant Camera: Louis Niemeyer. Musician: Jack Sheldon. Transportation: Mario Simon. Dialogue Coach: Bobby Hoffman. Running time: 98 minutes.

Song: "I'd Like to Be You for a Day" Words and Music by Al Kasha and Joel Hirschhorn.

Cast: Barbara Harris (Helen Andrews), Jodie Foster (Annabel Andrews), John Astin (Bill Andrews), Patsy Kelly (Mrs. Schmauss), Dick Van Patten (Harold Jennings), Vicki Schreck (Virginia), Sorrell Booke (Mr. Dilk), Alan Oppenheimer (Mr. Joffert), Ruth Buzzi (Opposing Coach), Kaye Ballard (Coach Betsy), Marc McClure (Boris Harris), Marie Windsor (Mrs. Murphy), Sparky Marcus (Ben Andrews), Ceil Cabot (Miss McGuirk), Brooke Mills (Mrs. Gibbons), Karen Smith (Mary Kay Gilbert), Marvin Kaplan (Carpet Cleaner), Al Molinaro (Drapery Man), Iris Adrian (Bus Passenger), Barbara Walden (Mrs. Benson), Shelly Juttner (Hilary Miller), Charlene Tilton (Bambi), Lori Rutherford (Jo-Jo), Jack Sheldon (Lloyd), Laurie Main (Mr. Mills), Don Carter (Delivery Boy), Fuddle Bagley (Bus Driver), Fritz Feld (Mr. Jackman), Dermott Downs (Harvey Manager), Jimmy Van Patten (Cashier), Allan Hunt (Car Cop), Robert Karvelas (Diner Customer), Jack Perkins (Car Cop), David Pollock (Student), Dick Winslow (Man in Pool).

After some colorful animated titles about body switching featuring the song "I'd Like to Be You for a Day," the film begins with Annabel sleeping in her bed on Friday the 13th and reluctantly getting up for the day at 7:30am.

Annabel is having teen troubles with braces, her developing figure, and messy habits. Annabel's younger brother Ben, who she calls 'Apeface,' is her complete opposite: very studious and neat.

Annabel is also into sports like waterskiing and field hockey. She also describes her dad, her mom, and the boy across the street that she has a crush on, Boris Harris with narration.

Annabel has her biggest difficulties with her mother, who is badgering Annabel about her cleaning habits, her eating habits, and remembering her appointments with her orthodontist and the aquacade, an event that Annabel will undertake a waterskiing performance. Bill, Annabel's father practices the speech that he will read at the aquacade with her mother, Helen.

After listening, Helen reveals that she has to go to school to speak with Mr. Dilk about Annabel's slipping grades.

Annabel is griping about her mother with her friend Virginia, while Helen gripes about Annabel with Bill. They both say "I wish I could switch places with her for just one day." They both get their wish.

The switch is really freaky as Annabel has to come to grips with her mind being in her mother's body and vice-versa.

Bill is in the other room wondering what strangeness is going on. The phone rings and Bill answers, but the transition has made Annabel refer to her father as "Bill" until she comes to terms with everything. Annabel asks

Bill to check on her mother, who is now dancing, chewing gum and listening to rock and roll music.

Helen says Annabel should try to do well on the typing test and also her field hockey game, and Bill, confused, relays this message.

Annabel tries to tell her friends that she's her mother, but her friends take it that she wants them to imitate their mothers and treat it as a game. Annabel tries to buy some cigarettes, but is laughingly rejected.

Helen gives Apeface Sugar-Coated Snappy Krackles to eat because she doesn't want to cook bacon and eggs. Then, she cringes when she has to give him a kiss when she sends him off to school.

She sends Bill off to work and hops on a skateboard while he's reminding her of some errands that she will need to do during the day.

Annabel gets on the bus with Virginia and gets money out of a lump held in her sock, spilling change all over the floor of the bus.

Helen sits at home, painting on tremendous amounts of make-up.

On the bus, Annabel shouts out while thinking about what Helen is going through, assuming she's eating and watching TV.

Helen is actually stuffing too many clothes into the washer while she chews bubble gum. Then she does go to watch TV with some potato chips.

She flips around the dial to see shows like *Romper Room* and a sewing program and a program in Spanish. The washer starts shaking and overflowing while the phone rings.

Bill is on the phone and asks Helen to pick up some liquor for some unexpected guests that he's bringing over that night. Helen has never purchased liquor or driven a car.

Annabel is still adjusting and checks the schedule. Her first class is photography and as she is late she comes into the darkroom and exposes all the film.

Back at home, Mrs. Schmauss, the maid, arrives while Helen is watching TV and working out to loud music. She asks Schmauss to help her with the laundry. Schmauss says that there are certain things that she doesn't do like clean up pig pens and run personal errands.

Annabel is in her next class taking the typing test, but is unable to type because the machine isn't turned on. She isn't used to an electric typewriter and soon she causes a chain reaction that short circuits all of the typewriters in the class.

Helen is cleaning up Annabel's room and the doorbell rings. Schmauss says that she doesn't answer doors either, so Helen answers the door to meet Floyd the car repairman who asks for a check, but Helen asks if cash will do.

The other doorbell rings and Helen answers it. It's the carpet cleaners. Helen doesn't have the $14.50 for the car repair and asks the carpet cleaners for the money.

The doorbell rings again and Mary Kay comes by to borrow the hair dryer, but Helen doesn't know where it is.

The repairman still wants his money, the carpet men need a pair of pliers, and the doorbell rings yet again. This time it's the drapery man who brings back the draperies after washing and repairing them.

Schmauss finds a bottle of liquor that Helen agrees was probably set out to incriminate her. The drapery man needs help, but the doorbell rings again and it's a young man with some groceries.

Schmauss is still complaining and so Helen fires her. The carpet man leaves in a huff and everyone else is still making their demands, so Helen drops to the floor and sucks her thumb.

Annabel is now at marching band practice, attempting to play her glockenspiel and march in formation, which she does horribly.

Bill gives a presentation at work about what will happen tonight with the aquacade. Harold, Bill's boss is not amused with the plans and hopes that everything goes well. Bill then receives a call from Helen who panics about everything that has gone wrong at home today.

Helen irons and starches a shirt to ultimate stiffness and then sits down to a hearty meal of macaroni and cheese and then calls Boris over. Boris agrees and so Helen changes her clothes into something more glamorous.

Boris comes in with some kibble that Helen requested. Boris is at home because he has adenoid problems and Helen gives him some vitamin C, acting overly formal in order to impress him.

Boris sees Annabel's room, but Helen says it's really Apeface's room. Meanwhile, Annabel is acing her history tests because of her firsthand knowledge of the Korean War.

Boris stays around to show Helen how to throw a boomerang. Boris is impressed with Helen, but she tries to steer him towards Annabel. Helen throws the boomerang and shatters a neighbor's window.

Annabel continues on about the Korean War and bores the other students with her long-windedness.

Boris is still impressed with Helen, who asks for him to come back over some time and play a board game or something.

Now it is time for the field hockey game and Coach Betsy gives a pep talk similar to being in the Marines. Annabel is nervous but Virginia says not to worry and to shoot her usual high number of goals. In fact, everyone is depending on Annabel to win the game.

The opposing coach knows this and gives her team a pep talk, telling them to get Annabel Andrews, which they do.

Helen picks up Apeface on foot since she can't drive. They have a talk about firing Mrs. Schmauss and Apeface reveals that he really likes Annabel and looks up to her.

In the field hockey game, the opposing team is downright abusive, so much so that Annabel decides to quit the game but then reconsiders.

Helen plays baseball with Apeface and his friends and does some spectacular hitting, catching, and pitching.

Annabel is now playing better, but unfortunately she scores a goal for the opposing team, causing them to win.

On the way home, Apeface compliments Annabel more and more and Helen explains why Annabel doesn't like Apeface.

Bill calls up wondering where Helen was, because there was another emergency. There is no food for tonight's event and Bill tells her to whip up something for 25 guests in three hours.

Annabel goes to Bill's office and sees Bill's new sexy secretary and gives a couple veiled threats. The secretary later comes in wearing a trench coat, flat shoes, and glasses, with her hair bound up.

Annabel asks Bill if she can borrow his credit card in order to purchase some new clothes, since she's getting her braces off today.

Helen hurriedly tries to stuff a turkey and cook it in record time. The phone rings and it is Mr. Dilk (Annabel's teacher) to say that Helen is 15 minutes late for the appointment about Annabel.

Helen calls Boris to watch Apeface and asks him to make a dessert while she goes off to the meeting on foot.

Annabel now gets her braces removed, then tries on some new clothes and purchases them. She also gets her nails done and her face and hair.

Afterwards, she is calmly walking down the street with her new purchases when her friends drive up and force her into the van as she is late for the water skiing event.

At the meeting, Mr. Dilk and everyone else are giving Annabel high marks, but things are starting to slip. The high approval shocks Helen. While defending Annabel, Helen inadvertently refers to her husband as her father.

While making the dessert, Apeface presses the blender without the lid being on and gets chocolate all over him. Helen gets home in time to find the turkey burning and chocolate all over the kitchen.

Bill calls in and wonders where Helen is and also where the food is. Helen starts again, using kibble and whatever is left around the kitchen.

Annabel is ready in her waterskiing outfit, but then chickens out at the last minute. Bill forces her into it by handing her the handlebar.

Helen decides to take the burnt turkey anyway, but needs Boris to drive the car because she can't and reveals that she is Annabel. Boris doesn't believe her, so she gets behind the wheel anyway and crashes through a fence before going forward. A high speed chase involving police cars ensues.

During this moment, both Annabel and Helen wish to be back in their own bodies, which happens but not in the way that they expect. Annabel ends up behind the steering wheel and Helen ends up on the water skis.

The car chase continues down stairs, around rotaries and on sidewalks, while Helen continues to water ski in her black dress, going so far as to grab a baton from another water skiing act and lighting fireworks.

Meanwhile, Mrs. Schmauss comes out of the liquor store on her bicycle only to be hit by Annabel in the car. Helen continues to water ski onto the beach and across a swimming pool.

The car chase continues as Helen grabs onto a hang glider and sails above the aquacade show, while Bill and everyone else viewing the show from a floating tent slowly sink into the water.

The chasing police cars get out of commission by tipping over, scrunching up like an accordion, and splitting in two.

Annabel finally arrives with Boris and Apeface and she drives into the water as Helen hang glides into some other water skiers and safely lands in the water next to them.

Mother and daughter are finally reunited and very happy to see each other and be themselves again.

Bill gets commended for a great water show as the floating tent sinks all the way.

Later, at home, Bill is trying to figure out what happened and Helen is not talking. Boris is more impressed with Annabel than before and they go out for pizza and bring Apeface with them.

Bill asks Annabel before she leaves what went wrong and Annabel won't talk, either.

Before everyone leaves for pizza, Bill and Apeface discuss their Saturday plans and each wishes they were each other. Helen and Annabel highly discourage this, but Bill and Apeface are adamant. They want to be each other and we leave on a freeze-frame knowing what's about to happen next.

This is one of the best latter-day Disney films and was so well received (grossing $26 million) that it aired on the anthology show in 1982, and was one of many that was remade for TV in 1995 and later theatrically with Lindsay Lohan and Jamie Lee Curtis in 2003.

Charlene Tilton appears here pre-*Dallas* as one of Annabel's friends.

On the DVD documentary, Jodie Foster said that Disney was really out of sync with the times, but that was what they set out to do. There is a real loyalty and family feeling with Disney. She said doing this film and *Candleshoe* at this time was really awkward for her, and that she actually had aspirations at this point to be a director rather than an actor.

As a result, it is very difficult for her to watch this movie and *Candleshoe* (1978), which she considers her transitional films as an actor.

What she liked best about *Freaky Friday* was the waterskiing. She says that she got sunburn while practicing and then was disappointed that all of her scenes were to be shot on a sound stage.

The field hockey scenes were heavily choreographed, and it was a smoggy day so they had to take many breaks. She loved working with John Astin, Dick Van Patten, and Ruth Buzzi, but her favorite scenes were the ones where she worked with Barbara Harris.

Foster feels that Harris got the hard part of the bargain on their switch because she had to do a lot of physical things like play baseball, ride a skateboard, and also fall a lot.

She also discusses doing the 1970 TV movie *Menace on the Mountain*, where she fell in the toilet. Then she discusses being mauled by a lion in *Napoleon and Samantha* (1972) and still has scars to prove it. On *One Little Indian* (1973) she sprained her ankle and delayed shooting. On *Candleshoe*, she loved working in England with the older actors like David Niven and Helen Hayes. It was kind of intimidating for her, because she respected those actors so much. She also mentions being under contract for *Freaky Friday* and *Candleshoe* at this time, which prevented her from doing Princess Leia in *Star Wars* (1977). Her mother made the decision to fulfill the Disney contract rather than break it for another film.

1977

After a couple years of half-hour reruns of *The Mickey Mouse Club*, *The New Mickey Mouse Club* debuted in January. A book based upon the show also appeared.

New films made for the anthology show include *The Golden Dog*, *Kit Carson and the Mountain Men*, *Barry of the Great St. Bernard*, *Go West, Young Dog*, *The Ghost of Cypress Swamp*, *The Track of the African Bongo*, *The Bluegrass Special*, *Halloween Hall O' Fame*, and *The Mouseketeers at Walt Disney World*. *A Tale of Two Critters* was a new theatrical featurette that made its way to the anthology show the following year.

Never a Dull Moment (1968) was re-released with *The Three Caballeros* (1945) as were *The Boatniks* (1970) and *Fantasia* (1940).

This year was also the first to have a serious challenger to the Disney anthology show when CBS aired *60 Minutes* opposite it. *60 Minutes* rose to become the number-one show of the season and stayed for many years.

There was also one all-new serial created for *The New Mickey Mouse Club*, called *The Mystery of Rustler's Cave* that originally aired in February. The follow-up to this year's successful *The Rescuers* was bandied about with *The Fox and the Hound* (1981) getting the final nod. One idea under consideration mentioned in Charles Solomon's *The Disney That Never Was* was *Scruffy*, but the idea was eventually considered too feeble and discarded.

Some of the biggest non-Disney hits of the year include *For the Love of Benji*, *Sinbad and the Eye of the Tiger*, the animated *Raggedy Ann and Andy*, and *Race for Your Life, Charlie Brown* and, surprise, surprise, *Star Wars* and *Close Encounters of the Third Kind*.

With these successes, Disney had to start to rethink its strategy of making every one of their films targeted to having a G-rating.

On the *Freaky Friday* DVD documentary, Jodie Foster reveals that she was contractually obligated to Disney and had to refuse the role of Princess Leia in *Star Wars*. On March 7, even before *Star Wars* made its May theatrical debut, Roy O. Disney's son, Roy E. Disney, tendered his resignation. His frustrations included the direction of Walt Disney Productions and its stagnant growth, paying particular attention to the declining quality of the studio's film output and his displeasure with the current management as led by Card Walker and Donn Tatum.

His resignation did not see immediate repercussions, but ultimately Roy did come back in 1984 to lead the crusade to take over Disney management and hand it off to Michael Eisner.

Still later, Roy had frustrations with Eisner and resigned again, then returned once moer before finally passing away in 2009.

Disney disbanded The Walt Disney Distributing Company to create merchandise of its own design rather than relying on licensees. It ran from 1971-1977.

At Disneyland, Space Mountain finally opened on May 4 after being a great hit since 1974 at Walt Disney World, while Nature's Wonderland and the Rainbow Caverns Mine Train closed for good to make room for the Big Thunder Mountain Railroad, scheduled to open in 1979.

While at Walt Disney World, the Empress Lilly riverboat opened and the Main Street Electrical Parade made its debut.

Non-soundtrack record releases included *The Magical Music of Walt Disney* and the soundtracks to various Rankin-Bass TV specials, including *Frosty's Winter Wonderland*, *Twas the Night Before Christmas*, and *The Hobbit*.

There were also record soundtracks to the various Charlie Brown TV specials including *A Charlie Brown Christmas* and *Charlie Brown's All-Stars*, and record readers for *Star Wars*.

Despite the fact that Disney missed the boat on the film, they seemed adamant about not making the same mistake again, which is why Disney joined forces with George Lucas for various records and theme park attractions in years to come.

A Charlie Brown Christmas was nominated for a Best Recording for Children Grammy, but lost.

In the comic book world, Gold Key continued to publish *Donald Duck, Mickey Mouse, Uncle Scrooge, Walt Disney's Comics and Stories, The Beagle Boys, Huey, Dewey and Louie Junior Woodchucks, Super Goof, Chip 'n' Dale, Scamp, Walt Disney Showcase, Daisy and Donald*, and *Moby Duck*. *Winnie the Pooh* started as a series.

Mickey Mouse Club Fun Book and *Walt Disney Christmas Parade* both appeared as one-shots.

Actor Paul Peterson told the story of how he got kicked off *The Mickey Mouse Club* in his tell-all book, *Walt, Mickey and Me*. An early salute to Mickey Mouse's 50th birthday in 1978 was issued, called *Mickey Mouse: Fifty Happy Years*.

Proctor and Gamble offered *Disney Magazine* to supermarkets, with issues provided free of charge to purchasers of certain P&G products. Eleven issues were produced and featured new and recycled articles from *Walt Disney's Magazine* from the 1950s and *The Wonderful World of Disney Magazine* from 1969-70.

The Littlest Horse Thieves

RELEASED BY BUENA VISTA ON March 11, 1977 (May 26, 1976 in UK as *Escape from the Dark*), Technicolor. Producer: Ron Miller. Associate Producer: Hugh Attwooll. Director: Charles Jarrott. Screenplay: Rosemary Anne Sisson. Story: Burt Kennedy, Rosemary Anne Sisson. Director of Photography: Paul Beeson, B.S.C. Art Director: Robert Liang. Editor: Richard Marden. Costume Designer: John Furniss. Set Dresser: Hugh Scaife. Production Manager: Robin Douet. Location Manager: Jake Wright. Assistant Director: Allan James. Continuity: Georgina Hamilton. Make-up: Roy Ashton, Harry Frampton. Hairdressing: Bobbie Smith, Joyce James. Casting: Maude Spector. Construction Manager: Leon Davies. Pony Trainer: James Prine. Technical Adviser (Mining): W.J. Charlton. Property Buyer: Bryn Siddall. Sound Editor: Rusty Coppleman. Sound Recordists: Claude Hitchcock, Ken Barker. Music Composer / Conductor: Ron Goodwin played by The Grimethorpe Colliery Band, recorded by Anvil Studios, filmed on location and at Pinewood Studios, London, England. Sound Recordist: Claude Hitchcock. Production Runner: Terry Bamber. Running time: 104 minutes.

Cast: Alastair Sim (Lord Harrogate), Peter Barkworth (Richard Sandman), Maurice Colbourne (Luke Armstrong), Susan Tebbs (Violet Armstrong), Andrew Harrison (Dave Sadler), Chloe Franks (Alice Sandman), Benjie Bolgar (Tommy Sadler), Prunella Scales (Mrs. Sandman), Leslie Sands (Foreman Sam Carter), Joe Gladwin (Bert), Jeremy Bulloch (Ginger), Derek Newark, Duncan Lamont, Ian Hogg, Richard Warner, Tom Laughlin, Don Henderson, Tommy Wright, John Hartley, Ken Kitson, Peter Geddis,

Roy Evans, Gorden Kaye, James Marcus, Donald Bisset, Gordon Christie, Walter Hill, Geraldine McEwan (Miss Coutt).

It is Yorkshire, England, in 1909, and coal mining is the main industry. Ponies are used to carry the coal through the tight mineways.

One of the dangers of mining in such tight spaces is that of tunnel collapse. New support beams need to be installed in order for the miners to not get buried alive.

The spaces are so tight so that the men have to walk hunched over and use the aid of a cane in order to walk through.

The ponies are sometimes stubborn as evidenced with Flash, who knows exactly when his shift is over and will not do any additional work after that point.

There are stable boys who feed hay to the ponies at the end of the shift, but the boys really are not supposed to be there due to child labor laws and so they have to hide from time to time when an inspection is held.

Every day the miners come home after feeding the ponies and the boys are paid for their work as well.

The boys are caught exiting the mine and the miners are questioned about them and advised to stop bringing the boys into the mine.

The new chief of the miners, Richard Sandman, is looking for ways to cut costs and the number one solution he comes up with is to get rid of the pit ponies.

He decides that the ultimate solution is to replace these ponies with machinery.

Dave and Tommy are two of the boys who work the stables and help Richard's daughter Alice down from a tree after being chased up there by a dog. They also help her get her kite out of the tree, and the three of them fly it.

After a little scuffle about whether Alice is a lady, the three become fast friends. Dave and Tommy tell Alice that they help with the pit ponies and Alice says that they'll miss the ponies when they are gone, which upsets the boys.

The boys' foster parents say at least it's just the ponies and not the people as well. Dave counters that if they cared about the people more, his dad would still be alive, almost earning a slap for his comment by Nile, his stepfather and one of the miners.

The next day, new shipments of machinery are sent by rail to the mine shaft. Alice really wants to see the ponies and the mine so Tommy and Alice exchange clothes so that she can pretend to be a boy for a day to see the goings-on. Sandman witnesses the boys going down and warns that if he sees the boys going down the mine again, someone will be dismissed.

Alice is excited to hear that the ponies will be set free so that they can run and play out in the fields. One of the miners tells her to ask her father what the fate really is for the pit ponies.

That night Dave has a dream about all the boys and Alice running the pit ponies through the fields and forests.

Alice is still concerned about the fate of the ponies, but no one has an answer. She is finally told that the ponies will probably be sent to the slaughterhouse. Alice is distressed and runs to the mine to talk with her father.

There are other, more pressing problems as the men cannot do their work while the cable is being laid, so the men are sent home.

Alice finally asks her father if the ponies will be sent to the slaughterhouse, but he refuses to answer and sends her home. Alice sees Dave and Tommy and tells them the horrible news.

They plan to steal the ponies to save them from their horrible fate, but it is more difficult as there are always people about the mines doing maintenance.

There are plans of all the workings and they decide to steal them out of Sandman's office once he leaves. Alice sneaks inside and there are plans, but they are not easily found and she almost gets caught sneaking about.

Eventually she does find the correct plans. She sneaks out and the three go to an alternate entrance shown on the plans. The alternate entrance is an abandoned mine shaft that is not entirely safe. They go through the old engine house which is now covered in spider webs, but if they can get it working, they can bring the ponies out.

Back at home, Alice asks her father how a winding engine works. This is so she can get the engine in the engine house working.

They need some grease, so they sneak into the present engine house and get some from a small oil can. They add coal and oil to the old engine house and get it working again.

They are spotted by a miner named Bert, and he asks what they are doing. Tommy reveals their plan to get the ponies out of the pit. Instead of being mad, the miner decides to help them.

After he helps to get the engine running, everyone agrees not to tell anyone else. Dave is the first one to go down into the mine. He descends with a single candle to see what he can find.

Dave is nervous because he doesn't know the exact direction in which he should be going. He uses a spool of twine in order to track his progress and not get lost. Dave does discover the correct way and he soon sees Flash.

Alice wonders if Dave will get to the right spot and Tommy scares her with tales of disaster. Eventually, Alice panics and wants to go down the mine as well to help find Dave. Tommy tells her not to.

Finally Dave gets back to the mine cart and Tommy and Alice lift him out. Dave almost did get lost, but he managed to find his way back.

After Dave is back on the surface, they find a perfect spot to keep the ponies after they rescue them.

Alice's teacher, Miss Glintz, has been looking all over for her and she brings her home. Alice has been with Dave and Tommy to see the ponies.

Dave and Tommy go home and they are told by Nile that the ponies will be sent to Barnsley. Dave and Tommy are told that they can go down to see the ponies one last time and Dave and Tommy act disinterested.

Nile goes to the mine and he's more concerned as to whether he will be able to keep his job than he is about the fate of the pit ponies.

Early the next morning, Alice, Dave, and Tommy meet in order to put their rescue plan to work. The men already in the mine think they hear the old winding engine, but Bert puts them off by saying that they are hearing things and that they couldn't pay him enough to go by there.

That night, Nile is concerned because the boys are not home and he feels that they have run away due to the ponies' impending fate. In reality, Dave and Tommy are hauling out the ponies to the surface with the old winding engine, with Alice on the surface making sure everything runs correctly.

Alice is not strong enough to run the machinery by herself, which worries Dave and Tommy, but Bert saves the day again by showing up and helping them out.

All works well as the boys get all the ponies up and out of the mine. Bert leaves and says again that he doesn't know anything about what's happening with the ponies and the mine.

The three continue on, taking all nine ponies to their special hiding place.

Meanwhile, Mr. Sandman goes in to check up on Alice, but she is not in her bed. Then, a couple of the miners knock on the front door and say that the ponies are missing.

All of the ponies are doing well in their new surroundings except Flash, who seems to be having difficulties. Soon they have greater troubles, as the three are caught by Mr. Sandman and brought home.

The next day, none of the miners are willing to go down into the mine and decide to defend the ponies and not allow them to be taken on the train to be slaughtered, much to Dave and Tommy's delight.

Sandman says that the machines have replaced the ponies and the machines are staying to protect their livelihood. The miners decide to go on strike. Sandman tells Alice what has happened and blames her for it.

Since the miners aren't working, they just sit around town. Sandman doesn't know what to do as everything is at a standstill.

It turns out Flash has pit blindness, which is why he can't make his way round on the surface world.

Sandman goes to the owner to see what he can do. The owner doesn't really care about how the pit is to be used, and that he can close it down at a moment's notice and start a new business.

In the meantime, the miners are having dog races and placing bets in order to kill time, because they have nothing else to do.

Sandman calls a special meeting and says that if no one comes back to work tomorrow the pit will be closed for good. He gives assurances that no one will be laid off, but there is still no place for the ponies.

Some of the men are willing to go back to work, because they would rather work with the machinery than not work at all.

Nile makes everyone take a vote about whether to go back to work and the majority of the men vote to go back to work, so the next day they go without the ponies.

Alice is so upset that she refuses to kiss her father again as long as he lives.

The men are back at work, but there is another explosion similar to the one that killed Dave and Tommy's father. There are eight men trapped down below in the mine, including Nile, with the threat of gases causing more explosions.

Dave and Tommy suggest using the old winding engine since it is working again and to also use Flash, since he doesn't need lights to know the way.

Dave wants to go down in the mine, but Sandman forbids it. Sandman goes down with a few others, including Flash and a canary who can detect the gasses before humans can.

Sandman doesn't know the way but Flash may, so they send the pony to lead the way. The gases are strong, so they don't have much time to get to the men and get them out.

Meanwhile, the eight men are surviving and trying to ration their water and help their injured.

Flash leads them to a blocked spot. Sandman starts tapping away on the walls and the trapped men tap back. Medical help is brought down into the mine.

The injured men are brought out by a stretcher hauled by Flash and the rest walk out after the hole is made. It's still a dangerous situation, as there could still be another explosion.

Sandman is the last man out and even Alice is happy to see him. The men all get out, but Flash goes back to his underground pen thinking his shift is over.

Nile plans to go down to rescue Flash, but just then another explosion occurs, causing the children to cry because they knew Flash was still down there.

A parade and picnic are held the next day for the miners and Nile tries to cheer Dave up, but there is happy news as the owner offers up a place for the other retired pit ponies to live out their lives.

Since this was a British production, many of the same people who worked on *One of Our Dinosaurs is Missing* (1975) worked on this film.

This is a remarkably well-done film and very moving, but unfortunately was not the type of film that filmgoers went to see in early 1977. Nowadays this would be a perfect film for the indie houses, but at the time, no one knew what to do about a sweet little film about pit ponies set in 1909 Yorkshire.

Prunella Scales is perhaps best known as Sybil Fawlty on *Fawlty Towers*. She did this film between the two series of that show.

This was Alastair Sim's final movie role. He is best known to US audiences for his role of Ebenezer Scrooge in the 1951 British version of *A Christmas Carol*, a.k.a. *Scrooge*.

Jeremy Bulloch later attained fame portraying Boba Fett in the *Star Wars* movies.

The working title for this film was *Pit Ponies*, and the UK release title was *Escape from the Dark*, which makes it sound like a horror film.

The Many Adventures of Winnie the Pooh

RELEASED BY BUENA VISTA ON March 11, 1977, Technicolor. Producer: Wolfgang Reitherman. Director: Wolfgang Reitherman, John Lounsbery. Story: Larry Clemmons, Vance Gerry, Ken Anderson, Ted Berman, Ralph Wright, Xavier Atencio, Julius Svendsen, Eric Cleworth. *Blustery Day* Story Supervision: Winston Hibler. Animators: Hal King, Milt Kahl, Ollie Johnston, John Lounsbery, Frank Thomas, Eric Cleworth, Art Stevens, Cliff Nordberg, Eric Larson, Gary Goldman, John Sibley, Don Bluth, Walt Stanchfield, Hal Ambro, Burny Mattinson, John Pomeroy, Chuck Williams, Richard Sebast, Dale Baer, Fred Hellmich, Bill Keil, Andrew Gaskill. Layout: Don Griffith, Basil Davidovich, Joe Hale, Dale Barnhart, Sylvia Roemer based on the books written by A.A. Milne, illustrated by Ernest H. Shepard, published in the U.S.A. and Canada by E.P. Dutton & Company, Inc. Background: Al Dempster, Bill Layne, Art Riley, Ann Guenther. Production Manager: Don Duckwall. Sound: Robert O. Cook, Herb Taylor. Film Editors: Tom Acosta, James Melton. Music Editor: Evelyn Kennedy. Assistant Directors: Ed Hansen, Dan Alguire, Richard Rich. Running time: 74 minutes.

Songs: "Winnie the Pooh," "Up, Down, Touch the Ground," "Rumbly in My Tumbly," "(I'm Just a) Little Black Raincloud," "Mind Over Matter," "What a Rather Blustery Day," "The Wonderful Thing About Tiggers," "Heffelumps and Woozles," "The Rain, Rain, Rain Came Down, Down, Down," "Hip Hip Pooh-ray" Music and Lyrics by Richard M. Sherman and Robert B. Sherman. Scored and Conducted by Buddy Baker.

Cast: Sebastian Cabot (Narrator), Junius Matthews (Rabbit), Howard Morris (Gopher), Ralph Wright (Eeyore), Clint Howard (Roo), Jon Walmsley

(Christopher Robin), Barbara Luddy (Kanga), John Fiedler (Piglet), Hal Smith (Owl), Bruce Reitherman (Christopher Robin), Timothy Turner (Christopher Robin), Dori Whitaker (Roo), Sterling Holloway (Winnie the Pooh), Paul Winchell (Tigger), Thurl Ravenscroft (Singer).

The Narrator begins telling the story of Winnie the Pooh, which leads to the "Winnie the Pooh" song introducing the various animal characters.

The Narrator explains that Pooh lived in a house with the name of Sanders above the door. Pooh stands at his mirror and tries to think and then sings "Up, Down, Touch the Ground" to remind him that he needs to do his stoutness exercises in order to build up an appetite and eat more honey.

Pooh gets his appetite but is sad to discover that he is desperately low on honey and he decides to follow a bee to a honey tree. Pooh climbs it while singing "Rumbly in My Tumbly."

Unfortunately, he loses his footing and drops down to the ground, hitting many branches on his way.

Pooh decides to see his friend Christopher Robin, who is in the process of nailing Eeyore's tail back on.

Pooh asks Christopher Robin for a balloon and also to help take him to a muddy place in order to roll around in and disguise himself as a little black raincloud.

Christopher Robin helps Pooh fly up to the beehive and they start singing "Little Black Raincloud." Pooh gets up to the beehive and reaches in with his paw for a large amount of honey. He places it in his mouth, taking in a number of bees in the process.

He starts shooting bees out of his mouth, but soon Pooh's disguise is dripping off and Pooh becomes the victim of many bee stings, being chased as the balloon deflates.

Pooh and Christopher Robin escape just in time by jumping into the mud puddle and covering themselves with an open umbrella.

Pooh's next plan is to visit his friend Rabbit for some honey. Rabbit is stingy with his honey until he gives up and offers Pooh some honey, which Pooh eats all up.

Unfortunately, all that eating has caused Pooh's belly to enlarge and he gets stuck as he tries to exit Rabbit's house. Owl comes to visit Pooh during his predicament as Rabbit scampers off to get help from Christopher Robin.

Owl is not of any particular help but he is soon displaced by Gopher, a character who claims, rightfully so, that "He's not in the book." Gopher says that he can dig Pooh out in three days.

Soon, Christopher Robin, Rabbit, and Eeyore arrive to try to pull Pooh out, but it's no use - Pooh's stuck. Christopher Robin suggests pushing Pooh back, but Rabbit is not having any of it. Unfortunately, Rabbit has to deal with viewing Pooh's rear end, but he redesigns it into a moose-hunting trophy.

Kanga and Roo stop by to offer Pooh a gift of honeysuckles, which makes Pooh sneeze and ruins Rabbit's decorating.

The Narrator describes the passage of time as Pooh remains stuck in Rabbit's hole. One night, Gopher comes out of the ground to have a midnight snack. He offers some to Pooh, until Rabbit stops it and pounds down a "Don't Feed the Bear" sign in front of the bear.

Eventually, Pooh loses a little weight and Rabbit budges Pooh, so everyone arrives to help tug Pooh out of the hole while they sing "Mind Over Matter."

The sheer force of pulling and pushing Pooh force him out of the hole like a gunshot and almost out of the book. Pooh lands in a high tree, which drives all the bees away. He is soon eating all the honey within arm's length. He sings "Rumbly in My Tumbly" again as we go on to another tale.

An east wind and a west wind are blowing and Pooh decides to visit his thoughtful spot while singing "What a Rather Blustery Day." When he arrives, he gets another visit from Gopher who warns that Pooh should leave because "it's Windsday."

Instead of leaving, Pooh decides to go visit his friend Piglet, who lives in a house with a sign that says "Trespassers Will," which is short for Trespassers William, according to Piglet.

Pooh visits with Piglet, but the sheer force of the winds causes Piglet to fly. His scarf unravels and Pooh flies Piglet like a kite. This sight is witnessed by Kanga, Roo, Eeyore, and Rabbit, and soon Pooh and Piglet fly up to Owl's house.

Owl lets Pooh and Piglet in and they all agree that it is a very blustery day outside. The winds make Owl's house rock back and forth, causing a mess when they try to sit down to eat a little honey.

Eventually the tree with Owl's house topples over, with everyone in it. Christopher Robin, Rabbit, and Eeyore stop by to see what happened and Eeyore says that he will find a new house for Owl. While Eeyore was gone, Owl kept prattling on for over 20 pages.

By this time, Pooh was back home in bed and he hears a growling and a knocking at his door and lets the new sound in. The new sound turns out to be Tigger, who introduces himself and sings his theme song, "The Wonderful Things About Tiggers."

Tigger says that he's the only one, but Pooh says there is another when he sees Tigger's reflection in the mirror. Next Tigger says he's hungry and he eats some of Pooh's honey, but realizes he doesn't like it.

Tigger warns Pooh about Heffalumps and Woozles, creatures who eat honey, and then bounces off, again singing his theme song.

Pooh is worried and marches around with his pop gun keeping on guard from the Heffalumps and Woozles. Eventually Pooh falls asleep and has a wild dream about Heffalumps and Woozles as their song is sung.

Pooh finally wakes up from his nightmare only to find the wind has changed to rain as the song "The Rain, Rain, Rain Came Down, Down, Down" plays in the background.

Piglet is having troubles of his own, as his house is filling up with water and flooding. Piglet manages to put a note in a bottle for someone to rescue him.

Meanwhile, Pooh gets stuck in one of his honey pots and floats downstream. The rest of the other animals float over to Christopher Robin's house, as it was built on higher ground.

Roo finds Piglet's message in the bottle. Christopher Robin reads it and sends Owl out to rescue Piglet. He ends up rescuing Piglet and Pooh, but not until after they go over a waterfall.

Everyone arrives at Christopher Robin's and he gives a hero party for Pooh's rescue of Piglet. At the party, Eeyore shows up with the house that he found. Everyone follows Eeyore to the house he proclaims as Owl's new house. It turns out that it is actually Piglet's house.

Rather than upsetting everyone, Piglet gives his house to Owl without issue, and Pooh saves the day for the crying Piglet by offering to let Piglet move in with him.

Pooh suggests making the one-hero party into a two-hero party, and everyone celebrates by singing "Hip Hip Pooh-ray," except Gopher who is sent down his gopher hole and not seen again for the remainder of the film.

After a brief linking narration, Pooh is back at his thinking spot only to be bounced on by Tigger. Tigger has made an annoying habit of bouncing on everyone and bounces on Piglet and then Rabbit.

Rabbit is not amused and wishes that Tigger would stop bouncing. Tigger says that bouncing is what Tiggers do best and sings his theme song about it.

Rabbit calls a meeting with Pooh and Piglet to protest Tigger's bouncing. Piglet agrees, but Pooh sleeps throughout the meeting. Ultimately, Rabbit decides to take Tigger on a long hike and lose him in the forest in order to take his bounce away.

The next day, the four go out on a hike and soon they leave Tigger behind by hiding in a hollow tree.

Soon they hear Tigger calling out for everyone, and then he bounces away. Rabbit leads Pooh and Piglet home, but he has lost his way and the three travel in circles as it gets darker and darker.

They keep ending up at the same pit and Pooh suggests that if they try to find the pit, they might find home. Rabbit thinks that this idea is ridiculous and sets off to prove him wrong.

Later, Pooh is hungry and his honey is calling him. He and Piglet go home by following his tummy. When the two get back home, they are bounced upon by Tigger, who has been home for quite some time.

Tigger asks where Rabbit is, and Pooh and Piglet say that he's still lost. Tigger offers to go back in the forest to rescue him.

Rabbit is scared by the various noises frogs and other creatures make, but suddenly Tigger bounces on Rabbit, rescuing him and taking him home.

Winter comes and Roo is waiting for Tigger to take him out to play, while Kanga tells Roo to be patient. Tigger finally shows up and Kanga advises him to have Roo back in time for his nap.

Rabbit is calmly skating on the icy pond when Tigger goes out and joins him. At first he skates fine, but then crashes into Rabbit.

Tigger and Roo go farther into the woods when Roo asks if Tiggers can climb trees. Tigger says that that's what Tiggers do best. He is able to bounce up, but getting down is another problem as Tigger hangs on for dear life from the top of the tree.

Pooh and Piglet are following tracks around in the snow. They hear a howl and they run and hide. Pooh says it's a jagular, but it's really Tigger and Roo calling down to them.

Roo's alright, but Tigger's stuck and Pooh and Piglet get Kanga, Rabbit, and Christopher Robin to help. They catch Roo first in Christopher Robin's splayed coat, but Tigger is too frightened to jump down.

Rabbit doesn't want Tigger to come down unless he promises not to bounce again. The Narrator finally helps Tigger down by rotating the book and he slides down the letters.

Tigger is grateful and decides to bounce, but Rabbit reminds him of his promise. Tigger is sad and walks away with his head hung low.

Everyone else is sad, but Rabbit is gloating and happy. Rabbit has to finally agree that he likes the old Tigger best and Tigger bounces him immediately, but instead of being mad, Tigger gets Rabbit to bounce himself and everyone else joins in.

Tigger sings his song one more time and then we come to the end of the book, where Christopher Robin and Winnie the Pooh must say goodbye because Christopher Robin has to go off to school.

Before he leaves, he has one final conversation with Pooh about doing just nothing. He also makes Pooh promise not to forget him. We close with a live-action stuffed Pooh winks at the camera.

Walt Disney originally envisioned Winnie the Pooh as a feature film in 1961 but wisely thought against it, realizing that Pooh was not a known quantity in the US (although Shirley Temple did air a marionette version on her *Shirley Temple Storybook Theatre* TV series). Instead, he decided to introduce American audiences to Pooh with a series of featurettes, the three of which comprise this movie with some new linking footage and a new ending to round out the story and make it a more cohesive feature.

As such, the film is really *Winnie the Pooh and the Honey Tree* (1966), *Winnie the Pooh and the Blustery Day* (1968), and *Winnie the Pooh and Tigger, Too!* (1974). Each of these had aired several times previously on TV as half-hour specials before being released in this feature.

Of course, due to Walt's keen foresight, Pooh has gone on to become the most popular Disney character since Mickey Mouse.

On the DVD, there is a documentary discussing the four children's books written by A.A. Milne.

Walt Disney Archivist Dave Smith says that Walt got the idea because of his two daughter's love for the stories when they were read to them as children.

Animators X. Atencio, Ollie Johnston, Frank Thomas, and Burny Mattinson talk about how Walt wanted to make the feature film with Wolfgang Reitherman directing.

The Sherman Brothers were brought in again to write new songs for the Pooh films. Walt wanted the songs to move the story along and be very simple. The brothers sing a few of them. Buddy Baker composed the score to match the characters.

Walt instructed the artists to try to stay as close to Ernest Shepherd's drawings as possible when animating and model sheets were created for the characters and also the backgrounds.

Some people disagreed with using Gopher as a replacement for Piglet, but they got away with it by having the character say that he's not in the book.

Paul Winchell, the voice of Tigger talks about voicing with Sterling Holloway as Pooh and Jon Walmsley talks about them and Jon's voicing of Christopher Robin. Voice artists Howard Morris, Ralph Wright, Sebastian Cabot, John Fiedler and Hal Smith are also mentioned.

The "Heffelumps and Woozles" segment, while well executed, pales in comparison to its inspiration of "Pink Elephants on Parade" from *Dumbo* (1941).

Originally, for each individual short, Christopher Robin was voiced by a different actor. For this film, Timothy Turner re-recorded all of Christopher Robin's lines so that the character's voice would sound consistent.

There have been many Pooh cartoons since and even a few theatrical features, such as *The Tigger Movie* (2000), *Piglet's Big Movie* (2003), *Pooh's Heffalumps Movie* (2005) and *Winnie the Pooh* (2011) and many direct-to-video films.

Winnie the Pooh and a Day for Eeyore (1983), which is included on the DVD as a bonus feature, was the first featurette to follow this film. It was also the first to feature the beginnings of a new voice cast as Narrator Sebastian Cabot passed away shortly after the release of the Pooh feature film.

The Rescuers

RELEASED BY BUENA VISTA ON June 19, 1977, Technicolor. Producer: Wolfgang Reitherman. Executive Producer: Ron Miller. Director: Wolfgang Reitherman, John Lounsbery, Art Stevens. Story: Larry Clemmons, Ken Anderson, Vance Gerry, Ted Berman, Burny Mattinson, Frank Thomas, David Michener, Fred Lucky, Dick Sebast suggested by *The Rescuers* and *Miss Bianca* by Margery Sharp. Directing Animators: Ollie Johnston, Frank Thomas, Milt Kahl, Don Bluth. Character Animation: John Pomeroy, Andy Gaskill, Art Stevens, Chuck Harvey, Bob McCrea, Cliff Nordberg, Gary Goldman, Dale Baer, Ron Clements, Bill Hajee, Glen Keane. Effects Animation: Jack Buckley, Dorse A. Lanpher, Ted Kierscey, James L. George, Dick Lucas. Key Assistant Animators: Stan Green, Chuck Williams, Walt Stanchfield, Dale Oliver, Harry Hester, Dave Sudling, Leroy Cross. Assistant Directors: Jeff Patch, Richard Rich. Art Director: Don Griffith. Layout: Joe Hale, Tom Lay, Guy Deel, Sylvia Roemer. Color Styling: Al Dempster. Background Painting: Jim Coleman, Ann Guenther, Daniela Bielecka. Titles: Melvin Shaw, Eric Larson, Burny Mattinson. Production Manager: Don Duckwall. Sound Editors: Herb Taylor, James Melton, Jim Koford. Music Editor: Evelyn Kennedy. Music Score Composed and Conducted by Artie Butler. Assistant Animators: Randy Cartwright, Ed Gombert, Tad Stones. Character Animation: Glen Keane, John Pomeroy. Animators: Heidi Guedel, Ron Husband. Directing Animators: Frank Thomas, Ollie Johnston, Milt Kahl. Running time: 76 minutes.

Songs: "The Journey," "Rescue Aid Society," "Tomorrow is Another Day" Carol Connors, Ayn Robbins. "Someone's Waiting for You" Music by Sammy Fain. Lyrics by Carol Connors, Ayn Robbins. Songs sung by Shelby Flint. "The U.S. Air Force" by Robert Crawford, "For Penny's a Jolly Good Fellow."

Cast: Bob Newhart (Bernard), Eva Gabor (Miss Bianca), Geraldine Page (Madame Medusa), Joe Flynn (Mr. Snoops), Jeanette Nolan (Ellie Mae), Pat Buttram (Luke), Jim Jordan (Orville), John McIntire (Rufus), Michelle Stacy (Penny), Bernard Fox (The Chairman), Larry Clemmons (Gramps), James MacDonald (Evinrude), George Lindsey (Rabbit), Bill McMillan (TV Announcer), Dub Taylor (Digger), John Fiedler (Owl), Ruth Buzzi (German Mouse).

Penny is being held captive and drops a message in a bottle into the water as "The Journey" is sung. The bottle is discovered by two mice, who take it to the United Nations Building where a meeting of the Rescue Aid Society is being held. Mice from all over the world have traveled via the suitcases of their human companions to attend this meeting.

Bernard the mouse custodian greets all the various mouse diplomats. The meeting is called to order and mention is made of the first mouse rescuer, Euripides Mouse, who took a thorn out of a lion's paw.

The group sings their anthem, "The Rescue Aid Society." Even Bernard is singing. Finally, Bianca the Hungarian representative arrives late, but singing the anthem.

Bernard is instructed to bring in a comb to use as a ladder to scale the bottle and open it. He almost decapitates other mice with his clumsiness. As he climbs the ladder he notices that it had 13 steps, but it's dismissed as superstitious nonsense.

Bernard lassos the bottle's cork and removes it. He gets inside the bottle and pushes the message out. It is from Morningside Orphanage and says that Penny is in terrible trouble, but the message is somewhat garbled.

Bianca asks to take the job, but she is frowned upon because usually it's a man's job. It is decided that she will have a co-agent go with her and everyone volunteers, but Bianca ends up taking Bernard, who is only the janitor.

Bernard and Bianca take a bus to the Morningside Orphanage, going through the zoo as a shortcut. Bernard is nervous as he's never been on a mission before. He stirs up a lion and they decide instead to avoid the zoo.

At the orphanage they find Penny's things, but no Penny. They attract the attention of an old cat named Rufus who tells them that Penny ran away.

Rufus remembers that Penny was sitting on the bed, depressed that she hadn't been adopted yet and how she had been constantly overlooked. After Penny had left, the police look for her, to no avail.

He reveals that a weird lady and her partner who run a sleazy pawn shop did look for her once. Bernard and Bianca go to Medusa's Pawn Shop. At the shop, they find a book that belonged to Penny.

The phone rings and Bernard and Bianca hide. It's Mr. Snoops. Madame Medusa is excited because she thinks they've found the diamond they're looking for, but it's really Mr. Snoops telling Medusa that he caught Penny dropping bottles into the water.

Medusa is upset and packs a bag to join them and get the job done right. Bernard and Bianca get into her suitcase and take the trip as well, or so they think. As Medusa takes a wild turn, the bag is thrown from the car.

Fortunately, the two mice know that Medusa is going to Devil's Bayou. They go to the airport to take a flight on Albatross Air Service. The flight they are going to take is Flight 13, which makes Bernard nervous.

An albatross is trying to land and is radioing in. No one is there to receive the message, so Bernard gives him clearance. The albatross' landing is very poor. He reveals himself to be Orville and he will be flying the mice.

As the mice climb the ramp to board Orville, Bernard discovers that there are 13 steps. After a somewhat difficult take-off, Orville and the mice are finally on their way. As they fly, "Tomorrow is Another Day" is sung.

At Devil's Bayou, Penny tries another escape, but Medusa sends her two alligators, named Nero and Brutus, to capture her.

Medusa tells Snoops to send up flares as she goes on her swamp-mobile to find Penny. The flares interfere with Orville's progress and the three fall from the sky.

They land at the house of Luke and Ellie Mae, two bayou mice. Luke loves to drink and he feeds a goodly amount into Bernard. With everyone safe, Orville is on his way back, but he encounters Medusa and her swamp mobile in the process.

Ellie Mae would love to give Madame Medusa a few whacks. The four mice see that Nero has caught Penny, who has tried to run away again.

Ellie Mae guides Bernard and Bianca to Evinrude, a mosquito who uses his powers to propel a leaf like a speedboat to get them to Penny. They travel until Evinrude poops out.

Snoops welcomes the alligators and Penny back. He sends out flares to Medusa instructing her to come back. Medusa asks why Snoops let her try to escape again and Snoops blames it on the alligator.

Medusa desperately wants the diamond to make her rich. It is in a tight spot that only Penny or some other small child can retrieve. They have tried already, but the tide keeps coming in and cramping their progress.

Meanwhile, Nero and Brutus smell the perfume on Bianca and capture Bernard, but Bianca rescues him and they escape from harm's way in Medusa's pipe organ, or so they think. The alligators play the organ and the mice are blown out of the various pipes, but they are still not captured.

Medusa comes in to stop the noise and screams when she encounters the mice, but they escape to the safety of Evinrude's speedboat leaf. The mice are almost ready to give up, but decide to continue as they would be letting down the Rescue Aid Society.

Medusa insists that Penny get the diamond. Penny wants to get back to the orphanage to get adopted, and Medusa says that no one would ever want to adopt a homely girl like Penny. Penny cries as "Someone's Waiting for You" is sung and then says her prayers, hoping that someone finds her bottle.

Bernard and Bianca show up to tell her that they got the bottle. Penny asks if they brought anyone bigger, and the mice say no.

Penny explains what has been happening and does a funny imitation of Medusa. Bernard tells Evinrude to get Ellie Mae for help, but Evinrude is chased by bats in the process.

Ellie Mae is already working on assembling help and she calls together the various bayou animals while waiting for word from Evinrude.

Medusa and Snoops take Penny back to the black hole where the diamond is and they send her down in a bucket. This time they take away her teddy bear to get her to do it. Bernard and Bianca go down with her.

They discover that the Devil's Eye diamond is buried inside an old skull, near a most perilous location where the tide comes in quickly. As they try to pry out the diamond, the tide keeps coming in higher and higher. They finally crack the skull with a pirate sword located nearby and dislodge the diamond.

Penny is brought up before she drowns and Medusa gets her diamond, refusing to share it with anyone including Snoops, who calls her a double-crosser.

Meanwhile, Evinrude gets through and gives the word to Ellie Mae and the other animals and they go to attack Medusa and Snoops. They capture Nero and Brutus and set off Medusa's fireworks while Penny and the mice escape on the swampmobile, but Medusa is not far behind and is waterskiing behind them. Nero and Brutus escape and become her water skis, but our heroes escape Snoops and Medusa, who is now being attacked by her traitorous alligators.

Bernard, Bianca, and Penny get back home and Penny finally gets her wish of being adopted and credits the Rescue Aid Society on a TV interview.

The Rescue Aid Society gets another call and Bianca volunteers herself and Bernard to go out again.

This was the most enjoyable of the three animated features made during the 1970s at Disney, but it would be the last hurrah of Disney's old guard of animation as many animators retired with this film. A few stayed on for *The Fox and the Hound* (1981), but inner turmoil at Disney, including a walk-out, disrupted the harmony that had existed since Walt's death.

Walt Disney suggested this as a possible animated feature back in 1962.

The design of the Rufus character was based on animator Ollie Johnston.

Jim Jordan is best-known as the voice of radio's Fibber McGee.

Joe Flynn recorded the voice of Mr. Snoops shortly before his death in 1974. This was his last work for Disney.

There is a short DVD documentary about villains, but it doesn't give any information about this film. The film was re-released in 2012 on DVD and Blu-ray, along with its 1990 sequel, *The Rescuers Down Under*. The 2012 release features an unreleased song called "Peoplitis" and additional storyboard ideas that didn't make it into the final film, including one featuring a bear character.

Cruella De Vil from *101 Dalmatians* (1961) was originally designed to be the villain, but this was changed.

Louis Prima recorded material for this film, but he lapsed into a coma during production and his contribution was left unused. He died in 1978.

Originally, an image of a topless woman appeared in a window as Bianca and Bernard flew by. It appeared on the original VHS tape releaser, but has since been removed on all subsequent releases.

This was a highly successful film for Disney, grossing $16 million domestically and $32.1 million internationally. It was reissued in 1983.

Herbie Goes To Monte Carlo

RELEASED BY BUENA VISTA ON June 24, 1977, Technicolor. Producer: Ron Miller. Director: Vincent McEveety. Writers: Arthur Alsberg, Don Nelson based on characters created by Gordon Buford. Art Directors: John B. Mansbridge, Perry Ferguson. Editor: Cotton Warburton, A.C.E. Set Decorator: Frank R. McKelvy. Special Effects: Eustace Lycett, Art Cruickshank, A.S.C., Danny Lee. Matte Artist: Peter S. Ellenshaw. Additional Photography: Charles F. Wheeler, A.S.C. Sound Supervision: Herb Taylor. Sound Mixer: Hal Etherington. Unit Production Manager: Don Guest. First Assistant Director: Paul "Tiny" Nichols. Second Assistant Director: Win Phelps. Costumes: Chuck Keehne, Emily Sundby. Make-up: Robert J. Schiffer. Hair Stylist: La Rue Matheron. Sound Editor: Raymond Craddock. Music Editor: Evelyn Kennedy. French Production Staff: Production Supervisor: Robert Velin. Production Manager: Michel Wyn. Unit Manager – 1st Unit: Jacques Perrier. Unit Manager – 2nd Unit: Jean Lara. Assistant Director: Marc Monet. Thanks to the City of Paris and the Principality of Monaco for their Cooperation in the Making of this Film. Second Unit Director: Arthur J. Vitarelli. Music:

Frank De Vol. Director of Photography: Leonard J. South, A.S.C. Associate Producer: Jan Williams. Set Dresser: Kurt V. Hulett. Assistant Property Master: Bob McLing. Sound Editors: George Fredrick, Ben Hendricks, Bill Wylie. Special Effects Foreman: Hans Metz. Special Effects Technician: Mike Reedy. Digital Asset Manager Remastering: Diane Wright. Stunt Drivers: Kevin N. Johnston, Jesse Wayne. Stunt Coordinator: Dick Warlock. Camera Operator: Jacques Mironneau. First Assistant Camera: Reggie Newkirk. First Assistant Camera, Second Unit: Louis Niemeyer. Assistant Editor: Barney Cabral. Picture Car Coordinator: Mario Simon. Dialogue Coach: Frawley Becker. Helicopter Pilot: Charles A. Tamburro. Running time: 105 minutes.

Cast: Dean Jones (Jim Douglas), Don Knotts (Wheely Applegate), Julie Sommars (Diane Darcy), Jacques Marin (Inspector Bouchet), Roy Kinnear (Quincey), Bernard Fox (Max), Eric Braeden (Bruno Von Stickle), Xavier Saint Macary (Detective Fontenoy), Francois Lalande (Monsieur Ribeaux), Alan Caillou (Emile), Laurie Main (Duval), Mike Kulcsar (Claude), Johnny Haymer (Race Official), Stanley Brock (Taxi Driver), Gerard Jugnot (Waiter), Jean-Marie Proslier (Doorman), Tom McCorry (Showroom M.C.), Lloyd Nelson (Mechanic), Jean-Jacques Moreau (Truck Driver), Yveline Briere (Girl Friend), Sebastien Floche (French Tourist), Madeleine Damien (Old Woman), Alain Janey (Man at Café), Raoul Delfosse (Police Captain), Ed Marcus (Exhibit M.C.), Richard Warlock, Kevin Johnston, Carey Loftin, Bill Erickson, Gerald Brutsche, Bob Harris, Jesse Wayne, Reg Parton (The Drivers), Josiane Balasko, Herbie (Itself), Andre Penvern (French Policeman).

Jim Douglas is car racing again and he enters a road race Monte Carlo with Herbie the VW. He is driving around with his friend, Wheeler. They ask directions from a French policeman on how to get to the race. When the policeman discovers that Herbie the VW is going to race, he laughs, prompting Herbie to squirt oil on the policeman's shoes.

Meanwhile, a magnificent diamond is being transported into a local museum by a number of top security guards.

At the race, Bruno Von Stickle and the other racers are being introduced. When Jim Douglas is introduced as driving Herbie, the people laugh.

Jim and Wheely reveal that they haven't won a race or even raced at all in the last 12 years. Bruno makes fun of Herbie along with everyone else.

The diamond is now in the museum, with the finest security system in place. It consists of a six-sided cage that descends from the ceiling if the diamond is disturbed in any way. Then the floor is activated as the curator and the guards leave the room. The curator says that the merest cigar ash will set off the alarm.

Two crooks named Quincey and Max are already prepared to take the diamond and are using an elaborate set of computerized items to deactivate the alarms. They easily steal the jewel, and at the critical time where Quincey is lifting the diamond with a claw, Max's watch goes off and he almost drops the diamond on the floor.

Quincey loses his patience with the claw and just grabs the diamond with his hand, setting off the alarm. The cage does not come all the way down as it is caught by wires that the thieves had strung up, and so Quincey and Max flee the scene.

Security is now frisking everyone in the area and so Max secretly slips the diamond into Herbie's gas tank.

Inspector Bouchet comes into town and the museum to check for clues and gets trapped in the cage that is designed for burglars.

The qualifying race is about to begin and Herbie falls in love with car #7, a light blue Lancia race car driven by Diane Darcy. The race begins and Herbie drives at top speed to catch up with #7. Herbie starts flirting by flipping his sun roof and waving his wipers and playing romantic music on the radio.

Herbie drives backwards, weaving back and forth to attract the other car's attention. Diane stops her car, angry about Herbie's antics. Diane feels that Jim and Wheely just doesn't want a woman in the race, which they claim is not true.

There is another qualifying race against Bruno, who will not let Herbie pass. Everything is fine until #7 is in Herbie's view and he starts gushing over her again.

Quincey and Max attend the car show in order to get their diamond back. They need to retrieve it or their leader XX (Double X) will cause them no end of troubles. They try to take the diamond while a short film is being shown about the car route, but before they can grab the diamond Herbie sees #7 yet again and leaves to be with her.

Quincey and Max keep backing up in the dark to try to find Herbie and in the process knock over the trophies for the race. When the film ends, Jim and Wheely wonder where Herbie has gone.

Herbie meets up with #7 again and flips his doors and trunk to try to attract her attention. Two men with a mirror walk by and Herbie notices that he's gotten filthy, so he leaves #7 and takes a dip in a nearby fountain to clean off. He then goes back to #7 with some flowers to resume his courtship. A waiter gets distracted watching the car's antics and upsets a couple dining by not paying attention to what he is doing and drops food on them.

Herbie and #7 go off together and Diane and Jim show up to look for their missing cars. Eventually they find their cars together on a passing boat, taking the equivalent of a romantic cruise.

Jim asks Diane out for dinner to explain everything, but she refuses. Later, Herbie is back at home and Quincey and Max make attempts to get the diamond back, but Herbie escapes before they can retrieve it.

It is another qualifying round the next day, but Herbie is not even trying. He's in last place. Jim makes threats to speed up, but Herbie ignores him until he sees #7 again and then he speeds up and wins the qualifying round in record time. Bruno is there to challenge.

Diane's car finally qualifies as well, with Herbie swooning on the sidelines. Jim congratulates her, but Diane is still disinterested in him and wants him to stay away.

Later, Quincey and Max try to follow Herbie in their car as Jim and Wheely panic because they feel that the thieves are killers. Herbie escapes through a narrow pipe that Quincey and Max can't fit into.

Wheely feels that the supposed killers were thugs hired by Diane. Jim goes and checks up on this and Diane angrily throws things at Jim for his accusations and is insulted that he would even suspect such a thing.

Jim and Wheely go to see Inspector Bouchet and ask if they can put Herbie in protective custody so that nobody will mess with him. It turns out that Bouchet is in cahoots with Max and Quincey, unbeknownst to his assistant Fontenoy, who drives Herbie to a secret place that even Bouchet doesn't know about. Bouchet tells Max and Quincey to be there the next day, when Herbie is filling up with fuel.

At the race the next day, Diane shows up to Jim to apologize for throwing all of those items and Jim apologizes for making accusations and wishes her good luck in the race.

Diane goes to her car and it doesn't start. Jim comes over to check it out and blames it on Herbie, but Diane doesn't want to hear about it. Jim and Wheely talk to #7 to help the car get over Herbie, but Diane gets angrier and feels that Jim and Wheely are crazy.

The race begins but Jim and Wheely aren't in it as they don't have Herbie and they watch the other contestants, including #7, start the race.

Finally, Fontenoy drives up in an armored car with Herbie inside. Wheely is angry, but they decide to press on and fill the gas tank with Quincey and Max at the pump, but Fontenoy says that this is not necessary because he filled the tank already.

Quincey, Max, and Bouchet are upset that they have missed yet another opportunity to retrieve the diamond from Herbie's gas tank.

Jim and Wheely are having trouble getting Herbie to race, so perform another "reverse psychology" pep talk that they gave #7 to make him race and it works. They tell Herbie to get over #7.

Fontenoy tells Bouchet that he has notified the Monte Carlo police to go over Herbie once he arrives, causing Bouchet to choke on his drink.

Herbie is racing, but still driving erratically. At one point Herbie is submerged under the water of a small lake with only Wheely's head visible, freaking out two men sitting on the lake in a small boat. Herbie finally crosses the lake and resumes the race, passing car after car and trying to get into first place. Reaching Bruno, Herbie is unable to pass, but at one crucial turn, Herbie manages to get ahead.

The race continues over the Alps. Quincey and Max fly in a helicopter to get in front of the cars in order to make another attempt at getting the diamond from Herbie. They put up a detour sign designed only for Herbie.

Jim and Wheely follow the detour and stop to try to figure out where they are. They become stranded on a narrow road at the top of a high cliff. Wheely discovers an echo which sets off an avalanche, pelting Herbie with tons of large rocks and boulders and burying them in the process.

Quincey and Max show up with a gun and direct Jim and Wheely to get out of Herbie. Herbie proceeds to squirt water in the thieves' eyes.

Herbie starts honking his horn, which causes another avalanche and covers the villains' car. Herbie then travels backwards to safety and back into the race. Jim now hears a knocking in the gas tank, but Wheely says to ignore it and keep racing.

Herbie comes up to Bruno again and he still tries to keep Herbie from passing, but Herbie is making too much noise and pulls off to the side of the road. Jim says that there is still a clunking sound. Wheely reaches in and pulls out the diamond thinking that it's just some old quartz. He almost hurls it away before Jim stops him.

While they look over the diamond, Quincey and Max show up again to take the stone but Herbie knocks the gun out of their hands and the four engage in a tussle, resulting in the crooks falling into a small pit. Jim and Wheely tie the crooks up and resume the race. They pass every car except #7, which they see submerged in water on the side of the road. Herbie refuses to stop until Jim says that Wheely had told Herbie lies about #7. With that, Herbie turns around and helps #7 out of the water and Jim and Wheely help a nearly-drowned Diane out of the car.

Diane finally sees it but doesn't believe it as Herbie hauls #7 out of the water in front of her. Herbie and #7 hold doors. Wheely wants to resume the race, but Herbie is not having it. Diane speaks to Herbie and tells him to go win the race for Jim, Wheely, and #7.

Herbie won't let Wheely back into the car until he gets down on his knees and apologizes for lying, which he does, and they finally resume the race.

Bouchet tells his superior Emile about what is going on and blames Fontenoy for what has happened.

Herbie is tailing Bruno again and once again he will not let Herbie pass. Herbie takes matters into his own hands…er…wheels and drives on the ceiling of the tunnel in order to finally pass Bruno and win the race. Bruno cannot believe it.

Jim and Wheely get the trophy and reveal that they have won a race for the 20th time and the first time in 12 years. Bouchet shows up to congratulate Herbie and Jim offers him the diamond. But before Bouchet can grab it, Fontenoy shows up with the museum curator and returns the diamond to him.

Fontenoy also reveals that only one man knew all the combinations for the alarm system, and that is Bouchet. Caught, Bouchet pulls a gun and takes the diamond, but before he can escape Herbie lifts his hood and knocks the gun away.

Fontenoy cuffs Bouchet, and Jim returns the diamond to the curator. The curator gives Herbie a kiss and he blushes a bright red.

Later, Jim escorts Diane to the curb after a nice dinner and the valet is dumbfounded as he says that he saw the cars drive off together without any drivers. Jim and Diane hop into a taxi and ask to be taken to the most romantic spot in Monte Carlo. There they find Herbie and #7 as well as Wheely and his new date.

This was Dean Jones' last feature film during the post-Walt, pre-Eisner period, though he did return for the five episodes of the *Herbie, the Love Bug* TV mini-series in 1981.

It is more than obvious that Disney was inspired by *The Return of the Pink Panther* (1975) in the making of this film. The inspectors in this film have strong French accents and the younger of the two inspectors is a bumbler in true Peter Sellers fashion.

The film is a pretty good entry in the Herbie series, but one thing that almost ruins it is Julie Sommars' acting ability, or lack thereof. She is immediately whiny and annoying and expounds about women's rights at length, making it hard to be sympathetic for her, especially when her car is supposedly stolen and when Jim's character says nothing negative about her race-driving abilities or indeed anything else negative about her, yet she overreacts anyway.

The gas cap on Herbie was totally fake, but necessary for the plot point of hiding the diamond. This is the only Herbie movie with this fake gas tank opening.

Jim Douglas had married Carol Bennett at the end of *The Love Bug* (1969), but no mention was made of this marriage or possible divorce in this film.

Goodyear was probably a sponsor for this as their tires are prominently displayed on Herbie, and Dean Jones makes mention in one scene of the Goodyear blimp. He also sports a Goodyear logo on his racing clothes.

The film was a box office success, grossing $29 million. It was re-released in 1981.

Pete's Dragon

RELEASED BY BUENA VISTA ON November 3, 1977, Technicolor. Producer: Ron Miller, Jerome Courtland. Director: Don Chaffey. Screenplay: Malcolm Marmorstein based on a story by Seton I. Miller and S. S. Field. Art Directors: John Mansbridge, Jack Martin Smith. Editor: Gordon D. Brenner. Costume Designer: Bill Thomas. Associate Choreographer: Martin Allen. Dance Arrangements: David Baker. Set Decorator: Lucien M. Hafley. Matte Artist: Peter Ellenshaw. Special Effects: Eustace Lycett, Art Cruickshank, A.S.C., Danny Lee. Production Manager: John Bloss. Unit Production Manager: Christopher Seiter. Assistant Director: Ronald R. Grow. Second Assistant Director: John M. Poer. Sound Supervisor: Herb Taylor. Sound Mixer: Frank C. Regula. Stunt Coordinator: John Moio. Costumes: Chuck Keehne, Emily Sundby. Make-up: Robert J. Schiffer. Hair Stylist: La Rue Matheron. Sound Editor: Raymond Craddock. Animation Editor: James Melton. Music Editor: Evelyn Kennedy. Elliott Created by Ken Anderson. Animation Director: Don Bluth. Animation Art Director: Ken Anderson. Layout: Joe Hale. Character Animators: John Pomeroy, Gary Goldman, Chuck Harvey, Cliff Nordberg, Ron Clements, Bill Hajee, Randy Cartwright, Glen Keane. Effects Animation: Dorse A. Lanpher. Assistant Animator Supervision: Chuck Williams. Choreography: Onna White. Music Supervised, Arranged and Conducted by Irwin Kostal. Director of Photography: Frank Phillips, A.S.C. Production Designer: John B. Mansbridge. Costume Designer: William Ware Theiss. Assistant Director: Gary LaPoten. DGA Trainee: Kate Tilley. Property Master: Kurt V. Hulett. Assistant Property Master: Bob McLing. Set Constructor: Steve Riley. Laborer: Frank White. Storyboard Artist: Peter Young. Sound Editors: Barney Cabral, George Fredrick, Ben Hendricks, Bill Wylie. Boom Operator: Ronald R. Cooper. Special Effects: David Domeyer. Special Effects Foremen: Hans Metz, Mike Reedy. Visual Effects Supervisor: Art Cruickshank. Matte Artist: John Emerson. Effects Animator: Ted Kierscey. Stunts: Bobby Porter, Jesse Wayne. Gaffer: Carl Boles. Electrician: Dan Delgado. Animator: Dale Baer. In between Artists: Leslie Gorin, Henry Selick. Assistant Animator: Don Hahn. Background Artist, Main Titles: Herbert Ryman. Orchestrator: Irwin Kostal. Transportation Co-Captain: Mario Simon. Production Assistant: Bill Hutchinson. Assistant Choreographer: Jerry Trent. Craft Service: John Wagner. Running time: 129 minutes.

Songs: "The Happiest Home in These Hills," "Boo Bop Bopbop Bop (I Love You, Too)," "I Saw a Dragon," "It's Not Easy," "Passamashloddy," "Candle on the Water," "There' Room for Everyone," "Every Little Piece," "Brazzle Dazzle Day," "Bill of Sale." Music and Lyrics: Al Kasha, Joel Hirschhorn.

Cast: Helen Reddy (Nora), Jim Dale (Dr. Terminus), Mickey Rooney (Lampie), Red Buttons (Hoagy), Shelley Winters (Lena Gogan), Sean Marshall (Pete), Jane Kean (Miss Taylor), Jim Backus (The Mayor), Charles Tyner (Merle), Jeff Conaway (Willie), Gary Morgan (Grover), Cal Bartlett (Paul), Charlie Callas (Elliott's Voice), Walter Barnes (Captain), Al Checco (Fisherman #1), Henry Slate (Fisherman #2), Jack Collins (Fisherman #3), Robert Easton (Store Proprietor), Roger Price (Man with Visor), Robert Foulk (Old Sea Captain), Ben Wrigley (Egg Man), Joe Ross (Cement Man), Rocky Bonifield (Townspeople / Dancer), Patrick Dennis-Leigh (Elderly Townsman), Debbie Fresh (Child / Dancer / Singer), George Golden (White-Haired Councilman), Ken Renard (African-American Townsman), Dinah Anne Rogers (Townsperson), Johnny Silver (Small Townsman), Dennis Stewart (Fisherman), Arthur Tovey (White-Haired Townsman).

A boy named Pete is running away from a group of ruffians called the Gogans, who want to keep him as an orphan. He is aided by an invisible entity that turns out to be a dragon named Elliott. The group sings "The Happiest Home in These Hills" as they try to recapture Pete while he hides.

Invisible Elliott flips several of the Gogans into the mud with his tail. This causes the four to fight with each other and eventually they all fall in. Lena Gogan warns the others that if they don't find Pete, they will have to take over the farm work.

After the four finally leave, Pete and Elliott decide to stay hidden and sleep. The next morning, Eliot finally reveals himself to be a dragon as he and Pete eat some apples from a tree. Pete feeds Elliott and then starts to sing "Boo Bop Bopbop Bop (I Love You, Too)" after Elliott bakes the final apple for Pete.

After singing, they decide to go to Passamaquoddy, a nearby town. Pete warns Elliott to stay out of trouble so that they can stay. Pete says that he has to be completely invisible and nothing else, even though Elliott tries to be partially visible.

Troubles start as they get into town, as a cat gets scared away and a man drops the eggs he is carrying. Elliott ruins a picket fence and also a freshly paved sidewalk. Pete then encounters a strict schoolmarm named Miss Taylor who is not impressed with Pete's antics.

The mayor comes out to praise his town and gets pummeled with the eggs that the man drops. Soon everyone else is complaining to the Mayor about Pete. Pete runs and hides and blames Elliott for everything.

Soon, a drunken man named Lampie emerges. He sees Elliott but is not fazed until he realizes that he is a dragon, at which point he runs into the local saloon to sing "I Saw a Dragon."

While singing, Lampie's daughter Nora comes into the bar looking for him. She continues the singing and dancing and barrel-rolling and later takes Lampie home.

At home, Lampie is still raving about Elliott, but Nora puts him to bed. She goes outside the lighthouse where they live and looks out at the ocean and spies Pete. Pete and Elliott hide in a nearby cave on the beach. Pete is mad at Elliott again, even when Elliott tries to play tic-tac-toe with him.

Nora shows up at the cave and asks what Pete is doing there. She sends Pete home, but discovers that Pete has no home to go to. Nora invites Pete to come back with her to the lighthouse. He tells Nora about the Gogans chasing him and about Elliott by singing "It's Not Easy."

The next day, Lampie wakes up and sees Pete. He starts screaming again about the dragon, but Nora and Pete calm him down.

Dr. Terminus and Hoagy come into town on his boat-shaped car with their medicine show and various medications. They rip up a picket fence and tear the steps off of the mayor's office. The mayor comes out and falls flat on his face.

The people of Passamaquoddy don't like Terminus and want him to leave. He begins to sing "Passamashloddy" in order to win over the people again, but fails when he messes up the name again and again.

Hoagy dons a number of disguises in order to fool the townspeople that he has faith in Terminus and his medicines, and he wins back the people's faith in Terminus.

Nora has a boyfriend named Paul, who is thought to have been lost at sea. Pete offers to take Paul's photo to Elliott in the cave in order to help find him. Nora is glad that Lampie is indulging Pete, but Lampie says again that he really saw a dragon. Nora goes out on the lighthouse by herself and starts singing "Candle on the Water."

Elliott, meanwhile, is warming himself by the fire in the cave. Pete shows up with a brand new suit provided by Nora and shows Elliott the photo of Paul.

Dr. Terminus and Hoagy are still prescribing their medicines. Hoagy is tired of responding to people who ask where Dr. Terminus' horses are. People assume that he and Terminus are rich because they are doctors and if so, where are their horses? It is explained, that the horses were given away to pay off a malpractice suit.

Lampie shows up drunk and asks Terminus about dragons. Terminus suggests Lampie ask a veterinarian. Lampie insists that he go see it, but Terminus is not interested. Hoagy has also been drinking and decides to indulge Lampie. The two are soon at the beach and heading towards the cave to see Elliott.

They find Elliott and start screaming, causing Elliott to scream as well. They all calm down and try to become friends. Hoagy offers Elliott a drink out of his flask, which he accepts. The result makes him a fire-breathing dragon and Lampie and Hoagy flee in terror.

Terminus is still concocting more medicines and Hoagy tells him that the dragon is real. Terminus doesn't believe him.

Nora says that Pete still has to go to school even though he is trying to get out of it. The students barrage Pete with a bunch of questions about Elliott.

Some fishermen see Pete and say that they have not been able to catch fish since he showed up, considering him bad luck. Nora says that they are all superstitious and she sings "There's Room for Everyone."

Miss Taylor reprimands Pete for making her students late. She doesn't want to add Pete to her class because he has no school records or birth certificate, but Nora persuades her to take him in.

The bell starts ringing and Pete says that it's Elliott, but Miss Taylor says that he's lying and cracks his knuckles. Elliott then pulls Miss Taylor's chair away. Miss Taylor decides to give Elliott a whipping, but Elliott stops her, but not before crashing through the schoolhouse wall.

Terminus wonders what happened and the students say that Pete's dragon wrecked the school. Terminus is now more curious about the dragon and wants to use him for his medications and sings "Every Little Piece." Afterwards, Hoagy takes Terminus to the lighthouse where Pete lives and he introduces himself.

He goes up to Pete and offers him five dollars to buy Elliott. Pete says that Elliott is not for sale since he doesn't own Elliott. He says that the dragon came to him because he was a child in need.

Terminus decides to withdraw his offer and just take Elliott, singing "Every Little Piece" again. Nora and Pete blow the foghorn to chase them off.

After they leave, Nora and Lampie offer to let Pete live with them. Pete accepts and sings "Brazzle Dazzle Day" as the three clean the lighthouse.

The Gogans show up to Passamaquoddy in search of Pete. Hoagy runs to Terminus to tell him about the Gogans. Hogan and Terminus race back over to the cave to make sure the Gogans don't get Elliott. Meanwhile, the Gogans find Pete and sing "Bill of Sale," claiming that they are Pete's rightful owners. Elliott disrupts their fun and they all end up in the water.

Terminus goes to see the Gogans and strikes up a deal. He will get them Pete if he is allowed to have Elliott. The Gogans laugh because they don't believe that the dragon exists, but they ultimately agree to help. Terminus then goes to the fishermen and tells them to construct a dragon trap so that the fishing will improve.

Later, the trap is set and the Gogans and the fishermen are ready while Terminus and Hoagy go and get Pete. Elliott tells Pete that he has found Paul. Pete tells Nora and Lampie says that that isn't fair to her.

Nora says that there are no dragons. Pete says that Elliott is real and asks Lampie if he's seen him. Lampie, now sober, says that he thought he saw him, but acted like it was an illusion when he was drunk.

The weather turns stormy and Nora is on the lighthouse with a telescope, looking out at sea. There is a ship nearby in need of lighthouse assistance, and the boat has Paul on board.

Meanwhile, Terminus and Hoagy capture Pete and give him to the Gogans, but they cannot have Pete completely yet as they need to use him as bait. They also need Hoagy to get Elliott to come to their dragon trap. Hoagy screams for dear life as he doesn't want to do it, but he eventually gives in and reluctantly agrees to do it.

Hoagy tells Elliott that the Gogans have Pete and so he follows Hoagy to the trap.

The ship at sea is still tossing and turning and the storm douses the light in the lighthouse, making things extremely dangerous for the ship.

Terminus, the Gogans, and the fishermen drop the net on Elliott, who becomes furious at being trapped. Terminus then lights the fuse on the harpoon he has set up to get Elliott. He aims it at Elliott, but Pete escapes the Gogans and aims the harpoon the other way.

Elliott finally gets out of the net and covers the harpoon and goes after the Gogans. He retrieves the bag that Pete is in. Lena Gogan shows Elliott the bill of sale proving that she owns Pete, but Elliot burns it with his fire breath.

The Gogans then fall into a barrel of oil and they run off before Elliott can breathe more fire on them, and Pete and Elliott start to laugh. While they are not paying attention, Terminus and Hoagy aim the harpoon at Elliott again, but as Hoagy notices the harpoon is wrapped around Terminus' foot, he loses his aim and he is shot high in the air.

While hanging upside down, Terminus asks Elliott if he has any spare parts for sale, like hair or nails or anything. Elliott says no and is not interested in money.

The mayor and Miss Taylor come outside and they are saved from a falling telephone pole by Elliott. They now see and believe in Elliott.

The ship is still rocking back and forth at sea and in danger of hitting the huge rocks. Nora and Lampie are still trying to relight the extinguished lighthouse, but everything is too wet and it's up to Elliott to breathe fire on the wick.

Finally, Nora and Lampie see Elliott and believe in him. Elliott tries to light the lighthouse, but has major difficulties, although he finally does it. The ship sees the light and sails past the rocks to safety. Nora gives Elliott a great big kiss.

Everyone in the village sings "I Saw a Dragon" and honors him for saving the town. Paul is reunited with Nora and explains that he survived the storm, but had amnesia. With his memory restored, he came back to Nora.

The mayor honors Pete and Elliott for their good works. Paul, Nora, Lampie, and Pete reprise "Brazzle, Dazzle Day" and Elliott tells Pete goodbye for good as he has to help someone else. Pete is sad, but he understands as Elliott flies away.

This was one of my favorite Disney films as a kid. I liked the animation and the characters. I didn't think the songs were as good as the ones in *Mary Poppins*, however.

This was the first real musical for Disney since 1971's *Bedknobs and Broomsticks* and was set up to emulate *Mary Poppins* (1964). It was actually moderately successful in comparison to what Disney was doing at this time and finished 17th for the year on the list of box office receipts. Elliott was also added to the Main Street Electrical Parade as a featured character.

Pete's Dragon was in planning since 1957 and was originally going to be filmed for the anthology show.

This was also the first animated film to not have any involvement by the "Nine Old Men", the group that Disney considered to be his top animators.

After being shelved for almost two decades, production for this film began in 1975. The clapboard in the DVD documentary says November 15, 1976. Sean Marshall hosts and tells of how he did most of the effects with the sodium screen process in front of a green screen, along with the traveling matte process. It's now done digitally, but at the time it was still a manual process.

Special note is made by Walt Disney himself of how the effects of live-action and animation combination were originated by Max Fleischer and later perfected by Disney.

Virginia Davis-McGee tells of how she worked with Disney on the original *Alice in Cartoonland* series.

Ub Iwerks was mentioned in this documentary for his technical advances besides animating Mickey Mouse and how Mickey was in the first sound cartoon, as well as *Flowers and Trees* for being the first full-color animated cartoon and *Snow White* (1937) for being the first full-length animated feature.

Roy E. Disney didn't remember Iwerks as an animator, but more as someone who solved technical problems at Disney. Iwerks developed the Disney Process Lab and created the state-of-the-art special effects for Disney.

Many examples are shown of Disney films that combined animation and live-action over the years, and the major technological advance that was made in 1959 that allowed for films like *Ten Who Dared* (1960), *The Absent-Minded Professor* (1961), *The Parent Trap* (1961), and *Mary Poppins*, and many later films for Disney.

The town of Passamaquoddy was built completely on the Disney back lot, but there were also scenes shot at Disney's Golden Oak Ranch in Santa Clarita.

Water was filmed in slow motion when it was splashing against the lighthouse and a full-sized lighthouse set was constructed on a rocky point in Morro Bay, California. Permission had to be granted by the Coast Guard in order for them to light the lamp.

Marshall reveals that he was not keen on the fame, but rather on everything else having to do with filmmaking. He also revealed that he didn't have any acting background and that he had to learn dancing and singing for the film.

Animator Ken Anderson reveals in another documentary the details of Elliott's fire-breathing and how he designed the dragon.

There is also a deleted storyboard sequence called "Terminus and Hoagy Hunt Elliott." It's somewhat different from what appeared in the actual film, but there are some similarities, too.

Also included on the DVD are the original song concept for "Boo Bop Bopbop Bop (I Love You, Too)" with the 1976 demo recording. There are original demo recordings for "Brazzle Dazzle Day" (an alternate song version), "Every Little Piece" (an alternate melody version) and "The Greatest Star of All" (a deleted song for a deleted character). All of these originate from February 11, 1976.

The songs from the Buena Vista Records promotional record are all included on the DVD. It features "It's Not Easy," "Brazzle Dazzle Day," "There's Room for Everyone," and "Candle on the Water." These are not the versions from the actual motion picture, as the actual original soundtrack was released on Capitol Records.

This was Jim Dale's first Disney movie. Prior to this, he was best known for appearing in a British series of *Carry On* films and for being a Broadway stage actor. Nowadays, he's best known as the narrator and story teller for the *Harry Potter* audio books.

This was Helen Reddy's first film. She was hired for her singing abilities after many hits like "I Am Woman" and "Delta Dawn."

Pete's Dragon was nominated for Academy Awards for Best Original Song Score and for Best Original Song with "Candle on the Water."

Excerpts from *The Plausible Impossible* and *The Disney Family Album* episodes from the anthology show are included on the DVD as well as the 1973 featurette *Man, Monsters and Mysteries*, about the Loch Ness monster.

The film grossed $18 million in the US and was reissued to theaters in 1984 in a 106-minute version. The original budget was $10 million. It also aired on the anthology show in 1986 and 1989.

It had many other firsts, mainly as the first Disney film to be released to home video, the first Disney film to be recorded in Dolby Stereo, and the first non-fully animated Disney film pre-1985 to be released to Blu-ray, barring *Tron* (1982).

Candleshoe

RELEASED BY BUENA VISTA ON December 16, 1977, Technicolor. Producer: Ron Miller. Director: Norman Tokar. Screenplay: David Swift, Rosemary Anne Sisson based on the book *Christmas at Candleshoe* by Michael Innes. Directory of Photography: Paul Beeson, B.S.C. Art Director: Albert Witherick. Editor: Peter Boita. Costume Designer: Julie Harris. Second Unit Director: Anthony Squire. Second Unit Photography: Ray Sturgess. Production Manager: Robin Douet. Special Effects: Cliff Culley. Camera Operator: Godfrey Godar. Set Dresser: Martin Atkinson. Sound Editor: Peter Best. Stunt Arranger: Bob Anderson. Assistant Director: Jack Causey. Continuity: Georgina Hamilton. Location Manager: Jake Wright. Casting: Maude Spector. Make-up: Roy Ashton, Bob Lawrence. Hairdressing: Joan Carpenter, Joyce Wood. Sound Recordists: Claude Hitchcock, Ken Barker. Music Composed and Conducted by Ron Goodwin recorded at Anvil Studios. Associate Producer: Hugh Attwooll. Filmed on location and at Pinewood Studios, London, England. Stunts: Peter Diamond, Kiran Shah. Running time: 101 minutes.

Cast: David Niven (Priory), Helen Hayes (Lady St. Edmund), Jodie Foster (Casey Brown), Leo McKern (Harry Bundage), Veronica Quilligan (Cluny), Ian Sharrock (Peter), Sarah Tamakuni (Anna), David Samuels (Bobby), John

Alderson (Jenkins), Midred Shay (Mrs. McCress), Michael Balfour (Mr. McCress), Sydney Bromley (Mr. Thresher), Michael Segal (Train Guard), Vivian Pickles (Clara Grimsworthy), Bob Anderson (Hood), Peter Diamond (Hood), January L'Angelle (Street Kid).

During the intro's snappy theme song we discover Casey, a tomboy troublemaker who causes mischief wherever she goes, like tossing a banana peel into the mailbox instead of the garbage can while she's hanging out with her friends. We see that she's also good at basketball.

She eventually attracts the attention of the police and manages to escape only to be turned in by her own family. The detective who takes her in checks Casey's shoulder for a scar. He then takes her away and pays the family off without explanation. It will be revealed during the course of the movie.

Casey is not taken to juvenile hall, but rather to a hotel, where she is directed to take a bath. After her bath, a man named Bundage takes over and asks Casey where she got her scars. She mouths off, saying she doesn't know. He gives her a slap for sassing him and then gives her a dress to wear.

Later, Casey and Bundage go out for a fancy dinner and he reveals who he is and what he knows about her. He is a con man and she is an heir to Candleshoe. He tells Casey that her parents are dead and she had gone missing and he has sent a letter to Lady St. Edmund about her.

Casey is not the missing child, but Bundage wants to use her in order to collect on a reward, by using her as a stand-in for the missing Margaret. Casey wants money for doing this and Bundage reluctantly agrees after some negotiations that include a Ferrari.

In England, Bundage coaches Casey on what she should know and how she should act. Bundage turns her over to Clara, who works for the family she will be going to.

Clara educates Casey about Margaret's likes and dislikes. They need to convince Lady St. Edmund that Casey is Margaret and in order to gain access to a treasure of Spanish doubloons.

After reading Bundage's letter, Lady St. Edmund agrees to meet Casey and soon they drive to Candleshoe, which is a huge mansion out in the country.

At Candleshoe they are greeted by Priory, the butler. As they wait for Lady St. Edmund, Casey notices a few differ-

ent children spying on her. Bundage points out the statue of Captain St. Edmund, the one who had all the gold in Lady St. Edmund's ancestry.

Lady St. Edmund tells Bundage that there is no reward for her return. Priory gives Casey some various foods to see if she likes them or dislikes them. At this point, St. Edmund takes Priory aside wondering what all the testing is for.

While they are out, Casey dumps the rest of the rice pudding she is eating. She doesn't like it even though Margaret is supposed to love it.

They return to the room and Casey drops a bombshell, telling the truth about everything that Bundage was trying to pull and the two excuse themselves. Bundage is dumbstruck for her sabotage of his devious plot.

Bundage is upset and tries to leave in a huff. Casey asks Bundage to act cool and to wait. Soon, Priory comes out and brings them back in because there really is a loose brick on the fireplace as Casey had suggested and St. Edmund embraces Casey, believing her to be Margaret. The story of the loose brick was originally told to her by Bundage.

Bundage goes back to Clara alone and tells her the good news that Casey has been accepted by St. Edmund. Casey's tactic worked in confirming her authenticity, despite the scam.

The next day, Casey takes a look in the massive library and remembers, as Bundage told her, that she has to go through every book to find information about the treasure. While there, Cluny discovers her and brings her to breakfast. Priory introduces Casey to Cluny, Peter, Anna, and Bobby: the adopted children of Candleshoe.

St. Edmund wants to take Casey for a walk, but first she notices that there are no roses in the hall vase and goes to tell Mr. Gippy, the gardener.

Mr. Gippy is actually Priory in disguise as he assumes the various roles to make St. Edmund believe that she has many people working on staff. Casey thinks that this is all nuts and finally they go on their walk.

After they get back and later that night, Bobby offers Casey some garlic to ward off ghosts. After bedtime, Casey goes back to the library to search through the books. She soon hears some noises, which turn out to be Priory taking a short cut to the room.

Priory reveals that there is no staff and barely enough money, which is why he plays multiple roles. Priory likes to keep up the illusion that they are rich for St. Edmund's sake. They do make a little money from cakes that they sell and tours that they give once a week.

The next day, Casey is back in the library again and discovers a clue that leads her closer to the treasure. She calls Bundage and tells him the good news. She said that she will have more news later.

Priory, now disguised as the chauffeur, takes St. Edmund to the village. Casey asks why they can't sell the car for money. The children say that Priory has already borrowed against the car for a loan.

Cluny tells Casey the chores that she is supposed to do that day. Casey refuses and it escalates into a fight that forces all of the children into the lake.

Later, St. Edmund asks Casey why she has a black eye and Casey makes up a tall tale, saying that she tripped over a rake and fell into the lake while she was trying to do some work that Cluny had asked her to do.

That night, Casey goes exploring in a nearby graveyard and invites Bundage and Clara. They discover the grave that they may have to dig up to discover more about the treasure.

The next day, Cluny cuts Casey some slack in order to keep the peace. Priory disguises himself as the Colonel to visit St. Edmund as he does once a month. The children reveal that Priory (disguised as the Colonel) brags about his horse riding skills, but in reality he cannot ride at all.

Casey begs the Colonel to ride since she now knows he can't and everyone else agrees. Priory reluctantly agrees, mounts the horse, and is sent off on a wild horse ride that knocks him to the ground.

Later, the children privately laugh with Priory about the incident. Priory says that they are still about $100 behind on the next tax payment, so Casey shows them some hustling and selling skills in order for them to sell more and fast. Soon, Cluny and the rest are joining in the fun and they earn more than enough than they needed.

Priory gives Casey the money to bring back to Candleshoe and as she puts the money in the cookie jar, Bundage shows up and wonders why Casey is wasting time selling wares and not looking for the treasure. Bundage sees the money and takes it and runs off.

Casey chases after him, but she gets hurt and ends up in the hospital with a bandage over her head. With the money gone, more items have to be put up for auction and the house is sold.

Priory and St. Edmund pack up their remaining offerings. St. Edmund wants to waltz to an old record before she packs it away but Priory refuses, claiming that it wouldn't be appropriate. St. Edmund asks if it would be more appropriate if she asked the Colonel, revealing that she knew that Priory was disguising himself as all the other characters all along.

Casey recovers from her injuries and the other children come to visit her. They have come to say goodbye as they are all going back to the children's home and St. Edmund is going to an old folks' home. Casey says she doesn't know anything about who stole the money, because she doesn't want to reveal that's it was Bundage.

Eventually, since everyone will be out on their ears, Casey decides to reveal all about the treasure. It leads them to a painting that unfortunately had just been sold by Priory. The man who has the painting is taking the train out, so they race to the train which has never, until now, been on time.

They are not giving up, so they chase the train as best they can and end up parking the car on the tracks in order to stop the train. Priory claims that the train will stop in time, which it does, but within an inch of Priory and the car.

They board the train and get a good look at the painting for another clue, which leads them back to the great hall at Candleshoe. They come in to discover that Bundage is already chipping away at the walls, trying to find the treasure.

St. Edmond says that they own Candleshoe for one more day and that everyone is trespassing. Bundage orders his men to take everyone hostage, which erupts into a battle, a chase, a fistfight, and finally a fight between Priory and Bundage using an umbrella and a battle axe and then with actual swords.

The children try to phone for help, but keep getting attacked while trying. Eventually, Peter and Cluny escape and run for the police.

The scuttle that had ensued had disturbed a major support beam, causing the statue to fall and the hidden treasure to fall from the ceiling. The police arrive with Peter and Cluny and the bad guys are arrested and Candleshoe remains with Lady St. Edmund, Priory, and the children.

The next day, Casey packs up her stuff to leave and goes to the train station to head back to L.A. St. Edmonds does not wish her to go, but Casey doesn't feel worthy of staying since she was trying to con her.

St. Edmonds asks her if Casey really wants to go back to L.A. After crying, she finally says no and stays at Candleshoe.

I remember seeing this and *Pete's Dragon* (1977) within a couple of months of each other and thought it interesting that both films had scenes where many of the characters slipped in and got covered with oil. I also thought this was (and still is) a great, but underrated, movie.

I loved David Niven's versatility in this movie in his portrayal of multiple characters. Laurence Olivier was originally considered for his role. Leo McKern replaced Harry Andrews and Veronica Quilligan replaced another actress for their roles.

On the *Freaky Friday* (1977) DVD documentary, Jodie Foster said that doing this film and *Freaky Friday* were really awkward for her, and that it is very difficult for her to watch these two movies, but also that she had total respect for the actors she worked with in this film, including David Niven and Helen Hayes.

The film was released at the tail end of 1977, for possible Oscar recognition. It didn't win any awards. It aired on the anthology show in 1986.

Screenwriter David Swift (*Pollyanna* (1960), *The Parent Trap* (1961)) was to be the original director of this film, but felt that Jodie Foster was all wrong for the part and quit.

1978

Mickey Mouse's 50th birthday this year made big news and a TV special called *Mickey's 50* appeared on the anthology show.

Other new films made for the anthology show include *Three on the Run, Journey to the Valley of the Emu, The Million Dollar Dixie Deliverance, Race For Survival, Trail of Danger, Child of Glass, The Young Runaways,* and *Christmas at Walt Disney World*. There was also the brand new special *NBC Salutes the 25th Anniversary of "The Wonderful World of Disney."*

After last year's successful *Rescuers* film, it was decided to start producing more new animation featuring the work of the younger animators joining Disney. One of their first completed projects was *The Small One*, released this year.

Film revenues alone were at their highest ever for Disney, grossing over $152 million.

Little Hiawatha, Donald's Fountain of Youth and *Bootle Beetle* were reissued this year as were *In Search of the Castaways* (1962), *The Jungle Book* (1967) and *Pinocchio* (1940). The Mr. Toad half of *The Adventures of Ichabod and Mr. Toad* (1949) was released with *Hot Lead and Cold Feet*. *The Black Hole* (1979) was in major production to be Disney's answer to *Star Wars* (1977).

Superman: The Movie was a successful Disney-type release from this year. There were no real new additions in the various theme parks, save for an abominable snowman added to Disneyland's Matterhorn and Jimmy Carter to Walt Disney World's The Hall of Presidents.

At the 1978 National Team Golf Championship in Walt Disney World, the purse was raised to $200,000.

Nothing really exciting was on the Disneyland record release schedule except the single of "Disco Mouse," which led to the release of the mega-successful *Mickey Mouse Disco* album in 1979. The Monkees' Davy Jones recorded a musical salute to Mickey Mouse's 50th birthday.

Charlie Brown's All-Stars and *The Hobbit* were both nominated for Best Recording for Children Grammys, but lost.

In the comic book world, Gold Key continued to publish *Donald Duck, Mickey Mouse, Uncle Scrooge, Walt Disney's Comics and Stories, The Beagle Boys, Huey, Dewey and Louie Junior Woodchucks, Super Goof, Chip 'n' Dale, Scamp, Walt Disney Showcase, Daisy and Donald*, and *Winnie the Pooh*. *Moby Duck* ended its run for the second and final time and a newspaper comic strip starring Winnie the Pooh made its debut.

The Wonderful World of Disney Digest appeared for two issues. Interest in the history of Disney comic books surged this year, with Abbeville Press publishing many volumes saluting the stories in large, white hardbound books; one starring Mickey Mouse and one starring Donald Duck.

More essential Disney books were issued this year, including *Walt Disney's America, Walt Disney's Treasury of Children's Classics* and *Walt Disney's Christmas Classics*.

Return From Witch Mountain

RELEASED BY BUENA VISTA ON March 10, 1978, Technicolor. Producer: Ron Miller, Jerome Courtland. Director: John Hough. Writer: Malcolm Marmorstein based on characters created by Alexander Key. Art Directors: John B. Mansbridge, Jack Senter. Editor: Bob Bring, A.C.E. Associate Producer: Kevin Corcoran. Special Effects: Eustace Lycett, Art Cruickshank, A.S.C., Danny Lee. Stop Motion Animation: Joe Hale. Set Decorator: Frank R. McKelvy. Production Manager: John Bloss. Unit Production Manager / Assistant Director: Michael Dmytryk. Second Assistant Director: Dorothy Kieffer. Sound Supervisor: Herb Taylor. Sound Mixer: Ron Ronconi. Costumes: Chuck Keehne, Emily Sundby. Make-up: Robert J. Schiffer. Hair Stylist: La Rue Matheron. Sound Editor: Ben F. Hendricks. Music Editor: Evelyn Kennedy. Music: Lalo Schifrin. Director of Photography: Frank Phillips, A.S.C. Stunts: Ted Duncan, Bobby Porter, Carey Loftin, A.J. Bakunas, May Boss, Donna Hall, Bob Harris, Norm Mont-Eton, Tony Brubaker, Gerald Brutsche, Gary Davis, Bob Drake, Richard Drown, Larry Dunn, Bud Ekins, Gary Epper, Beau Gibson, Norris Maxwell. Production Designer: John B. Mansbridge. Second Assistant

Director: Randy Carter. Props: Kurt V. Hulett. Foley Artist: Richard Partlow. Special Effects Technicians: Mike Edmonson, Hans Metz, Mike Reedy. Gaffer: Carl Boles. Assistant Editor: Barney Cabral. Running time: 94 minutes.

Cast: Bette Davis (Letha), Christopher Lee (Victor), Kim Richards (Tia), Ike Eisenmann (Tony), Jack Soo (Mr. Yokomoto), Anthony James (Sickle), Dick Bakalyan (Eddie), Ward Costello (Mr. Clearcole), Christian Juttner (Dazzler), Brad Savage (Muscles), Erik "Poindexter" Yothers (Crusher), Jeffrey Jacquet (Rocky), Stu Gilliam (Dolan), William H. Bassett (Operations Officer), Tom Scott (Monitor), Helene Winston (Dowager), Albert Able (Engineer), Denver Pyle (Uncle Bene), Brian Part (Goon #1), Pierre Daniel (Goon #2), Wally Brooks (Taxi Fare), Mel Gold (Security Guard), Bob Yothers (Cop), Casse Jaeger (School Patrolman), Larry Marmorstein (Guard #1), Bob James (Gate Guard), Ted Noose (Policeman), Ruth Warshawsky (Lady in Car), Adam Anderson (Man in Museum), Rosemary Lord (Woman in Museum), Lloyd Nelson (Museum Guard), Wally Berns (Man in Car), Gary Owens (Radio Announcer), Adam Roarke (Museum Security Guard).

A flying saucer carrying Tia, Tony, and Uncle Bene lands in a vacant football field (The Rose Bowl). Bene now sports a beard and warns Tony to energize only when absolutely necessary.
    Eddie, the taxi driver, is waiting to pick up Tia and Tony and takes them to an undisclosed location for a huge fare, but not without driving quickly and aggressively.
    Letha, Victor, and Sickle are three villains who arrive downtown to test a new appliance stuck behind Sickle's ear. Victor wants Sickle to climb up a fire escape, but he refuses. Victor turns on his machine and forces him to climb. Once the machine is turned on Sickle obeys all of Victor's commands without question.
    The taxi driver continues down the road but runs out of gas, so Eddie leaves the car to get some fuel. Tony has a vision of a man leaping off the roof of a building and he leaves the car to check things out.
    Letha is upset with Sickle walking along the ledge of the building and grabs the machine, causing Victor to drop it on the ground. The machine breaks and new commands are not followed. Sickle walks off the ledge, apparently to his death, but Tony saves him just before he hits the ground.
    Letha and Victor see Tony rescue him and decide that they need him for their work. They congratulate Tony and as they do, Victor sticks Tony with a needle. Tony passes out and the three leave with Tony in the car.
    Tia gets out of the taxi to check on things, but doesn't see anyone or anything. The taxi driver arrives with some gas at his abandoned cab and drives off in a huff since he's been stiffed on his fare.

Tia sees a group of four kids run by. They are being pursued by six other kids. The four plus Tia hide behind some barrels and then she uses her powers to roll the barrels and trash at the bullies and drop trash cans on top of them.

Tia and the four escape before the bullies free themselves. They thank Tia and introduce themselves as Crusher, Rocky, Muscles, and Dazzler of the Earthquake Gang.

They try to help Tia get back in touch with Tony when they see a green van drive up, driven by a man named Yoyo, a.k.a. Mr. Yokomoto, the truant officer who is trying to make the Earthquake Gang go back to school.

The gang eludes Yokomoto and they go into their hide-out, which is an abandoned house. While there, Tia gets a mental contact from Tony and the gang calls her weird and creepy. Tia can only see a light with her visions.

Tony sends a message to Tia while he sleeps on a gurney. Victor is trying to figure out Tony's power. Letha wants to know if Victor is going to follow her plans to make some money, but Victor claims that his scientific experiments are more important right now.

The Earthquake Gang goes home for the night and leaves Tia alone to fend for herself in the abandoned house.

Victor installs one of his sensors near Tony's ear, just like he did with Sickle, and tries to control him with a new machine. He speaks commands to take over Tony's mind and Tony reveals who he is and his powers without question. Letha and Sickle are not convinced that Tony has any powers, so Victor asks Tony to prove himself.

The gang comes back the next day and they continue to look for Tony. They decide to search every hospital in the area, but have no success.

Victor continues to have Tony do his bidding, which includes stacking wine barrels and filling two glasses with Burgundy.

Later, Sickle and Letha discuss the possibilities of taking Tony to Vegas and placing bets. They also contemplate having Tony help them to move gold bars. Sickle says that they would need an army to protect them, and Letha says that won't be necessary with Tony.

Victor goes off to get more equipment for his experiments and Letha says that everything is under control. She uses the machine after Victor leaves and takes Tony to the museum with Sickle, who waits for them at the car.

Tia has a vision about gold and the gang thinks that it's in the ground right in front of them. She says no, and that she also sees other things like a stagecoach and Western clothing. The gang says that that's in the museum, so they head over there.

Letha tells Tony to wheel the stagecoach around the museum as a diversion in order to distract everyone so that they can get the gold without being seen. She also tells him to short circuit the control system and to create general chaos. A guard hops aboard the stagecoach and tries to gain control but fails.

Victor returns to their hide-out and discovers that Letha, Sickle, and Tony are missing. He figures out that they are at the museum after reading a nearby newspaper headline about gold.

Tony burns a hole in the container holding the gold and then floats the gold to Sickle to put in the car, but it comes in too quickly for Sickle and it pummels him and the car.

Suddenly, Tony discovers that some of what he's doing is reversing on him, and that Tia is causing it to happen with her mental powers. Tony and Letha leave in a hurry. They go outside and see the car demolished by the gold bricks. Victor angrily comes up and orders them to get into his car. Sickle tries to start the car, but can't. Victor orders Tony to start the car without interference.

Mr. Yokomoto comes by, picking up Tia and the gang, who ask him to chase Tony and the others with his van. Victor commands Tony to place obstacles in Mr. Yokomoto's path, but Tia helps them to get through without harm.

Victor orders Tony to stop Tia and also asks to shine the sun into Mr. Yokomoto's eyes so that he will be blinded by it. Tony does so, and Mr. Yokomoto's van overturns and slides down the hill. The police come and write Yokomoto a ticket while Tia and the gang flee on foot.

Back at the hide-out, Victor says that he no longer trusts Letha because of what she did, but Letha said that she meant no harm. Tony reveals that he is in mental communication with Tia and guides her to the villain's secret hide-out where she is captured and put into a state of comatose hibernation.

The gang wonders where she went. Tia wakes from her sleep and tries to mentally communicate with Tony or with anyone. The gang goes out and tries to find her and Tia tries to communicate with her gang. She tells Alfred, the goat, an animal that is conveniently caged nearby to go find the Earthquakes.

Alfred escapes and tracks them down, running down city streets and over cars.

Victor takes Letha, Tony, and Sickle to an underground plutonium mine and wants to use Tony's powers to gain access to the plant and Victor's plan to become the most powerful man in the world. Victor tells Tony to put the satellite dishes atop the plant out of commission.

The goat hops into a cab driven by Eddie, the same cabbie from earlier in the film. Eddie has a conversation with Alfred, who answers with various bleats. When he discovers that he's been communicating with a goat, he crashes into a police car. When Eddie tries explaining himself to the policeman, the goat escapes and finally makes it to the gang's hideout.

Victor and the rest go into a secured area and he orders Tony to lift up the security guard and leave him there as they all file past.

The goat takes Tia's vest and the gang follows him to Victor's hide-out. Inside, they discover Tia lying under a glass lid and awaken her. Tia has a vision of a great ball and they all run off, leaving the goat behind.

Victor orders Tony to shut down the plant's cooling system, causing the reactor to overheat. Scientists try to override the heating but are unable to do so. Victor phones in to say that he's shut down the cooling system and will not turn it back on unless his demands are met.

The entire reactor is under emergency alert. People are evacuated and the scientists are told that they have to pay Victor, as they have no other choice.

Tia leads the gang to an auto wrecking yard when they see Mr. Yokomoto. They wonder why he doesn't want to chase them and he reveals that he will be losing his job. Yokomoto agrees to drive them wherever they want to go. Tia says to take them to the reactor. She uses her powers to get inside, just as Tony did earlier.

The temperature at the reactor keeps going up as the scientists are trying to raise the blackmail money, but they may be running out of time.

Tia asks what needs to be done to fix the cooling system and goes past the same security guard that Tony had elevated earlier. They are now face to face with Victor and the other bad guys.

Victor commands Tony to ignore anything that Tia says. Tia and the gang try to locate the cooling system themselves, but Sickle stands in their way.

Victor commands Tony to send a portable utility panel to run over Tia, but she intercepts it before any harm is done. Finally, the gang finds the cooling system just as the money arrives. Tia starts cooling everything, but Victor tells Tony to counter her powers and so they battle each other mentally.

Eventually Tia wins out and the temperature goes back to normal, but the bad guys aren't through yet, as Victor orders Tony to lure Tia to the middle of the room so that a large object can be dropped on her. Victor says to pretend that he can understand Tia, when he can't while under Victor's control. Tia stops the falling object before it lands on top of her.

Victor orders Tony to crush and kill Tia, but Tia focuses her energies on the control box, causing it to heat up and spark. With the control box out of commission, Tony regains his memory and Tia gets close enough to remove the transmitter hooked to his ear.

Victor comes back, demanding that Tony continue to take over the plant and Tony agrees, but elevates Victor instead. Letha arrives with two of the Earthquake Gang in her grasp, but she is elevated as well and the kids are released. Sickle arrives with the other two gang members, but he too is elevated to be with Victor and Letha and the kids are free to escape.

They all get back to Yokomoto's car and Tia and Tony fix and repair the car. Yokomoto proposes a deal that if the kids go back to school, he won't lose his job and he doesn't have to report that his van was wrecked. The gang agrees to go as all the kids leave the reactor by holding hands and floating over the fence.

Tia and Tony say goodbye, as their flying saucer is waiting for them at the Rose Bowl with Uncle Bene. They get back in the saucer and it flies away.

The Earthquake Gang gets into Yokomoto's van and he takes them and the goat back to school.

This film is ok, but the first film was much better. It probably helped that I saw the original back in the 70s on TV, whereas I saw this one for the first time in the 90s on tape and found it vastly inferior and stupid in comparison to the original, mainly due to the inclusion of the Earthquake Gang. They seemed really stupid to me, especially when they are introducing themselves.

Also, for some reason it seems like Kim Richards forgot how to act in the three years since the first film, as her delivery seems very stilted and forced. She seemed to do better a year later when she was cast in the ill-fated sitcom *Hello, Larry* with McLean Stevenson.

And Bette Davis seems drunk throughout the film as she has some of the corniest lines of dialogue in any Disney movie and delivers them in the strangest of ways.

The original working title for this film was *Escape to Witch Mountain, Part 2*.

There are many DVD extras, with new comments by Kim Richards, Iake Eissinmann, Brad Savage, Christian Juttner, Associate Producer Kevin Corcoran, and Director John Hough. Everyone was hesitant to do a sequel until they saw the script and storyline.

Eissinmann points out that he and Kim barely worked together on this film as they were separated by storyline for most of the film.

Richards points out that he didn't know how big Bette Davis and Christopher Lee were and what they had done previously.

Hough points out that casting Christopher Lee was his suggestion and that he felt that Lee would work well with Bette Davis. Interestingly, all three had at various times worked for Hammer Films. He also said that Anthony James was cast due to his excellent work in *In the Heat of the Night* (1967).

It was said that Bette Davis did the film because she wanted to do something that her grandchildren would enjoy. Eissinmann said that Davis had multiple handlers that did her bidding.

Corcoran said that Jack Soo was cast because of the dry humor that he exhibited so well on the then-currently-running *Barney Miller* TV show. This was Soo's last film.

There is a DVD reunion of The Earthquake Gang with Brad Savage, Erik Yothers, and Christian Juttner. They mentioned that they had the gang wear black leather-studded arm bands to make them look tough. They also talked about what it was like being on the Disney lot during the late 1970s. They reveal that the shoot lasted four months and they had hoped for a third film, but it did not materialize (at least not with them). According to John Hough, the missing member has become a lawyer.

On the DVD commentary, Iake and Kim reveal that many people confuse the titles. Is it *Escape to* or *Escape from* or *Return to* or *Return from*?

John Hough and the others reveal that the film was almost entirely shot in downtown Los Angeles, but scenes requiring special effects work were shot on the Disney back lot.

The Earthquake Gang's hide-out was an abandoned house on location except for the top floor, which was in-studio.

There was some difficulty in securing the Los Angeles Museum for location shooting, but ultimately Hough got his way.

The stuntman performed Anthony James' fall invented the air bag that he landed in. The part where James stopped in midair was shot in reverse.

Hough reveals that video assist and CGI were not used at the time that this film was being shot. One effect that he did use was Steadicam and he also created masks for the stunt doubles to use.

Eissinmann wonders how the harmonica, which was so critical to making his magic work in the first film, was somehow deemed unnecessary in this film. Also, he observes that there was only one animal, a goat, in this film compared to the first one, which had dogs, a cat and a horse.

Hough said in his commentary that this was the beginning of the end of traditional Disney. With the next film he directed for Disney (1980's *The Watcher in the Woods*), he had a lot more freedom with more mature subject matters. Soon after that, Touchstone Pictures was created so that adult films and children's films could be produced separately.

An amusing extra included on the DVD is an interview with Christopher Lee promoting this film. The interview is done completely in Spanish by interviewer Pepe Lupi and Lee speaking fluent Spanish, with some assistance on a few words until near the end. In the interview, Lee sports a big bushy mustache as he is working on his new film, *The Passage* (1979), and he sings a bit of opera.

The Cat From Outer Space

RELEASED BY BUENA VISTA ON June 9, 1978, Technicolor. Producer: Ron Miller. Co-Producer: Norman Tokar. Associate Producer: Jan Williams. Writer: Ted Key. Special Effects: Eustace Lycett, Art Cruickshank, A.S.C., Danny Lee. Matte Artist: Peter Ellenshaw. Second Unit Photography: Rexford Metz. Set Decorator: Norman Rockett. Animal Trainers: Rudy Cowl, Don Spinney. Orchestration: Jack Hayes. Production Manager: John Bloss. Unit Production Manager: Christopher Seiter. Assistant Director: Gene Sultan. Second Assistant Director: William Carroll. Sound Supervisor: Herb Taylor. Sound Mixer: Bud Maffett. Costumes: Chuck Keehne, Emily Sundby. Make-up: Robert J. Schiffer. Hair Stylist: Lola Kemp. Sound Editor: Ben F. Hendricks. Music Editor: Evelyn Kennedy. Second Unit Director: Arthur J. Vitarelli. Music: Lalo Schifrin. Editor: Cotton Warburton, A.C.E. Art Directors: John B. Mansbridge, Preston Ames. Director of Photography: Charles F. Wheeler, A.S.C. Pilots: Frank Tallman, Gavin James, Gary Bertz, Frank Pine, Tom Friedkin, Ross Reynolds. Stunt Coordinator: Richard Warlock. Stunts: Jack Verbois, Reg Parton, Bob Harris, Carey Loftin, Walter Robles, Fred Dale, Tom Steele, Gerald Brutsche, Julie Ann Johnson. Set Dresser: Eric A. Hulett. Assistant Property Master: Bob McLing. Sound Editor: George Fredrick. Special Effects: Gary D'Amico, Mike Edmonson, Allen Hurd, Mike Reedy. Special Effects Supervisor: Hans Metz. Running time: 103 minutes.

Cast: Ken Berry (Dr. Frank Wilson), Sandy Duncan (Doctor Liz Bartlett), Harry Morgan (General Stilton), Roddy McDowall (Mr. Stallwood), McLean Stevenson (Doctor Link), Jesse White (Earnest Ernie), Alan Young (Doctor Wenger), Hans Conried (Doctor Heffel), Ronnie Schell (Jake the Cat, Sergeant Duffy), James Hampton (Captain Anderson), Howard T. Platt (Colonel Woodruff), William Prince (Mr. Olympus), Ralph Manza (Weasel), Tom Pedi (Honest Harry), Hank Jones (Officer), Rick Hurst (Dydee Guard), John Alderson (Mr. Smith), Tiger Joe Marsh (Omar), Arnold Soboloff (NASA Executive), Mel Carter (1st Soldier), Dallas McKennon (Farmer), Alice Backes (Farmer's Wife), Henry Slate (Sandwich Man), Roger Pan-

cake (Red), Roger Price (1st E.R.L. Expert), Jerry Fujikawa (2nd E.R.L. Expert), Jim Begg (Dydee Driver), Pete Renaday (Bailiff), Rick Sorensen (Technician), Tom Jackman (Army Engineer), Fred L. Whalen (Sarasota Slim), Joe Medalis (Sucker), Gil Stratton (1st NASA Scientist), Jana Milo (2nd NASA Scientist), Sorrell Booke (Presiding Judge), Jackson Bostwick (Voices).

A strange spaceship lands in the yard of two farm folk. The farmer goes to investigate and runs off in fear. The spaceship opens up and a space alien resembling a small house cat emerges.

The military is called in to investigate and debrief the farmers. The military captures the spaceship and the scientists are stumped, but they do know that the ship is not man made. They are worried that some slimy creatures are finding their way into the White House, not knowing that the alien resembles a cat.

Another meeting is called, but Dr. Link is not paying attention as he's busy placing bets on the Lakers game. Dr. Heffel starts the meeting with General Stilton in charge and Dr. Liz Bartlett and other E.R.L experts in attendance. Mr. Stallwood is kicked out from this meeting, so he eavesdrops from a nearby telephone. He is also a spy.

A box marked Top Secret is opened and a floating artichoke-shaped, glowing object is revealed. Everyone is stumped as to what this is. Liz suggests bringing in her neighbor Dr. Frank Wilson, who is supposedly an expert on such things. He takes the object home to investigate it further.

The alien cat follows Frank to his office and Frank christens him Jake. Frank notices Jake's collar and makes reference to it, when Liz bursts in to his office and is upset that Frank is stumped as well.

Frank smooths everything out and invites Liz for dinner after her meeting. After Liz leaves, Jake speaks and reveals that his name is Zunar SJ190 Fourseven, but agrees to Jake for simplicity sake. He says that his collar amplifies brain power. He also says that he's communicating with Frank telepathically, which is why his mouth doesn't move.

Frank takes Jake home and after a short meal of cat food, Jake asks Frank to help him to repair his spaceship. Frank confirms that Jake really is from outer space and Frank agrees to help.

Frank asks Jake more about his collar and Jake shows off the collar's power by having Frank hold on to each side of Jake's collar causing him to float in mid-air.

Link bursts in to watch the basketball game and Frank loses his concentration and falls to the floor. Link wants the Lakers to win and it looks as if they are going to lose when Jake makes the ball go into the net and win the game for them.

Link leaves after the game ends and Liz stops by with her cat Lucy Belle for Jake to get acquainted with while they go out to dinner. Frank has forgotten and asks Liz if he can have a rain check on the dinner as Jake feigns illness and needs to run off to the vet.

Stallwood is lurking about the army base, trying again to get more information about the floating object and the spaceship and sneaks in after Frank and Jake do. A guard with a barking dog sees Frank and Jake, so Jake freezes them.

Frank and Jake get inside to the spaceship. Frank takes a spare collar from inside the ship and uses it to get on top of the ship to repair, but first decides to fly around the room with it, all the time being spied on by Stallwood.

After messing about, Frank finally makes the repair on top of the ship. The frozen guard starts moving again and signals the alarm so Frank and Jake flee the scene before their repairs are completely finished.

There's no way out on foot, so Frank jumps on a motorcycle with Jake and they elevate outside of the military barricade.

Back at Frank's house, Frank reveals that he cannot produce the $120,000 needed to purchase the gold that's needed to make the final repairs on the spaceship. Link bursts in to watch another sporting event, this time a horserace.

Link explains that he has a huge bet placed on this race on a horse called Sweet Jake. Jake the cat says that the money from the winnings will be what can get them the $120,000, but Frank says that it's just a bet. He's not guaranteed to win. Jake says that he will make the horse win and he does.

Jake says to Frank that they need to make more bets and to brink Link in on the action so that they can use his gambling skills to get the huge bets needed placed. Link is unconvinced while Stallwood starts spying again.

Jake makes Link's beer go back into the can and into his face while Stallwood is watching. Link still says that this doesn't prove anything so Jake tries again by retracting the paper towel roll and then wrapping the paper towels around Link.

Link is annoyed and decides to go home to watch opera with his wife instead of the games. This time Jake makes Link float and is finally convinced to help them out.

Bets are made with Earnest Ernie and his partner, Weasel. They agree to take the football bets using the horserace winnings.

General Stilton is still investigating the break-in to the spaceship and figures out that Frank is the one that caused the break-in so he's under suspicion.

The games are underway on TV and Liz stops by to see if Jake is better, but he sneezes and acts like he's still sick. Liz goes to get the vet and leaves Lucy Belle behind. Jake focuses on Lucy Belle instead of the game and delays doing anything to fix the game.

Dr. Wenger, the vet arrives and removes Jake's collar, but Frank manages to get the collar back on in time to interfere with the game, but Wenger has also given Jake a sedative, so he is out of commission and the vet leaves.

Frank and Link are upset and have to go to Ernie to stop the bets and tell Liz about what's been going on, on their way. Ernie will not refund the bet, but he does give Frank and Link a chance to break even by playing pool with their top player. Frank says that he can control the collar in this case as well as Jake. The odds are greater when Liz plays, so they all agree in order to achieve the largest winnings.

Liz does a wild break that flies all over the room, but ends up on the table with Frank's help. Nothing sinks and Slim, her competitor plays, sinking every ball. Soon, Jake comes to and Frank replaces the collar, but too late to win the game.

Frank takes out his final $60 and makes a wild bet where Slim gets 12 balls and the break and Liz plays blindfolded for ridiculous odds that will get them the $120,000 they need.

Slim breaks but Jake makes the balls go back into formation. Liz breaks with a blindfold and all 15 balls sink, winning them the game and the $120,000. Ernie and Weasel, Slim's buddies, are left crying.

Meanwhile, Stallwood plays back the film he has taken for Mr. Olympus and Omar. Unfortunately, since he filmed it upside down, it plays back upside down. Olympus says that he needs the collar.

Stilton is using his own spies called Dydee One to help track down Jake and they burst in and arrest Frank, Link and Liz in their home right after they've purchased the bar of gold. Jake freezes the intruders and reduces the bar of gold to the size that he needs for his ship.

Dydee One and Olympus, Omar and Stallwood arrive at Frank's house to see what's going on. Frank emerges dressed as Stilton in order to get back on base. Dydee One sees through the disguise and aims to shoot, but Jake freezes them too.

Frank leaves with Jake, but Liz and Link are captured by Olympus, Omar and Stallwood. Frank and Jake make it to the base and back to the ship. The gold is inserted into the ship and communication resumes between Jake and the mother ship.

Stilton and his men come to and they giggle when they see that Stilton is standing in his underwear. Stilton does not find this funny.

Link manages to escape and gets to the base to help Frank out and to say that Liz has been kidnapped. Frank says that Jake should just return home and not worry about this. The ship goes, but Jake has stayed behind.

Stilton and his men rush outside to their jeeps and see the Dydee One men still frozen. While driving, the military men see the ship taking off.

Olympus and his men with Liz wait in a helicopter as they see Link, Frank and Jake arrive. Stilton and the military men are arriving as well, so Olympus orders them to take off.

Jake hops aboard a nearby abandoned biplane with a broken propeller and gets it to fly. Frank hops in, but Link stays behind and gets captured by Stilton.

The biplane chases the helicopter. At one point, the helicopter doubles-back so Jake flips the biplane upside down and almost dislodges Frank in the process.

The helicopter tries to force the biplane to land and almost decapitates a farmer on a tractor in the process. Then they all narrowly escape crashing through a high bridge.

Eventually, shots are fired. Stallwood fires a tear gas gun which ruins the controls and everyone in the helicopter has to dive out. Everyone leaps out except Liz, who doesn't have a parachute. Stallwood doesn't have a parachute either, but grabs onto Olympus as he leaps out.

Liz is left to fly the helicopter herself. Frank tries to rescue her and Lucy Belle. It is a harrowing rescue, but Frank succeeds and they eventually land the plane. Olympus and the other spies are safe but all of their parachutes have been caught in the trees.

A hearing takes place to help Jake become a US citizen and he elevates the judge while he takes the oath.

This is another decent film in the Disney film canon marred by a very silly ending. It is noticeable at this point that the Disney people are really starting to lose their touch and changes have to be made soon.

Most people thought that *The Black Hole* was Disney's answer to the *Star Wars* science-fiction craze, but it really was this film that Disney originally responded with. Ironically, this is very similar to the upcoming *E.T.: The Extraterrestrial* (1982), which should have been a Disney film.

Though they never worked together on the series, this film stars both Harry Morgan and McLean Stevenson, best known for their portrayals on *M*A*S*H*.

This was Alan Young's first film in quite some time, but he would soon begin a long and rewarding career as a voice-over artist for Disney, doing the voice for Uncle Scrooge in *Mickey's Christmas Carol* (1983) and the later *DuckTales* TV series and movie.

Though uncredited, comedian and *Gomer Pyle U.S.M.C.* star Ronnie Schell was the voice of the cat. When I met him at one of his comedy benefits at San Francisco State University, Schell said that he had fond memories of doing this film and it was even more enjoyable for him than the other films he did for Disney.

Strangely, but probably to avoid confusion, Schell's voice was dubbed by another actor when portraying Sergeant Duffy.

This was Ted Key's third and final Disney movie story idea after *$1,000,000 Duck* (1971) and *Gus* (1976). Key is best-known for his *Saturday Evening Post* comic and later sitcom *Hazel* and *Jack and Jill* comic *Diz and Liz*.

Jake the cat was actually played by two cats: Rumple and Amber, both 15-month-old Abyssinian cats from the same litter. Animal trainers Rudy Cowl and Don Spinney were in charge of these cats and also Spot, the 3-year-old white Persian cat who played Lucy Belle. They also handled the sheep dog used in *The Shaggy D.A.*

This was longtime Disney Director Norman Tokar's final film before he died in 1979. He had been directing films for Disney since 1962 and may have known that this was to be his last film as virtually every existing Disney veteran appeared in this film who was still acting; even some who hadn't done a Disney film in quite some time.

The film aired on the anthology show in 1982.

Hot Lead and Cold Feet

RELEASED BY BUENA VISTA ON July 5, 1978, Technicolor. Producer: Ron Miller. Co-Producer: Christopher Hibler. Director: Robert Butler. Screenplay: Joe McEveety, Arthur Alsberg, Don Nelson based on a story by Rod Piffath. Production Manager: John Bloss. Unit Production Manager / Assistant Director: Paul "Tiny" Nichols. Second Assistant Director: Jerram Swartz. Special Effects: Eustace Lycett, Art Cruickshank, A.S.C., Danny Lee, Hal Bigger, Billy Lee. Set Decorator: Frank R. McKelvy. Sound Supervisor: Herb Taylor. Sound Mixer: Gregory Valtierra. Costumes: Chuck Keehne, Emily Sundby. Make-up: Robert J. Schiffer. Hair Stylist: Charlene Johnson. Sound Editor: Ben F. Hendricks. Music Editor: Evelyn Kennedy. Portions of this motion picture were filmed in Deschutes National Forest. Associate Producer: Kevin Corcoran. Costume Designer: Ron Talsky. Music: Buddy Baker. Orchestrations: Walter Sheets. Editor: Ray de Leuw, A.C.E. Art Directors: John B. Mansbridge, Frank T. Smith. Director of Photography: Frank Phillips, A.S.C. Stunt Coordinator: Buddy Joe Hooker. Stunts: Hugh Hooker, Dean Ferrandini, Bill Burton, Tom Huff, Steven Chambers, Dick Ziker, Hank Hooker, Fred Waugh, Donna Hall, David Ellis, Dave Rodgers, Chad Randall, Jean Coulter, Julie Ann Johnson, Gage Nelson. Set Dresser: Eric A. Hulett. Special Effects: David Domeyer, Allen Hurd. Running time: 90 minutes.

Songs: "May the Best Man Win" Al Kasha, Joel Hirschhorn, sung by Michael Dees. "Something Good is Bound to Happen" Buddy Baker, Arthur Alsberg, Don Nelson.

Cast: Jim Dale (Eli Bloodshy, Wild Billy Bloodshy, Jasper Bloodshy), Karen Valentine (Jenny Willingham), Don Knotts (Denver Kid), Jack Elam (Rattlesnake), Darren McGavin (Mayor Ragsdale), John Williams (Mansfield), Warren Vanders (Boss Snead), Debbie Lytton (Roxanne), Michael Sharrett (Marcus), Dave Cass (Jack), Richard Wright (Pete), Don "Red" Barry (Bartender), Jimmy Van Patten (Jake), Gregg Palmer (Jeff), Ed Bakey (Joshua), John Steadman (Old Codger), Eric Server (Cowboy 1), Paul Lukather (Cowboy 2), Hap Lawrence (Cowboy 3), Robert Rothwell (Cowboy 4), Terry Nichols (Prisoner), Dallas McKennon (Saloon Man 1), Stanley Clements (Saloon Man 2), Don Brodie (Saloon Man 3), Warde Donovan (Saloon Man 4), Ron Honthaner (Saloon Man 5), Norland Benson (Farmer 1), Jack Bender (Farmer 3), Jim Whitecloud (Indian Chief), Brad Weston (Indian), Russ Fast (Official 2), Mike Howden (Official 3), Art Burke (Official 4), James Michaelford (Dead-Eye).

Rustic footage of a stagecoach racing by is shown during the credits as "May the Best Man Win" is sung and played. The Denver Kid and Mayor Ragsdale witness this stagecoach coming into town.

Aboard is Jasper Bloodshy who has two sons Wild Billy and Eli who are about to inherit all of his land. But before they can confirm the will, Bloodshy throws himself off a cliff to his death.

Eli is a Good Samaritan type who sings on the street corner collecting money for the poor. Eli is not greeted with respect and the villagers throw vegetables at him when he gets the news about the land he is to inherit. He brings the two children named Roxanne and Marcus that help him with his charity work.

Wild Billy is a gunslinger and fires his guns randomly at the other cowboys to get his way. Mayor Ragsdale orders his men to take care of Eli before he gets into town as one Bloodshy is enough.

A stagecoach stops by Eli and the drivers confuse Eli with Billy and gladly take him and the kids to Bloodshy, for fear of his wrath. On their way, they meet Mayor Ragsdale's minions who want Eli, but they confuse him with Billy also and drop their guns. Eli gets out and chastises the men for aiming guns at him and accidentally sets off their Gatling gun. With Eli and the children no longer aboard, the stagecoach speeds off. The three set out on foot with the Gatling gun and soon meet Jenny, a schoolteacher who rides by with her horse and wagon.

Jenny invites them aboard and brings them to Bloodshy. The Denver Kid is the sheriff in town and he receives the will from the Bloodshy estate and he brings it to Mayor Ragsdale.

Eli and Jenny ride into town where there is a big gunfight underway. When anyone sees Eli, they think it is Billy and they run off and hide. Eli wants to know where the sheriff is and brings the Gatling gun into the saloon, which frightens everyone.

The sheriff wonders what Eli is doing with the huge gun and then congratulates him on becoming rich. He thinks that Eli is Billy, too, until the real Billy shows up in the same saloon. Finally, everyone realizes that Billy and Eli are twins as do Billy and Eli.

Billy challenges Eli to a race and the winner gets possession of all of their father's land.

There are other big problems as a lawbreaker named Rattlesnake also comes into town and he's mad at the sheriff for messing with his sister, and he challenges the sheriff to a gunfight.

Both men are incompetent as Rattlesnake gets his spurs locked together and the sheriff shoots himself in the foot.

Mayor Ragsdale befriends Eli and they discuss the challenge of winning over the land with a race. Jenny is leaving because the school and church has burnt down. Eli says that with the fortune, he can rebuild both.

Ragsdale goes back to his men and wants them to prevent Eli from winning the race. His men say that there shouldn't be any problem with Billy winning the race.

Meanwhile, it turns out that Jasper Bloodshy is not dead after all and he asks his butler Mansfield if he had delivered the will to the sheriff. Mansfield says that he has and wants to watch the race from afar to see how his sons battle it out.

Rattlesnake and the sheriff are continuing their fight and agree to shoot at ten paces, but they still keep messing up.

The children practice shooting guns to help Eli and Jenny shoos them off. Then she fires a gun and almost kills Eli in the process. She fires again and almost kills Jasper who is spying from atop a nearby roof.

Later, Rattlesnake and the sheriff are still at it and try to battle each other while trying not to slip in the mud. The sheriff stops and counts three to draw, but slowly sinks into the mud like quicksand.

Eli calls a meeting for the few men that are on his side and they feel that Eli doesn't have a chance. They discuss how Jasper ran the town with Jasper listening in from the rafters. They say that Bloodshy used to be a good town, but it went downhill. Eli says that there is not going to be a race and says that he will ask Billy to just split the inheritance. Jasper is disappointed.

Billy is in the saloon, drinking and firing shots at the piano when Eli comes in to discuss putting aside the contest and to split the inheritance. Billy is not interested and throws him out of the saloon and pours a bucket of water on his head.

The next day, the race is about to begin with the sheriff officiating. Rattlesnake shows up and says that their battle is not over yet, and the sheriff says later. The sheriff keeps blathering until everyone gets impatient and fires shots at him to get the race started.

The children and Jenny bring Eli some gifts to help him out including a white cowboy hat. The sheriff tries to fire a shot to begin the race, but someone else ends up doing it. Billy takes an easy lead and Eli starts off by going the wrong way in his steam engine.

Once he starts going the right way, Ragsdale's men try to stop him by lassoing his engine. Finally, Eli gets out in front, but Billy zips ahead again. Then Eli has problems with his steam engine falling apart and Ragsdale's men sending the engine on the wrong train route and then off the tracks totally through an Indian village and off a cliff.

Eli is down but not out and gets aboard a canoe, which soon springs a leak. Then he gets caught up in some rough rapids that send him downstream in a hurry. Billy thinks that he's won, but Eli is still going.

Ragsdale's men catch up with Eli again and tie him up with a rock and it looks as if they intend to toss him back into the river, but they are actually suiting him up to mountain climb. They do give him a drink from their canteen which gets him quite drunk.

Word gets back by carrier pigeon that Eli and Billy are virtually neck-a-neck. Jasper and the children overhear Ragsdale's plans about offing Eli. He adds that he wants the men to also off Billy as then the reward reverts to the executor of the will which is him.

Jasper wants to do something about this but Mansfield suggests staying back. The children and Jenny do take a horse to try to stop the killings.

Ragsdale's men toss large rocks towards Eli to stop him, but miss. Meanwhile, Billy is still ahead or so he thinks. Eli inadvertently keeps pulling ahead by using stunts like walking a tightrope, which is disrupted by Ragsdale's men who chop at the ropes.

Ragsdale's men are finally stopped by Jasper, who has had enough. Jenny sees Jasper and attacks him, not knowing that it's Jasper. The kids help.

The three catch up with Eli and warn him about Ragsdale's plans. They all leap aboard another horse and cart which splits in two as they ride. They stop at a spot where they see some more of Ragsdale's men and sneak up behind them and try to capture them before they can stop Billy. Eli yells out a warning for Billy, but he ends up getting captured.

Jasper and Mansfield are back on their feet, but are soon trapped by a branch that lands on Ragsdale's men as well as Jasper and Mansfield. The branch also lands on the dynamite plunger that was set to blow up Billy.

Eli goes to investigate to see what has happened. The people at the finish line feel that someone will show up very soon after hearing the blast. Eli finds Billy and is happy that Eli saved his life. Eli explains Ragsdale's plans and they team up to get him.

Jenny and the children arrive back in town with Ragsdale's men, who are all tied up in the back of another horse cart. Ragsdale announces that he is going to inherit the entire estate as neither brother seems to be coming back.

Eli comes into town and is angry at Ragsdale and starts shooting at him. It turns out that Eli and Wild Billy have switched clothes to impersonate each other in order to take care of Ragsdale.

Rattlesnake and the sheriff finally resume their gunfight now that the contest is over.

Jasper appears out of nowhere to tackle Ragsdale who thinks he's seeing a ghost. Finally, between the three they capture Ragsdale and get him locked up. The sheriff doesn't want to hear about it and tells his new deputy, Rattlesnake to take over while he goes to the meeting to see what will happen to the land now that Eli and Billy are getting along.

Eli leads the congregation to sing "Something Good is About to Happen" as they talk about missing their father, Jasper. Jasper decides not to reveal himself to the rest of the town and leaves town with Mansfield, but not before waving goodbye to the sheriff.

The versatility of Jim Dale is shown by the fact that he plays three different roles of Jasper, Billy and Eli.

Don Knotts returns to star in a film similar to those he made for Universal back in the 1960s. Prior to this, Knotts had only been teamed up for his Disney films or a featured player. This is the second teaming of Knotts and Darren McGavin in a film. They were last seen together in *No Deposit, No Return*.

This film shows how far special effects had gotten since *The Parent Trap* as many scenes show Jim Dale overlapping each other as Eli and Billy, whereas in the earlier film the two Hayley Mills characters tended to stay side by side.

This film was the first to use the new multi-colored Buena Vista logo. It didn't help in improving Disney's image at this point.

The original trailer included on the DVD features *The Madcap Adventures of Mr. Toad*, an excerpted cartoon featurette from *The Adventures of Ichabod and Mr. Toad* (1949).

1979

Something had to be done and everything was now riding on *The Black Hole* to save Disney, as revenues were now slipping.

Fewer new films were made for the anthology show: *Donovan's Kid*, *Shadow of Fear* (working title: *The Whisper in the Gloom*), *Born to Run*, *The Omega Connection* (working title: *The London Connection*), *The Sky Trap*, *Baseball Fever* and *Major Effects*. There was also the new half-hour special called *Black Holes: Monsters That Eat Space and Time*.

The Footloose Fox was a new live action featurette released to theaters. *The Love Bug* (1969) *101 Dalmatians* (1961) and *Sleeping Beauty* (1959) were also reissued.

Disney lost two of its major directors this year with the deaths of Norman Tokar and James Neilson. This contributed to more changes in tone of Disney pictures.

Another major problem occurred as Don Bluth and other animators walked out on *The Fox and the Hound* in September and decided to go it alone with the projects *Banjo, the Woodpile Cat* and the more ambitious *The Secret of NIMH*, which Disney passed on.

Big, non-Disney films that could have been made by them include *The Muppet Movie*.

At Disneyland, the big new attraction was the Big Thunder Mountain Railroad, opening on September 2 and replacing the boring old Rainbow Caverns Mine Train and all that area that used to have the mine train and the pack mules and such.

Also, all-attraction Disneyland Passports were tested this year and ultimately replaced the traditional A-E tickets.

Meanwhile, the purse at the Walt Disney World National Team Golf Classic was raised to $250,000.

Ground-breaking ceremonies were held for Epcot Center in October, while Walt Disney World honored its 100 millionth guest, Kurt Miller.

The biggest surprise success this year was the release of *Mickey Mouse Disco*. Though sales were initially slow, the decision was made to advertise the LP on TV and sales exploded, resulting in a double platinum record.

You're in Love, Charlie Brown was nominated for a Best Recording for Children Grammy, but lost.

In the comic book world, Gold Key continued to publish *Donald Duck, Mickey Mouse, Uncle Scrooge, Walt Disney's Comics and Stories, Huey, Dewey and Louie Junior Woodchucks, Super Goof, Chip 'n' Dale, Walt Disney Showcase, Daisy and Donald* and *Winnie the Pooh*. *The Beagle Boys* ended its run and was replaced by *The Beagle Boys vs. Uncle Scrooge*. *Scamp* also ended its run.

Mickey Mouse Surprise Party was a one-shot and a hardcover coffee table salute to *Snow White and the Seven Dwarfs* and one on Donald Duck similar to *Mickey Mouse: Fifty Happy Years* were issued this year. Abbeville continued its hardback comic book salute with a book featuring Goofy and one featuring Uncle Scrooge.

The *Air Pirates Funnies* copyright infringement case from 1971 took a strange turn as creator and artist Dan O'Neill fought back with more Disney copyright infringement by publishing Disney characters in *Coevolution Funnies*, defying the 1975 court ruling. O'Neill was threatened with real jail time and finally stopped. He always felt and still feels that he won…but won what?

Take Down

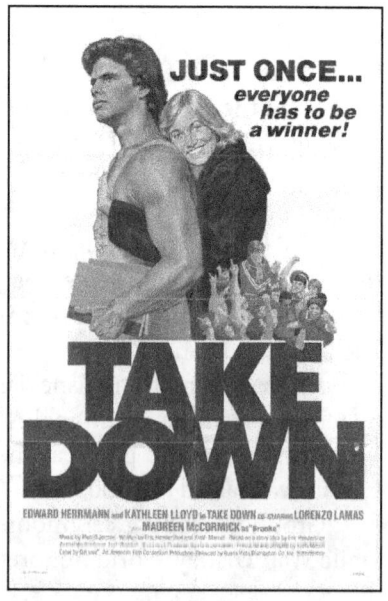

AN AMERICAN FILM CONSORTIUM production released by Buena Vista on January 1979, Color by Deluxe. Producer: Kieth Merrill. Associate Producer: Jack Reddish. Executive Producer: David B. Johnston. Director: Kieth Merrill. Writers: Kieth Merrill, Eric Hendershot based on a story idea by Eric Hendershot. Editor: Richard Fetterman. Music: Merrill Jenson. Director of Photography: Reed Smoot. Special thanks to Orem High School, Hillcrest High School, American Fork High School, Olympus High School, Box Elder High School, Viewmont High School. Thanks to Utah Athletic Association, Alpine School District. Production Manager: Jack N. Reddish. Art Director:

Douglas G. Johnson. Casting: Mike Fenton, Jane Feinberg. Executive Assistant to the Producer: Geneve Scott. Production Coordinator: Joan Arnold. Second Assistant Director: Douglas Wise. Controller: Sheldon Jew. Technical Advisor: Eric Hendershot. Script Supervisor: Terre Trelawney. Wardrobe: Michael Hoffman. Make-up: Randy Lowe, Catherine McClellan. Local Casting: Karl Wesson. Sound Mixer: Robert E. Sheridan. Sound Editors: Robert C. Dearberg, Jack T. Knight. Head Electrician: Richard Cronn. Property Master: Jan De Witt. Promotion: Will Whittle. Financial Advisor: Ronald A. Melanson, C.F.P. Montage Editor: Peter L. McCrea. Still Photographer: Erik Hein. Construction Coordinator: Marvin Stoutsenberger. Camera Operators: Michael O'Sullivan, T.C. Christensen. Camera Assistants: George Griner, Gordon Lonsdale, Stan Wadley. Boom Operator: Robert Heizer. Editorial Assistants: Michael Amundsen, C.W. Royer. Best Boy: David Schwartz. Dolly Grip: Bill Randall. Grips: Scott McGowan, Dennis Petersen, Dee Johnson. Electricians: Grant Williams, Fred Jones, John Tilton, William Van Hoek. Set Decoration: Trev Holmes, Chuck Anderson. Draftsman: Lowell Allen. Assistant Props: Roger Crandall. Craft Services: Clark Naisbitt, Alan Goresbeck. Post Production Secretary: Judy Christiansen. Transportation: Lee Carroll. Security: Lyn Nichols. Caterer: Bart's Catering. First Aide: Sheryl Pack. Secretary: Carol Ketchum. Production Assistant: David Fairbanks. Location Equipment: Productions Systems, Inc. Post Production Sound: Anvil Studios, England. Titles and Opticals: Master Film Effects. Music Score Performed by The National Symphony, London. Running time: 107 minutes. Rated PG.

Song: "I Tried for You" Written and Performed by Lorenzo Lamas.

Cast: Edward Herrmann (Ed Branish), Kathleen Lloyd (Jill Branish), Lorenzo Lamas (Nick Kilvitus), Maureen McCormick (Brooke Cooper), Nicholas Beauvy (Jimmy Kier), Stephen Furst (Randy Jensen), Kevin Hooks (Jasper Macgruder), Vincent Roberts (Bobby Cooper), Darryl Peterson (Ted Yacabobich), Toney Smith (Chauncey Washington), Salvadore Feliciano (Tom Palumbo), Boyd Silversmith (Jack "Notoe" Goss), Scott Burgi (Robert Stankovich), Lynn Baird (Doc Talada), Ron Bartholomew (Warren Overpeck), Kip Otanez (Zeno Chicarelli), Hyde Clayton (Principal), Oscar Rowland (Nick's Father), Elizabeth Grand (Nick's Mother), Prentiss Rowe (Referee), Christy Neal (Suzette Smith), Melvyn Pegues (Hood #1), David M. Thorne (Hood #2), Lucille Thorne (Band Teacher), Fred Rowland (Orem Coach), Carl Benett (Hillcrest Referee), Ron Tree (Viewmont Coach), Mary Pederson (Teacher), Kieth Merrill (Arnold), Jack Reddish (Announcer), Doug Johnson (Official), Lisa Gleave, Cindy Chipman, Julie Graves, Karen Frankenberry, Heidi Preston, Julie White (Mingo Junction Cheerleaders), Bob Kawa (Coach), Larry Miller (Leroy Barron), Gary Peterson (Thad Lardner).

A big football game is underway where the score is already 38-0. The Mingo Junction team gets into a huddle but decides to go against what the coach advises. The tactic doesn't work as Mingo Junction gets tackled by Rockville.

In the locker room, the team wants to wait until next year until one of the team says that they can win in wrestling. They set up a wrestling team of varying weights; some need to gain and some need to lose.

Nick works for a local company with a hard hat. Later, he hauls his father home from the local tavern. His father is dead drunk and Nick tells him to go to sleep. Nick is reprimanded by his mother for continuing to miss school.

The next day, Ed Branish is quickly grading papers for the remedial English class he teaches. Meanwhile, they are still trying to recruit athletes for the wrestling team and also to get permission from the school to have a team.

That night, Ed and his wife Jill have a fight as he wants to work on his thesis and his wife wants to talk about raising their family. His wife reveals that the principal wants Ed to coach the new wrestling team and there is no one else.

Nick shows up to school the next day and is chewed out by Ed for his failing grades and lousy attendance. They stop when Brooke, Nick's girlfriend shows up for class.

The wrestling team has its first meeting with Ed, who is ill-equipped for the job and says so. Again, he complains to the principal who insists that he at least give coaching a try.

Nick walks home when Brooke shows up to offer him a ride, but he initially refuses, then gets into the car and she takes him home. At home, Nick is mad at his father for slacking off at the job. His father is mad at Nick for doing poorly in school. Nick's mom asks about graduation and Nick reveals that he isn't going to graduate.

Ed comes home to a nice meal cooked by Jill and Ed says that he doesn't want to talk about having children. Jill says that they aren't going to talk about that and gives him a gift of a book called "Mastering Wrestling" wrapped in a Shakespeare book cover and another gift of shoes, a coach's sweater and a whistle.

The next day Ed really decides to give coaching a shot, but starts off miserably. Bobby asks if he should continue to keep the weight record and Ed says yes. He tells everyone to "work it up." He means to work out as he sneaks into the corner to read. Soon, water drips on him. It turns out to be one of the wrestlers sweating off some pounds.

Ed still complains to the principal, but he refuses to take Ed off as coach of the team and that it is not a request, but an order and that he needs to find a wrestler that weighs 185 pounds. Jill still encourages Ed to try and to see it as a new challenge.

At the fast food restaurant where they are eating, they see Nick throw down a man who is harassing his friends and Jill says that that should be his 185 pounder.

Others are still looking for someone who weighs 185 pounds and Randy is offered the position, but he says he weighs too much. They really just need 12 guys, so Randy reluctantly agrees, even though he really is a band major.

The referee weighs everyone and lets it slide this time when everyone is overweight, but not next time. He says to Ed that everyone will have to slim down.

The wrestling team is called the Bulldogs and they have their first bout against the Orem Tigers. Everyone does ok, although one of the Bulldogs gets disqualified for biting. Randy gets frightened and withdraws from the match.

After the match, Ed reveals to Jill his back story about sports that he had the desire to be a World Series champion for the New York Yankees, but that dream went away being a 6'3" 97-pound weakling who was always the last pick.

Ed uses his book knowledge to quote phrases about winning to the wrestling team. He has had a change of heart about being coach and feels that he actually can help.

Ed pays a visit to Nick's house and wants to talk to Nick about joining the wrestling team since Randy has chickened out. Nick says that he can't qualify because of his flunking English and his tardiness. Ed says that he can work things out, but Nick says no.

Nick sings "I Tried for You" while thinking things over. Ultimately, he changes his mind and decides to join the wrestling team after all.

Rockville High's wrestling team is getting a full workout with a strong coach. Mingo Junction's team is much less organized, but improving. The team is still not enamored with Ed as coach, but Ed keeps trying and reads his book, practicing some moves on Jill.

The next day, one of the students challenges Ed to a basic take down. This makes Ed nervous but he decides to take the challenge and knocks the student down.

There is another match and the referee is stricter this time about the weight so they have to take more extreme measures such as going to the bathroom to lose the weight in a hurry.

Mingo Junction does much better this time, winning most of their bouts. Nick is up next and he wrestles very well. He is reluctant to take praise from Ed, but eventually warms to him and teaches him while they work out together.

During the third match, Bobby takes a powerful throw, but he's ok. Brooke and Nick rush to his side to help him back to his seat.

Overall the Mingo Junction team keeps doing better and better. Ed pulls Nick aside and says that he still will not graduate and has to take English over again. Apparently, there are more hoops to jump. Ed offers to tutor Nick, but Nick is really upset and violently attacks his next partner in the wrestling match and causes a brawl and is eventually thrown off the mat by the referee.

Brooke tries to calm Nick down, but he cannot be consoled. Ed even tries to talk to Nick again, but Nick is not interested in being on the wrestling team again, so Randy is recruited again for the team, but is nowhere near the athlete that Nick was.

Nick finds out that Bobby has quit the team too, which upsets him. Bobby has quit because he is too ill and so Nick goes to see Bobby's sister, Brooke to offer condolences as to rejoin the team and not give up in Bobby's honor. He begins a strenuous workout routine.

At the championship bout, they give Bobby an honorary letterman's jacket. The referee doesn't want Nick to wrestle because of what happened last time, but both competing coaches agree to let him wrestle. The referee says that he will be keeping an eye on him. Nick may not wrestle anyway because he is overweight, so he heads for the toilets and the steam pipe.

Jill reveals to Ed at the competition that she is pregnant. At first the news doesn't faze him, but then it hits him.

The Mingo Junction team is doing exceptionally well and Nick still tries making the cut for the team. Randy is back in the band and plays his tuba to encourage the team to victory.

The score is tied at 27. The heavyweight bout is held before the 185-pound bout so that Nick can have a few more minutes to qualify. Finally, he does.

Nick's match gets underway and he wins after a lengthy battle. Even Nick's father is there to root him on.

This is a very pleasant film and somewhat of a surprise at this time for Disney movies. The students seem real instead of being the plastic Medfield College variety.

I saw this in the theater when it first came out and didn't realize that it was a film distributed by Disney. I only remembered that the film had Marcia Brady from *The Brady Bunch* and Flounder from *Animal House*, and there was a lot of bathroom going and sweating going on in order to make weight.

Lorenzo Lamas' song and singing isn't much, but it's interesting now as a strange sort of footnote.

For those used to seeing Maureen McCormick as just "Marcia, Marcia, Marcia," they might be pleasantly surprised that she has some acting chops in this film. Unfortunately, as described in her autobiography, this was a difficult time for her as she was in the midst of a long battle with drugs during this time.

This was the first film since Walt's death that was not produced by Buena Vista, only released by them. Though a common occurrence today, this was quite unusual for 1979. What's interesting is the number of additional credits for this film compared to the standard onscreen Disney credits at this time.

Disney must have been impressed with the work of Edward Herrmann and Stephen Furst as they signed them on for further pictures.

When *The Black Hole* came out at the end of 1979, a lot of attention was focused on the fact that it was the first PG-rated Disney film. This is technically true, as *Take Down* wasn't officially a Disney film, but it was released by Buena Vista, which makes this the first PG-rated release.

Actor Darryl Peterson went on to become professional wrestler Maxx Payne.

The North Avenue Irregulars

RELEASED BY BUENA VISTA ON February 9, 1979, Technicolor. Producer: Ron Miller. Co-Producer: Tom Leetch. Associate Producer: Kevin Corcoran. Director: Bruce Bilson. Screenplay: Don Tait based on the book by Reverend Albert Fay Hill. Set Decorator: Norman Rockett. Special Effects: Eustace Lycett, Art Cruickshank, A.S.C, Danny Lee. Stunt Coordinator: Eddy Donno. Titles: Art Stevens, Joe Hale. Production Manager: John Bloss. Unit Production Manager / Assistant Director: Christopher Seiter. Second Assistant Director: Randy Carter. Sound Supervisor: Herb Taylor. Sound Mixer: Bud Maffett. Costumes: Chuck Keehne, Emily Sundby. Make-up: Robert J. Schiffer, C.M.A.A. Hair Stylist: Eddie M. Baron. Sound Editor: Ben F. Hendricks. Music Editor: Evelyn Kennedy. Music: Robert F. Brunner. Orchestration: Walter Sheets. Editor: Gordon D. Brenner. Art Directors: John B. Mansbridge, Jack T. Collis. Director of Photography: Leonard J. South, A.S.C. Special Effects: Hans Metz. Running time: 100 minutes.

Songs: "Sunday Morning Music" Words and Music: Al Kasha, Joel Hirschhorn.

Cast: Edward Herrmann (Michael Hill), Barbara Harris (Vickie), Susan Clark (Anne Woods), Karen Valentine (Jane), Michael Constantine (Marv Fogelman), Cloris Leachman (Claire), Patsy Kelly

(Rose Rafferty), Douglas V. Fowley (Delaney Rafferty), Virginia Capers (Cleo), Steve Franken (Tom Voorhees), Dena Dietrich (Mrs. Carlisle), Dick Fuchs (Howard), Herb Voland (Doctor Fulton), Alan Hale (Harry, the Hat), Melora Hardin (Carmel), Bobby Rolofson (Dean), Frank Campanella (Max), Ivor Francis (Reverend Wainwright), Louisa Moritz (Mrs. Gossin), Marjorie Bennett (Mother Thurber), Ruth Buzzi (Doctor Rheems), Ceil Cabot (Pedestrian), Carl Ballantine (Sam), Linda Dee Lyons (Bette), Dave Morick (Policeman), Cliff Osmond (Big Chin), Damon Bradley Raskin (Danny), John Kerry (Roca's Lieutenant), Darrow Igus (Mechanic), Dennis Robertson (Truck Driver #1), Ed McCready (Truck Driver #2), Dave Ketchum (Captain Bamford), David Rode (Toby), Pitt Herbert (Mr. Thurber), Rickie Layne (Bettor), Tom Pedi (Bartender), John Wheeler (Clothier), Mickey Morton (Bootsie), Chuck Henry (TV Announcer), Jack Perkins (Bouncer), Bill McLean (Mr. Younger), Roger Creed (Mailman), Walt LaRue (Grandpa), Jack Griffin (Traffic Cop), Len Ross (Passerby), Douglas Hume (Driver), Gary Morgan, Jack Cameron White, Michael Lloyd, Kim Bullard (Strawberry Shortcake), Joan Hackett, Rachel Jacobs (Voice), Larry Moran (Jacob).

After an upbeat *Pink Panther*-like animated opening, a new pastor named Michael Hill shows up in town to the church with his two kids. The kids go investigating and pester Mr. Rafferty, who is painting the bell tower causing him to hold on to dear life on the bell cord.

The women of the church rush out, but it takes a while for a few of them to go retrieve a ladder. By this time, Rafferty is about to fall to the ground, but the ladder is propped up just in time.

The ladder is too short so the ladies take the ladder up to a higher floor, leaving Rafferty dangling. A crowd holding a large sheet is waiting to catch him from below as the ladies lower the ladder from above.

The ladder elongates as Rafferty climbs aboard and Rafferty falls to the sheet below as the ladder becomes unsafe.

Afterwards, the ladies welcome the new reverend to town and then go on their way. Anne Woods, one of the church ladies, stays behind and gives Michael her notes from the past few months. She hopes that she can remain secretary and Michael hopes so, too, but she is having difficulties since Michael is new and her father was the previous pastor.

Michael reveals that he has a lot of new plans for the church, but Anne says that it's probably better if he does it himself. Rose stops back in to pick up her scarf and Michael puts her in charge of the church singing fund, which she gladly accepts to the surprise of Anne.

Church is held the following Sunday and many of the regular patrons are shown in attendance, while the ladies sing a hymn, somewhat in tune.

Reverend Hill comes out to give his sermon as Mrs. Rafferty reveals that her husband bet the entire church fund on a horse race, enraging the pastor. Michael gives a speedy service and exits with Mrs. Rafferty and together they ride on his motorcycle to the betting parlor to stop the bet. The betting parlor is inside Sam the Tailor's shop. Sam says that gambler Harry the Hat is in back, and he also says that he has to press his pants as part of the deal before he sees Harry.

He removes his pants and goes in the back to discover a number of other people placing bets that aren't wearing their pants. Michael asks Harry for the money back and Harry refuses.

After the horse loses, Harry agrees to pay the money back and says to go through the door to get his money. The door leads to the outside and Michael goes around front to get back inside, but now the tailor shop door is closed and locked as well. Michael returns to the church without any pants.

Later, Michael returns back with new pants and the police, but when they get there, there is no funny business or gambling going on at all. As Michael leaves in disgust, Sam returns Michael's pants.

Still later, Michael performs a sermon on television on his show *Words to Live By* and accuses the police of being in cahoots with the gamblers. Everyone is watching the broadcast and realizes that this is a risky accusation.

The next day, Michael receives many death threats for his accusations of the town being ripped off by gamblers. He also gets a phone call from Dr. Fulton, the head of the Presbyterian Church telling him to leave politics out of his sermons and to just take care of recruiting new church members.

Michael takes this advice and goes door to door to former church members who give a variety of excuses as to why they no longer attend.

Michael comes across Strawberry Shortcake, a rock quartet who agrees to perform at the church in order to attract new members.

Marv Fogelman and Tom Voorhees from the Treasury Department come into town to speak with Michael about breaking up the gambling joints, but they will need spies, so he recruits Claire and five other women of the church to do the spying.

Fogelman shows up to the meeting and is shocked that Michael has only recruited women for the job. Marv explains that they need the women to place bets with the police watching in order to nab the crooks. They all agree to do it.

One of the church ladies named Jane is the first one to try and dresses up kind of trampy and enters a bar in order to nab their first crook. She places a bet at the bar in front of Marv.

Jane's fiancé, Howard and his mother come in wondering what Jane is doing looking all made up in a bar and she knocks him out rather than explain.

Meanwhile, Tom and Claire go to a flower shop to place a bet, but Claire speaks too loudly and their bet is rejected.

Church ladies Vickie, Cleo and Rose place a bet at a local diner, but when Rose presses the button on the tape recorder to incriminate the man at the diner, she presses play instead and "Roll out the Barrel" plays, scaring the man off.

All of the women fail and Marv and Tom are ready to pull the plug. The women all say they will do better next time and so Marv gives them all another chance.

On their second go round, Marv radios in to the ladies who are strategically placed around town in their cars to spy on various goings-on. They all use code names in order to not be traced so easily.

Vickie tries to be helpful but she has a carful of kids and dogs. Marv is still trying to send somebody to investigate and finally gets Cleo to do the job. She only does so much and Claire is then ordered to follow the man to a local park. He opens the contents of a suspected bag that only has a sandwich.

The next day, Vickie is given another chance and spies on the man in the grocery store. The bags are switched and then the man leaves, so Jane follows in her car as do the other ladies. Marv asks the women to "peel off" and they all do so that no one is following the man.

Claire eventually finds him again and starts following him, following so close as to hit the man's car. She takes a crow bar from his car and breaks the radio so that he cannot hear what Marv and Michael are saying.

The failure of the ladies lands Marv in the hospital. Michael visits Marv asking for yet another chance and Marv doesn't want to be involved, but if the women want to do it, they still can.

Michael takes over and radios the ladies to get them to try to find the gamblers. Anne wonders what Michael is doing and disagrees with it, and decides to resign.

Next Sunday, Strawberry Shortcake makes its debut performance at the church.

After church, Michael's kids wonder if he has to resign as pastor and Michael says no. Later that evening, the church is bombed and Anne and Michael discuss the fate of the church. Anne agrees to fight now that this has happened and she becomes a spy, too.

She is assigned to chase a cable TV van. At one point, the van ducks into a garage and the van's exterior and license plates are quickly changed.

In a meeting with the ladies, Michael reveals that they lose the cars that they are tailing in the same general area. Anne comes in with a note saying that the church will not be rebuilt and that Michael has been fired.

The next day, Michael tries to plead his case to Dr. Fulton. Anne picks up Dr. Reems and Reverend Wainwright (who is scheduled to replace Michael) and sees the refurbished van from the previous day and radios in to Michael.

Jane and Howard are about to get married, but they race off when Jane gets the emergency call from Anne. Dr. Reems reveals that she has done this sort of spy work herself and volunteers her services.

Vickie gets the call and tells her children that the pet show is off, but before she can get very far, dumps a crate containing a large snake in the middle of the street.

Claire gets the call while she is in the beauty parlor getting her hair done. She leaves with tin foil in her hair.

Wainwright is now in on the action and he and Reems and Anne track the van down to an abandoned warehouse.

Michael leaves Dr. Fulton and hops aboard his motorcycle to help as do the other ladies, kids and Howard. They all converge upon the gambling headquarters inside the warehouse.

The gamblers flee, but it is Cleo to the rescue with her truck and the other ladies surround the crooks with their cars, smashing and crashing them in the process. All the cars crash except Jane's, who keeps getting steered out of the way by Howard.

One of the crashes ruins Claire's new nails, who seeks revenge on the gambling king pin named Mr. Rocca and destroys his car.

Michael finally shows up, but Rocca is not finished and escapes with another car. Jane wants to smash the car into Rocca's again, but Howard still stops her. Rocca is finally foiled and he and the other crooks are taken to jail.

In the end, the car is unscathed, until another car topples on top of it smashing it to bits.

Michael gives his final address saying that the church will not be rebuilt and he will be done. Just then, the women drive up with Dr. Fulton who has changed his mind and the church with Michael will go on.

A very good movie again and somewhat more sophisticated than what was typically done at Disney at this time. The smash-up derby ending was typical Disney, but the fact that religion was even toyed with as a subject matter was new and different for Disney.

It was a reunion for Karen Valentine and Michael Constantine as they both appeared on *Room 222* and of course, Barbara Harris and Patsy Kelly appeared together in *Freaky Friday*.

Darrow Igus was soon to be a regular on the *Saturday Night Live* rip-off show called *Fridays*.

It aired on the anthology show in 1987. In the UK, the film was released as *Hill's Angels*.

The scene where the church blew up had to be reshot and the church rebuilt as there was no film in the camera, originally.

The Apple Dumpling Gang Rides Again

RELEASED BY BUENA VISTA ON June 27, 1979, Technicolor. Producer: Ron Miller. Co-Producer: Tom Leetch. Director: Vincent McEveety. Writer: Don Tait based on characters created by Jack M. Bickham. Director of Photography: Frank Phillips, A.S.C. Music: Buddy Baker. Orchestration: Walter Sheets. Art Directors: John B. Mansbridge, Frank T. Smith. Editor: Gordon D. Brenner. Unit Production Manager: Tom Leetch. Assistant Director: Robert M. Webb. Second Assistant Director: Alan Green. Production Manager: John Bloss. Sound Supervisor: Herb Taylor. Sound Mixer: Henry A. Maffett. Costumes: Chuck Keehne, Mary Dye. Make-up: Robert J. Schiffer, C.M.A.A. Hair Stylist: Chris Lee. Sound Editor: Ben F. Hendricks. Music Editor: Evelyn Kennedy. Set Decorator: Norman Rockett. Special Effects: Art Cruickshank, A.S.C., Danny Lee. Stunt Coordinator: Louis Elias. Technical Advisor: Monty Laird. Makeup Artist: Bron Roylance. Special Effects: David Domeyer, Hans Metz. Stunts: Larry Holt. Running time: 89 minutes.

Cast: Tim Conway (Amos), Don Knotts (Theodore), Tim Matheson (Private Jeff Reid Phillips), Kenneth Mars (Marshal Woolly Bill Hitchcock), Elyssa Davalos (Millie Gaskill), Jack Elam (Big Mac), Robert Pine (Lieutenant Jim Ravencroft), Harry Morgan (Major T.P. Gaskill), Ruth Buzzi (Tough Kate), Audrey Totter (Martha Osten), Richard X. Slattery (Sergeant Slaughter), John Crawford (Captain Sherick), Cliff Osmond (Wes Hardin), Ted Gehring (Hank Starrett), Morgan Paull (Corporal #1), Robert Totten (Blainey), James Almanzar (Lennie), Shug Fisher (Bartender), Rex Holman (Reno), Roger Mobley (Sentry #1), Ralph Manza (Little Guy), Stu Gilliam (The Cook), A.J. Bakunas (Henchman #1), Dave Cass (Henchman #2), Louie Elias (Henchman #3), Jimmy Van Patten (Soldier #1), Jay Ripley (Soldier #2), Nick Ramus (Indian Chief), George Chandler (Elderly Man), Bryan O'Byrne (Photographer), Jack Perkins (The Drunk), John Wheeler (Conductor) Art Evans (Baggage Master), Ed McCready (Citizen #1), Ted Jordan (Citizen #2), Pete Renaday (Jailer at Fort), Bobby Rolofson (Boy), Tom Jackman (Officer #1), Joe Baker (Prisoner Joe), Allan Studley (Prisoner Pete), Mike Masters (Cowboy), John Arndt (Cavalry Man #1), Bill Erickson (Cavalry Man #2), Vince Deadrick (Sentry #2), Gary McLarty (Corporal #2), Bill Hart (Officer #2), Mickey Gilbert (Tough #1), Wally Brooks, Stacie Elias, Mike Elias, Jessica Biscardi (Young Lady #1), Hank Robinson (Townsman), Arthur Tovey (Townsman Outside Bank).

Amos and Theodore, the bumbing bad guys turned good from *The Apple Dumpling Gang* (1975) ride around aimlessly on their donkey, Clarice. They comment on what happened to Dusty and Donavan from the first movie as they ride into the next town. They claim to be going straight.

Meanwhile, a covered wagon on fire is sent in by the Shawnee Indians to a Calvary camp. Major Gaskill is upset and wonders what is keeping supplies from getting through.

Private Reid meets Millie Gaskill as she arrives into town. She gives Reid the cold shoulder.

Amos and Theodore come out of a clothing shop sporting new duds and then go in to get a photo taken of themselves just as their donkey crashes into the photo and knocks everything over. Amos and Theodore are both stuck in their braces designed to keep them still during the older photography methods.

Now broke, they try to figure out what to do next and how to stay out of trouble. Meanwhile, a fight breaks out and Marshal Hitchcock comes in to say that he doesn't tolerate the fighting.

Theodore and Amos say they have nothing to worry about and go to the bank in order to open a bank account, not to rob the safe for the first time. However, they do not realize that the bank is being held up as they enter. One of the robbers pretends to be a teller and handles their deposit by taking it and they soon leave. With Amos and Theodore, the only ones left in the bank, they are accused of robbing the bank.

An elderly lady named Kate sees the bank being robbed and screams and fires a gun as the real robbers speed away. Reid pushes Millie out of the way of the getaway and gets covered in mud.

The Marshal goes in to the bank to take care of everything and arrests Amos and Theodore. He orders them to drop their guns, which fire accidentally and knocks the guns out of the Marshal's hands and Amos and Theodore flee the scene.

Kate rushes around telling everyone about what had happened and even went directly to Amos and Theodore bragging that she knows what they look like when they call for witnesses.

The Marshal shows back up to ask questions, now with his hands bandaged up. He gets a copy of Amos and Theodore's photo from the photographer as Amos and Theodore go into hiding. Their donkey shows up with the stolen money.

Later they decide that they will take the money back and decide to drop it in from a nearby roof into the bank. As they heave the heavy bags over, Amos lets go prematurely and Theodore goes sailing in through the bank window and knocks the Marshal over in the process.

The Marshal returns with a neck brace and vows to get The Apple Dumpling Gang despite the fact that they returned most of the money and goes out to find them.

Soon, Reid offers to take Millie to deliver some champagne. Millie is still not impressed with Reid and vows to report him to her father. Amos and Theodore are hiding in the cart with the exploding champagne bottles.

Their donkey is roaming free and the Marshal decides to follow the donkey as she will lead him to The Apple Dumpling Gang.

Sergeant Slaughter discovers The Apple Dumpling Gang in the back of the cart at the army fort and asks Reid who they are. Amos and Theodore cannot answer straight as they are drunk. Slaughter takes them in and makes them soldiers.

Soon, a trapper brings in some dead soldiers and is disappointed that he gets no money for his good deed as they were on duty. Major Gaskill asks Jim what was in the wagon and tells him to put it in storage with the other evidence of Indian attack.

Reid takes the arrows and is captured and thrown in the brig for his theft. Meanwhile, Amos and Theodore are still sleeping off their hangover despite showing up for arms inspection. Slaughter puts them on to kitchen, wood and stable detail for their insubordination.

Major Gaskill is finally reunited with his daughter at a Fort Concho function. Jim says that he plans to ask Millie's hand in marriage tonight.

Amos and Theodore are behind the scenes peeling potatoes. They are then asked to bring in a huge punch bowl into the main room and spill it all over the place.

The Marshal follows the donkey into the Fort and orders Amos and Theodore to drop everything. This includes the punch bowl which causes a chain reaction and the Marshal gets covered up with cake and the fort gets set on fire.

Everyone tries their best to put out the fire, but Amos and Theodore do everything wrong and end up blowing up the fort with gun powder and kerosene. Eventually everyone has to evacuate with the Marshal still in pursuit of Amos and Theodore and the fort explodes.

The next day, Millie and Reid are missing and Amos and Theodore are tied to two large wagon wheels to keep them out of further trouble. Slaughter says that Amos and Theodore will be rebuilding the entire fort with their own two hands.

Out of the rubble comes the Marshal who says that he will be putting Amos and Theodore out of their misery by shooting them between their eyes. Marshal decides to make the shooting challenging by spinning the wheels they are connected to and shooting at them. Slaughter stops him because he needs them to rebuild the fort.

Meanwhile, Reed brings Millie to meet Martha. Martha says that he's a good catch and she tells Millie privately that Reed loves her.

Amos and Theodore have been removed from the wheels and are now back in uniform in order to be court-martialed and Major Gaskill has been relieved of duties and Jim will be promoted to take his place.

The Marshal has gone batty and is locked up in a strait jacket vowing revenge on Amos and Theodore. Amos and Theodore are dressed now in stripes and sent to prison.

The other prisoners are afraid of Amos and Theodore who think The Apple Dumpling Gang as villains to reckon with. In prison, they are in charge of cleaning various metal items and inadvertently go the wrong way and come across Big Mac and his cronies, who have been meeting secretly in a nearby cave about a train robbery.

Major Gaskill apologizes to Millie that they will have to leave and postpone the wedding and Jim says that he will marry her as soon as he gets another leave.

Mac's gang decides to spare Amos and Theodore, thinking they are more competent and useful and make them part of the gang to rob the train and steal the army payroll.

They all ride to the new town of Buffalo Springs and Amos and Theodore try to find the sheriff. They are told that Hitchcock is the Marshal of the town here, too! Amos and Theodore now want to escape and hide from Mac and the Marshal by disguising themselves as showgirls. They end up on stage and put on a show, then dance with two of the local bar patrons.

Big Mac leaves in disgust as he figures that Amos and Theodore stood him up. Amos and Theodore's donkey once again causes a mess attracting the attention of the Marshal, who is strung up the minute he points his guns at Amos and Theodore in drag.

Amos and Theodore escape dressed in Indian blankets and pretend to be Indians. They board a train that is soon boarded by Big Mac and his men. Reid is still AWOL, but jumps onto the passing train in order to see Millie who is also on the train.

Reid plants a huge kiss on Millie and reveals that his real name is Jeff Phillips and that he is actually a special agent hired to watch the train.

Big Mac meets up with Jim Ravencroft. It turns out that Jim is a traitor and wants a cut of the army money that Big Mac is going to steal.

Reid is knocked out and Millie pushes the man who knocks him out off the train. Meanwhile, the train is also being attacked by Indians which is considered strange by Mac and Jim as they have been peaceful for years.

Amos and Theodore realize that they are probably safer being with Big Mac's men after all and reveal themselves. The train is finally stopped and the

Indians said that Amos and Theodore traded their donkey for two blankets, but the donkey ran off.

The Indians just want their blankets back and in removing them, reveal that Amos and Theodore are still wearing the dancing girl dresses. The Indians get their blankets and ride off.

Big Mac starts the robbery but Reid arrests everyone. Amos and Theodore are set free because of their bravery and the fact that they didn't rob the bank in the first place and they ride off reading the newspaper on the back of their donkey.

A lot of people don't seem to like this film, but I feel that it is every bit as good as the first. I suppose it depends on your tolerance of Conway and Knotts' shtick, but I feel that they do well together as they also did in *The Prize Fighter* (1979) and *The Private Eyes* (1980), two movies not made at Disney featuring the stars.

This is the first Disney movie (barring *Take Down*) that changed tradition by having the majority of the cast and credit roll at the end of the picture instead of the start. Disney was starting to make real films!

This film aired on the anthology show in 1982. The prison sets used in the film were the old *Zorro* sets.

Unidentified Flying Oddball

RELEASED BY BUENA VISTA ON July 26, 1979 (July 10, 1979 in UK as *The Spaceman and King Arthur*), Technicolor. Producer: Ron Miller. Associate Producer: Hugh Attwooll. Director: Russ Mayberry. Screen Story and Screenplay: Don Tait based on Mark Twain's *A Connecticut Yankee in King Arthur's Court*. Director of Photography: Paul Beeson, B.S.C. Art Director: Albert Witherick. Costume Designer: Phyllis Dalton. Editor: Pete Boita. Production Manager: Robin Douet. Casting Director: Maude Spector. Assistant Director: Vincent Winter. Location Manager: Barrie Melrose. Continuity: Georgina Hamilton. Camera Operators: Malcolm Vinson, Ray Sturgess. Sound Editor: Peter Best. Special Photographic Effects: Cliff Culley. Make-up: Roy Ashton, Ernie Gasser. Hairdressing: Joyce James, Betty Sherriff. Stunt Coordinator: Vic Armstrong. Assembly Editor: Jack Gardner. Sound Recordists: Claude Hitchcock, Ken Barker. Music composed and conducted by Ron Goodwin recorded at Anvil Studios. Assistant to the Producer: Don Tait. Filmed on location and at Pinewood Studios, London, England. Second Assistant Director: Terry Madden. Boom Operator: Keith Batten. Sound Re-Recording Mixer: John Hayward. Special Effects: Ron Ballanger, Michael Collins. Running time: 92 minutes.

Cast: Dennis Dugan (Tom Trimble / Hermes), Jim Dale (Sir Mordred), Ron Moody (Merlin), Kenneth More (King Arthur), John le Mesurier (Sir Gawain), Rodney Bewes (Clarence), Sheila White (Alisande), Robert Beatty (Senator Milburn), Cyril Shaps (Dr. Zimmerman), Kevin Brennan (Winston), Ewen Solon (Watkins), Pat Roach (Oaf), Reg Lye (Prisoner).

Stardust is a spaceship that's supposed to travel faster than the speed of light and NASA is having a meeting about it. This is supposed to be a manned flight, but this idea is rejected.

Scientist Tom Trimble is assigned to create a humanoid robot to go into space instead. The robot is designed to be an exact replica of Trimble. Trimble also has to educate his robot self-named Hermes.

Once built, Trimble demonstrates Hermes in front of the NASA staff. The staff agrees to use Hermes, but when the flight is scheduled to take off, Hermes gets cold feet. Trimble is called to talk to Hermes about it.

While talking to Hermes, the rocket takes off not allowing Trimble time to get off the ship. Trimble and Hermes are now on a space voyage that's scheduled to last 30 years.

The ship hurtles through space. What they don't know is that the ship is also hurtling through time. They end up in the time of King Arthur.

A young maiden named Alisande sees the spaceship land and Trimble emerges wearing a full space suit. He asks where he is and Alisande says that he's in England in the year 508.

Sir Mordred the knight and his assistant Clarence witness Alisande walking with Trimble and wonders where he comes from. Trimble looks especially spooky as he is not able to remove his space helmet and his face is obscured. They all go towards the castle of Camelot.

Inside Camelot, Merlin the magician is performing a series of magic tricks for King Arthur. Mordred brings Trimble to Arthur to turn him in and burn him at the stake.

Trimble requests help to remove his helmet and he is finally freed. He then proceeds to tell a lengthy story about the history of the world from King Arthur to the 20th Century and why and how he got there, boring everyone in the process.

Alisande visits Trimble in prison and tries to help Trimble escape until he freaks her out with the special features of his space suit which repels heat and flame. She leaves and Trimble begins to check on the other prisoners, many of whom are there by mistake.

Trimble is brought out to be burned at the stake and he looks as if he's gained weight. Actually, Trimble has blown up the suit so he doesn't get burned. He lets Clarence borrow his copy of *Playtime* magazine, a *Playboy* parody.

As they tie Trimble to the stake, they puncture his spacesuit and it deflates. Fire is set and Trimble escapes unharmed as his suit doesn't burn, but the ropes binding him do.

Afterwards, Mordred commands Clarence to fetch his sword. Trimble runs off in panic as he burns himself. Mordred gets his sword and challenges Trimble to a duel and they fight except Mordred's sword keeps getting more and more metal objects stuck to it and the added weight causes Mordred to fall off a precipice.

King Arthur decides to befriend Trimble and shows him the infamous Round Table. Trimble tells Arthur that Mordred has been arresting men under false charges.

The next day, Trimble offers to let Clarence keep the *Playtime* magazine if he helps him out by sabotaging Mordred's jousting costumes and swords.

Trimble is late to the joust, but he finally turns up, only it isn't Trimble, it is Hermes. Alisande is fooled and they begin to kiss. Trimble through radio control tells Hermes to knock it off.

The jousting begins and Mordred chops off Hermes arm. Trimble orders Hermes to keep going until he cannot go any longer. Next, Mordred chops off Hermes head. Arthur asks Mordred when he will quit and Mordred says that he must yield or die. In the next joust, Hermes is completely thrown from the horse and not able to move. Mordred claims victory.

Trimble reveals himself and offers proof to Arthur about Mordred's evil deeds. Mordred rides off before he can be captured. Hermes is repaired and Arthur offers his appreciation for being told of Mordred's treachery.

Trimble offers to take Alisande on a tour of his ship, but she refuses not sure if she has feelings for Trimble or Hermes. Trimble assures her that he is flesh and blood just like her and that Hermes is a robot.

Later, Arthur and Trimble take his laser weapon to try to find Mordred. Merlin, meanwhile, utilizes Oaf in order to capture Trimble so that he can get Hermes back. He lures Trimble by telling Alisande that he will help turn her pet gander back into her father, a fate that isn't true as Alisande's father is still in prison.

Merlin captures Alisande and then checks through Trimble's belongings. While looking through his stuff, Merlin takes Trimble's laser gun.

Trimble and Hermes test fly a smaller version of the spaceship with Arthur and Gawain looking on. A man discovers Alisande's gander and wants to cook it and Trimble figures out that Merlin and Mordred are in cahoots and they need to be captured.

Trimble says that he needs to wear Arthur's finest armor in order to capture them with his space vehicle. He catches up with Merlin and Mordred and orders them to release Alisande.

Alisande hops aboard Trimble's lap and he blasts off with his jet pack seat in order to return to Camelot. Mordred and his men also return to Camelot and Trimble knocks them all over as he flies on his chair. Then, an all-out sword fight ensues between Arthur and Mordred and their men.

Mordred gets in a lucky shot and disables Trimble's seat. Trimble is stuck and calls down to Clarence and Alisande to help him down. Then, Trimble uses his walkie-talkie to communicate to Hermes to do battle from within the spaceship and blow away Mordred and his men.

Merlin sneaks aboard the ship, but Hermes stops him just in time. Hermes turns on the ship's magnetic fields which smash all of Mordred's men against the ship, knocking them out one by one. The magnetic force is so strong that Trimble's armor is pulled off.

In the end, Trimble gives Arthur a pile of Mordred and his soldiers, Trimble is given a place at the Round Table and Trimble takes a Polaroid before he leaves.

Alisande's father and the other mistaken prisoners are released, even though Alisande feels that it was Merlin who changed the gander. Trimble would like to take Alisande back with her, but doesn't want to risk the possibility of her not surviving the trip back to the 20th Century.

Trimble and Hermes blast off of a wooden ramp and soars back into space. Alisande is saddened to lose her new friends.

While traveling back, Trimble and Hermes discover that the gander has been aboard all along and hasn't aged a bit, so they go back to retrieve Alisande to take her back to the 20th Century.

This film was retitled *A Spaceman in King Arthur's Court* when aired on the anthology show in 1982, probably because the story was ripped off from *A Connecticut Yankee in King Arthur's Court*. In Europe, the film was known as *The Spaceman and King Arthur*.

One more post-*Star Wars* space film released by Disney before they gave it the great guns with *The Black Hole* in December. It reminds me a lot of the Don Knotts feature *The Reluctant Astronaut* (1967).

This was yet another Disney production done in England, but as with the American arm of Disney, the days were numbered for films made exclusively by Disney in the UK.

The film was shot at Alnwick Castle in England. This location was chosen after scouting 20 other locations. Follow up on scenes and interiors were shot at Pinewood Studios in London.

The special effects team had to create a robot that could still function without a head and an arm. They also invented a laser gun, a jet pack and a magnetized sword. There was also a 25-foot-long space shuttle-type space craft created.

The largest set in the movie was the Camelot set which was 120 feet long and required one of the largest stages at Pinewood to house it.

There were over 600 garments created for the extras in the film and the NASA uniforms had to be made on spec, but also be able to expand and deflate on cue.

Ron Moody resumed the role of Merlin in Disney's *A Kid in King Arthur's Court* (1995).

The Black Hole

RELEASED BY BUENA VISTA ON December 20, 1979 (December 18, 1979 in UK), Technicolor. Technovision. Producer: Ron Miller. Director: Gary Nelson. Story: Jeb Rosebrook, Bob Barbash, Richard Landau. Screenplay: Jeb Rosebrook, Gerry Day. Music Composed and Conducted by John Barry. Production Designer: Peter Ellenshaw. Director of Photography: Frank Phillips, A.S.C. Art Directors: John B. Mansbridge, Al Roelofs, Robert T. McCall. Editor: Gregg McLaughlin, A.C.E. Unit Production Manager: Christopher Seiter. Assistant Director: Tom McCrory. Second Assistant Directors: Joseph P. Moore, Christopher D. Miller. Miniature Effects Creator and Supervisor: Peter Ellenshaw. Director of Miniature Photography: Art Cruickshank, A.S.C. Composite Optical Photography: Eustace Lycett. Mechanical Effects Supervisor: Danny Lee. Matte Artist and Matte Effects: Harrison Ellenshaw. Robots created by George F. McGinnis. Animation Special Effects: Joe Hale. Animators: Dorse A. Lanpher, Ted C. Kierscey. Optical Photography Coordinator: Robert Broughton. Production Illustrators: Fred Lucky, Gene Johnson, Robert Ayres, Leon R. Harris. Assistant Mechanical Effects: Hal Bigger. Assistant Matte Artists: David Mattingly, Constantine Ganakes. Sentry Robot Coordinator: Tommy McLoughlin. Sound Supervisor: Herb Taylor. Sound Mixer: Henry A. Maffett. Special Sound Effects: Ben F. Hendricks, William J. Wylie, James MacDonald. Sound Effects Editors: George Fredrick, Joseph Parker, Wayne A. Allwine, Louis Terrusa, John J. Jolliffe. Additional Special Sound Effects: Stephen Katz. Dialogue Replacement: Bernard P. Cabral, Norman Carlisle, Al Maguire. Rerecording Mixers: John Van Frey, Nick Alphin, Frank C. Regula, Bob Hathaway. Production Manager: John Bloss. Costume Supervisor: Chuck Keehne. Costume Designer: Bill Thomas. Make-up Supervisor: Robert J. Schiffer, C.M.A.A. Hair Stylist: Gloria Montemayor. Costumers: Jack

Sandeen, Mary Dye. Make-up: Nadia. Set Decorators: Frank R. McKelvy, Roger M. Shook. Property Master: Wilbur L. Russell. Camera Operator: Lloyd N. Ahern. First Assistant Cameraman: Robert La Bonge. Second Assistant Cameraman: Cecil R. Wilson. Orchestration: Al Woodbury. Supervising Music Editor: Evelyn Kennedy. Music Editor: Helen Sneddon. Music Scoring Mixer: Dan Wallin. Script Supervisor: Sandy Nelson. Assistant Film Editor: Nicholas Vincent Korda. Key Grip: Donald Capel. Second Grip: Howard L. Hagadorn. Gaffer: Carl Boles. Best Boy: Bernard F. Bayless. Miniatures Unit: Special Effects Photographed by A.C.E.S. Automatic Camera Effects Systems. Miniature Mechanical Effects and Chief Model Maker: Terence Saunders. A.C.E.S. Operators: Bill Kilduff, Robert R. Wilson. Matte Photography: Ed Sekac, Arthur Miller. Optical Printer Operators: Ray O. Hoar, Fred E. Branson, Philip L. Meador. Production Assistant: Stephen M. McEveety. Key Grip: Doc Reed. Gaffer: Roger E. Redel. Pitching Lens Relay System: Continental Camera. Stunts: Bill Couch, Alan Oliney, Conrad Palmisano, Bobby Sargent, Billy Jackson, Terry Nichols, Katee McClure, Bob Herron, Stevie Myers, Howard Curtis, Don Pulford, Regina Parton, Len Glascow, Melvin Jones, Ronald Oliney. Special Effects: Eric Allard, Gary D'Amico, Allen Hurd, Hans Metz, Mike Reedy, Ken Speed, Conrad E. Palmisano. Main Title Graphics: Thomas Baker. Special Effects Miniatures: Mike Edmonson. Graphic Artist, Opening Titles: Barry Seybert. Lighting Technician: Dan Delgado. Still Photographer: Wynn Hammer. Video Assist Operator: Brian L. McCarty. Set Lighting Technician: Peter McEvoy. Video Playback Services: Dana Winseman. Running time: 98 minutes. Rated PG.

Cast: Maximilian Schell (Doctor Hans Reinhardt), Anthony Perkins (Doctor Alex Durant), Robert Forster (Captain Dan Holland), Joseph Bottoms (Lieutenant Charles Pizer), Yvette Mimieux (Doctor Kate McCrae), Ernest Borgnine (Harry Booth), Tommy McLoughlin (Captain S.T.A.R.), Roddy McDowall (Voice of V.I.N.cent), Slim Pickens (Voice of Bob), Gary Nelson (Drone with Mask Removed).

A theatrical overture plays before the credits roll. Then, the film begins in earnest. It is the year 2130. The crew of a spaceship is speaking with V.I.N.cent, a robot that gives answers about their whereabouts. The crew feels that they are close to a real black hole, but V.I.N.cent has picked up something else, a large spaceship that is the United States Space Probe 1 or Signus, a ship that had been thought lost and also had Doctor Kate McCrae's father among her crew.

They decide to get closer so that they can climb aboard the ship which turns out to be piloted by Dr. Hans Reinhardt. Before they come aboard, they scan the ship for any hostile life forms. They don't pick up anything and then they signal for a response.

The Palomino goes into a tailspin and they are losing oxygen due to the nearby black hole which is sucking them in, so they have to get aboard the larger ship quickly.

While trying to stabilize, Kate utilizes her E.S.P. powers to communicate telepathically with V.I.N.cent, who has gone outside the ship to make repairs. The spinning ship causes the small robot to lose its grip and head towards the black hole, but soon the larger ship lights up and rescues the smaller ship and the robot with its tractor beam.

Captain Dan Holland is suspicious of the larger ship, but they aren't in the position to complain. Kate, Doctor Alex Durant, Lieutenant Charles Pizer and Harry Booth agree. They soon land in the larger ship's docking bay and exit. V.I.N.cent returns to the small ship and is ok. Charles stays behind in the ship, while the rest go out to explore, but soon V.I.N.cent is zapped, causing a little distress among the others.

The group encounters a number of humanoid robots carrying double-barreled laser weapons and they are led to a fast-moving transport that zips along the length of the larger ship.

They exit the transport and enter a room that is the main control center of the entire ship. The room is run by a number of robots and computers. One of the robots is called Maximilian who appears with spinning blades for hands.

At this point, they encounter the real Hans Reinhardt. The crew cannot believe it is him. Kate asks the whereabouts of her father, but Reinhardt reveals that he is dead. In fact, all of the crew except Reinhardt is dead.

Reinhardt explains how all the other crew died as they fled the ship and he stayed aboard along with Kate's father. In the intervening time, Reinhardt has created a number of robots to replace the human crew.

Charles appears in the elevator escorted by a number of Reinhardt's robots reuniting the entire crew. V.I.N.cent and Maximilian do not like each other and Dan orders Reinhardt to call off Maximilian. Reinhardt doesn't take well to orders, but agrees.

Maximilian leads Dan, Charles and V.I.N.cent on a tour of the ship and they encounter a beat-up robot similar in model to V.I.N.cent in their journeys.

The rest go on with Reinhardt and Alex wonders why he doesn't want to go back to Earth to glory in his successes. Reinhardt says that he has no interest. Dan sneaks off from his group and Harry sneaks off from his.

Dan snoops around and finds a closet full of old uniforms. Then he sees a grouping of some different looking robots walking in unison, but before he can investigate further, Maximilian retrieves him.

Harry is more successful in getting closer to these robots, and tries to get into a conversation with one of them, to no avail. He then rubs his arm on a window with condensation on it to reveal a greenhouse. As he looks through, the robot that he attempted conversation with leaves the room.

The rest of the group and Reinhardt view the black hole just outside of the ship's window.

Dan, Charles and V.I.N.cent come across some robots doing target practice in an elaborate form of a video game. V.I.N.cent finally speaks to the beat-up robot who reveals his name to be B.O.B.

Later, the two groups reunite with Reinhardt to have dinner. During dinner, Reinhardt holds a toast about space exploration and reveals that he plans to drive his ship into the black hole.

Harry says that his plans are crazy. Meanwhile, B.O.B. has a shooting match with one of the newer robots called S.T.A.R., but loses when the robot bumps him. Then V.I.N.cent steps up to the plate and soundly defeats him. This infuriates his opponent so much that he self-destructs.

Reinhardt reveals that he needs the Palomino (their small ship) to pilot the way into the black hole. Reinhardt leaves the room and the rest discuss everything. Harry suspects that the robots he saw are human. Dan just wants to get out of there.

The robots that Harry saw are being shown by B.O.B. to V.I.N.cent who reveals that they are not really robots, but human as Harry suspected. They are spotted, but they blast the robot that spots them.

The men continue to discuss things when V.I.N.cent requests that everyone return to the ship. Kate and Alex continue to talk before Reinhardt returns. He wonders where everyone else went and says that no one is allowed to go around his ship unescorted.

Reinhardt decides to go take a test trip out in space and he wants Alex to monitor his progress.

V.I.N.cent and B.O.B reveals all of the information about the humanoid robots to Harry, Dan and Charles. They decide to not leave because there are now humans aboard. Harry objects and they realize that they do have to leave as there is no hope for the human robots.

Kate reveals that she and Alex return to the ship, but Alex has been swayed by Reinhardt's convincing conversations. V.I.N.cent telepathically tells Kate to return to the ship with or without Alex.

Reinhardt starts up the reactors on the larger ship. Before Kate leaves, she pulls Alex aside and tells him the bad news about the humans. Alex goes to one of them and removes its mask revealing a grim sight of a dying man.

At this point, Alex and Kate know they have to leave, but Reinhardt orders Maximilian to retrieve them. Instead, he starts his rotating blades and kills Alex in the process. Kate is arrested and taken to the hospital.

Reinhardt says to the others that Kate and Alex are remaining behind to help him out. V.I.N.cent says that that's a lie and that Alex is dead and Kate is being taken to the hospital.

Rather than leave, Dan goes out to rescue Kate with the two robots. Reinhardt fires thrusters on the big ship. Charles and Harry wait behind. Kate is now in the rotating bed that has been zapping the brains of the other humans to make them robots and gets zapped as well, but Dan arrives just in time to rescue her from a doomed fate. They don disguises and leave the hospital.

Dan radios Harry that they will be returning to the Palomino. Reinhardt gives the order to fire upon any humans between the hospital and the Palomino. Dan and Kate remove their disguises as they are no longer useful.

An all-out laser gun battle ensues, with B.O.B. sustaining the most damage, but they do return to their ship. Reinhardt allows the Palomino to leave with the plan to destroy it after they get a little ways away.

Dan asks Charles to sneak up on the robots hindering him and Kate from returning to the ship, while Harry remains behind. Charles comes in blasting and the three plus the two robots rush back to the Palomino, but not before Harry blasts off by himself.

Harry gets a little ways away when Reinhardt blasts the Palomino and destroys it. Dan, Charles and Kate are safe and still alive, but now stuck on the larger ship.

New problems occur when a meteor shower hits the ship and destroys much of it. The three survivors and the two robots flee into the greenhouse area of the ship and another gun battle ensues with the robots. A large hole is blasted in the ceiling and everyone has to hold on for dear life before they are sucked out of the ship. The sudden climate change alters the greenhouse into a snowstorm freezing the robots.

Reinhardt gives the command of full speed ahead into the black hole as the meteor shower passes. Going towards the black hole ruins the structural integrity of the ship and it starts collapsing upon itself. The ship is now a dead form hurtling in space towards the black hole.

Reinhardt calls Maximilian to prepare the probe ship, but is suddenly crushed by a large metal plate. He calls out for Maximilian or anyone to help him, but no one answers his call. The rest get closer to where Reinhardt is, but Maximilian greets them with his spinning blades and laser beams. V.I.N.cent holds him off as the others escape.

V.I.N.cent and Maximilian battle it out and V.I.N.cent does his own version of a spinning blade, disrupting Maximilian's circuitry and destroying him in the process. Maximilian then floats out into space.

Dan, Charles and Kate find the probe ship and V.I.N.cent tries to convince B.O.B. to keep coming, but he says his days are done. Charles loses his footing and floats away, but V.I.N.cent rescues him. They start the probe ship and try to fly away, but they have no other choice, they must go through the black hole, per Reinhardt's pre-set course.

Inside the hole, time flashes by like a strobe light as the ship rotates out of control. Reinhardt floats in space and reencounters Maximilian, becoming Maximilian. In the end, he stands upon a high precipice looking over a valley of flames and the humanoid robots. This was his ship.

Through a crystal pathway, what appears to be an angel is sighted. Finally, the surviving crew of Kate, Don, Charles and V.I.N.cent get through the hole and are safely on the other side.

The super-spectacular event for Christmas 1979 competed with *Star Trek: The Motion Picture* at the box office. Disney pulled out all stops for this motion picture, going so far as to hire some top-notch talent like Maximilian Schell, Anthony Perkins and Ernest Borgnine, all of whom never worked for Disney before.

The other big news surrounding this film at the time it came out was that it was the first Disney film to earn a PG rating, though technically it wasn't true. *Take Down* earlier in the year had a PG rating and various pre-1968 Disney films were rated PG when rated upon reissue. These include *Treasure Island* (1950) and *The Moon-Spinners* (1964).

James Bond composer John Barry was brought on board to give the music and definite Bondish like sound. This was also the first digital soundtrack and on DVD it sounds really clear and fresh.

Effects artist Harrison Ellenshaw discusses the numerous special effects on the DVD documentary. He discusses his father Peter's excellent work on the film. There were over 150 matte paintings in the film, which is very high for a film.

All of the light effects like laser beams and rocket blasts were all hand animated.

V.I.N.cent and B.O.B. were usually hung by wires and many scenes were shot upside down so that you wouldn't look for the wires at the top, as they were at the bottom. They also moved the robots with armatures.

Again, these were the pre-CGI days, so miniature models of all the ships were created and used. In fact, this was the last major Disney visual effects film to be made this way as the next film to be made with extensive visual effects was *Tron* and that was done in the new way.

Ellenshaw reveals that the fire department had to be called each time they shot certain scenes that required a lot of fire effects.

The giant rolling meteor scene was reminiscent of the upcoming *Raiders of the Lost Ark*.

The black hole itself is made up of about 12-15 combined effects.

Many of the same people who worked on other Disney films, worked on this film, and in many cases outdid themselves. Yet the film still comes up short. One of the main reasons is the robots. I still contend that if you edited out the robots, you could make a decent, watchable film that isn't so hokey, similar to how certain fans edited out Jar-Jar Binks on Internet versions of *Star Wars Episode 1: The Phantom Menace* (1999).

It is strange that the film couldn't have been better, especially since it is essentially a rip-off of Disney's own *20,000 Leagues Under the Sea* (1954) set in space.

Another big problem is with the ending of the film with its angel / devil analogies. It's corny and also very confusing. I've had to watch the film many, many times to try to figure out what was going on at the end. There's imagery like Reinhardt having apparent sex with Maximilian and just lame effects as they go through the black hole.

Working titles for this film include *Space Station One* and *Space Probe*. The film was announced in 1976, before *Star Wars* was released.

The film did get Academy Award nominations for Cinematography and for Visual Effects.

In the DVD documentary, Harrison Ellenshaw reveals that they didn't have an ending originally, and unfortunately, it shows. There was an ending utilizing the Sistine Chapel that was ultimately scrapped.

On the real ending, even Ellenshaw says that he doesn't know what it means.

Ultimately, as with the upcoming *The Watcher in the Woods*, they didn't really know how to end it. You knew they had to go through the black hole, but if you are going to show something, it had better be exciting and what was shown was decidedly not. Most other adaptations changed the ending so that the crew entered an alternate universe.

Though the film featured the first digitally recorded soundtrack, a CD version of the soundtrack wasn't released until 2011.

John Hough was scheduled to direct this film, but turned it down.

Famous comic book artist Jack Kirby drew the comic strip adaptation of this film. There was also a lot of other merchandising.

Though the film grossed $35 million, Disney was now in serious trouble, so much so that the next film was released without the Disney name on it.

1980

This was *the* year of transition for Walt Disney Productions. Even before *The Black Hole* was released, Disney knew that things had to change in their feature film area, decidedly the weakest area of the entire Disney organization.

Disney promoted 1980 as having "A New Look" and considered the films *The Black Hole, Midnight Madness, Lady and the Tramp, A Watcher in the Woods, The Last Flight of Noah's Ark, Herbie Goes Bananas* and *The Fox and the Hound* proof of this new direction.

Part of the reason for the change also was due to the promotion of Card Walker to Chairman of the Board. He retained the position of CEO, a position he had held since 1976. Walker's previous position as President was filled by Ron Miller, Walt Disney's son-in-law, in February. Walker replaced Donn Tatum who in turn became Chairman of the Executive Committee.

Miller's first action as leader was to appoint Thomas Wilhite to their ailing film division. Wilhite was Disney's Publicity Director, but now he was promoted to Creative Developer for Motion Pictures and Television.

Wilhite tried to remedy their ailing film department in a number of ways. One was the removal of the Disney name on the film *Midnight Madness*. Once considered an asset, it was now considered a liability. It didn't help. Better movies were really the answer.

Unfortunately, the "better" movies were plagued with various problems from the special effects problems from *The Watcher in the Woods* to the teaming up with Paramount Pictures in an effort to produce better features. All attempts failed with Disney unable to produce a sizable hit until 1984.

Ending this year was *The New Mickey Mouse Club* after three years.

The strongest area in the past few years were the theme parks and that success continued with Disneyland's 25th Anniversary in July. A-E tickets were replaced by all attraction ticket books in November at both theme parks.

In Walt Disney World's Magic Kingdom, Big Thunder Mountain Railroad opened in November and the announcements were made for Disney to go ahead with Walt's plans for EPCOT, now renamed Epcot Center. The

$800 million project is scheduled to open in 1982. The Mickey Mouse Revue closed in September, to be reopened at Tokyo Disneyland in 1983.

The purse of the Walt Disney World National Team Championship Golf Classic was raised again to $350,000.

Strangely, with all of this transition going on, the biggest success of the year was actually an innocuous little record entitled *Mickey Mouse Disco* in which session musicians went in and sang disco themed songs based on the Disney characters. The tremendous success of the record album spawned a "brand new" Disney short featuring classic animation footage of the various characters dancing (especially Goofy) to the beat. The album rose to number 35 on the *Billboard* charts.

The great success of this album resulted in more albums of new material featuring Mickey, Donald and Goofy. Titles included *Yankee Doodle Mickey*, *Goin' Quackers*, *Pardners* and *Mickey's Christmas Carols*.

Other non-soundtrack albums released this year included the debut of the (eventually) four-volume *Children's Favorites* series featuring Larry Groce. These records proved to be almost as popular as *Mickey Mouse Disco* resulting in more gold and platinum records for the studio, and *The Official Album of Disneyland / Walt Disney World*.

New movies created for the anthology show include *Donald's Valentine Day Salute*, *The Kids Who Knew Too Much*, *Disney's Oscar Winners*, *Sultan and the Rock Star*, *The Secret of Lost Valley*, *The Mouseketeer Reunion* and *The Ghosts of Buxley Hall*. There were also the new specials: *Snow White Live*, *Kraft Salutes Disneyland's 25th Anniversary* and *Lefty*.

Song of the South (1946), *Bedknobs and Broomsticks* (1971), *Mary Poppins* (1964), *Lady and the Tramp* (1955) and *The Aristocats* (1970) were among the movies reissued this year.

Films this year that could have been made by Disney include *Bon Voyage, Charlie Brown (and Don't Come Back)* and *The Empire Strikes Back*.

Although Super 8 films and 16mm films had been available for years for purchase or rental, this year was the introduction of the first video cassettes with *Pete's Dragon* (1977), *The Black Hole* (1979) and *Mickey Mouse on Vacation* among the initial offerings.

In the comic book world, Gold Key continued to publish *Donald Duck*, *Mickey Mouse*, *Uncle Scrooge*, *Walt Disney's Comics and Stories*, *Huey, Dewey and Louie Junior Woodchucks*, *Super Goof*, *Chip 'n' Dale*, *Daisy and Donald* and *Winnie the Pooh*. *The Beagle Boys vs. Uncle Scrooge* and *Walt Disney Showcase* ended their runs. *The Black Hole* appeared as a mini-series comic book.

Abbeville continued its hardback salute to comic books with a book called *Animated Features and Silly Symphonies*.

The Mouse Club, a group of Disneyana collectors was formed in January.

Midnight Madness

RELEASED BY BUENA VISTA ON February 8, 1980, Technicolor. Producer: Ron Miller. Co-Producer: David Wechter, Michael Nankin. Director: David Wechter, Michael Nankin. Writer: David Wechter, Michael Nankin. Music: Julius Wechter. Orchestration: Bob Florence. Editors: Norman R. Palmer, A.C.E., Jack Sekely. Art Directors: John B. Mansbridge, Richard Lawrence. Director of Photography: Frank Phillips, A.S.C. Unit Production Manager: Don Henderson. Assistant Director: Bob Gossom. Second Assistant Directors: David Kahler, Don Newman. Additional Photography: Mike Sweeten. Production Manager: John Bloss. Sound Supervisor: Herb Taylor. Sound Mixer: Art Names. Costume Supervisor: Jack Sandeen. Men's Costumer: Milton G. Mangum. Women's Costumer: Nedra Rosemond-Watt. Make-up: Robert J. Schiffer, C.M.A.A. Hair Stylist: Gloria Montemayor. Set Decorators: R. Chris Westlund, Roger M. Shook. Matte Artists: Constantine Ganakes, David Mattingly. Special Effects: Danny Lee. Stunt Coordinator: Reg Parton. "Starfire" game by Technical Magic. Certain Game Techniques Inspired by Don Luskin, Patrick Carlyle, Cherie Chung. The producers wish to thank the City of Los Angeles and the City of Burbank for their cooperation in producing this fictional motion picture. Sound: Allen Hurd. Running time: 112 minutes. Rated PG.

Songs: "Midnight Madness," "Don't Know Why I Came," "Someone New" by David and Julius Wechter. "Midnight Madness" sung by Donna Fein.

Cast: David Naughton (Adam Larson), Debra Clinger (Laura), Eddie Deezen (Wesley), Brad Wilkin (Lavitas), Maggie Roswell (Donna), Stephen Furst (Harold), Irene Tedrow (Mrs. Grimhaus), Michael J. Fox (Scott Larson), Dirk Blocker (Blaylak), Andy Tennant (Melio), Marvin Katzoff (Debater #1), Alan Solomon (Leon), Joel P. Kenney (Flynch), David Damas (Marvin), Patricia Alice Albrecht (Lucille), Brian Frishman (Barf), Sal Lopez (Blade), Robyn Petty (Berie), Betsy Lynn Thompson (Peggy), Carol Gwynn Thompson (Lulu), Christopher Sands (Debater #2), Michael Gitomer (Debater #3), Curt Ayers (Armpit), Trevor Henley (Cudzo), Keny Long (Gerber), Debi Richter (Candy), Kirsten Baker (Sunshine), John Fiedler (Wally Thorpe), Ceil Cabot (Mrs. Thorpe), Charlie Brill (Jerry), Loretta Tupper (Elderly Lady), Eddie Bloom (Game Control Bookie), Dave Shelley (Harold's Father), Marvin Kaplan (Bonaventure Desk Clerk), Bert Williams (Security Captain), Arthur Adams (Police Sergeant), Tom Wright (Cop #1), Evelyn Havard (Cop #2), Ernie Fuentes (Miniature Golf Dad), Pillar Del Rey (Miniature Golf Mom), Georgia Schmidt (Old Lady in Car), J. Brennan Smith (Bratty Kid), Don Maxwell (Bratty Kid's Dad), Paul Reubens (Pinball City Proprietor), John Voldstad (Bellboy), Jack Griffin (Tow Truck Driver), Dick Winslow (Tourist), Emily Greet (Teenage Girl #1), Sheri Shepard (Teenage Girl #2), Paul Victor (Cashier), Tony Salome (Irving), Donna Garrett (Busty Waitress), Natalie Devis.

Two roller-skating hotties named Candy and Sunshine hand out invitations to an all-night scavenger hunt. One goes to Wesley, a bookworm nerd who shoos the girls away as soon as they give it to him. Another is Harold, a fat slob who dumps his fast food in disgust at the local drive-in when it doesn't meet with his expectations.

The final invitation goes to Adam, a clean-cut individual who wonders who it is from, but the girls reveal nothing.

Adam shows up at the specified location where the two girls who gave the invites welcome him and the four others selected to do a scavenger hunt including Wesley and Harold. After a short pre-filmed introduction, the man who sent out the invites turns out to be uber-nerd Leon.

Leon has a game he calls The Great All-Nighter featuring clues to follow to get from one location to another. After he explains his plans, no one is interested in participating and they all leave the room. Leon is not discouraged and tells the girls that they will be back by Friday when the game is set to begin.

Back at college, Wesley gives a powerful speech stating that football is unnecessary prompting the football team to throw food at him. Then the football team shoots a keg of beer at a girl's sorority where Donna is in charge.

Adam is tutoring a student when his girlfriend Laura comes to visit to say that she would like him to play Leon's game.

Harold is gorging on candy and his girlfriend and father tell him to stop being so messy. Harold's father goes so far as to chew him out for being lazy and not doing anything and ordering him to do Leon's game. Harold agrees to do it so that he can get back at Adam.

Wesley decides to go ahead and do it after what the football team did and the football team decides to do it just to pick on the others especially Wesley. Both Wesley and Donna want to get Lavitas for what he has done.

The five teams are formed and they all show up on Friday to start the game. Adam needs one more player and recruits Flynch when they see his "date."

Candy, Sunshine and Leon run the game from his house and requests that everyone phone in from each location as they arrive and they distribute the first clues to all the teams which are color coordinated.

Lavitas and his football buddies call a huddle and do a cheer. They wear great clothes and drive a VW subtitled The Meat Wagon.

Wesley and his nerdy debaters wear white and ride motor scooters. Donna and her sorority pals wear red and are riding in her red pick-up. Adam and his team ride in his yellow jeep and wear yellow, too. They try to solve the first clue as they drive as do the other teams.

All the teams solve the clue as "See the Stars," but then head off into different directions as to what they interpret what that clue really needs. Meanwhile, Harold's team in blue in his blue mini-van is taking it easy and types in the clue into his computer which gives him the answer to go to the Griffith Observatory.

Back at Leon's place, Candy and Sunshine place models of each team in their exact whereabouts on a huge map that covers the wall. Mrs. Grimhouse, the landlord, stops by and shows Leon his eviction papers.

The green team is at the Wax Museum. The white team is at the Chinese Theatre. The red team is at a disco. Harold calls in to Leon to say that they are at Griffith Observatory and that the game is too easy.

The yellow team is searching a map of the stars when they realize they were looking at the wrong type of stars and go to the observatory. They drive up just as the blue team is leaving.

Adam needs to look through the telescope, but a kid is looking at a woman undress first, saying that he needs to look at Venus. After he's caught, Adam gets a good eye view of the woman and then they reset the view to get the clue. The green team bursts in just as they get that clue, but the yellow team leads them astray by setting it back to the stripping woman.

Back at the headquarters, some of Leon's neighbors are complaining about the noise happening late at night. He calms them down by telling them what's going on, making them extremely interested about who's going to win.

The blue team is at the next clue, but Harold is sneaking marshmallows when he's not supposed to. The next clue refers to 8800 keys and they scour a piano shop. At one point they go into a rousing edition of "Heart and Soul," but finally find the next clue on the piano.

Adam and the yellow team drive by and see his kid brother Scott sitting at a bus stop waiting for a bus to San Francisco. Adam drags Scott into the Jeep and they continue on their way. The yellow and green teams both show up just as the blue team exits.

They get back into the van and plug in the next clue into their computer, but it doesn't work since the workings are now all gummed up with marshmallow since Harold hid them there.

Back at the piano store, all of the other teams are there. The green team plays the notes and one of them shouts that it's the Pabst Blue Ribbon Theme. Everyone on the other teams shouts, "Thanks!" as they now all know where the next clue will be…at the Pabst Blue Ribbon beer factory.

Donna drives by a carnival and the two twin heavy-set girls named Peggy and Lulu jump out, prompting Donna to park in a tow-away zone to go find them. She finally finds them after following the signs of all the closed restaurants.

Back at Pabst, the green team is having a field day with all the beer as they dive into one of the vats. The yellow team's Scott tries to sneak a beer and is arrested for being underage and the entire team is kicked out, fortunately near the next clue which is being spelled out in the warehouse. The clue leads them to Johnnie's Fat Boy Burgers.

The blue team is now falling behind as they feverishly try to fix the computer.

Donna finally finds Peggy and Lulu sitting on a Guess Your Weight attraction. The green team emerges from the vat totally intoxicated.

Back at headquarters, more neighbors complain until they see the other neighbors sitting and enjoying themselves watching the proceedings.

The blue team sees the yellow team drive by and they decide to just follow them and see where they are going. The red team gets back to their pickup only to find it being towed.

The yellow team goes into the burger joint, while the blue team punctures their tires and gas tank. When they finally go into the restaurant, they find the white team there as well. The clue is to look between two giant melons which turn out to be the waitress' breasts, not actual melons.

All of the teams try to get the waitress' attention in order to get a better look at the necklace around her neck which reads, "Hug Me," which translates to "Huge M." There is only one place that has a huge M, and that's the miniature golf place.

The yellow team figures this out first, but cannot go anywhere since their tires are flat. After the blue team taunts them and drives off, the yellow team sets out on foot.

The green team is still at Pabst and totally drunk. The red team knocks out the tow truck man and steals his truck which still has their truck hooked onto the back.

Laura is assigned to watch over Scott, who reveals that the reason that he is so upset is that Adam and everyone else has forgotten his birthday. Meanwhile, Adam and Flynch hop into an elderly couple's car to get to Miniature Golf World.

Mrs. Grimhouse comes back to Leon's apartment to serve him the eviction paper due to the neighbors' complaints, but none of the neighbors are complaining now, so she leaves.

Adam and Flynch are getting nowhere fast, so they abandon the elderly couple's car and Flynch flags down some young girls who drive them to golf.

The blue team reads that they must go play a full game of golf and not rush to the 18th hole. Harold wants to rush to the 18th hole anyway. They play and discover Leon's clue that they still have to play and that they've lost their ball, so they have to pay for another game.

The green team just happens upon the blue van while driving around in a daze and one of their members want to vomit. They stop and go into the miniature golf.

The green team, white team, reunited yellow team and blue team all play golf. The green team gets the clue first which is written on the underside of the drawbridge. They exit golf just as the red team arrives and the red team exits and follows them to the airport.

The yellow team figures this out too. They have gotten their car back and tire repaired, but now they are stalled because they have run out of gas. The other teams leave for the airport.

Leon radios in to say that the clue can be found near terminal #3. The white team comes in and is offered literature by some Hare Krishnas which turns out to be the next clue, but they discard it.

The blue team and green team also ignore the Hare Krishnas. The yellow team arrives and Laura tries to tell Adam to pay attention to Scott, which is why he acts so rebellious.

Harold slugs one of the Hare Krishnas causing him to drop all of his flyers and one of the other blue team members sees that there is a picture of Leon on it, prompting the attention of all the other teams, so everyone goes to the lockers to get the next clue, which is Pinball City.

The yellow team discovers Madam Leona at the arcade which tells them to play a video game called "Star Fire" (which is actually the *Star Wars* video game). They don't do well with the game. Scott looks on and says that he plays that game better than the rest.

Scott wins the game and they get the next clue to go to a hotel, but even then Adam belittles and ignores Scott which pisses him off. Then Scott leaves and everyone else exits the car. Adam drives on alone.

The red team gets Leon's clue and the green team overhears it and blocks their exit, but Peggy and Lulu fire machine gun balls at them. The pinball man tells everyone to act like adults, but no one listens and the red and green team battles each other.

The blue team drives up wondering where the finish line is and Scott reveals it to them. Meanwhile, Mrs. Grimhouse brings the police to arrest Leon, but he impresses the police with his police scanner that he's using to run the game.

Adam has second thoughts and drives back to pick up the team and Scott, but Scott is being interrogated by the blue team for information. Scott gives them the answer and drops him off and Adam rescues him and is grateful.

The white team shows up to the pinball arcade and inadvertently joins in the mayhem being caused by the red and green teams. The blue team discovers that they have dropped their Fat Boy doll and Harold's girlfriend insists that they go back and pick up the doll. When they arrive, they see the yellow team back in shape and ready to go so the race is on.

Mrs. Grimhouse breaks one of Leon's machines and she gets arrested instead of Leon. Since there is no more tracking, all of the neighbors drive over to the hotel to see who will be the winner in person. Everyone sets up at the Bonaventure Hotel in Los Angeles.

The red and white teams have an argument and then ultimately agree to team up because the white team's mopeds work and the red team has the directions. Meanwhile the green team arrives and messes up the travel folders. Then the blue and yellow teams arrive.

The desk man panics and tells the security guards, who arrest the red and white teams as they are most visible, and throw them out of the hotel, temporarily. The white team takes bellboy outfits and then helps a lady recklessly in order to get back into the hotel. Then they let the red team in who are now disguised as cleaning women.

Chaos ensues as all the teams are frantically trying to get to the correct hotel room where Leon and the neighbors are hanging out. Leon sends out a general page for all the teams and gives out a clue about the pool area.

Mrs. Grimhouse is not being watched at this point and she picks up the phone and dials security with her nose since she is still in handcuffs.

At the pool, now the red team and the green team are arguing and eventually both teams as well as the white team end up in the pool. The yellow team and the blue team race up in separate elevators and they see the clue of room 2704.

Unfortunately, the teams are both in express elevators that bypass the floor. The yellow team gets to the other elevator bank first and is soon rushing up to the 27th floor when there is a power outage instigated by Harold. The blue team then goes up the stairs, while the yellow team and the security guards are both trapped in separate elevators.

The yellow team discovers the manual override and uses Scott's retainer in order to try to make it work. Meanwhile, the blue team is tiring out walking up 27 flights of stairs and makes it to the 27th floor at the same time as the yellow team gets their elevator working again.

The blue team turns the fire hose on the yellow team, but they use the retainer to override the security guards' elevator and the fire hose hits the guards and they take the blue team off to jail.

The yellow team finally gets to room 2704 and eventually does the other three teams. At the party, Leon awards Adam with a plaque for being the first team. The blue team is escorted back by the room and Harold breaks free when he sees all the food and starts gorging.

Adam and Laura kiss as everyone else celebrates.

The movie originally was going to be called *The Great All-Nighter* and was based on a real underground campus game that the screen writers read about in the newspaper.

In this day of reality TV, this movie now plays like the TV series *The Great Race*.

Michael J. Fox made his screen debut in this film albeit by the name Michael Fox. He was used as he was 18, but looked years younger but could work the long hours not allowed by minors.

And Paul Reubens also makes his big screen debut at Pinball City portraying an early version of his later Pee-Wee Herman character.

The DVD trivia reveals it took 17 takes to get Mrs. Grimhouse to make a phone call with her nose.

The football players utilize the same jerseys that were used in *Gus*.

Though films like *The Cat from Outer Space* (1978), *Unidentified Flying Oddball* (1979) and *The Black Hole* (1979) were made to capitalize on the success of *Star Wars*, this film was made to capitalize on the success of *National Lampoon's Animal House* (1978) by even hiring Steven Furst (also seen in *Take Down*) as a sort of John Belushi-ish character.

By this time, the Disney name was severely tarnished. The failure of *The Black Hole* didn't help, so this film was released without any mention of the name "Disney" anywhere, although Buena Vista was mentioned, so knowledgeable individuals knew that this still was a good ol' Disney film anyway, except that it was another PG one. Disney didn't identify itself by name with this film until the 2004 DVD release.

It grossed a paltry $2.9 million and was filmed in July 1979.

The Watcher In The Woods

RELEASED BY BUENA VISTA ON April 17, 1980 (October 7, 1981 for Edited Version), Technicolor. Producer: Ron Miller. Co-Producer: Tom Leetch. Director: John Hough. Director on reshot ending: Vince McEveety. Screenplay: Brian Clemens, Gerry Day, Harry Spalding, Rosemary Anne Sisson from the novel *A Watcher in the Woods* by Florence Engel Randall. Production Designer: Elliot Scott. Art Director: Alan Cassie. Director of Photography: Alan Hume, B.S.C. Editor: Geoffrey Foot, G.B. F. E., Music Composed and Conducted by Stanley Myers, recorded at Anvil Studios. Associate Producer: Hugh Attwooll. Final sequence designed by Harrison Ellenshaw. Costume Designer: Emma Porteous. Set Decorator: Ian Whittaker. Additional Photography: Godfrey Godar, B.S.C. Production Supervisor: Basil Rayburn. Casting Director: Maude Spector. Sound Editor: Jim Shields, G.B.F.E. Filmed on location and at Pinewood Studios, London, England. Assistant Director: Richard Hoult. Location Managers: Rita Davison, Peter Bennett. Continuity: Kay Felton. Camera Operators: Jack Lowin, Malcolm MacIntosh. Special Effects: John Richardson. Photographic Processes: Robin Browne. Stunt Supervisor: Vic Armstrong. Make-up Chief: Ernie Gasser. Make-up for Miss Davis: Jill Carpenter. Make-up: Eileen Fletcher. Hairdressing Chief: Joyce James. Hairdresser for Miss Davis: Bobbie Smith. Hairdresser: Betty Sherriff. Sound Recordists: Claude Hitchcock, Gerry Humphreys. Final Sequence: Visual Effects: David Mattingly, Dick Kendall, Don Henry. Special Photographic Effects: Art Cruickshank, A.S.C., Bob Broughton. Special Effects Assistants: Neil Corbould, Ken Speed. Trainee Pyrotechnician: Tony Dunsterville. Special Effects Technicians: Ricky Farms, Garth Inns. Special Effects Artist: John Pohl. Model Effects: Tad Krzanowski. Visual Effects Camera: Jon Sorensen. Running time: 100 / 83 minutes. Rated PG.

Cast: Bette Davis (Mrs. Aylwood), Carroll Baker (Helen Curtis), David McCallum (Paul Curtis), Lynn-Holly Johnson (Jan Curtis), Kyle Richards (Ellie Curtis), Ian Brennan (John Keller), Richard Pasco (Tom Colley), Frances Cuka (Mary Fleming), Benedict Taylor (Mike Fleming), Eleanor Summerfield (Mrs. Thayer), Georgina Hale (Young Mrs. Aylwood), Katharine Levy (Karen Aylwood), Dominic Guard (Young John Keller).

ADDITIONAL CREDITS INCLUDED IN ORIGINAL ALTERNATE ENDING:

Other World Sequence Creator: Leon R. Harris. Animation Supervision: Joe Hale. Kinetic Light: Sam Nicholson, Brian Longbottom. Special Photographic Effects: Art Cruickshank, A.S.C. Special Mechanical Effects: Danny Lee. Alien Design: Joe Hale, C. Henry Selick, Andrew Gaskill, John Emerson, Rick Heinrichs. Animation Effects: Jack Boyd, Jane Boyd. Matte Artist: David B. Mattingly. Art Director: John B. Mansbridge.

The Curtis family is driving through the woods and is being watched. They stop at a mansion for rent. Parents Paul and Helen Curtis wonder why the rent is so cheap and the property is still available.

The elderly Mrs. Aylwood lives there and the family would have to live with her. She greets the realtor and is upset that she wasn't contacted before the family arrived, but allows them in anyway.

Daughters Jan and Ellie Curtis explore the house as dad plays the piano. Jan takes a look outside an upstairs window and sees a light flash. The window glass breaks and cuts her.

Mrs. Aylwood checks up on her and then says that the family can stay. Jan would like to keep looking, but mother asks why. Jan has had some weird feelings about the house, the woods and Mrs. Aylwood and suspects that something awful happened in the house at one time.

Back in the realtor's car, the realtor reveals that Mrs. Aylwood had a daughter at one point about Jan's age. Soon, the family moves in.

Jan takes a look in a mirror and does not see her reflection. The mirror shatters and reveals a hologram of a girl with a blindfold on. Later, Jan reads "The Green Light" in bed and Ellie frightens her.

Everyone is put to bed, but Jan witnesses some people outside her bedroom. Later, she cannot sleep and hears Ellie having a nightmare. Afterwards, Ellie asks if she can get into bed with Jan, who says yes.

The next day, at a nearby farm Ellie picks out a small puppy for sale. There is something moving in the barn and then Ellie falls into a trance and writes the name "Karen" in reverse on the window. Ellie says that she is going to name her dog "Narek."

A lady speaking with their mother sees the word Karen from afar and goes into distress. Back at the house, Jan sees a triangular piece of glass on the window as Ellie plays with her new dog. Jan looks again and Ellie and her dog are gone. Jan goes outside to look for Ellie and switches off a transistor radio that was left behind. Mrs. Aylwood is watching.

Jan goes deeper into the woods to see if she can find Ellie. She finally finds her deep in the woods after yelling for her. Jan then sees a bright flash and then two more and Jan is thrown into the water. Mrs. Aylwood comes to Jan's rescue, but it looked as if she was trying to drown her at first.

After rescuing her, Mrs. Aylwood reveals that her daughter's name was Karen and Jan says that she saw Karen in the mirror with the blindfold. Mrs. Aylwood explains where Karen went. She was blindfolded as part of a game and disappeared. Mrs. Aylwood believes that her daughter is still alive and out in the woods somewhere.

The next day, the family goes to a motorcycle race with their friend Mike as one of the contestants. Jan goes in for a closer look, but Ellie calls her away and a motorcycle flies off the tracks and lands exactly where Jan was standing.

Local Mary Fleming, who was freaked out about Karen's name earlier explains why she stays away from the woods and what happened to Karen to her son, Mike who begins asking her a lot of questions about Karen after speaking with Jan.

Ellie shows Jan her viewer for the upcoming eclipse. The parents leave to do some grocery shopping. Jan and Ellie go horseback riding with Mike and he reveals that his mother didn't want to talk about it much.

There is stranger goings on in the woods and when they ride towards them, they all flee in terror. There is a flash and it causes a truck to almost run over one of the horses and also to overturn.

Jan rides off and sees Karen's face in the chapel in a coffin and goes to investigate another part of the mansion and she encounters Tom, which startles her. Mike tells Jan that Tom was one of the three that saw Karen disappear, and tells her to calm down and to stop thinking there's anything supernatural going on.

Jan also says that the same triangle that is on her window is also on the coffin. Meanwhile Tom goes back to reveal to Keller that he saw Jan, who he mistakes for Karen. Keller says not to worry. He was just seeing things.

Meanwhile, Jan and Mike go to a local carnival and go to a fun house which has a room of mirrors. While looking in the mirrors, she sees Karen with the blindfold on instead of her own reflections for a few moments. She tells this to Mike who doesn't believe her.

Jan does her own investigations and comes upon the house of Keller to ask him for help. She explains that she sees Karen in mirrors and has to know what happened to Karen. Keller tells her to go away.

Jan decides to do an investigation in the woods and goes to see Tom. Tom says that he never found Karen when he looked for her. Jan asks why Karen was blindfolded and Tom says that he wasn't supposed to talk about it according to Mr. Keller.

Finally, he breaks and says that they were playing a game of "Ring around the Roses" and that he, Mary, John Keller guided Karen into an old church. Together, they did an initiation ceremony and when they were done, there was a bright flash and Karen had disappeared.

Back at the house, Mrs. Aylwood plays a music box for Ellie that plays the same tune as what was playing at the park. It was owned by Karen. Jan returns to tell Mrs. Aylwood about what happened to Karen.

The music box causes Ellie to go into a trance and starts speaking for Karen. Jan and Ellie's mother freaks and says that they are now going to leave the house. As they try to leave, the car starts to falter and Jan says that the spirits are trying to prevent them from leaving. Helen, their mom says nonsense, but soon they are completely stalled.

Helen tries to start the car, but Jan takes the keys and orders everyone to get out of the car and off the bridge where they stopped. Soon, there is a blinding flash and the bridge bursts into flames sending the car hurtling into the ravine below.

Everyone goes back to Mrs. Aylwood's home and Jan starts having nightmares, while Ellie sleepwalks. Ellie is in the bathroom and writes "Do Again Tomorrow" in reverse in the mirror. Ellie wakes up and doesn't know why she has written this.

The next day, Ellie can't find her eclipse viewer. As she looks for it, she starts saying similar phrases to Jan that Karen has said or had been said about her. Jan calls Mike and says that she needs to have Tom, John and Mary together again at the church during the eclipse in order to bring Karen back.

She reveals her plans to Mrs. Aylwood, who initially stops her, but then lets her go ahead and do it.

Jan asks John to join in the séance. He initially refuses, but eventually relents. Tom and Mary show up soon afterwards. The eclipse is starting so they have to hurry and repeat the ceremony, which initially happened during an eclipse.

This time they cannot run away or break the circle for it to work and Jan will replace Karen complete with blindfold. When they start, Ellie arrives speaking with Karen's voice. Mary wants to run, but they don't let her break the circle.

Bright lights surround Jan and the circle. Mike tries to break their circle, but they don't budge, so he rushes it and the circle is broken, but they have successfully brought her back.

Mrs. Aylwood arrives just in time to reunite with her daughter.

ALTERNATE ENDING #1:

The eclipse is starting so they have to hurry and repeat the ceremony, which initially happened during an eclipse.

This time they cannot run away or break the circle for it to work and Jan will replace Karen complete with blindfold. When they start, an alien arrives that zaps Mike. Jan removes her blindfold and sees the alien and is shocked. Mary and Tom start to run, but they end up backing up in fear as does John. The alien approaches Jan and takes her up with him and they disappear.

Helen appears and asks Mary, Tom and John where Jan has gone. They said that they did a séance that went awry, but soon Karen and Jan reappear.

Karen and Jan come home to find Ellie reuniting with her dog Narek and Karen is reunited with Mrs. Aylwood.

Jan explains to Ellie what had happened.

ALTERNATE ENDING #2:

Jan calls Mike and says that she needs to have Tom, John and Mary together again at the church during the eclipse in order to bring Karen back.

She reveals her plans to Mrs. Aylwood, who initially tries to stop her by pleading with her, but then lets her go ahead and do it.

Jan asks John to join in the séance. He initially refuses, but eventually relents. Tom and Mary show up soon afterwards. The eclipse is starting so they have to hurry and repeat the ceremony, which initially happened during an eclipse.

Ellie and her mother, Helen look through her eclipse viewer as the eclipse is about to begin. Then Helen goes inside and cannot find Jan. Helen tells Ellie and Mrs. Aylwood come in to tell Helen to stop the séance.

This time they cannot run away or break the circle for it to work and Jan will replace Karen complete with blindfold. When they start, an alien arrives that zaps Mike. Jan removes her blindfold and sees the alien and is shocked. Mary and Tom start to run, but they end up backing up in fear as does John. The alien approaches Jan and takes her up with him and they disappear.

We end up in the other world where Jan is dropped off to encounter Karen. Once they reunite they disappear to return into the real world.

Helen appears and asks Mary, Tom and John where Jan has gone. They said that they did a séance that went awry, but soon Karen and Jan reappear.

Karen and Jan come home to find Ellie reuniting with her dog Narek and Karen is reunited with Mrs. Aylwood.

Jan explains to Ellie what had happened.

Director John Hough is back with another tale of the supernatural. Unfortunately, unlike the two *Witch Mountain* movies, this one is really a misfire, mainly due to a lack of an ending with convincing special effects, of which the DVD presents two versions.

Bette Davis does a much better acting job here in comparison to *Return from Witch Mountain* (1978).

In the DVD commentary, Director John Hough reveals that this is really the first horror suspense thriller to bear the Disney name.

Ron Miller screened Hough's *The Legend of Hell House* (1973) and that's what prompted him to contact Hough to direct three films for Disney.

The farm in the film was also used in the 1960s *The Avengers* TV series which Hough also worked on. The writer on this film, Brian Clemens, also created *The Avengers*. His original script was much darker, so other writers were brought in to lighten it up.

Many scenes shot on location were also the same location used in the film *The Haunting* (1963), which is one of Hough's favorite films.

Three puppies were used in the making of the film, so that they could be ready at all times.

The film was 90% shot on location, but Hough believes that the interiors should have been shot on sets, as it was difficult to move cameras around.

Bette Davis tested to play herself as 40 years younger for one scene, but in the end, even she realized that she couldn't pull it off.

The motorbike stunts and crashes were all performed live by skilled stuntmen. They could have all gotten seriously hurt or worse.

If Kyle Richards looks like Kim Richards, it's because that Kyle is Kim's younger sister. She also had bit parts in the two *Witch Mountain* films.

All of the British actors and actresses in the film had Shakespearian stage acting experiences.

David McCallum of course is best known for his TV work on *The Man from U.N.C.L.E.*

The fun house mirror sequence was a total lift from Orson Welles' *The Lady from Shanghai* (1948). Hough is an admitted Welles fan and reveals that he borrowed the idea for this film.

The cat jumping scene was copied from Hough's own *The Legend of Hell House*.

Disney was still having issues with their movie audiences and issued their trailers with stern warnings that this is not a fairy tale and that parents should preview the movie before allowing pre-teens to watch.

The troubled production was released twice; both times without the proper ending that was desired. Hough considers the finished film a failure as he didn't have control over the effects of the final scenes and the ill-conceived alien was onscreen far too long as to be truly laughable by the critics.

The reshot ending cost $750,000 and was not directed by Hough because he had moved on to another film project that tied him up. Hough said that the alien should have been in, but only in the briefest of moments. The reshot ending had no alien at all.

In the DVD booklet, effects artist Harrison Ellenshaw said "I went through all these endings, which were all wretched."

Also, the movie was shortened considerably from 100 minutes to 83 minutes.

In the DVD booklet, actress Carroll Baker said that Hough was "under a lot of pressure" and "sometimes lost his patience."

Actress Lynn-Holly Johnson said that the entire production originally took three months, and then the new ending was shot a year later. Unlike *The Black Hole*, which had no ending to start, this film did have an ending, originally.

Alternate ending #1 was the version that Director John Hough preferred, but the alien was considered laughable so they had to go and reshoot.

This version was the one first released to theaters until it was pulled from distribution. It was never issued on home video until the 2002 Anchor Bay DVD version.

Alternate ending #2 is a combination of the two other endings, plus some other lame-looking Other World special effects footage. This footage was thought lost, but was also found and issued on video on the 2002 Anchor Bay DVD version.

The Anchor Bay DVD is the preferred version to own as when Disney reissued it on their own label, they cut the commentary and the extra scenes.

After all was said and done, the film grossed only $5 million.

Herbie Goes Bananas

RELEASED BY BUENA VISTA ON June 25, 1980, Technicolor. Producer: Ron Miller. Director: Vincent McEveety. Writer: Don Tait based on Characters Created by Gordon Buford. Music: Frank De Vol. Editor: Gordon D. Brenner. Art Directors: John B. Mansbridge, Rodger Maus. Director of Photography: Frank Phillips, A.S.C. Co-Producers: Kevin Corcoran, Don Tait. Unit Production Manager: Danny McCauley. Assistant Director: Win Phelps. Second Assistant Directors: Stephen M. McEveety, Christopher D. Miller. Second Unit Director: Michael Dmytryk. Additional Photography: Mike Sweeten. Production Manager: John Bloss. Sound Supervisor: Herb Taylor. Sound Mixer: Henry A. Maffett. Sound Editor: Ben F. Hendricks. Music Editor: Evelyn Kennedy. Costume Supervisor: Jack Sandeen. Men's Costumer: Milton G. Mangum. Women's Costumer: Mary Dye. Make-up Supervision: Robert J. Schiffer, C.M.A.A. Make-up: Nadia. Hair Stylist: Gloria Montemayor. Orchestration: Al Woodbury. Set Decorators: Norman Rockett, Roger M. Shook. Special Effects: Art Cruickshank, A.S.C., Danny Lee. Matte Artist: Constantine Ganakes. Stunt Coordinator: Buddy Joe Hooker. Stunt Players: Hank Bill Hooker, Steve Davison, Art Scholl, Bill Burton, Steve Vandeman, Bobby Porter, Donna Hall, Hugh Hooker, Bill Erickson, Richard Wright. Mexican Production Staff: Production Supervisor: Anuar Badin. Assistant Production Managers: Cesar A. Jimenez, David Prieto. Assistant Director: Mario Cisneros. Art Director: Agustin Ytuarte. Set Decorator: Enrique Estevez. Our thanks to the State of Jalisco, Mexico, City of Guadalajara, City of Puerto Vallarta, Secretary of Communications and Transport Ferry Service (Mexico), Republic of Panama. Assistant Production Manager, Mexico: Mario Cisneros. First Assistant Director, Second Unit: Peter L. Bergquist. Construction Coordinator: Richard J. Bayard. Sound Editor: Bill Wylie. Special

Effects: Gary D'Amico, Mike Edmonson, Hans Metz, Mike Reedy, Ken Speed. Stunts: James M. Halty, Ken Speed. Camera Operator: Lloyd Ahern II. Gaffer: Carl Boles. First Assistant Camera: Robert LaBonge. Camera Operator, Second Unit: Jim Luske. Second Assistant Cameras: Annie McEveety, Joe Valdez. Second Assistant Camera, Second Unit: Jeff Miller. First Assistant Camera, Second Unit: Randall Robinson. Gaffer, Second Unit: Jim Rose. Director of Photography, Second Unit: Mike Sweeten. Camera Operator, Second Unit, Mexico: Leon Sanchez. Assistant Camera, Second Unit: Harry Young. Transportation Co-Captain: Mario Simon. Helicopter Pilot, Second Unit: James W. Gavin. Diver: Ken Speed. Running time: 102 minutes.

Songs: "Look at Me," "I Found a New Friend" by Frank De Vol.

Cast: Cloris Leachman (Aunt Louise), Charles Martin Smith (D.J.), John Vernon (Prindle), Stephan W. Burns (Pete), Elyssa Davalos (Melissa), Joaquin Garay III (Paco), Harvey Korman (Captain Blythe), Richard Jaeckel (Shepard), Alex Rocco (Quinn), Fritz Feld (Chief Steward), Vito Scotti (Armando Mocci), Jose Gonzalez Gonzalez (Garage Owner), Ruben Moreno (Store Owner), Tina Menard (Store Owner's Wife), Jorge Moreno (Bus Driver), Allan Hunt (Canal Operator #1), Tom Scott (Canal Operator #2), Hector Morales (Mexican General), Iris Adrian (Loud American Wife), Ceil Cabot (Mrs. Purkiss), Patricia Van Patten (Cigarette Guest), Jack Perkins (Loud American), Henry Slate (Off-Watch Officer), Ernie Fuentes (Native), Antonio Trevino (Pigeon Owner), Dante D'Andre (Doctor De Morales), Alma Beltran (General's Wife), Dolores Aguirre (General's Daughter #1), Aurora Coria (General's Daughter), Alex Tinne (Local #1), Don Diamond (Local #2), Warde Donovan (Maître d'), Ray Victor (Guard Attendant), Bert Santos (Policeman #3), Buddy Joe Hooker (Chef), Steve Boyum (Panama Policeman), Kenny Endoso (Mexican Policeman), Mario Cisneros (Puerto Vallarta Policeman), Jeff Ramsey (The Matador), John C. Meier (Ship's Officer), Alejandro Aleman (Kid in Bus), Raul Gomez (Jeep Driver), Herbie (Itself), Gloria O'Brien (Singing Voice).

Pete has inherited his uncle's race car and he is with his friend D.J. in Puerta Vallarta to pick it up. While walking down the street, they meet Paco, a youthful con artist.

Three bad guys are also there to find an undiscovered Inca city. They are interested because they want to get all the riches.

Pete and D.J. find the car, which turns out to be a VW bug named Herbie. They don't have any money as Paco has pick-pocketed them.

Paco sees two of the bad guys and offers to carry their bag, but they reject him. He picks their pockets in the process. The third bad guy drives up to meet them.

Pete and D.J. find Paco and chase after him on foot, but before they can catch him, he takes a dollar and he tries to stuff the wallet in a mailbox, but D.J. stops him.

Paco still has the bad guys' wallets and they are still after him. They tell a local policeman who chases Paco into a shop. He hides in a basket. When the policeman leaves, he runs out and jumps into the back of Herbie.

Paco escapes, but the bad guys get their wallets back out of the mailbox, but missing a critical piece of film that was in the wallet.

Pete and D.J. get to the Sun Princess, a ship that will take them to their next destination which is Rio. Herbie is hoisted aboard carrying Paco. The three bad guys arrive too late to stop them.

On the ship, Captain Blythe tells his guests some exciting tales of his feats of daring.

A lady named Louise sitting nearby asks Pete and D.J. to sit at her table with her and her daughter, Melissa.

A man in the ship's cargo bay named Armando sits down to eat dinner, when he gets a phone call. When he returns to his dinner, he discovers that that his food has been taken by Paco, inside of Herbie. Herbie then appears to spit out the bones and the man demands Herbie to open his trunk. Herbie does and the man gets flipped. Then, Herbie leaves the scene.

Armando calls his superior for help. Help arrives and the man says that the car is running with no driver. The men prepare to pounce on Herbie, but Herbie drives away. Armando calls Captain Blythe to complain. Blythe chews him out, but eventually comes down to check on everything. The men capture Herbie and discover Paco as a stowaway inside.

Blythe calls Pete and D.J. into his office and asks them how they are going to pay for everything. If they don't pay, he says that their car will be impounded until then and Paco deported. They don't know where they are going to get their money.

That night there is a ship's costume dance and Pete dances with Melissa while D.J. sits with Louise while "Look at Me" plays.

Meanwhile, Paco who has been locked up in a holding cell in the hold gets Herbie to help him to escape. For helping Paco escape, Blythe orders Herbie to walk the plank.

Louise asks Blythe to reconsider his stance about making Herbie walk the plank, but he refuses and dumps Herbie into the sea. Paco sees this happen from a state room and sheds a tear.

At the ship's port, Pete and Louise discuss the car and Melissa, who has lightened up and removed her glasses. Melissa overhears Pete's somewhat negative comments about her and goes back into her shell, replacing her glasses.

The bad guys are at the port and reencounter Paco and try to take him. Paco escapes and soon discovers Herbie floating in the water. Paco has taken to calling Herbie "Ocho" and goes to rescue him.

Herbie seems to be unable to run, but he gets himself together and cleans himself up and soon he is up and running again with Paco at the wheel while "I Found a New Friend" plays.

Paco keeps reencountering the bad guys. He escapes again and runs back to Pete and D.J. for help, but they want nothing to do with him. Paco asks forgiveness. They do, but discover their wallets stolen again.

Louise and Blythe are both onshore and they jump into the same car, which is really Herbie disguised as a taxi. Herbie starts driving and Blythe discovers that the driver is Paco.

They try to escape the car, but can't. Melissa, Pete and D.J. try to flag down another car or bus to stop. Melissa stops a bus and pays the man $340 to buy it outright.

Blythe demands to stop, but Paco reveals that he cannot stop due to the men chasing them. Melissa, Pete and D.J. follow after them the best they can.

Herbie then drives into a bull fighting ring with the bad guys following them. The bull charges the bad guys' car and knocks it on its side.

The bull charges Herbie, but Herbie bullfights successfully. Blythe continues to plead for them to leave the bull ring, but Paco and Herbie still want to win, and they do. Then, they finally leave the ring, but first they want Blythe, Louise and Paco to step out and take a bow. When Blythe does, Herbie knocks him over.

Later, Melissa, Pete and D.J. finally see Blythe and Louise sitting by the side of the road and pick them up. They explain that Paco drove off with Herbie and the bad guys are still after them.

The bus breaks down so they try to fix it while Blythe phones his ship to try to get picked up, but he can't get through due to a language barrier. Then the operator is demanding money for more time on the telephone. Louise sneaks up and hangs up the phone and tries to console him.

Herbie and Paco keep driving and Paco wonders why the bad men want the film strip he still has. They are following him in an airplane from above.

The bus is now fixed and they continue on their way…for a while. They all try to either get their bus fixed again or try to get another ride.

A man comes up to Herbie and Paco who have now stopped and says that someone needs a taxi in the house ahead. Paco goes to see who it is, but it is a trap and the bad guys capture him, take him aboard their plane with Herbie driving after, but the plane takes off before Herbie can catch up.

Herbie comes back and picks up Pete, D.J., Melissa, Louise and Blythe to take them back to the ship.

The plane lands and the bad guys discover some gold and leave Paco behind. A storm has broken out. Herbie and the rest continue to travel.

Paco is now on his own to fend for himself until Herbie finally shows up.

Paco orders Herbie to go after the bad guys as it is Mayan gold. Herbie grabs the gold and drives off.

Soon, three banana trucks drive down the highway followed by Herbie covered in bananas so that the bad guys won't see them from their airplane.

Herbie drives to the world's foremost authority on Inca civilizations to turn in the gold, but it is taken again by the bad guys. Herbie and Paco see this and flip bananas in the tracks of the bad guys causing them to slip.

They finally recover and get the gold aboard their plane, but now they are covered in banana goop. With the extra weight, it is harder for the plane to take off and Herbie follows closely and "bites" the tail wing.

Still trying to take off, the airplane travels in circles as Herbie has bent the tail wing and is soon split in two. Then they lose their wings.

In the meantime, Melissa, Pete, D.J. and the doctor have finally loosened their ropes as they have been tied up all this time.

Police are chasing the bad guys by this point. Then, the propeller breaks off and the gold rolls out of the remaining fuselage. The bad guys are arrested.

Back on the ship, Louis still tries to lure Blythe, who finally notices her. It is a false alarm as he is really attracted to an older sailing ship from pirate times.

Herbie is cleaned up. Melissa and Pete fall in love. D.J. assures Louis that Herbie will win the race. Paco is the designated driver. D.J. asks why Paco calls Herbie "Ocho" when the number is 53. Paco explains that five and three are eight or ocho as a reprise of "I Found a New Friend" plays over the credits.

With that lame joke (and lame movie), the *Herbie, the Love Bug* series comes to an end except for the 1981 limited series, the TV movie and the 2005 Lindsey Lohan *Herbie: Fully Loaded* movie. The movie aired on the anthology show in 1987 and 1989.

This is pretty much the swan song of Walt Disney Productions as it was, even though I carry on with coverage until 1985 when Michael Eisner is by then fully involved.

This is also the last film featuring actress Iris Adrian, who was a mainstay at Disney since 1965 appearing in bit parts in many of their films. She died in 1994.

The choice was now to push full steam ahead with more adult features that were now typically rated PG, to utilize actors that were traditionally not used by Disney and to start using outside resources to complete their films.

The film grossed a passable $18 million and was re-released to theaters in 1981.

The Last Flight Of Noah's Ark

RELEASED BY BUENA VISTA ON June 25, 1980, Technicolor. Producer: Ron Miller. Co-Producer: Jan Williams. Director: Charles Jarrott. Story: Ernest K. Gann. Screenplay: Steven W. Carabatsos, Sandy Glass, George Arthur Bloom. Music Composed and Conducted by Maurice Jarre. Editor: Gordon D. Brenner. Art Director: John B. Mansbridge. Production Designer: Preston Ames. Director of Photography: Charles F. Wheeler, A.S.C. Unit Production Manager: William B. Venegas. Assistant Director: Richard Learman. Second Assistant Directors: Louis S. Muscate, Christopher D. Miller. Production Manager: John Bloss. Second Unit Manager: James W. Gavin. Sound Supervisor: Herb Taylor. Sound Mixer: Henry A. Maffett. Costume Supervisor: Jack Sandeen. Men's Costumer: Glenn T. Wright. Women's Costumer: Mary Dye. Make-up Supervisor: Robert J. Schiffer, C.M.A.A. Make-up: Robin Dee LaVigne. Hair Stylist: Eddie M. Barron. Orchestration: Richard Bowden. Sound Editor: Ben F. Hendricks. Music Editor: Evelyn Kennedy. Set Decorator: Norman Rockett. Special Effects: Danny Lee, Eustace Lycett, Art Cruickshank, A.S.C. Animals Handled by Jim Prine, Jay Fishburn, Don Spinney. Stunts: George Robotham, Arthur E. Stagg, Glenn Wilder, Clay Hodges, Calvin Fukushima, John F. Bylander, Bobby Porter, Orwin Harvey, Joe C. Hughes, Gordon Tadao Hirano. Prop maker / Welder / Fabricator: Gary Zink. Sound: Allen Hurd. Special Effects: Hans Metz, Ken Speed. Electrician: Dan Delgado. Composer, Additional Music: Richard Bowden. Musician: James Thatcher. Driver: Gilbert C. Pacheco. Running time: 97 minutes.

Song: "Half of Me" Sung by Alexandra Brown, lyrics by Hal David, music by Maurice Jarre.

Cast: Elliott Gould (Noah Dugan), Genevieve Bujold (Bernadette Lafleur), Ricky Schroder (Bobby), Vincent Gardenia (Stoney), Tammy Lauren (Julie), John Fujioka (Cleveland), Yuki Shimoda (Hiro), John P. Ryan (Coslough), Dana Elcar (Benchley), Ruth Manning (Charlotte Braithwaite), Arthur Adams (Leipzig Manager), Austin Willis (Slabotsky), Pete Renaday (Irate Pilot), Bob Whiting (Chaplain).

Two men barge into Noah Dugan's house for $5000 and beat him up. He tries to get a job in order to get some money in a hurry. He does get a job flying an airplane carrying a cargo of various wild animals for Stoney's Air Freight.

A young missionary named Bernadette is set to accompany him, but Noah says no. Noah says that he will do it for the $5000.

The plane is a very old prop plane called a B-29. After discovering how old the plane is, Noah turns down the offer again until he sees the bad guys show up. He quickly gets everyone aboard and takes off.

Stoney, the airport attendant stalls the bad guys until Noah and crew take off. The kids Julie and Bobby see Bernadette off, but then at the last minute climb aboard as stowaways.

The plane flies to Hawaii as the song "Half of Me" plays. Noah and Bernadette do not get along. Noah smokes a cigar and Bernadette plays Classical music. They both agree to stop in order to keep the peace.

The plane is not in the best shape. At one point, the automatic pilot burns out and Bernadette offers to fly if Noah gets tired. She lets him try, but is not very good. Julie and Bobby reveal their presence.

Noah checks out the animals in the back and gets kicked in the head and knocks him out. Bernadette can't come to his rescue, but he wakes up shortly.

In the morning, Noah mentions the beautiful sunrise that will appear behind them. When he sees the sunrise out the side window, he realizes that they have been flying off course the entire time due to interference from a tape recorder hanging nearby.

Bernadette and the children go in the back to pray. Noah feels that it won't do any good, but Bernadette says that it won't do any harm.

Soon, they start running out of gas and one engine quits. They find a small remote island to land on. Then, a second engine quits.

Bernadette lights another cigar for Noah, but they manage to land on the beach just as the final two engines conk out.

The landing is rough, but everyone is safe. They are on the island, but they are not alone as they are being watched by two Japanese soldiers named Cleveland and Hiro who did not know that World War II has ended.

Noah wants to relax on the beach, but Bernadette advises to get their camp established.

Bobby and Julie take Brutus the Brahma bull out for a walk and he runs away, so they go chasing after him.

Noah and Bernadette start looking for a good place to set up camp and settle and keep arguing all the way as they had in the plane.

Finally, Noah and the rest discover the encampment with the two Japanese soldiers still flying the Japanese war flag.

Bernadette wants to make friends with the soldiers and Noah warns that they shouldn't be too hasty as they might get killed.

Later, as the sun goes down, Bernadette offers to keep the peace with Noah and not be so argumentative with him. Noah agrees and they shake on it.

The next day, Bernadette takes a risk and confronts the Japanese soldiers directly. They aim their guns, but she is able to convince them to lower their guard and tell them that the war is over. The gamble works as they start laughing and eating together.

Noah goes after her to look for her and thinks that something is wrong and charges in. Hiro and Cleveland pull their swords on Noah, but Bernadette calms everyone down.

Cleveland explains he's named that because his mom visited there. They also explain that they lost their comrades and radio years ago, which is why they never heard the news about the end of the war.

Noah starts another fight with Bernadette as he was upset that she left to see the Japanese soldiers without telling him. Then, he shows his true feelings for her, by giving her a kiss.

The next day, Noah gets Bernadette and the kids to help haul the plane onto land. Cleveland and Hiro stop by and suggest converting the plane into a boat.

At first, Noah is not convinced until Hiro reminds him that they've been there for 35 years. Everyone, including Brutus helps convert the plane into a boat.

When done, Bobby and Julie bring the animals on board, but Noah doesn't think it's safe to bring them, and they think that Noah's mean and he wants to leave the animals on the island to die. Julie starts crying and Noah has a change of heart.

Bernadette paints "Noah's Ark" on the plane which initially annoys him, but then he changes his mind as he and Bernadette get closer.

Noah sets the ship sails with the animals on board and soon Cleveland and Hiro run out to the beach and want to come along too. They swim out to the boat and hurry out to sea.

Noah doesn't know why until he sees a series of explosions and Cleveland and Hiro have blown up their camp to leave no traces behind as per Japanese war rules.

Everyone takes a hand in steering the boat as they head out to sea. Once out there, they send out one of the ducks with a note to help them get rescued, but the duck flies the wrong way and heads towards China, not Hawaii.

They are out at sea a long time and they are soon running out of food. Bobby suggests that they could light up all of their lanterns in order to attract attention to their boat and be rescued.

Cleveland and Hiro manufacture some makeshift hooks and start fishing. Later, they use smaller fish they've caught as bait to attract larger fish including sharks.

At one point, Bobby falls into the water and Noah dives in to save him. It's a bit dicey at first but they both survive as Bernadette fires a shot at the shark, knocking him away. Bobby is grateful, but Noah is angry, but grateful to Bernadette. Later, Noah apologizes to Bobby for his outburst.

The next day, they are on their way again, but Bernadette is depressed, taking the blame for everything that has happened to them, since she had this outlandish missionary idea in the first place. Noah is sympathetic and they profess their love for each other.

Later, a storm brews and everyone makes sure that all of the animals are secure. Hiro shows photos of his children to Julie to calm her. The storm still does much damage to the boat, but Bernadette keeps praying.

The storm subsides, but Brutus has fallen during the storm and has hurt himself badly, so much so that Noah will have to shoot Brutus to put him out of his misery. Bobby strongly protests. Hiro takes the gun and assures him that it is for the best, but at the fatal moment, the coast guard arrives to save everyone.

Noah and Bernadette get married at sea as they are hauled to safety back to Hawaii. Brutus is nursed back to health and does not need to be euthanized.

I know that I've used this term to describe a lot of Disney films, but this film is very pleasant. My reasoning for using this term is that there is nothing really wrong with this film. In fact, it is quite entertaining, just not very memorable, unfortunately.

Elliott Gould had a similar situation that James Garner had in 1973-1974; his movie career was stalled, so he signed up to do this and *The Devil and Max Devlin* (1981) with similar results as Garner as neither film was very successful.

The film was shot in Victorville, California and on the islands of Kauai and Oahu in Hawaii.

They needed five B-29s for the movie to work, but found only two that worked and flew. They found four others that they could use in various forms.

In the end after their use, they had to return all of the planes back to the Navy as it is apparently the law.

Since the requirements and costs of shipping animals are astronomical, Disney decided to round up two sets of animals: one for use in California and one for use in Hawaii.

The film aired on the anthology show in 1981 and grossed $11 million. It was paired with a reissue of *101 Dalmatians* (1961) upon first release.

Popeye

RELEASED BY PARAMOUNT PICTURES CORPORATION ON December 6, 1980, Metrocolor, Technovision. Producer: Robert Evans. Director: Robert Altman. Screenplay: Jules Feiffer based on the "Popeye" characters created by E.C. Segar for King Features Syndicate. "Popeye" is a Trademark of The Hearst Corporation, King Features Syndicate Division. Music and Lyrics: Harry Nilsson. Additional Score: Tom Pierson. Costume Designer: Scott Bushnell. Supervising Editor: Tony Lombardo. Production Designer: Wolf Kroeger. Photography: Giuseppe Rotunno, A.S.C. Executive Producer: C.O. Erickson. Animation by Hanna-Barbera Productions, Inc. Choreography: Sharon Kinney, Dance; Hovey Burgess, Circus. Associate Producer: Scott Bushnell. First Assistant Directors: Bob Dahlin, Victor Tourjansky. Assistant Art Directors: Reg Bream, Stephane Reichel. Sound: Bob Gravenor. Location Manager: Robert Eggenweiler. Film Editors: John W. Holmes, A.C.E., David Alan Simmons. Additional Editing: Raja R. Gosnell. Assistant Editors: Eric Whitfield, Paul Rubell, Stephen Tucker, Bob Lederman, Jacque Toberen. Supervising Re-Recording Mixer: Michael Minkler, C.A.S. Music Re-Recording Mixer: Dan Wallin. Re-recording Engineer: Steve Brimmer. Supervising Sound Editor: Sam Gemette. Sound Effects Consultant: Rodney Holland. Sound Editors: Sam Shaw, John Larsen, Bill Phillips, Michael Ford, Hal Sanders. Loop Editor: Larry Singer, M.P.S.E. Sound Effects Editors: Teresa Eckton, Andy Patterson. Assistant Sound Editors: Edward A. Warschilka, Jr., John Benson, Roxanne Jones, Karen Rasch. Supervising Music Editor: Ted Whitfield. Music Editor: Richard Whitfield. Assistant Music Editor: Leslie A. Whitfield. Post Production Coordinator: Suzanne Hines. Post Production Sound and Editorial Facilities: Lions Gate Sound. Camera Operators: Giovanni Fiore, Gianfranco Transunto. Assistant Operators: Luigi Bernardini, Mauro Marchetti, Gian Maria Majorana. Underwater Camera Operator: Lorenzo Battaglia. Camera Assistants: Robert Reed Altman, Maurizio Zampagin. Gaffer: Rudolfo Bramucci. Key Grips: Vladimiro Salvatore, Alberto Emidi. Boom Man: Don Merritt. Recorder: Doug Shulman. Location Engineer: Randy Honaker. Special Effects Coordinator: Allen Hall. Assistant: Robert Willard. Technical Advisors: R.J. Hohman, Steve Foster. Stunt Coordinator: Roberto Messina. Wardrobe Supervisor: John Hay. Wardrobe Construction: Kate McDermott. Wardrobe Mistress: Yvonne Zarb Cousin. Property Master: Stephen Altman. Property Men: John Bucklin, Tony Maccario. Set Decorator: Jack Stephens. Construction Coordinator: Stephane Reichel. Construction Manager: Alvaro Belsole. Makeup Supervisor: Giancarlo Del Brocco. Makeup Artist: Alfred Tiberi. Assistants: Gilberto Provenghi, Alvaro Rossi. Chief Hairdresser: Maria Teresa Corridoni. Hairdressers: Aldo Signoretti, Gabriella Borzelli. Assistant: Rita Innocenzi. Script Supervisor: Luca Kouimelis. Talent Coordinator: Rick Sparks. Publicist: Bridget Terry. Publicity Assistants: Rita Galea, Cathy Keller. Unit Photographer: Paul Ronald. Unit Manager: Paolo Lucidi. Unit Coordinators: David Levy, Peter Bray. Title Design: Patty Ryan. Opticals: Cinema Research. Executive Assistant to Mr. Evans: Barbara Kalish. Assistants to Mr. Evans: Cathy Chazan, Stephanie Aranas. Mr. Williams' Dance Style Created by Lou Wills. Assistant to Mr. Williams: Mark Rutenberg. Locations Auditors: Richard Dubuque, Tim Engel. Assistant Accountant: Luciano Tartaglia. Master Carpenters: Gaetano Mirante, Bert Bowers. Master Painter: Guglielmo Modestini. Sculptors: Angelo Marta, Angelo Zaccaria, Michael Stroud. Draftsmen: Lester Smith, Stephen Bream. Animated Artifacts Created by Cosmekinetics, Ellis Burman, Bob Williams. Physical Therapist: James A. Rumsey, R.P.T. Caterer: Mickey Chonos. Production Manager-Europe: Frederick Muller. Transportation Captain: Bill Turner. Our gratitude to an international crew whose artistry helped to bring Sweethaven and the world of Popeye to life. Filmed on location in Malta in collaboration with Malta Film Facilities. Special Air Transportation by Alitalia Airlines. Original soundtrack album from the Boardwalk Entertainment Company. Assistant Sound Editor: Samuel C. Crutcher. Lead Sculptor: James Kagel. Stunt Double: Sergio Mioni. Underwater Assistant Camera: Adolfo Bartoli. Music Engineer, Mixer, Producer: Bruce Robb. Music Arranger: Bob Thompson. Singing Voice of Paul Smith: John Wallace. Production Assistant: Lary Crews. Personal Assistant, Robert Altman: Ed Horwitz. Running time: 113 minutes. Rated PG.

Songs: "Sweet Sweethaven," "Blow Me Down," "Everything is Food," "He's Large," "I'm Mean," "Sail With Me," "I Yam What I Yam," "He Needs Me," "Swee'pea's Lullaby," "It's Not Easy Being Me," "Kids," "Din' We." Music and Lyrics: Harry

Nilsson. Arranged and Conducted by Van Dyke Parks. Music and Lyric "I'm Popeye the Sailor Man": Sammy Lerner.

Cast: Robin Williams (Popeye), Shelley Duvall (Olive Oyl), Ray Walston (Poopdeck Pappy), Paul Dooley (Wimpy), Paul L. Smith (Bluto), Richard Libertini (Geezil), Donald Moffat (The Taxman), MacIntyre Dixon (Cole Oyl), Roberta Maxwell (Nana Oyl), Donovan Scott (Castor Oyl), Allan Nicholls (Rough House), Wesley Ivan Hurt (Swee'pea), Bill Irwin (Ham Gravy, the Old Boyfriend), Robert Fortier (Bill Barnacle, the Town Drunk), David McCharen (Harry Hotcash, the Gambler), Sharon Kinney (Cherry, his Moll), Peter Bray (Oxblood Oxheart, the Fighter), Linda Hunt (Mrs. Oxheart, his Mudder), Geoff Hoyle (Scoop, the Reporter), Wayne Robson (Chizzelflint, the Pawnbroker), Larry Pisoni (Chico, the Dishwasher), Carlo Pellegrini (Swifty, the Cook), Susan Kingsley (La Verne, the Waitress), Michael Christensen (Splatz, the Janitor), Ray Cooper (The Preacher), Noel Parenti (Slick, the Milkman), Karen McCormick (Rosie, the Milkmaid), John Bristol (Bear, the Hermit), The Steinettes: Julie Janney (Mena Walfleur), Patty Katz (Mina Walfleur), Diane Shaffer (Mona Walfleur), Nathalie Blossom (Blossom), Dennis Franz (Spike), Carlos Brown (Slug), Ned Dowd (Butch), Hovey Burgess (Mort), Roberto Messina (Gozo), Peitro Torrisi (Bolo), Margery Bond (Daisy), Judy Burgess (Petunia), Saundra MacDonald (Violet), Eve Knoller (Min), Peggy Pisoni (Pickelina), Barbara Zegler (Daphne), Paul Zegler (Mayor Stonefeller, the Official), Pamela Burrell (Mrs. Stonefeller), David Arkin (The Mailman / Policeman), Klaus Voormann (Von Schnitzel, the Conductor), Doug Dillard (Clem, the Banjo Player), Van Dyke Parks (Hoagy, the Piano Player), Stan Wilson (Oscar, the Barber), Roberto Dell'Aqua (The Chimneysweep), Valerie Velardi (Cindy, the Drudge), Jack Mercer (Voice of Popeye in Animated Prologue).

After a brief black and white nod to the old Fleischer Popeye cartoons, the film starts in earnest in widescreen color and live action with Popeye the sailor at sea during a storm in a small rowboat.

He rows himself into a small seaport town called Sweethaven. The villagers sing "Sweet Sweethaven" and we are introduced to the many various residents.

Popeye is approached by a tax collector who asks for a number of new taxes by just arriving. As soon as he pays, the tax collector is off to gather some new ones. Then, a piano almost clobbers Popeye as he sings "Blow Me Down."

Popeye meets Wimpy, a heavy-set hamburger eater and Geezil, a shady character always annoyed with Wimpy, and a number of suspicious people. He arrives at a rooming house and is greeted by a short old woman named Nana Oyl, who runs the house.

Inside, Popeye meets Nana's daughter, Olive who is trying on a new hat. Nana's son Castor is suspicious about Popeye. Olive then shows Popeye to his room.

The members of the Oyl family including father Cole Oyl along with Geezil, Wimpy and Popeye all sit down to dinner. They discuss where the Commodore of the town went and also Olive's boyfriend, Bluto, a rough and tumble sort. Soon, they all leave Popeye alone to fend for himself.

Later, Popeye is back in his room reading a book while lying on a hammock. Bluto comes blustering about and yells to everyone in Sweethaven to put their lights out for the night.

The next day, the town is up and at 'em and sings "Everything is Food." Wimpy tries to get a delayed payment on his hamburger from Rough House. When Rough House refuses, Wimpy chisels one away from someone else.

Popeye comes into Rough House's restaurant and explains that he's looking for his father, Poopdeck Pappy. The townspeople still don't like Popeye and they pick a fight with him, but they find out that they are no match for Popeye, who beats everyone up.

Back at the rooming house, Olive Oyl is holding a party, but it is evident that Popeye is not wanted. Bluto meanwhile is trying to find the best flower for Olive as she sings "He's Large" as an ode to Bluto.

Bluto arrives and is disturbed by a fly which he catches with his bare hand. Olive slips out and gets some more food and bumps into Popeye on her way back. He offers to help her carry her bags. Bluto is upset because Olive is not there and starts to get steamed.

Olive asks Popeye why he's there and he says he's looking for his pap. Along the way back, they come across an abandoned baby which turns out to be Swee'pea. Bluto loses his patience waiting and sings "I'm Mean."

Olive and Popeye finally show up with Swee'pea, but Bluto is still angry and he takes out his anger on Popeye and knocks him down and beats him up.

Later, Popeye tells Olive that he's going to adopt Swee'pea. A man posts a sign saying that there is going to be a fight with boxer Oxblood Oxcart. The winner will receive a small fortune. Castor is the first to enter the ring with Oxblood, but the Oyl family wants to get him out of the ring. Wimpy referees.

Castor is knocked out easily and is literally kicked out of the ring. Then, Popeye enters the ring. Popeye can't hit him due to Oxblood's mother being there, but Geezil advises him otherwise. Finally, Popeye gets mad at him to knock Oxblood out.

Later, Popeye checks on Swee'pea who is being fed by Olive. Popeye and Olive sing "Sail With Me." Olive is starting to fall for Popeye.

Swee'pea proves to be a bit of a psychic, which catches the attention of Wimpy who wants Swee'pea to predict the horse races.

Wimpy takes Swee'pea to the races and Olive and Popeye race to get him back and bring him home. Meanwhile, Swee'pea is accurately predicting the winners of the races.

When they find out that Swee'pea is picking the winners, Olive changes her tune, but Popeye is still upset that they are gambling and sings "I Yam What I Yam" and "I'm Popeye the Sailor."

Bluto is the owner of the gambling establishment and motions for Wimpy to come into his private office. After he gets Swee'pea back, Popeye leaves the rooming house.

The taxman tries to collect more taxes, but Popeye shoves him away and the taxman slides down a ramp into the sea and everyone cheers. Popeye is now the hero of Sweethaven, but Swee'pea is taken away from him again.

Olive comes to look for Popeye and sings "He Needs Me." Meanwhile, Swee'pea is now in the possession of Bluto. Popeye writes a letter about Swee'pea and sings "Swee'pea's Lullaby." He throws the note into a bottle and tosses it into the sea.

Wimpy is doing his own investigations and discovers that Swee'pea is still in Sweethaven. Olive Oyl discovers him spying and demands to know what he knows.

They spy through a window and discover an old man who resembles Popeye feeding Swee'pea spinach and hanging out with Bluto. The old man and Bluto sing "It's Not Easy Being Me."

Olive says to Wimpy that they have to rush to Popeye and tell him that they've found everyone; Swee'pea and Poopdeck Pappy. Olive says that Poopdeck is a crook and also the missing Commodore. Popeye doesn't believe them, but goes to look anyway.

When Popeye and Poopdeck meet each other, they cannot believe how much alike they look. Poopdeck says he doesn't have a son and to prove it, he asks Popeye to eat some spinach and he refuses.

Poopdeck has been tied up all this time and finally Popeye cuts him down. Bluto has left with a tied-up Olive Oyl and Swee'pea and steers his boat to leave the port and goes out to sea. Popeye and Poopdeck head after him as they go out to Scab Island. Wimpy, Geezil, Castor, Cole and Nana have joined them.

Now, Poopdeck tries to prove that Popeye is his son and Popeye refuses. Poopdeck does a rap about "Kids" and about how rotten they are.

Poopdeck fires shots upon Bluto's boat and eventually rams it, but Bluto has taken Olive and Swee'pea into a smaller row boat and takes them to Pirate's Cove. Wimpy uses Swee'pea to find a sunken treasure.

The sunken treasure is being guarded by a giant octopus. Meanwhile, Poopdeck has accidentally sunk his own ship and all the crew members swim for shore.

Popeye reencounters Bluto and picks a fight with him. Poopdeck tries to get the treasure himself and hauls it up.

The octopus pulls at Swee'pea in the boat, but he is pulled to safety by Poopdeck. Poopdeck finally opens the treasure chest and reveals that it is filled with cans of spinach and other mementos. Popeye and Bluto continue sword fighting. The octopus goes after Olive Oyl.

Poopdeck says that if he ate spinach, he wouldn't be losing the fight. Bluto decides to force feed Popeye spinach since he hates it so much. This was a mistake as Popeye achieves super-strength and pulverizes Bluto and the octopus. Olive is grateful and everyone sings "I'm Popeye the Sailor Man."

This is the first of two collaborations between Paramount Pictures and Walt Disney Productions; the second being *Dragonslayer* (1981). Paramount distributed the film domestically, while Disney distributed it internationally.

Though not known at the time, this was the first in a long line of Disney live-action features starring cartoon characters from other studios. It seemed that Disney was trying to do in the other characters as they never made a live-action *Mickey Mouse* film.

Other films to follow from Disney include *Dick Tracy* (1990), *Mr. Magoo* (1997), *Inspector Gadget* (1999) and *Underdog* (2009) among others.

One of the drawbacks of this film is screenplay writer Jules Feiffer's insistence on utilizing the Popeye comic strip as source material. The unfortunate reason being that Popeye as done by creator Elsie Segar was a very complex strip in comparison to the Fleischer animated cartoons. Audiences expected the typical Popeye-Olive-Bluto love triangle and instead got a jumbled mess of ideas and concepts and characters that were too numerous to effectively contain in a two hour film. It does look REALLY GOOD, however, and the casting is brilliant.

The film could have been improved with some judicious editing and faster pacing and maybe even some of the songs cut as this wasn't really Nilsson's most shining hour as a composer.

The Popeye cartoon at the beginning of the film was actually animated by Hanna-Barbera who had the animation rights at the time this film was released. Longtime Popeye voice artist Jack Mercer provided the voice for this brief animated appearance.

Popeye and Olive Oyl were originally to be portrayed by Dustin Hoffman and Gilda Radner, respectively. Mike Nichols, Arthur Penn and Arthur Ashby were all slated to direct this film.

Strangely, the song "Everything is Food" is in the film and not on the soundtrack album, while "Din' We" is on the soundtrack album and not in the film. The soundtrack has never been released to compact disc to date.

The budget was $20 million and the film grossed $50 million.

1981

The previous year's success with Disneyland's 25th anniversary continued with Walt Disney World's 10th anniversary. Disneyland also welcomed its 200 millionth guest with Gert Schelvis and Walt Disney World opened the Epcot Center Preview Center.

Disneyland was rather quiet with the closing of Fantasyland Theater with no fanfare. It was replaced by Pinocchio's Daring Journey in 1983.

Film revenues remained steady, but the revenue wasn't generated by the studios' new films, but rather the inroads the brand new home video market was making.

New films made for the anthology show include *Disney Animation: The Illusion of Life*, *A Disney Halloween*, *A Disney Storybook*, *The Cherokee Trail*, *A Magical Disney Christmas* and *Walt Disney ... One Man's Dream* (working title: *Walt Disney: The Man, The Artist, The Dreamer*). Fewer new shows were made and the most significant event is the anthology show changing networks for the first time in 20 years and changing its name to *Walt Disney*. There was also the new special called *Florida's Disney Decade*.

A feature film based on the life of Albert Einstein was mentioned in *Disney News*, but nothing ever came of it.

Cinderella (1950) and *Swiss Family Robinson* (1960) were reissued this year.

In his book, *The Disney That Never Was*, Charles Solomon reveals that the animated feature *Chanticleer* idea was revived as a follow up to *The Fox and the Hound*. *Chanticleer* had its origins as a Disney project as far back as 1937. Problems ensued in making a likable, sympathetic rooster character.

Work resumed during 1941 and then slowed during the war. Various treatments were introduced in 1945 and 1947 and then revived a decade later to be the follow-up feature to *101 Dalmatians* in 1961. Work on that stopped and replaced by *The Sword in the Stone* (1963).

Finally, a new treatment was tried in 1981 but was shelved again in favor of *The Black Cauldron* (1985), probably for the last time as ex-Disney animator Don Bluth released *Rock-a-Doodle* in 1992 which was a take on the *Chanticleer* story and didn't perform all that well, so the saga is probably over.

Herbie, the Love Bug came back once again, this time as a five episode mini-series that if successful, would have become a regular weekly show. The series marked the return of Dean Jones to Disney for the first time since 1977.

The success of last year's *Mickey Mouse Disco* compilation short prompted another compilation short called *Once Upon a Mouse*.

There was also an educational short produced called *Winnie the Pooh Discovers the Seasons*. This was the first time Hal Smith took over the role of Pooh and the first one made after narrator Sebastian Cabot's death.

Disney also released its first videocassettes of two of their fully animated features: *The Many Adventures of Winnie the Pooh* (1977) and *Dumbo* (1941). Live action releases include *Old Yeller* (1957), *Davy Crockett and the River Pirates* (1956), *The Absent-Minded Professor* (1961) and *Gus* (1976).

Three Herbie double-features were issued to theaters this year including *Herbie Goes Bananas* (1980) with *Freaky Friday* (1977), *Herbie Rides Again* (1974) with *Swiss Family Robinson* (1960) and *Herbie Goes to Monte Carlo* (1977) with *The World's Greatest Athlete* (1973).

The first edition of Walt Disney's World on Ice debuted in July. This was similar to the Disney On Parade show from a decade earlier.

The ongoing success of the *Mickey Mouse Disco* album and its follow-ups, led to more successful original albums this year including *Mousercise*, another platinum award-winning album. The success of this album also led to a daily series on The Disney Channel and merchandising.

There were also book and record sets released for *The Empire Strikes Back*, *Raiders of the Lost Ark* and *The Black Stallion*, all of which should have been Disney films, but weren't. *Clash of the Titans*, *Superman II* and *The Great Muppet Caper* could have also been made at Disney.

In fact, Disney was the first studio considered for *Raiders of the Lost Ark*, but the deal fell through when George Lucas and Steven Spielberg demanded too much of the profits. Ironically, *Raiders* was made by Paramount when Michael Eisner saw the script. Eventually, a ride based on the film was installed at Disneyland.

The Fox and the Hound soundtrack was nominated for a Best Recording for Children Grammy, but lost.

In the comic book world, Gold Key transitioned into Whitman and continued to publish *Donald Duck, Mickey Mouse, Uncle Scrooge, Walt Disney's Comics and Stories, Huey, Dewey and Louie Junior Woodchucks, Super Goof, Chip 'n' Dale, Daisy and Donald* and *Winnie the Pooh*.

The Fox and the Hound and *Condorman* appeared as mini-series as did *Dragonslayer* (published by Marvel).

Manuel Gonzales retired from the *Mickey Mouse* Sunday page that he had drawn since 1938.

More essential Disney books were first issued this year: *Great Moments from the Films of Walt Disney, Treasury of Stories from Silly Symphonies, The Fine Art of Disney's Donald Duck, Walt Disney's Uncle Scrooge McDuck: His Life and Times* and *Disney Animation: The Illusion of Life.*

The Devil and Max Devlin

RELEASED BY BUENA VISTA ON March 6, 1981, Technicolor. Executive Producer: Ron Miller. Producer: Jerome Courtland. Director: Steven Hilliard Stern. Screenplay: Mary Rodgers. Story: Mary Rodgers, Jimmy Sangster. Music: Buddy Baker. Editor: Raymond A. de Leuw, A.C.E. Art Directors: John B. Mansbridge, Leon R. Harris. Director of Photography: Howard Schwartz, A.S.C. Production Manager: John Bloss. Assistant Director: Irby Smith. Second Assistant Directors: Christopher D. Miller, Stephen M. McEveety. Sound Supervisor: Herb Taylor. Sound Mixer: Willie D. Burton, C.A.S. Sound Editor: Ben F. Hendricks. Music Editor: Jack Wadsworth. Costume Supervisor: Jack Sandeen. Costume Designer: Bill Thomas. Men's Costumer: Milton G. Mangum. Women's Costumer: Mary Dye. Make-up Supervisor: Robert J. Schiffer, C.M.A.A. Make-up: Nadia. Hair Stylist: Gloria Montemayor. Set Decorators: Norman Rockett, Roger M. Shook. Special Effects: Art Cruickshank, A.S.C., Danny Lee. Matte Artist: David Mattingly. Special thanks to Universal Studios Tour and the Universal Amphitheatre. The Grammy is a registered service mark, and used by permission of the National Academy of Recording Arts and Sciences. Special Effects: Hans Metz. Running time: 95 minutes. Rated PG.

Songs: Music: Marvin Hamlisch. "Roses and Rainbows" Lyrics: Carole Bayer Sager. "Any Fool Could See" Lyrics: Allee Willis.

Cast: Elliott Gould (Max Devlin), Bill Cosby (Barney Satin), Susan Anspach (Penny Hart), Adam Rich (Toby Hart), Julie Budd (Stella Summers), Sonny Shroyer

(Big Billy Hunniker), David Knell (Nerve Nordlinger), Charles Shamata (Jerry Nadler), Deborah Baltzell (Heidi), Ronnie Schell (Greg Weems), Jeannie Wilson (Laverne Hunniker), Stanley Brock (The Counterman), Ted Zeigler (Mr. Billings), Vic Dunlop (Brian), Reggie Nalder (Chairman of Devil Council), Lillian Muller (Veronica of Devil Council), Julie Parrish (Sheila), Sally K. Marr (Mrs. Gormley), Madelyn Cates (Mrs. Trent), Denise Du Barry (Stella's Secretary), Helene Wilson (Agent Hargraves), Susan Tolsky (Nerve's Mom), Vernon Weddle (Justice of the Peace), Ernest Harada (Motorcycle Scout #1), Bill Saito (Motorcycle Scout #2), Gustaf Unger (Gregory of Devil Council), Bertil Unger (Julian of Devil Council), Joseph Burke (Steven of Devil Council), Tak Kubota (Bruce of Devil Council), Army Archerd (Himself), Ruth Manning (Mrs. Davis), Bartine Zane (Blind Lady #2), Rahsaan Morris (Tremaine), Adam Starr (Kid at Carnival), Chip Courtland (Jock #1), Rene Lamart (Jock #2), Mark Andrews (Jock #3), Teri Landrum (Susie), Tracie Savage (Pammy), Nancy Bond (Mrs. Minushkin), Sheila Rogers (Mrs. Pepper), Robert Baron (Mr. Pepper), Pete Renaday (Studio Engineer), Albert Able (M.C. Announcer), Roger Price (Old Man), Robert S. Telford (Camper Owner), Wally K. Berns (Fan at Party), Mindy Sterling (Fan #1 at Grammy's), Richard Lasting (Fan #2 at Grammy's), Richard Crystal (Award Presenter), Steve Eastin (Larry Binder), James Almanzar (Ticket Taker), Nick Angotti (TV Reporter), Jackie Russell (Carnival Kid's Mom), Gary Morgan (Record Store D.J.), Ted Noose (Officer), Daley Pick (Orderly #2), Bari Roulette (Maid of Honor), Jan Jorden (Woman in Lounge), Madelyn Cates (Mrs. Trent), Jackson Bostwick (Additional Voices), Bartine Burkett (An Angel), Sean Kane (Kid in Playground).

Max Devlin is a landlord to an apartment complex where there is a rash of complaints from the tenants. He is a tough, harsh landlord that does not bend the rules at all. When he gets in a jam for not getting anything done, he blames the owner. Problem is, he is the owner.

Max sees a tenant sneak out before his eyes that hasn't paid this month's rent and goes out chasing after him. He bypasses a blind woman asking for help crossing the street and gets run over by a bus and killed. The bus was carrying a group of Hare Krishnas.

Max and others descend down into Hell. Max is silent while the others descend screaming, but he is still shocked at the sights he sees. He excuses it as having a bad dream.

In Hell, he meets Barney Satin and his group of advisors who welcome him. Max says that he doesn't belong there until he hears a list of his indiscretions he had done in his life.

The last indiscretion was failing to help Agent Hargraves. Max says he doesn't know anybody named Hargraves and the blind lady that he didn't help across the street appears on the screen.

Max says that that isn't fair, but Barney assures him that there is no such thing as fair and is ordered to Level 4 of Hell. Barney strikes a bargain that he'll let Max live for two more months, if he can find three souls to take his place.

Max mentions some horrible people he knows that could take his place, but they say that that's no good as they will get those people anyway. What they want are innocent people to sell their souls to the devil in order to achieve the goals that they have.

They show Max the three that they want. One is a child and Max hesitates and then agrees to the deal. He is returned to the bus accident and comes to with all the Hari Krishnas dancing about.

Max goes into a diner the next day and reencounters Barney dressed in a hard hat construction outfit. Max orders for Barney, but the cook can't see Barney, nor can anyone. Max freaks out and when he goes to pay for the coffees and leave, he doesn't see his or Barney's reflections in the mirror.

Barney explains that people can't see him, but they can see Max, but neither of them will appear in the mirror as they are both members of Hell.

Max asks Barney how he can find the three people that he needs to get and Barney says to just concentrate and he will magically appear there. He encounters the first victim in the ladies' room, which freaks both of them out.

Max comes back to his apartment complex and the tenants start screaming again, but he ignores them and locks the door. Barney tells Max to be more careful about where he appears and then Max goes back to the place where his first victim, a singer named Stella Summers is at.

Stella desires to be signed up by a top record executive named Jerry Nadler visiting the night club, but doesn't know how to get his attention. Max shows up and says that he can do it provided that she signs his agreement.

Stella goes out to sing and Max guarantees that she will be a success. She gives a boring introduction speech, but finally starts singing and does very well singing "Any Fool Can See" after a shaky start.

After she gets off the stage, she is a hit and is approached by Jerry and he wants to sign her right away.

We cut to Nelson "Nerve" Nordlinger who is a nerdy guy who aspires to ride in the motocross. Max appears and drives by in a car carrying a bike and a driver training school.

Nerve is willing to do anything including selling his soul in order to be a champion motocross rider. He gets on the bike and does really well until he rides out of Max's sight. Barney shows up to remind him that his magic powers to help don't work once the victim gets out of Max's sight.

We then go to a carnival where Max's third victim, a child named Toby Hart needs to get on a wild ride that needs an adult to ride with him. Max becomes Toby's uncle Max and starts discussing what his desires are after riding a number of thrill rides.

Toby doesn't really have any tremendous wants, until he reveals that his real father is dead and he would like Max to become his new father. Toby introduces Max to his mother, Penny, but she's not interested in getting married or Toby's matchmaking skills.

Stella is now in the studio recording some tracks, but her voice doesn't have the same power that it did on stage due to Max not being there.

Max realizes this and suddenly he isn't there and reappears with Stella and she records a perfect version of "Any Fool Can See" finally on take 43, but the first with Max present.

Max calls Toby and wants to speak with Penny to apologize for leaving all of a sudden and to tell her that he loves her, but she hangs up on him.

Max tries to get Stella to sign, but she keeps delaying. Barney asks how the others are doing and so Max checks up on Nerve. He's entered into a race and is nervous, but Max assures him that he has nothing to worry about and to just win.

Nerve is competing closely against a guy named Big Billy Hunniker, but Nerve comes out the victor.

Max comes back to Toby to try again courting Penny, but Toby warns her that Penny is interested in Larry, her tennis teacher.

Max decides to regrass the play area for her day care center in order to win Penny's heart. He explains that he has to manage Stella and Nerve and also be a landlord, so that's why he zips off so suddenly.

Unfortunately, Max almost loses Penny by revealing his true feelings about kids, but she reveals that she sometimes thinks the same way about kids even though she has the day care.

Stella goes out to perform her biggest concert yet and Max advises her not to sing until he gives the cue. Max has brought Penny to the concert which goes without a hitch.

Later, Penny drops Max off to another motocross event and she gives him a gift of an electric razor as Max has the tendency to cut his face while shaving.

Jumping back and forth between Stella, Nerve and Toby gets to be rather hectic and the pace starts taking its toll. Barney is also getting impatient. He's trying to get Max to finish his work. Max begs for more time.

Max still tries to get Stella to sign, but she says it's unnecessary. Then he tries again with Toby, but he won't sign until Max marries his mother.

Max tries again with Nerve, but he tries just as Nerve is at the starting line of another race and so his time runs out.

Max pops into Toby's party and then pops out again. Toby gets discouraged because Max comes and goes so quickly. He's having second thoughts.

Max goes back to Stella, but she's having a crisis about her goals. And now, Max is reconsidering what he's doing.

Max comes back to propose to Penny and she accepts. He's in a bind because he's getting married and has to attend Stella's concert and Nerve's motocross event all at the same time.

Max uses subterfuge to finally get Stella to sign. He disguises himself and pretends to be an autograph seeker. Stella changes instantly and becomes a darker persona, especially evident when she accepts her Grammy award.

Nerve finally signs a contract that Max place before him. He hesitates for a second as he says that "sole" has been misspelled as "soul." Max lies and says that he'll fix it later.

Next, Max gets married to Penny in a medium-sized outdoor ceremony. Afterwards, he gets Toby to sign the third and final agreement. Toby pulls Penny aside and says that he now hates Max.

Barney shows up and says that he needs the three now. Max says that he's done his obligations and that Barney will get the three at the end of their natural lives. Barney says that he lied and wants them now.

Max doesn't like what he hears and goes into the house to burn the contracts. Barney reveals himself to be the devil and says that Max will die and suffer eternal damnation if he burns the contracts. He burns the contracts anyway.

Max no longer has the ability to pop in and out, so he leaves Penny to check on Nerve and Stella. Nerve did not finish the race but it was because he never started. He was tripped by a little old lady. Max investigates and discovers that this little old lady was from upstairs, not down. Nerve is alright and admits that he was going to quit the racing scene.

Max says goodbye and says that he's going to be going away and not to a place where he can go. He goes to Stella and tells her the same thing and then goes home to Toby to tell him the same thing, too.

Toby doesn't want Max to leave, nor do the others. Penny comes in and says that Max's problem is that he has no self-image. He then looks into the mirror and he can see himself again. He realizes that Barney doesn't have him and that he will not die...at least not right away. So, he's not leaving.

He takes Penny and Toby to Stella's concert. Stella reveals at her concert that she will be taking a break for a year, and gives thanks to Max and sings "Roses and Rainbows." She can sing now with or without Max in attendance.

Nerve is also in the audience enjoying Stella's singing as Max, Penny and Toby enter the auditorium. Max looks up and thanks God for how everything turned out.

Elliott Gould's second and final film for Disney, playing essentially the same character he played in *The Last Flight of Noah's Ark* (1980).

Interestingly, Julie Budd was set to become the new Barbra Streisand and Elliott Gould was once married to Streisand. She has had a somewhat middling career since, even though she is a decent singer. She also sings the theme song to the next Disney film, *Amy*.

The story itself was essentially a rip-off of 1978's *Heaven Can Wait*, which in itself was a remake of *Here Comes Mr. Jordan* (1941).

Marvin Hamlisch returns to Disney as composer after *The World's Greatest Athlete* (1973) and a bunch of awards and world success later. He sadly died at age 68 in 2012.

Unfortunately, Bill Cosby has another flop with this film. Despite being a great success on records and TV, his movie career never really took off. He eventually made worse films like *Ghost Dad* (1990) and *Leonard, Part 6* (1987).

This film aired on the anthology show in 1987 and 1989 and grossed $16 million.

Amy

RELEASED BY BUENA VISTA ON March 20, 1981, Technicolor. Producer: Jerome Courtland. Director: Vincent McEveety. Writer: Noreen Stone. Music Composed and Conducted by Robert F. Brunner. Editor: Gregg McLaughlin, A.C.E. Art Directors: John B. Mansbridge, Mark W. Mansbridge. Director of Photography: Leonard J. South, A.S.C. Executive Producer: William Robert Yates. Unit Production Manager: Robert M. Webb. Assistant Director: Howard Grace. Second Assistant Director: James Turley, Linda Leigh Karjola. Sound Supervisor: Herb Taylor. Sound Mixer: Henry A. Maffett. Sound Editor: Ben E. Hendricks. Music Editor: Jack Wadsworth. Costume Supervisor: Jack Sandeen. Men's Costumer: John A. Anderson. Women's Costumer: Nedra Rosemond-Watt. Make-up Supervisor: Robert J. Schiffer, C.M.A.A. Make-up: Melanie Levitt. Hair Stylist: Chris Lee. Production Manager: John Bloss. Set Decorator: Roger M. Shook. Special Effects: Danny Lee. Technical Advisor: Todd Rutherford. Special thanks to the California School for the Deaf, Riverside. Stunts: Louie Nicholas, Jeffrey Dashnaw, Hank Hooker, Stacie Elias. Running time: 100 minutes.

Song: "So Many Ways" Sung by Julie Budd. Words: Bruce Belland. Music: Robert F. Brunner.

Cast: Jenny Agutter (Amy Medford), Barry Newman (Dr. Ben Corcoran), Kathleen Nolan (Helen Gibbs), Chris Robinson (Elliot Medford), Lou Fant (Lyle Ferguson), Margaret O'Brien (Hazel Johnson), Nanette Fabray (Malvina Dodd), Lance Legault (Edgar Winnback), Lucille Benson (Rose Metcalf), Jonathan Daly (Clyde Pruett), Lonny Chapman (Virgil Goodloe), Brian Frishman (Mervin Grimes), Jane Daly (Molly Tribble), Dawn Jeffory (Caroline Chapman), Frances Bay (Mrs. Lindey), Peggy McCay (Mrs. Grimes), Len Wayland (Mr. Grimes), Virginia Vincent (Edna Hancock), Norman Burton (Caruthers), Otto Rechenberg (Henry Watkins), David Hollander (Just George), Cory 'Bumper' Yothers (Wesley Moody), Alban Branton (Eugene), Ronnie Scribner (Walter Ray), Michelle Downey (Essie), Carson Sipes (Dwayne), Diana Boyd (Loretta), Flavia Fleischer (Iris), David Jacob Weiss (Glenn), Oscar Arturo Aguilar (Chester), Kevin Van Wieringen (Owen Corner), Seamon Glass (Mr. Watkins), Nancy Jeris (Mrs. Watkins), Randy Morton (Teenage Boy), Lance R. Gordon (Referee), John Arndt (Mr. Pool).

Amy Medford takes the wedding ring off her finger and leaves home as the song "So Many Ways" plays. She heads off by horse and buggy to the Parker School for the Deaf.

She has been brought in to see if she can help the deaf children speak. The head of the school, Lyle Ferguson, says that she will face some strong opposition.

Amy meets Henry Watkins, a deaf boy who is known as "H on the Eyes," and the only deaf child who plays with the blind children. She also meets Owen who gives Amy the name "A on the Lips" as she's the new speech teacher.

In class, Amy reveals that she doesn't know sign language and that her goal is to teach the deaf children to speak and to learn to read lips. Another teacher Malvina Dodd signs for her and is very skeptical.

Amy is introduced to Wesley and his doll named Mr. Moon, one of the blind children who believe that one day he will see.

Amy's husband Elliott is looking for her and doesn't understand why she ran away.

In class again, Amy tells Malvina to not sign so much and so Malvina leaves the class.

In the blind class, a student named Walter Ray is having stomach pains. He never goes anywhere without his friend Just George. Amy takes both of them to the office to see the school nurse or a doctor.

Principal Ferguson reveals that the school has no money for on staff doctors and only uses them in an extreme emergency. Amy finds this unacceptable.

They have no money for school repairs or good food for the children.

Amy sees Mr. Pruett, the custodian and asks her to help fetch the nearest doctor, Dr. Ben Corcoran. Amy keeps Walter and George company with stories until help arrives.

Pruett shows up with the doctor. They are both totally drunk. Dr. Corcoran continues Amy's story in his drunken state, and then does a check-up on Walter Ray.

Henry has a minor crush on Amy and gives her a drawing of her that he has made. The doctor concludes that Walter Ray has eaten some green apples and should be ok.

The doctor wants to give some of the deaf children a ride in his motorcar. Malvina protests, but he does it anyway.

Malvina reprimands Amy and claims again that they will not learn how to speak and that words will only confuse them.

The blind teacher asks why she is working there. She says that with Amy's looks, she would marry the first rich man she could meet. Amy says that that's what she did, but she wasn't happy. That is why she left.

The next day, Amy teaches the deaf children how to fly a kite and Dr. Corcoran arrives as he now has an interest in Amy. Amy is not interested in him…yet.

An investigator questions the staff at home as to why Amy might have left. A maid reveals that Mr. Medford is demanding, while Amy was not. The maid reveals that they had had a child who was deaf.

Amy has success with Henry who teaches him the word "kite." Malvina is not impressed, but the principal is.

The principal is being checked on after two months by Mr. Caruthers, the head of the school board, but reports of one word are not considered encouraging.

More troubles as Wesley has been diagnosed as having Rheumatic Fever.

The investigator goes to the Horace Mann School for the Deaf to find out information about the Medford's son.

Back at the Parker School, Amy drifts to sleep and has a nightmare. Dr. Corcoran wakes her up while Wesley gets steadily worse. They try everything to get his fever down, but nothing works and Wesley dies from his fever. Amy is very upset and Dr. Corcoran consoles her.

Amy reveals that her child was deaf and that he had a heart defect and that it was only a matter of time before he died. She revealed that her husband sent their child away to an institution and that Amy wasn't able to have normal children.

Mr. Grimes wants his deaf child Mervin, to be part of the school, but the principal wants to reject him because of the child's age, which is 19. Eventually, the principal reconsiders and lets him stay even though he's a big fella.

The investigator asks Mr. Medford if Amy would want to do teaching at any other school since she volunteered at the Horace Mann School.

Amy works the best with Henry and he takes to learning new words easily.

Dr. Corcoran arrives on a Sunday to see the principal conducting church services. The doctor has arrived to take Amy and some of the children on a picnic.

Later, they plan to go back, but they can't find Henry. Henry has taken an interest in a football game played by non-impaired children. Corcoran realizes that Henry and the other children would like to learn football, so he teaches them.

The investigator says to contact all of the deaf schools in the area in order to find Amy.

The principal and Amy approach Mr. Goodloe to have a football game against their team. There is concern about the deaf kids playing the non-deaf kids, but it is an unwarranted concern as both teams are good and professional.

Dr. Corcoran puts Mervin in the game and puts Amy at the goal in order for him to score a touchdown, as he has a tendency to run towards her, which he does, and Parker wins the game, handily.

The story of the winning team makes the papers and Mr. Medford and the investigator discover that that's where Amy went.

Corcoran invites Amy out to dinner and reveals his feelings for her. Amy says that she cannot do it as she is still married. Corcoran plants a kiss on her.

Amy continues teaching and Malvina fetches Henry as his parents have arrived for a visit. Henry wants to say "mother" and asks Malvina to review it with him before he sees his mom.

It turns out that Henry's mother is blind and now that he can say "mother," they can bond and now they have a way to communicate with each other.

The school board is angry because the principal has allowed the children to participate in football games. The principal defends his position and also requests a school doctor and has brought Amy and Henry to prove that she has taught Henry to speak some words.

Henry proves that he can speak, by answering a few questions. This changes the school board's mind.

Back at school, a drawing of Mervin as an ape is being handed around, causing Henry to get angry and fight one of the other kids in defense of Mervin. Henry and Mervin are friends and he doesn't want anyone to make fun of him, despite his advanced age and height.

The next day, Dr. Corcoran decides to teach Amy how to drive. Amy refuses but eventually reconsiders. She's not very good and they have to stop and repair a fence she's hit. They soon both profess their love for each other.

Back at the school, the principal has received a note from the investigator and Amy reveals that she forged her letter when she applied for the job at the school.

Amy says that she will do what it takes to succeed. It is now Christmas, and the blind children sing carols as the deaf children decorate the tree. There is an angel that is supposed to top the tree. Amy goes to fetch and accidentally drops it, shattering it into pieces.

Amy bursts into tears. Just George hears her crying and he consoles her. Just George explains his strange name and he says that he has no last name, it's just George.

The kid that drew the ape drawing of Mervin throws decorations at him and Henry punches the kid to stop him. Henry gives Mervin a star to place at the top of the tree, which he does.

Later, Amy plays Checkers with Henry and then gives him the Checker set to Henry. She says that it used to belong to her son. Then, she sends him off to bed.

Corcoran comes in dressed as Santa Claus and reads a poem to Amy that he has written for her.

At the Christmas performance the next day, the deaf children speak one word apiece to wish everyone a Merry Christmas. Then it's time for gifts and Mervin gives Henry a gift of a wooden snake he's carved for him, but that same other kid grabs it and breaks it, prompting another fight between the two.

This time Mervin steps in and really punches the bad kid hard. Mervin runs off in fear. The kid will be fine. He just got a bloody nose. Henry chases after Mervin to bring him back.

Elliott arrives to see Amy, but Malvina covers for her, but it's too late. Amy is in sight and husband and wife reencounter each other. Elliott reprimands her for running away and starts to pack her things.

Amy refuses to go back with him. She is alerted to the disappearance of Mervin and Henry and the concern is that they will be near the railroad tracks and not hear any approaching trains.

At one point, Henry trips and falls and feels the train track's vibrations, so he knows a train is coming through. Henry is lucky, but Mervin isn't.

Amy is distraught and wants to leave because she is tired of watching children die. Corcoran tries to convince her otherwise as Mervin's parents arrive to assess the damage. They are upset that they couldn't teach him, but Henry calls Mervin "friend."

It's too late for Mervin, but the couple has another deaf child named Pearl and request to make her talk like Henry.

They all go back to the school. Elliott is still there waiting, but Amy remains firm. She will not go back. Amy says that she taught Henry to speak, and that Henry taught her value.

She goes upstairs and Elliott leaves.

Amy is a very sweet and charming film, if highly underrated and largely forgotten in the Disney canon, and I defy anyone to watch it without shedding a few tears.

It's kind of a reworking of *The Miracle Worker* (1962). Nanette Fabray is deaf in real life as proof that a deaf person can learn to speak.

The actor who portrays Just George is the same child who also asked the girl in *Airplane* (1980) how she likes her coffee, to which she replies, "Black... like my men!"

Originally, this was to be aired on the anthology show with the title *Amy on the Lips*.

Dragonslayer

RELEASED BY PARAMOUNT PICTURES CORPORATION ON June 26, 1981, Color by Rank Film Laboratories. Panavision. Metrocolor. A Barwood / Robbins Production. Executive Producer: Howard W. Koch. Producer: Hal Barwood. Director: Matthew Robbins. Writers: Hal Barwood, Matthew Robbins. Music: Alex North. Film Editor: Tony Lawson. Production Designer: Elliot Scott. Director of Photography: Derek Vanlint. Made at Pinewood Studios, London, England and on location on the Isle of Skye, Scotland and in North Wales. Associate Producer: Eric Rattray. Assistant Director: Barry Langley. Continuity: Pamela Davies. Second Assistant Director: Roy Stevens. Third Assistant Director: Jerry Daly. Unit Production Manager: Donald Toms. Production Secretary: Norma Garment. Location Manager: Rita Davison. Production Accountant: John Sargent. Production Staff: Monica Rogers, Jennie Johnson, Paul Tucker, Deborah Vertue, Terry Needham, Roberta Johnson, Susan Axworthy, Susan Kane, Sally Forino, Davina Watson, Susie Harrod. Casting: Deborah McWilliams, Deborah Brown. First Unit Camera Operator: Eddie Collins. Second Camera Operator: John Golding. Camera Assistants: Brian Harris, John Keen, Tony Brown, Nick Schlesinger, Robin Carlyle. Grips: George Beavis, Albert Cowlard. Stand-by Crew: Trevor Nicol, Terry Newvell, Fred Meakin, Michael Spivey, Tony Jordon, Philip Connolly. Chief Electrician: Bert Bosher. Chargehand Electrician: Ron Hutton. Second Unit Director: Peter MacDonald. Second Unit Assistant Director: John Downes. Second Assistant Directors: Charles Marriott, Andrew Wood. Continuity: Doris Martin, Georgina Hamilton. Camera Operator: John Campbell. Camera Assistants: Beaumont Alexander, Mark Cridlin. Grip: Frank Batt. Stand-by Carpenter: Graham Britton. Dragon Design, Graphics and Titles: David Bunnett. Art Director: Alan Cassie. Property Master: Barry Wilkinson. Set Decorator: Ian Whittaker. Assistant Art Director: Ernest Archer. Chief Draughtsman: Ted Ambrose. Draftsmen: Peter Childs, Frank Walsh. Scenic Artist: Ernie Smith. Chief Sculptor: Derek Howarth. Sculptors: Arthur Healey, Brian Muir. Property Stand-by Crew: Wally Hill, Tommy Davies, Robert Sherwood. Dressing Props: Bernard Hearn, Nick Rivers. Property Storeman: Sid Alden. Property Maker: John Kijko. Property Buyer: Bryn Siddall. Construction Manager: Michael Redding. Assistant Construction Manager: Tony Morris. Chief Plasterer: Andrew Knapman. Chief Carpenter: Bill Evans. Chief Painter: Jock Campbell. Stunt Coordinator: Terry Walsh. Magic Adviser: Harold Taylor. Latin Adviser: Eric Watts. Choreographer: Peggy Dixon. Unit Publicist: Doreen Landry. Still Photographers: Laurie Ridley, Joe Pearce. Costume Designer: Anthony Mendleson. Wardrobe Master: John Hilling. Wardrobe Mistress: Dorothy Edwards. Wardrobe Assistants: Ken Crouch, Renee Heimer, Ken Lawton, Rene Leonard. Make-up: Graham Freeborn, Jane Royle. Hair: Barbara Ritchie, Bobbie Smith. Sound Designer: Dale Strumpell. Supervising Re-Recordist: Mark Berger. Re-Recordists: Walter Murch, Dale Strumpell. Production Sound Recordist: Anthony Dawe. Boom Operator: Nicholas Dunn. Production Sound Assistant: David Batchelor. Assistant Sound Designer: Louis Benioff. Dialogue Editor: Leslie Shatz. Sound Editors: Teresa Eckton, Jay Boekelheide, Tim Holland. Sound Effects Recordists: Andy Aaron, Douglas Hemphill. First Assistant Film Editor: David Spiers. Assistant Film Editors: Duwayne Dunham, Paul Hodgson. Sound Assistants: Dennie Thorpe, Barbara Ellis, Karen Wilson, Clifford Latimer, Carol Jean Appel, Ken Fischer. Sound Apprentices: George Budd, Daniel Kenney. Sound re-recorded at Zoetrope Studios, San Francisco, California. Music Recordist: Eric Tomlinson. Music Editor: June Edgerton. Period Music: Christopher Page. Music Contractor: Sidney Sax. The National Philharmonic Orchestra recorded at Anvil Abbey Road, London, England. Supervisor of Special Mechanical Effects: Brian Johnson. Special Effects Technicians: David Watkins, Philip Knowles, Neil Swann, John Gant, Peter Hutchinson, Andrew Kelly, Alan Bernard. Special Effects Crew: Barry Whitrod, Martin Gant, John Hatt, Norman Kerss, Ronald Hone, John Packenham, David Knowles. Special Effects Assistants: Clive Beard, Ian Corbould, Chris Gant, Guy Hudson, Digby Milner, Desmond Morgan, Daniel Murphy, Sean Nagle, Alan Poole, Peter Skehan,

Philip Smith, Anthony Speake, Mark Pickford. Dragon Action Props: Danny Lee. Halo Crane: Nick Allder, Dennis Low, Ray Evans. Traveling Matte Consultant: Dennis Bartlett. Aerial Photography: Continental Camera Systems. Pilot: Clay Lacy. Photographic Effects Produced at Industrial Light and Magic, Inc. Marin County, California. Supervisor of Special Visual Effects: Dennis Muren. Dragon Supervisors: Phil Tippett, Ken Ralston. Dragon Movers: Tom St. Amand, Stuart Ziff, Gary Leo. Close-up Dragon: Christopher Walas. Dragon Set Designs: Dave Carson. Dragon Consultant: Jon Berg. Optical Photography Supervisor: Bruce Nicholson. Optical Coordinator: Warren Franklin. Optical Printer Operators: Kenneth Smith, John Ellis, David Berry. Optical Line-up: Tom Rosseter, Mark Vargo, Ed Jones. Optical Technician: Duncan Meyers. Visual Effects Editors: Arthur Repola, Howard Stein. Effects Editorial Assistant: Peter Amundsen. Optical Laboratory: Alpha Cine Laboratory, Inc. Effects Production Supervisor: Thomas Smith. Effects Production Coordinator: Laurie Vermont. Administrative Coordinator: Chrissie England. Production: Laura Kaysen. Matte Painting Supervisor: Alan Maley. Matte Artists: Christopher Evans, Michael Pangrazio. Matte Photography: Neil Krepela. Matte Photography Assistant: Craig Barron. Effects Cameramen: Rick Fichter, Michael McAlister. Effects Camera Assistants: Selwyn Eddy III, Jody Westheimer, Ray Gilberti. Additional Photography: Jim Veilleux. Still Photographer: Terry Chostner. Still Photography Assistants: Roberto McGrath, Kerry Nordquist. Animation Supervisor: Samuel Comstock. Animators: Garry Waller, Loring Doyle, John Van Vliet, Kim Knowlton, Judy Elkins, Sylvia Keulen, Scott Caple, Dietrich Friesen. Additional Animation: Peter Kuran, Visual Concept Engineering. Additional Animators: Susan Turner, Kathrine Kean, Pam Vick, Chris Casady, Len Morganti. Animation Cameraman: Robert Jacobs. Optical Cameraman: James Hagedorn. Additional Optical Composites: RGB Film Processing, Lookout Mountain Films, Modern Film Effects. Ultra High Speed Camera: Bruce Hill Productions. Dragon Assistants: E. Eric Jensen, Bessie K. Wiley, Wesley Seeds, Marc Thorpe, Peter Stolz. Electronic Systems Designer: Jerry Jeffress. Computer Engineer: Kris Brown. Electronic Engineer: Mike MacKenzie. Equipment Engineering Supervisor: Gene Whiteman. Machinists: Udo Pampel, Conrad Bonderson. Model Shop Supervisor: Lorne Peterson. Model Makers: Scott Marshall, Ease Owyeung, Bruce Richardson, Charlie Bailey, Paul Huston, Mike Fulmer. ILM Effects Technicians T.E. Moehnke, William Beck, Dick Dova, Bobby Finley III, Edward Hirsh, Patrick Fitzsimmons, John McCleod. Pyrotechnics: Thaine Morris. Special thanks to The National Trust, North Wales, Snowdonia National Park and the Welsh Office, Ancient Monuments Branch. Stunts: Terry Walsh, Tony Smart, Vic Armstrong, Kiran Shah. Makeup Artist: Nick Dudman. Special Prop Fabricator: Trevor Cripps. Carpenters: Duncan Guest, Robert Jackson. ADR Mixer, UK: Lionel Strutt. Second Unit Effects: David Domeyer. Model Maker: Ken

Speed. Electronic Technician, ILM: Marty Brennies. Blue Screen and Optical Consultant, London: Roy Field. Special Visual Effects: Brian Johnson. Video Operator: Chris Warren. Soundtrack Producer: Dan Goldwasser. Puppeteers: David Claridge, Trevor Freeborn, Christopher Leith, Francis Wright. Running time: 109 minutes. Rated PG.

Cast: Peter MacNicol (Galen), Caitlin Clarke (Valerian), Ralph Richardson (Ulrich), John Hallam (Tyrian), Peter Eyre (Caslodorus Rex), Albert Salmi (Greil), Sydney Bromley (Hodge), Chloe Salaman (Princess Eispeth), Emrys James (Valerian's Father), Roger Kemp (Horsrik), Ian McDiarmid (Brother Jacopus), Ken Shorter (Henchman), Jason White (Henchman), Yolande Palfrey (Victim), Douglas Cooper, Alf Mangan, David Mount, James Payne, Chris Twinn (Urlanders).

A group of people with torches head towards a castle. Inside, Ulrich, a Merlin-type magician is working on some experiments. Ulrich puts various ingredients in a pot that elicits a wide variety of flashing lights and screaming sounds.

The group arrives at the castle and is turned away by Hodge, a man who answers the door. The group demands to see Ulrich and they say they won't leave until they see them.

Galen tells Ulrich of the visitors and Ulrich says to let them in and also that there is a task that needs to be done.

Galen is Ulrich's apprentice and he still expresses interest in becoming a sorcerer. Ulrich greets his visitors and requests to speak to Valerian, a young man. Ulrich already knows why they have come.

Valerian shows a dragon's claw, but it turns out to be a dragon's tooth. Ulrich reveals that he is not afraid of dragons, but he knows that the one terrorizing the village needs to be caught and Ulrich goes out to capture the dragon himself, but brings Galen along.

They are confronted by Tyrian who wonders if they are qualified to capture and kill a dragon. Ulrich shows that he has the correct tools and the correct skills, by showing off his special knife that Galen has retrieved for him.

Ulrich offers to let Tyrian stab him and when Galen goes to save him, the doors shut on him. Ulrich is stabbed and dies. Then the doors reopen for Galen to leave. It was all Ulrich's plan to have Galen slay the dragon.

Before they go, Galen sets Ulrich's lifeless body ablaze for a funeral ceremony. Galen goes through Ulrich's potions and takes the ones he feels he needs to get the dragon.

In using some of the potions, some of the items glow. Galen goes off with Hodge, Ulrich's elder assistant. Hodge complains, but Galen says that he's in charge now, so he must respect him.

Valerian and the villagers start complaining as they sit around the campfire. Suddenly, there is a flash and Galen and Hodge magically appear and Galen's states his intentions of fulfilling Ulrich's quest. So, off they go.

Meanwhile, a maiden is captured so that she can be sacrificed to the dragon. As the maiden frantically tries to free herself from her chains, the dragon appears and she barely succeeds.

The maiden rushes to leave, but the dragon captures her and burns her alive.

Back at the camp, Galen and Valerian separately get the idea to take a skinny dip swim, but Galen discovers the Valerian is not a he, but a she!

They get out of the lake, but Galen promises not to reveal Valerian's secret to anyone else.

Suddenly, an arrow sails through the air and stabs and kills Hodge. Galen, Valerian and the rest go on with their quest, and end up at the entrance to the dragon's lair.

Galen is warned not to go in alone, but does so anyway. He finds an entrance full of sulfuric smoke. He comes back outside and casts a magic spell on the dragon with the glowing amulet of Ulrich's.

His spell causes an avalanche of rocks, which buries everyone with him, which was not his attention. Everyone dives for safety. They seem to have defeated the dragon so they all celebrate.

Valerian tries on a dress as she reconsiders her sexual identity and approaches Galen, surprising everyone in the process. They proceed to dance and are soon joined by others.

Since Galen has proven himself to be quite a skilled magician, he is requested by the king to put on a performance. His skills are still somewhat in question due to his clumsiness.

The king asks if the dragon is really dead, because sometimes terrible things happen as the dragon just disappears instead of really dying.

As he is not truly sure, they decide to lock Galen up. Also in prison is the king's daughter, strangely held captive to protect her from dragons.

Many earthquakes start occurring and Galen uses his magic to escape and climb on to a horse to hasten his exit. He rides back to Valerian and the rest of the villagers.

The earthquakes turn out to be the dragon which has not been killed after all. A man of the cloth confronts the dragon, but is soon burnt to a crisp.

The dragon now flies in the air, spreading flames and havoc wherever he goes. The villagers start preparing new tools in order to attack the dragon. Since Valerian has shown that she's a girl, they no longer allow her to fight.

Galen doesn't care and works with Valerian and also is given a huge spear to stab the dragon. Galen says that he will still need the amulet as no one knows whether the spear will actually stab or kill the dragon.

Others are planning to try to kill the dragon as well. Meanwhile, another name has been drawn for a sacrifice and it turns out to be the king's daughter. The king refuses to accept the name and proceeds to draw another name, provoking the ire of the crowd.

It turns out that the king's daughter has been kept out of all the lotteries in the past, but she replaced all of the entries with her own, making it impossible to draw someone else's name.

The king gives Galen a special magical amulet of his own, so that he can save his daughter. Tyrian recommends not doing this as he feels that Galen will betray the king, but the king takes the chance anyway.

Galen takes the amulet and also speaks a few magic words towards his spear, which causes it to glow with magic powers. The smith pounds the spear into shape.

Meanwhile, Valerian collects some other items and encounters a small dragon in the process. The spear is sharpened and is strong enough to chop an anvil.

Valerian escapes and gives Galen a shield that she has constructed. She warns Galen that he will most assuredly die and that the dragon has little ones. Valerian feels that Galen is in love with the princess and also says that Galen will fail and be put in the lottery because she is a virgin.

Galen says that he is in love, but not with the princess, but with Valerian.

The princess, meanwhile, is put in chains and attached to the stake for the dragon's sacrifice. Galen arrives and stops the proceedings. Tyrian is also there to help the sacrifice proceed as normal.

Tyrian says that to stop the sacrifice, Galen will have to kill him and a sword duel begins. Galen is using his magic spear, so he can easily defend himself, despite Tyrian being the better swordsman.

Galen frees the princess and tells her to run, but she walks towards the dragon as Galen and Tyrian continue fighting. Galen gets in a powerful stab and kills Tyrian.

Galen gets closer to the large dragon, but has to encounter and kill many smaller dragons in the process. He finally gets to the large dragon's lair and takes out his amulet. He crosses a fire lake and finally encounters the humongous beast himself.

The dragon towers over Galen and breathes fire on him. Galen is protected by the shield, but killing the dragon isn't very easy since flames continue to shoot out of the dragon's mouth.

Eventually, Galen jumps on the back of the dragon and stabs him in the neck. The dragon is not that easy to kill as he writhes in pain and breathes more fire on Galen.

Valerian comes by later and finds a severely beaten Galen and his broken spear. She nurses him back to health and asks him to stop fighting the dragon and to leave the area. The smith agrees.

Galen and Valerian board a small boat to leave, when an eclipse shows Galen the real way to get the dragon according to Ulrich's plans.

The rest of the villagers still plan to slay the dragon. Galen and Valerian run back to the dragon's cave as he knows now what he did incorrectly before.

Galen performs another magic spell that causes the flames in the fiery pit to go out. One flame reappears and they manifest themselves into Ulrich. Galen tells Ulrich how he failed, but Ulrich says that Galen can still do it.

The dragon returns and Valerian is reunited with Galen. Ulrich orders Galen to destroy the amulet and Ulrich so that he can defeat the dragon, but first, Ulrich speaks some magic words to cause a tremendous hurricane and thunder and lightning storm.

The dragon swoops down to get Ulrich and he fires lightning bolts at the dragon. Valerian says to smash the amulet and Galen says no as he will know the right time.

The dragon breathes fire onto Ulrich and then lifts Ulrich high into the sky. The amulet glows brighter and Ulrich calls out for Galen. Galen smashes the amulet causing Ulrich and the dragon to explode.

The dragon has been destroyed and the villagers celebrate. The king arrives and credit for killing the dragon is given to him.

Galen and Valerian walk away. Galen wishes they had a horse and one suddenly appears and they ride off together.

This is the second of two collaborations between Paramount Pictures and Walt Disney Productions, the first being *Popeye* (1980). This film was the least successful of the two films. The budget was $18 million, but the film only grossed $14 million, although it has since become a cult classic.

Once again, Paramount distributed the film domestically, while Disney distributed it internationally.

I remember seeing it when it came out and thought it was a hit, but apparently it wasn't.

The special effects are highly impressive for a latter-day Disney film, thus far. A lot of this had to do with Paramount's involvement with Industrial Light and Magic (ILM), which by this time were ramping up their special effects department for films like *Raiders of the Lost Ark* (1981).

This was the first time that Disney used ILM. Who knew that 31 years later, Disney would purchase ILM?

The film was nominated for an Academy Award for Original Score and one for Visual Effects.

The Fox and the Hound

RELEASED BY BUENA VISTA ON July 10, 1981, Technicolor. Co-Producers: Wolfgang Reitherman, Art Stevens. Executive Producer: Ron Miller. Directors: Art Stevens, Ted Berman, Richard Rich. Story: Larry Clemmons, Ted Berman, David Michener, Peter Young, Burny Mattinson, Steve Hulett, Earl Kress, Vance Gerry based on the book by Daniel P. Mannix. Creative Assistant to the Producers: Melvin Shaw. Supervising Animators: Randy Cartwright, Glen Keane, Cliff Nordberg, Ron Clements, Frank Thomas, Ollie Johnston. Character Animation: Ed Gombert, Dale Oliver, Ron Husband, David Block, Chris Buck, Hendel S. Butoy, Darrell Van Citters, John Musker, Jerry Rees, Dick N. Lucas, Jeffrey J. Varab, Chuck Harvey, Phil Nibbelink, Michael Cedeno, Phillip Young. Effects Animators: Ted Kierscey, Jack Boyd, Don C. Paul. Coordinating Animators: Walt Stanchfield, Leroy Cross, Dave Suding, Chuck Williams. Key Assistants: Tom Ferriter, Sylvia Mattinson. Art Director: Don Griffith. Layout: Dan Hansen, Glenn V. Vilppu, Sylvia Roemer, Gus Vasilovich, Michael Peraza, Jr., Joe Hale. Color Styling: Jim Coleman. Background Painting: Daniela Bielecka, Brian Sebern, Kathleen Swain. Production Managers: Edward Hansen, Don A. Duckwall. Sound: Herb Taylor. Editors: James Melton, Jim Koford. Assistant Directors: Don Hahn, Mark A. Hester, Terry L. Noss. Music Editors: Evelyn Kennedy, Jack Wadsworth. Musical Score Composed and Conducted by Buddy Baker. Orchestration: Walter Sheets. Airbrush Artist: John Emerson. Animation Camera: Brian LeGrady, Rob Maine. Animators: Brad Bird, Don Bluth, Tim Burton, Lorna Cook, Andy Gaskill, Gary Goldman, Dan Haskett, Bill Kroyer, Linda Miller, John Pomeroy, Henry Selick. Assistant Animators: Ben Burgess, Leslie Gorin, Susan Kroyer, Harry Sabin. Inbetween Artist: Will Finn. Clean-up Artist: Rusty Stoll. Running time: 83 minutes.

Songs: "Best of Friends" Music: Richard O. Johnston. Lyrics: Stan Fidel. "Lack of Education," "A Huntin' Man," "Appreciate the Lady" Music and Lyrics: Jim Stafford. "Goodbye May Seem Forever" Music: Richard Rich. Lyrics: Jeffrey Patch.

Cast: Mickey Rooney (Tod), Kurt Russell (Copper), Pearl Bailey (Big Mama), Jack Albertson (Amos Slade), Sandy Duncan

(Vixey), Jeanette Nolan (Widow Tweed), Pat Buttram (Chief), John Fiedler (Porcupine), John McIntire (Badger), Dick Bakalyan (Dinky), Paul Winchell (Boomer), Keith Mitchell (Young Tod), Corey Feldman (Young Copper), "Squeeks" (The Caterpillar).

A fox is being chased by a pack of dogs with her baby in her mouth. The fox escapes, but this attracts the attention of Big Mama, the owl, who goes to see what all the noise is about.

The mother fox hides her baby, and is shot soon after. Big Mama goes down to comfort the fox. Big Mama elicits the help of Boomer and Dinky, two birds who try to find the fox a home.

They drop the fox off at Widow Tweed's house. She takes the fox in and names him Tod. Meanwhile, Amos Slade brings home a new hunting dog named Copper to accompany his older dog named Chief.

Tod plays with Abigail the cow's tail as Widow Tweed milks her. It turns out that Tod wanted a squirt of milk. Tod gets into other troubles by chasing the chickens and Widow Tweed reprimands him, temporarily.

Dinky and Boomer go back to what they were originally doing, which was trying to get Squeeks the caterpillar. Tod witnesses this and makes a funny face.

Copper smells a new smell. Chief sniffs and just says that it's Amos cooking. Copper knows it is something new and goes off to find what it is. It turns out to be Tod the fox. Big Mama sings about it with "Best of Friends" as the fox and hound do become best friends.

Amos goes out to fetch Copper and wants him to become a more reliable hunting dog. Amos ties him up to keep him from running away again. Tod comes by and wants to play again, but Copper says to not disturb Chief.

Tod disturbs Chief, Amos and a bunch of chickens. Chief chases after Tod and Amos fires shots at him. Tod escapes back home to find Widow Tweed driving away. Tod catches up with her as Amos fires shots at her.

She stops her car and grabs Amos' gun and fires a shot at his radiator and reprimands him for shooting at her and her fox. Amos gets angry. She keeps Tod inside in future in order to keep the peace.

Amos goes off onto a hunting trip with Chief and Copper. Tod is sad to see Copper go and vice versa. Big Mama sees that Tod is feeling down and sings "Lack of Education," and tells him that Copper is being trained into a good hunting dog.

Time passes and the seasons change from summer into winter. Dinky and Boomer continue to chase Squeaks, but give up and decide to fly south for the winter. Amos and his dogs continue to hunt through the snow and Copper grows to full size and has surpassed Chief as the better hunter.

Next spring, Big Mama emerges from her hibernation and Dinky and Boomer come back and resume hunting Squeaks. Tod has grown up, too.

Amos returns home with a number of pelts and sings "A Huntin' Man." Tod notices how big Copper has gotten, but Big Mama warns him that Copper is now a full-fledged hunting dog and that they are now natural enemies.

Later that evening, Tod goes to visit Copper, but Copper warns him that Tod will get both of them in trouble and sends him away.

Chief wakes up and starts barking at Tod causing Amos to wake up and fires shots at him. Chief chases after Tod with Copper also in pursuit. Copper catches up with Tod, but lets him go just once. Chief has not made any such promise and chases Tod on the railroad tracks. A speeding train hits Chief, but Tod escapes unharmed.

Copper is now mad at Tod for hurting Chief. Widow Tweed is out looking for Tod and finds him and takes him home before any more harm can be done. Amos comes to the door demanding to get Tod, but she won't let him in. Later, she takes Tod for a drive to take him away from the problems, takes off his collar and sets him free deep in the forest. "Goodbye May Seem Forever" plays in the background.

Tod must now brave the elements like a real fox as a rainstorm kicks in. Tod tries to find a place to live, and bothers a badger in his home, but a porcupine offers him shelter.

Chief is on the mend with a broken leg and craves sympathy from Amos and Copper, who sends Chief back to bed. Amos is now more determined than ever to get Tod and plans to set out larger traps.

Big Mama flies out to find Tod, but encounters another fox she knows named Vixie. Digger the badger still doesn't like Tod and sends him away, but Big Mama and Vixie catch up with him in the distance.

Vixie notices that Tod seems awfully downhearted and Big Mama and Vixie agree that Vixie should help cheer him up and get his mind off of being dropped off in the forest.

Tod sees Vixie and immediately falls head over heels in love with her. He introduces himself and she introduces herself and they spark up a conversation.

Vixie asks Tod to get her a fish, but he's too much in love. Then he professes to be an expert fisher fox, but really is not that good and catches a stick instead. Vixie laughs at him and they get snippy with each other. Big Mama sings "Appreciate the Lady." Vixie and Tod make amends.

Amos shows up with Copper at the restricted game reserve, but that's not stopping them. Amos cuts the barbed wire and they go in to get Tod. Amos sets up some of his traps. Tod and Vixie are in the area and set off some of the traps. Amos shoots at them and Copper catches up with them. They have a standoff.

Tod and Vixie run into a hole with Copper aggressively digging after them. Amos sets fire into the hole in order to smoke them out, but they manage to escape unharmed.

They cross over a felled tree bridge in front of a waterfall with Copper and Amos still in pursuit. Amos and Copper encounter a huge bear. They run and Amos gets trapped by one of his own traps. As he tries to escape, Copper fights the bear.

Amos tries to reach his gun but that's out of reach as well. Copper has been hurt so Tod comes to his rescue and battles the bear. The bear swipes at Tod, but the battle continues and the tree bridge falls as do the bear and Tod.

Tod survives, but just barely. Copper shows up and Amos points his gun at Tod. Copper puts himself between Tod and the gun and Amos cannot shoot. Amos and Copper go home. Tod is grateful for Copper's courage and the two part ways.

Big Mama is resting but is disturbed by Dinky and Boomer hunting Squeaks again, but Squeaks has transformed into a butterfly and flies away.

Widow Tweed bandages up Amos' leg, despite Amos' protests; Chief and Copper rest nearby. Chief says that Amos is making a lot of fuss about a hurt leg, while Copper dreams about his childhood friendship with Tod.

When I saw this upon original release, I found it disappointingly sugary sweet, especially in comparison to such meatier Disney cartoon fare as recent as even *The Rescuers* (1977). Upon rewatching it, it isn't too bad because it has what a lot of current animated cartoons being released today don't have, which is heart. It's still kind of sappy, though, and the songs save for "Best of Friends" are not very good, either.

I was more disappointed because also back then, they didn't make a feature or two a year as they do now, Disney made a feature every three or four years, thus making each on an event, but this one just wasn't.

On the DVD, there is a feature about passing the baton from the old guard Disney animators to the new guard. It wasn't an easy transition, but according to Disney animator Randy Cartwright, this was the beginning of the change that was eventually to produce *The Little Mermaid* (1989), *Beauty and the Beast* (1991) *Aladdin* (1992) and *The Lion King* (1994).

The old animators (Frank Thomas, Ollie Johnston and Wolfgang Reitherman) started the movie and then handed the project onto the new animators. Animator Glen Keane was shaking in his boots at the prospect and animators Ron Clements and John Musker offers their views as well. Everyone knew that the old guys were going to retire during the course of the picture. Singer Pearl Bailey helped by acting like her Big Mama owl character while singing in order to help the animators.

What they don't talk about in this documentary is how Don Bluth and a group of 17 other animators left the studio over this project. Bluth went on to release *Banjo, the Woodpile Cat*, *The Secret of NIMH* (1982), *An American Tail* (1986), *The Land Before Time* (1988) and a few other movies just to show how animated features COULD be done, but those films also have their shortcomings.

The fight with Copper and a bear is repeatedly considered the highlight of this film, but overall it is considered an uneven effort.

There are even mistakes as some footage was shot out of focus, but that has since been corrected with the advent of home video.

This film was originally touted as Disney's 20th full-length animated feature, but with the release of *The Black Cauldron* in 1985, suddenly this film became the 24th full-length animated release.

This was also the final G-rated film released during this era. Of course, Disney returned to making some G-rated films as Touchstone and Hollywood Pictures were established to take on those stronger pictures, but for now everything became PG from this point forward.

The film cost $12 million to make and production began in the spring of 1977. It grossed $63 million and was re-released to theaters in 1988.

Condorman

RELEASED BY BUENA VISTA ON August 7, 1981 (July 2, 1981 in UK), Technicolor. Producer: Jan Williams. Executive Producer: Ron Miller. Director: Charles Jarrott. Screenplay: Marc Stirdivant, Mickey Rose suggested by *The Game of X* by Robert Sheckley. Production Manager: John Bloss. Sound Supervisor: Herb Taylor. Sound Mixer: William Sivel. Costumes: Kent James, Jean Zay. Make-up Supervisor: Robert J. Schiffer, C.M.A.A. Make-up: Dan Striepeke. Hair Stylist: Alex Archambault. Sound Editor: Ben F. Hendricks. Music Editor: Jack Wadsworth. Associate Producer: Hugh Attwooll. Second Unit Director: Anthony Squire. Stunt Supervisor: Remy Julienne. Special Effects Supervisor: Art Cruickshank, A.S.C. Second Unit Camera: Godfrey Godar, B.S.C. Title Animation: Michael Cedeno. Animation Effects Supervisor: Jack Boyd. Our thanks to: The Principality of Monaco, The Village of Zermatt, The City of Paris, Societe Des Bains De Mer De Monte Carlo, Casino of Monte Carlo, Aeronavale Francaise French Naval Aviation for their cooperation in the making of this film. Production Manager (France): Philippe Modave. Assistant Directors: Richard Learman, Denys Granier-Deferre, Paul Feyder. Music: Henry Mancini. Editor: Gordon D. Brenner, A.C.E. Production Designer: Albert Witherick. Art Director (France): Marc Frederix. Director of Photography: Charles F. Wheeler, A.S.C. Production Managers: Antoine Compin, Charis Horton. Special Effects Technician: Chris Corbould. Post Special Effects: Ken Speed. Stunts: Dominique Julienne, Michel Julienne, Remy Julienne, Jean-Claude Lagniez, Colin Skeaping, Marc Wolf. Assistant Camera: Pierre Boffety. Assistant Camera, Second Unit: Philippe Houdart. Camera Operator: Jacques Mironneau. Production Runner: Callum McDougall. Running time: 90 minutes. Rated PG.

Song: "Condorman" by Henry Mancini.

Cast: Michael Crawford (Woody Wilkins), Oliver Reed (Krokov), Barbara Carrera (Natalia Rombola), James Hampton (Harry), Jean-Pierre Kalfon (Morovich), Dana Elcar (Russ), Vernon Dobtcheff (Russian Agent), Robert Arden (C.I.A. Chief), Gerard Buhr, David Pontremoli.

A fully-animated Condorman flies over the live-action background of Paris and highlights the title sequence as the "Condorman" theme plays.

Then, the live-action Condorman appears on the Eiffel Tower and surveys the land below. He sees his friend, Harry the photographer, who is set up to take photos of Condorman in action.

Condorman spreads his mighty wings and begins his descent as Harry photographs. The descent goes well until something happens and he drops into the sea.

Condorman is actually Woody Wilkins, who is a comic book artist and he likes to try out everything that Condorman is doing before he commits it to a comic book.

Harry tells Woody that he almost killed himself and for him to go back home to England to draw his comic books.

Later, Harry meets up with Russ as he's leaving on a business trip to Russia and puts Harry in charge. Russ tells Harry to get someone to help him out so he phones Woody.

Harry meets Woody at the train station. Woody is disguised in a hat and trench coat and Harry tells him he's supposed to be himself.

Woody is assigned to take the train to the end of the line which happens to be Istanbul. In Istanbul, Woody gets off and he's back in his Bogie disguise, but nowhere near as classy.

Woody trips and falls and falls over and into a conversation with Natalia Rombola, who is a Russian spy. She asks who he is and he reveals his name as Condorman.

Woody and Natalia are suddenly pursued by other spies and a fist fight breaks out. Woody successfully foils the crooks.

Next, they are off to Moscow. Natalia goes back home and encounters Krokov who has been waiting for her return and to know what information she has. Natalia reveals that the man she was speaking with is named Condorman.

Russ comes back and reveals what he has found out to Harry, which is Condorman. Harry says that Condorman is a made up creation of Woody, but Russ wants him to work with them. They go to Woody who balks at the offer to become a real spy.

Harry convinces him to change his mind by reminding him that he said that he won't put anything in the comic book unless he proves that it can work.

Woody comes up with an elaborate amount of equipment that he needs and now Russ balks, but both Woody and Harry convinces them otherwise.

Woody is then sent off to Yugoslavia. He is once again in disguise and scans the countryside wearing lederhosen and with abundant facial hair, looking for Natalia again. She appears hiding in the bushes disguised as a gypsy.

Woody and Natalia are both captured by more spies and held at gunpoint. Woody tries to talk himself out of their fix and then fires his gun at them which is disguised as a cane, although not very well as gunshot flies everywhere.

Woody and Natalia escape and drive off in a truck and then head off to Monte Carlo. Meanwhile, Krokov is pissed since the spies he sent out did not defeat Condorman.

In Paulownia, Yugoslavia, another spy is sent out; one with a silver eye. The clock in the town strikes 12 and everyone hides in their homes as a number of black sedans race through the streets. These sedans are seeking out Condorman, who is still driving their gypsy caravan truck. They don't understand why they don't see any people on the streets.

Natalia warns Woody about Krokov, but he isn't worried, but the sedans start surrounding their truck. Natalia says they can't outrun them in the truck and Woody agrees, so he drops them down into his Condor Car, which releases the truck shell and speeds off.

The Condor Car has a number of special features including laser beam bullets and a fully-charged surveillance system. The Condor Car outruns the sedans, but they gain up on them, so Woody sets fire to the pursuing sedans and they speed off the road.

There are two sedans left, one in front and one behind. The Condor Car raises a ramp on its front and the one sedan drives over the Condor Car and crashes onto the other pursuing sedan.

There is one more sedan left, which is in somewhat rough shape, but continues to pursue the Condor Car. It is driven by the man with the silver eye. Natalia sees him and knows exactly who he is. He's a spy named Morovich.

Woody tries to escape by driving through residential streets, but he cannot shake him. Then he drives off the pier and a rubber raft inflates and the Condor Car floats on the water and becomes a Condor Boat. They escape in style.

Krokov is tremendously angry at Morovich, but gives him one more chance to get them. Meanwhile, Woody and Natalia are now climbing the mountains of Italy, but are soon captured and thrown in jail for trespassing on private property.

Inspector Jean-Paul of Monaco comes by to bail them out and handcuffs them to himself as he releases them. Jean-Paul turns out to be Harry in disguise. He takes them away, but on their departure, they encounter Morovich, who has blocked the road. They flee on foot, but unfortunately are still handcuffed together.

The three bail into a local wedding. Natalia pretends to be affiliated with the groom and disrupts the wedding and gets the groom to punch Morovich and the other spies so Natalia, Woody and Harry can escape the room.

Krokov has taken to reading Condorman comic books which reveals what their plans are and shows them to Morovich.

Meanwhile, Woody, Harry and Natalia escape on a horse drawn hay cart into the Alps nearby the real Matterhorn Mountain. They drive up to an Inn and stay the night, finally freed from the handcuffs.

Natalia takes a little walk and is recognized by the local school children as Laser Lady, the Empress of Space from her comic books. Harry comes out to find Natalia and she is angry. She says that Woody is Condorman and that she is Laser Lady, so she demands to know what's going on, so Harry tells her.

That night the three have fun in the local pub and Natalia professes her love to Woody.

The next day, the three take the ski lift which, according to Woody, is their ticket to freedom by way of their zip line contraption that is jet-fueled.

They think that they are not seen, but they are seen by Krokov and Morovich, who shoot Woody and Harry from the sky and capture Natalia and take her away in a helicopter.

Woody and Harry are alright, but don't move until Woody gives the signal in order for Krokov and Morovich to believe that they are dead.

The next day, Krokov visits Natalia and explains why he captured her instead of killing her. He also explains that she will have to play the part of a perfect hostess for a party for the oil ministers that are scheduled to arrive the next day. If she doesn't obey, Krokov threatens to kill her.

Woody and Harry have been ordered back to Paris and the mission is considered a bust, but Woody doesn't want to quit and asks for two more days so that he can rescue Natalia.

At the Grand Casino in Monte Carlo, the Arab oil ministers arrive to thunderous applause. Krokov asks who one of the Arabs is, and it is revealed that he's the seventh richest man in the world. Krokov says to make sure that he shows up to the party.

This Arab turns out to be Woody in disguise. Harry is also in disguise as an Arab. Later, Woody catches up with Natalia and says that he's come to take her away, but she refuses due to Krokov.

Natalia also doesn't want to defect as Woody isn't worth dealing with since he's only a lowly comic book writer. Woody is severely disappointed, but then Natalia says something in code to him that he realizes is his cue to take her.

Harry sets off a pre-designated bomb and in the chaos drives off in one of the parked limos, while Woody and Natalia zip off upstairs and out the back way.

They are trapped on the back balcony, but Woody has another trick up his sleeve and takes off his Arab clothes to reveal his Condorman outfit. He asks Natalia to climb aboard and together they fly off the balcony, successfully.

Harry is still being followed and Woody and Natalia are shot at, but they all manage to escape and meet up together at their predetermined rendezvous.

Harry gets their first and doffs his disguise, but forgets to set the parking brake and the limo falls off the pier into the water.

Harry guides Woody and Natalia in for a landing and they all climb aboard a boat. Woody asks Natalia about her allegiance and what she thinks about comic books and she professes her love again.

They all speed off in the Condor Craft. Just as before with the black sedans, a number of black speedboats follow the Condor Craft.

The Condor Craft has another laser gun and Woody blows away the following speedboats. The Condor Craft successfully escapes, but not everyone just yet as Krokov and Morovich have their own speedboat which is larger and much more powerful than the other boats.

Woody fires, but the beams deflect off the boat and don't do any damage. Krokov and Morvich decide to ram the Condor Craft, but the Condor Craft is hoisted up at the last minute by a helicopter.

Krokov dives out of the boat, but Morovich is not so lucky and blows up in the explosion. Krokov is captured and taken to prison.

At Dodger Stadium in Los Angeles, Harry, Woody and Natalia watch a baseball game. The Good Year blimp flying overhead gives a message of welcome to Natalia.

Russ and other C.I.A. agents are flying in the blimp and they radio down to the three and offer to send them on to another mission.

This is not a bad film by any means, but it didn't really do that well at the box office, so tarnished was the Disney image by this point.

There were top quality cars and boats used in this production including seven Porsche 935 Turbo Carreras, two Group 5 Lemans Porsches and four modified Sterling racers to become the Condor Car.

The Condor Craft was a racing hydroplane and there was an Abati used by Morovitch and a number of Daycruisers.

Many of the people working on this film also worked on the *Pink Panther* films, *The Blue Max* (1966), *The Italian Job* (1969), *The French Connection II* (1975) and *Bobby Deerfield* (1977).

The film was shot on location in France, Monaco, Switzerland and Monte Carlo.

Michael Crawford went on to much greater success in the musical version of *The Phantom of the Opera.*

Disney did its typical push to make this film a success, complete with comic book adaptations and promotions through Baskin-Robbins, but it was to no avail. The film as with most Disney films of this era, was a disappointment.

They were to do better next with *Tron* (1982) but this was Disney's attempt to do another *Pink Panther* film even going so far as to hiring Henry Mancini to do the music for the film.

A Condorman action figure makes a cameo in the 2011 Pixar short *Toy Story Toons: Small Fry* in a support group for discarded kids' meal toys.

When Disney acquired Marvel Comics in 2009, *Amazing Spider-Man* editor Stephen Wacker lobbied to make Condorman part of the Marvel Universe.

1982

Disney continued to struggle for another year, even though more promising movies like *Tron* and *Tex* were released this year.

Disney executives were obsessed with the success of films like *Porky's* which turned in the high grosses and were produced very cheaply as Disney used to do. The only problem is that *Porky's* was a raunchy R-rated comedy of the type that Disney was still not willing to make at this point.

E.T.: The Extra-Terrestrial was yet another in a long line of highly-successful films that Disney should have made, although Card Walker and Ron Miller both agreed that the line "Penis breath" wouldn't have made the final cut in the film.

On Golden Pond was still another film that Disney felt they could have or should have made although they still wouldn't have been able to pull the star power of Henry and Jane Fonda and Katharine Hepburn.

There was also *Star Trek II: The Wrath of Khan* that a certain Michael Eisner was aggressively involved with at Paramount to revive the sagging *Star Trek* franchise.

New films produced for the anthology show include *Tales of the Apple Dumpling Gang, Donald and Jose, Olé!, A Disney Valentine, Beyond Witch Mountain, Pluto and his Friends, The Adventures of Pollyanna, A Disney Vacation, Epcot Center: The Opening Celebration, Disney's Halloween Treat, A Disney Christmas Gift* and *Winnie the Pooh and Friends*.

Totally original episodes are severely lacking at this point as all of the original programming produced are either one hour remakes of past films, compilations of old cartoons or the salute to the grand opening of Epcot Center. As such, in the fall the 29th and final season of the original run of the Disney anthology show premiered.

The only new all original shows appeared as half-hour specials including *Computers Are People, Too!* and *A Dream Called Walt Disney World*.

This was also the year that Disney tried some more new half-hour sitcoms. Unfortunately, none of them were successful and only lasted five or six episodes apiece. They were *Small & Frye*, *Gun Shy* (based on *The Apple Dumpling Gang* and *Zorro and Son*.

It was this latter series that was offered to Guy Williams who was comfortably in retirement. He was interested in doing the show until he found out that it was going to be a situation comedy and therefore declined.

Though new animated shorts were very sparse by 1982, two were actually produced this year: *Vincent*, a stop-motion animation by a young Tim Burton and *Fun with Mr. Future*, a standard cartoon with some live-action. *The Black Cauldron* was still in production.

It was also at this time, according to Charles Solomon's *The Disney That Never Was*, that Disney began developing *Musicana*, which would be a *Fantasia*-like presentation. One segment would have been *The Emperor's Nightingale* starring Mickey Mouse.

Musicana was shelved in favor of *Mickey's Christmas Carol* and the idea was revived for *Fantasia 2000*, but with none of the *Musicana* ideas included.

Darby O'Gill and the Little People (1959), *Alice in Wonderland* (1951), *Pollyanna* (1960), *Herbie Rides Again* (1974), *The Sign of Zorro* (1960), *Freaky Friday* (1977), *Justin Morgan Had a Horse* (1972), *The One and Only, Genuine, Original Family Band* (1968) and *A Tale of Two Critters* were released to home video for the first time and 1973's animated *Robin Hood*, *Bambi* (1942), *Peter Pan* (1953), *The Sword in the Stone* (1963) and *Fantasia* (1940) were reissued to theaters.

On the theme park front, the biggest news of the year was the grand opening of Walt Disney's EPCOT, now rechristened Epcot Center and redesigned to be a sort of permanent World's Fair, rather than the living, breathing city that Walt had envisioned. To the purists, this was a major letdown, but to everyone else, this was a tremendous step forward with a new concept from Disney as Walt Disney World up to this point was essentially the same as Disneyland surrounded by a lot of land and trees.

Passport tickets returned to the theme parks, but only for the summer months and Ronald Reagan was added to the Hall of Presidents.

At Disneyland, it was the end of the line for the Big Game Safari Shooting Gallery in Adventureland as well as the Chicken of the Sea Pirate Ship, which was supposed to be salvaged, but it was too water damaged after sitting in water for the past 25 years to be used for the New Fantasyland to open in 1983.

And, the original Golden Horseshoe Revue featuring Wally Boag ended after a world record 10 billion performances. Ok, maybe I'm exaggerating a tad.

Disney storyteller albums released this year include more based on movies that Disney should have been releasing such as *The Dark Crystal* and *E.T.: The Extra Terrestrial*.

Another film that Disney could have made and in fact was made by ex-Disney animators was Don Bluth's *The Secret of NIMH*. It wasn't as good as anticipated.

In the comic book world, Whitman continued to publish *Donald Duck, Mickey Mouse, Uncle Scrooge, Walt Disney's Comics and Stories, Huey, Dewey and Louie Junior Woodchucks, Super Goof, Chip 'n' Dale, Daisy and Donald* and *Winnie the Pooh*.

Cinderella appeared as a one-shot and more essential Disney hardbacks appeared including: *Treasures of Disney Animation Art, Walt Disney's World of Fantasy* and *Walt Disney's Fantasia*.

The Mouse Club held its first Disneyana in August in Anaheim and a magazine called *The Disneyana Collector* debuted.

Night Crossing

RELEASED BY BUENA VISTA ON February 5, 1982, Technicolor. Panavision. Executive Producer: Ron Miller. Producer: Tom Leetch. Director: Delbert Mann. Writer: John McGreevey based on the true story of the Strelzyk and Wetzel families. Music: Jerry Goldsmith. Editor: Gordon D. Brenner, A.C.E. Production Designer: Rolf Zehetbauer. Director of Photography: Tony Imi, B.S.C. Associate Producer: Marc Stirdivant. Production Manager: Dieter Meyer. Assistant Director: Don Roberts. Second Assistant Directors: Don French, Bettina Forg. Art Director: Herbert Strabel. Sound Mixer: Danny Daniel. Property Buyer: Adolf Nurschinger. Costume Supervisor: Ille Sievers. Costume Master: Ken Lawton. Costume Mistress: Friedel Schroeder. Make-up and Hairstylists: Evelyn Dohring, Gerhard Nemetz. Title Design: George Petlowany. Sound Effects: Ben F. Hendricks. Music Editor: Jack Wadsworth. Orchestration: Arthur Morton. Second Unit Director: James Gavin. Aerial Photography: Rexford Metz. Balloon Stunt Coordinator: Gary Cerveny. Balloon Crew Chief: Eugene Cerveny. Stunt Balloonists: Gary Cerveny, Diane Cerveny, Kinnie Gibson, Tommy Mercurio, Dawn Grant, Deborah Bryan, Harley V. Kinnamon. Filmed on location at Bavaria Studios, Munich, Germany. Conductor: Jerry Goldsmith. Running time: 107 minutes. Rated PG.

Cast: John Hurt (Peter Strelzyk), Jane Alexander (Doris Strelzyk), Glynnis O'Connor (Petra Wetzel), Doug McKeon (Frank Strelzyk), Beau Bridges (Gunter Wetzel), Ian Bannen (Josef Keller), Klaus Lowitsch (Schmolk), Anne Stallybrass (Magda Keller), Kay Walsh (Doris' Mother), Gunter Meisner (Major Koerner), Keith McKeon (Fitscher Strelzyk), Geoffrey Liesik (Little Peter Wetzel), Michael Liesik (Andreas Wetzel), Matthew Taylor (Lukas Keller), Sky Dumont (Ziegler), Jan Niklas (Lieutenant Fehler), Carola Hohn (Petra's Mother), Irene Prador (Mrs. Roseler), Jann Paulus Biczyzcki (Pharmacist), Osman Ragheb (Store Supervisor), Ursula Ludwig (1st Store Clerk), Jenny Thelen (2nd Store Clerk), Katharina Seyferth (Shopper), Gavin James (Pilot).

A short black-and-white prologue using actual stock footage describes the history of the Berlin Wall and how landmines and machine guns are set up to discourage escape from East Germany to West Germany.

The film opens in Poessneck, East Germany on April 4, 1978. Gunter Wetzel is riding his motorcycle home alongside his friend Peter Strelzyk, who is driving his car.

Neighbor Lukas Keller is requesting that they all sign a petition to condemn traitor and defector Herr Orson Mueller.

Gunter, Peter and father Josef Keller sign and then express regrets when they sit in a local pub. They feel that everyone has their bags packed ready to leave East Germany at any time as life in East Germany is very oppressive.

Peter advises his son, Frank to keep thoughts of escape to himself and the family and not express them publicly. They go and pick up Doris from the market.

They come home to find younger son Fitscher being reprimanded by grandmother for watching Western German television when he has homework.

The border is shown as proof to how heavily guarded it is both coming and going, especially at night when killer guard dogs are on patrol.

At night, Lukas hijacks a tractor with shovel in order to create a diversion. He drives the tractor into the guard tower, knocking it over and jumps out at the last moment to make a break on foot. While the guards observe the damage, Lukas makes his break, but the electric fence and gunshot kill him.

The next day, Hans comes by the Strelzek family to ask questions about their friendship with the Kellers, of which Lukas was their son. The Wetzels are also questioned as is Josef Keller.

Hans arrests Josef and Magda and their children and takes them away. After questioning, Magda and the children are set free, but Josef is still being held.

Josef's arrest prompts Peter and Gunter to reconsider their allegiance to the east and rekindles their desire to leave. Peter says to Doris that they should try before Frederick decides to do what Lukas did and find his body riddled with bullets.

On June 20, 1978, Peter tells Gunter his plans of building a hot air balloon to escape the east. Gunter feels that Peter is crazy, but is willing to try. They have to secure the materials from various sources and build everything from scratch.

Peter and Gunter go to a shop outside of town to get the material they need. When questioned why they need so much material, they say that they need it for tents as they do a lot of camping.

One of their nosy neighbors named Mrs. Roseler sees Peter and Gunter carrying in the large amount of material and tells her that it is a rug to keep her from snooping further.

Peter and Gunter measure out the material and cut it into smaller pieces and sew it together with a manual sewing machine. They work until the wee hours of the morning.

One night the buzzer rings and Peter and Gunter stop working. It turns out to be Mrs. Roseler with some chicken soup as she hasn't seen them go to work for at least two days, so she concludes that they are sick.

Petra warns them that in the future, they might not be as lucky as Mrs. Roseler may return with the police. Soon, they are done sewing and also very sore.

Next, they try to inflate the balloon, but they do not have enough propane or power to do it.

On October 14, 1978, Josef has finally been freed. Peter bumps into him at the drug store, but it is obvious that he is a weaker man. Josef advises that their families should no longer associate with each other and that the only way to be a friend is to not be a friend.

Hans stops by to talk to Peter again and says that he sees Peter coming and going so much and that he should take life a little easier. This is code saying that he is being watched.

That night, Peter and Gunter try to inflate their balloon again. They get farther along, but still fail. Peter is determined to keep working at it.

On December 16, 1978, Petra has a nightmare about the balloon and tells Gunter that she wants no more to do with the balloon. After pleading with Gunter, he agrees to tell Peter that they want out.

Peter says that Doris is having bad dreams as well, but he doesn't want to quit. Peter agrees and says that he needs to move the equipment to his house and that they should no longer be seen together in order to protect everyone.

Peter and Doris sit on a hill and discuss that he will continue working on the balloon and that the four of them will make it without Gunter and his family. Doris reluctantly agrees to continue.

On April 23, 1979, Peter finally secures a more powerful way to fill up the balloon and succeeds in filling up the balloon, but accidentally sets the balloon on fire.

They get the fire out and figure out another better way to control the flame and the gas pressure. This time they run out of gas and confirm that the next day they will go, but they don't actually leave until July 3, 1979.

Up until the last minute, Doris does not tell her mother that they plan to leave. At the time they are to leave, Doris cleans the bathroom as she doesn't want the police to know that she was a bad housekeeper.

They finally leave their house for what they feel will be the last time. The balloon is inflated and the family climbs aboard and the tethers cut.

The balloon slowly ascends higher and higher into the late night and gets as high as 800 feet up. The glowing object is not without its witnesses as it is observed from the now-repaired guard tower.

Dampness makes their journey somewhat difficult, but they successfully manage to stay up for quite a long while…approximately 34 minutes.

Eventually, there's nothing more that they can do and they abruptly land. Once they get out, the balloon floats off by itself and the family walks on foot, not sure of where they are.

Soon, they discover that they are right by the fence, but are they on the east or the west side? After careful observation, Peter realizes that they are in the zone on the east side. He informs the rest of the family that they must wait until daylight before they make their next move.

Next morning, Peter advises that they all walk single file and to watch out for wires along the way. Meanwhile, the deflated balloon has landed next to the fence and guards set off the alarms.

A jeep goes out to investigate the balloon, while the family manages to walk past security unnoticed. The investigators conclude that the people who manned the balloon should still be in the zone.

Helicopters are also sent out to investigate with Major Koerner aboard.

The family gets back to their abandoned car and luckily it has not been found yet, so they pack up their remaining things and drive home.

Once they get back, they realize that they have to make absentee notices for the children and for them. Doris also notices that she's lost her prescription blood pressure medicine bottle.

The telephone rings and it is Doris' mother. She's concerned about their whereabouts and Peter explains that the children have been ill and that Doris had to stay home from work to care for them.

Everyone tries to sleep, but they are all on edge since their escape attempt failed. Peter is upset for his failure and Doris consoles him. The children come in and offer their help and say that they didn't do so badly for their first try.

Frank and Fitscher say that they cannot give up because now the SSD will be looking for them. Frank has made arm bands for the family. With this vote of encouragement, Peter agrees to try again. The first thing he does is get a new car as to not have the old one traced.

On July 11, 1979, life seems to be back to normal and Peter goes to visit Gunter and his family. Peter explains that the balloon really worked, but landed a few hundred feet away from the border. Peter wishes that they could come with them.

Major Koerner is still on the search and concludes that the balloon could have only flown for only about 20-30 minutes and that their best lead is to check all the local fabric shops and see who bought a huge quantity of fabric in recent times.

Gunter says to Peter to make room for eight in the next balloon. His change of heart is due to Petra's mother being sick in the west and the family not allowed to visit her.

Gunter and Peter obtain more fabric, but it is more difficult this time to get it without being seen and in such large amounts. They sew day and night. The newspapers report and show the found items from the first balloon such as gauges.

The SSD are closing in and they still don't have enough material. The SSD knows that Peter and Gunter are purchasing more material.

This time Doris and Petra help in every way that they can in order to get everything done quicker.

On September 15, 1979, Doris' prescription bottle is found. The SSD goes to the pharmacist to find out who has prescriptions for blood pressure medicine and to go through all the records. The pharmacist complies and finds the addresses of all the people requiring the medication in the area.

This turns out to be the same night that the two families decide to leave. It is now or never.

Hans and Major Koerner are now working together and the next prescription pulled is that of the Strelzyks. The SSD visits their abandoned home and the abandoned home of the Wetzels.

The SSD questions Mrs. Roseler who rats on the two families. Reports of a small car pulling a trailer and driving on the road are broadcast.

The Strelzyks arrive at the predestined meeting place, but the Wetzels are late. Gunter finally shows up saying that his motorcycle was stalling.

Koerner puts all lookout towers on full alert as they feel that another balloon escape attempt will happen and they want to be ready to capture the families.

The balloon is inflated and is much larger than the last one. Everyone climbs aboard, the ropes cut and they float up again. As they ascend the balloon catches on fire, but it is extinguished quickly. The families sustain some injuries, but they are floating high above the ground again – this time higher than before – well over 6000 feet.

They keep flying, but progress is slow as they have a huge rip near the top of the balloon. They are witnessed again by one of the lookout towers and Koerner is informed and he boards a helicopter.

The families are running out of fuel and start their descent. They are basically free floating and hoping for the best that they are floating in the right direction.

They have been up 27 minutes and Peter says that that is not enough. They barely escape hitting some telephone wires, but eventually crash down to the ground below. As before, they walk single file and do not know exactly where they are.

Gunter Meisner and Peter scout ahead and tell everyone else to stay put. They cautiously keep walking until they arrive at a nearby house. They duck when they see flashing police lights, but they are seen.

Peter asks if they are in the west and the officer says yes. Gunter lights a flair signaling to the families that they have done it and they are free.

Peter and Gunter are let go and reunite with the families.

A final postscript states: *The Strelzyk and Wetzel families now live in West Germany. Peter owns an electrical supply store. Gunter has realized his dream of becoming an auto mechanic. And the children are free to reach for the sky... without the help of a balloon.*

The happy thing is, in 1992, the Berlin Wall was finally taken down after 30 years, so their freedom to come and go as they please is now truly secure.

This is an excellent film and very atypical for Disney prior to this time, but Disney was in flux, so very different and experimental and more mature films were attempted.

If Major Koerner looks familiar, he is portrayed by Gunter Meissner, who portrayed Otto Slugworth in *Willy Wonka and the Chocolate Factory* (1971).

John Hurt was approached on set to lend his voice to the horned king for the upcoming *The Black Cauldron* (1985).

The film grossed $8 million.

The original title was to be *The Last Flight to Freedom*, but it was changed to *Night Crossing* because of its similarity to *The Last Flight of Noah's Ark* (1980).

Tron

RELEASED BY BUENA VISTA ON July 9, 1982, Technicolor. Panavision 70. Executive Producer: Ron Miller. Producer: Donald Kushner. Associate Producer: Harrison Ellenshaw. Director: Steven Lisberger. Screenplay: Steven Lisberger. Story: Steven Lisberger, Bonnie MacBird. Director of Photography: Bruce Logan. Production Designer: Dean Edward Mitzner. Film Editor: Jeff Gourson. Music: Wendy Carlos. Conceptual Artists (Electronic World): Syd Mead, Jean "Moebius" Giraud, Peter Lloyd. Music and Sound Design Supervisor: Michael Fremer. Music Performed by Los Angeles Orchestra. Conductor: Richard Bowden. The London Philharmonic Orchestra Conductor: Douglas Gamley. Orchestrations: Jorge Calandrelli. Unit Production Manager: Ralph Sariego. First Assistant Director: Lorin B. Salob. Second Assistant Director: Lisa Marmon. Costume Designers: Elois Jenssen, Rosanna Norton. Sound Effects Design and Synthesis: Frank Serafine, Serafine FX Studios. Music Synthesizer Performances and Processing: Wendy Carlos. Sound Department Supervisor:  Bob Hathaway. Supervising Sound Editor: Gordon Ecker, Jr. (WallaWorks). Sound Effects Editors: Anthony Milch, Randy Kelley, Marvin Walowitz, Vince Melandri. Production Sound Mixer: Jim Larue. Scoring Recordist: John Mosely, C.A.S. Re-Recording Mixers: Michael Minkler, C.A.S., Bob Minkler, C.A.S, Lee Minkler, C.A.S. "MCP" Voice Processing: Champ Davenport, Jack Manning (Synthefex). Assistant to the Composer: Annemarie Franklin. Post Production Facilities: Lions Gate Sound. Executive in Charge of Production: Thomas L. Wilhite. Studio Production Manager: Ted Schilz. Art Directors: John Mansbridge, Al Roelofs. Set Decorator: Roger Shook. Script Supervisor: Edle Bakke. Casting: Pam Polifroni. Electronic Conceptual Design: Jean "Moebius" Giraud, Richard Taylor. Costume Supervisor: Jack Sandeen. Men's Costumes: Lorry Richter. Women's Costumes: Nedra Rosemond-Watt. Make-up Supervisor: Robert J. Schiffer, C.M.A.A. Make-up: Gary Liddiard. Hair Stylist: Joy Zapata. Mechanical Special Effects: R.J. Spetter. Production Storyboards: Bill Kroyer, Jerry W. Rees, John Norton, Andy Gaskill. Pre-Production Concepts: John Norton, Roger Allers, Chris Lane, Peter Mueller. Assistant Editors: Walter Hekking, Baylis Glascock. Negative Cutting: Ed Capuano. Dialogue Editing: Stan Gilbert, M.P.S.E., Robert Bradshaw, Bill Shenberg. Foley Editor: Mike Wilhoit. Music Layout: Jeffrey Gussman. Special Record Coordination: Michael Dilbeck. Assistant Sound Editors: Bob Newlan, John M. Lowry. Camera Operators: Ron Vargas, Greg Heschong, Rexford Metz. First Assistant Camera Operators: Horace Jordan, Mike Weldon, Lynn Tomes, James Anderson. Second Assistant Camera Operator: Mario Zavala. Draftsmen: Bob Stahler, Bob Beall, John Dail,

Eugene Harris, Antoinette Gordon. Propmaster: Wilbur Russell. Production Painter: Shelley Phillips. Grip Supervisor: Owen Crompton. Key Grip: Stan Reed. Second Grip: Ron Peebles. Electrician Supervisor: Herbert Hughes. Gaffer: Roger Redel. Best Boy: Bernie Bayless. Visual Effects Unit: Visual Effects Concepts: Steven Lisberger. Visual Effects Supervisors: Richard Taylor, Harrison Ellenshaw. Effect Technical Supervisor: John Scheele. Scene Coordinators: Deena Burkett, Michael Gibson, John Grower, Peter Blinn, Don Button, Clint Colver, Linda D. Stokes, Craig Newman, Jim Keating, Kerry Colonna. Assistant Scene Coordinators: Jacqui Hooks, Cynthia Rush, Laura Lieben, Lynda Ellenshaw, Scott Russo, James Valentine, Dana Duff, Ron Rae, Shelley Hinton, Paul La Mori, Denise Wethington. Background Design: Peter Lloyd. Background Composite Supervisor: Marta Russell. Background Painting Supervisor: Jesse Silver. Background Artists: Christopher D. Andrews, Gary Conklin, Larry Grossman, Corey Harris, Tia W. Kratter, Peter Mueller, Donald Towns, Thomas Woodington. Background Composite Assistants: Catherine Eby, John Bates, Sandra Harper, Lorraine Schweizer. Background Technical Inker: Carolyn Bates. Background Plate Photography: Dave Iwerks, Bernie Gagliano, Gene Larmon. Background Plate Processing: Tom's Chroma Lab. Effects Animation Supervisor: Lee Dyer. Effects Animation: John Van Vliet, John Norton, Barry Cook, Michael Wolf, Chris Casady, Gail Finkeldei, Darrell Rooney. Assistant Effects Animators: Allen Blyth, Ed Coffey, Eric Durst, Peter Gullerud, Maria Ramocki, Ron Stangl, Dave Stephan, Maureen Trueblood, John Tucker, Dennis Edwards, Vicki Banks, Byron Werner. Airbrush Supervisor: Greg Battes. Airbrushers: Andy Atkins, William Arance, James Walter Shaw. Effects Ink and Paint Supervisor: Auril Pebley. Inkers: May Kong, Lillian Fitts, Christina Caspary, Bonny Nardini, Janette Downs, Maria Luisa Alvarez. Lab Coordinator: Rob Hummel. Color Timer: Martin Welsh. Camera Schedule Coordinators: Valerie Hagenbush, Christopher Keith. Film Logging: Eileen Kuramoto. Photographic Process Lab Supervisors: Art Cruickshank, A.S.C., Peter Anderson. Photo-Rotoscope Supervisor: Ron Osenbaugh, Frank Amador, Gayl Kelm, Roger Rinati, Dave Scott. Photo-Rotoscope Coordinator: Marian Guder. Opticals: Bob Broughton. Matte Production Supervisor: Arnie Wong. Matte Production: Lynn Singer, Jan Browning, Animation Camera Services. International Cel Coordination: Raulette Woods, Julian Pena, Paul Hernandez, Peter Aries. Sample Art Supervisor: Stephanie Burt. Inking / Painting: Ann Marie Sorenson, Cathy Crum, Ronnie Prinz, Alison DeCecio, Lisa Adams, Flavia Mitman, Priscilla Alvarez, Elaine Robinson. Effects Unit Managers: David V. Lester, Steven McEveety. Secretaries to Mr. Linsberger: Anna-Lisa Nilsson, Margaret Flook. Production Assistants: Debra DeVito Jackson, Wendy Williams, Denise Olivo, Michael G. Craig, Mical Morrish, Michael Schilz. Mechanical Designs and Conversions: Don Iwerks, Bob Otto, Don Porterfield, Mechanical Concepts. Computer Systems and Software Development: Dave Inglish, Mark Kimball, Dave Barnett, Marty Prager, Bill Tondreau, Cinetron Inc. Effects Transportation: Katy Johnson, Dyke Johnson. Lithographic Production: G2 Graphic Service Inc. Production Ink and Paint Matting by Cuckoo's Nest Productions, Taipei, Taiwan (numerous names written in Taiwanese). Animation Compositing Camera Supervisor: Jim Pickel. Animation Compositioning Camera: Don Baker, Glenn Campbell, Neil Viker, John Aardal, Dana Ross, Brandy Whittington, Annie McEveety, Kieran Mulgrew, Dick Kendall, Douglas Eby, George Epperson, Paul Wainess. Additional Animation Compositing Cameras: All Electric Cameraworks / R&B EFX, Praxis Filmworks, Cruise and Co., Pacific Art and Title, Movie Magic, Van Der Veer Photo Effects, Robert Abel and Associates. Computer Generated Images Unit: Computer Effects Supervisor: Richard Taylor. Computer Image Choreography: Bill Kroyer, Jerry W. Rees. Magi Synthavision: Technology Concepts: Phillip Mittelman, Ph.D. Scene Creation Concepts: Lary Elin Popielinski. Scene Programmers: Nancy Hunter Campi, Christian Wedge. Synthavision Technologists: Martin O. Cohen, Ph.D., Herbert Steinberg, Ph.D., Eugene Troubetzkoy, Ph.D., Kenneth Pierlin. Synthavision Production: John Beach, Tom Bisogno. Information International, Inc.: Scene Programmers: Craig W. Reynolds, William Dungan, Jr., Larry Malone, Jeremy Schwartz, Mal McMillan. Object Digitizing: Art Durinski. Computer Production Coordination: Lynn Wilkinson. Transition to Electronic World and Main Title: Robert Abel and Associates: Design Supervisor: Kenny Mirman. Systems Programmers: Frank Vitz, Bill Kovacs, Richard Baily, Tim McGovern. Systems Supervisor: Robert Abel. Camera: Patric Kenly, Kris Gregg. "Tron" Formation and the "Bit": Digital Effects, Inc.: Systems Supervisor: Judson Rosebush. Computer Production Supervisor: Jeffrey Kleiser. Computer Animators: Donald Leich, Gene Miller. Stunt Coordinator: Richard E. Butler, Jr. Stunt Players: Al Jones, Bill Burton, Fred Lerner, Glenn Wilder, Bennie E. Dobbins, Rita Egleston, Hank Hooker, Donna Garrett, Gary Epper, James Winburn, Gary Jensen, Walter Scott, Larry Holt, Ross Reynolds, James Deeth. Photographed at Walt Disney Studios, Burbank, California and Lawrence Livermore Lab, Livermore, California. Special thanks to: Anicam, Atari Corp., Apple Computer Inc., Mountain Hardware Corp., Crown International, Goodyear Rubber and Tire Corp., Pacific Telephone, Federal Screw Works, Electro Voice Inc., Eastern Acoustical Works, APT Holman Corp., Fairlight Corp., E. Rotberg, Morgan Renard, Daimon Webster, BTX Corp., Audio and Design Recording, Inc., Delta Labs Inc., Syntauri Corp., L. Bassett, Charles Haas, Jetcopters Inc., Lexicon Inc., Olympia USA, After Image Inc., Gary Demos, John Whitney, Jr., TBS / Video H&A Landaker, Sam Schatz Disc Co-Coordinator, E.E.G., Music Technology Inc., Cinema Air, Advanced Music Systems, RH and AHK Associates. Original Motion Picture Soundtrack album available on CBS Records and Tapes. Sound: Allen Hurd. Foley Artist: John Roesch. Sound Recordist: Philip Rogers. Supervising Sound Editor: Wylie Stateman. Special Effects: Gary D'Amico, David Domeyer, Mike Edmonson, Hans Metz, Mike Reedy. Animation Compositing Camera: Thomas Baker, Bill Kent. Animation Camera: William Cruse. Camera System Design Team, Robert Abel and Associates: Christopher Dusendschon. Rotoscope: Jammie Friday. Digital Artists: David Mattingly, Liza Moon. Stunts: Charlie Picerni. Animation Camera Operators: Peter McEvoy, Steven Wilzbach. Animators: Tim Burton, Rick Moore. Ink and Paint Artist: David Halver. Music Supervisor, Songs: Tom Bocci. Running time: 96 minutes. Rated PG.

Songs: "Only Solutions" "1990's Theme" Written and Performed by Journey.

Cast: Jeff Bridges (Kevin Flynn / Clu), Bruce Boxleitner (Alan Bradley / Tron), David Warner (Ed Dillinger / Sark / Master Control Program), Cindy Morgan (Lara / Yori), Barnard Hughes (Dr. Walter Gibbs / Dumont), Dan Shor (Ram / Roy Kleinberg, Popcorn Co-Worker), Peter Jurasik (Crom), Tony Stephano (Peter / Sark's Lieutenant), Craig Chudy (Warrior #1), Vince Deadrick (Warrior #2), Sam Schatz (Expert Disc Warrior), Jackson Bostwick (Head Guard), Dave Cass (Factory Guard), Gerald Berns (Guard #1), Bob Neill (Guard #2), Ted White (Guard #3), Mark Stewart (Guard #4), Michael Sax (Guard #5), Tony Brubaker (Guard #6), Charles Picerni (Tank Commander), Pierre Vuilleumier (Tank Gunner #1), Erik Cord (Tank Gunner #2), Loyd Catlett (Conscript #1), Michael J. Dudikoff, II (Conscript #2), Richard Bruce Friedman (Video Game Player), Loyd Catlett (Video Game Cowboy), Rick Feck, John Kenworthy (Boys in Video Game Arcade), Lisette Kremer (Video Gamer), Jerry Maren.

Kevin Flynn is an excellent video game player and creator and shows his expertise with video games at a local arcade. The games are shown in their natural form and also as part of a real-life video game universe with light cycles and Recognizers.

The evil Sark is trying to gain control of this universe with the help of Master Control. Another program victim named Rom is forced into playing according to Ram. Rom reveals that Master Control is controlling everything by taking other programs over.

Meanwhile back in the real world, Flynn is working on his computer and talks back and forth with the computer world. He types in commands for the computer world to follow.

The computer Flynn drives a tank and shoots at a number of flying arcs, blowing them away with the help of his friend Bit.

When something happens to the computerized Flynn, it shows up as a crash on the real world Flynn. The computerized Flynn has been captured by Master Control and tortured until he talks and reveals his owner and is destroyed.

The real world Sark as Ed Dillinger flies in by helicopter to his corporate headquarters and logs into his computer. He has recently attended a computer trade show and is back. Master Control reveals that Flynn was trying to break in and Master Control said that he was successful in blocking his entry.

Meanwhile, computer programmer Alan Bradley tries to access the computer and is also blocked, being told to speak with Mr. Dillinger about it.

Dillinger reveals that everyone with Group 7 access had to be blocked out for a few days. Alan says that he's created a program called Tron that is a security program that monitors any illegal entry into the system.

After Alan leaves, Master Control scolds Dillinger for allowing Alan to create programs like Tron.

In another area of the building, two scientists named Lara and are attempting a transfer of an orange from one spot to another in the form of a transporter. The experiment is tried and the orange digitized and it disappears and then reappears in another location.

Alan comes in to check in on the progress of these experiments and reveals his frustration with Dillinger blocking his Tron program.

Alan speaks with Lara privately and she reveals what Flynn has been doing and Lara says that she needs to see him to let him know that Dillinger is on to him and watch his step.

Alan and Lara drive to Flynn's video arcade where Journey's "Only Solutions" plays in the background. They catch up with Flynn who is close to beating the world record on Space Paranoids. He does and is cheered on as a hero.

Alan, Lara and Flynn meet up and Lara says that they have to talk. Lara asks if Flynn's been trying to sneak into the Encom System. Flynn reveals that he has been doing a little hacking.

Alan asks why and Flynn says that he's trying to find out some information about who's trying to take away the rights to his video games that he's invented. The person who has taken away his rights didn't change the names of the games and stole them from him. Flynn says that he wants to break into the system because he knows that in the system somewhere is the evidence that he is correct.

After his explanation, Lara and Alan agree that what he did was correct and also they agree to help him.

The older scientist pleads with Dillinger to allow the staff to regain access into the system. He feels that it is truly unfair that it has been blocked. Dillinger says not to worry that he doesn't need to worry about gaining access anymore, despite being the one to originally create the Master Control program.

Dillinger continues his discussion with Master Control who now feels that he's superior to any human and keeps getting incrementally smarter for a computer.

Back at Encom, Flynn says that he can only upload Alan's Tron program for a few minutes before Master Control detects that the program is there so they have to work fast or they will be blocked out again.

Master Control orders Dillinger to keep all of the programmers out of the system. Meanwhile, Lara and Flynn sneak around the back way to a special computer hidden in the back where Lara was working on the laser. Flynn sits down and starts trying to gain access into the system.

Master Control detects immediately that Flynn is trying to change the program and with the laser beam pointed directly at Flynn, he is scanned and digitized and sucked into the computer and placed onto the gaming grid.

Flynn's new form is as one of the players and he is forced by Sark's guards into a cell. Master Control tells Sark that Flynn is a user, which makes Sark a little bit nervous.

Sark asks what would happen if he refuses and Master Control shows him by sapping him of his strength, so he agrees to battle him.

Flynn meets Ram and Tron and they tell him that he's a guest of the Master Control program. The guards come and take all of the players and line them up into the game.

Sark gives a short speech about what they are supposed to do on the game grid. He says that all players will receive an identity disc that records all of their information. If it is lost, they will be subject to immediate deresolution.

Tron is in a disc game fighting for the users, while Ram and Flynn discuss their backgrounds. Flynn is assigned to battle Rom in another disc game utilizing rings and large scoops on their hands.

While they battle, Ram and Tron discuss Flynn. Rom is quite good, but Flynn takes over. Sark commands for Flynn to finish the game by killing Rom. Flynn refuses, so Sark kills him and Master Control orders Flynn to play games until he breaks.

Flynn meets Tron and calls him Alan. Tron says that Alan is his user. Ram, Tron and Flynn now are part of a light cycle race. Flynn successfully beats his opponents and escapes the game grid and invites Ram and Tron to follow him.

After they escape, Sark sends every tank and Space Paranoid after them. When they have gone as far as they can go, they revert back to their humanoid form and they travel on foot. Flynn says that they need to get to Master Control to take over.

On their way, they discover a body of water. They all drink from it and the water gives them extra power. Soon, they are on their way again and they revert back into cycles.

The tank fires shots and blows up Ram and Flynn's cycles. It is up to Tron to keep going and he drives off into the next sector.

The tanks keep scanning, but they cannot find Ram and Flynn and presume that they're dead. Ram is weak and Flynn carries him on his back to a safe spot where they can rest.

After they rest, Flynn realizes that he can reconstruct and repower things and forms his own Space Paranoid. Ram says that he shouldn't be able to do that, but he forgets that Flynn is a user.

Flynn drives the Recognizer slowly through the computer. Ram tries to go on, but he is just too weak and soon he disappears as Master Control disintegrates him. It is now up to Tron and Flynn to get to Master Control and take over.

Flynn is not the best driver of the Recognizer and keeps hitting the walls. Meanwhile, Tron meets up with Yori, the program who has Lara as a user. They embrace and then he explains his plans.

Flynn meets up with Bit who tries to help him out, but all she can say is yes and no. Finally, Flynn crashes and destroys the Recognizer in an area with strange and outdated programs.

Flynn thought he could meet up with Tron, but he cannot find him. Flynn encounters a guard and knocks him out. He gets the guards' power and he disintegrates.

Tron and Yori are getting closer to Master Control, but keep encountering more guards. They are still followed by the Recognizers.

They arrive to meet Dumont and ask if they can contact Tron's user, Alan.

Dumont says that he can't really help, but then decides to anyway and allows Tron and Yori to pass.

Sark is aware of Dumont helping them and orders the logic probe to be brought in.

Tron gets in to the MCP and sends his disc to take over the program. In doing so, the code disc means freedom and all of the grids start changing from red into blue.

Sark is not finished yet and goes to Dumont and demands to know where Tron went. Dumont cries dumb.

Tron and Yori board a flying butterfly-looking ship and traverse through space, still being pursued by Sark.

Master Control is upset with Sark's performance and starts torturing him. Flynn finally meets up with Tron who is hanging by a thread. They bring him aboard and his power is switched back from red to blue.

Flynn reveals that he is a user. They next encounter some grid bugs, which are bad news if they touch them, but more imminent are Recognizers who have gotten onto the same beam as their ship. They have to switch beams and fast.

Sark captures Dumont and tortures him for his treason. Dumont fearlessly faces him and says that he remembers Master Control when he just was a chess program.

Eventually, Sark intercepts the beam and Yori and Flynn are reunited with Dumont, and they tell him that Tron has been erased. Sark reveals that everyone will begin to de res, which means they will be destroyed.

It turns out that Tron isn't dead after all. Flynn reveals that he still has more power than Sark knows and transfers some of that power to Yori to make her stronger.

The rest of the programs are assimilated into the Master Control and all seems lost, but Tron reveals himself. This time Sark and Tron battle with their disc tossing game. The battle seems lost until Tron gets in a lucky shot that breaks Sark's disc in two.

Then Tron flings his disc directly at Master Control, but gets repeatedly blocked. Master Control gives Sark extra power and he regains strength and becomes a giant.

Flynn says he needs to jump directly into the Master Control program. Yori says that he will be de resed and he is willing to take that risk. In doing so, he stops Master Control long enough for Tron to get his disc in. This also allows the enlarged Sark to fall.

In doing so, Tron is finally able to overtake the computer universe and it completely changes everything from red to blue. Tron is reunited with Yori and Flynn is sent back into the real world. A printout of his accomplishments appears on the printer.

Flynn is excited and runs to tell everyone else. Dillinger tries to log in, but now he's being kept out and also alerted that Flynn is the creator of the programs. Flynn reunites with Alan and Lara on the Encom rooftop to tell them the good news that he is now running the company.

This is a strong turning point film for Disney for instead of being behind the times on some fad like science-fiction fantasy film, they were at the forefront of something new. I really like this film, but admit I was a little confused when I first saw it, so far ahead of its time it was.

On the DVD, there are numerous features. One has an interview with writer and creator Steve Lisberger, who claimed that he was inspired by *Star Wars* (1977) and *Jaws* (1975) for his work. He also said that this was a film that had to be computer-generated.

Producer Donald Kushner said that the difficult part was making the fantasy world and the reality world cohesive to each other.

Effects Technical Supervisor, John Scheele, explains this technique utilizes traditional animation cels. There were different layers used for the different colors.

Computer Image Choreography Bill Kroyer said a problem was that the creators of computer programs at the time were not filmmakers and did not necessarily think visually. The makers of *Tron* pushed the computer people faster than they would have had they not been working on this film.

The DVD also has early traditional on it by Steven Lisberger Studios that featured a character called Tron and early video tests of how the computer effects in the final movie would work.

An excerpt of a May 1982 special entitled *Computers Are People Too* is included where Lisberger explains his computer world and how Jeff Bridges' character Flynn is sucked into the computer.

Richard Taylor, Co-Supervisor of Special Effects explains how the computer-generated objects were created when there are no physical three-dimensional objects at work. He claimed the hardest part was marrying the computer-generated effects with the live-action effects.

Another special of the time called *Beyond Tron* featured the Founder of MAGI, Dr. Phillip Mittelman discussing the uses and origins of three-dimensional photography and computer animation with Synthavision. Also, later developments were discussed such as texture and contrast.

The *Triple I Demo* reel is also included and is significant because this is the reel that encouraged Disney to give *Tron* the green light in the first place that a film like this could be done. It reminds me a lot of Kraftwerk.

As for the music for the film, the utilization of music written by Wendy Carlos was significant as Wendy (formerly Walter) created the iconic *Switched-On Bach* album that took synthesized music to a new level the way that *Tron* took movie-making to a new level.

The DVD also presents the original end credits featuring Carlos' entire score. When the film was ultimately released, part of the Carlos score was replaced by a song called "Only Solutions" by Journey.

The Making of Tron tells how Michael Lisberger began his interests in animation and computer-generated images. Conceptual Artist Roger Allers said that early Lisberger Productions included stuff for TV commercials and TV shows like *Sesame Street*.

Producer Donald Kushner tells of the animated Olympic shorts called *Animalympics* that predated *Tron* and were sold to NBC. At the time, they didn't have enough animators to complete everything, so they moved to Venice, California and added staff. This added staff was lucrative for *Tron*.

Tron was planned as an independent movie, but when the 1980 Summer Olympics were canceled by the US, Lisberger suddenly was scrambling to get *Tron* made and they now needed the help of a major studio by this point.

Storyboard Artist Andy Gaskill also provides comments. The storyboards were all created by the time Disney was approached.

Disney Chairman Dick Cook remember when Lisberger came in to discuss the film, but the initial hesitation was more about if it could be done than whether it was a good movie script or not. He said that they were looking for something new and felt that this was it.

This was a gamble for all, but the age old "What would Walt do?" question arose again and ultimately that was the reason that Disney went ahead with it.

Visual Effects Supervisor Richard Taylor agrees that it was that plus the video game craze of the day.

Harrison Ellenshaw was a valuable Disney ally to make the film work because of his work on *Star Wars* and because of his father Peter's matte work on numerous Disney films.

To ease Disney's fears of production problems, a test film was made for Disney utilizing costumes from *The Black Hole* (1979) and a Frisbee champion named Sam Schatz to show the Kodaliths and the backlighting.

Director of Photography Bruce Logan said that the change was made from a white background to a black background to save on lighting costs.

Syd Mead, Peter Lloyd and Jean "Moebius" Giraud were essential to help make the film work and were hired for their design work. Moebius ended re-storyboarding everything that everyone else did and it his imprint that is all over this film.

Casting the film was somewhat difficult for this movie since Disney didn't have the clout in the early 80s that they do today, but actor Jeff Bridges was on board because of the potentially innovative ideas presented on the film.

Actor Bruce Boxleitner read the script while doing another Western TV movie and turned it down because it was totally out of his element, but eventually came around when he saw the storyboards, the fact that it was a feature and that Jeff Bridges had already signed on.

Actor Barnard Hughes, on the other hand, had a great feeling about the script and easily agreed to do it.

Actor David Warner's role was originally envisioned for Peter O'Toole and unlike Bruce Boxleitner, didn't get it and so Warner was given the nod.

Actress Cindy Morgan said that Warner was ultimately an excellent choice and she easily went in for her role as well.

Actor Dan Shor was a young new actor, but performed very well in his first major role.

Initially many of the actors were hesitant about the costumes as they tended to reveal everything. The costumes were also very tight so that there was not much sitting down on the set. Video games were also brought onto the set in order to set a mood.

The all-black set was a frustrating problem for the actors because they had to look offstage at pieces of tape and imagine they were talking to a large object or another computer-generated character. The actors had to create the world for their audience.

Some scenes were shot at Lawrence Livermore Lab for authenticity's sake and the actors had a lot of fun doing those scenes.

Boxleitner talks of a lucky scene where he caught a flying disc over his head. It looks really good and was done on the first take and is in the final print.

The film was made in a somewhat rudimentary way and they knew it could be done, but they realized that everything was going to take a lot longer than they envisioned to complete the processing, so it had to be shipped overseas for help, but another problem arose that they didn't allow the cels to completely dry and they stuck together.

There was another problem that the Kodaliths weren't exposed together and this created small flashes of light. This was covered up with sound effects giving the impression that the computer program had glitches in them causing the flashes. The reality was that the Kodaliths should have been exposed from the same box, so that the variations of up to an entire F-stop wouldn't be seen.

Background Painter Tia Kratter said that a difficulty with *Tron* was with everything being painted in values rather than colors and painting everything with an airbrush.

Another problem was that computer animation at the time couldn't recognize lens distortion, so everything that required this had to be hand done.

There are scenes that are completely computer-animated and others that were composites and still others that were done to look like computer animation, but were actually done with traditional animation and various camera tricks.

Magi Synthevision did the three-dimensional objects such as the light cycles and the tanks.

Information International (Triple I) did the more elaborate three-dimensional objects with a wire mesh type model for items with multi curves and shapes. The translucent solar sailor is their greatest accomplishment for the film. The two company's effects were intermingled throughout the film.

Completed frames were sent over the phone lines one by one from Burbank to the East Coast to check the progress on the footage becoming basically an early form of emailing.

Pixar's John Lasseter was an animator on *Mickey's Christmas Carol* while *Tron* was being made. The light cycle footage was the first computer animation that he had ever seen, and was fascinated by this. The rest is history. Basically, without *Tron*, there would be no *Toy Story* (1995).

Tron ultimately had over 27 minutes of computer animation and was overlooked by the Academy of Motion Pictures Arts and Sciences for an Oscar as they considered using this amount of digital effects as "cheating."

It was, however, nominated for Sound and for Costume Design.

A five-minute sampler film was created at the time to promote the uniqueness and high quality of the computer effects to film exhibitors.

The DVD has a couple of deleted scenes that featured a love scene between Tron and Yori that was cut because it was deemed that it didn't work. Other people feel that it should have been kept in. In my opinion, the scenes look nice but really add nothing to the story and I tend to agree with Bruce Boxleitner's assessment that these are supposed to be computer people and not real, so they shouldn't be falling in love. These scenes were cut so late that they feature completed special effects.

Also, an alternate explanatory opening is presented that was cut in later showings as people became more knowledgeable about computers.

The 2011 DVD has an audio commentary with Director Steve Lisberger, Producer Donald Kushner, Associate Producer and Visual Effects Supervisor Harrison Ellenshaw and Visual Effects Supervisor Richard Taylor. Here are some highlights of their conversations:

The character Alan was named after Alan Kaye, who invented the Powerbook. He claimed that everyone would have a computer one day and apparently no one believed him. They should have asked me. I would have believed him, because here we are. Everyone has a cell phone and most have Smartphones.

Originally, they were going to do this film independently, but barring that because they didn't have enough money to do it properly, Disney was their first and most logical choice, but they didn't know if Disney would do it as they had been notorious in recent times for turning down innovative film ideas like *Star Wars* (1977) and *Raiders of the Lost Ark* (1981).

Strangely, the central idea of using another program to hack into an existing program to find out information hasn't really gotten mainstream use until very recently according to the filmmakers.

The touchscreen desk used by Dillinger in the film was made by traditional rear screen projection. This also has only attained mainstream acceptance in recent times.

David Warner's voice was used for that of Master Control.

The main concern at the time was a company like IBM was going to take over the other smaller friendlier computer companies and discard them, which became the central theme of the movie.

The name Encom was the only name that they could find that wasn't already a registered corporate name.

Disney was the only film company ever allowed access to film inside the Lawrence Livermore Lab.

This was the first film shot in quite some time in 65mm. Apparently the last time an entire film was shot in 65mm was for *Ryan's Daughter* (1970).

There were more 65mm cameras available than Vista Vision cameras which is why it was shot this way. The cameras are huge and bulky and they work better in high light levels than low light levels. As such the actors had to be completely shot separately and they were composited.

Some scenes were reshot ostensibly because the lighting didn't match, but actually it was done to improve the dialogue.

Peter O'Toole really wanted to play Tron, but he had auditioned for Dillinger. Regardless, he was not in the film.

Otherwise, it was somewhat difficult to get actors for this film as it wasn't considered desirable at the time to work for Disney.

The face of the juggling man from the Triple I sample reel is what was used for the Master Control Program.

Actual Frisbees were used for the discs in the movie and is the deadliest weapon in the film.

There are 75,000 frames of traditional animation in this film which is low compared to a fully animated picture, but Disney was used to it.

Spartacus (1960) was a big influence for *Tron*.

The light cycle sequence was created by Magi and was virtually all CGI. The Recognizers were also created by Magi and loosely based on King Kong in design. Every piece had to be animated individually to replicate reality. The bubbles and the grid bugs were also Magi Synthevision.

There are 1100 composite effects shots in this film and 900 of those had human beings in the shot.

There were 600,000 cels that needed to be housed and painted and sent to Asia.

There were four computer animation companies used for the film and at the time, they apparently were the only four computer animation companies in existence at the time.

Informational Technology animated the solar sailor and the walls. Digital Effects Incorporated animated the "bit."

Cindy Morgan was the last person cast in a role that Blondie's Debbie Harry had auditioned for.

It was impossible to do perspective movement shots due to all of the special effects compositing. In fact, the camera was locked to the floor in order for nothing to move.

The designs on the costumes were done by Moebius and Syd Mead.

The giant Mickey Mouse head appears at the 72 minute mark when the solar sailor sails by.

MCP was completely designed by Informational International.

Sark's brain splitting open is what got the film the PG rating.

The film was ahead of its time and even if one was to attempt it now, it wouldn't be done in the exact same way again.

The film ultimately wasn't a great success at the time in comparison to other blockbusters like *E.T.* (1982) or *Star Wars* (1977), but now has attained a cult following. It did set the stage for the future of Disney and with filmmaking, in general.

This all seems rudimentary today, but in 1982, this was very much the state of the art. It's also amazing to note that this film came out less than a year from the guard-changing *The Fox and the Hound* (1981). One wonders what the Disney Nine Old Men would have made with computer animation if they had needed to learn it to further their craft.

An entire book could be written on the significance and of the making of this film and indeed one has been, called *The Making of Tron* by William Kallay.

Tron was ahead of its time and a major leap ahead for Disney. Eventually, a sequel was made with Jeff Bridges and Bruce Boxleitner called *Tron Legacy* that was released in 2011. Shortly after that there was an animated TV series.

The film had a budget of $17 million and grossed $74 million.

Journey was recruited to contribute songs when Supertramp pulled out. Wendy Carlos provided the majority of the soundtrack.

A comic book adaptation of this film did not appear until 2010, published by Marvel.

The film is the first live-action film produced by Disney before 1985 to appear in Blu-ray format.

Tex

RELEASED BY BUENA VISTA ON July 30, 1982, Technicolor. Panaflex. Panavision. Executive Producer: Ron Miller. Producer: Tim Zinnemann. Director: Tim Hunter. Screenplay: Charlie Hass, Tim Hunter based on the novel by S.E. Hinton. Music: Pino Donaggio. Conductor: Natale Massara. Editor: Howard Smith. Production Designer: Jack T. Collis. Director of Photography: Ric Waite. Unit Production Manager: Jerry A. Baerwitz. Assistant Director: Tom Connors III. Second Assistant Director: Christopher D. Miller. Second Unit Director / Stunt Coordinator: Nate Long. Additional Music: The Fabulous Thunderbirds. Casting: Pam Polifroni. New York Casting: Margery Simkin. Tulsa Casting: Lisa Clarkson. Costume Supervisor: Jack Sandeen. Costumes: Dan Moore. Make-up Supervisor: Robert J. Schiffer, C.M.A.A. Make-up: Jim Scribner. Art Director: John B. Mansbridge. Set Decorators: Don Ramacle, Roger M. Shook. Sound Supervisor: Bob Hathaway. Sound Design: Lon E. Bener (WallaWorks). Sound Mixer: Henry A. Maffett. Music

The Feature Films – 1982

Editor: Jack Wadsworth. Postproduction Consultant: Joe Dante. With special thanks to the Oklahoma Film Commission for their help and cooperation. Sound Recordist: Allen Hurd. Sound Re-Recording Mixer: Michael Minkler. Assistant Sound Editor: Bob Newlan. Gaffer: Carl Boles. Best Boy: Dan Delgado. Lighting Technician: Jeff Stanman. Script Supervisor: Judi Brown. Running time: 102 minutes. Rated PG.

Cast: Matt Dillon (Tex McCormick), Jim Metzler (Mason McCormick), Meg Tilly (Jamie Collins), Bill McKinney (Pop McCormick), Frances Lee McCain (Mrs. Johnson), Eric Ben Johnson (Cole Collins), Phil Brock (Lem Peters), Emilio Estevez (Johnny Collins), Jack Thibeau (Coach Jackson), Zeljko Ivanek (Hitchhiker), Tom Virtue (Bob Collins), Pamela Ludwig (Connie), Jeff Fleury (Roger), Suzanne Costallos (Fortune Teller), Marilyn Redfield (Ms. Carlson), Mark Arnott (Kelly), Jill Clark (Marcie), Sheryl Briedel (Lisa), Lisa Mirkin (Shelly), Rod Jones (Doctor), Richard Krause (Ride Operator), Don Harral (Doctor at Hospital), Janine Burns (Nurse), Mark Huebner (Orderly), Ron Thulin (Anchorman), Mary Simons (Ms. Germanie), Francine Ringold (Lady Reporter), Darren Cates (Kid Near Tex), Robin Winters (Girl on Bike), Lance Parkhill (Boy), Wayne Dorris (Kid #2), Mike Coats (Dave), Charlie Haas (Lee), Larry Stallsworth (Patrolman), Adam Hubbard (Kid #1), Scott Smith (Biker #1), Eric Beckstrom (Biker #2), S.E. Hinton (Mrs. Barnes), Buddy Joe Hooker (Stunt Double), Coralie Hunter (Lukie), Toyota (Tex's Horse), Tammy Borland (Girl on Horse), Marlo Holly (Basketball Fan), James P. Rice (Basketball Fan).

Tex McCormick takes a ride on his horse named Rowdy. His brother Mason is filling out a form for a basketball scholarship at Indiana.

The two are just scraping by and there is barely food in the refrigerator and the electric bill has not been paid. Their father has been out of town working on the rodeo but he will be home soon.

Tex's friend Johnny Collins stops by on his motorcycle. Tex hops on and they ride to Bixby High School. At school, they bump into Johnny's sister, Jamie.

Mrs. Johnson gives the assignment for a book report and tells Tex to read a different book this time as he has read and reported on the same book twice.

At the end of the school day, Johnny drops Tex off at home. The heat is back on as Mason finally has paid the electric bill. The way Mason was able to pay the bill was to sell Tex's horse. Tex is upset and wants Mason to get the horses back. Mason refuses and Tex picks a fight.

After the fight, Tex walks away seeing if he can find who Mason sold the horses to. Johnny and Jamie ride up and ask him what happened. Tex explains that he is determined to find who has his horse. Johnny and Jamie ride away.

Mason drives up in the truck and demands that he get in the truck. Tex initially refuses, but eventually gets in.

Back at home, Mason's friend Bob Collins checks in on the two to see what's going on. Mason has regrets about hitting Tex, but what is done is done and ultimately he blames everything on their father. Tex overhears everything from the other room and is still upset.

Tex's friend Lem Peters stops by to celebrate the birth of his son and wants Tex and Mason. First, they stop by Cole's place to steal some liquor. Cole is Johnny and Jamie's father.

Johnny and Bob wake up and they all start celebrating but are told to keep it down because their dad is still up.

Tex goes to get Jamie and she squirts him with water. Cole walks in wondering what the noise is and Jamie blames it on the window being open while Tex hides.

Cole closes the window and tells her not to reopen it and leaves. Tex comes out and he and Jamie join the rest of the party.

After a few minutes of conversation again, Cole asks what all the noise is and everyone except for Johnny, Bob and Jamie jumps out the window and leaves the room. The lights are turned out.

Back at home, Mason tells Tex that Lem is a fool for having a baby and that Jamie has more sense for not rushing into anything. Tex doesn't understand why.

The next day, Tex and Johnny go to the carnival and anger the Ferris wheel man for rocking the cars.

They bump into Jamie and her friends and she wants to get her fortune told. Tex thinks it's a bunch of bunk. Jamie says that she'll pay for it. Tex says he'll pay and reluctantly goes in.

The fortune teller reads Tex's palm and says that he's a fourth generation cowboy and she advises that he should and shouldn't change. Then she says he can think of one yes or no question. Just then a horse walks by the tent and the fortune teller says that unfortunately, the answer is no.

Tex gets home late and Mason wonders where he's been. Tex lies and says he was at a party. Mason says that Tex is drunk.

Mason asks if Tex can get undressed by himself for bed. Tex says yes and then plops into bed fully dressed. Mason helps Tex off with his boots.

Next morning, Tex wakes up with a hangover. Cole stops by and was wondering why Johnny and Jamie came home drunk last night. Mason says he doesn't know and he doesn't want Cole to speak with Tex. Next, Cole wonders where their father is and says that he would appreciate it if he and Tex stay away from his kids.

Mason comes back inside to speak with Tex and Tex is underneath his bed. Tex says he feels sick and wants to stay home from school, but Mason says that he's missed too much school and so he must go.

Tex asks if he can go to Indiana. Mason says that he can't take him because where would he stay and yells at him for not thinking it through.

At school, Mason continues to practice his basketball. He is determined to win that scholarship.

In art class, everyone is making sculptures out of Popsicle sticks, making houses or some other structure. Tex felt it would be great fun to build the sticks into a pile and set it on fire.

Tex is immediately sent to the principal's office and she wonders what he was thinking by setting fire to his sculpture. She also asks about Tex's father and lets Tex off without suspension, but says that he won't be so lucky next time if she sees him in her office one more time this semester.

The next day at lunch, Jamie wants to have a talk with Tex. She wonders why he and Johnny are not speaking. It's because he made a crack about Tex's dad.

Tex gets a ride out to where Johnny is riding motorcycles with his other cycle friends. Johnny rides off and takes a nasty spill. After he gets up, Tex takes a spin on Johnny's bike and also takes a nasty spill. Johnny and Tex make up.

Back at home, Mason says that he's going to Tulsa to the hospital if Tex wants to come. Tex says ok and is dropped off at the mall, but wonders why Mason needs to go to the hospital. Mason doesn't want to tell him.

At the mall, Tex bumps into Jamie. They speak a few minutes and then she leaves. Mason picks up Tex and the diagnosis is that Mason has an ulcer. Tex is concerned.

On the way back, Tex and Mason stop by to visit Lem and Connie and their new baby, Luke. Lem shows off his new car. Mason asks how much he's been dealing since he knows that he would normally not have enough money to buy a car.

On the way back home, Tex and Mason stop their truck and pick up a hitchhiker. The hitchhiker pulls a gun on them and points it at Mason's chest while Tex keeps driving.

A police car starts following them and Tex decides to do a wild swerve to dislodge the gun and attract attention to the cops.

The ploy works as the police surround and capture the hitchhiker after they shoot him at the side of the road. The police explain that the hitchhiker was a wanted man for quite some time.

Later that evening, Mason and Tex watch their news report where they were interviewed by reporters. The phone rings and it is their father. He says that he's finally back in town.

Tex is happy to see their dad, but Mason is not. He's angry that he had to sell the horses to pay the bills. Pop says that he won't be leaving again and wants to help them get the horses back. Mason says he doesn't need his horse back, but they can go get Rowdy.

Tex, Mason and Pop drive out to the man who has the horse that Mason sold them to. While Pop and Mason try to negotiate a deal, Tex goes out to see Rowdy for the first time in months. Tex is greeted by a small girl who says that the horse is hers now.

Tex goes back to Mason and Pop. Mason says that the family doesn't want to sell the horses back and Tex gets angry at Mason all over again.

Back at home, Tex opens the letter from Indiana with the financial aid forms that need to be filled out so that Mason can attend.

To get their mind off things, everyone goes to see Mason play in the school basketball game. At one point during the game, a fight between the two teams erupts. The referees try to stop it.

Back in the locker room, Mason doesn't understand why he didn't get his letter answered from Indiana. Tex walks in, but doesn't say anything.

Later, Tex is back with Jamie in the truck. They start making out. When things get a little hot and bothered, Jamie stops everything, because she's not ready for sex yet. Tex drives her home.

The next day, Tex and Johnny pull another prank and replace the typewriter ribbons with caps. When they explode, Tex and Johnny start laughing a little bit early and are both sent to the principal's office. Cole and Mason show up to discuss everything.

Cole wants Johnny to stay away from Tex and takes him home. Pop shows up late and Cole tells him to stick around and father's his children.

Pop laughs when he hears about Tex's prank and the principal pulls Tex aside and offers him a job as punishment. She feels that will keep him out of trouble.

Tex leaves the office and Mason and Pop are fighting over him and Mason reveals that Pop isn't really his father.

Tex runs out of the school and sees Lem at the side of the road sitting in his car. Tex gets in and they drive off. Lem says he's off to get some more weed. Lem says that he also has to make amends with one of his clients named Kelly and needs Tex as a backup.

Kelly is upset that Lem didn't bring the proper drugs and he starts yelling at him. Tex doesn't want any part of this and gets up to leave.

Kelly pulls a gun thinking that Tex is a narc. Tex slugs him and grabs the gun and pulls it on Kelly, almost pulling the trigger. A shot had been fired.

After they get back in the car, it is obvious that Tex is bleeding from his side. Lem panics because he has stuff in his trunk. Tex gets annoyed and asks to be let off. He gets to a pay phone and calls Jamie and asks her what his phone number is, so that he can call home. Cole intervenes and asks Tex to hang up the phone. Tex continues bleeding and hangs up and staggers to the curb.

Lem drives back and picks Tex up and takes him to a doctor. At the hospital, Mason shows up to check in on Tex. Tex is woozy with an IV in him.

Later, Tex wakes up and Pop and Mason are in the hospital room with him. Mason tells Tex that he will be postponing college for a while to take care of him.

Pop explains the family situation. He said that he went to prison around the time before Tex was born and while he was in there, his wife got pregnant with another man and that man was Tex's real father.

Later, Johnny and Jamie sneak in with a gurney to visit Tex in the hospital.

Still later, Tex pulls out the Indiana application and fills it out and sends it in for Mason without telling him. A few days later, Mason is congratulated, but he doesn't know why as he never filled out the form.

Tex comes home and he and Mason discuss the application and they make up. Tex insists that Mason goes to school and not babysit him, regardless as to whether Pop is around or not. Tex goes back to attend the horses at the job that his principal got him.

This was a much more mature type of teenager film than typically made by Disney up to this point. The teenagers in this film wouldn't be caught dead with the squeaky clean teens of the Dexter Riley films or even the Jodie Foster films. Things were changing with discussions about sex and drugs and drinking and guns.

Strangely, Disney got the rights to this S.E. Hinton novel, but not the other two that were made into films around the same time (*The Outsiders* (1983), *Rumble Fish* (1983)), which Francis Ford Coppola made into films.

The film grossed $7 million, a respectable, but disappointing box office response, despite the film being a favorite of critics.

1983

The Disney Studio celebrated its 60th anniversary with a more muted celebration than the "50 Happy Years" celebration from 1973.

More changes occurred this year in regards to Disney management. Donn Tatum stepped down as Chairman of the Executive Committee and stayed on as a Member of the Board of Directors, a role he held until he retired in 1992, at which time he was known as Director Emeritus. Tatum died in 1993.

Card Walker retired as Chairman of the Board and CEO shortly after the openings of Epcot Center and Tokyo Disneyland. He died in 2005.

Raymond Watson succeeded Walker as Chairman of the Board, until Michael Eisner arrived in 1984.

Ron Miller continued on as President and also became CEO on February 24, until Michael Eisner took over in 1984.

The final threads of the original Disney organization were truly beginning to unravel, but Miller wasn't going to go down without a fight. Miller decided to replace Tom Wilhite with Richard Berger. Miller liked Wilhite's ideas and films over the past two years, but their performance was left with much to be desired.

Wilhite's final lasting contribution was to encourage Disney to start a separate movie label to issue movies with more mature content. Miller championed this idea which eventually spawned Touchstone Pictures.

Disney was in a severely weakened position. This is not to say that they were going to go bankrupt, but their value was so low at this point, that it would have been easy for a wealthy person to buy up shares of stock and take over the company…and that's exactly what was happening.

The people at Disney had to fight back or surely someone would buy up the company and piecemeal it out, selling off the theme parks to one buyer, the movie studio to another, the animation department to yet another. Or, it was possible that Disney would be swallowed by the like of Coca-Cola or some other major conglomerate similar to what happened to other movie studios.

The entire saga is told in great detail in the book *Storming the Magic Kingdom* by John Taylor, and is better explained in that book, than I can even attempt here.

New episodes made for the final season of the anthology show include *Walt Disney's Mickey and Donald, Ferdinand the Bull and Mickey, A Valentine from Disney, Mickey and Donald Kidding Around* and *A Disney Vacation*. All were compilations of older cartoons. The next all-new made-for-TV movie ended up debuting on The Disney Channel and was later briefly released to theaters, *Tiger Town*.

Walt Disney was canceled after 29 seasons on the air, including the titles *Disneyland, Walt Disney Presents, The Wonderful World of Color, The Wonderful World of Disney* and *Disney's Wonderful World*. At the time, it was the longest running prime-time show in television history. The reason for cancellation was two-fold: it was not getting the ratings it once had and, with the advent of The Disney Channel, more attention was paid to the fledgling cable channel in order to get it established. Disney figured that people would not want to pay for the channel if they could get the same material for free on Saturday nights.

The show was to resume in 1986 under the title *The Wonderful World of Disney* with a predominance of newly- produced made-for-TV films and for the first time since Walt's death, a regular host in the form of Michael Eisner.

Strangely, at this time, there was an increase of many new specials that aired in syndication and on the networks: *Believe You Can…And You Can!, Walt Disney's Mickey and Donald Presents Sport Goofy, The Fairest of Them All, Winnie the Pooh and Friends, U.S. Junior Tournament World Tennis Tournament, Walt Disney's Mickey and Donald Presents Sport Goofy #2, Walt Disney's Mickey and Donald Presents Sport Goofy #3, U.S. Junior Tournament World Tennis Tournament #2* and *Walt Disney World Very Merry Christmas Parade (1983 Version)*.

A number of *Sport Goofy* specials were created stringing together footage from those old Goofy cartoons that instruct you how to ski, etc. Some new footage was produced for these.

Animation made a minor comeback in 1983 with the release of *Winnie the Pooh and a Day for Eeyore*, the fifth Winnie the Pooh cartoon and the second since 1977's *Many Adventures of Winnie the Pooh* compilation, and *Mickey's Christmas Carol*, nominated for an Academy Award and the first new Mickey Mouse theatrical cartoon since 1953. Work continued on *The Black Cauldron* (1985).

Snow White and the Seven Dwarfs (1937), *The Sword in the Stone* (1963) and *The Rescuers* (1977) were reissued to theaters this year and *Tron* (1982) and *The Black Hole* (1979) were released to home video for the first time.

Successful films this year that could have been made by Disney include *Superman III* and *Return of the Jedi*.

On the theme park front, Tokyo Disneyland opened up by the Oriental Land Company. In a strange move, Disney licensed out their Disneyland concept to Japan rather than just build their own. Disney has since changed this policy and every subsequent Disney theme park is owned and operated by Disney. The cost of Tokyo Disneyland was $300 million. The Mickey Mouse Review was transplanted from Walt Disney World to this park.

The purse for the Walt Disney World Golf Classic was raised to $450,000.

Horizons opened at Epcot Center.

Disneyland reopened with a new Fantasyland on March 25, complete with refurbished attractions as well as one completely new ride called Pinocchio's Daring Journey and a Sword in the Stone presentation. They also opened an entertainment center around the Disneyland Hotel with many free attractions, shops and restaurants.

The original Disneyland record albums continued this year with the successful *Mickey Mouse Splashdance* and *Mousetronics* albums.

The Charlie Brown albums based on TV shows increased to 10 and one for 1972's *Snoopy, Come Home* and the current TV special *It's Flashbeagle, Charlie Brown* which begat the album *Flashbeagle* (this and *Splashdance* both based on the hit non-Disney movie *Flashdance*).

In the comic book world, Whitman continued to publish *Donald Duck, Mickey Mouse, Uncle Scrooge, Walt Disney's Comics and Stories, Huey, Dewey and Louie Junior Woodchucks, Super Goof, Chip 'n' Dale, Daisy and Donald* and *Winnie the Pooh*.

Walt Disney's Comics and Stories reached a major milestone unique to comic books in April when the 500th issue was published.

Abbeville concluded its hardback salute to Disney comic books with *Donald Duck and his Nephews*.

The Disney Channel Magazine also debuted for subscribers of the cable station.

Trenchcoat

RELEASED BY BUENA VISTA ON March 11, 1983, Technicolor. Producer: Jerry Lieder. Associate Producer: Joel Morwood. Director: Michael Tuchner. Writers: Jeffrey Price, Peter Seaman. Music: Charles Fox. Editor: Frank J. Urioste, A.C.E. Production Designer: Rodger Maus. Director of Photography: Tonino Delli Colli. Unit Production Manager: E. Darrell Hallenbeck. First

Assistant Director: Carlo Cotti. Second Assistant Director: Michael Kissaun. First Assistant Director, U.S.A.: Mark Schilz. Second Assistant Director, U.S.A.: Doug Metzger. Filmed on location in Malta in collaboration with Mediterranean Film Facilities Ltd. Production Coordinator: Simon Benzakein. Second Unit Director of Photography: Isidore Makofsky, A.S.C. Script Supervisor: Rachel Griffiths. Camera Operator: Carlo Tafani. Set Decorator: Harry Cordwell. Special Effects: George Iaconelli. Costumes: Gloria Mussetta. Hairstyling: Leonard Drake. Make-up: Pierantonio Mecacci. Sound Supervisor: Jean-Louis Ducarme. Casting: Pam Polifroni. London Casting: Maude Spector. Rome Casting: Guidarino Guidi. Costume Supervisor: Jack Sandeen. Make-up Supervisor: Robert J. Schiffer, C.M.A.A. Casino sequence filmed at The Dragonara Palace Hotel and Casino, Malta, courtesy of the Kursaal Company. Art Director: John B. Mansbridge. Set Decorator: Roger Shook. Sound Supervisor: Bob Hathaway. Supervising Sound Editor: Joseph A. Parker. Sound Editor: George Fredrick. Re-recording Mixers: Richard R. Portman, Nick Alphin, Frank C. Regula. Music Editor: Jack Wadsworth. Assistant Film Editor: Derek Brechin. Production Assistant, U.S.A.: Harriet Greenberg. Production Assistant, Rome. Albamaria Ruggieri. Titles: Wayne Fitzgerald Modern Film Effects. Stunt Coordinator: Remy Julienne. Stunts: Michel Julienne, Dominique Julienne, Christian Bonnichon, J.C. Bonnichon, Brigitte Magnin. Sound: Allen Hurd. Running time: 91 minutes. Rated PG.

Song: "Stop! In the Name of Love" Words and Music by Eddie Holland, Lamont Dozier, Brian Holland.

Cast: Margot Kidder (Mickey Raymond), Robert Hays (Terry Leonard), David Suchet (Inspector Stagnos), Gila Von Weitershausen (Eva Werner), Daniel Faraldo (Nino Tenucci), Ronald Lacey (Princess Aida), Pauline Delaney (Lizzy O'Reilly), John Justin (Marquis De Pena), P.G. Stephens (Sean O'Reilly), Leopoldo Trieste (Esteban Ortega), Brizio Moninaro (Corporal Lascaris), Martin Sorrentino (Afro-Dite), Luciano Crovato (Taxi Driver), Massimo Sarchielli (Boss Arab), Jennifer Darling (Laurie), Kevork Malikyan (Arab), Vic Tablian (Achmed), Brian Coburn (Burly Salt), Fifi Moyer (Mother), Marcello Krakoff, Philip Alexander, Brian Eubanks (Children), Saviour Tanti (Passport Agent / Officer), Nadine Azzopardi (Stewardess), Emanuel Abela (Man at Museum Post Card Rack), Charles Saliba, Benny Farrugia (Bartenders), Margaret Von Brockdorff, Ruth Borthwick, Freda Camilleri,

Lilly Harding (Nuns), Narcy Calamatta (Tour Guide), Anthony Spiteri (Bald Man), Joe Quattromani (Man in Fez), Eddie Baldacchino (Wheelman at Dragonara Casino), Joe Coppini (Fish Monger), Michael Kissaun (Backstage Man), Charles Darmanin, Joe Abela (Museum Guards), David Suchet (Inspector Stagnos), Anna Cachia (Dancer).

Mickey Raymond is a court stenographer who also wants to be a writer, so she goes to Malta to write her first book, a mystery novel. She starts writing on the plane ride over.

Terry Leonard flirts with a stewardess and is posing as a doctor. Mickey observes this behavior while waiting for the airplane lavatory. Terry then tries to flirt with Mickey, but she thwarts his advances.

In Malta, Mickey gets her bags taken in the airport by a random taxi driver, who is quite a wild driver. He gets her to her hotel in record time.

The hotel clerk says that the hotel is full. Mickey says that she has a reservation. The clerk warns her that this may not be the hotel for her, but Mickey says that she'll stay anyway.

From her hotel, Mickey tries to see if she can observe a mystery story, so that she can turn it into her novel. There are many suspicious looking people about.

A strange man with a beret leaves a restroom behind that has another man who is bleeding while sitting in the toilet stall.

Mickey is nearby, but unaware of all this as she calmly looks at picture postcards for inspiration. In the market square, she observes Terry again, but this time he's wheeling and dealing.

Meanwhile, the man in the beret approaches Mickey from behind and steals her purse.

Mickey goes to the police station and explains that her purse has been stolen and even explains how it was probably done. As the police don't typically have major crimes to deal with in Malta, they are largely unconcerned.

Back in the hotel, Mickey starts writing "Malta Wants Me Dead," based on this experience with the police. She takes a shower and as she's freshening up, the man with the beret breaks into her room. She takes her deodorant and sprays it into the man's eyes and the man falls out of the window two floors down to his death. Mickey is so shocked, she can't even scream, until she goes down to the hotel lobby wearing just a towel.

The same police detective from the station appears at the hotel to question her. Problem is, they find no trace of the man on the ground below. The detective reveals that he has Mickey's manuscript and starts reading from it revealing where she called the police and the hotel clerk as idiots and they don't believe her now as she is just fictionalizing things that are supposedly happening to her.

Mickey insists that there was a murdered man, but the police do not believe her. They give back her manuscript and they leave.

Mickey decides to take a break to sunbathe on the beach and an Italian man named Nino comes up to speak with her and make a play for her. Mickey is not interested and decides to go for a swim to get away from him.

A small boy starts digging into the sand to build a sand castle and discovers a man buried in the sand, the same man that Mickey had killed. She contacts the police again and this time they have the body, but it is not the same man she killed.

The police reveal that the dead man is Harry Benjamin. Mickey says that she didn't kill this man and the detective says that she killed the man that killed Harry. Mickey wants to throw up and then passes out when the detective demands to know where Mickey put the drugs.

The next day in prison, Mickey is greeted by Terry, who has been brought in by the detective. Terry says that he's a lawyer and Mickey agrees, even though they are both lying.

The detective lets the two go free and later Mickey and Terry go out to dinner to discuss what Terry really does for a living. Terry explains himself, but his explanations don't make any logical sense and Mickey calls him on it.

Terry finally admits the truth, which is much more ordinary. He's driven a taxi and bought and sold jewelry. He asks if he's going to appear in Mickey's book. Mickey asks why and Terry says that he's the guy that sprung her from jail.

Later, Mickey and Terry go to the gambling casino and while they place bets at the roulette wheel, Mickey is rejoined by Nino and Terry is rejoined by the woman named Eva that he sold a piece of jewelry to earlier in the market square.

Both people raise the suspicions of each other, but eventually Mickey and Terry leave together despite the fact that she still feels that she's in grave danger. Terry wants to join her for the night, but Mickey turns him down as she still does not completely trust him.

The next day, Mickey calls the American Embassy and is trying to see if she can get help to get her passport back which is currently being held by the police as they don't want her to leave the country.

She doesn't get anywhere on the phone, so she goes out for a walk and encounters the same taxi driver from earlier who takes her to the Embassy.

As soon as she gets out of the car, another car with some Arabs smash into the taxi and kidnap Mickey and force her into their car. The taxi driver picks up his bumper and goes chasing after the other car.

The taxi smashes into the other car repeatedly until he is forced up a steep incline and his hood falls off.

The Arabs give Mickey some sodium penethol to get her to speak. Under the influence of the drug, Mickey says that she's a court stenographer.

During the interrogation, the taxi driver comes back and smashes into the other car and sends it into the wall. Mickey gets out and walks in a daze down the road.

She is seen by Terry, who picks her up and takes her to have a picnic. Still under the influence of the drug, Mickey is so out of it, she just sits silently as Terry puts a gold necklace around her neck that says "Trouble."

Mickey reveals that she likes Terry and also says that she felt that he was obnoxious when she first met him. Then she passes out.

Terry drags Mickey back to her hotel room as Eva happens to be there checking into another room. Mickey is still out of it and says that she was kidnapped.

Back in her room, Terry asks about the Arabs since she is somewhat awake. She mentions something about 10 kilos of drugs, but then passes out again.

The Arabs, meanwhile, are back at their hide-out aboard a yacht. They plan to light a hookah, but the hookah is filled with gun powder and not tobacco causing the boat to explode when lit.

Next morning, Mickey goes down to the hotel restaurant and is alert, but very groggy. She looks at the newspaper and sees the article about the Arabs' explosion. Terry shows up and Mickey asks for him to take her to the cops.

Terry advises that this wouldn't be a good idea as she is already the suspect for murder and drug-dealing. This wouldn't look good and she'd just be thrown in prison. Terry advises that she play detective to clear her name.

Mickey dons a hat and trench coat and decides to go it alone. She walks down the street and is picked up by Eva who asks about Terry. Mickey says that she doesn't know much, so Eva drops her off but gives her the invitation to get together soon to discuss things further.

Mickey goes to the docks and offers money to anyone who has information about Harry Benjamin. One ship captain takes her up on the offer and takes her to Harry's last place of residence. The lead leads her to a dead end.

Then she looks underneath a bunk and discovers a signed photo of Princess Aida. Aida was a dancer who used to strut her stuff onstage every night, so Mickey went to the club. Along the way, Mickey discovers that she is being watched and followed, so she takes back alleys to get around.

One man captures her. It turns out to be Nino. Nino reveals that everyone is after the 10 kilos and shows photos of the boat explosion, and the Arabs and of Eva. Nino says that Eva and Terry were the cause of the explosion.

Mickey doesn't know exactly who to believe, but she shows Nino the photo of Princess Aida. Nino suggests that they both go to Aida's show that evening.

Nino goes to the men's room, but doesn't come out for a while, so Mickey goes to check up on him and finds him outside with a knife in his belly. Another man grabs Mickey, but she runs off.

She gets to a phone booth and makes a phone call to the U.S. Embassy, but as before she is put on hold. Mickey gets to the Nicia Club where Aida is performing and sneaks in the back way and into her dressing room.

Before she can get in the dressing room, a man with a gun sneaks up behind her and wonders what she wants. She tells the man what she wants, that she needs to ask Princess Aida about Harry Benjamin.

The man with the gun turns out to be Princess Aida! Mickey and Aida discuss things for a couple of minutes when Aida is called on stage for another performance.

As Aida prepares to exit, Mickey puts two and two together, but then there are some gunshots and Mickey runs onto the stage where another female impersonator is performing "Stop! In the Name of Love."

Mickey leaps off stage and runs into the alley and encounters Eva with a gun. Eva is no longer being friendly and plans to kill Mickey, but before Eva can pull the trigger, Terry pulls the trigger on Eva and kills her. Mickey runs off.

Back at the hotel, Terry waits in the lobby reading a newspaper. The couple named Sean and Lizzie that have met with Mickey in the hotel's restaurant every day, now are protecting her.

Terry asks Lizzie where Mickey is and she finally takes him to her. When Mickey encounters Terry again, she pulls a gun on him.

Mickey asks Sean to keep the gun on Terry as she escapes, but he uses the gun on both Terry and Mickey. It seems that Sean and Lizzie are in with Arab friends, and they tie Mickey and Terry up in the hotel greenhouse and set a bomb to go off and blow them up as Sean and Lizzie get away.

Terry tells Mickey to kick the table to knock the shears off and make them within reach. Mickey asks why she should trust Terry and he reveals that he is a secret agent.

While kicking, the pair of shears lands perilously near Terry's groin. Mickey frees Terry and he grabs the bomb and tosses it away. Terry leaves Mickey tied up so she won't run away, but finally sets her free.

Sean and Lizzie drive away with the hotel clerk and they hear an explosion, believing that Terry and Mickey are now dead. They go to a secluded area by the coast, but Mickey and Terry are in hot pursuit.

Sean and Lizzie discover that they are being followed and so Lizzie starts firing shots at them, causing Mickey and Terry to crash.

Mickey and Terry switch seats. Mickey reveals that she doesn't know how to drive stick shift. Terry guides her, but she hits the clutch instead of the brake. This causes a chain reaction where all of the cars waiting to board the ferry including the one with Sean and Lizzie bump into each causing Sean and Lizzie's car to fall into the water.

The Maltese detective arrives and everything is cleared up. Sean and Lizzie are sent to prison and Mickey goes home to San Francisco to finish her mystery novel.

Mickey writes that Terry went on to solve another case in Tangiers, but in reality he comes back to be with Mickey in San Francisco.

A fairly enjoyable if underrated film. As with *Midnight Madness* (1980), there was once again no mention of Disney made on this film.

Unlike *Midnight Madness*, this film is a little less slapstick and somewhat more realistic with the appearances of dripping blood and murder and corpses and transvestitism.

And let's give a round of applause for the first time the word "shit" is uttered in a Disney film!

Leonard Maltin acts like this is a traditional Disney film minus a shaggy dog in his *Movie Guide*, but this film is really nothing like the Disney films of yore.

The film grossed $4.3 million.

Ray Bradbury's Something Wicked This Way Comes

RELEASED BY BUENA VISTA ON April 29, 1983, Technicolor. Panaflex. Panavision. A Bryna Company Production. Producer: Peter Vincent Douglas. Director: Jack Clayton. Screenplay: Ray Bradbury based on his novel. Music: James Horner. Special Visual Effects: Lee Dyer. Costumes: Ruth Myers. Unit Production Manager: Richard Learman. First Assistant Director: Dan Kolsrud. Second Assistant Director: Lisa Marmon. Film Editor: Argyle Nelson, A.C.E. Production Designer: Richard MacDonald. Director of Photography: Stephen H. Burum, A.S.C. Film Editor: Barry Mark Gordon. Creative Consultant: Jeanie Sims. Casting: Pam Polifroni, Virginia Higgins. Script Supervisor: Edle Bakke. Costumer Supervisor: Jack Sandeen. Men's Costumer: Tony Faso. Women's Costumer: Jennifer Parsons. Creative Make-up: Robert J. Schiffer, C.M.A.A. Make-up: Gary Liddiard, C.M.A.A., Jim Scribner. Hair Stylist: Edie Panda. Art Directors: John B. Mansbridge, Richard James Lawrence. Production Illustrator: Joe Hurley. Set Decorator: Rick Simpson. Contruction Coordinator: Dennis DeWaay. Associate Producer: Dan Kolsrud. Additional Second Assistant Directors: Christopher D. Miller, Scott Cam-

eron. Camera Operator: Elliott Davis. Assistant Film Editor: Axel Anton Hubert. Sound Supervisor: Bob Hathaway. Special Sound Effects Created by Richard R. Portman, David M. Horton. Supervising Sound Effects Editor: Joseph A. Parker. Supervising Music Editor: Jack Wadsworth. Music Editor: Dennis Ricotta. Dialogue Editor: Al Maguire. Production Mixer: Bruce Bisenz, C.A.S. Re-recording Supervisor: Richard R. Portman. Re-recording Mixers: Nick Alphin, Frank C. Regula. Effects Animation Supervisor: Michael Wolf. Animation Production Coordinator: Ron Stangl. Animators: William Allen Blyth, Ed Coffey, Gail Fox, Allen Gonzales, John Norton, Darrell Rooney, Scott Santoro. Composite Supervisor: Clint Colver. Scene Planning: Richard T. Sullivan. Airbrush: W.L. Arance. Special Effects Consultant: Harrison Ellenshaw. First Assistant Director Special Effects: Steve McEveety. Additional Photography: Jan Kiesser. Special Photographic Effects: Art Cruickshank, A.C.E., Peter Anderson, Phil Meador. Special Kaleidoscopic Effect: Symmetricon. Additional Visual Effects: Van Der Veer Photo Effects, Visual Concepts Engineering. Opticals Supervisor: Bill Kilduff. Mechanical Special Effects Supervisor: Roland Tantin. Mechanical Special Effects: Allen Hall, Hans Metz, Isidoro Raponi, Willard Livingston. Matte Artists: Jesse Silver, Michael Lloyd. Production Coordinators: Bayard Veiller, Susan Recton, Cardon Walker. Tarantulas supplied by Animal Actors of Hollywood. With special thanks to the people of Vermont for their help and cooperation. Stunts: Gary Combs, George Robotham, Charles Tamburro, Bobby Porter, Patrick Romano, Jeff Viola. Special Makeup Effects: Stan Winston. Production Illustrator: Jesse Silver. Assistant Property Master: Alan Sims. Foreman: Daniel Turk. Sound Editors: Wayne Allwine, George Fredrick, George Probert, Roger Sword, Allen Hurd. ADR Editor: Al Maguire. Cable Person: Douglas J. Schulman. Special Effects: Gary D'Amico, John Palmer, Robert G. Willard. Miniatures: George Paine. Rotoscope Artist: David Halver. Visual Effects: George Muhs, Susan Turner. Visual Effects Assistant Scene Coordinator: Lynda Thompson. Stilt Walker: Scott Land. Gaffer: Carl Boles. First Assistant Camera: Michael R. Marquette. Set Lighting Technician: Peter McEvoy. Conductor: James Horner. Composer, Additional Music / Orchestrator: Greig McRitchie. Score Mixer: Shawn Murphy. Animal Trainer: Mark Harden. Aerial Coordinator / Pilot: Charles A. Tamburro. Running time: 94 minutes. Rated PG.

Cast: Jason Robards (Charles Halloway), Jonathan Pryce (Mr. Dark), Diane Ladd (Mrs. Nightshade), Royal Dano (Tom Fury), Vidal Peterson (Will Halloway), Shawn Carson (Jim Nightshade), Mary Grace Canfield (Miss Foley), Richard Davalos (Mr. Crosetti), Jack Dengel (Mr. Tetley), Jack Dodson (Doctor Douglas), Bruce M. Fischer (Mr. Cooger), Ellen Geer (Mrs. Halloway), Pam Grier (Dust Witch), Brendan Klinger (Cooger as a Child), James Stacy (Ed, the Bartender), Angelo Rossitto (Little Person #1), Peter D. Risch

(Little Person #1), Tim T. Clark (Teenage Boy), Jill Carroll (Teenage Girl), Tony Christopher (Young Ed), Sharan Lea (Young Miss Foley), Scott De Roy (Cooger as a Young Man), Sharon Ashe (Townswoman), Arthur Hill (Narrator), Phil Fondacaro (Demon Clown), Jerry Maren.

It is an autumn day in October. Two boys run named Will Halloway and Jim Nightshade play through the fields of 10,000 pumpkins waiting to be cut.

A seller of lightning rods was coming into town as a storm was heading into Greentown. We are introduced to the various townsfolk including the bartender who was an ex-football jock who was now missing an arm and a leg as well as the barber and the tobacconist.

Miss Foley is the school teacher who was believed to be beautiful when she was much younger. She was also very stern and strict and had kept the two boys after school for whispering in class.

Jim Nightshade was Will Halloway's best buddy. They were born on the same night. They run into town and say hi to all the townspeople and witness the man selling the lightning rods.

Jim and Will go to visit Will's father Charles who works in a library. Afterwards, they bump into the lightning rod salesman who recommends that Jim's father purchase a rod, but Jim's father is dead. Jim decides to buy one anyway and purchases one with two beetles on it.

Mr. Halloway goes to the tobacconist to purchase a cigar and then meets up with the barber, Mr. Crosetti, who smells that visitors are going to be coming into town. Crosetti also suggests that Halloway should put some color in his hair.

Halloway goes to the bar and throws a pass with Ed, who catches it with his good arm and his stump.

Jim and Will install the lightning rod and a flyer blows up that says that a carnival will be coming into town the next day called Darks Pandemonium.

Halloway also discovers this flyer blowing in the breeze on the street and also sees a man distributing these flyers by randomly throwing them into the breeze.

When he turns to look at a casket in a window, it is briefly replaced with a woman lying there with a red glowing ring.

Halloway comes home and talks with Will and tosses the carnival flyer into the fire. Halloway regrets that he can't play catch with his son, but cannot due to his heart condition.

At night, Will sees his dad leave the house. Downtown, the lightning rod salesman also sees the woman lying there with the red glowing ring.

Will and Jim both open their windows and shout to each other that the carnival is coming into town by train in the middle of the night. They both get dressed and go outside to see it arrive.

The train says Dark's Temple of Temptations on the side. As they watch the train pull in to the station, strange things happen like lights bursting from a nearby statue.

The carnival is set up with a Ferris wheel and other amusements. Will and Jim investigate things closer and discover an abandoned railway carriage filled with cobwebs. A tarantula crawls against one of their hands and they run out screaming.

Mr. Halloway, meanwhile, is still strolling around and goes back to the window where he saw the woman, but now the woman is gone and only the red ring remains.

Halloway goes home and finds Jim is up, too. They talk about the carnival coming into town and wonder if it is real and then decide to go back to bed.

The next day, the carnival is up and running. Everyone in town seems to go to it, but Jim and Will feel that it's just a plain old carnival with nothing special.

Ed hits the bell with a hammer and gets a free pass to the mirror maze. He goes to the mirrors and it shows Ed with two good arms and legs.

At the exit of the mirror maze, Jim and Will encounter Miss Foley who is in kind of a daze after going through the maze.

Crosetti the barber gets his palm read by the woman with the red ring. She says that he is missing something from his life…a woman.

Mr. Tetley, the tobacconist places a bet on the spinning wheel and wins $1,000, a cigar and a free pass to the Ferris wheel. At the wheel, a beautiful lady is waiting and they ride the wheel together.

Jim and Will come across some exotic dancers. Jim is interested, but Will is not. Jim even goes so far as to peer through a small hole in the tent to see what's inside.

The exotic dancers dance with Mr. Crosetti who soon appears nude with the dancers. Just as it is getting interesting, a small man whacks the tent telling the boys that they are too young to watch the show.

Meanwhile, the Ferris wheel stops and Mr. Tetley is nowhere to be seen and the ride operator takes the woman with the red ring by the hand and guides her off the ride.

Jim and Will sneak in and climb aboard the merry-go-round, but before they can ride, the ride operator lifts them off the ride and takes them to Mr. Dark, the owner of the carnival.

Dark shows them some magical tricks and then offers them free passes to other attractions and sends them on their way.

Jim and Will decide to stay after the park closes and they see the merry-go-round start up, but it travels backwards.

Ride operator Mr. Cooger rides it and he regrows his hair and becomes a young man and eventually a small boy. Mr. Dark lifts him off and tells him to go about his work. Jim and Will run off.

They pass by Crosetti's barber shop as they go home and it has a sign that says "Closed Due to Illness."

They also pass by Miss Foley's house to see if she's alright. Foley is visited by her nephew Robert, who is actually Mr. Cooger. Will wants to warn Miss Foley, but they chicken out and say that they won't be in school on Monday.

As they leave, Robert comes outside and flings a rock at Miss Foley's window. Foley yells out to Will that she will tell his mother on him for breaking her window.

The boys run off and encounter Mr. Halloway and scream. Will explains the weird things he has seen.

Mr. Halloway explains to his son how Mr. Nightshade rescued Will from the water when he was much younger and he always regretted that he didn't do it himself.

At Jim's house, he asks his mother about his father and if he looks like him.

Meanwhile, Miss Foley peers into the mirror and becomes a beautiful young woman. The only side effect of this transformation is that Miss Foley can no longer see. Robert stands over her, grinning.

Jim and Will get back together. Jim plans to go on the merry-go-round and run it forward to grow older.

Mr. Dark tells Mr. Cooger (now back at his normal age) to not let the boys interfere with his work.

Jim and Will come back and witness that Mr. Crosetti has been turned into a bearded lady statue and Mr. Tetley has been turned into a cigar store Indian statue and the lightning rod salesman is being tortured with an electric chair until he tells them when the storm is coming back as it will wash the carnival away.

The woman with the red ring appears in a bridal gown to show his reward for telling Dark when the storm is coming. He refuses to tell and gets zapped. The boys yell for Dark to stop and then run off.

Dark says to the woman with the ring that the boys have seen too much and asks her to bring them back to him.

The woman transforms into a green mist and surrounds the boys' homes.

Will is reprimanded for being out so late and his mother says to get upstairs and go to bed. Dad has a talk with Will and he warns him to be careful as something strange is going on.

The strange mist surrounds the homes and Jim asks Will to climb into his house as the lightning rod is protecting them. However, the protection isn't perfect as the ceiling starts cracking and the room starts filling with tarantulas.

The tarantulas crawl all over them as they try to smash them, but eventually a lightning bolt hitting the rod stops everything…or was it all just a nightmare as the boys wake up in a sweat and screaming.

The next day in church, the boys sing hymns with their families. Afterward, Jim and Will realize that they can't go home as Mr. Dark is after them. They can't go home as Dark will kill their families. Will calls his dad and he asks him to come home, but he tells his dad that he can't.

Dark leads the parade with the young Miss Foley, the Crosetti bearded lady, the Tetley Indian and the electrocuted lightning rod salesman among those walking in the parade along with a number of midgets and Cooger back as a child looking for Jim and Will.

Dark goes into the bar and speaks with Mr. Halloway and his buddy, the doctor. Dark explains that he has some prizes for them. He shows Halloway what they look like as tattoos on the palms of his hands.

Halloway lies and makes up names of who the kids are, but Dark sees through Halloway's lies. As he squeezes his hand in anger, it begins to bleed and it drips on Will, who is hiding with Jim in the sewer below. Dark goes on his way.

Next, Halloway meets up with Ed who is now able-bodied and a boy and does a quick football toss with him. Halloway drops his cigar purposefully and whispers to the boys to meet him at the library.

At the library, the boys reveal that the parade procession was actually a funeral and that they had two caskets ready for the boys. Halloway looks through the books to research more information about this strange carnival.

They hear a noise, so the boys go to hide. The visitor is Mr. Dark who knows that the two boys are in the library somewhere. Dark says that he has free rides on the merry-go-round to lure them back to the carnival.

Halloway reveals to Mr. Dark that he now knows who he and his people are and the evil that they do. Dark turns to Halloway and says that he can make him young again if he just reveals where the boys are. Dark takes a book and tears the pages out as years that he can never live again.

Halloway is almost lured into Dark's clutches when Will shouts out to not listen. Dark rips out the pages to his present age and then he literally throws the book at him. Dark then clutches Halloway's hand and begins to crush it.

With Halloway out of commission, Dark continues to search the stacks for the boys and finally nabs them from behind and drags them out of the library. Dark reveals the woman with the red ring is to become their new mother.

The woman removes the boys' tongues so that they no longer have the ability to speak. Dark also commands her to give Halloway a brief taste of death so that he will know what it's like when it comes again.

Dark plans to send Will forward on the merry-go-round to become an adult and make him a partner and to ride Jim backwards to make him a baby.

Halloway regains his strength and goes back to the carnival. At the entrance he meets up with Jim's mother who has a free pass. Halloway takes the ride pass, tears it up and sends her home.

Halloway and Will enter into the hall of mirrors. Dark shows what happened to Crosetti, Tetley and Ed and then shows a different life he can have: one without regrets.

Will tells his dad that he loves him and is shown drowning. This time Halloway smashes through the glass and rescues his own son. This causes a chain reaction of supernatural changes as the lightning salesman takes a rod and shoves it through the woman with the red ring, killing her.

Jim is still lured onto the merry-go-round, but Will rescues and pulls him off at the last moment and Mr. Dark gets pulled aboard.

As Dark goes round and round, he gets older and older. Halloway acts younger, but doesn't get younger and Jim and Will are fine, so they eventually flee the scene.

Mr. Dark rots away and as he does so, the carnival tears apart and the townspeople revert back to their normal selves and also flee. Dark is rescued too late by one of his midget accomplices and the entire carnival is swirled up like a tornado into the sky.

Halloway and the boys make it home, running as they go. Halloway feels younger than he has felt in years.

The movie is very creepy in a good way, and is somewhat confusing at times, but overall is a major step forward for Disney in becoming a modern studio. It did so-so business at the box office.

Besides being a Ray Bradbury book, this story was also adapted back in the 1950s in one of the EC horror comics.

Mary Grace Canfield was Ralph Monroe on *Green Acres*. She also appeared years ago in *Pollyanna*.

An opening sequence about the carnival's arrival in town and featuring extensive computer animation was deemed not convincing enough and so was cut.

Ray Bradbury gave his blessing for Disney to make this film in 1981. He wanted Jason Robards to play the father, a character based on Bradbury's own father. He also wanted British director Jack Clayton. Bradbury also wanted special effects kept at a minimum. Clayton got Bradbury to cut his 240-page screenplay down to 120, much to Bradbury's annoyance.

David Lean and Steven Spielberg were both considered for directing this film, and Darren McGavin, Dick Van Dyke, Dean Jones, Walter Matthau, Jack Lemmon, James Garner and Hal Holbrook were all considered to play Charles Halloway.

Bradbury wrote this story in 1952 after seeing Gene Kelly in *Singin' in the Rain*. He showed the story to Kelly and he considered making it back then, but nothing happened.

EC Comics produced a comic book adaptation in *The Haunt of Fear* #18, March-April 1953. The story was called "The Black Ferris" and was illustrated by Jack Davis.

Bradbury published the novelization in 1962.

The budget was $18 million and the film grossed $8.4 million. In an episode of the animated TV show *Freakazoid!*, they mention that it was this film and not *The Black Hole* or *Tron* which put Disney's finances in serious jeopardy and at risk for a corporate takeover.

Never Cry Wolf

RELEASED BY BUENA VISTA ON October 6, 1983, Technicolor. Panaflex. Panavision. An Amarok Productions, Ltd. Production. Executive Producer: Ron Miller. Associate Producer: Walker Stuart. Producers: Lewis Allen, Jack Couffer, Joseph Strick. Director: Carroll Ballard. Screenplay: Curtis Hanson, Sam Hamm, Richard Kletter based on the book by Farley Mowat. Narration Writers: Charles Martin Smith, Eugene Corr, Christina Luescher, Ralph Furmaniak. Music: Mark Isham. Sound: Alan R. Splet. Editors: Peter Parasheles, A.C.E., Michael Chandler. Art Director: Graeme Murray. Director of Photography: Hiro Narita. Production Managers: Robert Steinbrecher, Wanda Mull. Unit Manager: Fitch Cady. First Assistant Directors: John Houston, Scott Maitland. Second Assistant Directors: Anthony Cookson, Colin Michael Kitchens. Script Supervisors: Barbara Parker. Casting: Jennifer Shull. Costumers: Deborah Scott, Trish Keating. Camera Operator: Paul Marbury. Camera Assistants: Mindaugas Bagdon, Dan Heather, Brent Spencer, Curtis Peterson. Second Unit Camera Operator: Stephen St. John. Third Unit Camera Assistant: Walter Lloyd. Sound Mixers: David Parker, Randy Thom. Sound Assistant: Martin Fossum. Key Grip: Gabriel Kruks. Best Boy: Scott Robinson. Grips: Dillard Brinson, James Hurford. Electrician: John Bartley. Best Boy: William Thum. Property Masters: Wayne McLaughlin, Grant Swain. Art Department: John Wright, William Shumow, Richard Wilcox. Associate Editor: Jeffrey Friedman, Assistant Editors: Michael Rosenthal, Jenny Stein. Apprentice Editors: Martha J. Goode, Michael Levin, Sharon Wood. Sound Editors: Teresa Ekton, Robert Shoup. Dialogue Editor: Vivian Hillgrove Gilliam. Associate Sound Editor: Rob Fruchtman. Assistant Sound Editors: Suzanne Meyers, Claire Schoen, Michael Silvers, Wendy Zheutlin. Apprentice Sound Editors: Alan Abrams, Robert Epstein. Music Production and Supervision: Todd Boekelheide. Additional Arrangements and Production: Mark Adler. Synthesizer Programming and Performance: Mark Isham. Main Title Design: Carrie De Ruiter. Wildlife Consultant: Peter Matthiessen. Driver Captains: Alois Stranan, Robert Bowe. Animal Trainers: Gary Kenwood, Cheryl Shawver, Kenneth Beebe, Sieuwke Bisleti, Deborah Coe, Karen Dew, Gary Gero, Mark Hardin, Madeline Holmes, Donna Loptsom, Kelley Pratt, Ronald Raffler, Julian Sylvester. Domestic Animals: North American Guard Dog and Kenneling Service Ltd. Trained by H.J. McCullough. Special Effects: John Thomas. Stunt Coordinator / Double: John Wardlow. Production Coordinators: Patricia Allen, Claudette Laurencelle. Assistant Production Coordinator: Diane Richwine. Location Auditors: Diana Austin, John Morrissey. Production Liason: Douglas White. Production Assistants: Bayard Carey, Lamme Hemphill, Patty Proud-  foot, William Mizel, Lane Starling. Underwater Unit: Ocean Films Ltd. Cameraman: Al Giddings: Assistants: Arlette Greenfield, Douglas Laughlin, Terry Thompson. Additional Divers: Harry Lowry, Daniel Swanstrom. Special Thanks to: The People of Atlin, British Columbia, The Fraternal Order of the Eagles, The Red Onion, Skagway, Alaska, The Museum of Natural History, New York City, The Zoology Department, University of California, Berkeley, Brown, Farris and Associates, Vancouver, British Columbia. Additional Music: Robert Hughes. Props / Set Dresser: Douglas Freeman. Sound Re-Recording Mixer: Luther Greene. Sound: Allen Hurd, Jeff Kliment. Apprentice Sound Editor: Cliff Latimer. Sound Technician: Ewa Sztompke. Still Photographer: Bruno Engler. Music Recordist: Gary Clayton. Running time: 105 minutes. Rated PG.

Cast: Charles Martin Smith (Tyler), Brian Dennehy (Rosie), Zachary Ittimangnaq (Ootek), Samson Jorah (Mike), Hugh Webster (Drunk), Martha Ittimangnaq (Woman), Tom Dahlgren (Hunter #1), Walker Stuart (Hunter #2).

The opening text on film reads: *In recent years, the Arctic region has been the scene of biological catastrophe. The great, caribou herds that only a few years ago numbered in the millions have all but vanished.*

A Government agency orders a biological report be prepared that would scientifically justify extermination of the suspected culprit—a creature known from story, myth and legend as a ferocious killer. <u>Canis Lupis</u>—*the wolf.*

Because of the extreme difficulties involved, no scientist had ever actually observed wolves in the act of attacking and killing caribou. So the major task of "The Lupine Project" was for someone to travel to the Arctic, track down a pack of wolves and observe this behavior in detail.

A train travels up to the Arctic carrying Tyler, a man assigned to watch and gather information about wolf behavior. The train drops him off in Knutsak at The Caribou Hotel, but he needs to go another 40 miles north.

Tyler is warned that the wolves will tear him apart. Rosie is the pilot that flies him the rest of the way to his final destination. The plane has difficulty getting off the ground as there is too much weight on the plane, so much is tossed overboard.

Finally, they get off the ground, barely. While flying, there seems to be nothing but snow on the Earth below. Tyler has some serious doubts about his mission. Tyler is worried, but Rosie is not. Soon, the engine is overheating and stalling. Rosie goes outside to fix the plane while Tyler flies, barely. Rosie gets the engine running again and gets back inside.

They make a safe landing on the snow. Tyler gets out and Rosie quickly dumps all of Tyler's stuff onto the snow and flies away. Tyler is literally out in the middle of nowhere.

Tyler looks around with all of his stuff strewn about and sees absolutely nothing nearby. He takes out a pipe and has a smoke and tries to decide his next move.

He tries to drink a beer, but the beer is frozen. He goes through the other boxes and finds such useless items as light bulbs and multiple cans of asparagus. He does use a heating element to defrost the beer and gets the radio working, which picks up a Russian radio station.

Tyler tries to set up camp and type his reports, but the weather keeps getting colder and colder. He finally witnesses his first wolves running across the snow. He hides under his canoe to avoid detection.

It turns out that the wolves are actually sled dogs with an Eskimo named Ootek. Tyler asks Ootek to help him with his equipment, but Ootek ignores him and drives off. Tyler makes the decision to chase after him as he is the only person in the area.

Eventually, Ootek speeds off and Tyler passes out from exhaustion. Ootek comes back to rescue him and the sled dogs take him back to Ootek's place.

Ootek is initially a mysterious sort of fellow as he doesn't communicate with Tyler very well. Ootek comes and goes and Tyler decides to relax for a while before doing anything further.

Eventually, Tyler decides to brave the cold to look for his stuff and actually witnesses some wolves that attack him. It turns out to be a nightmare.

Tyler is actually still at Ootck's place witnessing a small group of newborn mice, but he does get his equipment and starts searching for Canis Lupis.

At one point while walking, the ice breaks and Tyler is trapped underneath the ice. He breaks through with his rifle which he had fortunately held on to and pulls himself out of the trap.

Tyler builds a fire to dry out his clothes and stands naked in the wilderness.

Later, with his clothing back on, Tyler hears many wolf calls, but doesn't witness a wolf for over a month. Finally, he sees one not too far off and tries to follow it. His first sighting is of one of the largest and rarest of the wolf species.

Tyler watches through a crudely constructed telescopic lens, but later decides to attract the wolf's attention by making a lot of noise and setting up a tent inside his territory.

This proves to be a good thing as far as attracting the wolf's attention, but also brought him too close as the wolf came right up to the tent and wet on some of Tyler's stuff.

Tyler fights back by urinating all over the surrounding area of his tent for over a two acre area. The wolf came back to smell the urine and to mark his territory implying that Tyler was ok to be in his territory.

In Tyler's notebook, he names the male wolf, George and another female wolf, Angeline. Soon, George and Angeline become a family of five and their interest in Tyler becomes secondary.

Wolves mate for life. George goes out to hunt or to do something while Angeline waits behind with the children. And, a lot of howling goes on.

Tyler says that the reason he is out there to prove that the wolves are killing and eating the caribou population, but in analyzing the wolves' scat, he discovers that only a few small bones are in it and no caribou remains. Tyler is mystified by his findings.

Tyler also discovers that mice are literally everywhere in the Arctic. He realizes that this is what the wolves actually subsist on. The idea that a large animal can live entirely on mice may be treated with skepticism, so Tyler decides to conduct an experiment. He decides to eat mice himself and does so with vigor.

Tyler continues making his wolf observations, sometimes watching as many as five at a time playing with each other. He also observed George's return to the wolf pack. With George's return, Angeline joins George on his nightly rounds.

Tyler also sees a strange wolf that he only sees fleetingly. He assumes that he's part of the pack, but also another watcher. He also takes a lot of photographs of his observations.

One time Tyler got so caught up in his observations that he was startled when Ootek and his friend Mike show up. Mike offers Tyler some fish and Tyler turns it down, telling him he's currently eating mice as an experiment. The two agree that this is a good idea.

Tyler tells the two about his studies of wolf scat. He figures that if he studies what came out of a wolf, he'll know what went into a wolf. Again, they say that this is a good idea.

The three decide to hang out together. Mike has a bassoon and practices on it, occasionally. Ootek is knowledgeable about wolves, but Tyler doesn't want to press him too much about what he knows and let him reveal it naturally.

Tyler still has nightmares about wolves coming and tearing him up. Mike tells Tyler that wolves howl when they are lonely. He says that you howl in order to attract a wolf so that you can kill it. Wolf pelts command $350.

Summer is ending, so Tyler has to make his final observations. At one point, Tyler meets the rest of Ootek's family (his wife and son) as they travel north.

Mike tells Tyler that the caribou are currently travelling south and will soon be there. Mike goes south and Ootek takes Tyler to a place further north to observe wolves before they too part ways.

Alone once again, Tyler runs around naked, diving into a lake and taking a nap. The observant wolves start running around, but it is not to get Tyler, but to get away from the caribou stampede. Tyler runs with the stampede fully naked observing the wolves chasing after them.

He does observe the wolves going in for one kill and they all feast on the caribou. Afterwards, Tyler puts his clothes back on and observes the bones and discovers disease in the marrow of the caribou bones.

Soon, Tyler overhears gunfire and the smell of gasoline and comes across a camp with Rosie and they excitedly reencounter each other. Rosie is with two other men and they all eat food with Tyler observing.

The men load up their new plane with wolf skins and antlers and Rosie asks Tyler to get on the plane, but Tyler refuses in disgust. Living amongst the wolves has changed him.

Tyler hikes back to the base which will take him three days, but only minutes for Rosie by plane.

Later, Rosie comes back for Tyler, but he shoos him away with rocks and bullets, so Rosie takes off again and flies off.

Next, Tyler stumbles across a camp of Mike's. He says that he's heading back north. He tells him to stop worrying about the wolf pups and to start worrying about himself. Mike flashes a grin of brand new teeth and then goes on his way.

Ultimately, Tyler chronicles all of his observations about the wolves and this helped change man's perception about them. Tyler didn't watch the wolves leave as he teaches Ootek how to juggle.

I think over again my small adventures. My fears, those small ones that seemed so big, for all the vital things I had to get and to reach. And yet there is only one great thing. The only thing. To live to see the great days that dawns and the light that fills the world. – Old Inuit Song

This caption closes the film.

Officially, this is the final film in wide theatrical release by Walt Disney Productions. On the teaser poster, the legend reads Walt Disney Productions. By the time the movie was actually released, the revised poster above stated Walt Disney Pictures. On the actual film itself, it still says Walt Disney Productions.

This is a really great, if uncharacteristic movie to be released by Disney at this time.

Actor Charles Martin Smith says that this was the loneliest film shoot that he had ever done.

This movie features the first male nudity in a Disney film, actually any nudity of any kind in a Disney film.

Other reviewers observed at the time, the irony of having the main character of this film consume mice, since it was a film made by Disney and the home of Mickey Mouse.

The film was nominated for an Academy Award for Sound and was budgeted at $11 million and grossed $27.6 million.

Running Brave

AN ENGLANDER PRODUCTION released by Buena Vista Distribution on November 4, 1983, Medallion Film Laboratories, Toronto. Panavision. An Englander Productions in Association with The Ermineskin Band Presentation. Producer: Ira Englander. Associate Producer: Maurice Wolfe. Director: D.S. Everett. Writers: Henry Bean, Shirl Hendryx. Casting: Mike Fenton, Jane Feinberg, A.S.C.D., Marci Liroff. Director of Photography: Francois Protat. Production Designer: Carol Spier. Supervising Editor: Peter Zinner, A.C.E. Music: Mike Post. Production Manager: Don Bucksbaum. Production Executive: Martha Moran. First Assistant Director: Martin Walters. Production Coordinator: Angela Heald. Editors: Tony Lower, Earle Herdan. Business Affairs: J. Wilton Littlechild, Douglas McCleod, Dennis Gavin. Camera Operator: Cyrus Block. First Assistant Cameraman: Theo Eleseuer. Second Assistant Cameraman: Christopher J. Harris. Unit Manager: Nick Gray. Second Assistant Director: Mac Bradden. Third Assistant Director: Bill Mizel, Deborah Lefaive, Karen Grugon. Script Supervisor: Christine Wilson. Production Assistant: Shirley J. Gill. Production Accountant: Linda Jeffery-Ludlow. Art Department Accountant: Wendy P. Kraft. Assistant Accountant: Lyn Lucibello. Art Director: Barbara Dunphy. Assistant Art Director: Alfred. Wardrobe Designer: Wendy Hugglin. Assistant Wardrobe Designer: Christopher Ryan. Wardrobe Supervisor: Trish Keating. Wardrobe Assistants: Linda Langdon, Tish Monaghan, Nancy Englander. Seamstress: Joan Olsen. Set Decorators: Rose Marie McSherry, Jim Erickson, Jacques Bradette. Assistant Set Decorators: Tedd Muchera, Don Mackenzie, Daniel Brauette. Property Master: Hilton Rosemarin. Assistant Property Master: Ian Thomas. Prop Buyer: Shirley Ingey. Head Makeup Artist: Phyllis Newman. Makeup Artist: Marlen Schneider. Head Hairstylist: James Brown. Hairstylist: Donna Bis. Sound Mixer: Rob Young. Boom Operator: Graham Crowell. Gaffer: John Berrie. Best Boy: Randy Tomiuk. Electricians: Don Metz, Martin Wilde. Generator Operator: Rodger Dean. Key Grip: Dave Humphreys. Best Boy: Brian Kuchera. Grips: Richard M. Allen, Christopher Tate, Clarence Brown. Construction Manager: Brian Cockroft. Head Carpenter: Del Embree. Assistant Head Carpenter: Bruce Robinson, Martin Shustak. Carpenters: Michael Ellsworth, Peter Gerrie, Christopher Good, Cindy Gordon. Head Scenic Painter: Nick Kusonic. Assistant Head Painter: Patricia Mackenzie. Scenic Painters: James McAteer, Brent Lane, Barbara Becker, Sylvie Bouchard, Laurie Dobbie, Michael Heinrich, Linda Pelttari. Graphic Artist: John Blackie. Draftsman: Dan Davis. Sketch Artist: Nancy Pearce. Creative Consultant: Dorothea Moore. Track Sequence Consultant: Bill Easton. Research: Michael Date, Mark Trahant. Casting-Canada: Deirdre Bowen. Location Casting: Bette Chadwick. Publicist: Mahoney / Wasserman and Associates. Publicist Unit Representative: Richard Leary. Location Publicist: Jami Drake. Stills Photographer: Joseph Lederer. Transportation Coordinator: Don Metzer. Driver Captain: Nick Muchera. Drivers: Dennis Fitzgerald, Blake Patterson, Barry Kraft, Alan Wightmore, John Aushead, Avery King, Eddie Washington, George Prabucki, Ann McGaw. Picture Vehicles: John McEwan. Wranglers: Norm Edge, Duane Edge. Location Managers: David McAree, Glenn Ludlow, Brian Ross. Office P.A.: Norm Fassbender. Production Secretary: Donna Waring. Art Department Trainee: Liz Amsden. Casting P.A.s: Roseline Richardson, Sandra Cowan. Production Trainees: Milton McDougall, Charlene Pearce, Tracy Galbraith. Craft Service: Bill Gawryluk. Music Supervisor: Don Perry. Music Editor: Allan K. Rosen for La Da Productions. First Assistant Editor: Bev Neal. Second Assistant Edi-

tor: Robin Leigh. Post Production Creative Sound: Neiman-Tillar Associates. Sound Re-recording: Ryder Sound Services Inc. Re-recording Mixers: Gary C. Bourgeois, C.A.S., Neil Brody, C.A.S., Robert L. Harman, C.A.S., T.A. Moore, Jr., C.A.S. Titles and Optical Effects: Modern Film Effects. With Thanks to: The City of Edmonton, Commonwealth Stadium and Clarke Stadium, Edmonton, Alberta, Canada, The University of Alberta, Edmonton, Alberta Economic Development Film Industry Office, Via Mail Canada, Inc., The City of Drumheller, Alberta. Special thanks to the following organizations for their support of the Billy Mills Indian Youth Leadership Program: Atlantic Richfield Corporation, Adolf Coors Company, Anheuser-Busch Companies, Inc., Castle and Cooke, Inc., First Interstate Bank of California Foundation, Gannett Foundation, General Electric Company, General Foods Fund, Inc., Rockwell International Corporation Trust, Times Mirror Foundation, Whitaker Corporation. This true story based on the life of Billy Mills includes some fictional events and people. In such cases any similarity to actual events or people, living or dead is purely coincidental. Running time: 106 minutes. Rated PG.

Songs: "I'm a Jayhawk" Written by George Bowles. "Hey Liley, Liley Lo (Married Man Gonna Keep Your Secret)" Words and Music by Elizabeth Austin and Alan Lomax. "Tom Dooley" Words and Music Collected. Adapted and Arranged by Frank Warner, John A. Lomax and Alan Lomax. "Sound Off (Duckworth Chant)" Written by Willie Lee Duckworth and Bernard Lezir. "Theme from a Summer Place" Music: Max Steiner. "Summertime Blues" Words and Music: Eddie Cochran and Jerry Capahari. "Tequila" Words and Music: Chuck Rio. "Auld Lang Syne" and "The American National Anthem" Performed by the Aruza High School Band.

Cast: Robby Benson (Billy Mills), Pat Hingle (Coach Bill Easton), Claudia Cron (Pat Mills), Jeff McCracken (Dennis Riley), August Schellenberg (Billy's Father), Denis LaCroix (Frank Mills), Graham Greene (Eddie Mills), Michael J. Reynolds (Roger Douglas), Kendall Smith (Young Billy), George Clutesi (Ben), Margo Kane (Catherine), Derek Campbell (Fight Bookmaker), Maurice Wolfe (Uncle Chester), Albert Angus (Bud), Barbara Blackhorse (Young Catherine), Carmen Wolfe (Jen American Horse). William Berry (Carny Barker), Kaye Corbett (Viking), John Littlechild (Pine Ridge Boy), Tantoo Martin (Caroline), Gail Omeasoo (Roseanne), Billy Runsabove, Seymour Eaglespeaker, Maurice Wolfe, Merrill Bendoff (Indian Singers / Drummers), The Ermineskin Band (Pow-Wow Dancers), Chris Judge (Schwartz), Paul Hubbard (Pebbly), Jack Ackroyd (High School Coach), Tommy Banks (Campus Cop), Clare Drake (Assistant Coach), Rob Roy (Frat President), Graham MacPherson (Stan Larson), Francis Damberger (Wilson), Ray

Kelly (Trainer), Thomas Peacocke (Mr. Harris), Barbara Reese (Mrs. Harris), Douglas Marquardt (Drill Sergeant), Bonar Bain (University Protester), Donna Devore (Girl Student), Wendell Smith (Chris Mitchell), Daryl Menard (Ron Clarke), Greg Coyes (Mohamed Gemmaroli), Kim Maser (Gerry Lindgren), Walter David (Mimi Wolfe), Bryan Hall (Bob Richards), Greg Rogers (American Sportscaster), Christopher Gaze (Aussie Sportscaster), William Fisher (British Sportscaster), Fred Keating (TV Sportscaster), Brendan Hughes (American Coach), Will Reese (Town Official), Harvey Haugen (Mayor), Gary Poon (Japanese Official).

A scout named Coach Easton is brought out to see Billy Mills, a top runner. Problem is, Billy is an Indian and that doesn't sit well with Easton as he feels that Indians are irresponsible. Billy wins the Custer County Cross Country Championship in record time.

Billy defends himself and Easton decides to give him a chance. Easton asks why Billy eased up at the end. Billy says he knew he would win. Easton says to not do that anymore and he will sign him up.

Billy continues practicing his running. Billy's family is excited except Billy's brother Eddie, who feels that he will be coming back soon, because they will try to make him white. The family waves him goodbye as he takes the long bus trip to the University.

Billy has been running his entire life and this was the first time he had ever left the reservation.

In flashbacks, Billy gets a haircut and sees Frank come home from prison and his father telling Billy that he can go anywhere he wants with a positive attitude like he has.

Back to the present, Billy arrives at the Lawrence Campus of the University of Kansas. He is somewhat lost and somewhat clumsy, but finally makes it to his orientation with Coach Easton.

After the pep talk, the running team is taken to the track to run. Billy is called over by Easton after his practice race and wonders why he came in second. Billy said that it was just practice, not a race. Easton says that everything should be treated as a race.

In the locker room after the showers, a fight almost breaks out between Billy and one of his other fellow runners. Billy is still adjusting to being around white people, especially ones that tease him.

Billy goes into his dorm room and is surprised to discover that someone is also there in his room. He introduces himself as Dennis Riley and tries to be friendly with him.

In another flashback, Billy remembers when his father used to box in order to earn easy cash. Billy's father would act weak until Billy made a 5 to 1 bet and then his father would knock out his opponent, giving Billy big winnings.

Afterwards, Billy and his dad take a walk with his dad giving him some advice. Billy's dad then suffers a fatal heart attack and a funeral ceremony is performed complete with authentic Indian music and drumming.

Back to the present, Easton is still driving his runners hard in order to make them the best they can be. Easton sends the runners to the showers but also announces that there is a party the upcoming weekend that everyone should attend.

At the party, Billy is introduced to an insurance salesman who is also the sponsor for Billy's scholarship. He also meets a pretty girl, but keeps getting introduced to people by Coach Easton. He's introduced to Mr. and Mrs. Harris.

The day of the big track meet is at hand and the runners are on the bus to Nebraska. Easton reminds his runners that last year Nebraska won, but this year he wants to win.

The cross country race begins. At first Nebraska and Kansas runners are intermixed, but then Billy pulls way out in front and wins the race. After he wins, one of his fellow runners asks if the win was for his team or his tribe. This prompts a slug from Billy.

Billy sends his sister a letter expressing his loneliness about being the only Indian on campus.

Easton has a frank talk with Billy expressing his pleasure with him and tells him about his experiences with other Indian runners. He asks Billy what he would like to do and Billy says that he wants to compete and win in the Olympics.

Easton reminds him that he still is slowing up near the end, but he needs to stop doing that in order to become a true Olympic hopeful for the 1964 Tokyo Olympics.

Billy and his team begin training harder and harder. Easton posts articles about champion runners in order to encourage his team.

It is rush week and many of the men from the University of Kansas are trying to get into the fraternities. Billy shows up and all is fine until he is reminded that Indians are not allowed in the fraternity. Billy leaves in disgust.

Billy then goes to the sorority to meet up with the girl that he met at the party. She smiles at him, but is quickly told to get inside by the sorority leader for the night. Afterwards a campus policeman harasses him, forcing Billy to show his ID.

Billy has a frank discussion with his roommate and they discover that they have one thing in common that they both lost their parents when they were young.

Billy continues to win races and the girl he admires starts showing up to watch him run. After the race, she invites him for a soda. Her name is Pat.

Billy writes more letters to his sister revealing his declining interest in running, but he says he will renew his spirit thanks to the support from his girlfriend Pat and roommate Dennis.

Billy continues to win awards and gets through four years of college. Reporters ask him what's next, like the Olympics. Easton continues to push Billy, but Billy is beginning to get burnt out. Dennis says that Billy should say something, but he chickens out.

Later, with Pat, she reveals that her parents are having difficulties with Billy because of prejudice. Billy is upset, but Pat requests that she works with him in order to have a united front against their prejudices.

Roger Douglas, the insurance man from earlier offers Billy a job selling insurance, and Billy is interested.

Some of Billy's family comes to the University to visit and to meet Pat. Frank asks Pat if he's coming back home. Billy says that he's saving money up so that Pat and he can find a place to live together.

Eddie is bored and wants to leave the "white man's world." Billy gets upset and sends Eddie off. Frank is ok to stay, but he leaves as well. Billy is more depressed.

Billy keeps running races, but his stamina is not there and he starts losing. Easton chews him out for having a bad race, but eases up on him, but he continues to do poorly, even coming in last place. Easton tells him that he's either a runner or a quitter.

To clear his mind, Billy caddies for Roger. Since Billy is starting to lose races, he threatens rescinding his offer of a job.

Billy goes to meet Pat and asks if she would want to run away with him. He wants to do it to get away from the running, the insurance salesman and to get away from being an Indian. Pat asks for clarification of what he means and Billy drives off.

Easton says that Roger is there, but Billy doesn't want to speak with him. Billy says that he doesn't want to run anymore as well and leaves the locker room.

Billy takes the bus back home to be with his family. He is greeted by a young boy who is happy to meet him. He says he knows him from the papers and hopes that Billy competes in the Olympics.

Billy meets up with Eddie who welcomes him home. Billy calls him a jerk, but gets in his truck anyway. He can't be too mad at him. Eddie and Billy go over to see Frank, who is drunk. Billy and Frank have a heart to heart talk and Frank says that Billy has to go to the Olympics as well.

Billy also meets up with his sister and participates in the Indian tribal dancing and singing going on. Billy misses Pat the entire time he's back at home.

The next day, Billy races Frank who's driving a truck. He admits that it feels good to be running again. Billy's sister reveals that she has been keeping a scrapbook of Billy's accomplishments and she asks if he's going to the Olympics. Billy wonders why everyone is asking him that.

Billy decides to go to Tokyo and he wants to take Frank with him. Pat sends Billy a telegram asking him to come back. Billy goes to visit Frank to pick him up, but Frank is dead, having shot himself. Billy is angry.

After the funeral, Billy joins the Marines in order to cope. The Marines help Billy to train for the Olympics. Eventually, he gets the courage to go back to Pat. Pat is hurt by Billy's running away.

Now a couple again, Billy keeps training and runs at the Olympic trials in Los Angeles. Billy makes it and flies to Tokyo. Ron Clarke of Australia is considered the favorite. No one is predicting that Billy will win. In fact, no American is favored to win.

The gun is fired for the 10,000 meter race. Early on, the contestants are sticking together in a pack. Easton is in Tokyo watching from the wings and Pat is in the stands.

Soon, Billy makes his move and moves up to second place behind Clarke, but then takes the lead. Eventually, Billy falls into second, then third place, but then he pulls back into first with an extra burst of speed.

Clarke once again moves into first place. The various announcers place some side bets on who will win.

Billy once again pulls into first place. At the two lap mark, Billy and Clarke are neck a neck.

On the final lap, Billy puts on the speed, but Billy is pushed into the third lane and falls into fourth place. Billy regains his composure and regains the lead and wins the race.

Easton sheds tears as he is overwhelmed as Billy wins the gold medal in record time. Pat is excited, too, and they both congratulate him.

Billy comes back home to Lawrence, Kansas a hero. Even his enemies congratulate him.

The film ends with the caption: *Billy Mills is now a successful business executive living in Sacramento, California with his wife, Pat, and their three daughters. He devotes much of his time working with Native American youth to help them realize their goals.*

As with *Take Down* (1979), this was not a film made by Disney; it was only distributed by Buena Vista.

Even though virtually all of this film was supposed to take place in Kansas and Nebraska, it actually was completely shot in Alberta, Canada.

The film grossed $3 million.

1984

Michael Eisner took over The Walt Disney Company on September 22, 1984, forever changing Disney as we knew it, some for the better, some not. He replaced Ron Miller as CEO and Raymond Watson as Chairman of the Board. Frank Wells replaced Ron Miller as President. The Disney family's management of the company had already ended in June.

Prior to this, the long legal battle for Disney which included various other resignations, corporate takeover attempts and Disney's purchase of other companies such as Gibson Greeting Cards, ended. The dust had finally settled, but Eisner and company had a lot of work cut out for them.

Also, prior to this, Eisner was instrumental behind the success of *Star Trek III: The Search for Spock* released this year by Paramount.

New specials made for TV include *Disney's All-Star Valentine Party*, *Disney's All-Star Mother's Day Album*, *Walt Disney Presents Sport Goofy Olympic Games Special*, *Walt Disney's Mickey, Donald and Sport Goofy: Getting Wet*, *Donald Duck's 50th Birthday*, *Walt Disney's Mickey, Donald and Sport Goofy: Snowtime*, *Walt Disney's Mickey, Donald and Sport Goofy: Happy Holidays* and *Walt Disney World Very Merry Christmas Parade (1984 Version)*.

New movies produced for The Disney Channel include *Gone Are the Dayes*, *Circus* and *Love Leads the Way: A True Story*. There were also series premieres with *Steve Allen's Music Room* and *Superted*. The cablecast day stretched from 16 to 19 hours to accommodate the new shows.

Tim Burton, who had made the animated *Vincent* in 1982, released a live-action featurette called *Frankenweenie*, which was remade by him as an animated feature in 2012.

Trenchcoat (1983) and *Johnny Tremain* (1957) were released to home video and *Pete's Dragon* (1977), *Pinocchio* (1940) and *The Jungle Book* (1967) were reissued to theaters. Work was almost complete on *The Black Cauldron* (1985) and preliminary work began on *The Great Mouse Detective* (1986).

Wildside was the last attempt by Disney to create a weekly TV series before the Eisner takeover. As with the other weekly TV show attempts of this period, this show was short-lived, only lasting six episodes.

Also, Disney was in charge of designing the Sam the Eagle character for the 1984 Summer Olympics held in Los Angeles, who bore more than a passing resemblance to Sam in America Sings.

The Morocco pavilion opened at Epcot Center after a name change from Equatorial Africa.

Mickey Mouse celebrated his 50th birthday in 1978, so this year Donald Duck followed suit with his 50th birthday celebration with June 9 declared Donald Duck Day.

PSA becomes the new sponsor for Circle-Vision with new films called *All Because Man Wanted to Fly* and *American Journeys,* and the 3-D *Magic Journeys* made its debut at Disneyland.

The Country Bear Christmas Special made its debut at both parks to change up the long-running Country Bear Jamboree, and Mr. Lincoln was reprogrammed to give the audio-animatronic character more lifelike movements.

New non-soundtrack albums released this year included *Paint a Rainbow in Your Heart* based on the popular non-Disney toy character and animated series *Rainbow Bright.* They also released a record reader for *Indiana Jones and the Temple of Doom* which could have been a Disney film.

Flashbeagle was nominated for a Best Recording for Children Grammy, but lost. And, Edna Disney, widow of Roy O. Disney died at the age of 84 on December 19.

In the comic book world, Whitman continued to publish *Donald Duck, Mickey Mouse, Uncle Scrooge, Walt Disney's Comics and Stories, Huey, Dewey and Louie Junior Woodchucks, Super Goof, Chip 'n' Dale, Daisy and Donald* and *Winnie the Pooh,* but all were canceled by mid-year as Western Publishing decided to cease publishing all comic books in 1984. Many Disney titles resumed publication by a new company called Gladstone, but apart from a couple one-shots in 1985, they didn't resume properly until 1986.

A little known, long-running magazine finally ended this year, *Disneyland Vacationland*, also known as simply *Vacationland*. The magazine was a 3x a year AAA and travel agency giveaway that originally started in 1956 shortly after Disneyland opened. It featured articles not just about Disneyland, but the surrounding Los Angeles area attractions such as Knotts Berry Farm.

After *Disney News* premiered in 1965 for Magic Kingdom Club members, articles and covers tended to appear in tandem, but some were unique to either title.

Disney News carried on for another decade, but was eventually renamed *The Disney Magazine* before being canceled in 1996. An updated version now appears on newsstands called *Disney23*.

Alice in Wonderland, Peter Pan, Bambi and *Snow White* all appeared as one-shot comic books.

Splash

A TOUCHSTONE FILM RELEASED by Buena Vista on March 9, 1984. Technicolor. Panaflex. Panavision. Executive Producer: John Thomas Lenox. Producer: Brian Grazer. Director: Ron Howard. Screen Story: Bruce Jay Friedman. Screenplay: Lowell Ganz, Babaloo Mandel, Bruce Jay Friedman based on a story by Brian Grazer. Music: Lee Holdridge. Casting: Bill Shepard. Costume Designer: May Routh. Editors: Daniel P. Hanley, Michael Hill. Production Designer: Jack T. Collis. Director of Photography: Don Peterman. Production Manager: John Thomas Lenos. First Assistant Director: Jan R. Lloyd. Second Assistant Directors: Doug Metzger, Christopher Griffin, Hans Anthony Beimler. Sound Mixer: Richard S. Church, C.A.S. Chief Lighting Technician: Kalani Manning. Property Master: Wilbur L. "Rusty" Russell. Costume Supervisor: Jack Sandeen. Key Costumer: Sandy Berke Jordan. Make-up Supervisor: Robert J. Schiffer, C.M.A.A. Make-up Artist: Bruce Hutchinson. Swimming Choreographer: Mike Nomad. Unit Publicist: Lyla Foggia. Assistant to Mr. Grazer: Sam Crespi. Assistant to Mr. Howard: Louisa Marie. Transportation Coordinator: Gary D. Paulsen. Production Coordinator: Bobby Kronowitz. Script Supervisor: Terry Terrill. Men's Costumer: Charles De Muth. Hair Stylist: Carol Pershing. Art Director: John B. Mansbridge. Set Decorator: Norman Rockett. Special Effects Supervisor: Roland Tantin. Special Mechanical Effects: Hans Metz. Camera Operator: John Connor, S.O.C. Still Photographer: Ron Ratzdorff. Key Grip: Jerry King. Nautical Coordinator: Motion Picture Marine. Location Manager: William T. Schneider. Stunt Coordinator: Fred Waugh. Script Supervisor: Susan Preston. Men's Costumer: Jody Berke. Hair Stylist: Judi Goodman. Set Decorator: Philip Smith. Property Master: Bob Wilson, Sr. Camera Operator: John Fauer, S.O.C. Panaglide Operator: Craig DiBona. Still Photographer: S. Karen Epstein. Key Grip: Louis Cappeto. Chief Lighting Technician: Jon Tower. Production Coordinators: Cleve Kingston, Jane Raab. Location Manager: Harry Grier. Stunt Coordinators: Victor Magnotta, Edgard Mourino. New York Casting: Pat McCorkle. New York Extra Casting: Dan Tyra-Danico Casting. New York Production Services: Theatre Vision International, Inc. Production Su-

pervisors: Ira Marvin, Joseph P. Kane. Underwater Director of Photography: Jordan Klein. Underwater Still Photographer: David Doubilet. Nautical Coordinators: James Steven Claridge, Gavin A McKinney. Location Manager: BJ Johnson. Stunt Coordinator: Hubie Kerns, Inc. Special Visual Effects Supervisor: Mitch Suskin. Mermaid Design and Construction: Robert Short. Sound Supervisor: Bob Hathaway. Supervising Sound Effects Editor: Joseph Parker. Sound Effects Editor: George Fredrick. Supervising Music Editor: Jack Wadsworth. Music Editor: Richard S. Luckey. Additional Orchestrations: Alf Clausen. Music Coordinator: Sidney James. Dialogue Editor: Al Maguire. Assistant Editors: Roger W. Tweten, Carol Ann Jackson. Music Scoring Mixer: Shawn Murphy. Re-recording Mixers: Richard Portman, Nick Alphin, Frank Regula, Tom Gerard. Special Photographic Effects Supervisor: Philip Meador. Title Design: Wayne Fitzgerald, David Oliver. Sequence from *Bonanza* provided by National Telefilm Associates, Inc., Los Angeles, California, through the courtesy of NBC. Statue of Liberty National Monument, National Park Service, United States Department of the Interior. Filmed on location in New York City, Los Angeles, California, Nassau, Bahamas. Stunts: Daniel Aiello, Bill Anagnos, Jophery Brown, John Cade, Al Cerullo, Jr., John De Bello, Len De Virgilio, Tim Gallin, Jery Hewitt, Erik Koniger, Lisa Loving, Michael Mirkin, Erick E. Mourino, Catherine Schultz, Anne Senelly, A.L. Sheppard, Alex Stevens, Mark Sutton, Roy Thomas, Jesse Wayne, Peggy Westmoreland, Tom Wright, Scott Leva, Michael M. Vendrell. Special Makeup Effects Artists: John Naulin, Robert Short. DGA Trainee: Jay Tobias. Props: Dennis J. Parrish. Painter: Richard Shelton. Sound: Allen Hurd. Boom Operator: Linda Murphy. Assistant Camera: Lawrence Grauman. Underwater Camera Operator, Second Unit: Jordan Klein, Jr. First Assistant Camera: Keith Peterman. Second Assistant Camera, New York: Scott Rathner. Dolly Grip: Tim Ryan. Music Arranger, Source Arrangements: Brad Dechter. Musician: George Doering. Drivers: Nick D'Elia, Patrick Hogan. Marketing Consultant: Craig Miller. Running time: 110 minutes. Rated PG.

Songs: "Wooly Bully" Performed by Sam the Sham and the Pharaohs. "Love Came for Me" Performed by Rita Coolidge. Lyric: Will Jennings. Music: Lee Holdridge. "She Works Hard for the Money" Performed by Donna Summer.

Cast: Tom Hanks (Allen Bauer), Daryl Hannah (Madison), Eugene Levy (Walter Kornbluth), John Candy (Freddie Bauer), Dody Goodman (Mrs. Stimler), Shecky Greene (Mr. Buyrite), Richard B. Shull (Doctor Ross), Bobby Di Cicco (Jerry), Howard Morris (Doctor Zidell), Tony Di Benedetto (The Doorman), Patricia Cronin (Michaelson), Charles Walker (Michaelson's Partner), David Knell (Claude), Jeff Douccttc (Junior), Royce D. Applegate (Buckwalter), Tony Longo (Augie), Nora Denney (Ms. Stein), Charles Macaulay (The President),

Ronald F. Hoiseck (Doctor Johannsen), Lou Tiano (Bartender), Joe Grifasi (Manny), Rance Howard (McCullough), Corki Corman-Grazer (Wife), Fred Lerner (Husband), David Lloyd Nelson (Lieutenant Ingram), Al Chesney (Fat Jack), Lowell Ganz (Stan, the Tour Guide), James Ritz (TV Department Manager), Maurice Rice (TV Salesman), Babaloo Mandel (Rudy), Pierre Epstein (Doctor Hess), Cheryl Howard (Girl at Wedding), Louisa Marie (Girl at Wedding), Valerie Wildman (Wedding Guest), Christopher Thomas (Wedding Guest), Richard Dano (Wedding Guest), Clint Howard (Wedding Guest), Ron Kuhlman (Man with Date), Lori Kessler (Girl with Date), Joe Cirillo (Sergeant Munson), Tom Toner (Parilli), Lee Delano (Sergeant Lelandowski), Migdia Varela (Wanda), Jack Denton (Man by Elevator), Nick Cinardo (George), Fil Formicola (Policeman), Than Wyenn (Mr. Ambrose), Clare Peck (TV Reporter), Eileen Saki (Dr. Fujimoto), Jodi Long (Reporter), Victoria Lucas (Reporter), Jeffrey Dreisbach (Reporter), Amy Ingersoll (Reporter), Daryl Edwards (Reporter), Jack Hallett (Reporter), Bill Smitrovich (Ralph Bauer), Nancy Raffa (Mary Bauer), David Kreps (Young Allen), Jason Late (Young Freddie), Shayla MacKarvich (Young Madison), April Adams (Skater), Margaret Benczak (Skater in Ski Sweater), Jill Jacobson (Jill, Girl in Bar), Vincent Jerman-Jerosa (Vinny), Charles Mitchell (National Guard Soldier), Ilana Rapp (Apartment Dweller), Lilian Sasson (Guest at Presidential Banquet), Nick Vallelonga (News Photographer), Emmanuel Lewis (Boy in Toothpaste Commercial).

The story begins in Cape Cod, 20 years ago. "Wooly Bully" is playing as a young Freddie Bauer drops coins to look up women's skirts while riding on a boat cruise. His parents reprimand him. Brother Allen is not interested in Cape Cod, but rather the water. He dives from the boat and happily swims in the water, encountering a mermaid. He is soon rescued and taken back aboard.

20 years later in New York, Allen is working at the docks purchasing fruit. Allen is stuck with a shipment of bad cherries and the man selling it says he made a deal with his brother Freddie. It turns out to be a bad poker debt.

Mr. McCullough wants some cherries, but Allen sells him bananas instead. Freddie announces his first published work in *Penthouse* magazine.

Mrs. Stimler is their ditzy receptionist who can't take a proper message to save her life.

Freddie and Allen have vastly different opinions about how they run their produce company and have an argument about it.

Allen gets a call from Victoria, his girlfriend, who breaks up with him.

Later, Allen and Freddie attend a wedding as ushers. Freddie still drops coins to look up ladies' dresses and Allen stops him. Allen is depressed about being alone and later gets drunk after the wedding.

At the same bar, Freddie works his way with the ladies and offers one to Allen, who isn't interested. Allen says that he's going to go back to Cape Cod. Allen takes a taxi and takes the 300 mile trip.

At Cape Cod, Allen meets up with Dr. Walter Kornbluth, who is an ocean scientist setting up an experiment.

Allen takes a small motorboat run by a man named Fat Jack to an island. The boat conks out in the middle of the ocean and Fat Jack dives overboard to swim back and get the other boat.

Allen cannot swim, so he's stuck in the boat all by himself with nowhere to go. He somehow manages to get the motor running again, but is tossed overboard. The boat hits him in the head and he starts sinking.

Underwater, he is rescued by the same mermaid as before and set on shore. Allen now has a tremendous hangover and headache. The mermaid observes him from afar, but Allen sees her.

Allen starts to talk to her, but she runs off as she has legs on land and a fish tail under water. Allen signals her to come back, but as he cannot swim, he doesn't go after her.

The mermaid rescues Allen's wallet which was lost when he was drowning underwater. The mermaid then encounters Dr. Kornbluth who is scuba diving and she swims off before he can snap a photo.

The mermaid goes back to her home, which is inside a sunken ship. She later comes back onto land fully nude to join a tour group at the Statue of Liberty. This causes quite a stir and the mermaid is captured by police. They try to question her, but she speaks no English.

Allen gets a phone call and rushes off to the police station. They contacted him as he is the only form of ID that she has on her.

Allen shows up and meets up with the mermaid again. She is now wearing a large T-shirt and gives Allen a big kiss when she sees him. Allen takes her home to his place. She keeps kissing him.

Back at home, Allen is so happy, he sings "Zip-a-dee-doo-dah" while he prepares her food. He leaves to go back to work, but decides to make love to her before going back.

Back at work, Allen is very happy and excited. The mermaid stays at home and watches TV, then emerges from Allen's apartment wearing some of Allen's clothes. The doorman asks her where she's going and she says "Bloomingdale's" after watching a commercial.

At Bloomindale's, a sales associate helps her buy the latest fashions. After her purchases, she goes by the TV department and sees more items such as a Crazy Eddie commercial.

Allen gets back home with a bouquet of flowers but rushes out when he can't find her. He asks the doorman and he says that he sent her in a cab to Bloomingdale's.

The mermaid has been in the TV department for six hours. Allen says to the man behind the counter that he's come to take her home and that she doesn't speak any English. By watching all the TV, she now does speak English.

Allen asks the mermaid her name and she says that it's hard to say in English. Allen says to say it anyway and she lets out a piercing shrieking sound that busts all the TV sets' picture tubes.

They walk home and Allen asks her a lot of questions. While she explains things, she gets distracted by many of the sights of New York. Eventually, she says that she's only going to be around for six days.

Allen asks her to take on an English name and she asks for suggestions. While saying examples, they arrive at Madison Avenue and she says that she likes the name Madison.

Later, back at Allen's place, Madison decides to take a bath and fills the tub with water and Morton salt. When her legs touch the water, they turn back into a fish tail.

Allen wakes up concerned and asks if he can come into the bathroom. She says to not bother, but he insists. She turns her tail back into legs just in the nick of time.

Dr. Kornbluth is still at sea doing undersea exploration. His two stupid partners are not of much help to him. One of them is reading a scandal newspaper that has an article about the mysterious naked girl at the Statue of Liberty. Kornbluth gives orders to take the boat back to shore.

Allen and Madison spend more time together and go out for another walk and encounter a mermaid statue. He says that he really likes it. Allen explains the time when he was a child and fell overboard on the boat and thought he saw a mermaid.

The next day, Allen and Freddie get together and play racquetball and discuss Madison and her peculiarities and strange inconsistencies in her stories.

Kornbluth is back on shore being chewed out by a panel of fellow scientists for writing a paper on mermaids.

Madison gives Allen the mermaid statue as a present and they express their love for each other.

Back on the street, Kornbluth sees Allen and Madison walking together and tosses water on her, but he has made a mistake. It was another couple and Kornbluth gets slugged.

At dinner, Allen tells Madison that she doesn't have to leave. He offers her a job and offers to marry her in order to keep her in the country. Dinner is served and is full Maine lobsters which Madison eats with relish, shell and all.

Madison tells Allen no on his proposal for marriage, but refuses to tell him why. They go ice skating, but Allen is visibly upset that Madison has rejected him. Madison doesn't understand why Allen is so angry and runs away.

Eventually, she comes back and decides to accept Allen's offer for marriage.

Kornbluth is sneaking around Allen's apartment pretending to be a custodian, albeit with a huge cast on his arm. This time he sees the couple go up to Allen's apartment and Kornbluth rushes up and turns the fire hose on the elevator, spraying the wrong couple and Kornbluth gets beat up again.

Allen and Madison attend a Presidential gala. Kornbluth is there posing as a busboy with a huge broken arm. He hides a tank of water on his back ready to spray, but he is spotted by the Secret Service and taken away.

Madison wants to tell Allen everything about her and they leave the dinner. They see Kornbluth outside and he sprays her with his hose and Madison falls to the ground and turns back into a mermaid.

Allen is shocked but he cannot get to her as the press photographers and interviewers surround her and carry her away. Allen is taken away as well.

Kornbluth's scientists have Allen under observation and underwater and he screams out again that he's not a fish. Finally, Madison is dropped into the water alongside him.

The scientists conclude that Allen is not a fish and so they drop him off at home, where he is surrounded by reporters and photographers. Freddie comes to his rescue saying that they will only talk to *Penthouse* magazine.

Freddie takes Allen back to work and Allen says that he's upset that she's a mermaid and not a human. Freddie tells him he should be so lucky to have someone like Madison, regardless.

Dr. Ross tells Kornbluth that they are going to go so far as to dissect Madison to see how she tics. Kornbluth thinks that this is going too far and now also sympathizes with Madison, expressing regret for how he treated her.

Allen gets upset and meets up with Kornbluth who is now at the dentist getting his teeth fixed from all of the fights and together they start battling it out. Kornbluth apologizes for his behavior and says that he can take Allen back to Madison, but they must do it in disguise.

Allen and Freddie pose as Swedish scientists. The guard speaks to them in Swedish and Freddie responds with the only Swedish phrase that he knows from Swedish porn that he has a 12-inch penis.

Finally, they get back together. Allen tells Madison that he's still in love with her despite the fact that she's a mermaid.

Allen and Kornbluth kidnap Madison to sneak her out and tell the guard that laser beams came out of the mermaid's eyes and to get help. When he does, the three run out.

Soon, the real Swedish scientists arrive at the Natural History Museum with Dr. Ross and all they encounter is Freddie, sitting atop the tank with a fishing pole.

Allen, Madison and Kornbluth think that they have escaped, but as soon as they feel that they've gotten away, a group of soldiers approach the car that they are in. They are also being pursued by various military trucks and a helicopter.

Kornbluth gets the idea to drop him off and let Allen and Madison escape in order to create a diversion. It doesn't work and he gets run over.

Allen and Madison get to the dock with everyone still in hot pursuit. Madison reveals that she was the mermaid that Allen saw when he was a child and they both remember that he was safe when she was with him underwater.

But Alan cannot go with her because he will have to stay with her underwater forever. At first he declines, but at the last minute he changes his mind and jumps in despite not being able to swim.

Madison rescues him under water and they embrace, but there are scuba divers ready to take them and they do. Madison and Allen pull out their breathing hoses and together they swim away as "Love Came for Me" plays.

This was the very first Touchstone Film and the first Disney film to feature female nudity; male nudity first appeared previously in *Never Cry Wolf* (1983).

This is a very funny and entertaining film and one of the best comedy films ever made, Disney or otherwise. With this film, Ron Howard really proved himself to be a great director, even though he had directed a few films prior to this.

Amazingly, Disney had great success again with this story in about five years with the all-animated *The Little Mermaid* (1989) utilizing some of the same elements from this film. There was also a 1988 made-for-TV sequel called *Splash, Too* that had none of the same cast members from this film.

Howard Morris used to perform with Ron Howard on *The Andy Griffith Show*. Rance Howard is Ron's father and Clint Howard is Ron's brother. Both are usually in Ron Howard films.

On the DVD documentary Ron Howard, producer Brian Grazer and writers Babaloo Mandel and Lowell Ganz discuss the making of *Splash*. It was apparently in turnaround for about seven years which meant that studios were interested in it, but not enough to green light it.

Mandel and Ganz were the writers on Howard's previous film *Night Shift* (1982) and they decided to take them on to rewrite this film.

Another mermaid film starring Warren Beatty and directed by Herbert Ross was being shopped around at the same time called *Mermaid*, which complicated *Splash* being made.

Eugene Levy concurs that every studio turned them down on this movie until Disney came along and took a chance on it.

Mandel and Ganz's impression of Disney at this time was that the studio seemed to be stuck in 1941 and they joked to Ron if he saw *Splash* being a talkie.

Disney asked about *Mermaid* and Grazer and Howard said that they would make this movie cheaper, faster and better.

Howard was concerned that they would cut the movie to get a G rating and make it like all of the other Disney movies that had come before.

Grazer recalls that Michael Eisner had taken over Disney and started the Touchstone label, which is totally untrue. The fact is that Ron Miller created Touchstone and Eisner wasn't even in the picture at Disney until six months after *Splash* was released.

Daryl Hannah recalled that they released it on Touchstone because they didn't want the Disney name to be associated with something as scandalous as her naked bottom (even though Charles Martin Smith's naked bottom appeared in *Never Cry Wolf* (1983) five months before with the Disney name on it).

Tom Hanks recalls more accurately and jokingly said that Ron Miller (who was a USC football player) wanted the company to be called Touchdown Pictures, but was misunderstood.

Howard and Hanks recalls that every A-list actor was offered *Splash*, but turned it down because of the Disney name and it was to be directed by Ronny "Opie" Howard.

Howard said that Hanks was approached to play Freddie at first, the part that ultimately went to John Candy. They wanted Michael Keaton or John Travolta to play the part of Allen.

Hanks was considered after he played a part on *Happy Days* in the years after Howard had left the show but Mandel and Ganz were still affiliated with it. Hanks wasn't doing anything as *Bosom Buddies* had already been canceled, so he said yes to the guest spot. It was a character that wanted vengeance against Fonzie from childhood and wanted to beat him up.

Grazer was amazed at Hanks' confidence during his audition. Hanks said he was confident because Disney at the time looked so run down and tacky, he felt that he had the role in his hands.

In an amazing statement in retrospect, Howard said that no one would go to a Tom Hanks movie, but he decided that it was better to cast the role with a good actor rather than a big name star.

Tom Hanks was cast and then they decided to get John Candy because he was funny. Grazer and Howard also decided to not worry about the fact that Hanks and Candy look nothing alike as brothers. Hanks was thrilled to be working with Candy and Levy as they both came from *SCTV*, one of his favorite TV shows.

Candy in a 1984 interview said that Ron Howard is a rough man to work for and Tom Hanks too. The only one he liked was Daryl Hannah. He made these statements totally straight, but he was really joking.

Hannah reveals that she loved the Hans Christian Andersen fairy tale of *The Little Mermaid* since she was a child and actually practiced swimming like a mermaid by binding her feet together when she was young. Hannah was spotted for the role from *Blade Runner* (1982).

Strangely, there was amazing resistance from the Disney studio to hiring Hannah, so according to Grazer, he hired her when the Disney head went to Switzerland (which was Miller, not Eisner).

Levy recalls that he drove up with Candy and that they were both impressed to be working for Howard, who had been working in the industry since about age 2.

Hanks said that during read-throughs that he tried too hard to be funny. Afterwards, Howard pulled him aside and said that they had Candy and Levy for laughs and what Hanks needed to do was to love the girl. Otherwise, they didn't have a movie.

The scene where Candy speaks Swedish took many takes as he arrived drunk to the set and was somewhat unpredictable causing everyone to laugh and ruin takes.

Hannah recalls her toughest scene was eating the lobster as she has been a vegetarian since age 11. Even though they made part of it fake for her to eat it, it still was difficult for her to do.

They tried to use stunt doubles for Hannah, but Hannah revealed that she was the best at holding her breath, not letting out bubbles and swimming like a mermaid.

There was a scene that was shot but ultimately cut out involving a sea hag, but it was removed because it added an air of mystery to Madison and deemed unnecessary.

The movie itself was a monumental success; something that Disney had not seen in quite some time.

Incidentally, *Mermaid* never got made.

The DVD also included Hanks and Hannah's audition tapes.

Here are some additional observations from the DVD audio commentary:

Splash was so big at the time that Daryl Hannah made the cover of *People Weekly* dressed as a mermaid.

Howard said that he was depressed to discover that Disney was to make this movie and he was terrified that Disney was going to come in and chop his film up. It turned out ok and they let the film go as is.

The flashback prologue was added as, once the film was completed, they realized that the mermaid did not appear until over a half hour into the film.

Ron Howard's dad Rance appears in one of the opening scenes chewing out Tom Hanks.

John Candy was the "star" they signed when they did the movie. The adult John Candy looks up Ron Howard's wife's dress.

Ron Howard's brother Clint makes a cameo as a wedding guest.

The movie was made with a very small crew of only about eight people. The first cut of the movie was about two hours and forty-five minutes.

Lowell Ganz, the writer, appeared as Stan the tour guide.

The fountain in the movie now resides at Walt Disney World.

Jodie Foster, Brooke Shields, Rosanna Arquette, Tatum O'Neal, Michelle Pfeiffer, Julia Louis-Dreyfus, Melanie Griffith, Diane Lane, Kathleen Turner, Debra Winger, Lisa Whelchel, P.J. Soles and Sharon Stone were all considered for the role of Madison.

Chevy Chase, Dudley Moore, Bill Murray were also considered for Allen Bauer. Tom Hanks says that he was the 11th choice.

John Candy hitting himself on the head with the handball wasn't planned and shot in one take. Candy also was suffering from a hangover after hanging out with Jack Nicholson all night.

The ice skating rink was not real, just a constructed set built on location. Babaloo Mandel had a cameo as Rudy the skate man. Brian Grazer had a cameo as a man hailing a taxi, but he couldn't say his line.

There were 66-68 shooting days on this movie and the budget was $10 million and grossed $70 million.

The film was nominated for an Academy Award for Screenplay written directly for the screen. It aired on the anthology show in 1986, 1987 and 1996.

Tiger Town

A THOMPSON STREET PICTURES FILM released by Buena Vista on June 8, 1984, T.V.C. Panaflex. Panavision. Producer: Susan B. Landau. Director: Alan Shapiro. Writer: Alan Shapiro. Additional Material: Bobby Fine. Costumer Designer: Gary Jones. Production Designer: Neil J. Spisak. Music: Eddy L. Manson. Film Editors: Richard A. Harris, John F. Link. Director of Photography: Robert Elswit. Production Associate: Forrest Murray. Production Manager: Joanne Mallas. Second Assistant Directors: Steve Novack, Mary Ellen Woods. Casting: Lynn Kressel / New York, Nancy Kelly / Detroit. Sound Mixer: Alan Byer. Sound Boom: Jeff Jones. First Assistant Camera: Frank Perl. First Assistant Camera: Kim Marks. Camera Assistant: Michael Menlo. Still Photographer: Linda Solomon. Assistant to Director: Evan Dunsky. Assistant to Producer: Janice Yarbrough. Property Master: Michael Foxworthy. Props: Brian Hartley. Location Manager: Corinne Saarahen. Location Scout: Kimberly Conley. Storyboard Artist: Bill Bryan. Script Supervisor: Susan Malerstein. Location Auditor: Marianne Scanlon. Production Office Coordinator: Maria Petrella. Trainee: Elizabeth Wetzel. Technical Advisor: Gates Brown. Stunt Coordinator: Sandra Gimpel. Assistant Editor: Toni Morgan. Apprentice Editor:

Pamela Easley. Post Production Assistant: Mary Ellen Woods. Make-up and Hair: Felice Fassnacht. Casting Assistant: Jane Ann Lowther. Assistant to Costume Designer: Anne Saunders. Costume Assistant: Michaelene Cristini. Sound Editors: Sound Flash, Inc. Supervising Sound Editor: Jim Troutman. Re-recording Mixers: Christopher L. Haire, John L. Anderson, Andy Bass. Music Editor: Ted Roberts. Re-recording Services: Compact Sound Services. Musicians: Eddy Manson, Mel Tax, Abe Most, Tony Terran, Chauncey Welsch, Mundell Lowe, Louis Kabok, Claire Fisher, Victor Feldman.
Gaffer: Robert Hayward. Grips: Gordon Connelly, William T. Strachan, Jr., Jim Troutman, Jack Tobin. Title Design: Dan Curry. Titles and Opticals: Modern Film Effects. Opticals: Exceptional Opticals. Negative Cutter: Larry Mischel. Lab Timer: Angelo Russo. Craft Service: Candice Dana. Production Assistants: Alan Davidson, Michael Jody, Nancy M. Williams, Brian Cheatham, Robert Edwards, Philip Mulliner, Barry Sloan. Teamster Driver: Patrick Mulligan. Still Photographs Supplied by: National Baseball Library, Cooperstown, New York. Made with the cooperation of the American League and its Member Teams. Special Thanks to Annette Handley. Dedicated to The Detroit Tigers, who helped make this film possible. Running time: 76 minutes.

Songs: "On the Sunny Side of the Street" Written by D. Fields, J. McHugh. Performer: Louis Armstrong. "Go Get 'Em Tigers" Composed and Arranged by Artie Fields. Lyrics: Ernie Hartwell. "Take Me Out to the Ball Game" Written by Jack Norworth. Performer: James Boutell. "In the Good Old Summertime" Writer: E. Eianes, Leland Gillette. Performer: James Boutell.

Cast: Roy Scheider (Billy Young), Justin Henry (Alex), Ron McLarty (Buddy), Bethany Carpenter (Mother), Noah Moazezi (Eddie), Mary Wilson (National Anthem Singer), Sparky Anderson (Tigers Manager), Ernie Harwell (Radio Announcer), Al Ackerman (Sportscaster), Ray Lane (Radio Announcer), Lindsay Barr (Peanut Vendor), Dave Bokas (Crusty Man), Chris Bremer (Loud Kid), Katie Delozier (Little Girl), Jack Fish (Stadium Guard), Gerald L. Monford (Lunch Room Kid), Leon Smith (Druggist), Ralph Valatica (Hot Dog Vendor), Whit Vernon (Mr. Cullen), Von Washington (Souvenir Vendor), Larry Williams (Bus Driver), Eric Tuchelske (Baseball Fan).

Detroit Tiger Billy Young is up at bat after the previous batter gets a walk. The announcers discuss that the fans are enthusiastic despite the fact that the Tigers are currently in last place.

Billy Young is the oldest Tiger in his final season with his dreams of playing in the World Series now unrealized. Alex is one of his young fans in the stands cheering him on.

It is strike one. Then, it's strike two. And finally, strike three. Alex and his dad leave the stadium a little bit sadder, but Alex is still hopeful.

There is a montage of great Tiger moments and players of the past as well as non-Tiger players as the credits roll.

Alex is asleep. Many Tigers photos and souvenirs adorn his walls. Alex's mother comes in to wake him up by playing a record of "The Star Spangled Banner" and shouting, "Play ball!"

At school, Alex's friends tease him for liking baseball so much and they tear up his Tigers magazine. Alex's father works at a car manufacturing plant. Father and son meet up after work by the waterline and they walk home.

On the way home they pass by a fancy restaurant and even though dad cannot afford it and the fact that mom was scheduled to make macaroni, he takes Alex to it anyway.

The next day, dad stays home as he doesn't feel too good. He gives Alex some money and asks him to not tell his mother. He reminds Alex that if he believes something with all his heart, he can make it happen.

Later, Alex comes home from school and discovers a lot of people at his home. His dad has died and apparently was worse off that he claimed. Alex's mom comforts him.

Alex is sad and lonely, but still takes the bus to the ball games. He watches the Tigers practice and also witnesses Billy getting teased.

At the next game, Billy comes up to bat again, but continues his losing streak of strike-outs until Alex prays really hard and Billy hits a home run.

The next day, Alex reads the positive reviews in the paper and even some of his fellow students are excited.

At another game, Billy comes up to bat again and Alex prays really hard again and Billy hits a triple. That night, Alex catches Billy on the TV news.

At school, Alex tries to use his prayer power, but the other students wonder why he's acting so weird.

Later, Alex sneaks into the Tigers locker room and slips Billy a note that says, "You're going to do it, Billy. You've just gotta believe," and slips out. Billy reads it later.

At dinner with his mother, Alex plays with his mashed potatoes. His mom is still sad and goes to bed early. Billy's success is what keeps Alex going.

Alex sees Billy practice and actually calls out to him. Alex asks Billy if he still wears his good luck bracelet. Alex says that he doesn't need it. All he needs to do is believe.

At the next game, mom is listening on the radio at home while Alex is at the stadium praying. Billy comes through with another homer and wins the game again for the Tigers.

That night, mom asks Alex how he knew that Billy was going to hit a home run and he explains his powers. Then, he says that the Tigers will win the pennant. His mother doesn't believe him.

Another game and Alex is watching at home using his powers, but this time it doesn't work as Billy strikes and then grounds out.

That night, in an interview with Manager Sparky Anderson, he claims that the Tigers do have a shot at winning the pennant with only 50 more games to play.

Alex realizes that his powers work only at home games and if he actually is in the stands. He cuts out of school early and is caught by the hall monitor, who phones his mother.

His mother is upset with Alex for cutting school and orders him not to go to the game. He goes anyway, but his heart isn't in it and he gets up to walk away as Billy comes up to bat. On the first pitch, Billy gets hit in the head.

Alex comes home and mom is concerned. She had been watching the game and saw Billy get hit and talks with Alex about beliefs. Alex still insists that he has to get out of school early in order for the Tigers to win the games.

In a montage of Tigers hitting and running with "Go Get 'em, Tigers" playing in the background, Billy does a promo and a shaving commercial.

At the end of the season, there is a TV interview with Billy discussing his amazing turnaround during the season.

The entire city is excited and business and schools close early in order to attend the game. Alex is on his way, and gets pulled aside by the street gang that has harassed him before, delaying him from attending and taking his money and ticket.

Bands play and the National Anthem is sung while Alex is still being held against his will and harassed. At one point a teacher walks by. Alex calls out to him and he escapes and runs to the ball park.

Billy gets up to bat and strikes. Alex is still running to the game. He misses a bus and tries to borrow a bike from a girl, who finally lets him have it to get to the game faster. At one point, he almost gets run over.

Back to the game, Billy isn't even fielding very well and missed a very lucrative play in the outfield. Alex tries for another bus, but doesn't have the 50 cent fare, so he grabs onto the back of the bus.

The game continues. Alex finally gets to the game during the ninth inning where the Orioles lead the game 3-1. Once again it is up to Billy to come through.

Alex literally runs under the turnstile, totally ignoring the guard and running full speed to the seats.

Billy swings and misses. Then, Billy swings and connects, but it is a foul ball. Strike two. Billy's good luck bracelet falls off. Alex is still running to the seats and finally arrives.

Once there, he sees Billy swing and connect with the ball, but the ball is in field, so it is possible to throw him out. The fielder misses it, but throws it home. The score is 3-2 as Billy rounds the bases. Then the score is 3-3.

Running for home, Billy slides into home plate and touches it before the catcher can tag him, winning the game and the pennant for the Tigers.

Excitement for everyone ensues. Alex is the last to leave the stadium.

The final Disney movie released under the original regime until Michael Eisner took over on September 22, 1984. There were still a few movies left over in the pipeline from the old regime. This was also the final theatrical movie released bearing the legend Walt Disney Productions as all subsequent films say Walt Disney Pictures. This is due to the fact that the film was originally produced for The Disney Channel and aired on October 9, 1983.

Theatrically, the film was released only in the Detroit area for obvious reasons. It actually plays like a Disney film of yore mainly because it's a little bit far-fetched, a little bit too slick where it should be a little bit grittier, despite the fact that there is a death.

It aired later on the anthology show in 1986 and 1988.

Country

A TOUCHSTONE FILM RELEASED by Buena Vista on September 28, 1984, Technicolor. Panavision. A Far West Productions Pangaea Corporation Production. Producer: William D. Wittliff, Jessica Lange. Director: Richard Pearce. Writer: William D. Wittliff. Music: Charles Gross. Casting: Bill Shepard, C.S.A., Liz Keigley. Editor: Bill Yahraus. Production Designer: Ron Hobbs. Director of Photography: David M. Walsh. Line Producer: William Beaudine, Jr. Stunt Coordinator: Whitey Hughes. Stunts: J. Mark Donaldson, Beth Nufer, Al Jones. Production Manager: William Beaudine, Jr. First Assistant Director: Al Nicholson. Second Assistant Director: Craig A. Beaudine. Additional Photography: Roger Shearman. Sound Supervisor: Bob Hathaway. Production Sound: Jim Webb, C.A.S., Scott Senechal. Camera Operator: Jim Blanford. First Assistant Cameraman: Gary Jay. Lighting Gaffer: Norman Harris. Best Boy: Danny Delgado, Jr. Key Grip: Robert Miller, Sr. Best Boy: John Lubin. Costume Department Supervisor: Jack Sandeen. Costumes: Tommy Welsh, Rita Salazar. Make-up Supervisor: Robert J. Schiffer, C.M.A.A. Make-up: Mark Bussan. Hair Stylist: Toni-Ann Walker. Art Director: John B. Mansbridge. Set Decorator: John Franco, Jr. Property

Master: Bill Dietz. Livestock: Bobby Davenport. Craft Service: Al Freeman. Location Set Construction: Wynands Productions Inc. Special Effects Supervisor: Roland Tantin. Special Effects: D. Mike Paris., Al Broussard. Special Photographic Effects: Philip Meador. Special Visual Effects: Michael Lloyd. Special Photographic Effects Cameraman: Dick Kendall. First Process Engineer: Don Henry. Effects Cinematographer: Peter Anderson. Re-recording Mixers: Richard Portman, Nick Alphin, Frank C. Regula. First Assistant Editor: Stephen Mark. Second Assistant Editor: Marty Stanovich. Supervising Sound Effects Editor: Joseph Parker. Sound Effects Editors: George Fredrick, Wayne Allwine, Dave Horton, Roger Sword, George Probert. A.D.R. Editor: Al Maguire. Additional Second Assistant Director: Regina Gordon. Production Coordinator: Sheila A. Warner. Script Supervisor: Jan Kemper. Unit Publicist: Robert Werden. Still Photographers: Dean Williams, Elliott Marks. Transportation Coordinator: Gary D. Paulsen. Transportation Captain: Chuck Jeglinski. Main Title Design: Paul Pascarella. Catering: Guinea Up Catering. Iowa Casting: Doster, Keigley and Rhodes. Extra Casting: Karen Standard. Music Supervisor: Jay Lawton. Music Editor: Jack Wadsworth. Music Scoring Mixer: Shawn Murphy. Orchestrations: Gary Anderson. Thanks to Rural American Organization, David L. Ostendorf, Daniel Levitas, Iowa Film Commission, Bill Lindstrom. Sound: Allen Hurd. Composer, Additional Music: Gary Anderson. Publicity Writer: David Hakim. Running time: 110 minutes. Rated PG.

Songs: Piano Solos: George Winston. "Crying My Heart Out Over You" Performed by Ricky Skaggs. "I'll Find it Where I Can" Performed by Waylon Jennings.

Cast: Jessica Lange (Jewell Ivy), Sam Shepard (Gil Ivy), Matt Clark (Tom McMullen), Therese Graham (Marlene Ivy), Levi L. Knebel (Carlisle Ivy), Jim Haynie (Arlon Brewer), Sandra Seacat (Louise Brewer), Alex Harvey (Fordyce), Wilford Brimley (Otis), Stephanie-Stacie Poyner (Missy Ivy), Jim Ostercamp (Cowboy), Robert Somers (Grain Elevator Operator), Frank Noel, Jr. (Semi Driver), Reverend Warren Duit (Preacher), Conrad Doan (Auctioneer), James Harrell (Bank Officer), Dean French (Bartender), Betty Smith (Secretary), Vern Porter (Longley), Sandra J. Hughes (Mrs. McAdams),

Rudy Newhoff, Ambrose Knebel, Bernard Larimer, Norbert W. Bruns, Albert B. Schmitt, Norman Bennett, Roy Rechkemmer, Roland F. Miller, Ralph E. Deuhr (Farmers), Curtis Siemens, Donna Manbeck, Edwin Manbeck, Robert Growney, John Jones (Band), Robert Heiple (Farmer at Auction), Raleigh Magee (Farmer at Auction), Will Schmitz, Jr. (Young Boy).

Farmer Jewell Ivy is making hamburgers on white bread. Her daughter Marlene shows her a condom she's found in her brother Carlisle's room.

Jewell is concerned and tells her husband, Gil. Gil is not concerned and says that Carlisle is probably carrying it for show like he did when he was younger.

Marlene practices putting make-up on the baby while her parents are plowing through the fields on a tractor before a storm kicks in. Jewell's father Otis is there to help as well.

Suddenly, Jewell sees a giant twister tornado and screams and hits the dirt. After it passes, Gil gets up to rescue Otis, who was in an overturned truck, but Carlisle is still missing.

Feverishly, they sort through a huge pile of grain and dig him out. Everyone goes home to safety.

The next day, everyone eats breakfast and then heads off to work or school. Otis, Gil and Carlisle sit in the truck and tell funny and slightly dirty stories. Gil gives Carlisle his first chew, but he spits it out the first chance he gets.

Gil gets a grain check, but this time he discovers that he's on an FHA list which means that the money has to be paid on his FHA loan. He is upset about this.

Gil goes to the bank to discuss why he's on the list. The reason that he's on the list is that he didn't get pre-approval when he got the last 100 sacks of feed to feed his sheep.

Gil needs to make amends on all this before he can get any money, which is going to mess things up, since he owes money to people.

After Gil leaves, the two bankers discuss Gil and that he's moments away from being foreclosed on and kicked off his farm.

At the dance that night, Gil discusses the issues with the feed and the FHA with Jewell.

The next day, Jewell tries to find the paperwork about the purchase, but can't seem to find anything. Eventually, she does find something and Gil says that he needs to take that to the FHA.

Carlisle is angry because Marlene has been in his room. He doesn't want to mention the condom so he acts as if he's been mistaken.

Gil tells Jewell that he will tell Carlisle the "Honor" speech, which is "Get on her and stay on her!"

On Sunday, the family goes to church. Later that day, their friend Arlon drives up while the family is trying to watch a football game. He wants to lease part of Gil's land for a couple of months. They think the request is odd, but agree to it.

The next day, Jewell and Gil are back at the FHA to discuss things. The news is bad that he's losing money on his farm and has all the loans and interest to pay on.

They are informed that they are not making a decent living and that the land is not worth as much as it was when they first got the loans.

Gil says that they shouldn't look at things short-term, that things will turn around. Gil demands the money he's owed, but he's told that the money has already been applied to his loans.

That night, Jewell stays up late poring over the books to see if there's anything she can do to change the numbers to make them look better.

Much later that night, Arlon shows up with his sheep and drops them off.

The next day, Gil gets a mysterious phone call that he doesn't want to discuss at the dinner table. Later, he reveals that it was an auctioneer. They are to be foreclosed and liquidated.

The mail arrives and it is more bad news. They have 30 days to pay off every loan they've got. Jewell calls the FHA wanting to discuss things again.

They are advised to get an auctioneer. They would literally have to sell everything including the land to pay everything which is $96,000.

Tensions now run high with the family and everyone starts snapping at each other.

Gil tries to get a new loan to pay off the old loan, but is turned down.

McMullen comes in to take Arlen's sheep without his permission, because Arlen has been hiding them because he had already been foreclosed on by the FHA. Jewell tries to shoo the sheep away, but they FHA gets them anyway.

Arlen and his son drive up and try to stop them, but it is to no avail. The sheep are taken away in a large truck.

The next day, Gil is in a bar and sees McMullin and tries to understand why they are taking everyone's land. McMullen explains that Gil is sitting on great land, but that he's a lousy farmer.

Jewell offers to get a job, but Gil doesn't want her to be a waitress. Jewell says that they have no choice. Gil says that he's spoken with the auctioneer and that's that.

Otis is pissed and he says that he wouldn't have borrowed the money in the first place if he were Gil.

Jewell tells Gil that Arlen is in trouble and for Gil to come along, but he says to go on without him, so she goes herself.

It turns out that they've taken Arlen's farm away. Jewell asks Arlen to come back to the house and talk. Arlen agrees, but instead shoots himself with a rifle.

At the funeral, Arlen's boy and Louise his wife mourn their loss. At FHA, McMullen finally quits as a result of this tragedy.

Gil goes to Carlile and asks him if he wants to be a farmer, and he says no and to hell with him because he's drunk. Gil starts beating him up and they get into a fight.

Jewell sees this and tries to break it up and Gil hits her. She hits him with a big stick and kicks him off the farm, taking Carlile away.

Finally, Jewell confides to the children exactly what has happened and they pray a big prayer at dinner. Later that night as everyone else sleeps, Jewell begins to cry.

The next day, Jewell goes to see the FHA list and wants to see it, but Marvin says that she's not allowed to see it. Finally, he relents and copies the names on the list down by hand.

Jewell then takes it upon herself to contact all of the families on the list and see if she can help work things out between them all.

The family, meanwhile start auctioning off their stuff, but Jewell has asked all the families to show up in unity. A man asks where the money goes at the auction and it is explained that they go to the FHA for repayment of debt.

Once they realize this, most people are no longer interested in bidding but Carlile does bid high and wins a harness that belonged to Otis and gives it back to him.

People bid lowball bids like a nickel and the auctioneer gets frustrated and eventually the townspeople order the FHA to go and start chanting "No sale!"

The auctioneers close up shop and are harassed as they leave. The FHA says that they can legally take their stuff to sell at a proper auction in another county. Jewell says that they can take their things, but they can't take them off their land.

McMullen says that the family can file an appeal and could actually win the lawsuit against the FHA.

Gil finally returns and Jewell says that he needs to apologize to Carlile before he does anything else. Gil says that Carlile did a good thing for Otis and does apologize.

Otis says that everyone has to keep up the good spirits and remain united in their fight.

A postscript: *Feb. 16, 1984 – A Federal Judge in North Dakota ordered the U.S. Government to stop all FMHA farm foreclosures until the farmers of this country receive their rights of due process under the law.*

This movie was released only days after Michael Eisner's ascension, so it definitely was in production during the Ron Miller period, but boy, what a depressing movie.

It has the feel of more serious films that Disney produced earlier, but the major difference is in the lighting and the style. Disney films traditionally had really bright, flat lighting, whereas here the lighting is more muted and modern.

Jessica Lange was nominated for Best Actress.

The film grossed $9.64 million.

1985

With Michael Eisner and Frank Wells firmly in place, the transition of Walt Disney Productions into The Walt Disney Company came swiftly and surely, although the name change didn't take effect until February 6, 1986.

The old Disney organization breathed its last with the release of the disappointing *The Black Cauldron*, which was Ron Miller's final major contribution to the company, although the final remainders of the old guard continued through *My Science Project*. The rest of the movie schedule was filled out by Touchstone Picture releases and the first of the new Walt Disney Pictures banner with *Return to Oz*. Apart from *Cauldron*, none of the newer releases even remotely resembled Disney film releases of yore, and in fact could have been released by any of the major studios. Also, Roy E. Disney returned to the fold and work on *The Great Mouse Detective* (1986) resumed.

Silver Screen Partners II was established in 1985 to help finance the films made at Disney and helped secure larger budgets for their films as a result. The larger budgets did not help initially as Disney sustained a series of box office flops like *Return to Oz*, *The Black Cauldron*, *My Science Project*, *One Magic Christmas* (working titles: *Father Christmas* and *One Night Before Christmas*), *The Journey of Natty Gann* and *Off Beat*(1986).

Not until 1986 did they finally have their first bonfire box office hit with the $91 million grossing *Down and Out in Beverly Hills* (working title: *Jerry Saved from Drowning*), which also turned out to be Disney's first R-rated film.

Ron Miller once said, "The day we make an R picture is the day I'm gone from this company." Miller was long gone by this point.

Fantasia (1940) and *101 Dalmatians* (1961) were reissued this year.

The Muppets Take Manhattan and *Back to the Future* could have been made by Disney.

New specials produced for television include: *Disneyland's 30th Anniversary Celebration* and *Walt Disney World Happy Easter Parade (1985 Version)*.

New movies produced for The Disney Channel include *Black Arrow*, *Lots of Luck*, *The Undergrads*, *The Caldecott Story* and *The Blue Yonder* and series like *Dumbo's Flying Circus*, *Still the Beaver* and *The Dr. Joyce Brothers Program*.

On network TV, Disney finally broke into Saturday morning programming with the animated *Disney's Adventures of the Gummi Bears* and *The Wuzzles* featuring all-new material and primetime with *The Golden Girls*.

Disneyland celebrated its 30th birthday with a 30-hour party similar to 1980's 25-hour party. This would be the last time to my knowledge that Disneyland would be open for such an extended day and I was in attendance.

And (cry), they closed Adventure Through Inner Space to make room for Star Tours, a ride based on *Star Wars* (1977). While I like Star Tours, I wish that they didn't have to sacrifice such a cool ride for it. I always felt they should have closed Mission to Mars instead due to the similarity of subject matter of a space mission that has to be aborted, but oh well...

Comic books were pretty much out of the picture this year, but a new company called Gladstone managed to publish two one-shot reprint books: *Disneyland Birthday Party* and *Uncle Scrooge Goes to Disneyland*.

Yet another biography of Disney came out this year with Leonard Mosley's *Disney's World*, but the accuracy of this work is more suspect as even the author's name is misspelled inside!

Baby... Secret of the Lost Legend

A TOUCHSTONE FILM RELEASED by Buena Vista on March 22, 1985, Technicolor. Executive Producer: Roger Spottiswoode. Producer: Jonathan T. Taplin. Associate Producer: E. Darrell Hallenbeck. Director: B.W.L. Norton. Writers: Clifford and Ellen Green. Music: Jerry Goldsmith. Editors: Howard Smith, David Bretherton, A.C.E. Production Designer: Raymond G. Storey. Director of Photography: John Alcott, B.S.C. Unit Production Manager: E. Darrell Hallenbeck. First Assistant Director: Steve McEveety. Second Assistant Director: Craig A. Beaudine. Production Supervisor: Alex DeGrunwald. Casting: Bill Shepard, C.S.A., Rose Tobias Shaw. United States Crew: Camera Operator: Jamie Anderson. First Assistant Cameraman: Dana Christiaansen. Costume Department Supervisor: Jack Sandeen. Costume Supervisor: Susie S. McEveety. Make-up Supervisor: Robert J. Schiffer, C.M.A.A. Art Director: John B. Mansbridge. Production Illustrator: John Jensen. Set Decorator: Roger Shook. Property Master: Wilbur "Rusty" Russell. Production Coordinator: Chip Fowler. Assistant to the Producer: Anastasia St. Amand. Production Liaison: Michael J. Schilz. Special Effects Supervisor: Roland Tantin. Dinosaur

Technicians: Paul Vigil, Philip Bartko, Willard Livingston, Kenneth Clark, Gary D'Amico, Steve Debs, Jeff Karpe. Dinosaur Body Motion: Paula Crist, Terri Girvin, Richard Aguirre, Jerrol Gower. Miniature Consultant: Paul Houston. Mechanical Effects: David Domeyer, Joe DiGaetano, Hans Metz, Michael Reedy, Richard Hill, John Parker. Special Photographic Effects Supervisor: Philip Meador. Special Effects Cinematography: Peter Anderson. Special Effects Cinematography Assistant: Richard Mosier. Matte Artist: Michael Lloyd. Dinosaur Sculptures: James Kagel. Optical Department Supervisor: William Kilduff. Assistant Editors: Baylis Glascock, Mark Eggenweiler. Orchestrations: Arthur Morton. Music Supervisor:
Jay Lawton. Music Editor: Ken Hall. Music Scoring Mixer: Shawn Murphy. Sound Supervisor: Bob Hathaway. Sound Mixer: Kirk Francis. Re-recording Mixers: Richard Portman, Nick Alphin, Frank C. Regula. Supervising Sound Editor: Joe Parker. Sound Editors: George Fredrick, Dave Horton, Roger Sword, George Probert, Colin Mouat, Don Warner, Jim Isaacs. Foley Artists: Paul Holzborn, Wayne Allwine. A.D.R. Editor: Al Maguire. Script Supervisor: Joanie Blum. Unit Publicist: Howard E. Green. Still Photographer: Graham Attwood. Miss Young's Wardrobe Designer: Bill Kaiserman. Titles: Ed Garbert. United Kingdom Crew: Assistant Director: Augustin Dahouet-Boigny. Second Assistant Director: Steve Harding. Production Consultant: Gladys Pearce. Liaison: Joane Artaud. Liaison and Casting: Paul Wassaba. Costumers: Sally Downing, Paddy Sharkey. Make-up / Hair Stylist: Karen Dawson. Make-up Artists: Maureen Stevenson, Kevin Board. Art Director: Steve Spence. Set Decorator: Julie Graysmark. Property Master: John Graham. Camera Operator: Salvador Gil. First Assistant Camera: Juilio Leiva. Boom Operator: Mike Tucker. Clapper / Loader: Paul Kenward. Camera Engineer: Nobby Godden. Gaffer: Lou Bogue. Best Boy: Glen Parsons. Grip: Jimmy Walters. General Operator: Harry Bisson. Construction Manager: Len Furey. Standby Carpenter: Mick Law. Catering Supervisor: Dominic Clooney. Transportation Coordinator: Stephan Singer. Post-Production Coordinator: Horace Bishop. United Kingdom Crew Second Unit: Director / Cameraman: Egil Woxholt. Assistant Directors: Lee Cleary, Jeannot Banny. First Assistant Cameraman: Ian Smith. Camera Grip: Ray Hall. Best Boy: Tim O'Connell. Continuity: Lyn Norton. Dinosaurs Created and Engineered

by Isidoro Raponi and Roland Tantin. Producers extend their thanks to the Government and the people of the Ivory Coast for their cooperation during the making of this film. Stunts: Coordinator: Dicky Beer. Andy Bradford, Gareth Milne, Graeme Crowther, J. Mark Donaldson, Natasha Bauman, Tracey Eddon, Jim Dowdall, Andy Epper, Melvin Jones, Kirk Elam. Dinosaur Voices: Mark Mangine, George Budd. Sound: Allen Hurd. Mechanical Effects: Bill McCarney. Marketing Consultant: Craig Miller. Running time: 95 minutes. Rated PG.

Cast: William Katt (George Loomis), Sean Young (Susan Matthews-Loomis), Patrick McGoohan (Doctor Eric Kiviat), Julian Fellowes (Nigel Jenkins), Kyalo Mativo (Cephu), Hugh Quarshie (Kenge Obe), Olu Jacobs (Colonel Nsogbu), Eddie Tagoe (Sergeant Gambwe), Edward Hardwicke (Doctor Pierre Dubois), Julian Curry (Etienne), Alexis Meless (Guide), Susie Nottingham (Baki, the Laboratory Assistant), Stephane Krora (Port Captain), Anthony Sarfoh (Village Chief), Jeannot Banny (Killed Solder), Roger Carlton (Old African), Therese Taba (Colleague).

In the Equatorial Rain Forest of West Africa, rumors persist of a huge reptile-like creature. Said to be larger than an adult elephant, the natives call it Mokele – Mobembe. Numerous expeditions have been mounted in its pursuit. So far none has met success.

There is a parade of soldiers and others in their traditional native garb dancing down the street, playing and singing.

Dr. Eric Kiviat, who is on the sidelines, receives some important documents and photos of a dinosaur that's been discovered.

Meanwhile, scientist George Loomis is trying to teach some of the African natives the game of baseball. He gets a phone call from America offering him a job with a newspaper.

His wife, Susan, shows Dr. Kiviat a skull that she's found. Unfortunately, it is a giraffe's skull, not a dinosaur's, dating only about 80 years. Kiviat reminds her to be patient with her digging.

Kiviat keeps his photos secret and tells the others not to tell George and Susan. At dinner, George tells Susan that once they go home, they can start their real life and a family.

Kiviat congratulates George on his new job and requests that Susan speak with Pierre Dubois before they leave. He pulls out a skull that is larger but similar to Susan's.

The night before they are to leave, Susan cannot sleep and takes a helicopter flight for one last attempt to get a dinosaur bone, leaving George a note.

After he wakes up, George tries to charter a plane to follow her. It is difficult, but a flight is finally arranged. The plane is not in the greatest condition, but it gets him there. While flying, George complains about what Susan has done to the pilot.

When George arrives, he asks the natives where Susan is and they point in her direction. He is annoyed that she wrote a note and left, but this is soon forgotten when keeping a man alive where she is becomes a higher priority; a man who has encountered a dinosaur.

George and Susan take another flight to find the dinosaur and Susan is grateful that George is willing to come along.

Meanwhile, Dr. Kiviat is upset that they know where the dinosaur is and also that he is looking in the wrong place for dinosaurs.

Once George and Susan arrive in their destination, the pilot takes a rowboat and rows away from the scene, leaving George and Susan to fend for themselves.

They walk through the jungle but are soon surrounded by a group of natives brandishing spears. They do not speak English. George offers his watch in exchange for leaving them alone, but the natives are not interested.

Susan takes a flash photo, which startles the natives and they raise their spears again. After Susan gives the natives the Polaroid photo, they calm down and realize what a photo is and would like to have many photos taken of their tribe.

Now friends, the natives offer George and Susan food such as a soup made out of ants. George offers one of the natives a granola bar, but he too, is equally unimpressed.

George and Cephu exchange names as well and everyone is relaxed with each other despite the language barrier. George tries to teach Cephu some basic English words as the natives dance around a fire.

George and Susan start feeling a little strange after drinking a little more of the liquid. Susan shows Cephu a drawing of a dinosaur and tries to explain that they are looking for it, when suddenly the entire tribe stops dancing and disappears. George and Susan set up a tent and call it a night after hearing a strange trumpet-like sound.

In the tent, George wants to make love. Susan asks now and George says that the natives can watch if they are still out there. Susan isn't sure if she's in the mood, but soon the dinosaur that they are looking for removes their tent.

Meanwhile, Dr. Kiviat has taken a boat steered by a group of rowdy African soldiers up to the area where George and Susan are.

The next day, George and Susan look for the dinosaur on foot and finally witness him firsthand. Susan asks George for her camera so that she can get photos. Soon, they discover that there is more than one dinosaur.

The dinosaurs see George and Susan, but they gather up a lot of fruit in order to attract the dinosaurs and to get them used to them. As they get friendlier, Susan instructs George to put a transmitter on the baby dinosaur that they've christened Baby.

George tries to do so underwater, but he cannot see very well and George and Baby actually meet up nose to nose and startle each other. Eventually, Baby comes to the surface and Susan starts petting her.

Dr. Kiviat and his crew finally arrive and shoot a tranquilizer gun into the neck of one of the larger dinosaurs, eventually causing it to pass out. This incites the wrath of the other large dinosaur and the soldiers fire live ammunition at the dinosaur as they panic and run away.

The dinosaur turns its attentions to the tranquilized dinosaur and eventually he is shot dead. Kiviat is angry at the soldiers for killing one of the dinosaurs.

George and Susan witness Kiviat and the soldiers, but they hide Baby. George goes out and yells at Kiviat wondering what he's doing and he's slapped down to the group.

The soldiers plan to kill George when Cephu hits the soldier with an arrow. George escapes and Kiviat plans to take the remaining dinosaur back to civilization.

After they leave, Baby goes to investigate the body of his dead father and gets emotional about it. George and Susan come out of hiding and check up on their stuff, some of it damaged.

George and Susan would like Baby to come with them, since he has no one else to rely on and Susan suggests that they race Kiviat back home to beat him to the punch on the discovery.

To capture Baby, they lure her into their tent, but Baby runs off with the tent in tow. After they capture her, George and Susan reassure Baby that everything is alright.

Meanwhile, Kiviat is hauling the mother dinosaur, but the soldiers keep shooting tranquilizers into her, which makes Nigel, Kiviat's assistant angry as they are using too much tranquilizer.

Night falls and George, Susan and Baby try to sleep, but Baby is still sad and hungry and lonely. Baby wants to sleep inside the tent with George and Susan and comes inside.

The next day, the three continue their trek. George climbs trees in order to retrieve fruit for Baby and disturbs a beehive and gets numerous bee stings. Susan covers the bee stings with mud to help soothe the pain and Susan and George start making love with Baby disrupting their fun.

Eventually, Baby wanders off. George and Susan finish making love and go out to look for Baby. Fortunately, Baby has the tracking bracelet and they use the scanner to follow Baby. While following, they spy Kiviat and Nigel preparing to ship the dinosaur mother. She is strapped down to a wooden raft.

The soldiers see George and Susan trying to free the dinosaur mother and start firing their weapons. The soldiers don't kill them this time, but instead hold them captive.

Kiviat goes to talk to the couple in order to suss out the whereabouts of Baby, as he wants to take that dinosaur, too. Nigel is still concerned as the soldiers are still firing tranquilizers.

Kiviat prepares a new tranquilizer, but instead of giving it to the dinosaur, he uses it on the soldier that keeps tranquilizing the dinosaur.

The soldiers get to their helicopter to try to tranquilize Baby from above with George and Susan aboard. As they fire upon Baby, George and Susan kick all of the soldiers out of the helicopter and then jump themselves into the water and swim towards Baby.

George and Susan recapture Baby and the three of them hide in a cave with Kiviat, Nigel and some of the soldiers in pursuit.

George and Susan keep running and encounter a huge amount of bats living in the cave. The soldiers start firing shots, but Kiviat stops them, because they might hit Baby.

George and Susan are up against a waterfall, but instead of surrendering, the two along with Baby decide to ride the waterfall down. They flow with the water, which leads all three of them outside of the cave and away from Kiviat and his men.

Kiviat and his men decide to press on with taking the dinosaur mother away, but he makes an announcement via loudspeaker that he is leaving and for George and Susan to take care.

George and Susan are stuck, but they don't mind as Kiviat has left them alone. They will worry about getting home later. Cephu stops by and leads them to their plane with the same pilot.

Kiviat and Nigel are preparing to leave by their plane when a fire erupts. It turns out that George has set fire to their camp and the soldiers desperately try to put the fire out quickly.

George and Susan still cannot leave because they've lost track of where Baby is again and they don't have their tracking equipment with them, so they will have to wait.

Cephu and some of the natives capture some of the soldiers and Cephu gets ahold of one of the soldier's guns and starts firing on the soldiers.

The natives and the soldiers battle each other, while George and Susan free the dinosaur mother. Kiviat has captured Baby and has him in a cage on his truck.

The dinosaur mother is free and starts destroying Kiviat's camp. George and Susan hop onto a motorcycle to chase after Kiviat. The dinosaur mother chases after him as well, since Baby is aboard.

George and Susan catch up to Kiviat and force him off the road. The car tips over and Kiviat stumbles out of the car. Baby has been thrown and it looks as if she's dead when Kiviat checks on her. He can't check for long as the dinosaur mother bites and kills Kiviat.

George and Susan go to check up on Baby. Baby still appears to be dead, but then comes to when her mother sniffs at her. Mother and daughter are reunited.

George and Susan decide to leave Baby and her mother behind and leave the dinosaurs up to legend.

This was actually a pretty amazing film when it came out in 1985, but it was soon overshadowed and forgotten when Steven Spielberg came out with his *Jurassic Park* masterpiece in 1993.

This film grossed $15 million.

It's nice to see Patrick MacGoohan back in the Disney fold for one more go round. He was seen previously in Disney's *The Three Lives of Thomasina* (1964) and *Dr. Syn, Alias the Scarecrow* a.k.a. *The Scarecrow of Romney Marsh* (1963).

It is one of the first live-action Disney movies to be released on Blu-ray, albeit on the Mill Creek label.

Return To Oz

RELEASED BY BUENA VISTA ON June 21, 1985, Technicolor. Produced in association with Silver Screen Partners II. Producer: Paul Maslansky. Executive Producer: Gary Kurtz. Director: Walter Murch. Screenplay: Walter Murch, Gill Dennis based on the books *The Land of Oz* and *Ozma of Oz* by L. Frank Baum. Director of Photography: David Watkins. Production Designer: Norman Reynolds. Editor: Leslie Hodgson. Music: David Shire. In Charge of Production: Bruce Sharman. Claymation: Will Vinton Productions. Production Manager: Stephen Lanning. Associate Producer: Colin Michael Kitchens. Unit Manager: Phil Kohler. Production Coordinator: Barbara Allen. Assistant Production Coordinator: Moyra Simpson. Location Manager: Grania O'Shannon. Casting: Mike Fenton, C.S.A., Jane Feinberg, C.S.A., Susie Figgis, Marci Liroff. Supervising Art Director: Charles Bishop. Art Director: Fred Hole.

Set Decorator: Michael Ford. Illustrator and Story Board Artist: Mike Ploog. Story Board Artists: Denis Rich, Henry Selick, Harley Jessup. Chief Draughtsman: Reg Bream. Draughtsman: Richard Holland. Modelers: Brian Muir, Derek Howarth, Roy Rodgers. Art Department Models: George Djurkovic. Scenic Artists: Ted Michell, Robert Walker. Production Buyer: David Lusby. Construction Manager: Bill Welch. H.O.D.'s Contruction: Albert Long, Kenneth Clarke, William Beecham, L.F. Lawrence, Michael Driscoll, Peter Collins. Operating Cameraman: Gordon Hayman, John Palmer, Ken Worringham. Camera Assistants: Roger McDonald, David Budd, Shane O'Neill. Camera Grips: Ken Atherfold, Jim Dawes. Gaffers: Maurice Gillett, Roy Larner. Video Coordinator: Christopher Warren. Video Technicians: Robert Bridges, Christopher Kenny. Assistant Directors: Michael Murray, Ray Corbett. Second Assistant Directors: Ian Hickinbotham, Kieron Phipps. Continuity: Sally Jones. Producer's Secretary: Anne Britten. Director's Secretary: Sue Matthews. Executive Producer's Secretary: Glynis Robertson. Unit Nurse: Muriel Murch. Tutors: Mary Jo Macvey, Cathy McMahon. Stunt Arranger: Colin Skeaping. Stunts: Andy Bradford, Tip Tipping, Gareth Milne. Mime Movement Arranger: Pons Maar. Supervising Accountant: Sam Williams. Assistant Accountants: Linda Gregory, Michael Yell. Publicity: Alan Arnold. Publicity Assistant: Rebecca West. Stills Photographer: Barry Peake, Richard Blanshard. Costume Designer: Raymond Hughes. Assistant Costumer Designer: William B. McPhail. Wardrobe Supervisor: Paul Vachon. Wardrobe Assistants: Hilary Watson, Rosemary Worth, Anthony Allen. Make-up Supervisor: Robin Grantham. Make-up Artists: Beryl Lerman, Magdalen Gaffney. Chief Hairdresser: Patricia McDermott. Property Master: Peter Hancock. Property Master (Locations): Philip McDonald. Unit Props: William Coggon, Robert Hill, Bruce Cheesman, Ron Higgins. Dressing Props: Doug Purdie, Alan Adams, Christopher Sheehan. Prop Management: Timothy Ibbetson. Animal Trainer: Mike Culling. Second Editor: Peter Boita. Senior Assistant Editor: Kerry Kohler. Assistant Editor: Daniel Farrell. Sound Editors: Peter Musgrave, G.B.F.E., Michael Hopkins, G.B.F.E., Martin Evans. Assistant Sound Editors: Walter Nelson, Geoff R. Brown, Tony Morris. Music Editor: Stan Witt. Assistant Music Editor: Gordon Greenaway. Production Sound: Robert Allen. Sound Crew: Martin Trevis, Tim Blackham. Re-recording Mixer: Bill Rowe. Assistant Re-recording Mixer: Ray Merrin. Music Recording Mixer: Eric Tomlinson. ADR Recording Mixer: Lionel Strutt. Music Performed by The London Symphony Orchestra. Conductor: Harry Rabinowitz, David Shire. Soloists: Violin: Michael Davis. Cello: Douglas Cummings. Orchestration: Herbert W. Spencer. Second Unit: Director / Cameraman: James Devis, B.S.C. Assistant Director: Peter Waller. Second Assistant Director: Waldo Roeg. Continuity: Doris Martin, Melinda Rees. Mechanical Characters: Characters based on original drawings by John R. Neill with additional drawings by Gary Frutkoff. Creative Design Supervisor: Lyle Conway. Senior Designer: Tim Rose. Designers: Nick Rayburn, Stephen Norrington, John Coppinger, Chris Ostwald, Chris Eveleigh, Richard Padbury. Mechanical Design: John Stephenson, H.W. Hamilton Smith. Fabrid Design: Val Jones, Lesja Liber, Cas Willing. Hair Design: Stuart Artingstall. Textile: Helen Lewis. Patternmaker: Brian Archer. Technicians: Ian Rolph, Hean Scanlan, Colin Hurry, Roger Nichols, Derek Frampton, William Plant. Foam Latex Supervisor: Tom McLaughlin. Supervising Plasterer: Paul Jiggins. General Assistant: David Sainty. Production and Mechanical Effects Unit: Model and Special Effects Supervisor: Ian Wingrove. Senior Effects Technicians: Trevor Neighbour, Brian Morrison, David Watkins, Barry Whitrod. Effects Technicians: Mike Dawson, David Watson, Peter Davey, Ren Gittens, B. Frank Richardson, Brian Lince, Ray Lovell. Model and Process Effects Unit: Director of Model and Process Unit – Visual Effects Consultant: Zoran Perisic. Model Cameraman: John H. Harris. Camera Operator: David Worley. Assistant Cameraman: Richard Craske. Matte Photography Consultant: Stanley Sayer, B.S.C. Optical Effects and Matte Painting Unit: Optical Editorial Supervisor: Peter Krook. Assistant Optical Editor: Nicholas Moore. Optical Effects: Optical Film Effects Ltd. Additional Opticals: General Screen Enterprises Ltd., Rank Film Laboratories, Peerless Camera Co. Ltd., Westbury Design and Optical Ltd., Peter Govey Film Opticals, Oxford Scientific Films Ltd., Carl Willat. Title Designs: Richard Morrison. Matte Artist: Charles Stoneham. Matte Camera: Peter Hammond, B.S.C. Matte Paintings and Additional Opticals: Disney EFX. Supervision: Phillip Meador. Matte Supervision: Michael Lloyd. Matte Artist: Robert Scifo. Effects Animation: Allen Gonzales. Camera Operators: Carl Frith, Robert Hill. Matte Camera Assistant: Tim McHugh. First Process Engineer: Don Henry. Claymation Unit: Claymation Director: Will Vinton. Claymation Producer: David Altschul. Claymation Art Director: Barry Bruce. Claymators: Joan C. Gratz, Tom Gasek, Craig Bartlett, Bruce McKean, Gary McRobert, William Fiesterman, Mark Gustafson, Douglas Aberle, Joanne Radmilovich. Claymation Technical Supervision: Gary McRobert. Special thanks to Robert Watts and George Lucas. Music Recorded at Anvil-Abbey Road Studios, London. ADR by Mayflower Recording Ltd. Produced and Re-recorded at Thorn-EMI Elstree Studios, Hertfordshire, England, produced by Oz Productions Limited. Supporting Puppeteers: Susan Dacre, Geoff Felix, David Greenaway, Swee Lim. Cinematographer: Freddie Francis. Original Executive in Charge of Production: Thomas L. Wilhite. Assistant Directors: Steve Lanning, John Speer. Assistant Art Director: Gavin Bocquet. Painter: Michael Finlay. Supervising Dressing Props: Dave Midson. Sculptor: Brian Muir. Plasterer: Jay Pales. Special Effects Assistant: David Hunter. Optical Camera Operator: Alan Church. Additional Opticals: Peter Govey. Claymation Camera, Motion Control Engineer: Sam Longoria. Electrician: Dean Kennedy. Assistant to Director: Francis Ford Coppola. Marketing Consultant:

Craig Miller. Assistant Accountants: Tony Miller, Stefano Priori. Preliminary Artwork: Maurice Sendak. Running time: 110 minutes. Rated PG.

Cast: Nicol Williamson (Doctor Worley / Nome King), Jean Marsh (Nurse Wilson / Mombi), Piper Laurie (Aunt Em), Matt Clark (Uncle Henry), Fairuza Balk (Dorothy), Michael Sundin and Tim Rose (Tik-Tok), Sean Barrett (Tik-Tok Voice), Mak Wilson (Billina), Denise Bryer (Billina Voice), Brian Henson and Stewart Larange (Jack Pumpkinhead), Brian Henson (Jack Pumpkinhead Voice), Lyle Conway and Steve Norrington (Gump), Lyle Conway (Gump Voice), Justin Case (Scarecrow), John Alexander (Cowardly Lion), Deep Roy (Tin Man), Emma Ridley (Ozma), Sophie Ward (Mombi II), Fiona Victory (Mombi III), Pons Maar (Lead Wheeler / Nome Messenger), John Alexander, Rachel Ashton, Robbie Barnett, Ailsa Berk, Peter Elliot, Roger Ennals, Michael Hine, Mark Hopkins, Colin Skeaping, Ken Stevens, Philip Tan, Robert Thirtle (Wheelers), Bruce Boa (Policeman), Nicola Roche, Cheryl Brown, Alison Lynn, Sarah White (Dorothy's Doubles), Tansy (Toto), Cherie Hawkins (Polychrome), Kevin Hudson (Munchkin), Jon Jacobs (Cage Carrier).

We join young farm girl Dorothy and her small dog Toto lying in bed staring at the sky. Her Aunt Em and Uncle Henry come in concerned as she is still up past 1:30 in the morning. Henry is reading a newspaper ad about shock therapy to help Dorothy sleep, since she hasn't for the past six months and only talks about Oz. Meanwhile, Dorothy sees a shooting star.

The next day, Dorothy tries to see if Belina the hen is laying eggs again. Outside, she discovers a key that has "OZ" on the handle. She shows it to Em, who reminds her that this is just part of her imagination.

Dorothy says that her Oz friends are in trouble. Em says that they are in trouble as winter is coming along. To get Dorothy's mind off things, Em takes her for a ride. Toto follows behind even though he is supposed to stay home.

Em and Dorothy arrive at a doctor's office and Dorothy talks about Oz and shows him the key she has found. The doctor asks how she got back home and Dorothy says she came back with the ruby slippers.

The doctor asks where the ruby slippers are now and Dorothy says that she lost them on the way back home.

The doctor reveals his electro-shock therapy device in order to help Dorothy sleep and to forget about Oz. While he is talking about this, Dorothy sees a reflection of Ozma, an Oz princess in the mirror.

Em leaves Dorothy at the doctor's office and says that she will be back the next day and to do everything the doctor and the head nurse says.

Dorothy is led by the head nurse down a narrow corridor and is left alone in a waiting room. She looks out a window to see Em riding away, when Ozma appears and gives Dorothy a pumpkin.

Ozma asks Dorothy why she's there and Dorothy explains, then Ozma zips off. Dorothy begins to carve the pumpkin.

Hours later, the head nurse who's called Miss Wilson arrives and takes her by a gurney to the operating room. She is strapped down.

In the operating room, the doctor turns on his electro-shock machine and Miss Wilson puts on a head set like device onto Dorothy's ears and head.

Just as the doctor flips the switch, a thunderclap causes a power outage. In the background, many screams are heard.

The doctor and nurse leave the room to check on everything and to get the power back on.

While they are away, Ozma returns and helps Dorothy off the operating table and removes the head set. Together, they run away, but are discovered by Miss Wilson.

They leave the doctor's office and run through the forest during a dark and rainy night with Miss Wilson in pursuit.

Ozma and Dorothy end up in a nearby river and Miss Wilson falls in, but Dorothy and Ozma are swept away by the rushing waves.

Dorothy grabs onto a wooden cage and floats to calmer waters, but Ozma is nowhere to be seen and Miss Wilson makes it back to shore and watches Dorothy get away.

The waters calm and recede. Dorothy starts having a conversation with Billina, her chicken, who now has the power to speak. Dorothy reasons that if they were in Oz, Billina's speech wouldn't be strange at all.

Dorothy says that if that they are in Oz, they would be in the deadly desert, but if they touch the sand, they will turn into dust themselves. Dorothy skips stones to a grassy area while holding Billina and they are safe.

Dorothy picks some strange looking fruits as food for now and for later. The fruit contains sandwiches inside and she and Billina eat as the rocks spy on them, knowing that it is Dorothy that has returned.

Dorothy and Billina come across her old house; the one that survived the cyclone the first time she came to Oz. Dorothy wonders where all the munchkins have gone.

Dorothy then discovers that the yellow brick road has been uprooted and is in a shambles. She decides to follow it to see what has happened to the Emerald City.

When she gets there, Emerald City is still standing, but basically is destroyed. The citizens have been turned into stone. A piece of graffiti warns them to "Beware the Wheelers."

Looking further, she discovers the Tin Woodsman and the Cowardly Lion in stone. Soon, Dorothy and Billina encounter the Wheelers, men who have wheels in place of hands or feet.

Dorothy pulls out her key which unlocks a wall and they escape the Wheelers temporarily. The Wheelers say that the Nome king doesn't allow chickens in Oz, but doesn't explain who the Nome king is. Then they leave.

After the Wheelers leave, Dorothy discovers another metal man, this one made out of copper; a wind-up man named Tik Tok. Dorothy winds his keys and Tik Tok explains that he is a one-man army of Oz and he will not turn to stone because he is not alive.

Tik Tok opens the door and looks out for Wheelers before they all leave. They don't get very far before they encounter Wheelers again, but Tik Tok takes care of them.

A Wheeler says that the Nome king conquered the Emerald City and turned everyone into stone. He also mentions a witch named Mombi. Then they let him go after the Wheeler takes them to Mombi's house.

Dorothy, Tik Tok and Billina meet a lady playing a mandolin and ask if she's Mombi. The lady takes Dorothy by the hand and leaves the others behind. Dorothy asks where the Scarecrow is.

The lady removes her head and replaces it with a different one, shocking Dorothy in the process. She then wants to have Dorothy's head, but Tik Tok and Billina come to the rescue to stop her.

Unfortunately, Tik Tok's action runs down and the lady takes Dorothy away and locks her up with Billina. Dorothy peers out the window and sees the Nome king's mountain. Then, she discovers a painting of the Tin Man and the Scarecrow.

In the corner, a pumpkin man named Jack Pumpkinhead comes alive to talk to Dorothy. He is in a few pieces, but is not rotting after asking Dorothy to check and to help put Jack back together.

Jack explains that the woman is Mombi and that she hasn't used her real head in years and also that she has forgotten about him. Jack and Dorothy sneak out to leave and help wind Tik Tok back up.

Tik Tok, Jack and Billina go upstairs and take a Gump stuffed animal head off the wall, while Dorothy sneaks into Mombi's room and takes a key that's tied to her hand. She has to sneak through the room that stores all of Mombi's heads in order to get to the powder of life.

Mombi wakes up, but as she has no head currently attached, is not able to chase Dorothy very well. Dorothy gets back to Jack, Tik Tok and Billina, but Tik Tok's brains have run down so he isn't very effective until Dorothy winds it up again. Then, Dorothy pours the powder of life on the Gump's head and he comes to life and speaks.

With the power, the Gump is able to make their makeshift palm leaves fly as well as the sofa they are sitting on and everyone flies out of Mombi's castle. Mombi finally gets a head on and directs the Wheelers to go after Dorothy.

Dorothy and everyone keep flying in the night sky, while Dorothy and Billina fall asleep as they are exhausted. They don't really care where they go at this point, just as long as they get some rest.

Mombi tells Ozma who appears in Mombi's mirror that no one will be able to rescue her as no one knows that she is trapped and in trouble.

The Wheelers continue their pursuit until they come upon the deadly desert. The desert stops the Wheelers as well, while Dorothy and everyone else fly over the desert. This is not the safest place for them to be as they could land in the desert and turn to stone.

Jack loses his head at this point and Dorothy asks the Gump to retrieve it. They do, but then the entire apparatus they are flying on falls apart and they all fall, but land on a high snowy cliff instead of in the deadly desert.

They put the Gump's sofa back together, when they encounter the Nome King. Dorothy asks for the Nome King to give everything back like the Scarecrow and to turn the Tin Man and Cowardly Lion and everyone else back to the way they were and not stone.

The Nome King refuses her request and starts laughing. He shows Dorothy the inside of the rocks and the precious emeralds contained therein and says that if everyone else stops stealing from him, he'll stop stealing from everyone else.

Dorothy also re-encounters the Scarecrow at this point, but is now trapped inside the rock with him. The Scarecrow is trapped for stealing emeralds. Dorothy starts to cry and tells the Nome King that the Scarecrow had nothing to do with the emeralds. They were already there when he became king.

The Nome King puts Dorothy and everyone up to a test. If the correct door is touched, the Scarecrow will be released and everyone will be freed. If not, Dorothy and everyone else will become the Nome King's prisoners.

The Gump goes first and while he's away, the rest of them partake in some refreshments provided by the Nome King, but they are basically inedible for non-rock creatures.

The Gump has failed and turns into a permanent part of the Nome King's collection as an ornament. Jack goes next, but he's not afraid, since he's not alive.

Meanwhile, Mombi is feverishly trying to catch up to Dorothy. Jack fails and Tik Tok goes next. He asks Dorothy to wind him up tight before he tries. He feels that he will guess correctly.

While Tik Tok tries, the Nome King asks as to why Dorothy came back to Oz. It wouldn't be for the Scarecrow would it, but rather for the ruby slippers and he reveals that he is wearing them.

Tik Tok fails and now it is up to Dorothy to guess. Before she tries, the Nome King offers to send Dorothy home with the ruby slippers where she will never return to Oz and also forget about it ever existing.

Dorothy decides to not take this exchange and goes into the room to find the correct object to touch. She calls out for Tik Tok, but he does not answer. He has pretended to run down in order to bring in Dorothy and together they can work as a team to find the correct object.

Tik Tok concentrates and touches a silver cup, but it too, is not correct. Dorothy is all alone, as Mombi shows up with the Wheelers at the Nome King's door. Mombi goes in and the Nome King requires her to bow before him.

Dorothy goes through two incorrect guesses and only has one guess left. Dorothy spins around and with closed eyes uses her intuition to guide herself to the correct item, which turns out to be a green emerald. She says "Oz" and the emerald turns into the Scarecrow.

The Nome King tells Mombi that after Dorothy is turned into an ornament, no one will be left who will remember Oz and he will be turned into a human, but the plan backfires.

Dorothy and the Scarecrow embrace. She says that people from Oz must have turned into green ornaments, so they search the room for other green items. Dorothy says "Oz" while touching another green item and it turns into the Gump.

Suddenly an earthquake happens, sending debris and rubble to topple onto them. The earthquake was created by the Nome King who does not allow Dorothy to get the rest of her friends, despite her protests. They do find another green object and get Jack back, at least, but Billina and Tik Tok are still missing.

The Nome King picks up the sofa and eats it and then tries to pick up Jack and eat him. The Scarecrow carries the Gump's head as they all try to escape. The Nome King sends his Nome statues to help capture them.

The Nome King picks up Jack to eat him, but an egg falls into his mouth from Jack's head as Billina was still inside of Jack's head all this time and laid the egg.

The egg turns out to be poison for the Nome King and he sets down Jack as the Nome King starts to decay and disappear, leaving only the ruby slippers which Dorothy takes and puts on.

Dorothy wishes with the slippers that everyone from Oz and the Emerald City be restored to the way they were and Mombi be captured. She gets her wish and everyone is back to the way it was except the whereabouts of Tik Tok. Fortunately, the Gump had a green item hidden in his antlers and when Dorothy touches it and says "Oz," Tik Tok reappears back to normal.

In Emerald City, a parade is held featuring the Cowardly Lion, the Tin Man, Dorothy, Billina, Jack, the Gump a shined and polished Tik Tok, some Munchkins and Mombi in a cage.

Everyone wants Dorothy to become the Queen of Oz, but she has to go back home. Dorothy wishes that she could be in both places at the same time and Ozma appears in a mirror. Ozma asks Dorothy to help her step through the glass.

Jack, who has been calling Dorothy "Mom" the entire time, realizes that Ozma is her true mom. Mombi was the one who put Ozma into the mirror. Ozma forgives Mombi, becomes Queen of Oz and tells Dorothy that she can come back to Oz anytime she wishes.

Billina decides to stay behind in Oz as Dorothy says goodbye to everyone and goes back home.

Back at home, Dorothy reappears lying by the river with Toto by her side. Uncle Henry shows up next and is happy to see her along with Aunt Em. Henry carries her home.

It is explained that the clinic burnt to the ground after the lightning storm and the doctor perished trying to save his equipment.

Just then a paddy wagon goes by with Nurse Wilson inside.

Back at home, Dorothy summons Ozma and she appears in her mirror. Dorothy calls Aunt Em to look, but Ozma quiets her. Dorothy says to never mind, it was just her reflection. Dorothy then goes outside to play with Toto.

The film should have been a delightful sequel to the classic 1939 feature film *The Wizard of Oz*. Instead, it was a dark, scary and disturbing sequel that should mostly be avoided. I mean, really, electro-shock therapy on Dorothy in the first 10 minutes of the film?

The only saving grace is certain characters like Tik Tok, and the film is pretty faithful to the second and third Oz books, but again Dorothy getting electro-shock therapy has got to be one of the lowlights of Disney cinematic history, and that part should have been removed.

This film had a budget of $28 million of which it grossed only $11 million. Apparently, many felt that this was too scaring and disturbing in comparison to the relatively sweet 1939 film.

This was the first Disney film to bear the new "Walt Disney Pictures" tag onscreen.

Actress Fairuza Balk explains on the DVD interview that she went to a cattle call in Vancouver, then cut it down to 12 girls in LA, did more screen tests, got down to two girls and then one.

It was a long shoot of about eight or nine months and Fairuza was tired of it by the end.

She is a fan of the Oz books.

There was Claymation and animatronics done for the film at the time. Fairuza said that it wasn't really a scary experience for her, but more fun.

The film was nominated for an Academy Award for Visual Effects. Disney did win an Oscar this year for Scientific or Technical for the development of and animation photo transfer process. It wasn't specifically attached to any one film, but I'm sure it was a process used for this film.

Walter Murch was a special director to Fairuza and she's still in contact with him to this day. She felt like an equal and not like a kid.

She felt Nicol Williamson is a great actor and loves him in *Excalibur* and that Piper Laurie and Jean Marsh were great, too.

The man inside of Tik Tok was completely upside down to do the role. Jack Pumpkinhead was an incredibly complicated figure when shown in full shot. It was very intricate puppetry.

The very last scene of the movie was about 130 degrees and everyone was sweating because there was this huge crowd and Fairuza fainted at one point.

The man in the lion suit was boiling.

The premiere was a big deal and she flew around the world to Japan and other places.

The film has its fans. Fairuza says that she's pretty anonymous nowadays, but does get noticed from time to time. She has been in other films as an adult.

She loves the music and the effects of the film.

Production began on this film as far back as 1980, but the main filming was in February 1984.

Actors Leo McKern and Christopher Lloyd were both considered for the role of the Nome King. Emma Ridley, who played Ozma, was also considered for Dorothy.

No fees had to be paid for the use of the Oz stories as they had fallen into the public domain by this time, even though Disney had had the rights to the stories for quite some time. Disney did have to pay a fee to MGM for the use of the ruby slippers as the ruby slippers were an invention of theirs created for the 1939 film. In the Oz books, Dorothy's slippers were silver.

The Black Cauldron

RELEASED BY BUENA VISTA ON July 24, 1985, Technicolor. Produced in Association with Silver Screen Partners II. Executive Producer: Ron Miller. Producer: Joe Hale. Director: Ted Berman, Richard Rich. Story: David Jonas, Vance Gerry, Ted Berman, Richard Rich, Al Wilson, Roy Morita, Peter Young, Art Stevens, Joe Hale based on the Chronicles of Prydain series by Lloyd Alexander. Music: Elmer Bernstein. Additional Dialogue: Rosemary Anne Sisson, Roy Edward Disney. Animators: Andreas Deja, Hendel Butoy, Dale Baer, Ron Husband, Jay Jackson, Barry Temple, Phil Nibbelink, Steven Gordon,

Doug Krohn, Shawn Keller, Mike Gabriel, Phillip Young, Tom Ferriter, Jesse Cosio, Ruben Procopio, Viki Anderson, David Block, Charlie Downs, Sandra Borgmeyer, Ruben Aquino, Cyndee Whitney, George Scribner, Mark Henn, Terry Harrison, David Pacheco. Key Coordinating Animator: Walt Stanchfield. Effects Animators: Don Paul, Mark Dindal, Jeff Howard, Patricia Peraza, Scott Santoro, Glenn Chaika, Barry Cook, Ted Kierscey, Kelvin Yasuda, Bruce Woodside, Kimberly Knowlton, Allen Gonzales. Layout Styling: Mike Hodgson. Layout: Don Griffith, Guy Vasilovich, Dan Hansen, Glenn Vilppu, William Frake III. Color Styling: James Coleman. Background: Donald Towns, Brian Sebern,  Tia Kratter, John Emerson, Lisa Keene, Andrew Phillipson. Character Design: Andreas Deja, Mike Ploog, Phil Nibbelink, Al Wilson, David Jonas. Key Cleanup Artists: Retta Davidson, Dave Suding, Chuck Williams, M. Flores Nichols, Martin Korth, Tom Ferriter, Fujiko Miller, Isis Thomson, Lureline Weatherly, Wesley Chun. Executive in Charge of Production: Edward Hansen. Production Manager: Don Hahn. Assistant Directors: Mark Hester, Terry Noss, Randy Paton. Picture and Sound Effects Editors: James Melton, Jim Koford, Armetta Jackson. Sound Effects Designer: Mike McDonough. Sound Effects: Paul Holzborn, Wayne Allwine. Re-Recording Mixers: Richard Portman, Nick Alphin, Frank C. Regula. Music Scoring Mixer: Shawn Murphy. Re-Recorded at International Recording. Sound Supervisor: Bob Hathaway. Orchestrations: Peter Bernstein. Music Editor: Kathy Durning. Music Supervisor: Jay Lawton. Supervising Music Editor: Jack Wadsworth. Music Preparation: Norman Corey. Music Contractor: Regnal Hall. Special Photographic Effects: Philip Meador, Ron Osenbaugh, Bill Kilduff. Additional Animation: Kathy Zielinski, Jill Colbert, Kevin Wurzer, Sylvia Mattinson, Sue Dicicco, Richard Hoppe, Dave Brain, Maurice Hunt. Additional Story Contributions: Tony Marino, Mel Shaw, John Musker, Steve Hulett, Burny Mattinson, Ron Clements, Doug Lefler. Animation Consultant: Eric Larson. Assistant Layout: David Dunnet, Greg Martin, Karen Keller, Kurt Anderson, Carol Holman Grosvenor, Frank Frezzo. Assistant (in Alphabetical Order): Tony Anselmo, Dorthea Baker, Bil Berg, Reed Cardwell, Jesus Cortes, June Fujimoto, Ray Harris, Mauro Marcssa, Jim Mitchell, Gilda Palinginis, David Pruiksma, Toby Shelton, Russ Stoll, Jane Baer, Philo Barnhart, Ben Burgess, Brian Clift, Rick Farmiloe, Terrey Hamada, Jeffery Lynch, Michael McKinney, Brett Newton, Phil Phillipson, Natasha Selfridge, David Stephan, George Sukara, Larry White. Assistant Effects Animators: Gail Finkeldei, Joe Lanzisero, Steve Starr, Tom Hush, Rolando Mercado, John Tucker. Breakdown Artists: Sue Adnopoz, Barbara DeRosa, Edward Goral, Christine Liffers, Kaaren Spooner, Peggy Tonkonogy, Anthony DeRosa, Denise Ford, Tina Grusd, Elyse Pastel, Louis Tate, Jane Tucker, Maria Ramocki-Rosetti, Stephan Zupkas. Effects Breakdown Artists: Ed Coffey, Peter Gullerud, Christine Harding. Animation Camera: Jim Pickel, John Aardal, Frank Tompkins, James Catania, Kieran Mulgrew, Jere Kepenek, Steve Hale, Rick Taylor, Ed Austin, Errol Aubry, Brandy Whittington, Paul Wainess, Roy Harris, Niel Viker, Brian Holecheck, Dan Bunn. Inbetween Artists: Kelly Asbury, Michael Horowitz, Eileen Lambert, Stephen Hickner, Mona Hosbjor, Robert Minkoff, Alex Topete. Effects Inbetween Artists: Vicki Banks, Dave Bossert, Esther Barr, Gary Trousdale. Blue Sketch Artists: Roxy Novotny Steven, Cathy Zar. Ink and Paint Manager: Becky Fallberg. Animation Check: Janet Bruce, Lisa Poitevint, Karen Paat, Jill Stirdivant, Mavis Shafer. Color Model Artists: Sylvia Roemer, Debbie Jorgensborg, Brigitte Strother, Ann Paeff. Xerox / Animation Photo Transfer: Bill Brazner, Dede Faber, Raffi Koumashian, Carmen Sanderson, Jean Pierre Gagnon, Robyn Roberts, Bert Wilson. Effects Photo Transfer: Bernie Gagliano. Key Xerox Checkers: Margaret Trindale, Cherie Miller, Darlene Kanagy, Tatsuko Deramirez, Maria Fenyvesi. Painting: Gretchen Albrecht, Penny Campsie, Ginni Mack, Karen Comella. Final Check: Hortensia Casagran, Wilma Baker, Robin Police. Paint Lab: Dodie Roberts, Betty Stark, Ray Owens. Scene Planning: Dave Thomson, Brian Legrady, Don Bourland, Bob Mills, Rick Sullivan. Title Graphics: Ed Garbert. End Title Design: David Jonas. Publicist: Howard E. Green. Production Secretaries: Lorraine Davis, Charles Rogers. Administrative Supervisor: Joanne Phillips. Administrative Office Staff: Phyllis Losie, Susan Vessiny. Production Coordinators: Joseph Morris, Dennis Edwards, Ronald Rocha. Still Camera: Dave Spencer. Art Props: Dale Alexander. Conceptual Artist: Tim Burton. Storyboard Artist: Peter Young. Sound: Allen Hurd. CGI Animator: Lem Davis. Motion Control Photography: Richard Mosier. Cel Painter, Xerox Checker: Daryl Carstensen. Assistant Animator: Michael Giaimo. Character Designer: Milt Kahl. Painter: Madlyn O'Neill. Assistant Animator: Lenord Robinson. Musician: Cynthia Millar. Marketing Consultant: Craig Miller. Running time: 80 minutes. Rated PG.

Cast: Grant Bardsley (Taran), Susan Sheridan (Eilonwy), Freddie Jones (Dallben), Nigel Hawthorne (Fflewddur Fflam), Arthur Malet (King Eidilleg), John Byner (Girgi / Doli), Lindsay Rich, Brandon Call, Gregory Levinson (Fairfolk), Eda Reiss Merin (Orddu), Adele Malis-Morey (Orwen), Billie

Hayes (Orgoch), Phil Fondacaro (Creeper), Pete Renaday, James Almanzar, Wayne Allwine, Phil Fondacaro, Steve Hale, Phil Nibbelink, Jack Laing (Henchmen), John Hurt (The Horned King), John Huston (Narrator).

The narration explains the story of an evil king that was thrown into a black cauldron. The cauldron was hidden while evil men were out searching for it in order to get the cauldron's evil powers.

Elderly Dallben is discussing what's going on while his young apprentice named Taran is daydreaming looking out the window. Dallben reminds him that the horned king could get back into power and that's why he has to continue to do his chores.

Taran believes that Dallben doesn't understand. Taran would rather be doing heroic deeds and be a famous warrior than doing what he's doing.

Taran practices his sword fighting skills against the various barnyard animals including geese, a goat and a pig, when he's discovered goofing off by Dallben.

Dallben tells Taran to wash the pig, Hen Wen, but Taran's having difficulties. Dallben tells Taran to bring the pig inside because it possesses magic powers when it puts its snout inside of a small pool of water.

Images show up in the water of the horned king and the black cauldron. The images show that if the Horned King finds the black cauldron, he will be all powerful.

Taran goes off with Hen Wen, but Dallben is worried for him because of these new revelations.

The Horned King is excited to discover that he is close to finding the black cauldron.

Taran talks with the mute Hen Wen and says that he's impressed with Hen Wen's powers. Taran starts daydreaming again of being a powerful knight. His daydreaming gets himself into trouble again as Hen Wen has gone missing.

While searching for Hen Wen, Taran is pounced upon by a small scavenging creature named Gurgi, who takes Taran's apple. After Taran gets the apple back, he asks Gurgi if he's seen Hen Wen. Gurgi says no.

Taran eventually sees Hen Wen being pursued by a giant flying dragon. Hen Wen outruns the dragon for a time, but eventually the dragon captures the pig.

Taran vows to go to the castle to get Hen Wen back, but Gurgi advises him not to go and doesn't want to go himself.

Taran does go to the castle and sneaks inside. At first, he is greeted by a snarling, barking dog of a sleeping guardsman.

Deeper inside the castle, there are many men and creatures eating and drinking and flirting with a dancing girl. The festivities are short-lived when the Horned King makes his appearance.

A prisoner is brought out and it turns out to be Hen Wen. A small troll creature tries to force Hen Wen to show off the visions of where the black cauldron is.

Hen Wen escapes her chains and rushes back to Taran's arms. The Horned King wants to see the visions, but Taran says no. In that case, the Horned King says that he has no further use for the pig and orders his head to be chopped off.

Taran rescues Hen Wen and decides to cooperate with the Horned King. Hen Wen sticks her nose in the water and the visions start, but nothing is revealed before Taran grabs the pig and runs off.

Taran and Hen Wen climb up to a high tower and Taran throws Hen Wen into the moat below, but Taran is captured and thrown into the dungeon.

In the dungeon, Taran relives the events of the day and is upset that he is now imprisoned. A lady named Princess Eilonwy comes out of the dungeon floor accompanied by a floating light source called Bobble.

Eilonwy invites Taran to accompany her into the area below the dungeon, where many rats live. She takes him to an abandoned area covered with cobwebs that houses a sword.

Eilonwy asks where Taran got a sword when they spy a minstrel named Fflewddur being arrested and thrown in the dungeon. They rescue him and then Taran plays with his sword.

Taran and Eilonwy run up the stairs and he uses his sword which turns out to have magical powers which allow them to escape much easier.

The three are surrounded, but Taran is still able to defeat the pursuers as the sword is more powerful and the three escape by the skin of their teeth.

The troll goes to the Horned King and decides to tell him what happened, proactively, but the king doesn't want to hear that Taran and the other two have escaped and that Hen Wen is also still missing.

The Horned King spares him, but tells him to get them all back.

Hiding out in the forest, Fflewddur starts singing about their adventures with Taran and Eilonwy. Taran says that he saved everyone, but Eilonwy says that it's only the sword that did everything.

Later, Eilonwy apologizes for her sarcasm and they decide to join forces to find Hen Wen. Meanwhile, Fflewddur is being harassed by Gurgi, who is trying to take his hat and harp.

Taran introduces Gurgi as a coward and a thief, but Gurgi says that he's seen Hen Wen's tracks. Taran doesn't believe him, but they all decide to follow Gurgi anyway.

It turns out that Gurgi is telling the truth, but as they try to follow the tracks into a small lake, a whirlpool develops and sucks them all down to the bottom.

There, they are encountered by little fairy creatures called the Fairfolk. The Fairfolk reveal that they have their pig and they return her to them.

The Fairfolk ask if the Horned King is still doing his dirty work. They feel that he will never find it, because it is very well hidden.

Taran suggests that they all go to the cauldron first and destroy it before the Horned King gets there. The Fairfolk use their powers to float everyone to where the cauldron resides in Morva.

Taran bursts into a seemingly abandoned house. It is actually the home to multiple toads that actually used to be human. Then, they discover an entire room filled with cauldrons.

The home also is the home to three witches, one of whom makes an amorous play to Fflewddur before he too, is turned into a toad, by one of the other witches.

Taran asks the witches if they know the whereabouts of the black cauldron. They are not very keen about revealing where the cauldron is and send the other cauldrons his way. Taran's sword starts splitting the cauldrons in two by itself.

The witch sisters discuss everything and offer to trade the black cauldron in exchange for Taran's sword. Taran refuses and then relents. Eilonwy tries to talk him out of it, but he gives it to them anyway in exchange for the black cauldron.

The witches appear to be lying, but actually live up to their promise. The black cauldron cannot be destroyed, but its evil powers can be stopped if someone gets inside to stop them, but they cannot get back out. Otherwise, essentially the cauldron is useless.

Taran gets depressed, but Eilonwy cheers him up saying that she still believes in him. Just as she says this, flying dragons and the Horned King's armed guards surround and capture everyone.

The three and the cauldron are all taken back to the dungeon. They are offered the chance to go inside the cauldron, but it will cost them their lives.

The Horned King now has possession of the black cauldron and calls out his army of the dead called the cauldron born.

The black cauldron bubbles and burbles and shoots out flames and sparks and various images of skulls and creatures. A green mist floats out amongst the dead and brings them back to life to become the Horned King's army.

The Horned King sends out these warriors to destroy everything in their path. They cross the castle drawbridge into the village.

Gurgi is still free, but still cowardly, but he gets into the dungeon and frees the three others. Taran leaves to defeat the army, even though Eilonwy objects. Even Gurgi objects to Taran jumping into the cauldron, and jumps in instead.

The effect is immediate and the Horned King's army starts to decompose and die again. The green mist floats back into the cauldron. Taran wants to find out if there's another chance for Gurgi, but he cannot get close to the cauldron without getting sucked in himself.

The Horned King discovers that Taran is the cause of the army's defeat and threatens to kill Taran, but the cauldron's effect is too great and he gets sucked into the cauldron himself, decomposing along the way.

It is a horrible death, but all is quiet after the Horned King is sucked in. Then the cauldron glows a bright yellow and sinks into the ground causing the castle to fall apart. Taran, Eilonwy and Fflewddur run out of the castle as fast as they can.

They escape in the nick of time as the castle completely collapses and explodes. The trio is adrift on a raft and is circled by one of the remaining dragons, who fly away.

They end up on a small spot of land. Just then, the black cauldron emerges from the water, empty and harmless. The witches come back to take the cauldron back, but Fflewddur says that they don't give away, they trade.

Taran says that they will trade the cauldron back, not for the sword, but for Gurgi. The witches do return Gurgi to them. He seems apparently dead, but not for long and everyone rejoices.

On the DVD, there is a 10-minute deleted scene called The Fairfolk. The scene doesn't add anything to the movie as it mainly consists of trying to find Hen Wen the pig and spiraling down into a whirlpool and meeting King Adolade and the rest of the Fairfolk.

Actor John Byner as Gurgi has to be one of the most annoying voices ever to grace a Disney cartoon. It is the same kind of annoying voice that Elmo has in *Sesame Street*. *The Black Cauldron* eventually did inspire a theme park attraction at Tokyo Disneyland.

Actress Hayley Mills was originally considered for Eilonwy.

This movie was the last animated Disney film to use the multi-plane camera and the first one since *The Jungle Book* (1967). The camera is unnecessary today as multi-plane effects can be created in the computer.

This is the first animated film from Disney to receive a PG rating. I never really cared for it upon first viewing in 1985, but it has grown on me, not to be my favorite, but an acceptable Disney cartoon feature.

This film grossed $21 million which would have normally made it a hit by 1985 standards, but the film cost $25 million to make.

The film would have been issued in 1984, had there not been delays made by editing and reshooting by Jeffrey Katzenberg.

This was the last animated film by Disney to be completed at the Walt Disney Studios in Burbank as the animation department was moved to Glendale for subsequent films.

Author Lloyd Alexander said that he enjoyed the film, but it was nothing like his book and wishes that anyone who watches this film would go back and read his book.

My Science Project

A TOUCHSTONE FILM RELEASED by Buena Vista on August 9, 1985, Technicolor. Associate Producer: E. Darrell Hallenbeck. Producer: Jonathan Taplin. Associate Producer: E. Darrell Hallenbeck. Director: Jonathan R. Betuel. Writer: Jonathan R. Betuel. Original Music: Peter Bernstein. Director of Photography: David M. Walsh. Film Editor: Timothy O'Meara. Casting: Bill Shepard. Production Designer: David L. Snyder. Art Director: John B. Mansbridge. Set Decoration: Jerry Wunderlich. Costume Design: Betsy Jones. Makeup Effects: Lance Anderson. Makeup Artist: Zoltan. Hair Stylist: Ramsey. Makeup Supervisor: Robert J. Schiffer. Unit Production Manager: E. Darrell Hallenbeck. Second Assistant Director: Carole Keligian. DGA Trainee: Michael Schilz. First Assistant Director: Jerry Sobul. Leadman: Nigel A. Boucher. Production Illustrator: Tom Cranham. Assistant Art Director: Stephen Dane. Construction Coordinator: Dennis DeWaay. Production Illustrator: Marty Kline. Storyboard Artist: Paul Power. Property Master: David Quick. Sound Editors: Wayne Allwine, James J. Isaacs, Joe Parker, George Probert, David A. Whittaker. Sound Re-Recording Mixers: Nick Alphin, Thomas Gerard, Andy MacDonald. Foley Artist: Paul L. Holzborn. Special Sound Effects: Alan Howarth. ADR Editor: Al Maguire. Assistant Sound Editor: Edward Malone. Supervising Sound Editor: Colin C. Mouat. Production Sound: Scott Senechal, Jim Webb. T-Rex Crew: Michael Burnett, Tony Gardner. Special Effects: Gary D'Amico. Mechanical Effects: Michael Lantieri. Special Effects Foreman: Hans Metz. Special Effects Technician: Mike Reedy. Special Effects Assistant, Post Production: Ken Speed. Special Effects, First Unit: Brian Tipton. Photographic Effects: John Aardal, Ed Austin, Michael Bishop, Oscar Fatur, Bernie Gagliano, Rusty Geller, John Godden, Allen Gonzales, Robert Hill, Philip Huff, Robert Mills, Francis O'Connell, Ron Os-

enbaugh, Joe Parra, Jim Pickel, Michael Reed, Richard Rippel, Gail Venturelli, Neil Viker, John White, Robert Wilson. Effects Animators: Bill Arance, Esther Barr, Christine Harding, Chris Casady, Glenn Chaika, Ed Coffey, Barry Cook, Gail Fox, Peter Gullerud, Jeff Howard, Kimberly Knowlton, Scott Santoro, Gary Trousdale, Bruce Woodside. Special Effects Animator: Craig Clark. Animation Photography Supervisor: Clint Colver. Special Lighting Effects Consultant: Michael Fink. Matte Unit: Carl Frith, Don Henry, Richard Kendall, Tim McHugh, Robert Scifo. Additional Animators, Available Light Limited: Katherine Kean, Candace Lewis, Byron Werner. Animation Camera Coordinator: Christopher Keith. Optical Effects Supervisors: William Kilduff, Greg Van Der Veer. Supervising Matte Artist: Michael Lloyd. Photographic Effects Supervisor: Philip Meader. Visual Effects Supervisors: Richard Mosier, John Scheele. Ink and Paint Animation Cameraman, Available Light Limited: Joseph Thomas. Animation Designer and Supervisor: John Van Vleit. Stunts: Michael Adams, Alonzo Brown, Jr., John Cade, Michael Cassidy, Larry Duran, David Michael Graves, Tracy Hutchinson, Max Kleven, Joel Kramer, Walt La Rue, Steven Lambert, Al Leong, Anderson Martin, Rex Pierson, Bill Saito, Glenn Wilder, Eddie Wong. Second Assistant Camera: G. Martin Beazell. Dolly Grip: Danny E. Boldroff. Camera Operator: Bob Edesa. Lighting Gaffer: Norman Harris. Lamp Operator: Harold Hathaway. Best Boy: Ron Kenyon. Grip: Hugh Langtry. Key Grip: Richard Moran. First Assistant Camera: Michael S. Nash. Still Photographer: Ralph B. Nelson. Lamp Operators: Bruton Peterson, Robert Wilhoit. Costumer: Susie S. McEveety. Costume Department Supervisor: Jack Sandeen. Costumer: Don Vargas. Assistant Editors: Mark Eggenweiler, Lynne Bailey Smith. Orchestrators: Alf Clausen, Brian Mann, Joel Rosenbaum, David Spear. Music Supervisor: Jay Lawton. Music Editor: Curtis Roush. Script Supervisor: Faye Brenner. Location Manager: Rolf Darbo. Assistant to the Producer: Anastasia St. Amand. Assistant, Mr. Betuel: Robert Wait. Unit Publicist: Bob Werden. Special Makeup Effects Artist: Rick Baker. Makeup Supervisor: David B. Miller. Sound: Allen Hurd. Production Estimator: Julianna Arenson. Marketing Consultant: Craig Miller. Running time: 94 minutes. Rated PG.

Songs: "My Science Project" Words and Music by Bob Held, Michael Colina, Bill Heller. Performer: The Tubes. "Hard to Believe" Words and Music: Bob Held, Bill Heller, Matthew Hill. Performer: The Tubes. "Hit and Run" Words and Music: Jeff Gordon, Bob Held, Bill Heller. Performer: David Johansen. "My Mind's Made Up" Words and Music by Bob Held, Bill Heller. Performer: Steve Johnstad. "Fish Cheer and I-Feel-Like-I'm Fixin' to Die Rag" Written by Country Joe McDonald. Performer: Country Joe and the Fish. "The Warrior" Writer: Holly Knight and Nick Gilder.

Cast: John Stockwell (Michael Harlan), Danielle von Zerneck (Ellie Sawyer), Fisher Stevens (Vince Latello), Raphael Sbarge (Sherman), Dennis Hopper (Bob Roberts), Richard Masur (Detective Isadore Nulty), Barry Corbin (Lew Harlan), Ann Wedgeworth (Dolores), Candace Silvers (Irene), Beau Dremann (Matusky), Pat Simmons (Crystal), John Vidor (Jock #1), Vincent Barbour (Jock #2), Jaime Alba (Jock #3), Robert Beer (President Eisenhower), John Carter (General), Cameron Young (General's Aide), Noel Conlon (Secret Service Man), Jackson Bostwick (Sentry), Robert DoQui (Desk Sergeant), Elven Havard (Fireman), Linda Hoy (Librarian), Robin Allyn (Ellie's Friend), Michael Berryman (Mutant #1), Chuck Hemingway (Coy), Pamela Springsteen (Hall Monitor / Ellie's Friend), Matt Hoescher (Preppie), Jack O'Leary (Sentry at Air Force Guardhouse), Clare Peck (Policewoman), Joel Harrison (Wno), Ann Culotta (Trucker's Wife), Hank Calia (Neanderthal Man), Scott Bailey Spangler (Guard #2 at Air Force Guardhouse), Frank Welker (Aliens Voice), Donna Lee Heising (Sorceress) Al Leong (Vietnamese Soldier), Lyza Reese (Student).

In 1957, a motorcade carrying President Eisenhower leaves Dawson Air Force Base. The President is shown a mysterious alien discovery. Eisenhower orders the discovery to be disposed.

In 1985, at a high school, Mr. Bob Roberts, the school science teacher, asks his students what their science projects will be. Bob comes up to Michael Harlen and asks what he's going to do, but Michael has no clue and says that he's working on it. Bob reminds him that no project, no diploma.

After school, Michael bugs his girlfriend Crystal, who wants more than he is willing to offer, and she breaks up with him.

Nerdy Shermy asks Ellie out, but she puts him off, as she's trying to interview Michael for the school yearbook.

After the interview, Michael goes back to work on his car. His friend Vince asks what happened between him and Crystal.

Soon, there is a line-up of students trying to leave school. They are all behind Ellie, who has faked a broken down car in order to catch the attention of Michael again, so he'll notice her.

Michael asks her why she did this and Ellie says that she wants to go out on a date with him. After thinking about it, and seeing Crystal with someone else, he agrees.

Michael drives off and goes home, which resides above his dad's hardware store. His dad is caught fooling around with Dolores.

After being introduced, Michael leaves again to go out on his date with Ellie. He uses the date as an excuse to break into a top secret junk yard of the military to find something useful for his science project.

Ellie is kind of upset at Michael's choice of location for dating until he reminds her that everything has a story and she's a reporter.

While walking, Michael falls through a hole in the floor and discovers a secret room with various items including a live snake and items from a fallout shelter.

Ellie wants him to come back to the surface, but Michael ignores her, insisting upon investigating his whereabouts.

Michael comes upon a box that should not be opened except by authorized personnel under controlled conditions. He breaks into it anyway and discovers a small machine that glows and sparks.

Meanwhile, a security guard takes his dog to investigate who is trespassing. Ellie sees a mouse and screams, calling attention to the guard who orders them to stop.

Michael grabs the glowing box and takes it with him as they both flee the military junk yard.

While driving away, the item that Michael has grabbed saps the electricity from his car and they stop. Michael and Ellie open the hood to investigate and they are hit by a number of sparks.

A moving van drives by and Michael flags it down. He asks to use the van's CB radio and radios Vince to help him out. Vince is in the middle of making love to his date, but agrees to rescue Michael and Ellie.

They are rescued and Vince pushes Michael's car to Ellie's home and he drops her off, and then pushes Michael to his repair shop.

Vince's date complains what a bad date this is, but Vince tells her to take a hike as he helps Michael fix his car, all the time the glowing box is still in the back seat.

The next day in school, Michael and Vince lamely practice their typing in class in order to kill the time until the period is over.

Back at the auto repair, Micheal decides to clean the glowing box and discovers other working features of it, while Vince works on the car.

Once he gets it going, Michael shows Vince and they witness the glowing orb of the box absorb the power from some batteries in a nearby radio.

They hook the orb up to a car battery and it sucks up the power of it and of the ceiling lights. The orb then materializes an ancient Egyptian vase, and then they shut it off.

Still not sure what they have, they hide the machine and the vase. After they leave, they realize that they have been zapped ahead two hours in the future.

Michael and Vince decide to do some more investigations and go to the library to find a book on the subject. Nerdy Shermy is the librarian and helps them find a book about time warps.

Bob asks Michael and Vince what they're working on, but they don't want to say anything yet that they have discovered a time warp machine.

Michael calls Ellie for another date and she asks if they're going to another junk yard. Michael says no.

Michael hasn't been home for a bit, but when he comes home, he discovers his dad and Dolores have now gotten married and have redecorated the house.

Finally, Michael decides to reveal his science project to Bob, who is amazed by the fact that it is generating energy without power or heat.

Michael and Bob, together with Ellie and Vince decide to do a little experimenting with the glowing orb to see what it can do.

Bob is convinced that this discovery is bigger than anything ever discovered, bigger than the universe: a time space warp.

Ellie says that they should call the police, but Bob says no and he gets too excited about the potential power of the orb and gets sucked into it.

The rest of them say that they have to stop the warp in order to bring Bob back. Meanwhile, the energy of the orb keeps increasing and absorbing energy from a series of power poles and Michael, Ellie and Vince race their car in order to stay ahead of a power surge until they crash into a dead end.

The three of them hook up sticks of dynamite onto a makeshift rocket. The power surge is coming and the three detonate the dynamite with their car battery.

There is now an investigation at the high school and as the three return, they wonder how they are going to get the orb out of the high school.

There is also an investigation into the downed power lines and the three really decide to lay low for a while, but Michael starts to really fall for Ellie and they kiss.

Michael goes into his room, only to be greeted by the police who say that he has three eyewitnesses about missing dynamite and also asks Michael the whereabouts of Bob.

Before they go down to the police station, Michael phones Ellie and tells her to bring the gizmo to the police station.

The police also arrest Vince. Michael's dad and new stepmother accompany them to the station.

As Ellie goes into get the glowing orb, she is greeted by Sherman, who wonders what it is and won't let her take it before he experiments with it a bit.

Of course, everything goes awry and in the chaos, Michael and Vince grab a police car and flee the scene.

They drive to the high school to see a huge swirling mass engulfing the sky. The warp is now expanding with people from the past and the future. While they are observing this, they are attacked by their new visitors.

The warp gets bigger and Michael, Vince and Sherman must battle the increasing amount of strange visitors from the past and future.

Then, they encounter a large dinosaur that resembles Godzilla. Things seem to increasingly get out of hand until they discover Ellie as apparently dead.

She is not, but the glowing orb must be stopped, so Michael goes in to the center of the storm to try to shut everything off.

He succeeds and everything returns back to the orb and shuts off. They all go outside and see fire fighters hosing down the school and rescuing people.

Everyone is worse for wear, but alive, when suddenly Bob appears out of nowhere. He has traveled to the 1960s and back to 1985, and is questioned by the police and taken away. The kids are all set free.

Michael goes to the junk yard and returns the glowing box to where it came from.

Afterwards, Michael and Ellie are driving home and his car breaks down again, this time because he has run out of gas.

They decide to walk back to town and as they leave, leftover sparks emanate from the car.

This really was the last film commissioned by the previous Disney administration, even though it was released almost a year after Michael Eisner took office.

The movie is ok, but nothing remarkable and is much more vulgar in tone than any previous teen comedy made at Disney to this point, including *Midnight Madness* (1980).

Although the Walt Disney Productions saga continued in name only until February 6, 1986, *My Science Project* is really the final film that bears any resemblance or continuity of Disney of old, with longtime Makeup Artist Robert J. Schiffer, Art Director John B. Mansbridge, Costumer Jack Sandeen and Special Effects men Hans Metz, Mike Reedy, Gary D'Amico and Ken Speed on board before they were dismissed by Eisner, as well as character actor Jackson Bostwick.

Schiffer did work one last time for Disney on *Tough Guys* (1986) and Speed on *Down and Out in Beverly Hills* (1986). D'Amico did some effects for the revived anthology show in 1986-1987.

The film was also a flop, grossing $4 million.

The Rest of the Story

The *Black Cauldron* (1985) was the final animated film instigated by Ron Miller and the former Disney regime. Michael Eisner was firmly in place by this time and his changes were already becoming apparent, but this film still needed to see release, and ultimately was a major disappointment to all those anticipating it. Among Disney animated features, it is largely forgotten today.

In the DVD documentary *Waking Sleeping Beauty* (2009), much was discussed about the rebirth of Disney animation. Ironic, since the same arguments happened at the tail end of Walt's career. Of course, after this new nadir of *The Black Cauldron*, there was a slow rebirth and eventual death again of Disney animation, but at this point, things were bound to get better. After passable animated features such as *The Great Mouse Detective* (1986) and *Oliver and Company* (1987), Disney finally hit the big time again with *Who Framed Roger Rabbit?* (1988) and *The Little Mermaid* (1989).

As far as the remaining line-up for 1985 live-action features, there was *The Journey of Natty Gann* and *One Magic Christmas*, projects green lit after Eisner's ascension.

I could have reviewed these and 1986's *Down and Out in Beverly Hills* which were all released before the Walt Disney Productions name change to The Walt Disney Company, but as seen by virtually all Disney films made after about 1982, the changes to the company management and the way they made films had already been completed. The company name change was merely a formality.

Eisner also changed WED Enterprises to Walt Disney Imagineering.

More hit albums were released including *Totally Minnie* and *Rock Around the Mouse* among others and of course, the very successful soundtracks for many of Disney's animated feature films beginning with *The Little Mermaid*.

Comic books made a comeback in 1985 by a new company called Gladstone, which had published hardcover reprints under the moniker of Another Rainbow previously.

The long-running *Disneyland Vacationland* was canceled and *Disney News* was revamped and sold on newsstands. It too, was canceled eventually, but the Disney newsstands now carry *Disney 23* which basically serves the same function.

The success of Gladstone prompted Eisner to pull in the comic book publishing to create the Disney Comics label. Though the line started off with good intentions, eventually since comic books are not the dominant force they once were, the line was severely curtailed in what has been dubbed the Disney implosion.

Eventually, the characters were licensed back out again to Gladstone and later Marvel, and finally Boom. As of 2011, the long-running titles of *Walt Disney's Comics and Stories* and *Uncle Scrooge* (amazingly retaining their original numbering) have possibly breathed their last, but stranger things have happened, but Disney's highest priority in the 21st century are not comic books.

Most currently, Fantagraphics are reprinting the classic Carl Barks and Floyd Gottfredson stories for the umpteenth time, but this time in classy hardback volumes with excellent reproduction.

Throughout the rest of the 1980s and the 1990s, Michael Eisner grew the company into a strong empire. However, in doing so he virtually erased all memories of the mom and pop charm that originally existed when it was Walt Disney Productions. The films now could be made by anyone at any studio and no longer have that Disney stamp on them, even the animated ones.

Michael Eisner stayed in charge until 2005 when Robert Iger took over. At that point, Disney had become such a major force that virtually all animated properties are either owned by Disney, Warner Bros. or Dreamworks.

Disney now owns Marvel Comics and George Lucas' Industrial Light and Magic and is strongly connected to Apple, The Muppets and Pixar and seems destined to rule the world. It is no longer the family-owned company that was on the verge of a stock buy-out in 1984.

The Short Subjects

The amount of newly produced short subjects virtually dried up during the period of 1967-1985, but of the 15 produced, two won Academy Awards and two more were nominated, all animated.

In total, 11 of the 15 were animation, with two of those being compilations. The rest were live-action, with one of those being a theatrical issue of a short originally aired on the anthology show.

On the animated shorts, with the exception of *Mickey's Christmas Carol* (1983) which brought back many of the Disney stable of animation stars to the theater for the first time since the 1960s (in the case of Mickey himself, since the 1950s), Winnie the Pooh starred in three shorts, two of those being part of *The Many Adventures of Winnie the Pooh* compilation from 1977.

In fact, Winnie the Pooh became the biggest rival to Mickey Mouse for most popular character. So popular, that the first three of the four shorts aired as half hour specials at various times from 1970-1977 independent of the anthology show.

Many older shorts were also reissued during this period, some with new feature films and some with the usual reissues of the Disney classic animated features and some live-action reissues. Some shorts were compiled into feature films such as the various sports related Goofy films produced during the 1940s and 1950s.

Though Disney had a goodly amount of original TV programming created during this period, the bulk of the filmed product from Walt Disney Productions was for theatrical feature films, with the majority of them being live-action.

1967
Scrooge McDuck and Money – cartoon
The Legend of the Boy and the Eagle – live action

1968
Winnie the Pooh and the Blustery Day – cartoon (Academy Award Winner)

1969
Hang Your Hat in the Wind – live action
It's Tough to Be a Bird – cartoon (Academy Award Winner)

1970
Dad, Can I Borrow the Car? – live action and animation

1972
The Silver Fox and Sam Davenport – live action (originally released to TV, 1962)
The Magic of Walt Disney World – live action
Superstar Goofy – compilation cartoon

1973
Man, Monsters and Mysteries – live action and animation

1974
Winnie the Pooh and Tigger Too – cartoon (nominated for Academy Award)

1975
Fantasy on Skis – live action (originally released to TV, 1962)

1977
A Tale of Two Critters – live action

1978
The Small One – cartoon

1979
The Footloose Fox – live action

1980
Mickey Mouse Disco – compilation cartoon

1981
Once Upon a Mouse – compilation cartoon
Winnie the Pooh Discovers the Seasons – cartoon

1982
Vincent – stop-motion animation
Fun with Mr. Future – live action and animation

1983
Winnie the Pooh and a Day for Eeyore – cartoon
Mickey's Christmas Carol – cartoon (nominated for Academy Award)

1984
Frankenweenie – live action

Disney on TV

During the 1967-1985 period, the anthology showed plowed on at least until 1983. Walt Disney Productions didn't really attempt any new shows until 1972's *The Mouse Factory*.

In 1975, there was a half-hour revival of the original *Mickey Mouse Club*, which soon paved the way for *The New Mickey Mouse Club* in 1977.

From 1982-1985, Walt Disney Productions tried a number of short-lived TV series based on various theatrical properties. None of which were particularly successful. Disney would have to wait until 1985 and *The Golden Girls* to have their first bona fide hit TV series since *Zorro*.

In 1983, The Disney Channel debuted on cable. Originally, a haven for the huge backlog of Disney product, but soon after those shows were depleted, new programming was created.

In the fall of 1985, Disney entered the Saturday Morning TV market for the first time ever, but these are not documented as they fall outside the scope of this book, but there apparently was talk about Disney doing a series as early as the 1967-1968 season and again during the 1978-1979 season.

All along, various specials and movies that aired independently of the anthology show were aired including a number starring Winnie the Pooh.

All shows listed below are one hour in length unless mentioned otherwise.

(Note: Please consult Leonard Maltin's *The Disney Films* for anthology episodes prior to Walt's death. The April 2, 1967 was the final new anthology episode to feature a brand new introduction by Walt Disney.)

WALT DISNEY'S WONDERFUL WORLD OF COLOR
1966-1967, NBC, SUNDAY, 7:30 PM

12/18/66 *Disneyland Around the Seasons* (new)
12/25/66 *The Truth About Mother Goose* (1963)
1/1/67 *The Silver Fox and Sam Davenport* (1962)

1/8/67 *Willie and the Yank*, part one (new)
1/15/67 *Willie and the Yank*, part two (new)
1/22/67 *Willie and the Yank*, part three (new)
1/29/67 *Gallegher Goes West*, part three (new)
2/5/67 *Gallegher Goes West*, part four (new)
2/12/67 *The Coyote's Lament* (1961)
2/19/67 *The Boy Who Flew with Condors* (new)
3/5/67 *Atta Girl, Kelly*, part one (new)
3/12/67 *Atta Girl, Kelly*, part two (new)
3/19/67 *Atta Girl, Kelly*, part three (new)
3/26/67 *Man on Wheels* (new)
4/2/67 *A Salute to Alaska* (new)
4/9/67 *Joker, the Amiable Ocelot* (1966)
4/16/67 *The Prince and the Pauper* (1962), part one
4/23/67 *The Prince and the Pauper* (1962), part two
4/30/67 *The Prince and the Pauper* (1962), part three
5/7/67 *The Legend of El Blanco* (1966)
5/14/67 *For the Love of Willadean* (1964), part one
5/21/67 *For the Love of Willadean* (1964), part two
5/28/67 *The Boy Who Flew With Condors* (1967)
6/4/67 *The Horsemasters* (1961), part one
6/11/67 *The Horsemasters* (1961), part two
6/18/67 *Disneyland Around the Seasons* (1966)
6/25/67 *Gallegher Goes West* (1966), part one
7/2/67 *Gallegher Goes West* (1966), part two
7/9/67 *Gallegher Goes West* (1966), part three
7/16/67 *Gallegher Goes West* (1966), part four
7/23/67 *The Horse Without a Head* (1963), part one
7/30/67 *The Horse Without a Head* (1963), part two
8/6/67 *Man on Wheels* (1967)
8/13/67 *A Salute to Alaska* (1967)
8/20/67 *The Moon-Spinners* (1964), part one
8/27/67 *The Moon-Spinners* (1964), part two
9/3/67 *The Moon-Spinners* (1964), part three

1967-1968, NBC, SUNDAY, 7:30 PM

9/10/67 *The Tattooed Police Horse* (1964) (new to TV)
9/17/67 *The Not So Lonely Lighthouse Keeper* (new)
9/24/67 *How the West Was Lost* (new)
10/1/67 *The Fighting Prince of Donegal* (1966), part one (new to TV)

10/8/67 *The Fighting Prince of Donegal* (1966), part two (new to TV)
10/15/67 *The Fighting Prince of Donegal* (1966), part three (new to TV)
10/22/67 *Run, Appaloosa, Run* (1966) (new to TV)
10/29/67 *Pollyanna* (1960), part one
11/5/67 *Pollyanna* (1960), part two
11/12/67 *Pollyanna* (1960), part three
11/19/67 *One Day on Beetle Rock* (new)
11/26/67 *The Monkey's Uncle* (1965), part one (new to TV)
12/3/67 *The Monkey's Uncle* (1965), part two (new to TV)
12/10/67 *A Boy Called Nuthin'*, part one (new)
12/17/67 *A Boy Called Nuthin'*, part two (new)
12/24/67 *From All of Us to All of You* (1958)
1/7/68 *Way Down Cellar*, part one (new)
1/14/68 *Way Down Cellar*, part two (new)
1/21/68 *Disneyland: From the Pirates of the Caribbean to the World of Tomorrow* (new)
1/28/68 *Pablo and the Dancing Chihuahua*, part one (new)
2/4/68 *Pablo and the Dancing Chihuahua*, part two (new)
2/11/68 *My Family is a Menagerie* (new)
2/25/68 *The Young Loner*, part one (new)
3/3/68 *The Young Loner*, part two (new)
3/10/68 *Wild Heart* (new)
3/17/68 *The Ranger of Brownstone* (new)
3/24/68 *The Horse With the Flying Tail* (1960)
3/31/68 *The Mystery of Edward Sims*, part one (new)
4/7/68 *The Mystery of Edward Sims*, part two (new)
4/14/68 *Ten Who Dared* (1960) (new to TV)
4/21/68 *Jungle Cat* (1960)
4/28/68 *Nature's Charter Tours* (new)
5/5/68 *Johnny Shiloh* (1963), part one
5/12/68 *Johnny Shiloh* (1963), part two
5/19/68 *The Not So Lonely Lighthouse Keeper* (1967)
5/26/68 *Run, Appaloosa, Run* (1966)
6/2/68 *One Day on Beetle Rock* (1967)
6/9/68 *Disneyland: From the Pirates of the Caribbean to the World of Tomorrow* (1968)
6/16/68 *This is Your Life Donald Duck* (1960)
6/23/68 *Pablo and the Dancing Chihuahua* (1968), part one
6/30/68 *Pablo and the Dancing Chihuahua* (1968), part two
7/7/68 *Greta, the Misfit Greyhound* (1963)
7/14/68 *The Mystery of Edward Sims* (1968), part one
7/21/68 *The Mystery of Edward Sims* (1968), part two

7/28/68 *On Vacation* (1956)
8/4/68 *Ten Who Dared* (1960)
8/11/68 *Sancho, the Homing Steer* (1962), part one
8/18/68 *Sancho, the Homing Steer* (1962), part two
8/25/68 *The Legend of Two Gypsy Dogs* (1964)
9/1/68 *Sammy, the Way-Out Seal* (1962), part one
9/8/68 *Sammy, the Way-Out Seal* (1962), part two

1968-1969, NBC, SUNDAY, 7:30 PM

9/15/68 *The Legend of the Boy and the Eagle* (1967) (new to TV)
9/22/68 *Boomerang, Dog of Many Talents*, part one (new)
9/29/68 *Boomerang, Dog of Many Talents*, part two (new)
10/6/68 *Pacifically Peeking* (new)
10/13/68 *Toby Tyler* (1960), part one
10/20/68 *Toby Tyler* (1960), part two
10/27/68 *Brimstone, the Amish Horse* (new)
11/3/68 *The Ugly Dachshund* (1965), part one (new to TV)
11/10/68 *The Ugly Dachshund* (1965), part two (new to TV)
11/24/68 *The Treasure of San Bosco Reef*, part one (new)
12/1/68 *The Treasure of San Bosco Reef*, part two (new)
12/15/68 *The Owl That Didn't Give a Hoot* (new)
12/22/68 *The Mickey Mouse Anniversary Show* (new)
12/29/68 *A Country Coyote Goes Hollywood* (1965)
1/5/69 *Solomon, the Sea Turtle* (new)
1/12/69 *Those Calloways* (1965), part one (new to TV)
1/19/69 *Those Calloways* (1965), part two (new to TV)
1/26/69 *Those Calloways* (1965), part three (new to TV)
2/2/69 *Pancho, Fastest Paw in the West* (new)
2/9/69 *The Secret of Boyne Castle*, part one (new)
2/16/69 *The Secret of Boyne Castle*, part two (new)
2/23/69 *The Secret of Boyne Castle*, part three (new)
3/2/69 *Nature's Better Built Homes* (new)
3/16/69 *Ride a Northbound Horse*, part one (new)
3/23/69 *Ride a Northbound Horse*, part two (new)
3/30/69 *The Legend of the Boy and the Eagle* (1967) (new to TV)
4/6/69 *An Otter in the Family* (1965)
4/13/69 *Mediterranean Cruise* (1964)
4/20/69 *Bristle Face* (1964), part one
4/27/69 *Bristle Face* (1964), part two
5/4/69 *The Wahoo Bobcat* (1963)

5/11/69 *Kilroy* (1965), part one
5/18/69 *Kilroy* (1965), part two
5/25/69 *Kilroy* (1965), part three
6/1/69 *Kilroy* (1965), part four
6/8/69 *Three Tall Tales* (1963)
6/15/69 *The Horse of the West* (1957)
6/22/69 *Escapade in Florence* (1962), part one
6/29/69 *Escapade in Florence* (1962), part two
7/6/69 *The Owl That Didn't Give a Hoot* (1968)
7/13/69 *Boomerang, Dog of Many Talents* (1968), part one
7/27/69 *Boomerang, Dog of Many Talents* (1968), part two
8/3/69 *The Treasure of San Bosco Reef* (1968), part one
8/10/69 *The Treasure of San Bosco Reef* (1968), part two
8/17/69 *Little Dog Lost* (1963)
8/24/69 *Davy Crockett - Indian Fighter* (1954)
8/31/69 *Davy Crockett Goes to Congress* (1955)
9/7/69 *Davy Crockett at the Alamo* (1955)

THE WONDERFUL WORLD OF DISNEY
1969-1970, NBC, SUNDAY, 7:30 PM

9/14/69 *Wild Geese Calling* (new)
9/21/69 *My Dog, the Thief*, part one (new)
9/28/69 *My Dog, the Thief*, part two (new)
10/5/69 *The Three Lives of Thomasina* (1963), part one
10/12/69 *The Three Lives of Thomasina* (1963), part two
10/26/69 *The Feather Farm* (new)
11/2/69 *Charlie, the Lonesome Cougar* (1967), part one (new to TV)
11/9/69 *Charlie, the Lonesome Cougar* (1967), part two (new to TV)
11/16/69 *Varda, the Peregrine Falcon* (new)
11/23/69 *The Secrets of the Pirates Inn*, part one (new)
11/30/69 *The Secrets of the Pirates Inn*, part two (new)
12/7/69 *Inky, the Crow* (new)
12/21/69 *Babes in Toyland* (1961), part one (new to TV)
12/28/69 *Babes in Toyland* (1961), part two (new to TV)
1/4/70 *Yellowstone Cubs* (1963)
1/11/70 *Bon Voyage* (1962), part one (new to TV)
1/18/70 *Bon Voyage* (1962), part two (new to TV)
1/25/70 *Bon Voyage* (1962), part three (new to TV)
2/1/70 *Smoke*, part one (new)
2/8/70 *Smoke*, part two (new)

2/15/70 *Big Red* (1962), part one
2/22/70 *Big Red* (1962), part two
3/1/70 *Menace on the Mountain*, part one (new)
3/8/70 *Menace on the Mountain*, part two (new)
3/22/70 *Disneyland Showtime* (new)
3/29/70 *Nature's Strangest Oddballs* (new)
4/5/70 *The Hound that Thought He Was a Raccoon* (1960)
4/12/70 *The Adventures of Chip 'n Dale* (1959)
4/19/70 *Almost Angels* (1962), part one
4/26/70 *Almost Angels* (1962), part two
5/3/70 *Man is His Own Worst Enemy* (1962)
5/10/70 *The Scarecrow of Romney Marsh* (1964), part one
5/17/70 *The Scarecrow of Romney Marsh* (1964), part two
5/24/70 *The Scarecrow of Romney Marsh* (1964), part three
5/31/70 *One Day at Teton Marsh* (1964)
6/7/70 *Music for Everybody* (1966)
6/14/70 *Flash, the Teenage Otter* (1961)
6/21/70 *Run, Light Buck, Run* (1966)
6/28/70 *Disneyland Showtime* (1970)
7/5/70 *The Secrets of the Pirates Inn* (1969), part one
7/12/70 *The Secrets of the Pirates Inn* (1969), part two
7/19/70 *Inky, the Crow* (1969)
7/26/70 *In Shape with Von Drake* (1964)
8/2/70 *Menace on the Mountain* (1970), part one
8/9/70 *Menace on the Mountain* (1970), part two
8/16/70 *Varda, the Peregrine Falcon* (1969)
8/23/70 *Willie and the Yank* (1967), part one
8/30/70 *Willie and the Yank* (1967), part two
9/6/70 *Willie and the Yank* (1967), part three

1970-1971, NBC, SUNDAY, 7:30 PM

9/13/70 *Cristobalito, the Calypso Colt* (new)
9/20/70 *The Boy Who Stole the Elephant*, part one (new)
9/27/70 *The Boy Who Stole the Elephant*, part two (new)
10/4/70 *Westward Ho the Wagons!* (1956), part one
10/11/70 *Westward Ho the Wagons!* (1956), part two
10/18/70 *The Wacky Zoo of Morgan City*, part one (new)
10/25/70 *The Wacky Zoo of Morgan City*, part two (new)
11/1/70 *Snow Bear*, part one (new)
11/8/70 *Snow Bear*, part two (new)

11/15/70 *Monkeys, Go Home!* (1967), part one (new to TV)
11/22/70 *Monkeys, Go Home!* (1967), part two (new to TV)
11/29/70 *Hang Your Hat on the Wind* (1969) (new to TV)
12/13/70 *It's Tough to Be a Bird* (1969) (new to TV)
12/20/70 *From All of Us to All of You* (1958)
12/27/70 *Minado, the Wolverine* (1965)
1/3/71 *Three Without Fear*, part one (new)
1/10/71 *Three Without Fear*, part two (new)
1/17/71 *The Adventures of Bullwhip Griffin* (1967), part one (new to TV)
1/24/71 *The Adventures of Bullwhip Griffin* (1967), part two (new to TV)
1/31/71 *The Adventures of Bullwhip Griffin* (1967), part three (new to TV) / *Project Florida* (new)
2/7/71 *Bayou Boy*, part one (new)
2/14/71 *Bayou Boy*, part two (new)
2/21/71 *Moon Pilot* (1962), part one
2/28/71 *Moon Pilot* (1962), part two
3/7/71 *Hamad and the Pirates*, part one (new)
3/14/71 *Hamad and the Pirates*, part two (new)
3/21/71 *Kidnapped* (1960), part one
3/28/71 *Kidnapped* (1960), part two
4/4/71 *Operation Undersea* (1954)
4/11/71 *Von Drake in Spain* (1962)
4/25/71 *The Ballad of Hector the Stowaway Dog* (1964), part one
5/2/71 *The Ballad of Hector the Stowaway Dog* (1964), part two
5/9/71 *Emil and the Detectives* (1965), part one
5/16/71 *Emil and the Detectives* (1965), part two
5/23/71 *The 101 Problems of Hercules* (1966)
5/30/71 *The Boy Who Stole the Elephant* (1970), part one
6/6/71 *The Boy Who Stole the Elephant* (1970), part two
6/20/71 *It's Tough to be a Bird* (1969)
6/27/71 *Cristobalito, the Calypso Colt* (1970)
7/4/71 *A Square Peg in a Round Hole* (1963)
7/11/71 *The Wacky Zoo of Morgan City* (1970), part one
7/18/71 *The Wacky Zoo of Morgan City* (1970), part two
7/25/71 *Hang Your Hat on the Wind* (1969)
8/1/71 *The Waltz King* (1963), part one
8/8/71 *The Waltz King* (1963), part two
8/15/71 *A Boy Called Nuthin'* (1967), part one
8/22/71 *A Boy Called Nuthin'* (1967), part two
8/29/71 *Comanche (Tonka)* (1958), part one
9/5/71 *Comanche (Tonka)* (1958), part two

1971-1972, NBC, SUNDAY, 7:30 PM

    9/19/71 *Charlie Crowfoot and the Coati Mundi* (new)
    9/26/71 *Hacksaw*, part one (new)
    10/3/71 *Hacksaw*, part two (new)
    10/10/71 *Summer Magic* (1963), part one
    10/17/71 *Summer Magic* (1963), part two
    10/31/71 *The Strange Monster of Strawberry Cove*, part one (new)
    11/7/71 *The Strange Monster of Strawberry Cove*, part two (new)
    11/14/71 *The Horse in the Gray Flannel Suit* (1968), part one (new to TV)
    11/21/71 *The Horse in the Gray Flannel Suit* (1968), part two (new to TV)
    11/28/71 *Lefty, the Dingaling Lynx*, part one (new)
    12/5/71 *Lefty, the Dingaling Lynx*, part two (new)
    12/19/71 *Disney on Parade* (new)
    12/26/71 *Cavalcade of Songs* (1955)
    1/2/72 *The Tattooed Police Horse* (1964)
    1/9/72 *Mountain Born* (new)
    1/23/72 *The Family Band (The One and Only, Genuine, Original Family Band)* (1968), part one (new to TV)
    1/30/72 *The Family Band (The One and Only, Genuine, Original Family Band)* (1968), part two (new to TV)
    2/6/72 *Justin Morgan Had a Horse*, part one (new)
    2/13/72 *Justin Morgan Had a Horse*, part two (new)
    2/20/72 *The City Fox* (new)
    3/5/72 *Banner in the Sky (Third Man on the Mountain)* (1959), part one
    3/12/72 *Banner in the Sky (Third Man on the Mountain)* (1959), part two
    3/19/72 *Chango, Guardian of the Mayan Treasure* (new)
    3/26/72 *Michael O'Hara the Fourth*, part one (new)
    4/2/72 *Michael O'Hara the Fourth*, part two (new)
    4/9/72 *Dad, Can I Borrow the Car?* (1970) (new to TV)
    4/16/72 *At Home With Donald Duck* (1956)
    4/23/72 *The Light in the Forest* (1958), part one
    4/30/72 *The Light in the Forest* (1958), part two
    5/7/72 *Joker, the Amiable Ocelot* (1966)
    5/14/72 *Atta Girl, Kelly!* (1967), part one
    5/21/72 *Atta Girl, Kelly!* (1967), part two
    5/28/72 *Atta Girl, Kelly!* (1967), part three
    6/4/72 *Wild Burro of the West* (1960)
    6/11/72 *Way Down Cellar* (1968), part one
    6/18/72 *Way Down Cellar* (1968), part two
    6/25/72 *Nature's Better Built Homes* (1969)
    7/2/72 *Disney on Parade* (1971)

7/9/72 *Hacksaw* (1971), part one
7/16/72 *Hacksaw* (1971), part two
7/23/72 *Charlie Crowfoot and the Coati Mundi* (1971)
7/30/72 *The Goofy Sports Story* (1956)
8/6/72 *The Strange Monster of Strawberry Cove* (1971), part one
8/13/72 *The Strange Monster of Strawberry Cove* (1971), part two
8/20/72 *Pablo and the Dancing Chihuahua* (1968), part one
8/27/72 *Pablo and the Dancing Chihuahua* (1968), part two
9/3/72 *Davy Crockett's Keelboat Race* (1955)
9/10/72 *Davy Crockett and the River Pirates* (1955)

1972-1973, NBC, SUNDAY, 7:30 PM

9/17/72 *The Computer Wore Tennis Shoes* (1969), part one (new to TV)
9/24/72 *The Computer Wore Tennis Shoes* (1969), part two (new to TV)
10/1/72 *The Nashville Coyote* (new)
10/8/72 *Savage Sam* (1963), part one
10/15/72 *Savage Sam* (1963), part two
10/22/72 *The High Flying Spy*, part one (new)
10/29/72 *The High Flying Spy*, part two (new)
11/5/72 *The High Flying Spy*, part three (new)
11/19/72 *Nosey, the Sweetest Skunk in the West* (new)
11/26/72 *Chandar, the Black Leopard of Ceylon*, part one (new)
12/3/72 *Chandar, the Black Leopard of Ceylon*, part two (new)
12/17/72 *Salty, the Hijacked Harbor Seal* (new)
12/24/72 *A Present for Donald* (1954)
12/31/72 *One Day on Beetle Rock* (1967)
1/7/73 *The Mystery in Dracula's Castle*, part one (new)
1/14/73 *The Mystery in Dracula's Castle*, part two (new)
1/21/73 *Fifty Happy Years* (new)
1/28/73 *The Monkey's Uncle* (1965), part one
2/4/73 *The Monkey's Uncle* (1965), part two
2/11/73 *Rascal* (1969), part one (new to TV)
2/18/73 *Rascal* (1969), part two (new to TV)
3/4/73 *Chester, Yesterday's Horse* (new)
3/11/73 *The Little Shepherd Dog of Catalina* (new)
3/18/73 *The Boy and the Bronc Buster*, part one (new)
3/25/73 *The Boy and the Bronc Buster*, part two (new)
4/1/73 *Call it Courage* (new)
4/15/73 *The Boy Who Flew With Condors* (1967)
4/22/73 *Ride a Northbound Horse* (1969), part one

4/29/73 *Ride a Northbound Horse* (1969), part two
5/6/73 *The Coyote's Lament* (1961)
5/13/73 *The Young Loner* (1968), part one
5/20/73 *The Young Loner* (1968), part two
5/27/73 *Brimstone, the Amish Horse* (1968)
6/3/73 *Fifty Happy Years* (1973)
6/10/73 *Chandar, the Black Leopard of Ceylon* (1972), part one
6/17/73 *Chandar, the Black Leopard of Ceylon* (1972), part two
6/24/73 *Ida, the Offbeat Eagle* (1965)
7/1/73 *The Mystery in Dracula's Castle* (1973), part one
7/8/73 *The Mystery in Dracula's Castle* (1973), part two
7/15/73 *How the West Was Lost* (1967)
7/22/73 *Andrew's Raiders (The Great Locomotive Chase)* (1956), part one
7/29/73 *Andrew's Raiders (The Great Locomotive Chase)* (1956), part two
8/5/73 *Pancho, the Fastest Paw in the West* (1969)
8/12/73 *Toby Tyler* (1960), part one
8/19/73 *Toby Tyler* (1960), part two
8/26/73 *The Nashville Coyote* (1972)
9/2/73 *A Tiger Walks* (1964), part one
9/9/73 *A Tiger Walks* (1964), part two

1973-1974, NBC, SUNDAY, 7:30 PM

9/16/73 *The Barefoot Executive* (1971), part one (new to TV)
9/23/73 *The Barefoot Executive* (1971), part two (new to TV)
9/30/73 *Fire on Kelly Mountain* (new)
10/7/73 *Mustang!*, part one (new)
10/21/73 *Mustang!*, par two (new)
10/28/73 *King of the Grizzlies* (1970), part one (new to TV)
11/4/73 *King of the Grizzlies* (1970), part two (new to TV)
11/11/73 *Flight of the White Stallions (Miracle of the White Stallions)* (1963), part one
11/18/73 *Flight of the White Stallions (Miracle of the White Stallions)* (1963), part two
11/25/73 *Run, Cougar, Run* (1972), part one (new to TV)
12/2/73 *Run, Cougar, Run* (1972), part two (new to TV)
12/16/73 *The Proud Bird From Shanghai* (new)
12/23/73 *From All of Us to All of You* (1958)
12/30/73 *An Otter in the Family* (1965)
1/6/74 *The Whiz Kid and the Mystery at Riverton*, part one (new)
1/13/74 *The Whiz Kid and the Mystery at Riverton*, part two (new)

1/20/74 *Hog Wild*, part one (new)
1/27/74 *Hog Wild*, part two (new)
2/3/74 *Carlo, the Sierra Coyote* (new)
2/10/74 *The Ugly Dachshund* (1965), part one
2/17/74 *The Ugly Dachshund* (1965), part two
3/3/74 *Ringo, the Refugee Raccoon* (new)
3/10/74 *Diamonds on Wheels*, part one (new)
3/17/74 *Diamonds on Wheels*, part two (new)
3/24/74 *Diamonds on Wheels*, part three (new)
3/31/74 *The Magic of Walt Disney World* (1972) (new to TV)
4/14/74 *The Secrets of the Pirate's Inn* (1969), part one
4/21/74 *The Secrets of the Pirate's Inn* (1969), part two
4/28/74 *Run, Appaloosa, Run* (1966)
5/5/74 *Charlie, the Lonesome Cougar* (1967), part one
5/12/74 *Charlie, the Lonesome Cougar* (1967), part two
5/19/74 *The Whiz Kid and the Mystery at Riverton* (1974), part one
5/26/74 *The Whiz Kid and the Mystery at Riverton* (1974), part two
6/2/74 *Jungle Cat* (1960)
6/9/74 *For the Love of Willadean* (1964), part one
6/16/74 *For the Love of Willadean* (1964), part two
6/23/74 *The Not So Lonely Lighthouse Keeper* (1967)
6/30/74 *Mustang!* (1973), part one
7/7/74 *Mustang!* (1973), part two
7/14/74 *The Adventures of Chip 'n Dale* (1959)
7/21/74 *Bristle Face* (1964), part one
7/28/74 *Bristle Face* (1964), part two
8/4/74 *Carlo, the Sierra Coyote* (1974)
8/11/74 *The Ranger of Brownstone* (1968)
8/18/74 *The Magic of Walt Disney World* (1972)
8/25/74 *Davy Crockett - Indian Fighter* (1954)
9/1/74 *Davy Crockett Goes to Congress* (1955)
9/8/74 *Davy Crockett at the Alamo* (1955)

1974-1975, NBC, SUNDAY, 7:30 PM

9/15/74 *The Million Dollar Duck* (1971), part one (new to TV)
9/22/74 *The Million Dollar Duck* (1971), part two (new to TV)
9/29/74 *Shokee, the Everglades Panther* (new)
10/6/74 *Return of the Big Cat*, part one (new)
10/13/74 *Return of the Big Cat*, part two (new)
10/20/74 *Two Against the Arctic*, part one (new)

10/27/74 *Two Against the Arctic*, part two (new)
11/3/74 *Adventure in Satan's Canyon* (new)
11/10/74 *Those Calloways* (1965), part one
11/17/74 *Those Calloways* (1965), part two
11/24/74 *Those Calloways* (1965), part three
12/1/74 *Runaway on the Rogue River* (new)
12/8/74 *Stub, the Best Cow Dog in the West* (new)
12/22/74 *The Truth About Mother Goose* (1963)
12/29/74 *The Legend of the Boy and the Eagle* (1967)
1/5/75 *Greyfriar's Bobby* (1961), part one
1/12/75 *Greyfriar's Bobby* (1961), part two
1/19/75 *The Sky's the Limit*, part one (new)
1/26/75 *The Sky's the Limit*, part two (new)
2/2/75 *Johnny Tremain* (1957), part one
2/9/75 *Johnny Tremain* (1957), part two
2/23/75 *The Wild Country* (1971), part one (new to TV)
3/2/75 *The Wild Country* (1971), part two (new to TV)
3/9/75 *The Footloose Goose* (new)
3/16/75 *Deacon, the High Noon Dog* (new)
3/23/75 *Welcome to the "World"* (new)
4/6/75 *Kids is Kids* (1961)
4/13/75 *The Yellowstone Cubs* (1963)
4/20/75 *One Day at Teton Marsh* (1964)
4/27/75 *My Dog, the Thief* (1969), part one
5/4/75 *My Dog, the Thief* (1969), part two
5/11/75 *Wild Geese Calling* (1969)
5/18/75 *Return of the Big Cat* (1974), part one
5/25/75 *Return of the Big Cat* (1974), part two
6/1/75 *Nature's Charter Tours* (1968)
6/8/75 *My Family is a Menagerie* (1968)
6/15/75 *Two Against the Arctic* (1974), part one
6/22/75 *Two Against the Arctic* (1974), part two
6/29/75 *Inky, the Crow* (1969)
7/6/75 *Adventure in Satan's Canyon* (1974)
7/13/75 *Greta, the Misfit Greyhound* (1963)
7/20/75 *Runaway on the Rogue River* (1974)
7/27/75 *Three Without Fear* (1971), part one
8/3/75 *Three Without Fear* (1971), part two
8/10/75 *Run, Light Buck, Run* (1966)
8/17/75 *Snow Bear* (1970), part one
8/24/75 *Snow Bear* (1970), part two
8/31/75 *Solomon, the Sea Turtle* (1969)

1975-1976, NBC, SUNDAY, 7:00 PM

9/14/75 *The Boy Who Talked to Badgers*, part one (new)
9/21/75 *The Boy Who Talked to Badgers*, part two (new)
9/28/75 *The Outlaw Cats of Colossal Cave* (new)
10/5/75 *The Secret of the Pond*, part one (new)
10/12/75 *The Secret of the Pond*, part two (new)
10/19/75 *Seems There Was This Moose* (new)
10/26/75 *Now You See Him, Now You Don't* (1972) (2 hours) (new to TV)
11/2/75 *Napoleon and Samantha* (1972) (2 hours) (new to TV)
11/9/75 *Big Red* (1962) (2 hours)
11/16/75 *Smoke* (1970) (2 hours)
11/30/75 *Sammy, the Way-Out Seal* (1962) (2 hours)
12/7/75 *Monkeys, Go Home!* (1967) (2 hours)
12/21/75 *Three Tall Tales* (1963)
12/28/75 *The Pigeon That Worked a Miracle* (1958)
1/4/76 *Twister, Bull From the Sky* (new)
1/11/76 *The Whiz Kid and the Carnival Caper*, part one (new)
1/18/76 *The Whiz Kid and the Carnival Caper*, part two (new)
1/25/76 *The Legend of Sleepy Hollow* (1949)
2/1/76 *The Bears and I* (1974), part one (new to TV)
2/8/76 *The Bears and I* (1974), part two (new to TV)
2/15/76 *Superdad* (1973) (2 hours) (new to TV)
2/22/76 *Goofing Around with Donald Duck* (1963)
2/29/76 *The Survival of Sam the Pelican* (new)
3/14/76 *The Flight of the Grey Wolf*, part one (new)
3/21/76 *The Flight of the Grey Wolf*, part two (new)
3/28/76 *Dad, Can I Borrow the Car?* (1970)
4/4/76 *The 101 Problems of Hercules* (1966)
4/11/76 *A Ranger's Guide to Nature* (1966)
4/18/76 *Chico, the Misunderstood Coyote* (1961)
4/25/76 *Sammy, the Way-Out Seal* (1962) (2 hours)
5/9/76 *Ducking Disaster with Donald Duck and His Friends* (1962)
5/16/76 *The Parent Trap* (1961) (2½ hours)
5/23/76 *The Boy Who Talked to Badgers* (1975) (2 hours)
5/30/76 *Killers of the High Country* (1959)
6/6/76 *Little Dog Lost* (1963)
6/13/76 *The Outlaw Cats of Colossal Cave* (1975)
6/20/76 *Goofy's Salute to Father* (1961)
6/27/76 *Seems There Was This Moose* (1975)
7/11/76 *The Secret of the Pond*, part one (1975)
7/18/76 *The Secret of the Pond*, part two (1975)

7/25/76 *Superstar Goofy* (1972) (new to TV)
8/1/76 *Menace on the Mountain* (1970), part one
8/8/76 *Menace on the Mountain* (1970), part two
8/15/76 *The Owl That Didn't Give a Hoot* (1968)
8/22/76 *Summer Magic* (1963), part one
8/29/76 *Summer Magic* (1963), part two
9/5/76 *A Country Coyote Goes Hollywood* (1965)
9/12/76 *Davy Crockett's Keelboat Race* (1955)
9/19/76 *Davy Crockett and the River Pirates* (1955)

1976-1977, NBC, SUNDAY, 7:00 PM

9/26/76 *One Little Indian* (1973), part one (new to TV)
10/3/76 *One Little Indian* (1973), part two (new to TV)
10/10/76 *The Biscuit Eater* (1972), part one (new to TV)
10/17/76 *The Biscuit Eater* (1972), part two (new to TV)
10/24/76 *20,000 Leagues Under the Sea* (1954) (2 hours)
10/31/76 *The Secret of Old Glory Mine* (new)
11/7/76 *Happy Birthday Donald Duck* (1956)
11/14/76 *The Apple Dumpling Gang* (1975) (2 hours) (new to TV)
11/28/76 *Disney's Greatest Dog Stars* (new)
12/5/76 *Goofy Takes a Holiday* (1961)
12/19/76 *Babes in Toyland* (1961), part one
12/26/76 *Babes in Toyland* (1961), part two
1/2/77 *The Golden Dog* (new)
1/9/77 *Kit Carson and the Mountain Men*, part one (new)
1/16/77 *Kit Carson and the Mountain Men*, part two (new)
1/23/77 *Cristobalito, the Calypso Colt* (1970)
1/30/77 *Barry of the Great St. Bernard*, part one (new)
2/6/77 *Barry of the Great St. Bernard*, part two (new)
2/13/77 *This is Your Life Donald Duck* (1960)
2/20/77 *Go West, Young Dog* (new)
2/27/77 *The Strongest Man in the World* (1975) (2 hours) (new to TV)
3/6/77 *Call it Courage* (1973)
3/13/77 *The Ghost of Cypress Swamp* (new)
3/20/77 *The Horse in the Gray Flannel Suit* (1968), part one
3/27/77 *The Horse in the Gray Flannel Suit* (1968), part two
4/3/77 *The Track of the African Bongo*, part one (new)
4/10/77 *The Track of the African Bongo*, part two (new)
4/17/77 *Nosey, the Sweetest Skunk in the West* (1972)
4/24/77 *Michael O'Hara the Fourth* (1972), part one

5/1/77 *Michael O'Hara the Fourth* (1972), part two
5/8/77 *The Castaway Cowboy* (1974) (2 hours) (new to TV)
5/15/77 *Disney's Greatest Villains* (1956)
5/22/77 *The Bluegrass Special* (new)
5/29/77 *The Little Shepherd Dog of Catalina* (1973)
6/5/77 *The High Flying Spy* (1972), part one
6/12/77 *The High Flying Spy* (1972), part two
6/19/77 *The High Flying Spy* (1972), part three
6/26/77 *Fire on Kelly Mountain* (1973)
7/3/77 *Mustang!* (1973), part one
7/10/77 *Mustang!* (1973), part two
7/17/77 *The Secret of Old Glory Mine* (1976)
7/24/77 *Lefty, the Dingaling Lynx* (1971), part one
7/31/77 *Lefty, the Dingaling Lynx* (1971), part two
8/7/77 *On Vacation with Mickey Mouse and Friends* (1956)
8/14/77 *The City Fox* (1972)
8/21/77 *The Horse With the Flying Tail* (1963)
8/28/77 *It's Tough to be a Bird* (1969)
9/4/77 *The Ranger of Brownstone* (1968)
9/11/77 *The Mystery of Dracula's Castle* (1973) (2 hours)

1977-1978, NBC, SUNDAY, 7:00 PM

9/18/77 *Gus* (1976) (2 hours) (new to TV)
9/25/77 *King of the Grizzlies* (1970) (2 hours)
10/2/77 *Treasure of Matecumbe* (1976) (2 hours) (new to TV)
10/9/77 *The Hound that Thought he was a Raccoon* (1960)
10/16/77 *Charley and the Angel* (1973) (2 hours) (new to TV)
10/23/77 *The Incredible Journey* (1963) (90 minutes) (new to TV)
10/30/77 *Halloween Hall O' Fame* (new)
11/13/77 *The Computer Wore Tennis Shoes* (1969) (2 hours)
11/20/77 *The Mouseketeers at Walt Disney World* (new)
11/27/77 *The Adventures of Bullwhip Griffin* (1967), part one
12/4/77 *The Adventures of Bullwhip Griffin* (1967), part two
12/11/77 *Run, Cougar, Run* (1972) (2 hours)
12/25/77 *From All of Us to All of You* (1958)
1/1/78 *The Spy Busters* (1969) (2 hours)
1/8/78 *Three on the Run* (new)
1/22/78 *Journey to the Valley of the Emu* (new)
1/29/78 *The Shaggy Dog* (1959) (2 hours)
2/5/78 *The Million Dollar Dixie Deliverance* (2 hours) (new)

2/19/78 *The Ugly Dachshund* (1965), part one
2/26/78 *The Ugly Dachshund* (1965), part two
3/5/78 *Race For Survival* (new)
3/12/78 *Trail of Danger*, part one (new)
3/19/78 *Trail of Danger*, part two (new)
3/26/78 *Mixed Nuts* (1959)
4/2/78 *The Barefoot Executive* (1971), part one
4/9/78 *The Barefoot Executive* (1971), part two
4/16/78 *Adventure in Satan's Canyon* (1974)
4/23/78 *Those Calloways* (1965), part one
4/30/78 *Those Calloways* (1965), part two
5/7/78 *Those Calloways* (1965), part three
5/14/78 *Child of Glass* (2 hours) (new)
5/21/78 *Jungle Cat* (1960)
5/28/78 *The Young Runaways* (2 hours) (new)
6/4/78 *A Tale of Two Critters* (1977) (new to TV)
6/11/78 *Disney's Greatest Villains* (1956)
6/18/78 *The Scarecrow of Romney Marsh* (1964), part one
6/25/78 *The Scarecrow of Romney Marsh* (1964), part two
7/2/78 *The Boy and the Bronc Buster* (1973), part one
7/9/78 *The Boy and the Bronc Buster* (1973), part two
7/16/78 *The Whiz Kid and the Carnival Caper* (1976), part one
7/23/78 *The Whiz Kid and the Carnival Caper* (1976), part two
7/30/78 *Nature's Strangest Oddballs* (1970)
8/6/78 *Hog Wild* (1974), part one
8/13/78 *Hog Wild* (1974), part two
8/20/78 *The Three Lives of Thomasina* (1963), part one
8/27/78 *The Three Lives of Thomasina* (1963), part two
9/3/78 *Shokee, the Everglades Panther* (1974)
9/10/78 *Donald Duck Quacks Up* (1961)

1978-1979, NBC, SUNDAY, 7:00 PM

9/17/78 *Dumbo* (1941) (2 hours)
9/24/78 *The Shaggy D.A.* (1976) (2 hours) (new to TV)
10/1/78 *In Search of the Castaways* (1962), part one (new to TV)
10/8/78 *In Search of the Castaways* (1962), part two (new to TV)
10/15/78 *Now You See Him, Now You Don't* (1972), part one
10/22/78 *Now You See Him, Now You Don't* (1972), part two
10/29/78 *The Gnome-Mobile* (1967), part one (new to TV)
11/5/78 *The Gnome-Mobile* (1967), part two (new to TV)

11/12/78 *The Boatniks* (1970) (2 hours) (new to TV)
11/19/78 *Mickey's 50* (90 minutes) (new)
11/26/78 *Superdad* (1973), part one
12/3/78 *Superdad* (1973), part two
12/10/78 *Christmas at Walt Disney World* (new)
12/31/78 *Three Tall Tales* (1963)
1/7/79 *Donovan's Kid*, part one (new)
1/14/79 *Donovan's Kid*, part two (new)
1/21/79 *The Nashville Coyote* (1972)
1/28/79 *Shadow of Fear*, part one (new)
2/4/79 *Shadow of Fear*, part two (new)
2/11/79 *Ride a Wild Pony* (1975), part one (new to TV)
2/18/79 *Ride a Wild Pony* (1975), part two (new to TV)
3/4/79 *Never a Dull Moment* (1968) (2 hours) (new to TV)
3/18/79 *The Omega Connection* (2 hours) (new)
3/25/79 *Born to Run*, part one (new)
4/1/79 *Born to Run*, part two (new)
4/8/79 *The Boy from Dead Man's Bayou* (*Bayou Boy*) (1971), part one
4/15/79 *The Boy from Dead Man's Bayou* (*Bayou Boy*) (1971), part two
4/22/79 *The Legend of the Boy and the Eagle* (1967)
4/29/79 *The Tattooed Police Horse* (1964)
5/6/79 *The Parent Trap* (1961) (2 hours)
5/13/79 *The Sky Trap* (2 hours) (new)
5/20/79 *Goofing Around with Donald Duck* (1963)
5/27/79 *The Million Dollar Dixie Deliverance* (1978) (2 hours)
6/3/79 *A Tiger Walks* (1964), part one
6/10/79 *A Tiger Walks* (1964), part two
6/17/79 *Goofy's Salute to Father* (1961)
6/24/79 *The Survival of Sam the Pelican* (1976)
7/1/79 *Charlie, the Lonesome Cougar* (1967), part one
7/8/79 *Charlie, the Lonesome Cougar* (1967), part two
7/15/79 *Salty, the Hijacked Harbor Seal* (1972)
7/22/79 *My Dog, the Thief* (1969), part one
7/29/79 *My Dog, the Thief* (1969), part two
8/5/79 *The Ranger of Brownstone* (1968)
8/12/79 *Justin Morgan Had a Horse* (1972), part one
8/19/79 *Justin Morgan Had a Horse* (1972), part two
8/26/79 *The Sky's the Limit* (1975), part one
9/2/79 *The Sky's the Limit* (1975), part two

DISNEY'S WONDERFUL WORLD
1979-1980, NBC, SUNDAY, 7:00 PM

9/9/79 *The Absent-Minded Professor* (1961), part one
9/16/79 *The Absent-Minded Professor* (1961), part two
9/23/79 *The Love Bug* (1969) (2 hours) (new to TV)
9/30/79 *The Million Dollar Duck* (1971), part one
10/7/79 *The Million Dollar Duck* (1971), part two
10/14/79 *Baseball Fever* (new)
10/21/79 *Gus* (1976), part one
10/28/79 *Gus* (1976), part two
11/4/79 *20,000 Leagues Under the Sea* (1954) (2½ hours)
11/11/79 *The Strongest Man in the World* (1975) (2 hours)
11/25/79 *Duck for Hire* (1957)
12/16/79 *Major Effects* (new)
12/23/79 *From All of Us to All of You* (1958)
12/30/79 *Dad, Can I Borrow the Car?* (1970)
1/6/80 *Donald Duck Quacks Up* (1961)
1/13/80 *That Darn Cat!* (1965) (2 hours)
1/20/80 *Mickey's Greatest Adventures* (1955)
1/27/80 *The Computer Wore Tennis Shoes* (1969), part one
2/3/80 *The Computer Wore Tennis Shoes* (1969), part two
2/10/80 *Donald's Valentine Day Salute* (new)
2/17/80 *Escape to Witch Mountain* (1975) (2 hours) (new to TV)
2/24/80 *The Apple Dumpling Gang* (1975) (2 hours)
3/2/80 *The Monkey's Uncle* (1965) (2 hours)
3/9/80 *The Kids Who Knew Too Much* (2 hours) (new)
3/16/80 *Son of Flubber* (1963) (2 hours) (new to TV)
3/23/80 *The Shaggy D.A.* (1976), part one
3/30/80 *The Shaggy D.A.* (1976), part two
4/6/80 *Pluto's Day* (1956)
4/13/80 *Disney's Oscar Winners* (new)
4/20/80 *Sultan and the Rock Star* (new)
4/27/80 *The Secret of Lost Valley*, part one (new)
5/4/80 *The Secret of Lost Valley*, part two (new)
5/11/80 *Goofy Takes a Holiday* (1961)
6/1/80 *The Young Runaways* (1978), part one
6/8/80 *The Young Runaways* (1978), part two
6/15/80 *Goofy's Salute to Father* (1961)
6/22/80 *Donovan's Kid* (1979), part one
6/29/80 *Donovan's Kid* (1979), part two
7/6/80 *Fire on Kelly Mountain* (1973)

7/13/80 *Treasure Island* (1950), part one
7/20/80 *Treasure Island* (1950), part two
7/27/80 *The Misadventures of Chip 'n Dale* (1959)
8/3/80 *The Omega Connection* (1979), part one
8/10/80 *The Omega Connection* (1979), part two
8/17/80 *Child of Glass* (1978), part one
8/24/80 *Child of Glass* (1978), part two
8/31/80 *Twister, Bull From the Sky* (1976)
9/7/80 *Mickey's Greatest Adventures* (1955)
9/14/80 *Disneyland's 25th Anniversary Show* (1980)

1980-1981, NBC, SUNDAY, 7:00 PM

9/28/80 *The Shaggy Dog* (1959), part one
10/5/80 *The Shaggy Dog* (1959), part two
10/12/80 *Escape to Witch Mountain* (1975) (2 hours)
10/26/80 *Disney's Greatest Villains* (1956)
11/2/80 *The Apple Dumpling Gang* (1975) (2 hours)
11/9/80 *Old Yeller* (1957), part one
11/16/80 *Old Yeller* (1957), part two
11/23/80 *The Mouseketeer Reunion* (new)
12/14/80 *From All of Us to All of You* (1958)
12/21/80 *The Ghosts of Buxley Hall*, part one (new)
1/4/81 *The Ghosts of Buxley Hall*, part two (new)
1/18/81 *Pluto's Day* (1956)
2/1/81 *This Is Your Life, Donald Duck* (1960)
2/22/81 *Disney's Oscar Winners* (1980)
3/8/81 *Duck for Hire* (1957)
3/15/81 *The Castaway Cowboy* (1974), part one
3/22/81 *The Castaway Cowboy* (1974), part two
3/29/81 *That Darn Cat!* (1965), part one
4/5/81 *That Darn Cat!* (1965), part two
4/19/81 *Lefty* (1980)
4/26/81 *Disney Animation: The Illusion of Life* (new)
5/3/81 *Disney's Greatest Dog Stars* (1976)
5/10/81 *The Boatniks* (1970), part one
5/17/81 *The Boatniks* (1970), part two
5/24/81 *Pollyanna* (1960) (3 hours)
5/31/81 *Baseball Fever* (1979)
6/7/81 *The Wild Country* (1971), part one
6/14/81 *The Wild Country* (1971), part two

6/21/81 *Napoleon and Samantha* (1972), part one
6/28/81 *Napoleon and Samantha* (1972), part two
7/5/81 *Goofy Takes a Holiday* (1961)
7/12/81 *Now You See Him, Now You Don't* (1972), part one
7/19/81 *Now You See Him, Now You Don't* (1972), part two
7/26/81 *The Misadventures of Chip 'n Dale* (1959)
8/2/81 *Follow Me, Boys!* (1966), part one (new to TV)
8/16/81 *Follow Me, Boys!* (1966), part two (new to TV)
8/23/81 *Big Red* (1962), part one
8/30/81 *Big Red* (1962), part two
9/6/81 *The Barefoot Executive* (1971), part one
9/13/81 *The Barefoot Executive* (1971), part two

WALT DISNEY
1981-1982, CBS, SATURDAY, 8:00 PM

9/26/81 *The Love Bug* (1969), part one
10/3/81 *The Love Bug* (1969), part two
10/10/81 *Herbie Rides Again* (1974), part one (new to TV)
10/17/81 *Herbie Rides Again* (1974), part two (new to TV)
10/24/81 *A Disney Halloween* (new)
10/31/81 *The Last Flight of Noah's Ark* (1980), part one (new to TV)
11/7/81 *The Last Flight of Noah's Ark* (1980), part two (new to TV)
11/14/81 *A Disney Storybook*, part one (new)
11/21/81 *A Disney Storybook*, part two (new)
11/28/81 *The Cherokee Trail* (new)
12/5/81 *A Magical Disney Christmas* (new)
12/12/81 *Walt Disney ... One Man's Dream* (2 hours) (new)
12/19/81 *Escape to Witch Mountain* (1975), part one
12/26/81 *Escape to Witch Mountain* (1975), part two
1/2/82 *Man's Hunting Instinct* (1961)
1/16/82 *Tales of the Apple Dumpling Gang* (new)
1/23/82 *Donald and Jose, Olé!* (90 minutes) (new)
1/30/82 *The Cat from Outer Space* (1978), part one (new to TV)
2/6/82 *The Cat from Outer Space* (1978), part two (new to TV)
2/13/82 *A Disney Valentine* (new)
2/20/82 *Beyond Witch Mountain* (new)
2/27/82 *A Spaceman in King Arthur's Court (Unidentified Flying Oddball)* (1979), part one (new to TV)
3/06/82 *A Spaceman in King Arthur's Court (Unidentified Flying Oddball)*, part two (new to TV)

3/13/82 *The Moon-Spinners* (1964), part one
3/20/82 *The Moon-Spinners* (1964), part two (90 minutes)
4/10/82 *The Adventures of Pollyanna* (new)
4/17/82 *Treasure Island* (1950), part one
4/24/82 *Treasure Island* (1950), part two
5/1/82 *A Disney Vacation* (new)
5/8/82 *The Million Dollar Duck* (1971), part one
5/15/82 *The Million Dollar Duck* (1971), part two
5/22/82 *Smoke* (1970), part one
5/29/82 *Smoke* (1970), part two
6/5/82 *The Treasure of San Bosco Reef* (1968), part one
6/12/82 *The Treasure of San Bosco Reef* (1968), part two
6/19/82 *The Cherokee Trail* (1981)
6/26/82 *The Ranger of Brownstone* (1968)
7/3/82 *The Little Shepherd Dog of Catalina* (1973)
7/10/82 *Kidnapped* (1960) (2 hours)
7/17/82 *Duck for Hire* (1957) (30 minutes)
7/31/82 *Pluto and his Friends* (30 minutes) (new)
8/7/82 *The Strange Monster of Strawberry Cove* (1971) (2 hours)
8/21/82 *Fire on Kelly Mountain* (1973)
9/4/82 *Beyond Witch Mountain* (1982)
9/11/82 *Gus* (1976), part one
9/18/82 *Gus* (1976), part two

1982-1983, CBS, SATURDAY, 8:00 PM

9/25/82 *The Apple Dumpling Gang Rides Again* (1979), part one (new to TV)
10/2/82 *The Apple Dumpling Gang Rides Again* (1979), part two (new to TV)
10/9/82 *Freaky Friday* (1977), part one (new to TV)
10/16/82 *Freaky Friday* (1977), part two (new to TV)
10/23/82 *Epcot Center: The Opening Celebration* (new)
10/30/82 *Disney's Halloween Treat* (new)
11/6/82 *No Deposit, No Return* (1976), part one (new to TV)
11/13/82 *No Deposit, No Return* (1976), part two (new to TV)
11/20/82 *Blackbeard's Ghost* (1968), part one (new to TV)
11/27/82 *Blackbeard's Ghost* (1968), part two (new to TV)
12/4/82 *A Disney Christmas Gift* (new)
12/11/82 *Winnie the Pooh and Friends* (new)
1/1/83 *Walt Disney's Mickey and Donald* (30 minutes) (new)

1/4/83 *The World's Greatest Athlete* (1973), part one (new to TV)
1/11/83 *The World's Greatest Athlete* (1973), part two (new to TV)
1/18/83 *Ferdinand the Bull and Mickey* (new)
1/25/83 *The Shaggy D.A.* (1976), part one
2/1/83 *The Shaggy D.A.* (1976), part two
2/08/83 *A Valentine from Disney* (new)
2/15/83 *The Hunter and the Rock Star* (*Sultan and the Rock Star*) (1980)
5/3/83 *Mickey and Donald Kidding Around* (new)
5/21/83 *Disney's Greatest Villains* (1956)
7/9/83 *A Disney Vacation* (new)
7/16/83 *The Kids Who Knew Too Much* (1980), part one
7/23/83 *The Kids Who Knew Too Much* (1980), part two
7/30/83 *The Sky Trap* (1979), part one
8/6/83 *The Sky Trap* (1979), part two
9/03/83 *The Omega Connection* (1979), part one
9/10/83 *The Omega Connection* (1979), part two
9/17/83 *Baseball Fever* (1979)
9/24/83 *Walt Disney's Mickey and Donald* (1983)

DISNEY CHANNEL PREMIERE FILMS

10/9/83 *Tiger Town*
5/6/84 *Gone Are the Dayes*
10/7/84 *Love Leads the Way: A True Story*
1/6/85 *Black Arrow*
2/3/85 *Lots of Luck*
5/5/85 *The Undergrads*

SPECIALS

3/10/70 *Winnie the Pooh and the Honey Tree* (1966) (30 minutes) (new to TV)
11/30/70 *Winnie the Pooh and the Blustery Day* (1968) (30 minutes) (new to TV)
3/22/71 *Winnie the Pooh and the Honey Tree* (1966) (30 minutes)
10/29/71 *The Grand Opening of Walt Disney World* (90 minutes) (new)
12/1/71 *Winnie the Pooh and the Blustery Day* (1968) (30 minutes)
3/14/72 *Winnie the Pooh and the Honey Tree* (1966) (30 minutes)
11/22/72 *The Julie Andrews Hour* (1 hour)
11/29/72 *Winnie the Pooh and the Blustery Day* (1968) (30 minutes)

4/4/73 *Winnie the Pooh and the Honey Tree* (1966) (30 minutes)
10/25/73 *Walt Disney – A Golden Anniversary Salute* (90 minutes) (new)
11/28/73 *Winnie the Pooh and the Blustery Day* (1968) (30 minutes)
2/23/74 *20,000 Leagues Under the Sea* (1954) / *Beaver Valley* (1950) (2 hours) (new to TV)
3/26/74 *Winnie the Pooh and the Honey Tree* (1966) (30 minutes)
4/10/74 *Sandy in Disneyland* (1 hour) (new)
7/11/74 *Herbie Day at Disneyland* (1 hour) (new)
9/20/74 *Walt Disney – A Golden Anniversary Salute* (90 minutes)
10/26/74 *The Parent Trap* (1961) / *Mysteries of the Deep* (1959) (2 hours) (new to TV)
11/26/74 *Winnie the Pooh and the Blustery Day* (1968) (30 minutes)
12/14/74 *The Three Lives of Thomasina* (1963) / *It's Tough to Be a Bird* (1969) / *Arizona Sheepdog* (1955) (2 hours) (new to TV)
3/8/75 *Pollyanna* (1960) / *Nature's Strangest Creatures* (1959) (2 hours) (new to TV)
11/1/75 *The Absent-Minded Professor* (1961) / *Hurricane Hannah* (1962) (2 hours) (new to TV)
11/28/75 *Winnie the Pooh and Tigger Too* (1974) (30 minutes) (new to TV)
2/14/76 *Old Yeller* (1957) / *Pecos Bill* (1948) / *A Country Coyote Goes Hollywood* (1965) (2 hours) (new to TV)
4/3/76 *Monsanto Night Presents Walt Disney's America on Parade* (1 hour) (new)
5/1/76 *That Darn Cat!* (1965) / *Bear Country* (1953) (2 hours) (new to TV)
10/16/76 *The Great Locomotive Chase* (1956) / *Nikki, Wild Dog of the North* (1961) (2 hours) (new to TV)
11/25/76 *Winnie the Pooh and Tigger Too* (1974) (30 minutes)
11/26/76 *The Moon-Spinners* (1964) / *Prowlers of the Everglades* (1953) (3 hours) (new to TV)
12/6/76 *Christmas in Disneyland* (1 hour) (new)
12/11/76 *Lt. Robin Crusoe, U.S.N.* (1965) / *Nature's Half Acre* (1951) (2 hours) (new to TV)
1/29/77 *A Horse Called Comanche* (*Tonka*) (1958) / *Wonders of the Water World* (1961) (2 hours) (new to TV)
11/25/77 *Winnie the Pooh and the Honey Tree* (1966) (30 minutes)
9/13/78 *NBC Salutes the 25th Anniversary of "The Wonderful World of Disney"* (2 hours) (new)
9/17/78 *Dumbo* (1941) (2 hours)
12/1/78 *Winnie the Pooh and the Blustery Day* (1968) (30 minutes)

4/4/79 *Happy Birthday Donald Duck* (1956) (1 hour)
4/11/79 *On Vacation with Mickey Mouse and Friends* (1956) (1 hour)
11/79 *Black Holes: Monsters That Eat Space and Time* (30 minutes) (new)
1980 *Snow White Live* (90 minutes) (new)
2/22/80 *This is Your Life, Donald Duck* (1960) (1 hour)
3/6/80 *Kraft Salutes Disneyland's 25th Anniversary* (1 hour) (new)
10/22/80 *Lefty* (1 hour) (new)
10/2/81 *Florida's Disney Decade* (1 hour) (new)
11/22/81 *Mary Poppins* (1964) (3 hours) (new to TV)
5/1/82 *The Strongest Man in the World* (1975) (2 hours) (new to TV)
5/23/82 *Computers Are People, Too!* (30 minutes) (new)
9/19/82 *A Dream Called Walt Disney World* (30 minutes) (new)
11/25/82 *Mary Poppins* (1964) (3 hours)
4/21/83 *Believe You Can…And You Can!* (30 minutes) (new)
5/27/83 *Walt Disney's Mickey and Donald Presents Sport Goofy* (30 minutes) (new)
6/3/83 *The Fairest of Them All* (30 minutes) (new)
8/30/83 *Winnie the Pooh and Friends* (1 hour)
9/10/83 *U.S. Junior Tournament World Tennis Tournament* (2 hours) (new)
9/16/83 *Walt Disney's Mickey and Donald Presents Sport Goofy #2* (30 minutes) (new)
10/29/83 *Disney's Halloween Treat* (1982) (1 hour)
11/24/83 *Walt Disney's Mickey and Donald Presents Sport Goofy #3* (30 minutes) (new)
12/3/83 *U.S. Junior Tournament World Tennis Tournament #2* (2 hours) (new)
12/20/83 *A Disney Christmas Gift* (1982) (1 hour)
12/25/83 *Walt Disney World Very Merry Christmas Parade (1983 Version)* (new)
2/14/84 *Disney's All-Star Valentine Party* (1 hour) (new)
5/11/84 *Disney's All-Star Mother's Day Album* (1 hour) (new)
6/8/84 *Walt Disney Presents Sport Goofy Olympic Games Special* (30 minutes) (new)
9/14/84 *Walt Disney's Mickey, Donald and Sport Goofy: Getting Wet* (30 minutes) (new)
11/15/84 *Donald Duck's 50th Birthday* (1 hour) (new)
11/30/84 *Walt Disney's Mickey, Donald and Sport Goofy: Snowtime* (30 minutes) (new)
12/10/84 *Mickey's Christmas Carol* (1983) (1 hour) (new to TV)
12/14/84 *Walt Disney's Mickey, Donald and Sport Goofy: Happy Holidays* (30 minutes) (new)

Disney on TV   525

12/25/84 *Walt Disney World Very Merry Christmas Parade (1984 Version)* (90 minutes) (new)
2/18/85 *Disneyland's 30th Anniversary Celebration* (2 hours) (new)
4/7/85 *Walt Disney World Happy Easter Parade (1985 Version)* (1 hour) (new)
8/11/85 *Disneyland's 30th Anniversary Celebration* (2 hours)

30 MINUTE TV SERIES

THE MOUSE FACTORY
SYNDICATED, 1971-1972

1/26/72 *Vacations* (Charles Nelson Reilly)
2/2/72 *Women's Lib* (Jo Anne Worley)
2/9/72 *Folk Tale Favorites* (Johnny Brown)
2/16/72 *Spooks and Magic* (Phyllis Diller)
2/23/72 *Physical Fitness* (Don Knotts)
3/1/72 *The Great Outdoors* (Dom DeLuise)
3/8/72 *Water Sports* (Joe Flynn)
3/15/72 *Man at Work* (John Byner)
3/22/72 *Music* (Skiles and Henderson)
3/29/72 *Interplanetary Travel* (Jonathan Winters)
4/5/72 *Homeowners* (Jim Backus)
4/12/72 *Spectator Sports* (Charles Nelson Reilly) (Note: George Carlin was originally scheduled to host this show.)
4/19/72 *Horses* (Jo Anne Worley)
4/26/72 *Aviation* (Johnny Brown)
5/3/72 *Back to Nature* (Wally Cox)
5/10/72 *Bullfighting to Bullfrogs* (Pat Buttram)
5/17/72 *Sports* (Pat Paulsen)

SYNDICATED, 1972-1973

9/20/72 *Alligators* (Johnny Brown)
9/27/72 *Paul Bunyan* (Jim Backus)
10/4/72 *Bullfighting* (Bill Dana)
10/11/72 *Knighthood* (Henry Gibson)
10/18/72 *Pluto* (John Astin)
10/25/72 *Goliath II* (Kurt Russell)
11/1/72 *The Mouse Show* (Dave Madden)

11/8/72 *Cats* (Shari Lewis)
11/15/72 *Ben Franklin* (Wally Cox)
11/22/72 *Mickey* (Annette Funicello)
11/29/72 *Lions* (Henry Gibson)
12/6/72 *Consciences* (Harry Morgan)
12/13/72 *Noah's Ark* (Bill Dana)
12/20/72 *Hunting* (John Astin)
12/27/72 *Sports*
1/3/73 *Tugboats* (Dave Madden)
1/10/73 *Automobiles* (Ken Berry)
1/17/73 *Trains* (Harry Morgan)
1/24/73 *Homes* (Jim Backus)
1/31/73 *The Reluctant Dragon* (Wally Cox)
2/7/73 *Wheels* (Johnny Brown)
2/14/73 *Winter Fun* (Kurt Russell)
2/21/73 *Penguins* (Annette Funicello)
2/28/73 *Elephants* (Nipsey Russell)
3/7/73 *Mickey and the Beanstalk* (Shari Lewis)
3/14/73 *Dancing* (Ken Berry)

THE MICKEY MOUSE CLUB
SYNDICATED, 1974-1975 AND 1975-1976

1/20/75-9/76

THE NEW MICKEY MOUSE CLUB
SYNDICATED, 1976-1977 AND 1977-1978

1/14/77-12/1/78

HERBIE, THE LOVE BUG
CBS, 1981-1982

3/17/82 *Herbie, the Match Maker*
3/24/82 *Herbie to the Rescue*
3/31/82 *My House is Your House*
4/7/82 *Herbie, the Best Man*
4/14/82 *Calling Doctor Herbie*

SMALL & FRYE
CBS, 1982-1983

3/7/83 *Fiddler on the Hoof*
3/14/83 *Endangered Detectives*
3/21/83 *The Case of the Street of Silence*
6/1/83 *Small & Frye Pilot*
6/8/83 *Schlocky Too*
6/15/83 *The Case of the Concerned Husband*

GUN SHY
CBS, 1982-1983

3/15/83 *Western Velvet*
3/22/83 *Pardon My Boy, Is That the Quake City Choo Choo?*
3/29/83 *What Do You Mean "We," Amigo?*
4/5/83 *You Gotta Know When to Hold 'Em*
4/12/83 *Reading, Writing and Robbing*
4/19/83 *Mail Order Mommy*

ZORRO AND SON
CBS, 1982-1983

4/6/83 *Zorro and Son Pilot*
4/13/83 *Beauty and the Mask*
4/20/83 *A Fistful of Pesos*
4/27/83 *Wash Day*
5/4/83 *The Butcher of Barcelona*

WILDSIDE
ABC, 1984-1985

3/21/85 *Well Known Secret*
3/28/85 *Delinquency of a Miner*
4/4/85 *The Crimea of the Century*
4/11/85 *Don't Keep the Home Fires Burning*
4/18/85 *Buffalo Who?*
4/25/85 *Until the Fat Lady Sings*

Bibliography

Building a Company: Roy O. Disney and the Creation of an Entertainment Empire by Bob Thomas, Hyperion, 1998

Comix: A History of Comic Books in America by Les Daniels, Bonanza, 1971

The Comic- Book Book by Don Thompson and Dick Lupott, Nostalgia Books, 1974

Disney A to Z by Dave Smith, Hyperion, 1996, 1998

Disney Films, The by Leonard Maltin, Hyperion, 1973, 1984, 1995

Disney News Magazine, Walt Disney Productions, 1967-1985

Disney Studio Story, The by Richard Hollis and Brian Sibley, Crown Publishing, 1988

Disney That Never Was, The by Charles Solomon, Hyperion, 1995

Disney Trivia from the Vault by Dave Smith, Disney Editions, 2012

Disneyland Encyclopedia, The by Chris Strodder, Santa Monica Press, 2008

Golden Age of Walt Disney Records 1933-1988, The by R. Michael Murray, Antique Trader Press, 1997

I Was a TV Horror Host by John Stanley, Creatures at Large Press, 2007

Leonard Maltin's 2012 Movie and Video Guide by Leonard Maltin, Signet, 2012

Making of Tron, The by William Kallay, CreateSpace, 2011

Married to the Mouse: Walt Disney World and Orlando by Richard E. Foglesong, Yale University Press, 2001

Mouse Tracks: The Story of Walt Disney Records by Tim Hollis and Greg Ehrbar, University Press of Mississippi, 2006

100 Years of American Newspaper Comics by Maurice Horn, Gramercy Books, 1996

Overstreet Comic Book Price Guide #42, The by Robert M. Overstreet, Gemstone Publishing, 2012

Rebel Visions: The Underground Comix Revolution 1963-1975 by Patrick Rosenkranz, Fantagraphics Books, 2002

Since the World Began, Walt Disney World: The First 25 Years by Jeff Kurtti, Hyperion, 1996

Storming the Magic Kingdom by John Taylor, Knopf Publishing, 1987

Tomart's Illustrated Disneyana Catalog and Price Guide, Volume 1-3 and *Supplement Edition* by Tom Tumbusch, Tomart Publications, 1985, 1987

Walt Disney & Recollections of the Disney Studios: 1955-1980 by Charles Tranberg, BearManor Media, 2012

The Wonderful World of Disney Television: A Complete History by Bill Cotter, Hyperion Publishing, 1997

"Working for Mickey Mouse," *Inside Comics #2* by David Marlow, Galaxy News Service, Summer 1974

Index

AAA 444
Aardal, John 397, 483, 488
Aaron, Andy 370
Abel, Robert 397
Abela, Emanuel 418
Abela, Joe 419
Abbeville Press 282, 300, 326, 417
Abbey Road, 370
ABC 7, 86
Abercrombie, Ian 172
Aberle, Douglas 474
Able, Albert 231, 283, 360
Abrams, Alan 430
Absent-Minded Professor, The 58, 164, 274, 358
Academy Awards 20, 50, 103-104, 116, 138, 150, 176, 204, 215, 230, 275, 279, 324, 375, 405-406, 416, 435, 454, 463, 480-481, 497
Ackerman, Al 455
Ackerman, Bettye 50
Ackland, Joss 199
Ackroyd, Jack 437
Acosta, Tom 70, 147, 252
Acting Out the ABC's 20
Adam, Scott 90
Adams, Alan 473
Adams, April 447
Adams, Arthur 328, 346
Adams, Lisa 396
Adams, Michael 489
Adams, Nancy 147
Addison, John 212
Adler, Mark 430
Adnopoz, Sue 483
Adolph Coors Company 437
Adrian, Iris 39, 82, 87, 192, 219, 228, 231, 237-238, 341, 345
Advanced Music Systems 397
Adventure in Satan's Canyon 158
Adventure Through Inner Space 13, 466
Adventureland 388
Adventures of Bullwhip Griffin, The 11
Adventures of Ichabod and Mr. Toad, The 281, 298
Adventures of Pollyanna, The 387
Aeronvale Francaise French Naval Aviation 380
African Lion, The 205
After Image Inc. 397
"Age of Not Believing, The" 97, 99, 103

Aguilar, Oscar Arturo 365
Aguirre, Dolores 341
Aguirre, Richard 467
Agutter, Jenny 365
Ahern II, Lloyd N. 319, 340
Ahn, Philip 134
Aiello, Danny 446
Air Pirate Funnies 81, 179, 300
Airplane! 8, 369
Aladdin 379
Alaska 59
Alba, Jaime 490
Albert, Eddie 185, 190-191
Alberta, Canada 441
Alberta Economic Development Film Industry Office 437
Albertson, Jack 376
Albrecht, Gretchen 483
Albrecht, Patricia Alice 327
Albright, Lynne 125, 185
Alcott, John 466
Alden, Sid 370
Alderson, John 275-276, 289
Aldrich, Fred 47, 54
Aldridge, James 212
Aleman, Alejandro 341
Aletter, Frank 117, 122
Alexander, Beaumont 369
Alexander, Dale 483
Alexander, Elizabeth 212
Alexander, Jane 390
Alexander, John 475
Alexander, Judy 223
Alexander, Lloyd 481, 488
Alexander, Philip 418
"Alexander's Ragtime Band" 212
Alguire, Dan 252
Alice in Cartoonland 274
Alice in Wonderland 158, 388, 444
Alitalia Airlines 350
Alfinsen, Tom 82
Alfred 436
Algar, James 50, 121, 204
Alguire, Dan 70, 147
All Because Man Wanted to Fly 444
All Electric Cameraworks 397
All in the Family 121
Allard, Eric 319

Allder, Nick 371
Allen, Anthony 473
Allen, Barbara 472
Allen, Lewis 430
Allen, Lowell 301
Allen, Martin 268
Allen, Patricia 431
Allen, Rex 15, 17
Allen, Jr., Rex 17
Allen, Richard M. 436
Allen, Robert 473
Allen, Steve 443
Allers, Roger 395, 403
All-Star Movies Resort 44
Allwine, Wayne A. 318, 424, 459, 467, 482, 484, 488
Allyn, Robin 490
Almanzar, James 160, 172, 228, 310, 360, 484
Alnwick Castle 317
Alpha Cine Laboratory, Inc. 371
Alphin, Nick 318, 418, 446, 459, 467, 482, 488
Alpine Gardens 13
Alpine School District 300
Alsberg, Arthur 218, 227, 262, 294
Altman, Reed 350
Altman, Robert 349-350
Altman, Stephen 350
Alton, Leon 82, 97
Altschul, David 474
Alvarez, Maria Luisa 396
Alvarez, Priscilla 396
Amador, Frank 396
"Amanda" 87
Amarok Productions, Ltd., An 430
Amazing Spider-Man, The 385
Ambro, Hal 252
Ambrose, Ted 370
Ameche, Don 66
America on Parade 178, 217
America the Beautiful 79, 178
America Sings 132, 159, 444
America Sings 159
American Film Consortium 300
American Fork High School 300
American Heritage 20
American Humane Association 74
American Journeys 444
American League 455
"American National Anthem, The" 437
American Tale, An 380
Ames, Preston 289, 345
Amos, John 133, 138
Amsden, Liz 436
Amsterdam, Morey 35
Amundsen, Michael 301
Amundsen, Peter 371
Amy 364-369
Amy on the Lips 369

Anagos, Bill 446
Anaheim, California 389
Anchor Bay 340
Andersen, Hans Christian 452
Anderson, Adam 283
Anderson, Bill 26, 46, 53, 81, 90, 109, 138, 150, 179, 192, 206, 223, 230
Anderson, Bob 198, 275-276
Anderson, Christina 139, 151, 179, 231
Anderson, Chuck 301
Anderson, David 165
Anderson, Gary 459
Anderson, Herbert 50, 53
Anderson, Hillyard 54
Anderson, James 395
Anderson, Jamie 466
Anderson, John A. 364
Anderson, John L. 455
Anderson, Ken 70, 73, 146, 252, 258, 268, 274
Anderson, Kurt 482
Anderson, Lance 488
Anderson, Peter 396, 423, 459, 467
Anderson, Shelby 81, 96, 192, 223
Anderson, Sparky 455
Anderson, Viki 482
Andrews, Christopher D. 396
Andrews, Edward 91, 117, 139
Andrews, Harry 279
Andrews, Julie 105, 108
Andrews, Mark 360
Andy Griffith Show, The 77, 451
Angotti, Nick 360
Angus, Albert 437
Anheuser-Busch Companies, Inc. 437
Anicam 397
Animal Actors of Hollywood 424
Animal House (see *National Lampoon's Animal House*)
Animalympics 403
Animated Features 326
Animation Camera Services 396
Another Rainbow 495
Ansara, Michael 165
Anselmo, Tony 482
Anspack, Susan 359
Anthology Show (See *Wonderful World of Disney, The*)
Anthony, Piers 3
Anthrax 5
Anvil-Abbey Road Studios 474
"Anvil Chorus" 205
Anvil Studios 198, 212, 247, 275, 301, 314, 333, 370
"Any Fool Could See" 359, 361-362
Appel, Carol Jean 370
Apple Computer Inc. 397, 496
Apple Dumpling Gang, The 192-198, 310, 388
"Apple Dumpling Gang, The" 192

Index   533

Apple Dumpling Gang Rides Again, The 230, 310-314
Applegate, Royce D. 446
"Appreciate the Lady" 376, 378
APT Holman Corp. 397
Aquino, Ruben 482
Arambula, Roman 178
Aranas, Stephanie 350
Arance, William (W.L.) (Bill) 396, 424, 489
Archambault, Alex 380
Archer, Brian 474
Archer, Ernest 370
Archerd, Army 360
Arches National Park 122
Arctic, The 176
Arden, Eve 179, 184
Arden, Robert 381
Arends, Harry 98
Arenson, Julianna 489
Aries, Peter 396
Arlis, George 211
Aristocats, The 7, 11, 19, 45, 61-62, 70-74, 80, 105, 150, 326
"Aristocats, The" 70
Aristokittens, The 80, 108, 133, 159, 178
Arizona Game and Fish Department 204
Arkin, David 351
Armentrout, John 98
Armstrong, Andy 198
Armstrong, Louis 20, 73, 455
Armstrong, Vic 314, 334, 371
Arndt, John 310, 365
Arnold, Alan 473
Arnold, Denny 90, 117, 179, 223, 228
Arnold, Joan 301
Arnold, Mark 1
Arnold, Phil 21
Arnott, Mark 409
Arou, Alfonso 87, 122
Arquette, Rosanna 454
Art of Walt Disney, The 133
Artaud, Joane 467
Artingstall, Stuart 474
Aruza High School Band 437
Asbury, Kelly 483
Ashby, Arthur 355
Ashby, Jack 179
Ashby, John 223
Ashe, Sharon 425
Ashley, Edward 160
Ashton, Rachel 475
Ashton, Roy 247, 275, 314
Askin, Leon 134
Askins, Monroe P. 113
Asner, Edward 228
Aspercel 35-38
Astin, John 238, 243
Atari Corp. 397

Atencio, Xavier 252, 257
Atherfold, Ken 473
Atkins, Andy 396
Atkinson, Martin 275
Atlantic Richfield Corporation 437
Atta Girl, Kelly 11
Attmore, Billy 224, 227
Attwood, Graham 467
Attwooll, Hugh 198, 206, 247, 275, 314, 333, 380
Aubry, Errol 483
Audio and Design Recording Inc. 397
Audio-animatronics 12
Audley, Eleanor 31
"Auld Lang Syne" 437
Austin, Elizabeth 437
Automatic Camera Effects Systems 319
Auer, Greg 90
Aushead, John 436
Austin, Diana 431
Austin, Ed 483, 488
Austin, Holly 97
Autopia 13
Avalon, Frankie 44
Avengers, The 189, 338
Axworthy, Susan 369
Ayers, Curt 327-328
Ayres, Lew 109
Ayres, Robert 318
Azzopardi, Nadine 418

Baar, Tim 35
Babes in Toyland 86
Baby…Secret of the Lost Legend 466-472
Bachmann, Conrad 97
Back to the Future 465
Backdraft 77
Backes, Alice 126, 289
Backus, Jim 117, 121, 269
Bacon III, William W. 14, 62
Bad News Bears, The 217-218
Bad News Bears in Breaking Training, The 218
Bad News Bears Go to Japan, The 218
Baddeley, Hermoine 70, 73
Badin, Anuar 340
Baer, Dale 147, 252, 258, 269, 481
Baer, Jane 482
Baerwitz, Jerry A. 408
Bagdon, Mindaugus 430
Bagley, Fuddle 238
Bahler, Olsson, Murray and Haas 224
Bailey, Alfred M. 204
Bailey, Charlie 371
Bailey, Jack 180
Bailey, Pearl 376, 379
Bailey, Raymond 160, 179-180, 184
Baily, Richard 397
Bain, Bonar 438

Baird, Lynn 301
Bakalyan, Richard (Dick) 31, 53, 117, 121, 139, 179, 231, 283, 377
Baker, Ben 87
Baker, Bob 96
Baker, Buddy 50, 62, 90, 113, 122, 138, 151, 165, 192, 204, 219, 223, 230, 252, 257, 294, 310, 339, 359, 376
Baker, Carroll 334
Baker, David 268
Baker, Diane 35
Baker, Don 397
Baker, Dorthea 482
Baker, Elsie 21
Baker, Frank 161
Baker, Joby 21, 151, 255
Baker, Joe 98, 310
Baker, John 98
Baker, Kirsten 328
Baker, Rick 489
Baker, Thomas 319, 398
Baker, Wilma 483
Bakery, The 98
Bakewell, William 180
Bakey, Ed 295
Bakke, Edle 185, 395, 423
Bakunas, A.J. 282, 310
Balasko, Josiane 264
Balchowsky, Max 38-39
Baldacchino 419
Baldwin, Bill 35
Balfour, Michael 276
Balk, Fairuza 475, 480-481
"Ballad of Smith and Gabriel Jimmyboy, The" 47
Ballanger, Ron 314
Ballantine, Carl 306
Ballard, Carroll 430
Ballard, Kaye 238
Ballard, Terry 74
Ballew, Jerry 185
Balogh, George 165
Baloo and Little Britches 20
Baltzell, Deborah 360
Bamber, Dickie 198
Bamber, Terry 247
Bambi 204, 388, 444
Bamford, Tom 38
Band of Angels 108
Banjo, the Woodpile Cat 299, 380
Banks, Tommy 437
Banks, Vicki 396, 483
Bannen, Ian 390
Banny, Jeannot 467-468
Baracchi, Gilda 212
Barbash, Bob 318
Barbour, Tim 98
Barbour, Vincent 490

Bardon, John 199
Bardsley, Grant 483
Barefoot Executive, The 81-86, 137, 236
Barker, Ken 198, 212, 247, 275, 314
Barkley, Dorothy 74
Barks, Carl 14, 81, 159, 496
Barkworth, Peter 247
Barnes and Barnes 53
Barnes, Walter 185, 269
Barnett, Dave 397
Barnett, Robbie 475
Barney Miller 288
Barnhart, Dale 252
Barnhart, Philo 482
Baron, Eddie 305
Baron, Robert 360
Barr, Esther 483, 489
Barr, Lindsay 455
Barrett, Sean 475
Barrie, Amanda 199, 203
Barron, Craig 371
Barron, Eddie M. 345
Barry, Don "Red" 295
Barry, Ivor 160, 172
Barry, John 318, 323
Barry of the Great St. Bernard 245
Bartko, Philip 467
Bartholomew, Ron 301
Bartlett, Cal 269
Bartlett, Craig 474
Bartlett, Dennis 371
Bartley, John 430
Bartoli, Adolfo 350
Bart's Catering 301
Barwood, Hal 369
Barwood / Robbins Production, A 369
Baseball Fever 299
Baskin-Robbins 385
Bass, Andy 455
Bassett, L. 397
Bassett, William H. 283
Batchelor, David 370
Bates, Jeanne 228
Bates, John 396
Batman 58
Batt, Frank 369
Battaglia, Lorenzo 350
Batten, Keith 314
Battes, Greg 396
Baum, L. Frank 46
Bauman, Natasha 468
Bavaria Studios 390
Baxley, Craig R. 138
Bay, Frances 365
Bayard, Richard J. 340
Bayless, Bernard F. (Bernie) 319, 396
Baylor, Hal 82, 144, 160, 165

Index 535

Bayly, Lorraine 212
Bayou Boy 80
Beach, James 180
Beach, John 397
Beagle Boys, The 14, 20, 46, 62, 80, 108, 132-133, 159, 178, 218, 246, 282, 300
Beagle Boys vs. Uncle Scrooge, The 300, 326
Beall, Bob 395
Bean, Henry 435
Bear Country 80, 107
Bear Country 204-205
"Bear Necessities, The" 211
Beard, Clive 370
Bears and I, The 165-168
Beatles, The 19, 131, 211
Beatty, Robert 315
Beatty, Warren 451
Beaudine, Craig A. 458, 466
Beaudine, Jr., William 458
"Beautiful Briny, The" 97, 100, 103
Beauty and the Beast 7, 379
Beauvy, Nicholas 301
Beaver Valley 204
Beavis, George 369
Beazell, G. Martin 489
Beck, William 371
Becker, Barbara 436
Becker, Frawley 263
Beckstrom, Eric 409
Bedford, Brian 147
Bedknobs and Broomsticks 5, 7, 29-30, 79, 96-105, 107, 150, 197, 273, 326
Beebe, Ford 14
Beebe, Kenneth 431
Beebe, Lloyd 14, 62, 122, 204
Beecham, William 473
Beer, Dicky 468
Beer, Robert 490
Beeson, Paul 198, 206, 247, 275, 314
Beetlebomb 43
Begg, Jim 290
Begley, Jr., Ed 54, 58, 117, 139, 151
Beimler, Hans Anthony 445
Belasco, Leon 151
Believe You Can...And You Can! 416
Bell, Alfred 212
Belland, Bruce 53, 65, 82, 364
Belle Fourche, South Dakota 58-59
Belling, Andy 97
Belsole, Alvaro 350
Beltran, Alma 341
Belushi, John 333
Benczak, Margaret 447
Bender, Jack 82, 91, 117, 295
Bendoff, Merrill 437
Bener, Lon E. 408
Benett, Carl 301

Benioff, Louis 370
Benji 159
Benji, the Hunted 159
Bennett, Jeff 98
Bennett, Marjorie 306
Bennett, Norman 460
Bennett, Peter 334
Benson, Hugh 169
Benson, John 349
Benson, Lucille 365
Benson, Norland 295
Benson, Robby 437
Benton, Robert 230, 237
Benzakein, Simon 418
Berg, Bil 482
Berg, Jon 371
Berger, Mark 370
Berger, Richard 415
Bergquist, Peter L. 340
Berk, Ailsa 475
Berke, Jody 445
Berlin Wall 394
Berlinger, Warren 231
Berman, Ted 90-91, 96, 252, 258, 376, 481
Bernard, Alan 370
Bernardi, Herschel 219, 223
Bernardini, Luigi 350
Berns, Gerald 398
Berns, Wally K. 192, 283, 360
Bernstein, Elmer 481
Bernstein, Peter 482, 488
Berrie, John 436
Berry, David 371
Berry, Ken 160, 164, 289
Berry, William 437
Berryman, Michael 490
Bertz, Gary 289
Best of Donald Duck, The 14
"Best of Friends" 376-377, 379
Best of Uncle Scrooge, The 14
Best of Walt Disney Comics, The 159
Best of Walt Disney's True-Life Adventures, The 17, 204-206, 211
Best, Peter 198, 212, 275, 314
Bettles, Robert 212
Betuel, Jonathan R. 488
Beverly Hillbillies, The 29
Bewes, Rodney 315
Bewitched 130
Beyond Tron 403
Beyond Witch Mountain 191, 387
Bicentennial 159, 178, 217
Bickham, Jack M. 192, 310
Biczyzcki, Jann Paulus 390
Bielecka, Daniela 258, 376
Big Game Safari Shooting Gallery 388
Big Thunder Mountain Railroad 246, 299, 325

Bigger, Hal 125, 185, 294, 318
Biggest Bongo of the World, The 132
Biography of a Grizzly, A 62
"Bill of Sale" 269, 272
Bill, Tony 31
Billboard 326
Billett, Stewart C. 81
Billy Mills Indian Youth Leadership Program 437
Bilson, Bruce 305
Bird, Brad 376
Bis, Donna 436
Biscardi, Jessica 310
Biscuit Eater, The 109-113
Bisenz, Bruce 424
Bishop, Charles 472
Bishop, Horace 467
Bishop, Michael 488
Bisleti, Sieuwke 431
Bisogno, Tom 397
Bisset, Donald 248
Bisson, Harry 467
Bixby, Bill 192, 197
Black Arrow 465
Black Cauldron, The 150, 357, 380, 388, 394, 416, 443, 465, 481-488, 495
"Black Ferris, The" 430
Black Hole, The 176, 281, 293, 299, 305, 317-326, 333, 339, 404, 416, 430
Black Holes: Monsters That Eat Space and Time 299
Black Stallion, The 358
Blackham, Tim 473
Blackhorse, Barbara 437
Blackbeard's Ghost 20-24, 30, 235
Blackie, John 436
Blade Runner 453
Blair, Janet 26
Blake, Larry J. 26, 39, 160, 180
Blanford, Jim 458
Blanshard, Richard 473
Blazing Saddles 237
Blevins, Bret 210
Blinn, Peter 396
Block, Cyrus 435
Block, David 376, 482
Blocker, Dirk 327
Blondie 407
Bloom, Eddie 328
Bloom, George Arthur 345
Bloss, John D. 35, 50, 81, 90, 96, 143, 185, 230, 268, 282, 289, 294, 305, 310, 318, 327, 340, 345, 359, 364, 380
Blossom, Nathalie 351
"Blow Me Down" 350, 352
Blue Max, The 385
Blue Yonder, The 466
Bluegrass Special, The 245
Blu-ray 70, 150, 262, 275, 408, 472

Bluel, Richard 169
Blum, Joanie 467
Blumenthal, Herman Allen 26
Bluth, Don 147, 252, 258, 268, 299, 358, 376, 380, 389
Blyth, William Allen 424
Blythe, Allen 396
Boa, Bruce 475
Boag, Wally 39, 388
Board, Kevin 467
Boardwalk Entertainment Company 350
"Boatniks" 65
Boatniks, The 65-69, 108, 238
Bob McGrath Sings for All the Boys and Girls 132
Bob Newhart Show, The 86, 235, 237
Boba Fett 252
Bobby Deerfield 385
Bocci, Tom 398
Bochner, Lloyd 35
Bocquet, Gavin 474
Boekelheide, Jay 370
Boekelheide, Todd 430
Bofferty, Pierre 381
Bogue, Lou 467
Boita, Peter 198, 206, 212, 275, 314, 473
Bokas, Dave 455
Boldroff, Danny E. 489
Boles, Carl 117, 125, 172, 185, 219, 224, 228, 268, 283, 319, 341, 409, 424
Boles, Jim 192
Bolgar, Benjie 247
Bonanza 446
Bon Voyage, Charlie Brown (and Don't Come Back) 326
Bond, Margery 351
Bond, Nancy 360
Bonderson, Conrad 371
Bondi, Beulah 82
Bone, Jackie 74
Bonifield, Rocky 269
Bonney, Gail 54, 160
Bonnichon, Christian 418
Bonnichon, J.C. 418
"Boo Bop Bopbop Bop (I Love You, Too)" 269-270, 274
Booke, Sorrell 238, 290
Boom Comics 496
Boomerang, Dog of Many Talents 19
Booth, Jimmie 192
Bootle Beetle 281
Borden, Dick 204
Borgmeyer, Sandra 482
Borgnine, Ernest 319, 323
Borland, Tammy 409
Born to Run 299
Borthwick, Ruth 418
Borzellli, Gabriella 350

Index   537

Bosher, Bert 369
Bosley, Tom 228, 230
Bosom Buddies 452
Boss, May 228, 231, 282
Bossert, Dave 483
Bostwick, Jackson 172, 192, 228, 290, 360, 398, 490, 493
Bottoms, Joseph 319
Bouchard, Sylvie 436
Boucher, Nigel A. 488
Bourgeois, Gary C. 437
Bourland, Don 483
"'Bout Time" 26, 28-29
Boutell, James 455
Bowden, Richard 345, 395
Bowe, Robert 431
Bowen, Deirdre 436
Bowers, Bert 350
Bowles, Billy 91
Bowles, George 437
Box Elder High School 300
Boxleitner, Bruce 398, 404-406, 408
Boy and the Bronc Buster, The 132
Boy and the Runaway Elephant, The 61
Boy Called Nuthin', A 12
Boy/Car/Girl 43
Boy Named Charlie Brown, A 46
Boy Who Stole the Elephant, The 61
Boy Who Talked to Animals, The 177
Boy Who Talked to Badgers, The 177
Boyd, Diana 365
Boyd, Jack 62, 96, 113, 138, 334, 376, 380
Boyd, Jane 113, 334
Boyum, Steve 341
Bradbury, Ray 423, 429
Bradden, Mac 435
Braddock, Martin 161
Bradette, Jacques 436
Bradford, Andy 468, 473
Bradley, Paul 21, 54, 82, 109, 117
Bradshaw, Robert 395
Brady Bunch, The 304
Braeden, Eric 263
Brain, Dave 482
Bramucci, Rudolfo 350
Branson, Fred E. 319
Branton, Alban 365
Brauette, Daniel 436
Bray, Peter 350-351
Brazner, Bill 483
"Brazzle Dazzle Day" 269, 272-274
Breaking Smith's Quarter Horse 46
Bream, Reg 349, 473
Bream, Stephen 350
Brechin, Derek 418
Bremen Town Musicians, The 19
Bremer, Chris 455

Brennan, Ian 334
Brennan, Kevin 315
Brennan, Walter 26, 30, 164
Brenner, Faye 489
Brenner, Gordon D. 121, 204, 268, 305, 310, 340, 345, 380, 389
Brennies, Marty 372
Brent, Eve 82
Bresslaw, Bernard 199, 203
Bretherton, David 466
Brewer, Kim 38
Bridges, Beau 390
Bridges, Jeff 398, 403-404, 408
Bridges, Robert 473
Briedel, Sheryl 409
Briere, Yveline 263
Brill, Charlie 21, 328
Brill, Richard 38
Brimley, Wilford 459
Brimmer, Steve 349
Brimstone, the Amish Horse 19
Bring, Bob 138, 230, 282
Brinson, Dillard 430
Bristol, John 351
British Columbia 168
Britten, Anne 473
Britton, Graham 369
Britton, Tony 206
Brock, Hall 38
Brock, Phil 409
Brock, Stanley 263, 360
Brodhead, James E. 180, 192, 224
Brodie, Don 185, 295
Brody, Neil 437
Bromley, Sydney 276, 372
Bronson, Betty 21
Brooke, Walter 143
Brooks, Wally 283, 310
Brost, Fred 185
Brotherson, Eric 97, 180
Broughton, Robert (Bob) 318, 334, 396
Broussard, Al 459
Brown, Alexandra 345
Brown, Jr., Alonzo 489
Brown, Deborah 369
Brown, Carlos 351
Brown, Cheryl 475
Brown, Clarence 436
Brown, Farris and Associates 431
Brown, Gates 454
Brown, Geoff R. 473
Brown, Hilyard 65
Brown, James 228, 436
Brown, Jophery 446
Brown, Judi 409
Brown, Kris 371
Brown, Robert 207

Brown, Ron 15, 122, 165
Brown, Timothy 228
Brown, Tony 369
Browne, Robin 334
Browne, Roscoe Lee 133
Browning, Jan 396
Brubaker, Tony 282, 398
Bruce, Barry 474
Bruce Hill Productions 371
Bruce, Janet 483
Brugman, James 97
Brummer, Susan 217
Brunetti, Argentina 82
Brunner, Robert F. 20, 31, 46, 53, 65, 74, 81-82, 109, 116, 125, 169, 179, 228, 305, 364
Bruns, George 35, 38, 70, 147, 160
Bruns, Norbert W. 460
Brutsche, Jerry (Gerald) 138, 185, 219, 231, 263, 282, 289
Bryan, Bill 454
Bryan, Deborah 389
Bryant, Anita 61
Bryant, William 47
Bryer, Denise 475
Bryna Company Production, A 423
BTX Corp. 397
Buchanan, William 206
Buck, Chris 376
Buck, David 207
Buckley, Jack 96, 147, 258
Bucklin, John 350
Bucksbaum, Don 435
Budd, David 473
Budd, George 370, 468
Budd, Julie 359, 363-364
Buena Vista Distribution 14, 20, 26, 30, 35, 38, 46, 50, 53, 62, 65, 70, 74, 81, 86, 90, 96, 109, 113, 116, 121, 125, 133, 138, 143, 146, 150, 160, 165, 169, 172, 179, 184, 192, 198, 204, 206, 212, 218, 223, 227, 230, 237, 247, 252, 258, 262, 268, 275, 282, 289, 294, 298, 300, 304-305, 310, 314, 318, 327, 333, 340, 345, 359, 364, 376, 380, 389, 394, 408, 417, 423, 430, 435, 441, 445, 454, 458, 466, 472, 481, 488
Buena Vista Imaging 97
Buena Vista Records 20, 274
Buena Vista Sound 98
Buford, Gordon 38, 160, 262, 340
Buhr, Gerard 381
Building a Company 13, 159
Bujold, Genevieve 346
Bull from the Sky, A 217
Bullard, Kim 306
Bulloch, Jeremy 247, 252
Bunn, Dan 483

Bunnett, David 369
Burbank, California 230, 327, 397, 405, 487
Burbank, Jeffrey 82
Burden, Hugh 199
Bureau of Indian Affairs and the Crow Indian Tribe 204
Burgess, Ben 376, 482
Burgess, Hovey 349, 351
Burgess, Judy 351
Burgi, Scott 301
Burke, Art 295
Burke, Joseph 360
Burke, Patrick Sullivan 97, 169
Burkett, Bartine 360
Burkett, Deena 396
Burman, Ellis 350
Burnett, Michael 488
Burnett, Steven 38, 231
Burns, Forrest 109
Burns, Janine 409
Burns, Stephan W. 341
Burrell, Larry 228
Burrell, Pamela 351
Burt, Stephanie 396
Burton, Norman 365
Burton, Willie D. (Bill) 143, 294, 340, 359, 397
Burton, Corey 98
Burton, Tim 376, 388, 398, 443, 483
Burum, Stephen H. 423
Bush, Jeff 126
Bush, Owen 192
Bushman, Richard 151
Bushnell, Scott 349
Bussan, Mark 458
Butkus, Dick 228, 230
Butler, Artie 258
Butler, Gae Clark 125
Butler, Jr., Richard E. 237, 397
Butler, Robert 53, 81, 86, 116, 294
Butoy, Hendel S. 376, 481
Butterfield, Roy 38
Button, Don 396
Buttons, Red 269
Buttram, Pat 70, 73, 147, 258-259, 377
Buzzi, Ruth 70, 238, 243, 259, 306, 310
Byatt, Walter 198
Byer, Alan 454
Bylander, John F. 345
Byner, John 483, 487
Byron, Kathleen 199

Cabot, Ceil 238, 306, 328, 341
Cabot, Sebastian 218, 252, 257
Cabral, Barney 219, 231, 237, 263, 268, 283
Cabral, Bernard P. 318
Cachia, Anna 419
Cactus Flower 29

Cade, John 446, 489
Cady, Fitch 430
Cady, Frank 91, 95
Caffey, Dick 109, 169, 179
Caffey, Melissa 179
Cagny, James 237
Caillou, Alan 263
Calamatta, Narcy 419
Calandrelli, Jorge 395
CalArts 13, 61, 80, 159
Calconda, Jack 74, 90, 96
Caldecott Story, The 466
Caldwell, Russ 39
Calia, Hank 490
California 349
California Highway Commission 13
California Institute of the Arts (see CalArts)
California School for the Deaf, Riverside 364
Call, Brandon 483
Call it Courage 132
Callahan, Pepe 192
Callas, Charlie 269
Calvert, Bill 179
Camarata Conducts Man of La Mancha 13
Cambridge, Godfrey 109, 113
Camelot 104, 318
Cameron, Ian 172
Cameron, Paul L. 20, 26, 38, 86
Cameron, Scott 423-424
Camilleri, Freda 418
Camlin, Peter 91
Campanella, Frank 306
Campbell, Derek 437
Campbell, Glenn 397
Campbell, Jock 370
Campbell, John 369
Campbell, Mike 212
"Campfire is Home, The" 62
Campi, Nancy Hunter 397
Campsie, Penny 483
Canadian Wildlife Service 204
Canada 437
Canary, David 54
Candido, Candy 147, 160
"Candle on the Water" 269, 271, 274-275
Candleshoe 146, 164, 222, 243, 275-279
Candy, John 446, 452-454
"Candy Man" and Other Sweet Songs 132
Canfield, Mary Grace 424, 429
Cangary Limited 15, 62, 122
Capahari, Jerry 437
Capel, Donald 319
Capers, Virginia 134, 306
Capina, Lito 169
Capitol Records 274
Caple, Scott 371
Cappeto, Louis 445

Captain Clegg 211
Captain Ron 184
Capuano, Ed 395
Car-Boy-Girl 38
Car 54, Where Are You? 69
Carabatsos, Steven W. 345
Cardiff, Jack 212
Cardwell, Reed 482
Carey, Bayard 431
Carey, Jr., Harry 122
Carey, Michele 87
Carlin, Ed 125
Carlisle, Norman 318
Carlyle, Robin 369
Carlo, the Sierra Coyote 158
Carlos, Wendy 395, 403, 408
Carlson, Steve 50
Carlton, Roger 468
Carlyle, Patrick 327
Carmel, California 190
Carne, Judy 105
Carney, Alan 21, 160
Carney, Fox 98
Carnival of the Animals 13
"Carnival of the Animals – The Swan" 160
Caron, Leslie 105
Carothers, A.J. 30
Carousel of Progress, The 13, 132, 158-159, 178
Carpenter, Bethany 455
Carpenter, Jill 334
Carpenter, Joan 275
Carr-Glyn, Neva 212
Carrera, Barbara 381
Carrick, William 204
Carroll, Jill 425
Carroll, Lee 301
Carroll, Pete 134
Carroll, William 289
Carry On 203, 275
Carry On Dick 211
Carson, Dave 371
Carson, Robert S. 161
Carson, Shawn 424
Carstensen, Daryl 483
Carter, Beverly 160
Carter, Don 151, 179, 238
Carter, Jimmy 281
Carter, John 490
Carter, Mel 289
Carter, Randy 283, 305
Cartwright, Randy 258, 268, 376, 379
Caruso, Anthony 31
Caruso, Dee 133
Casady, Chris 371, 396, 489
Casagran, Hortensia 483
Case, Justin 475
Casino of Monte Carlo 380

Caspary, Christina 396
Casper, Billy 117
Cass, Dave 224, 295, 310, 398
Cassidy, Michael 489
Cassie, Alan 333, 369
Castaway Cowboy, The 146, 169-171
Castle and Cooke, Inc. 437
Cat from Outer Space, The 95, 229, 289-294, 333
Catania, James 483
Cates, Darren 409
Cates, Madelyn 360
Catlett, Loyd 398
Causey, Jack 275
CBS 86, 211, 245
CBS Records and Tapes 398
CD 104, 108
Cedeno, Michael 376, 380
Celtic Frost 5
Cerullo, Jr., Al 446
Cervantes y Saavedra, Miguel de 90
Cerveny, Diane 389
Cerveny, Gary 389
Cerveny, Eugene 389
Ceseri, Charles 74
CGI 104, 191, 288, 323, 407
Chadwick, Bette 436
Chaffey, Don 212, 268
Chaika, Glenn 482, 489
Chainsaw 15
Chambers, John 98
Chambers, Steven 294
Chambliss, Woodrow 75
Chandar, the Black Leopard of Ceylon 108
Chandler, George 185, 310
Chandler, Michael 430
Chango, Guardian of the Mayan Treasure 108
Chanticleer 150, 357-358
Chapman, Lonny 122, 365
Charley and the Angel 138-143
Charlie 15, 17
Charlie Brown 246, 417
Charlie Brown Christmas, A 246
Charlie Brown's All-Stars 246, 281
Charlie the Duck 91-95
Charlie Crowfoot and the Coati Mundi 80
Charlie, the Lonesome Cougar 14-17
Charlotte's Web 131
Charlton, W.J. 247
Charone, Irwin 160, 180, 228
Chase, Chevy 454
Chazan, Cathy 350
Chateau Bon Vivant 125
Cheatham, Brian 455
Checco, Al 134, 269
Cheesman, Bruce 473
Cherokee Trail, The 357
Chesney, Al 447

Chester, Yesterday's Horse 132
Chevalier, Maurice 61, 70, 73
Chicken of the Sea Pirate Ship 388
Child of Glass 281
Childs, Peter 370
Chilling, Thrilling Sounds of the Haunted House 132
Chip 'n' Dale 14, 20, 46, 62, 80, 108, 133, 159, 178, 218, 246, 282, 300, 326, 358, 389, 417, 444
Chipman, Cindy 301
Chitty, Erik 199
Chitty Chitty Bang Bang 5, 19
Chonos, Mickey 350
Chostner, Terry 371
Christensen, Michael 351
Christensen, T.C. 301
Christiaansen, Dana 466
Christian, Leigh 134
Christiansen, Judy 301
Christie, Gordon 248
Christmas at Candleshoe 275
Christmas at Walt Disney World 281
Christmas Carol, A 252
Christmas in Disneyland 217
Christopher Syn 206, 211
Christopher, Tony 425
Chronicles of Prydain 481
Chudy, Craig 398
Chulay, John C. 31
Chun, Wesley 482
Chung, Cherie 327
Church, Alan 474
Church, Richard S. 445
Cinardo, Nick 447
Cinderella 132, 357, 389
Cinema Air 397
Cinema Research 350
Cinetron Inc. 397
Circle-Vision 13, 79, 158, 444
Cirillo, Joe 447
Cisneros, Mario 340-341
City of Drumheller, Alberta, The 437
City of Edmonton, The 437
City of Guadalajara 340
City of Paris, The 262, 380
City of Puerta Vallarta 340
City Fox, The 108
Claridge, David 372
Claridge, James Steven 446
Claridge, Shaaron 66
Clark, Carroll 20, 26, 30, 35, 38
Clark, Craig 489
Clark, David F. 165
Clark, Dean 70
Clark, Fred 35
Clark, Jill 409
Clark, Kenneth C. 467

Clark, Matt 459, 475
Clark, Roydon 143, 169
Clark, Susan 192, 197, 305
Clark, Tim T. 425
Clark, Tom 97
Clarke, Alexander 53
Clarke, Caitlin 372
Clarke, Kenneth 473
Clarke Stadium 437
Clarkson, Kate 212
Clarkson, Lisa 408
Clash of the Titans 358
Clatworthy, Robert 74, 86, 169, 223
Clausen, Alf 446, 489
Clavering, Eric 47
Claymation 480
Clayton, Gary 431
Clayton, Hyde 301
Clayton, Jack 423, 429
Cleary, Lee 467
Clegg, Terry 198
Clemens, Brian 333, 338
Clements, Jr., Calvin 74
Clements, Ron 258, 268, 376, 379, 482
Clements, Stanley 295
Clemmons, Larry 70, 146, 252, 258-259, 376
Cleworth, Eric 70, 146, 252
Cliff, John 31, 35, 39, 54
Clift, Brian 483
Clinger, Debra 327
Clooney, Dominic 467
Close Encounters of the Third Kind 245
Club 33 13
Clutesi, George 437
Coats, Mike 409
Cobb, Peggy 74
Coburn, Jr., Bob 74, 90, 96, 125
Coburn, Brian 418
Coca-Cola 415
Cochran, Eddie 437
Cockroft, Brian 436
Cody, Kathleen 126, 130, 139, 151, 155
Coe, Deborah 431
Coevolution Funnies 300
Coffey, Ed 396, 424, 483, 489
Coffin, Tris 82
Coggon, William 473
Cohen, Martin O. 397
Colbert, Jill 482
Colbourne, Maurice 247
Cole, George 206
Coleman, James (Jim) 258, 376, 482
Colina, Michael 489
Colley, Don Pedro 134, 160
Colli, Tonino Delli 417
Collier, Dave 74
Collier, Richard 21

Collins, Eddie 369
Collins, Jack 269
Collins, Michael 314
Collins, Peter 473
Collins, Winnie 91, 117
Collis, Jack T. 305, 408, 445
Colman, Edward 20, 38, 90
Colman, Booth 87
Colonna, Kerry 396
Colver, Clint 396, 424, 489
Combs, Gary 138, 424
Comella, Karen 483
Comic-Book Book, The 159
Comix: A History of Comic Books in America 81
Commonwealth Stadium 437
Compact Sound Services 455
Compin, Antoine 381
Computer Wore Tennis Shoes, The 53-59, 117, 121, 184
"Computer Wore Tennis Shoes, The" 53
Computers Are People, Too! 387, 403
Comstock, Samuel 371
Conaway, Jeff 269
Concors, Dave 97
Condorman 380-385
Condorman 358, 380-385
"Condorman" 381
Condylis, Paul 31
Conkline, Gary 396
Conley, Kimberly 454
Conlon, Noel 490
Connecticut Yankee in King Arthur's Court, A 314
Connelly, Gordon 455
Connolly, Philip 369
Connor, Carol 258
Connor, John 445
Connors III, Tom 408
"Conquistador" 87
Conrad, Michael 21
Conried, Hans 231, 236, 289
Constantine, Michael 305, 309
Continental Camera Systems 319, 371
Conway, Lyle 473, 475
Conway, Russ 134
Conway, Tim 131, 133, 137-138, 192, 197-198, 228, 230-231, 236-237, 310, 314
Cook, Barry 396, 482, 489
Cook, Dick 404
Cook, Lorna 376
Cook, Robert O. 14, 20, 26, 31, 35, 38, 46, 50, 53, 62, 65, 70, 74, 81, 86, 90, 96, 109, 116, 204, 252
Cookson, Anthony 430
Coolidge, Philip 31
Coolidge, Rita 446
Cooper, Clay (see O'Brien, Clay)
Cooper, Douglas 372

Cooper, Jack C. 204
Cooper, Ray 351
Cooper, Ronald R. 185, 268
Cooperstown, New York 455
Coppini, Joe 419
Coppinger, John 474
Coppleman, Rusty 247
Coppola, Francis Ford 413, 474
Corbett, Kaye 437
Corbett, Ray 473
Corbin, Barry 490
Corbould, Chris 381
Corbould, Ian 370
Corbould, Neil 334
Corby, Ellen 113, 116
Corcoran, Kevin 197, 223, 282, 287-288, 305, 340
Cord, Erik 398
Cordell, Ricky 47
Cordwell, Harry 418
Corey, Norman 482
Coria, Aurora 341
Corman-Grazer, Corki 447
Cornick, James F. 74
Corr, Eugene 430
Correia, Marinho 14, 62, 122
Corridoni, Maria Teresa 350
Cortes, Jesus 482
Cosby, Bill 359, 364
Cosell, Howard 134, 136-138
Cosio, Jesse 482
Cosmekinetics 350
Costallos, Suzanne 409
Costello, Ward 283
Cotti, Carlo 418
Couch, Bill 38, 319
Couffer, Jack 430
Coulter, Jean 294
Country 458-463
Country Bear Christmas Special, The 444
Country Bear Jamboree 79, 107, 444
Country Bear Jamboree 80
Country Joe and the Fish 489
Courtland, Chip 360
Courtland, Jerome 121, 184, 212, 268, 282, 359, 364
Cousin, Yvonne Zarb 350
Cow Dog 158
Cowan, Sandra 436
Cowl, Henry L. 50, 90, 109, 122, 125, 185, 231
Cowl, Rudy 289, 294
Cowlard, Albert 369
Cox, Wally 26, 66, 82, 86, 107
Coyes, Greg 438
Craddock, Raymond 223, 230, 237, 262, 268
Craig, Ivan 122
Craig, John 26
Craig, Michael G. 212, 396
Crane, Bob 151, 155, 228, 230

Crandall, Cecil A. 20, 31
Crandall, Robert H. 204
Crandall, Roger 301
Cranham, Tom 488
Craske, Richard 474
Crawford, John 113, 310
Crawford, Michael 381
Crawford, Robert 258, 385
Crazy with the Heat 177
Creach, Everett 38
Creber, William J. 150
Creed, Roger 306
Crespi, Sam 445
Crested Butte, Colorado 125
Crew, Lary 350
Cridlin, Mark 369
Cripps, Trevor 371
Crisler, Herb 204
Crist, Paula 467
Cristini, Michaelene 455
Cristobalito, the Calypso Colt 61
Crompton, Owen 396
Cron, Claudia 437
Cronin, Patricia 446
Cronjager, William 121
Cronn, Richard 301
Crosby, Bing 30
Crosby, Cathy 82
Crosby, Joan 231
Cross, Jimmy 35
Cross, Leroy 258, 376
Crothers, Scatman 70, 73
Crouch, Ken 370
Crovato, Luciano 418
Crow, Don 74
Crowell, Graham 436
Crowly, Patricia 109
Crown International 397
Crowther, Graeme 468
Cruella De Vil 262
Cruickshank, Art 125, 133, 138, 160, 172, 179, 184,
    192, 218, 223, 227, 230, 237, 262,
    268, 282, 289, 294, 305, 310, 318,
    334, 340, 345, 359, 380, 396, 424
Cruise and Co. 397
Crum, Cathy 396
Cruse, William 398
Crutcher, Samuel C. 350
"Crying My Heart Out Over You" 459
Crystal, Richard 360
Cuckoo's Nest Productions 397
Cuka, Frances 334
Culley, Cliff 198, 275, 314
Culley, Wilf 62
Culling, Mike 473
Culotta, Ann 490
Culp, Robert 169

Culver, Howard 54, 82, 91
Cummings, Douglas 473
Curb, Mike 108
Curry, Dan 455
Curry, Julian 468
Curtis, Gene 38
Curtis, Howard 319
Curtis, Jamie Lee 243
Curtis, Ken 147
Curtis, Michael W. 191
Curzon Jill 207
Cushing, Peter 211

Dacre, Susan 474
Dad, Can I Borrow a Car? 61, 498
DaGradi, Don 20, 38, 86, 96, 103
Dahlgren, Tom 431
Dahlin, Bob 249
Dahouet-Boigny, Augustin 467
Daigler, Gary 169
Dail, John 395
Daily, Bill 82, 86
Daisy and Donald 159, 178, 218, 246, 282, 300, 326, 358, 389, 417, 444
"Dakota" 26-27
Dale, Fred 289
Dale, Jim 269, 275, 295, 298, 315
Dallas 243
Dallimore, Maurice 91
Dalton, Phyllis 314
Daly, Jane 365
Daly, Jerry 369
Daly, Jonathan 50, 91, 151, 180, 224, 231, 365
Damas, David 327
Damberger, Francis 437
D'Amico, Gary 289, 319, 341, 398, 424, 467, 488, 493
Damien, Medeleine 263
Dana, Candice 455
D'Andre, Dante 341
Dane, Stephen 488
Danico Casting 445
Daniel, Danny 198, 389
Daniel, Pierre 283
Daniels, Eugene 185
Daniels, Les 81
Dano, Richard 447
Dano, Royal 424
Dante, Joe 409
Darbo, Rolf 489
Darby O'Gill and the Little People 388
Dark, Christopher 87
Dark Crystal, The 388
Dark Shadows 130
Darling, Jennifer 418
Darmanin, Charles 419
Dashnaw, Jeffrey 364

Date, Michael 436
Davalos, Elyssa 310, 341
Davalos, Richard 424
Davenport, Champ 395
Davenport, Robert (Bobby) 227, 459
Davey, Peter 474
David, Bill 74
David, Hal 345
David, Walter 438
Davidovich, Basil 70, 147, 252
Davidson, Alan 455
Davidson, John 26, 29-30
Davidson, Retta 482
Davies, Leon 247
Davies, Pamela 369
Davies, Tommy 370
Davis, Bette 283, 287, 334, 338-339
Davis, Dan 436
Davis, Elliott 424
Davis, Gary 282
Davis, Jack 430
Davis, Jim 144
Davis, Lem 483
Davis, Lorraine 483
Davis, Michael 473
Davis, Walt 231
Davis-McGee, Virginia 274
Davison, Leonard 81
Davison, Rita 334, 369
Davison, Steve 340
Davy Crockett 210
Davy Crockett 46
Davy Crockett and the River Pirates 358
Davy Crockett Explorer Canoes 80
Dawe, Anthony 370
Dawes, Jim 473
Dawkins, Monica 212
Dawson, Karen 467
Dawson, Mike 474
Dawson, Ron 74
Day, Gerry 318, 333
Day, Tilly 198
De Bello, John 446
De Benning, Jeff 180
De Leuw, Raymond A. 109, 138, 150, 192, 294, 359
De Muth, Charles 445
De Roy, Scott 425
De Ruiter, Carrie 430
De Sales, Francis 180
De Vargas, Val 165
De Virgilio, Len 446
De Vol, Frank 262, 340-341
De Witt, Jan 301
De Wolfe, Billy 133, 138
Deacon, Richard 21, 26
Deacon, the High Noon Dog 177
Dead Horse State Park 122

Deadrick, Vince 310, 398
Dean, Fabian 54, 82
Dean, Rodger 436
Deane, Leroy G. 143, 165
Dearberg, Robert C. 301
Debny, John 179
Debs, Steve 467
DeCecio, Alison 396
Dechter, Brad 446
Deel, Guy 179, 230, 258
Deeney, Catherine 126
Dees, Michael 294
Deeth, James 397
Deezen, Eddie 327
Degeneres, Bill 74, 185
DeGrunwald, Alex 466
Deja, Andreas 481-482
DeKova, Frank 75
Del Brocco, Giancarlo 350
Del Conte, Ken 228
Del Ray, Pillar 328
Del Ruth, Thomas 74
Delamain, Aimee 199
Delaney, Pat 117, 139
Delaney, Pauline 418
Delano, Lee 447
Delfosse, Raoul 263
Delgado, Jr., Danny (Dan) 219, 268-269, 319, 345, 409, 458
Delgado, Luis 169
Delevanti, Cyril 97
D'Elia, Nick 446
Dell Comics 14
Dell, Paula 237
Dell'Aqua, Roberto 351
Delozier, Katie 455
"Delta Dawn" 275
Delta Labs Inc. 397
Deluxe 300
Demos, Gary 397
Dempster, Al 70, 96, 147, 252, 258
Dengel, Jack 424
Dennehy, Brian 431
Denney, Nora 446
Dennis, Gill 472
Dennis, John 31
Dennis the Menace 53
Dennis-Leigh, Patrick 97, 268
Denton, Jack 447
Denver, John 165, 168
Denver Museum of National History 204
Depardieu, Gerard 155
Department of the Interior, The 19, 204
DePatie-Freleng 46
Depp, Johnny 12
Deramirez, Tatsuko 483
Derfus, Dana 38

DeRosa, Anthony 483
DeRosa, Barbara 483
Deschutes National Forest 192
"Desert Lullaby" 87
Destino 7
Detroit, Michigan 454, 458
Detroit Tigers, The 455-458
Deuhr, Ralph E. 460
Deusingn, Murl 204
DeVargas, Val 224
Devil and Max Devlin, The 348-349, 359-364
Devine, Andy 147
Devis, James 473
Devis, Natalie 328
Devore, Donna 438
Devry, Elaine 160
Dew, Karen 431
DeWaay, Dennis 423, 488
DeWitt, Faye 98
Di Cicco, Bobby 446
Di Benedetto, Tony 446
Diamond, Don 341
Diamond, Peter 275-276
Diamonds on Wheels 158
Diaz, Rudy 143
DiBona, Craig 445
Dicicco, Sue 482
Dick Tracy 34, 191, 354
Dickens' Christmas Carol Featuring the Walt Disney Players 178, 218
"Die Fledermaus" 39
Dietrich, Dena 306
Dietz, Bill 459
DiGaetano, Joe 467
Digital Effects, Inc. 397, 407
Dignam, Mark 207
Dilbeck, Michael 395
Dillard, Doug 351
Dillon, Brendan 172
Dillon, Matt 409
"Din' We" 350, 355
Dindal, Mark 482
Dirty Mary, Crazy Larry 189
"Disco Mouse" 281
Discovery Bay 158-159
Discovery Island 158
Disney (see Walt Disney Productions)
Disney Animation: The Illusion of Life 357, 359
Disney Channel, The 104, 358, 416, 443, 458, 466, 501, 522
Disney Channel Magazine, The 417
Disney Character Voices 98
Disney Christmas Gift, A 387
Disney College Program 2, 4-5
Disney Comics 496
Disney Dollars 2
Disney, Edna 444

Index   545

Disney EFX 474
Disney Family Album, The 275
Disney Films, The 8, 11, 14, 17, 25, 125, 133, 501
Disney Magazine, The 444
Disney/MGM Studios Tour, The 44
Disney News 150, 206, 357, 444, 496
Disney on Ice 46, 108
Disney on Parade 44, 46, 108, 358
Disney on Parade 80
Disney That Never Was, The 11, 19, 45, 245, 357, 388
Disney, Roy Edward 245-246, 274, 465, 481
Disney, Roy O. 13, 19, 73, 79, 245-246, 444
Disney Songs the Satchmo Way 20
Disney Storybook, A 357
Disney Vacation, A 387, 416
Disney Valentine, A 387
Disney Version, The 20
Disney, Walt 1-2, 5-8, 11-14, 17, 19-21, 24-25, 29-30, 34, 43, 58, 61, 73, 90, 103-104, 107, 131, 150, 178, 184, 189, 191, 197-198, 203-206, 210-211, 217-218, 223, 246, 257, 261-262, 267, 273-274, 304, 325, 357, 388, 404, 416, 466, 495, 501
Disney World (see Walt Disney World)
Disney's Adventures of the Gummi Bears 466
Disney's All-Star Mother's Day Album 443
Disney's All-Star Valentine Party 443
Disney's Greatest Dog Stars 217
Disney's Halloween Treat 387
Disney's Oscar Winners 326
Disney's World 466
Disney's Wonderful World (see *Wonderful World of Disney, The*)
Disneyana 326, 389
Disneyana Collector, The 389
Disneyana Collectors Club 109
Disneyana Shop, The 217
Disneyland 12-13, 43, 45, 79-80, 107, 131-132, 158-159, 164, 178, 217, 246, 281, 299, 325, 357-358, 388, 417, 444, 466
Disneyland Birthday Party 466
Disneyland: From the Pirates of the Caribbean to the World of Tomorrow 19
Disneyland Hotel 417
Disneyland Magazine 109, 133, 159
Disneyland Passports 299
Disneyland Showtime 61
Disneyland Vacationland 444, 496
Disneyland's 30th Anniversary Celebration 465
Disney23 444, 496
Divison of Fish and Game, State of Utah 122
Dixon, Glenn 82
Dixon, MacIntyre 351
Dixon, Peggy 370
Diz and Liz 294

Djurkovic, George 473
Dmytryk, Michael J. 65, 122, 133, 282, 340
Doan, Conrad 459
Dobie, Alan 207
Dobbie, Laurie 436
Dobbins, Bennie E. 397
Dobtcheff, Vernon 381
Doctor Dolittle 12
Dods, Marcus 212
Dodson, Jack 424
Doering, George 446
Dohring, Evelyn 389
Domeyer, David 185, 237, 268, 294, 310, 371, 467
Dominick, Rex 31
Don Quixote 90
Donaggio, Pino 408
Donald and Jose, Ole! 387
Donald Duck 204, 282, 300, 326, 444
Donald Duck 14, 20, 46, 62, 80, 108, 132, 159, 178, 218, 246, 282, 300, 326, 358, 389, 417, 444
Donald Duck and his Nephews 417
Donald Duck Day 444
Donald Duck's 50th Anniversary 443
Donald's Diary 45
Donald's Dream Voice 45
Donald's Fountain of Youth 281
Donald's Valentine Day Salute 326
Donaldson, J. Mark 458, 468
Donovan, Warde 224, 228, 295, 341
Donovan's Kid 299
"Don't Know Why I Came" 327
Don't Raise the Bridge, Lower the River 34
DoQui, Robert 224
Dornfeld, Mark 98
Domeyer, David 398
Donno, Eddie 305
Dooley, Paul 351
DoQui, Robert 490
Doran, Johnny 224
Dorosh, John 4
Dorris, Wayne 409
Dorsman, Judith 212
Doster, Keigley and Rhodes 459
Doubilet, David 446
Double Trouble 223
Doucette, Jeff 446
Doucette, John 143
Doucette, Rudy 38
Douet, Robin 247, 275, 314
Douglas, James B. 82
Douglas, Kirk 116
Douglas, Michael 113, 116
Douglas, Peter Vincent 423
Dova, Dick 371
Dove, Andrew 199
Dowd, Ned 351

Dowdall, Jim 468
Down and Out in Beverly Hills 465, 493, 495
Downes, John 369
Downs, Charlie 482
Downs, Janette 396
Downey, Cheryl 237
Downey, Michelle 365
Downing, Sally 467
Downs, Dermott 185, 189-191, 238
Doyle, Loring 371
Dozier, Lamont 418
Dr. Jekyll and Mr. Hyde 210
Dr. Joyce Brothers Show, The 466
Dr. Syn, Alias the Scarecrow 206-211, 472
Dragonara Palace Hotel and Casino, The 418
Dragonslayer 354, 358, 369-375
Drake, Bob 38, 282
Drake, Clare 437
Drake, Jami 436
Drake, Leonard 418
Draper, Charles L. 14
Dream Called Walt Disney World, A 387
Dreamworks SKG 496
Dreisbach, Jeffrey 447
Dremann, Beau 490
Driscoll, Bobby 5
Driscoll, Michael 473
Drown, Richard 282
"Drummin' Drummin' Drummin'" 26, 28
Dryer, Fred 228
Drysdale, Don 43
Du Barry, Denise 360
Duarte, Edward 74
Dubin, Gary 70
Dubin, Joseph 204
Dubuque, Richard 350
Ducarme, Jean-Louis 418
DuckTales 178, 293
Duckwall, Don A. 70, 147, 252, 258, 376
Duckworth, Willie Lee 437
Dudikoff II, Michael J. 398
Dudman, Nick 371
Duff, Dana 396
Dugan, Dennis 315
Duggan, Andrew 165
Duggan, Gerry 212
Duit, Reverend Warren 459
Duke, Stan 39
Dumbo 108, 204, 217, 257, 358
Dumbo's Flying Circus 466
Dumont, Sky 390
Dunbar, Bill 192
Dunbar, Olive 219
Duncan, Sandy 91, 158, 289, 376
Duncan, Ted 38, 282
Dungan, Jr., William 397
Dunlap, Al 185

Dunlop, Vic 360
Dunn, Larry 282
Dunn, Liam 134, 139, 160, 228, 235, 237
Dunn, Matthew Conway 179
Dunn, Nicholas 370
Dunne, Steve 151
Dunnet, David 482
Dunphy, Barbara 435
Dunsky, Evan 454
Dunsterville, Tony 334
Duran, Larry 489
Durham, Duwayne 370
Durinski, Art 397
Durning, Kathy 482
Durst, Eric 396
Dusendschon, Christopher 398
Duvall, Shelley 351
DVD 8, 29-30, 43, 69, 73, 103-104, 116, 125, 137, 146, 150, 175, 189, 191, 197, 203, 206, 210-211, 236, 243, 245, 257-258, 262, 273-275, 279, 287-288, 298, 323-324, 333, 338-340, 379, 402-403, 406, 451, 453, 480, 487, 495
Dye, Mary 97, 310, 318, 340, 345, 359
Dyer, Carolyn 96
Dyer, Lee 396, 423

Eaglespeaker, Seymour 437
Easley, Pamela 455
Eastern Acoustical Works 397
Eastin, Steve 360
Eastman, Peter Paul 35, 54, 82, 151, 228
Easton, Bill 436
Easton, Robert 269
Ebsen, Buddy 26, 29-30
Eby, Catherine 396
Eby, Douglas 397
EC Comics 429-430
Eccles, Robin 35
Eckemyr, Agneta 172
Ecker, Jr., Gordon 395
Eckton, Teresa 349, 370
Ed Sullivan Show, The 211
Eddie, Golden 109
Eddon, Tracey 468
Eddy III, Selwyn 371
Edesa, Bob 489
Edge, Duane 436
Edge, Norm 436
Edgerton, June 370
Edimi, Alberto 350
Edmonson, Mike 283, 289, 319, 341, 398
Edmonton, Alberta 437
Edwards, Cliff 13
Edwards, Daryl 447
Edwards, Dennis 396, 483
Edwards, Dorothy 370

Edwards, Robert 455
Edwards, Sam 87, 109, 185
Egerton, Mark 212
Eggenweiler, Robert 349, 467, 489
"Eglantine" 97, 100, 104
Egleston, Rita 397
Eianes, E. 455
Einstein, Albert 357
Eisenmann, Ike 185, 189-191, 283, 287-288
Eisner, Michael 7-8, 246, 267, 345, 358, 387, 415-416, 443, 452-453, 458, 462, 465, 493, 495-496
Eissinmann, Iake (see Eisenmann, Ike)
Ekins, Bud 282
Ekton, Teresa 430
El Cid 104
Elam, Kirk 468
Elcar, Dana 346, 381
Electric Company, The 132
Electro Voice Inc. 397
Eleseuer, Theo 435
Elkins, Bud 38
Elkins, Judy 371
Elam, Jack 31, 75, 295, 310
Elias, Louie (Louis) 224, 310
Elias, Mike 310
Elias, Stacie 310, 364
Ellenshaw, Harrison 191, 318, 323-324, 333, 394, 396, 404, 406, 424
Ellenshaw, Linda 396
Ellenshaw, Peter S. 20, 38, 96, 169, 172, 191, 218, 227, 230, 262, 268, 289, 318, 323, 339, 404
Elliot, Jack 26
Elliot, Peter 475
Elliott 268-275
Ellis, Barbara 370
Ellis, David Richard 179, 294
Ellis, John 371
Ellison, Joy 151
Ellsworth, Michael 436
Elson, Donald 87
Elswit, Robert 454
Elwyn, Michael 199
Ely, Ron 116
Emerson, John 70, 86, 268, 334, 376, 482
Emhardt, Robert 50
E.M.I. Studios 198
Embree, Del 436
Emperors Nightingale, The 388
Empire Strikes Back, The 326, 358
Empress Lilly River Boat 246
Enberg, Dick 228, 230
Enchanted Tiki Room, The 20
Endoso, Kenny 341
Engel, Roy 139
Engel, Tim 350

England 243, 301, 317
England, Chrissie 371
Englander, Ira 435
Englander, Nancy 436
Englander Production, An 435
Engler, Bruno 431
English, Liz 70
Ennals, Roger 475
E.P. Dutton & Company, Inc. 252
EPCOT 13, 80, 178, 325, 388
Epcot Center 7, 80, 299, 325, 357, 387-388, 415, 444
Epcot Center: The Opening Celebration 387
Epper, Andy 468
Epper, Gary 282, 397
Epperson, George 397
Epstein, Pierre 447
Epstein, Robert 430
Epstein, S. Karen 445
Equatorial Africa 444
Equinta, Sam 74
Erdman, Richard 50
Ericson, John 97
Erickson, Bill 263, 310, 340
Erickson, C.O. 349
Erickson, Jim 436
Ermineskin Band, The 437
Ermineskin Band Presentation, The 435
Essoe, Gabe 143
Escape from the Dark (see *Littlest Horse Thieves, The*)
Escape to Witch Mountain 5, 184-192, 338-339
Escape to Witch Mountain, Part 2 287
Estevez, Emilio 409
Estevez, Enrique 340
Etherington, Hal 262
Eubanks, Brian 418
Eustral, Anthony 97
Evans, Art 310
Evans, Bill 370
Evans, Christopher 371
Evans, Martin 473
Evans, Mike 117, 121
Evans, Monica 70, 147
Evans, Ray 371
Evans, Robert 349
Evans, Roy 248
Eveleight, Chris 474
Everglades National Park 204
Everett, D.S. 435
Everitt, Jim 98
"Every Little Piece" 269, 271-272, 274
"Everything is Food" 350, 352, 355
"Ev'rybody Wants to Be a Cat" 70-71, 73
Ewing, Roger 47
Excalibur 480
Exceptional Optics 455

Exodus 5
Eyre, Peter 372

Faber, Dede 483
Fabray, Nanette 365, 369
Fabulous Thunderbird, The 408
Fain, Sammy 258
Fairbanks, David 301
Fairest of Them All, The 416
Fairlight Corp. 397
Faith in Physics 4
Fallberg, Becky 483
Family Affair 112
Family Band: From the Missouri to the Black Hills, The 26
Family Band, The (See *One and Only, Genuine, Original Family Band, The*)
Family is a Menagerie, My 19
Fankboner, Sarah 151, 231
Fannon, William 125
Fant, Lou 365
Fantagraphics 496
Fantasia 45, 245, 388, 465
Fantasia 2000 388
Fantasy on Skis 177, 498
Fantasyland 417
Fantasyland Theater 357
Far West Productions 458
Faraldo, Daniel 418
Farley, Morgan 82, 97
Farmer, Philip Jose 3-4
Farmiloe, Rick 483
Farms, Ricky 334
Farnsworth, Richard 31, 192
Farrell, Daniel 473
Farrelly Brothers, The 17
Farruglia, Benny 418
Faso, Tony 423
Fassbender, Norm 436
Fassnacht, Felice 455
Fast, Russ 295
Father Christmas 465
Fatur, Oscar 488
Fauer, John 445
Faulkner, Edward 82, 87, 117
Fawcett Publications 109, 133, 159
Fawcett, William 21, 54
Fawlty Towers 252
Faye, Herbie 21
Feck, Rick 398
Federal Screw Works 397
Fegan, John 212
Feiffer, Jules 349, 354
Fein, Donna 327
Feinberg, Jane 301, 435, 472
Feld, Fritz 54, 161, 179, 238, 341
Feldman, Corey 376

Feldman, Victor 455
Feldon, Barbara 219
Feliciano, Salvadore 301
Felix, Geoff 474
Fell, Noman 65
Fellowes, Julian 468
Felton, Kay 334
Fenton, Mike 301, 435, 472
Fenyvesi, Maria 483
Ferdin, Pamelyn 26, 29
Ferdinand the Bull and Mickey 416
Ferguson, Perry 230, 262
Ferrandini, Dean 294
Ferriter, Tom 376, 482
Fetterman, Richard 300
Feyder, Paul 380
Fibber McGee 262
Fichter, Rick 371
Fidel, Stan 376
Fiedler, John 50, 147, 151, 218, 231, 235, 237, 253, 257, 259, 328, 377
Field, Roy 372
Field, S.S. 268
Fields, Artie 455
Fields, D. 455
Fiesterman, William 474
50 Happy Years 131, 415
Fifty Happy Years 132
Figgis, Susie 472
"Fight On" 147
Fimple, Dennis 192
Finch, Christopher 133
Fine Art of Disney's Donald Duck, The 359
Fine, Bobby 454
Fink, Michael 489
Finkeldei, Gail 396, 483
Finlay, Michael 474
Finley III, Bobby 371
Finn, Will 376
Fiore, Giovanni 350
Fire on Kelly Mountain 132
Fireball 500 44
Firestorm 132
First Interstate Bank of California Foundation 437
Fischer, Bruce M. 424
Fish and Wildlife Service 204
"Fish Cheer and I-Feel-Like-I'm Fixin' to Die Rag" 489
"Fish Heads" 53
Fish, Jack 455
Fishburn, Jay 345
Fishcher, Ken 370
Fisher, Claire 455
Fisher, Shug 169, 310
Fisher, William 438
Fitts, Lillian 396
Fitzgerald, Dennis 436

Fitzgerald, Wayne 446
Fitzpatrick, Pat 179
Fitzsimmons, Patrick 371
Flashbeagle 417, 444
Flashdance 417
Flavin, James 82
Fleischer, Flavia 365
Fleischer, Max 273
Fleischer Studios 351, 354
Fletcher, Eileen 334
Fleury, Jeff 409
Flight of the Grey Wolf, The 217
Flight to the Moon, The 13, 178
Flinn III, John C. 90, 143, 224
Flint, Shelby 258
Flintstones, The 131
Flocke, Sebastien 263
Flook, Margaret 396
Florence, Bob 327
Florida 2, 13, 108
Florida's Disney Decade 357
Flowers and Trees 274
Flying Saucers 12
Flynn, Eric 207
Flynn, Gertrude 21
Flynn, Joe 39, 53, 58, 82, 91, 117, 121, 151, 155, 179, 184, 258, 262
Foggia, Lyla 445
Fonda, Henry 387
Fonda, Jane 387
Fondacaro, Phil 425, 484
Fong, Benson 39, 43, 179
Fong, Brian 39
Fong, Harold 39
Fonzie 452
Foot, Geoffrey 333
Footloose Fox, The 299, 498
Footloose Goose, The 177
Footloose Goose from Saskatchewan, The 177
"For He's a Jolly Good Fellow" 21
"For Penny's a Jolly Good Fellow" 258
For the Love of Benji 245
Ford, Denise 483
Ford, Gerald 178
Ford, Glenn 47, 50
Ford, Michael 349, 473
Fordney, Alan 39
Forg, Bettina 389
Forino, Sally 369
Forman, Joey 66
Formicola, Fil 447
Fornoles, Romeo 97
Forrest, David 198
Forrest, Steve 50, 75, 350
Forster, Robert 319
Forsyth, Bruce 97
Forsythe, Rosemary 144

Fort Wilderness Campground 79
Fortier, Robert 351
Fossum, Martin 430
Foster, Jodie 113, 116, 131, 143, 146, 190, 238, 243, 245, 275, 279, 413, 454
Foulger, Bryon 21
Foulk, Robert 39, 54, 269
Four Media Company 97
Fowler, Chip 466
Fowley, Douglas V. 122, 306
Fox and the Hound, The 150, 159, 184, 245, 261, 299, 325, 357-358, 376-380, 408
Fox, Bernard 91, 259, 263
Fox, Charles 417
Fox, Gail 424, 489
Fox, John J. 91
Fox, Michael J. 327, 333
Foxcroft, Les 212
Foxworth, Robert 224, 227
Foxworthy, Michael 454
Frake III, William 482
Frampton, Derek 474
Frampton, Harry 206, 247
Francis, Freddie 474
Francis, Ivor 134, 151, 306
Francis, Kirk 467
Franco, Jr., John 458
Franco, Larry 179
Franken, Steve 306
Frankenberry, Karen 301
Frankenweenie 443, 499
Franklin, Annemarie 395
Franklin, Warren 371
Franks, Chloe 247
Franz, Dennis 351
Fraternal Order of the Eagles, The 431
Frates, Melvin W. 185
Freakazoid! 430
Freaky Friday 116, 146, 237-243, 245, 279, 309, 358, 388
Frederix, Marc 380
Fredrick, George 219, 223, 228, 231, 237, 263, 268, 318, 418, 424, 446, 459, 467
Freeborn, Graham 370
Freeborn, Trevor 372
Freeman, Al 459
Freeman, Douglas 431
Freeman, Kathleen 180
Fremer, Michael 395
French Connection II, The 385
French, Dean 459
French, Don 389
Fresh, Debbie 269
Frezzo, Frank 482
Friday, Jammie 398
Friedman, Jeffrey 430
Frisbee 404, 407

Frishman, Brian 327, 365
Fridays 309
Friedkin, Tom 289
Friedman, Bruce Jay 445
Friedman, Richard Bruce 398
Friesen, Dietrich 371
Frith, Carl 474, 489
Fritz the Cat 108
Frome, Milton 180, 228, 231
Frommer, Ben 26, 39
Frosty's Winter Wonderland 246
Fruchtman, Rob 430
Frutkoff, Gary 473
Fuchs, Dick 306
Fuentes, Ernie 328, 341
Fujikawa, Jerry 91, 290
Fujimoto, June 482
Fujioka, John 346
Fukushima, Calvin 345
Fulmer, Mike 371
Fun with Mr. Future 388, 499
"Fundamental Elements" 104
Funicello, Annette 44, 107
Furey, Len 467
Furmaniak, Ralph 430
Furniss, John 247
Furst, Stephen 301, 327, 333
Further Adventures of Jiminy Cricket, The 13

Gable, Clark 108
Gabor, Eva 70, 73, 258
Gabriel, Mike 482
Gaffney, Magdalen 473
Gagliano, Bernie 396, 483, 488
Gagnon, Jean Pierre 483
Galbraith, Tracy 436
Galea, Rita 350
Gallin, Tim 446
Game and Fish Department, State of Arizona 122
Game Departments of Kenya, Uganda and Tanzania, The 204
Game of X, The 380
Gamley, Douglas 395
Ganakes, Constantine 318, 327, 340
Gann, Ernest K. 345
Gannett Foundation 437
Gant, Chris 370
Gant, John 370
Gant, Martin 370
Ganz, Lowell 445, 447, 451-452, 454
Garay III, Joaquin 341
Garberti, Ed 230, 467, 483
Gardenia, Vincent 346
Gardner, Gerald 133
Gardner, Jack 314
Gardner, Richard 86
Gardner, Tony 488

Garment, Norma 369
Garner, James 131, 143, 146, 169, 171, 197, 348-349, 429
Garrett, Donna 328, 397
Garrett, Lyla 81
Gasek, Tom 474
Gaskill, Andrew (Andy) 252, 258, 334, 376, 395, 403
Gaspar, Chuck 172
Gasser, Ernie 314, 334
Gausman, Hal 20, 26, 38, 46, 53, 74, 90, 96, 109, 133, 143, 160, 172, 184
Gavin, Dennis 435
Gavin, James W. 341, 345, 389
Gawryluk, Bill 436
Gaze, Christopher 438
Gear, Les 74, 90
Geary, Richard 38
Geddis, Peter 247
Geer, Ellen 424
Geer, Will 113, 116
Gehring, Ted 82, 310
Geiger, Charles W. 126
Geller, Rusty 488
Gelman, Larry 117, 151, 180
Gemette, Sam 349
General Electric Company 437
General Foods Fund, Inc. 437
General Screen Enterprises Ltd. 474
Genge, Paul 21
George, Chief Dan 47, 50, 165
George, James L. 258
George, John 97, 126
Gerard, Anthony 204
Gerard, Thomas (Tom) 446, 488
Gero, Gary 431
Gerrie, Peter 436
Gerry, Vance 70, 146, 252, 258, 376, 481
Ghost Dad 364
Ghost of Cypress Swamp, The 245
Ghosts of Buxley Hall, The 326
Giamo, Michael 483
Gibson, Beau 282
Gibson Greeting Cards 443
Gibson, Kinnie 389
Gibson, Mary Ann 231
Gibson, Michael 396
Giddings, Al 431
Gifford, Frank 134
Gil, Salvador 467
Gilbert, Mickey 310
Gilbert, Stan 395
Gilberti, Ray 371
Gilder, Nick 489
Gill, Shirley J. 435
Gillespie, Jean 219
Gillett, Maurice 473
Gillette, Leland 455

Gillette, Ruth 231
Gilliam, Stu 219, 283
Gilliam, Vivian Hillgrove 430
Gilmore, Andrew 113, 125
Gilkyson, Terry 70, 122, 206, 211
Gilliam, Stu 91, 310
Gimpel, Sandra 454
Giorgio, Tony 185
Giraud, Jean "Moebius" 395, 404, 407
Girvin, Terri 467
Gitomer, Michael 327
Gittens, Ren 474
Gladstone Comics 444, 466, 495-496
Gladwin, Joe 247
Glascock, Baylis 395, 467
Glascock, Bill 90
Glascow, Len 319
Glasow, Betty 198
Glass, Ned 21, 31, 39
Glass, Sandy 345
Glass, Seamon 365
Gleave, Lisa 301
Glendale, California 487
Glover, Bruce 87, 143
Gnome-Mobile, The 11
"Go Get 'Em Tigers" 455
Go West, Young Dog 245
Godar, Godfrey 198, 275, 334, 380
Godden, John 488
Godden, Nobby 467
Godey, John 30
Goelz, Al 74
Goin' Quackers 326
Gold Key Comics 14, 20, 46, 62, 80, 108, 132, 159, 178, 218, 246, 282, 300, 326, 358
Gold, Mel 283
Goldberg, Art 126
Goldberg, Mike 126
Golden Oak Ranch 274
Golden Books 178
Golden Dog, The 245
Golden Evenings of Summer, The 138
Golden, George 21, 82, 269
Golden Girls, The 466, 501
Golden Globe Awards 143
Golden Horseshoe Revue, The 388
Golden Voyage of Sinbad, The 158
Goldilocks 46
Golding, John 369
Goldman, Danny 133
Goldman, Gary 252, 258, 268, 376
Goldsboro, Bobby 151
Goldsmith, Jerry 143, 389-390, 466
Goldwasser, Dan 372
Golf Resort Hotel 132, 158
Gombert, Ed 258, 376
Gomer Pyle U.S.M.C. 293

Gomez, Raul 341
Gone Are the Dayes 443
Gone with the Wind 43
Gonzales, Allen 424, 474, 482, 488
Gonzales, Manuel 359
Gonzalez Gonzalez, Jose 341
Gonzalez-Gonzalez, Pedro 39
Good, Christopher 436
Good Morning World 155
Good Samaritan Hospital 7
"Goodbye May Seem Forever" 376, 378
Goode, Martha J. 430
Goodman, Dody 446
Goodman, Judi 445
Goodwin, Ron 198, 247, 275, 314
Goodyear Rubber and Tire Corp. 268, 397
Goodyear Grand Prix Raceway 158
Goofy 108, 300, 326, 416, 497
Goral, Edward 483
Gordon, Antoinette 396
Gordon, Barry Mark 423
Gordon, Cindy 436
Gordon, Jeff 489
Gordon, Lance R. 365
Gordon, Regina 459
Gordon, Steven 481-482
Goresbeck, Alan 301
Gorin, Leslie 269, 376
Gosnell, Raja R. 349
Gossom, Bob 327
Gostelow, Gordon 207
Gottfredson, Floyd 159, 178-179, 496
Gould, Elliott 346, 348, 359, 363
Gould, Harold 179, 228
Gould, Ina 97
Gould, Sandra 82
Gould-Porter, Arthur E. 97
Gourson, Jeff 395
Government of Brazil 204
Govey, Peter 474
Gower, Jerrol 467
Grabowski, Norman 21, 35, 160
Grace, Bud 151, 223, 228
Grace, Howard 364
Graf, Allan 228
Graham, John 467
Graham, Therese 459
Grammys, The 13, 62, 159, 218, 246, 281, 300, 358-359, 444
Granatelli, Andy 39
Grand, Elizabeth 301
Grand Opening of Walt Disney World, The 80
Granier-Deferre, Denys 380
Grant, Cleveland P. 204
Grant, Dawn 389
Grantham, Robin 473
Grate, Lynn 38

Gratz, Joan C. 474
Grau, Doris 90, 126
Grauman, Lawrence 446
Gravenor, Bob 349
Graves, David Michael 489
Graves, Ed 81
Graves, Julie 301
Gray, Nick 435
Graysmark, Julie 467
Grazer, Brian 445, 451-454
Great All-Nighter, The 333
Great Dinosaur Robbery, The 198
Great Moments from the Films of Walt Disney 359
Great Moments with Mr. Lincoln 132, 178, 444
Great Mouse Detective, The 443, 465, 495
Great Muppet Caper, The 358
Great Race, The 333
"Greatest Star of All, The 274
Green Acres 73, 95, 429
Green, Alan 310
Green, Clifford 466
Green, Ellen 466
Green, Howard E. 98, 467, 483
Green Bay Packers 230
Green, Stan 147, 230, 258
Greenaway, David 474
Greenaway, Gordon 473
Greenberg, Barry 180
Greenberg, Harriet 418
Greene, Graham 437
Greene, Luther 431
Greene, Shecky 446
Greenfield, Arlette 431
Greenslade, Arthur 86
Greet, Emily 328
Gregg, Kris 397
Gregory, James 91, 179
Gregory, Linda 473
Grier, Harry 445
Grier, Pam 424
Grifasi, Joe 447
Griffin, Christopher 445
Griffin, Jack 117, 134, 139, 151, 180, 219, 306, 328
Griffith, Don 70, 96, 147, 252, 258, 376, 482
Griffith, Eva 212
Griffith, Melanie 47, 454
Griffiths, Lucy 199
Griffiths, Rachel 418
Grigg, Gene 125
Grimes, Gary 228
Grimethorpe Colliery Band, The 247
Griner, George 301
Grist, Hal 38
Groce, Larry 218
Gross, Charles 458
Grossman, Harry S. 197-198
Grossman, Larry 396

Grosvenor, Carol Holman 482
Groves, Herman 179
Grow, Ronald R. 90, 125, 138, 172, 192, 227, 237, 268
Grower, John 396
Growney, Robert 460
Grugon, Karen 435
Grundeen, Frank 46
Grundt, Gregory 98
Grusd, Tina 483
G2 Graphic Service Inc. 397
Guard, Dominic 334
Guder, Marian 396
Guedel, Heidi 258
Guenther, Ann 147, 252, 258
Guest, Don 262
Guest, Duncan 371
Guidi, Guidarino 418
Guinea Up Catering 459
Gulf Oil 12-13, 20, 45
Gullerud, Peter 396, 483, 489
Gummi Bears (see *Disney's Adventures of the Gummi Bears*)
Gun Shy 198, 388, 527
Gus 227
Gus 198, 227-230, 294, 333, 358
Guss, Louis 219
Gussman, Jeffrey 395
Gustafson, Mark 474
Gutierrez, Joseph 87
Guyler, Deryck 199
Gwillim, David 172
Gwynne, Peter 212

Haas, Charles (Charlie) 397, 409
Hack, Dorothy 109
Hackett, Buddy 39, 43
Hackett, Joan 224, 306
Hacksaw 80
Haddon, Dayle 133
Haddrick, Roy 212
Hafley, Lucien M. 268
Hagadorn, Howard L. 319
Hagedorn, James 371
Hagenbush, Valerie 396
Haggard, Nathan 90
Haggerty, Dan 74
Hahn, Don 269, 376, 482
Haire, Christopher L. 455
Hajee, Bill 258, 268
Hakim, David 459
Hale, Alan 306
Hale, Georgina 334
Hale, Joe 96, 147, 252, 258, 268, 282, 305, 318, 334, 376, 481
Hale, Richard 87, 144
Hale, Steve 483-484

"Half of Me" 345-346
Hall, Allen 350, 424
Hall, Bryan 438
Hall, Don 62
Hall, Donna 192, 282, 294, 340
Hall, Huntz 160
Hall, Ken 467
Hall of Presidents. The 178, 281, 388
Hall of Presidents, The 80
Hall, Ray 467
Hall, Regnal
Hallam, John 372
Hallenbeck, E. Darrell 417, 466, 488
Hallett, Jack 447
Halloween Hall O' Fame 245
Halver, David 398, 424
Hamad and the Pirates 80
Hamada, Terrey 483
Hammer, Alvin 117
Hammer, Wynn 319
Hamilton, Georgina 198, 247, 275, 314, 369
Hamilton, William 74
Hamlisch, Marvin 133, 138, 150, 359, 364
Hamm, Sam 430
Hammer Films 211, 287
Hammond, Nicholas 151
Hammond, Peter 474
Hampton, James 289
Hanalei, Ralph 169
Hancock, Peter 473
Handley, Annette 455
Hang Your Hat on the Wind 45, 498
Hanks, Tom 446, 452-454
Hanley, Daniel P. 445
Hanly, Margaret 165
Hanna-Barbera 58, 131, 349, 354
Hannah, Daryl 446, 452-453
Hannemann, Nephi 169
Hannon, Chick 74
Hansel and Gretel 11-12
Hansen, Dan 376, 482
Hansen, Edward 70, 147, 252, 376, 482
Hanson, Curtis 430
"Happiest Girl Alive, The" 26-27
"Happiest Home in These Hills, The" 269
Happiest Millionaire, The 11, 14, 17, 25, 29-30
"Happy Birthday" 147
Happy Birthday Party for Winnie the Pooh, A 13
Happy Days 77, 452
Harada, Ernest 360
Harcourt, David 206
"Hard to Believe" 489
Harden (Hardin), Mark 424, 431
Hardin, Melora 306
Harding, Christine 483, 489
Harding, Fred 212
Harding, Lilly 419

Harding, Steve 467
Hardwicke, Edward 468
Harmon, John 82
Harmon, Robert L. 437
Harmon, Steve 26
Harness Fever 158
Harral, Don 409
Harrell, James 459
Harris, Ray 482
Harrod, Susie 369
Harrington, Pat 54
Harris, Barbara 238, 243, 305, 309
Harris, Bob 38, 263, 282, 289
Harris, Brian 369
Harris, Christopher J. 435
Harris, Corey 396
Harris, Eugene 395-396
Harris, John H. 474
Harris, Julie 275
Harris, Leon R. 318, 334, 359
Harris, Max 199
Harris, Norman 458, 489
Harris, Phil 20, 70, 73, 147
Harris, Richard A. 454
Harris, Roy 483
Harrison, Andrew 247
Harrison, Joel 490
Harrison, Terry 482
Harry, Debbie 407
Harry Potter 275
Hart, Bill 310
Hartigan, Ben 74, 90, 126
Hartley, Brian 454
Hartley, John 247
Hartman, David 172
Hartstone, Graham V. 198, 212
Hartwell, Ernie 455
Harvey, Alex 459
Harvey, Chuck 258, 268, 376
Harvey Comics 1
Harvey, Harry 21
Harvey, Orwin 345
Harveyville Fun Times!, The 1
Harwell, Bert 204
Harwell, Ernie 455
Haskett, Dan 376
Hass, Charlie 408
Hastings, Bob 66, 139, 219
Hatch, Eric 35
Hathaway, Bob 318, 395, 408, 418, 424, 446, 458, 467, 482
Hathaway, Harold 489
Hatt, John 370
Haugen, Harvey 438
Haunt of Fear, The 430
Haunted Mansion, The 7, 45, 61
Haunted Mansion, The 46

Haunting, The 338
Havard, Elven 490
Havard, Evelyn 328
Hawaii 59, 171, 349
Hawkins, Cherie 475
Hawley, Lowell 26
Hawn, Goldie Jeanne 26, 29
Hawthorne, Nigel 483
Hay, John 350
Hayes, Billie 483-484
Hayes, Helen 131, 160, 164, 198, 203, 243, 275, 279
Hayes, Jack 289
Hayes, John 224, 231
Hayman, Gordon 473
Haymer, Johnny 263
Haynie, Jim 459
Hays, Robert 418
Hayward, John 314
Hayward, Robert 455
Hazel 95, 229, 294
"He Needs Me" 350, 353
"He's Gonna Make It" 82
"He's Large" 350, 352
Heald, Angela 435
Healey, Arthur 370
Healey, Myron 54
Hearn, Bernard 370
Hearn, Chick 39
Hearst Corporation, The 349
Heath, John 212
Heather, Dan 430
Heaven Can Wait 364
"Heffalumps and Woozles" 252, 255, 257
Heidi 20
Heimer, Renee 370
Hein, Erik 301
Heinrich, Michael 436
Heinrichs, Rick 334
Heiple, Robert 460
Heisling, Donna Lee 490
Heizer, Robert 301
Hekking, Walter 395
Held, Bob 489
Heller, Bill 489
Hellmich, Fred 70, 96, 147, 252
Hello, Larry 287
"Hello, My Baby" 143
Helmsman 2
Hemingway, Chuck 490
Hemphill, Douglas 370
Hemphill, Lamme 431
Hendershot, Eric 300-301
Henderson, Don 247, 327
Hendricks, Ben F. 38, 81, 160, 263, 268, 282, 289, 305, 310, 318, 340, 345, 359, 364, 380, 389
Hendry, Marsh 30

Hendryx, Shirl 435
Henley, Trevor 328
Henn, Mark 482
Henry, Chuck 306
Henry, Don 334, 459, 474, 489
Henry, Justin 455
Henson, Brian 475
Hepburn, Katharine 387
Herbert, Percy 199, 207
Herbert, Pitt 151, 306
Herbie Day 164
Herbie Day at Disneyland 158
Herbie: Fully Loaded 344
Herbie Goes Bananas 325, 340-345, 358
Herbie Goes to Monte Carlo 230, 235, 262-268, 358
Herbie Rides Again 158, 160-164, 358, 388
Herbie, the Love Bug 39-43, 95, 121, 158, 160-165, 263-268, 340-345, 358
Herbie, the Love Bug 267, 344, 358, 526
Herdan, Earle 435
Here Comes Mr. Jordan 364
Hernandez, Fred 74, 87
Hernandez, Paul 396
Herrmann, Edward 301, 305
Herron, Bob 319
Hertelendy, Hanna 228
Hertfordshire, England 474
Heschong, Greg 395
Hester, Harry 258
Hester, Mark A. 376, 482
Hewitt, Alan 35, 53, 82, 117
Hewitt, Jery 446
Hewlett, Arthur 199
"Hey Liley, Liley Lo (Married Man Gonna Keep Your Secret)" 437
Hibler, Christopher 35, 38, 50, 53, 65, 90, 96, 116, 125, 138, 151, 169, 228, 294
Hibler, Winston 14, 35, 62-63, 70, 113, 143, 165, 169, 172, 175, 204, 252
Hickinbotham, Ian 473
Hickman, Bill 38, 138
Hickner, Stephen 483
Hickson, Joan 199, 203
Higgins, Ron 473
Higgins, Virginia 423
High Flying Spy, The 108
Hiken, Nat 69
Hilditch, Robert 212
Hill, Reverend Albert Fay 305
Hill, Arthur 425
Hill, Dave 117
Hill, Matthew 489
Hill, Michael 445
Hill, Richard 467
Hill, Robert 473-474, 488
Hill, Willy 370
Hill, Walter 248

Hilling John 370
Hill's Angels 309
Hillcrest High School 300
Hine, Michael 475
Hines, Suzanne 350
Hingle, Pat 143, 437
Hinrichsen, Niels 172
Hinton, S.E. 408-409, 413
Hinton, Shelley 396
"Hip Hip Pooh-ray" 252, 255
Hirano, Gordon Tadao 345
Hirsch, Edward 371
Hirschhorn, Joel 238, 269, 294, 305
"Hit and Run" 489
Hitchcock, Claude 247, 275, 314, 334
Hluhuwe Game Reserve of Zululand 204
Hoar, Ray O. 319
Hobbit, The 246, 281
Hobbs, Ron 458
Hobelman, Ed 97
Hodges, Clay 345
Hodgson, Leslie 472
Hodgson, Mike 482
Hodgson, Paul 370
Hoescher, Matt 490
Hoffman, Bobby 31, 237
Hoffman, Dustin 355
Hoffman, Michael 301
Hofstein, Ricquette 212
Hog Wild 158
Hogan, Patrick 446
Hogan's Heroes 155, 230
Hogg, Ian 247
Hohman, R.J. 350
Hohn, Carola 390
Hoiseck, Ronald F. 447
Holbrook, Hal 429
Holcombe, Harry 180, 185
Holdridge, Lee 445-446
Hole, Fred 472
Hole, Jonathan 54, 91
Holecheck, Brian 483
Holland, John 180
Holland, Richard 473
Holland, Rodney 349
Holland, Tim 370
Hollander, David 365
Holleywell, Tom P. 165
Holliman, Earl 109
Holloway, Sterling 70, 218, 253, 257
Holly Marlo 409
Hollywood Pictures 380
Holman, Rex 113, 185, 224, 310
Holmes, John W. 349
Holmes, Madeline 431
Holmes, Trev 301
Holt, Larry 310, 397

Holt, Robert 97
Holter, Bob 133
Holter, Gene 133, 143
Holton, Jack 74, 185
Holzborn, Paul L. 482, 488
Homel, Bob 31
Hompton, James 381
Honaker, Randy 350
Hone, Ronald 370
Hong, James 219
Hong Kong Phooey 73
Honthaner, Ron 295
Hooker, Hank 294, 397
Hooker, Hugh 294
Hooker, Buddy Joe 169, 179, 224, 227, 294, 340-341, 409
Hooker, Hank Bill 340, 364
Hooker, Hugh 340
Hooks, Jacque 396
Hooks, Kevin 301
Hootsie the Owl 45
Hopkins, Mark 475
Hopkins, Michael 473
Hoppe, Richard 482
Hopper, Dennis 490
Hordern, Michael 206
Horizons 417
Horn, Stephen 109
Horner, James 424
Horse in the Gray Flannel Suit, The 17, 35-38
Horton, Charis 381
Horton, David M. (Dave) 424, 459
Horton, Howard "Dutch" 126, 185
Horwitz, Ed 350
Hosbjor, Mona 483
Hot Lead and Cold Feet 281, 294-298
Hodart, Philippe 381
Holland, Brian 418
Holland, Eddie 418
Holzborn, Paul 467
Horner, James 423
Horowitz, Michael 483
Horton, Dave 467
Hough, John 184, 189-191, 282, 287-288, 324, 333, 338-339
Hoult, Richard 334
Hound of Florence, The 230
House of the Future 12
Houston, John 430
Houston, Paul 467
How to Play Baseball 45
How to Swim 45
Howard, Arthur 199
Howard, Cheryl 447
Howard, Clint 75, 77, 252, 447, 451-453
Howard, Jeff 482, 489
Howard, Rance 74-75, 447, 451, 453

Howard, Ronny (Ron) 75, 77, 445, 451-453
Howard, Vince 82
Howarth, Alan 488
Howarth, Derek 370, 473
Howden, Mike 295
Hoy, Linda 490
Hoy, Robert 38
Hoyle, Geoff 351
Hoyle, Lester 126
Hubbard, Andy 409
Hubbard, Gordon 20, 26, 31
Hubbard, John 160
Hubbard, Paul 437
Hubert, Axel Anton 424
Huddleston, Floyd 70, 147
Hudson, Guy 370
Hudson, Kevin 475
Hudson, Lord Tim 70
Hudson's Bay Company 204
Huebner, Mark 409
Huey, Dewey and Louie Junior Woodchucks 14, 20, 46, 62, 80, 108, 133, 159, 178, 218, 246, 282, 300, 326, 358, 389, 417, 444
Huff, Philip 488
Huff, Tom 294
Hugglin, Wendy 436
Hughes, Barnard 398, 404
Hughes, Brendan 438
Hughes, Herbert 396
Hughes, Joe C. 345
Hughes, Raymond 473
Hughes, Robert 431
Hughes, Sandra J. 459
Hughes, Whitey 458
Hulett, Eric A. 289, 294
Hulett, Kurt V. 219, 237, 263, 268, 282
Hulett, Ralph 70, 86, 147
Hulett, Steve 376, 482
Hume, Alan 333
Hume, Douglas 306
Hummel, Rob 396
Humphrey, Nick 74
Humphreys, Dave 436
Humphreys, Gerry 334
Hunicutt, Arthur 91
Hunt, Allan 238, 341, 345
Hunt, Linda 351
Hunt, Maurice 482
Hunter, Coralie 409
Hunter, David 474
Hunter, Tim 408
"Huntin' Man, A" 376, 378
Hurd, Allen 289, 294, 319, 327, 398, 409, 424, 431, 446, 459, 468, 483, 489
Hurford, James 430
Hurley, Joe 423

Hurry, Colin 474
Hurst, Rick 289
Hurt, John 390, 394, 484
Hurt, Wesley Ivan 351
Hush, Tom 483
Husband, Ron 258, 376, 481
Huston, John 484
Huston, Paul 371
Hutchinson, Bill 231, 269
Hutchinson, Bruce 445
Hutchinson, Peter 370
Hutchinson, Tracy 489
Hutton, Ron 369

"I Am Woman" 275
I Dream of Jeannie 86
"I Found a New Friend" 341, 343-344
"I Saw a Dragon" 269-270, 273
"I Tried for You" 301, 303
"I Yam What I Yam" 350, 353
"I'd Like to Be You For a Day" 238
"I'll Find it Where I Can" 459
"I'm a Jayhawk" 437
"(I'm Just a) Little Black Raincloud" 252-253
"I'm Mean" 350, 352
"I'm Popeye the Sailor Man" 351, 353-354
Iaconelli, George 418
Ian and Sylvia 122
Ibbetson, Timothy 473
IBM 406
If You Had Wings 107
Iger, Robert 7, 496
Igus, Darrow 306, 309
IMDB 17, 34, 58, 74
Imi, Yony 389
In Search of the Castaways 61, 281
"In the Good Old Summertime" 212, 455
In the Heat of the Night 287
Incident at Hawk's Hill 158
Incredible Journey, The 45
Indian Village, The 80
Indian War Canoes 80
Indiana Jones 2
Indiana Jones and the Temple of Doom 444
Indrisano, John 35
Industrial Light and Magic, Inc. (ILM) 371, 375, 496
Informational International (Triple I) 405, 407
Ingersol, Amy 447
Ingey, Shirley 436
Inglish, Dave 397
Inky, the Crow 45
Innes, Michael 275
Innocenzi, Rita 350
Inns, Garth 334
Inside Comics 157
Inspector Gadget 354
International Recording 482

Ion, Bill 90, 125
Iowa Film Commission 459
"Iris and Fido" 87
Irwin, Bill 351
Isaacs, James J. (Jim) 467, 488
Isbell, Lloyd 185
Isham, Mark 430
Island at the Top of the Word, The 158-159, 172
Isle of Skye, Scotland 369
Italian Job, The 385
It's a Small World 12
It's a Small World 20
It's a Small World: Walt Disney's Greatest Hits 108
It's Flashbeagle, Charlie Brown 417
"It's Not Easy" 269-270, 274
"It's Not Easy Being Me" 350, 353
It's Tough to Be a Bird 8, 45, 61, 498
Ittimangnaq, Martha 431
Ittimangnaq, Zachary 431
Ivanek, Zelijko 409
Ivory Coast 468
Iwerks, Dave 396
Iwerks, Don 396
Iwerks, Ub 104, 274

Jack and Jill 294
Jack Benny Program, The 237
Jackman, Tom 310
Jackson, Andrew 150, 169, 179
Jackson, Armetta 482
Jackson, Billy 319
Jackson, Carol Ann 446
Jackson, Debra DeVito 396
Jackson, Gene 90
Jackson, Jay 481
Jackson, Robert 371
Jackson, Sammy 66, 91
Jackson, Tom 290
Jacobs, Eylia 65
Jacobs, Jon 475
Jacobs, Olu 468
Jacobs, Rachel 306
Jacobs, Robert 371
Jacobson, Jill 447
Jacquet, Jeffrey 283
Jaeger, Casse 283
Jaeger, Frederick 199
Jaeckel, Richard 341
Jaffe, Nicole 39
Jaffe, Sam 97
Jaffer, Melissa 212
Jagger, Dean 47
Jake the cat 289-294
Jalbert, Joe Jay 125
James, Allan 247
James, Anthony 283, 287-288
James, Bob 283

James Bond 323
James, Brion 224
James, Clifton 109
James, Emrys 372
James, Gavin 289, 390
James, Joyce 247, 314, 334
James, Kent 74, 97, 185, 380
James, Peter 206
James, Robert 38
James, Sidney 446
Janey, Alain 263
Jann, Gerald 38
Janney, Julie 351
Janov, Ellen 35
Japan 417, 481
Jar-Jar Binks 324
Jarre, Maurice 172, 176, 345
Jarrott, Charles 247, 345, 380
Jaws 402
Jay, Gary 458
Jeffersons, The 121
Jeffery-Ludlow, Linda 435
Jeffory, Dawn 365
Jeffress, Jerry 371
Jeglinski, Chuck 459
Jennings, Waylon 459
Jennings, Will 446
Jensen, E. Eric 371
Jensen, Elois 395
Jensen, Gary 397
Jensen, Howard 38, 96
Jensen, John 138, 237, 466
Jenson, George 185
Jenson, Merrill 300
Jeris, Nancy 365
Jerman-Jerosa, Vincent 447
Jerry Saved from Drowning 465
Jessup, Harley 473
Jetcopters Inc. 397
Jew, Sheldon 301
Jewell, Austen 74, 160, 172
Jewell, Stuart V. 204
Jewkes, Delow 97
Jiggins, Paul 474
Jiminez, Cesar A. 340
Jobs, Steve 2
Jody, Michael 455
Johansen, David 489
Johnny Tremain 443
Johnson, Arch 113
Johnson, Bill 74
Johnson, BJ 446
Johnson, Brian 370, 372
Johnson, Claude 113
Johnson, Clay 2
Johnson, Dee 301
Johnson, Douglas G. 301

Johnson, Dwayne, 191
Johnson, Dyke 397
Johnson, Eric Ben 409
Johnson, Gene 318
Johnson, Jennie 369
Johnson, Julie Ann 289, 294
Johnson, Katy 397
Johnson, Lynn-Holly 334, 339
Johnson, Roberta 369
Johnson, Ruth Anna 2
Johnstad, Steve 489
Johnston, David B. 300
Johnston, Kevin N. 237, 263
Johnston, Ollie 70, 146, 252, 257-258, 262, 376, 379
Johnston, Richard O. 376
Jolliffe, John J. 318
Jonas, David 96, 481-483
Jones, Al 397, 458
Jones, Betsy 488
Jones, Davy 281
Jones, Dean 17, 21, 25, 35, 38-39, 43, 91, 95, 126, 129-131, 164, 217, 231, 235, 263, 267-268, 358, 429
Jones, Ed 371
Jones, Freddie (Fred) 301, 483
Jones, Gary 454
Jones, Hank (Henry) 21, 25-26, 30, 50, 82, 86, 91, 113, 161, 219, 231, 289
Jones, Jeff 454
Jones, John 460
Jones, Melvin 319, 468
Jones, Rod 409
Jones, Roxanne 349
Jones, Rusty 14
Jones, Sally 473
Jones, Terry 150
Jones, Val 474
Jorah, Samson 431
Jordan, Horace 395
Jordan, Jim 259, 262
Jordan, Judy 66
Jordan, Sandy Berke 445
Jordan, Ted 91, 310
Jordan, Tony 369
Jorden, Jan 360
Jorgensborg, Debbie 483
Josephson, Les 228
Journey 398, 403, 408
Journey of Natty Gann, The 465, 495
"Journey, The" 258-259
Journey to Matecumbe, A 223
Journey to the Valley of the Emu 281
Judge, Chris 437
Jugnot, Gerard 263
Julian, Arthur 65
Julie Andrews Hour, The 108
Julienne, Dominique 418

Julienne, Michel 381, 418
Julienne, Remy 380-381, 418
Jung, Allen 39
Jungle Book, The 11, 13-14, 17, 20, 73, 150, 211, 281, 443, 487
Jungle Cat 204
Jungle Cruise 2-6
Junior Woodchucks Guide 133
Junk Food Junkie 218
Jurasik, Peter 398
Jurassic Park 472
Justin, John 418
Justin Morgan Had a Horse 108, 388
Juttner, Christian 283, 287-288
Juttner, Shelly 238

Kabok, Louis 455
Kagel, James 350, 467
Kahana, Kim 169, 192
Kahl, Milt 70, 96, 146, 252, 258, 483
Kahler, David 327
Kahn, Bernie 81
Kaiserman, Bill 467
Kalfon, Jean-Pierre 381
Kalish, Barbara 350
Kalley, William 408
Kamins, Harry 74
Kamins, Richard 74
Kanagy, Darlene 483
Kane, Joseph P. 446
Kane, Margo 437
Kane, Sean 360
Kane, Sid 97
Kane, Susan 369
Kansas 441
Kaplan, Marvin 238, 328
Kapp, Joe 134
Karjola, Linda Leigh 364
Karp, Bob 46
Karpe, Jeff 467
Karvelas, Robert 238
Kasha, Al 238, 269, 294, 305
Katt, William 468
Katz, Patty 351
Katz, Stephen 318
Katzenberg, Jeffrey 487
Katzoff, Marvin 327
Kauai 171, 349
Kaufman, Monique 199
Kauppi, Pekka 165
Kawa, Bob 301
Kaye, Alan 406
Kaye, Gorden 248
Kaysen, Laura 371
Kean, Jane 269
Kean, Katherine (Kathrine) 371, 489
Keane, Glen 258, 268, 376, 379

Index   559

Kearney, Gene 74
Keating, Fred 438
Keating, Jim 396
Keating, Trish 430, 436
Keaton, Michael 452
Keehne, Chuck 20, 26, 31, 35, 38, 46, 50, 53, 65, 74, 81, 86, 90, 96, 109, 113, 116, 121, 125, 133, 138, 143, 151, 160, 165, 169, 172, 179, 185, 192, 219, 223, 228, 230, 237, 262, 268, 282, 289, 294, 305, 310, 318
Keen, Geoffrey 206
Keen, John 369
Keene, A. 97
Keene, Lisa 482
Kehoe, Pat 179, 192, 228
Keigly, Liz 458
Keil, Bill 252
Keith, Brian 87, 90
Keith, Christopher 396, 489
Keligian, Carole 488
Keller, Cathy 350
Keller, Karen 482
Keller, Shawn 482
Kelley, Barry 39
Kelley, Randy 395
Kelley, Richard A. 109
Kelly, Andrew 370
Kelly, Gene 429
Kelly, Nancy 454
Kelly, Patsy 238, 305, 309
Kelly, Ray 437-438
Kelly, Ron 62
Kelly, Scott 98
Kelm, Gayl 396
Kelsey, Dick 96
Kemp, Kenner G. 35, 54, 117
Kemp, Lola 289
Kemp, Roger 372
Kemper, Jan 459
Kendall, Richard (Dick) 334, 397, 459, 489
Kenly, Patric 397
Kennedy, Burt 247
Kennedy, Dean 474
Kennedy, Evelyn 20, 26, 31, 35, 38, 46, 50, 53, 62, 65, 70, 74, 81, 86, 90, 96, 109, 113, 116, 125, 133, 138, 143, 147, 151, 160, 165, 169, 172, 179, 185, 192, 204, 219, 223, 228, 230, 237, 252, 258, 262, 268, 282, 289, 305. 310, 319, 340, 345, 376
Kennedy, Frank 86
Kennedy, Robert 43
Kenney, Daniel 370
Kenney, Joel P. 327
Kenny, Christopher 473
Kent, Bill 398

Kenward, Paul 467
Kenwood, Gary 431
Kenworthy, John 398
Kenworthy, Jr., Paul 204
Kenyon, Ron 489
Kepenek, Jere 483
Kerns, Hubie 446
Kerry, John 306
Kerss, Norman 370
Kerwin, Lance 185
Kessler, Lori 447
Ketchum, Carol 301
Ketchum, Dave 306
Keulen, Sylvia 371
Key, Alexander 184, 190, 282
Key, Ted 90, 95, 227, 229, 289, 294
Kid in King Arthur's Court, A 318
Kidd, Jonathan 26
Kidder, Margot 418
"Kids" 350, 354
Kids Who Knew Too Much, The 326
Kieffer, Dorothy 90, 96, 125, 151, 160, 172, 230, 282
Kiel, Richard 228
Kierscey, Ted 258, 268, 318, 376, 482
Kiesser, Jan 424
Kijko, John 370
Kilduff, William (Bill) 319, 424, 467, 482, 489
Kimball, Mark 397
Kimball, Ward 90-91, 96, 107
Kimble, Greg 104
Kimmel, Bruce 192
King, Avery 436
King, Bill 74, 97
King, Brian 98
King Features Syndicate 349
King, Hal 70, 96, 146, 252
King, Jerry 445
King Kong 407
King Louie and Mowgli 20
King, Jr., Martin Luther 43
King of the Grizzlies 62-65
King, Robert L. 116
Kingsley, Susan 351
Kingston, Cleve 445
Kinnamon, Harley V. 389
Kinnear, Roy 199, 263
Kinney, Sharon 349, 351
Kirby, Bruno 151, 155
Kirby, George 231
Kirby, Jack 324
Kirk, Claude 13
Kirkpatrick, George 126
Kiser, John 125
Kissaun, Michael 418-419
Kissimmee, Florida 2
Kit Carson and the Mountain Men 245
Kitchens, Colin Michael 430, 472

Kitson, Ken 247
Klein, Jr., Jordan 446
Kleiser, Jeffrey 397
Kletter, Richard 430
Kleven, Max 31, 489
Kliment, Jeff 431
Kline, Marty 488
Klinger, Brendan 424
Knapman, Andrew 370
Knebel, Ambrose 460
Knebel, Levi L. 459
Knell, David 360, 446
Knight, Don 192, 224
Knight, Holly 489
Knight, Jack T. 301
Knoller, Eve 351
Knotts Berry Farm 444
Knotts, Don 192, 197, 219, 228, 230, 263, 295, 298, 310, 314, 317
Knowles, David 370
Knowles, Philip 370
Knowlton, Kimberly (Kim) 371, 482, 489
Koch, Howard W. 369
Kodaliths 404-405
Koester, John 165
Koford, Jim 258, 376, 482
Kogan, Milt 219
Kohler, Kerry 473
Kohler, Phil 472
Kolden, Scott 139
Kolstad, Lasse 172
Kolsrud, Dan 423
Komar, Bill 98
Kong, May 396
Koniger, Erik 446
Konrad, Dorothy 161
Korda, Nicholas Vincent 319
Korman, Harvey 341
Korth, Martin 482
Koslo, Paul 87
Kostal, Irwin 96-97, 268-269
Kouimelis, Luca 350
Koumashian, Raffi 483
Kovace, Bill 397
Kraft, Barry 436
Kraft Salutes Disneyland's 25th Anniversary 326
Kraft, Wendy P. 435
Kraftwerk 403
Krakoff, Marcello 418
Kramer, Joel 489
Kratter, Tia W. 396, 405, 482
Krattiger, Bob E. 74
Krause, Richard 409
Kremer, Lisette 398
Krepela, Neil 371
Kreps, David 447
Kress, Earl 376

Kressel, Lynn 454
Kroeger, Wolf 249
Krohn, Doug 482
Krone, Fred 38
Kronowitz, Bobby 445
Krook, Peter 474
Krora, Stephane 468
Kroyer, Bill 376, 395, 397, 403
Kroyer, Susan 376
Kruger National Park of South Africa 204
Kruks, Gabriel 430
Kruschen, Jack 91
Krzanowski, Tad 334
Kubota, Tak 360
Kuchera, Brian 436
Kuhlman, Ron 447
Kulcsar, Mike 263
Kulp, Nancy 70
Kuramoto, Eileen 396
Kuran, Peter 371
Kuri, Emile 20, 26, 31, 35, 38, 46, 50, 53, 65, 74, 81, 86, 90, 96, 109, 113, 116, 125
Kuri, John A. 81, 150, 169, 192, 197-198
Kuri, Joseph 185
Kursaal Company, The 418
Kurtz, Gary 472
Kushner, Donald 394, 402-403, 406
Kusonic, Nick 436

La Bonge, Robert 319, 341
La Da Productions 436
La Mori, Paul 396
La Rue, Walt 31, 489
Lacey, Ronald 418
"Lack of Education" 376-377
Lack, Simon 207
LaCrois, Denis 437
Lacy, Clay 371
Ladd, Diane 424
Lady and the Tramp 14, 80, 108, 325-326
Lady from Shanghai, The 339
Lafaive, Deborah 435
Lagniez, Jean-Claude 381
Lai, Rick 210
Laing, Jack 484
Laird, Monty 310
Lake Buena Vista 61
Lake Buena Vista Village Marketplace 178
Lake Buena Vista Village Townhouses 132
Lalande, Francois 263
Lamart, Rene 360
Lamas, Lorenzo 301, 304
Lamb, Gil 21, 35, 39, 66
Lambert, Eileen 483
Lambert, Hugh 26
Lambert, Steven 489
Lamont, Duncan 247

Lamping, Frank 74, 81
Lanchester, Elsa 21, 50
Land Before Time, The 380
Land of Oz, The 472
Land, Scott 424
Landau, Richard 318
Landau, Susan B. 454
Landon, Ted D. 165
Landrum, Bill 97
Landrum, Teri 360
Landry, Doreen 370
Lane, Brent 436
Lane, Charles 70
Lane, Chris 395
Lane, Diane 454
Lane, Dick 231
Lane, Ray 455
Langdon, Linda 436
Lange, Jessica 458-459, 463
L'Angelle, January 276
Langley, Barry 369
Langtry,Hugh 489
Lanning, Stephen (Steve) 472, 474
Lanpher, Dorse A. 258, 268, 318
Lansburgh, Larry 35
Lansbury, Angela 97-98, 103
Lantieri, Michael 488
Lanzisero, Joe 483
Lapotaire, Jane 199
LaPoten, Gary 230, 268
Lara, Jean 262
Larimer, Bernard 460
Larmon, Gene 396
Larner, Roy 473
LaRocca, Charles 74
Larsen, John 349
Larson, Eric 70, 96, 147, 252, 258, 482
Larson, Milt 96-97
Larue, Jim 395
LaRue, Walt 306
Lasseter, John 405
Lassie 58
Last Flight of Noah's Ark, The 325, 345-349, 363, 394
Last Flight to Freedom, The 394
Lasting, Richard 360
Late, Jason 447
Latimer, Clifford 370, 431
Lating, Manfred 96-97
Laughlin, Douglas 431
Laughlin, Tom 247
Lauren, Tammy 346
Laurencelle, Claudette 431
Laurie, John 199
Laurie, Piper 475, 481
Laurita, Dana 147
LaVigne, Robin Dee 345

Law, Mick 467
Lawrence, Bob 275
Lawrence, Hap 295
Lawrence, Harry 212
Lawrence, L.F. 473
Lawrence Livermore Lab 397, 405-406
Lawrence, Richard James 327, 423
Lawrence, Robert 62
Lawson, Tony 369
Lawton, Jay 459, 467, 482, 489
Lawton, Ken 370, 389
Lay, Tom 258
Layne, Bill 70, 96, 147, 252
Layne, Rickie 306
Le Mesurier, C.F. 206
Le Mesurier, John 315
Lea, Sharan 425
Leachman, Cloris 139, 143, 155, 305, 341
Lean, David 429
Learman, Richard 345, 380, 423
Leary, Richard 436
Lebanon, Kansas 58-59
Lederer, Joseph 436
Lederman, Bob 349
Lee, Billy 294
Lee, Chris 310, 364
Lee, Christopher 283, 287-288
Lee, Danny 38, 96, 116 125, 133, 138, 160, 165, 172, 179, 184, 190, 192, 218, 223, 227, 230, 237, 262, 268, 282, 289, 294, 305, 310, 318, 327, 334, 340, 345, 359, 364, 371
Lee, Michele 39, 43
Lee-Sung, Richard 192
Leetch, Tom 31, 46, 65, 86, 113, 125, 143, 237, 305, 310, 333, 389
Lefler, Doug 482
Lefty 326
Lefty, the Dingaling Lynx 80
Legault, Lance 365
Legend of Hell House, The 189, 338-339
Legend of the Boy and the Eagle, The 11, 497
LeGrady, Brian 376, 483
Liech, Donald 397
Leigh, Robin 436-437
Leith, Christopher 372
Leiva, Juilio 467
Lemmon, Jack 429
Lennie, Angus 199
Lenox, John Thomas 445
Lenz, Rick 87
Leo, Gary 371
Leonard, Part 6 364
Leonard, Rene 370
Leong, Al 489-490
Lerman, Beryl 473
Lerner, Fred 397, 447

Lerner, Sammy 351
Leslie, Robert Franklin 165
Lester, David V. 396
Lester, Robie 70, 73
"Let Her Alone" 122, 125
"Let's Put it Over with Grover" 26-28
Leva, Scott 446
Levin, Michael 430
Levinson, Gregory 483
Levitas, Daniel 459
Levitt, Melanie 364
Levy, David 350
Levy, Eugene 446, 451, 453
Levy, Katharine 334
Lewis, Al 66, 69
Lewis, Candace 489
Lewis, Emmanuel 447
Lewis, Harold 26
Lewis, Helen 474
Lexicon Inc. 397
Lezir, Bernard 437
Liang, Robert 247
Liber, Lesja 474
Libertini, Richard 351
Liddiard, Gary 395, 423
Lidsville 30
Lieben, Laura 396
Lieder, Jerry 417
Liesik, Geoffrey 390
Liesik, Michael 390
Liffers, Christine 483
Lilly, Jack F. 74
Lim, Swee 474
Lince, Brian 474
Lincoln, Abraham 6
Lindsey, George 70, 126, 130, 139, 147, 224, 259
Lindstrom, Bill 459
Link, John F. 454
Linke, Paul 179
Lion King, The 379
Lions Gate Sound 350, 395
Liroff, Marci 435, 472
Lisberger, Steven 394, 396, 402-404, 406
Lisberger Studios 403
Little Britches 74
Little Gems from Big Shows 132
Little Hiawatha 281
Little Mermaid, The 104, 379, 451-452, 495
Little Shepherd Dog of Catalina, The 132
Little Sky, Dawn 192
Littlechild, John 437
Littlechild, J. Wilton 435
Littlest Horse Thieves, The 247-252
Livermore, California 397
"Livin' One Day at a Time" 138
Living Desert, The 204-205
Livingston, Willard 424, 467

Llewellyn, Russell 46
Lloyd, Christopher 481
Lloyd, Jan R. 445
Lloyd, Kathleen 301
Lloyd, Michael 306, 424, 459, 467, 474, 489
Lloyd, Peter 395-396, 404
Lloyd, Walter 430
Lofgren, George 74
Loftin, Carey 38-39, 263, 282, 289
Logan, Bruce 394, 404
Lohan, Lindsay 243, 344
Lomax, Alan 437
Lomax, John A. 437
Lombardo, Tony 349
Lomprakis, Peter 74
London Connection, The 299
London, England 206, 247, 275, 301, 314, 317, 334, 369-370, 372, 474
London Philharmonic Orchestra 395
London Symphony Orchestra, The 473
Long, Albert 473
Long, Jodi 447
Long, Keny 328
Long, Nate 408
Longbottom, Brian 334
Longo, Tony 446
Longoria, Sam 474
Lonsdale, Gordon 301
"Look at Me" 341-342
Lookout Mountain Films 371
Looney Tunes 143
Lopez, Sal 327
Loptsom, Donna 431
Lord, Rosemary 283
"Los Angeles" 151
Los Angeles, California 86, 95, 230, 288, 327, 444, 446, 480
Los Angeles Memorial Coliseum 230
Los Angeles Museum 288
Los Angeles Orchestra 395
Los Angeles Rams 230
Los Angeles Sports Arena 230
Los Padres National Forest 192
Losie, Phyllis 483
Lost in Space 52, 95
Lost Ones, The 172, 176
Lots of Luck 466
Louis-Dreyfus, Julia 454
Lounsbery, John 70, 96, 146, 252, 258
"Love" 147, 150
Love Bug, The 20, 38-45, 95, 121, 158, 268, 299
"Love Came for Me" 446, 451
Love Leads the Way: A True Story 443
Lovell, Ray 474
Loving, Lisa 446
Low, Dennis 371
Lowe, Mundell 455

Lowe, Randy 301
Lower, Tony 435
Lowers, Herman 74
Lowin, Jack 334
Lowitsch, Klaus 390
Lowry, Harry 431
Lowry, John M. 395
Lowry, Judith 151, 155
Lowther, Jane Ann 455
Lt. Robin Crusoe, U.S.N. 34, 158
Lubin, John 458
Lucas, Dick N. 70, 258, 376
Lucas, George 246, 358, 474, 496
Lucas, Victoria 447
Lucibello, Lyn 435
Lucidi, Paolo 350
Luckey, Richard S. 446
Lucky, Fred 258, 318
Luddy, Barbara 147, 253
Ludlow, Glenn 436
Ludwig, Pamela 409
Ludwig, Ursula 390
Luescher, Christina 430
Lukas, Karl 160, 231
Lum, Susie 98
Lupi, Pepe 288
Lupott, Dick 159
Lupton, John 113, 134
Lusby, David 473
Luske, Cecil 185
Luske, Jim 65, 97, 125, 185, 340
Luskin, Don 327
Luthaker, Paul 295
Lycett, Eustace 20, 31, 38, 50, 65, 81, 90, 96, 116, 125, 133, 138, 151, 160, 218, 223, 227, 230, 237, 262, 268, 282, 289, 294, 305, 318, 345
Lydon, James 87
Lye, Reg 315
Lynch, Jeffery 483
Lynch, Ken 31
Lynn, Alison 475
Lyons, Linda Dee 306
Lytton, Debbie 295

M*A*S*H 293
Maar, Pons 473, 475
Maccario, Tony 350
Macaulay, Charles 446
MacBaird, Bonnie 394
MacDonald, Andy 488
MacDonald, James 26, 96, 147, 259, 318
MacDonald, Kenneth 26
MacDonald, Peter 369
MacDonald, Richard 423
MacDonald, Saundra 351
MacIntosh, Malcolm 334

Mack, Ginni 483
MacKarvich, Shayla 447
Mackenzie, Don 436
MacKenzie, Mike 371
Mackenzie, Patricia 436
MacManus, Dan 70, 147
MacMichael, Florence 35
MacMurray, Fred 34, 139, 142-143
MacNicol, Peter 372
MacPherson, Graham 437
MacQueen, Scott 98, 104
Macvey, Mary Jo 473
Madcap Adventures of Mr. Toad, The 298
Madden, Peter 199
Madden, Terry 314
Maffett, Bud 74, 289, 305
Maffett, Henry A. 90, 96, 310, 318, 340, 345, 364, 408
Magee, Raleight 460
Magi Synthevision 403, 405, 407
Magic Carpet 'Round the World 158
Magic Journeys 444
Magic Kingdom, The 2, 6, 132, 158, 325
Magic Moments 133
Magic of Walt Disney World, The 108, 498
Magic Volksy, The 43
Magical Disney Christmas, A 357
Magical Music of Walt Disney, The 246
Magnin, Brigitte 418
Magnotta, Victor 445
Maguire, Al 318, 423-424, 446, 459, 467, 488
Mahoney, Jack 38
Mahoney / Wasserman and Associates 436
Main, Laurie 180, 238, 263
Main Street, U.S.A. 4, 43, 217
Main Street Electrical Parade 6, 107, 178, 246, 273
Maine, Rob 376
Maitland, Scott 430
Major Effects 299
Major the Lion 113
Majorana, Gian Maria 350
Making of Tron, The 403, 408
Makofsky, Isidore 418
Mako 172
Malanowski, Tony 97
Malcolm, Otis 35, 38, 46, 50
Malerstein, Susan 454
Malet, Arthur 97, 483
Maley, Alan 26, 31, 35, 38, 46, 50, 53, 62, 65, 74, 81, 86, 96, 109, 125, 133, 151, 160, 172, 185, 371
Malikyan, Kevork 418
Malis-Morey, Adele 483
Mallas, Joanne 454
Malone, Edward 488
Malone, Larry 397

Malta 350, 418
Malta Film Facilities 350
Maltin, Leonard 8, 11, 13-14, 17, 25, 98, 107, 125, 133, 155, 203, 210, 423, 501
Man from U.N.C.L.E., The 339
Man, Monsters and Mysteries 132, 275, 498
Manbeck, Donna 460
Manbeck, Edwin 460
Mancini, Henry 223, 380-381
Mandel, Babaloo 445, 447, 451-452, 454
Mandel, Johnny 185, 237
Mangan, Alf 372
Mangano, Stephanie 98
Mangine, Mark 468
Mangum, Milton G. 327, 340, 359
Manley, Peter 206
Mann, Brian 489
Mann, Burch 223
Mann, Delbert 389
Mann, George 97
Mann, Larry D. 75, 87, 139
Mann, Pamela 206
Manning, Jack 109, 117, 151, 160, 180, 228, 395
Manning, Kalani 445
Manning, Ruth 219, 346, 360
Manning, Stacy 192, 197
Mannix, Daniel P. 376
Manser, Kevin 212
Mansbridge, John B. 20, 30, 35, 38, 46, 50, 53, 74, 81, 86, 90, 96, 109, 113, 116, 121, 125, 133, 138, 143, 150, 160, 165, 169, 172, 179, 184, 192, 218, 223, 227, 230, 237, 262, 268, 282, 289, 294, 305, 310, 318, 327, 334, 340, 345, 359, 364, 395, 408, 418, 423, 445, 458, 466, 488, 493
Mansbridge, Mark W. 364
Manson, Eddy L. 454-455
Many Adventures of Winnie the Pooh, The 158, 252-258, 358. 416, 497
Manza, Ralph 289, 310
Manzy, David 134
Marbury, Paul 430
March of the Penguins 206
Marchetti, Mauro 350
Marcus, Ed 263
Marcus, James 248
Marcus, Sparky 238
Marden, Richard 247
Maren, Jerry 398, 425
Maressa, Mauro 482
Margetts, Monty 113
Margolin, Arnold 125
Marie, Louisa 445, 447
Marin County, California 371
Marin, Jacques 172, 263
Marino, Tony 482

"Mariposas D'Amora" 87
Mark, Stephen 459
Markland, Ted 21
Marks, Chris 97
Marks, Elliott 459
Marks, Franklyn 14-15, 62, 65, 74, 81, 125, 169
Marks, Kim 454
Marlow, David 157
Marmon, Lisa 395, 423
Marmorstein, Larry 283
Marmorstein, Malcolm 268, 282
Marquardt, Douglas 438
Marquette, Michael R. 424
Marr, Sally K. 360
Marriott, Charles 369
Mars, Kenneth 310
Marsac, Maurice 161
Marsh, Jean 475, 481
Marsh, Tiger Joe 185, 289
Marshall, Ann 151, 179
Marshall, Joan 35
Marshall, Sean 269, 273-274
Marshall, Scott 371
Marta, Angelo 350
Martin, Alexander 489
Martin, Doris 369, 473
Martin, Greg 482
Martin, Tantoo 437
Marvel Comics 6, 358, 385, 408, 496
Marvin, Ira 446
Mary Poppins 19, 29-30, 43, 79, 103, 105, 132, 273-274, 326
Maser, Kim 438
Maslansky, Paul 472
Maslowski, Karl H. 204
Massara, Natale 408
Massinburg, Essil 185
Master Film Effects 301
Masters, Bill 74
Masters, Dorothy 90
Masters, Mike 310
Masur, Richard 490
"Matecumbe" 224
Matheron, La Rue 20, 26, 31, 35, 38, 46, 50, 53, 65, 74, 90, 96, 109, 116, 125, 133, 138, 151, 160, 169, 172, 179, 185, 192, 219, 228, 230, 262, 268, 282
Matheson, Tim 310
Mathews, Jim L. 65
Mativo, Kyalo 468
Matterhorn 12, 281
Mattey, Robert A. 20, 31, 38, 65, 74, 81, 86
Matthau, Walter 429
Matthews, Junius 252
Matthews, Sue 473
Mattiessen, Peter 430-431
Mattingly, David 318, 327, 334, 359, 398

Index

Mattinson, Burny 147, 252, 257-258, 376, 482
Mattinson, Sylvia 376, 482
Maude-Roxby, Roddy 70
Maury, Darrel 179
Maus, Rodger 340, 417
Maverick 146
Maxwell, Don 328
Maxwell, Norris 282
Maxwell, Roberta 351
"May the Best Man Win" 294-295
Mayberry R.F.D. 130
Mayberry, Russ 314
Mayflower Recording Ltd. 474
Mayo, Marvin 97
McAlister, Michael 371
McAree, David 436
McAteer, James 436
McBride, Robert D. 172, 219
McCain, Frances Lee 409
McCall, Robert T. 318
McCallum, David 334, 339
"McCanless County" 87
McCann, Chuck 160
McCarney, Bill 468
McCarty, Brian L. 319
McCarty, Floyd 65
McCary, Rod 160
McCauley, Danny 340
McCay, Peggy 365
McCharen, David 351
McClellan, Catherine 301
McClelland, Ian 207
McCleod, Douglas 435
McCleod, John 371
McClure, Katee 319
McClure, Marc 238
McCorkle, Pat 445
McCormick, Karen 351
McCormick, Larry 228
McCormick, Maureen 301, 304
McCormick, Pat 231
McCorry, Tom 263
McCracken, Jeff 437
McCrea, Bob 147, 258
McCrea, Peter L. 301
McCready, Ed 306, 310
McCrory, Tom 237, 318
McCullough, H.J. 431
McDermott, Kate 350
McDermott, Patricia 473
McDiarmond, Ian 372
McDonald, Country Joe 489
McDonald, Jimmy 43
McDonald, Philip 473
McDonald, Roger 473
McDonough, Mike 482
McDougall, Callum 381

McDougall, Milton 436
McDowall, Roddy 97-98, 104, 289, 319
McEveety, Annie 341, 397
McEveety, Bernard 113, 143, 165
McEveety, James 179
McEveety, Joseph L. (Joe) 20, 26, 53, 81, 116-117, 150, 218, 294
McEveety, Steven M. (Steve) 319, 340, 359, 396, 424, 466
McEveety, Susie S. 466, 489
McEveety, Vincent 90, 95, 109, 138, 150, 169, 179, 223, 227, 229-230, 262, 310, 333, 340, 364
McEvoy, Peter 319, 398, 424
McEwan, Geraldine 248
McEwan, John 436
McGavin, Darren 219, 295, 298, 429
McGaw, Ann 436
McGinnes, George F. 318
McGiver, John 192, 197
McGoohan, Patrick 206, 211, 468, 472
McGovern, Tim 397
McGowan, Scott 301
McGowan, Tom 70
McGrath, Bob 132
McGrath, Roberto 371
McGreevey, John 389
McGreevy, Michael 53, 59, 117, 121, 126, 130, 179, 184, 231, 236
McHugh, J. 455
McHugh, Tim 474, 489
McHugh, Tom 204
McInnes, James 96
McIntire, John 160, 259, 377
McKay, Allison 151
McKay, Jim 134
McKayle, Donald 96
McKean, Bruce 474
McKelvy, Frank R. 31, 35, 50, 65, 81, 86, 116, 125, 138, 218, 223, 227, 262, 282, 294, 319
McKennon, Dallas 97, 289, 295
McKeon, Doug 390
McKeon, Keith 390
McKern, Leo 275, 279, 481
McKinley National Park 204
McKinley, Richard 224, 231
McKinney, Bill 409
McKinney, Gavin 446
McKinney, Michael 483
McKuen, Rod 86-87, 89-90
McLarty, Gary 310
McLarty, Ron 455
McLaughlin, Gregg 14, 62, 165, 204, 318, 364
McLaughlin, Tom 474
McLaughlin, Wayne 430
McLean, Bill 306
McLing, Bob 90, 96, 113, 185, 263, 268

McLoughlin, Tommy 318-319
McMahon, Cathy 473
McMillan, Bill 259
McMillan, Man 397
McPhail, William B. 473
McReady, Ed 151
McRitchie, Greig 424
McRobert, Gary 474
McSherry, Rose Marie 436
McVey, Tyler 31, 180
McWilliams, Deborah 369
Me, Myself and Irene 17
Mead, Syd 395, 404, 407
Meador, Philip L. 319, 424, 446, 459, 467, 474, 482, 489
Meakin, Fred 369
Mecacci, Pierantonio 418
Mechanial Concepts 396-397
Medalis, Joe 290
Medallion Film Laboratories, Toronto 435
Meddock, Larry 237
Medfield, Massachusetts 184
Mediterranean Film Facilities Ltd. 418
Meillon, John 212
Meillon, Jr., John 212
Meisner, Gunter 390, 394
Melandri, Vince 395
Melanson, Ronald A. 301
Meless, Alexis 468
Mello, Albert 96
Melrose, Barrie 314
Melton, James (Jim) 147, 252, 258, 268, 376, 482
Memphis State University 2
Menace on the Mountain 61, 116, 243
Menard, Daryl 438
Menard, Tina 341
Mendleson, Anthony 198, 206, 370
Mendoza, Margarito 87
Menges, Joyce 117
Menlo, Michael 454
Menzies-Urich, Heather 54
Mercado, Rolando 483
Mercer, Jack 351, 354
Mercer, Johnny 147
Mercurio, Tommy 389
Merin, Eda Reiss 483
Mermaid 451-453
Merrill, Kieth 300-301
Merrin, Ray 473
Merritt, Don 350
Messina, Roberto 350-351
Metrano, Art 180
Metrocolor. 349
Metz, Don 436
Metz, Hans 86, 90, 96, 117, 125, 133, 138, 151, 160, 169, 172, 179, 185, 192, 219, 223, 228, 231, 237, 263, 268, 283, 289, 305, 310, 319, 341, 345, 359, 398, 424, 445, 467, 488, 493
Metz, Rexford 289, 389, 395
Metzer, Don 436
Metzger, Doug 418, 445
Metzler, Jim 409
Metzler, Robert F. 14, 62
Mexico 340
Meyer, Dieter 389
Meyer, Otto 35, 65, 90, 97
Meyers, Duncan 371
Meyers, Suzanne 430
MGM 481
Micale, Paul 161
Michael O'Hara the Fourth 108
Michaelford, James 295
Michaels, Phillip 74
Michel, Ted 473
Michener, Dave 70, 146, 258, 376
Michigan J. Frog 143
Mickey and Donald Kidding Around 416
Mickey Mouse 2, 12, 20, 81, 158, 204, 246, 257, 274, 281-282, 326, 388, 407, 416, 435, 444, 497
Mickey Mouse 14, 20, 46, 62, 80, 108, 132, 159, 178, 218, 246, 282, 300, 326, 354, 358, 389, 417, 444
Mickey Mouse and his Friends 20
Mickey Mouse Anniversary, The 19
Mickey Mouse Club 107, 132, 177, 217, 245-246, 501, 526
Mickey Mouse Club Fun Book 246
Mickey Mouse Club Scrapbook, The 177
Mickey Mouse Disco 281, 300, 326, 358, 498
Mickey Mouse: Fifty Happy Years 246, 300
Mickey Mouse March 159
Mickey Mouse Mini-Comic 218
Mickey Mouse on Vacation 326
Mickey Mouse Revue, The 79-80, 326, 417
Mickey Mouse Splashdance 417
Mickey Mouse Surprise Party 46, 300
Mickey Mouse: This is My Life 80
Mickey's Christmas Carol 178, 293, 388, 405, 416, 497, 499
Mickey's Christmas Carols 326
Mickey's 50 281
Mickey's Mellerdrammer 158
Midnight Cowboy 43
Midnight Madness 325, 327-333, 423, 493
"Midnight Madness" 327
Midori 66
Midson, Dave 474
Meier, John C. 341
Mike Curb Congregation, The 108
Mikkelson, Ralph 90, 96, 125
Milch, Anthony 395
Miles, Vera 75, 143, 169

Mill Creek 472
Milland, Ray 185, 190
Millar, Cynthia 483
Miller, Arthur 319
Miller, F. Ben 75
Miller, Cherie 483
Miller, Christopher D. 318, 340, 345, 359, 408, 423
Miller, Craig 446, 468, 474, 483, 489
Miller, David B. 489
Miller, Denny 172
Miller, Fujiko 482
Miller, Gene 397
Miller, Jeff 341
Miller, Kurt 299
Miller, Larry 301
Miller, Linda 376
Miller, Sr., Robert 458
Miller, Roger 147
Miller, Roland F. 460
Miller, Ron 30, 65, 74, 116, 125, 169, 184, 212, 218, 223, 227, 230, 237, 247, 258, 262, 268, 275, 282, 289, 294, 305, 310, 314, 318, 325, 327, 333, 338, 340, 345, 359, 376, 380, 387, 389, 394, 408, 415, 430, 443, 452-453, 462, 465, 481, 495
Miller, Seton I. 268
Miller, Tony 475
Millhollin, James 31
Milliken, Sue 212
Million Dollar Dixie Deliverance, The 281
Million Dollar Duck, The 90-95, 229, 294
Mills, Billy 437
Mills, Robert (Bob) 483, 488
Mills, Brooke 238
Mills, Hayley 298, 487
Milne, A.A. 252, 257
Milne, Gareth 468, 473
Milner, Digby 370
Milo, Jana 290
Milotte, Alfred 204
Milotte, Elma 204
Mimieux, Yvette 43, 319
"Mind Over Matter" 252, 254
Mineral King 13, 19, 45-46, 107, 159, 178
Minkler, Bob 395
Minkler, Lee 395
Minkler, Michael 349, 395, 409
Minkoff, Robert 483
Minner, Kathryn 21, 39
Minnesota Division of Game of Fish 204
Minnie Mouse 12
Mioni, Sergio 350
Miracle of the White Stallions 191
Miracle Worker, The 365
Mirante, Gaetano 350
Mirkin, Lisa 409

Mirkin, Michael 446
Mirman, Kenny 397
Mironneau, Jacques 263, 381
Misadventures of Merlin Jones, The 58, 108
Mischel, Larry 455
Miss Bianca 258
Mission to Mars 178, 466
Misty the Michievous Mermaid 46
Mitchell, Charles 447
Mitchell, Jim 482
Mitchell, Keith 376
Mitchell, Pat 125
Mitman, Flavia 396
Mittelman, Phillip 397, 403
Mitzner, Dean Edward 394
Mizel, William (Bill) 431, 435
Moazezi, Noah 455
Mobley, Roger 310
Moby Duck 19
Moby Duck 14, 20, 46, 62, 218, 246, 282
Modave, Philippe 380
Modern Film Effects 437, 445
Modestini, Guglielmo 350
Moebius (See Giraud, Jean "Moebius")
Moehnke, T.E. 371
Moffat, Donald 351
Moio, John 268
Molen, Gerald R. 185
Molinaro, Al 238
Moller, Edward C. 15
Monaghan, Tish 436
Monet, Marc 262
Monford, Gerald L. 455
Moninaro, Brizio 418
Monkees, The 281
Monkeys, Go Home! 11, 197
Monkey's Uncle, The 58
Monorail 12
Monsanto Night Presents Walt Disney's America on Parade 217
Mont-Eton, Norm 282
Montaigne, Lawrence 185
Montana Fish and Game Department 204
Montash, Henry 206
Montemayor, Gloria 237, 318, 327, 340, 359
Montgomery, Lee Harcourt 91
Montgomery, Ralph 21
Monty Python 150, 158
Monty Python and the Holy Grail 158
Moody, Ralph 74
Moody, Ron 105, 315, 318
Moon, Liza 398
Moon Pilot 236
Moon-Spinners, The 323
Mooney, David 161
Moore, Alvy 161
Moore, Dan 408

Moore, Dorothea 436
Moore, Dudley 454
Moore, Joanna 31
Moore, Joseph P. 318
Moore, Nicholas 474
Moore, Rick 398
Moore, Jr., T.A. 437
Moortgat, Ron 97
Morales, Hector 341
Moran, Larry 219, 306
Moran, Martha 435
Moran, Richard 489
More Jungle Book 20
More, Kenneth 315
Moreau, Jean-Jacques 263
Moreland, Mantan 109, 113
Moreno, Jorge 341
Moreno, Robert C. 46
Moreno, Ruben 341
"Moreover and Me" 109
Morgan, Boyd "Red" 143
Morgan, Cindy 398, 404, 407
Morgan, Desmond 370
Morgan, Gary 269, 306, 360
Morgan, Harry 82, 87, 126, 139, 192, 197, 289, 293, 310
Morgan, Read 144
Morgan, Toni 454
Morgan, William 62
Morganti, Len 371
Morick, Dave 306
Morita, Roy 481
Moritz, Louisa 306
Mork and Mindy 137
Morocco 444
Morris, Howard 252, 257, 446, 451
Morris, Joseph 483
Morris, Rahsaan 360
Morris, Reginald 62
Morris, Thaine 371
Morris, Tony 370, 473
Morrish, Mical 396
Morrison, Barbara 97
Morrison, Brian 474
Morrison, Richard 474
Morrissey, John 431
Morrow Bay, California 274
Morrow, Bryon 54
Morrow, Vic 224
Morse, Robert 65
Morton, Arthur 143, 389, 467
Morton, Gregory 54
Morton, Mickey 306
Morton, Randy 365
Morwood, Joel 417
Mosely, John 395
Mosier, Richard 467, 483, 489

Mosley, Leonard 466
Moss, Raymond 74
Most, Abe 455
Motion Picture Marine 445
Mouat, Colin C. 467, 488
Mount, David 372
Mountain Born 108
Mountain Lion, The 121
Mourino, Erick E. 446
Mouse Club, The 326, 389
Mouse Factory, The 8, 107, 121, 132, 501, 525-526
Mouseketeer Reunion, The 326
Mouseketeers at Walt Disney World, The 245
Mousercise 358
Mousetronics 417
Mountain Hardware Corp. 397
Mourino, Edgard 445
Movie Guide 155, 203, 423
Movie Magic 397
Mowat, Farley 430
Moyer, Fifi 418
Mr. Magoo 354
Mr. Toad 281
Muchera, Nick 436
Muchera, Tedd 436
Mueller, Peter 395-396
Muhs, George 424
Muir, Brian 370, 473-474
Mule Pack 132
Mulgrew, Kieran 397, 483
Mull, Wanda 430
Muller, Frederick 350
Muller, Lillian 360
Mulligan, Patrick 455
Mulliner, Philip 455
Mumy, Billy 50, 52-53
Munich, Germany 390
Muppet Movie, The 299
Muppets Take Manhattan, The 465
Muppets, The 496
Murch, Muriel 473
Murch, Walter 370, 472, 480
Murdock, George 21
Muren, Dennis 371
Murphy, Daniel 370
Murphy, Linda 446
Murphy, Pat 74
Murphy, Robert 121
Murphy, Shawn 424, 446, 459, 467, 482
Murray, Bill 454
Murray, Forrest 454
Murray, Graeme 430
Murray, Michael 473
Muscate, Louis S. 345
Muse, Clarence 134
Museum of Natural History, The 431
Musgrave, Peter 473

Index 569

Music Technology Inc. 397
Musicana 388
Musker, John 376, 379, 482
Mussetta, Gloria 418
Mustang! 132
Mustin, Burt 117, 160, 180
My Dog, the Thief 45
My Father, the Hero 155
"My Mind's Made Up" 489
My Science Project 465, 488-493
"My Science Project" 489
My Three Sons 142
Myers, Ruth 423
Myers, Stanley 333
Myers, Stevie 319
Myhers, John 117, 126, 160, 180, 224, 231
Mystery in Dracula's Castle, The 129, 132
Mystery of Edward Sims, The 19
Mystery of Rustler's Cave, The 245

Nadia 319, 340, 359
Nagle, Sean 370
Nahan, Stu 228, 230
Naisbitt, Clark 301
Nalder, Reggie 360
Names, Art 327
Nankin, Michael 327
Napoleon and Samantha 112-116, 131, 243
Nardini, Bonny 396
Narita, Hiro 430
NASA 318
Nash, Michael S. 489
Nassau, Bahamas 446
Nashville Coyote, The 108
National Academy of Television Arts and Sciences, The 81
National Audubon Society 204
National Baseball Library 455
National Football League 228, 230
National Lampoon's Animal House 304, 333
National Park Service 122, 204, 446
National Park Service of Canada 204
National Philharmonic Orchestra, The 370
National Symphony, The 301
National Team Golf Championship 281
National Telefilm Associates, Inc. 446
National Trust, The 371
Nature's Better Built Homes 45
Nature's Charter Tours 19
Nature's Strangest Oddballs 61
Nature's Wonderland 246
Naughton, David 327
Naulin, John 446
Navrides, Ginger 98
NBC 86, 211, 403, 446
NBC Salutes the 25th Anniversary of "The Wonderful World of Disney" 281

Neal, Bev 436
Neal, Christy 301
Nebraska 441
Needham, Terry 369
Neighbour, Trevor 474
Neill, Bob 398
Neill, John R. 473
Neilson, James 206, 399
Neise, George N. 54, 82
Nelson, Argyle 423
Nelson, David Lloyd 447
Nelson, Don 218, 227, 262, 294
Nelson, Gage 294
Nelson, Gary 237, 318-319
Nelson, Lloyd 74, 90, 263, 283
Nelson, Ralph B. 489
Nelson, Sandy 319
Nelson, Walter 473
Nemetz, Gerhard 389
Never a Dull Moment 30-34, 245
Never Cry Wolf 430-435, 451-452
New Adventures of Robin Hood, The 159, 178
New Fantasyland 388
New Mickey Mouse Club, The 132, 217, 227, 245, 325, 501, 526
New Orleans Square 13
New York 157, 431, 446, 454
New York 157
New York World's Fair 12, 14
New Zoo Revue, The 132
Newark, Derek 247
Newhart, Bob 258
Newhoff, Rudy 460
Newkirk, Reggie 263
Newlan, Bob 395, 409
Newman, Barry 365
Newman, Christopher 198
Newman, Craig 396
Newman, Don 327
Newman, Phyllis 436
Newsies 30
Newton, Brett 483
Newvell, Terry 369
Nibbelink, Phil 376, 481-482, 484
Nicol, Trevor 369
Nicholas, Louie 364
Nicholls, Allan 351
Nichols, Barbara 139
Nichols, Lyn 301
Nichols, M. Flores 482
Nichols, Mike 355
Nichols, Paul "Tiny" 74, 223, 262, 294
Nichols, Roger 474
Nichols, Terry 295, 319
Nicholson, Al 458
Nicholson, Bruce 371
Nicholson, Jack 454

Nicholson, Sam 334
Niemela, Al 62, 165
Nieman-Tillar Associates 437
Niemeyer, Louis 231, 237, 263
Nieto, Jose 87
Night Creatures 211
Night Crossing 389-394
Night Shift 447
Niklas, Jan 390
Nilsson, Anna-Lisa 396
Nilsson, Harry 349-351, 354
Nimmo, Derek 199
Nine Old Men, The 149, 273, 408
"1990's Theme" 398
Niven, David 219, 222-223, 243, 275, 279
Nixon, Richard 107
No Deposit, No Return 218-223, 298
Noad, Jessica 212
"Nobody's Problems" 97, 102, 104
Noel, Jr., Frank 459
Nolan, Jeanette 258, 377
Nolan, Kathleen 365
Nomad, Mike 445
Noose, Ted 283, 360
Nordberg, Cliff 146-147, 252, 258, 268, 376
Nordquist, Kerry 371
Norman, Floyd 147
Norrington, Stephen (Steve) 474-475
North, Alex 369
North American Guard Dog and Kenneling Service Ltd. 431
North Avenue Irregulars, The 305-309
North, Heather 82
"North Pole Polka" 103
North, Sterling 50
North Wales 369, 371
Norton, B.W.L. 466
Norton, John 395-396, 424
Norton Lyn 467
Norton, Mary 96
Norton, Rosanna 395
Norworth, Jack 455
Nosey, the Sweetest Skunk in the West 108
Noss, Terry L. 376, 482
"Not in Nottingham" 147, 149
Nottingham, Susie 468
Nova, Lou 21
Novack, Dan 74, 126, 185
Novack, Steve 454
Now You See Him, Now You Don't 57, 116-121, 184
Nudity 435, 451
Nufer, Beth 458
Nurschinger, Adolf 389

Oahu 349
Oakland, Simon 87
Oates, Warren 47
O'Brien, Clay 143, 192, 197
O'Brien, Gloria 341
O'Brien, Margaret 365
O'Brien, Richard 219, 231, 237
O'Brien, Virginia 228
O'Byrne, Bryan 91, 228, 310
O'Callaghan, Cindy 97
Ocean Films Ltd. 431
Ocherman, Leon 81
O'Connell, Francis 488
O'Connell, Tim 467
O'Connell, William 87
O'Connor, Glynnis 390
Odd Couple, The 29-30
O'Dell, Rosemary 50
Of Mice and Mickey 177
Off Beat 465
Official Album of Disneyland / Walt Disney World, The 326
"Oh, Benjamin Harrison" 26
O'Hanlon, George 91, 95, 117, 139
O'Herlihy, Michael 26, 46
Ohlund, Gunnar 172
Oklahoma Film Commission 409
"Old Home Guard, The" 97-98, 103
Old Yeller 158, 358
O'Leary, Jack 490
Oliney, Alan 319
Oliney, Ronald 319
Oliver and Company 495
Oliver, Dale 147, 258, 376
Oliver, David 446
Olivier, Laurence 279
Olivo, Denise 396
Olsen, Joan 436
Olson, Nancy 47, 126, 129
Olympia USA 397
Olympic Stadium 237
Olympics 403, 439-441, 444
Olympus High School 300
O'Malley and the Alley Cats 80, 108, 133, 159
O'Malley, J. Pat 147
O'Meara, Timothy 488
Omeasoo, Gail 437
Omega Connection, The 299
On Golden Pond 387
"On the Sunny Side of the Street" 455
"On Wisconsin" 147
Once Upon a Mouse 358, 498
One and Only, Genuine, Original Family Band, The 26-30, 388
"One and Only, Genuine, Original Family Band, The" 26-27, 29
One Day in Beetle Rock 12
101 Dalmatians 45, 262, 299, 349, 357, 465
One Little Indian 143-146, 197, 243

Index 571

One Magic Christmas 465, 495
$1,000,000 Duck (see *Million Dollar Duck, The*)
One Night Before Christmas 465
One of Our Dinosaurs is Missing 164, 198-203, 218, 251
O'Neal, Tatum 454
O'Neill, Dan 81, 179, 300
O'Neill, Madlyn 483
O'Neill, Shane 473
"Only Solutions" 398, 403
"Oo-de-lally" 147
Oppenheimer, Alan 238
Optical Film Effect Ltd. 474
Orange Bird, The 61
Orchard, John 97, 228
O'Rear, Frankie 125
O'Rear, John 125
Orem High School 300
Oriental Land Company, The 417
Orlando, Florida 4
Orrison, George 74
Ortega, John 113
Oscar (see Academy Awards)
Osenbaugh, Ron 396, 482, 489
O'Shannon, Grania 472
O'Shea, Mike 125
O'Shea, Tessie 97
Osmond, Cliff 306, 310
Ostendorf, David L. 459
Ostercamp, Jim 459
Ostwald, Chris 474
O'Sullivan, Michael 301
O'Sullivan, Richard 207
Otanez, Kip 301
O'Toole, Peter 404, 407
Otto, Bob 396
Ousdal, Sverre 172
Outlaw Cats of Colossal Cave, The 177
Outsiders, The 413
Owen, Reginald 97
Owens, Gary 39, 283
Owens, Ray 483
Owl That Didn't Give a Hoot, The 19
Owyeung, Ease 371
Oxford Scientific Film Ltd. 474
Oz books 46, 472, 480
Oz Productions Limited 474
Ozma of Oz 472

Paat, Karen 483
Pablo and the Dancing Chihuahua 19
Pacheco, David 482
Pacheco, Gilbert C. 345
Pacific Telephone 397
Pacific Title Digital 97
Pacific Title and Art Studio 97, 397
Pacifically Peeking 19

Pack, Sheryl 301
Packenham, John 370
"Paco the Brave" 87
"Paco, the Great Engineer" 87
Padbury, Richard 474
Padilla, Robert 87
Paeff, Ann 483
Page, Christopher 370
Page, Geraldine 258
Paine, Debbie 53
Paine, George 424
Paint a Rainbow in Your Heart 444
Pales, Jay 474
Palfrey, Yolande 372
Palinginis, Gilda 482
Palmer, Bud 134
Palmer, Gregg 47, 295
Palmer, John 424, 473
Palmer, Norman R. 50, 204, 230, 327
Palmer, Roger 62
Palmisano, Conrad E. 319
Palo Alto, California 190
Pampel, Udo 371
Panaflex 408, 423, 430, 445, 454
Panavision 86, 90, 369, 389, 394, 408, 423, 430, 435, 445, 454, 458
Pancake, Roger 289-290
Pancho, Fastest Paw in the West 45
Panda, Edie 423
Pangaea Corporation Productions 458
Pangrazio, Michael 371
Paniolo 171
Paramount Pictures 7, 325, 349, 354, 358, 369, 375, 387
Parasheles, Peter 430
Pardners 326
Parent Trap, The 19, 274, 279, 298
Parenti, Noel 351
Paris, D. Mike 459
Paris, Jerry 30-31, 34
Parish, Roger 46
Parker, Barbara 430
Parker, David 430
Parker, Jim 125
Parker, John 467
Parker, Joseph A. (Joe) 318, 418, 424, 446, 459, 467, 488
Parkhill, Lance 409
Parks, Van Dyke 351
Parra, Joe 489
Parrish, Dennis J. 446
Parrish, Julie 360
Parsons, Glen 467
Parsons, Jennifer 423
Part, Brian 283
Partlow, Richard 283
Parton, Regina (Reg) 38, 263, 289, 319, 327

Partridge Family, The 116
Pascarella, Paul 459
Pasco, Richard 334
Passage, The 288
"Passamaschoddy" 269-270
Pastel, Elyse 483
"Pastures Green" 87, 89-90
Patch, Jeffrey 147, 258, 376
Paton, Randy 482
Patrick, Butch 26, 30
Patterson, Andy 349
Patterson, Blake 436
Patterson, Dick 180
Patterson, George 211
Paul, Don C. 376, 482
Paul, Lee 172
Paul Lynde Show, The 116
Paull, Morgan 310
Paulsen, Gary D. 445, 459
Payne, James 372
Payne, Maxx 305
PBS 132
Peacocke, Thomas 438
Peake, Barry 473
Peanuts 29
Pearce, Charlene 436
Pearce, Gladys 467
Pearce, Joe 370
Pearce, Nancy 436
Pearce, Richard 458
Pearson, Richard 199
Peary, Robert 176
Pebley, Auril 396
Peck, Clare 447, 490
Pederson, Mary 301
Pedi, Tom 289, 306
Peebles, Ron 396
Peel, Richard 97
Peerless Camera Co. Ltd. 474
Pee-Wee Herman 333
Pegues, Melvyn 301
Pellegrini, Carlo 351
Pelletier, Louis 35, 46, 121
Pelttari, Linda 436
Pena, Julian 396
Penis breath 387
Penn, Arthur 355
Penthouse 447, 450
Penvern, Andre 263
People of Atlin, British Columbia, The 431
People Weekly 453
PeopleMover 13
"Peoplitis" 262
Peraza, Jr., Michael 376
Peraza, Patricia 482
Perisic, Zoran 474
Perkins, Anthony 319, 323

Perkins, Jack 38, 91, 238, 306, 310, 341
Perkins, Les 98, 104
Perl, Frank 454
Perri 17, 65
Perrier, Jacques 262
Perry, Don 305
Perry, Harold 139
Perry, Joseph V. 161
Pershing, Carol 445
Pertwee, John 199, 203
Peter Govey Film Opticals 474
Peter Pan 45-46, 217, 388, 444
Peterman, Don 445
Peterman, Keith 446
Peters, Jon 30
Petersen, Dennis 301
Peterson, Bruton 489
Peterson, Clifford 15
Peterson, Curtis 430
Peterson, Darryl 301, 305
Peterson, Gary 301
Peterson, Lorne 371
Peterson, Paul 246
Peterson, Rod 62
Peterson, Vidal 424
Pete's Dragon 30, 121, 268-275, 279, 326, 443
Petlowany, George 389
Petrella, Maria 454
Petticoat Junction 95
Pettingill, Jr., Olin Sewall 204
Petty, Robyn 327
Peverall, John 206
Pfeiffer, Michelle 454
Phantom of the Opera, The 385
Phantom Tollbooth, The 62
Phelps, Win 262, 340
Phillips, Barney 219
Phillips, Bill 349
Phillips, Frank 26, 53, 74, 86, 96, 116, 125, 133, 160, 172, 185, 192, 219, 223, 228, 230, 268, 282, 294, 310, 318, 327, 340
Phillips, Joanna 483
Phillips, Joanne 126
Phillips, John 65
Phillips, Shelley 396
Phillipson, Andrew 482
Phillipson, Phil 483
Phipps, Kieron 473
Phyllis 155
"Phony King of England, The" 147, 149
Picerni, Charlie 165, 398
Pick, Daley 59
Pickel, Jim 397, 483, 489
Pickens, Slim 31, 192, 319
Pickford, Mark 371
Pickles, Vivian 276

Pidgeon, Walter 50
Pierlin, Kenneth 397
Pierce, Reggie 90
Pierson, Rex 489
Pierson, Tom 349
Piffath, Rod 294
Piglet 218, 252-258
Piglet's Big Movie 258
Pine, Frank 289
Pine, Robert 143, 165, 310
Pinero, Federico 35
Pinewood Studios 198, 206, 247, 275, 314, 317-318, 334, 369
"Pink Elephants on Parade" 257
Pink Panther, The 198, 223, 306, 385
Pinkley, Price 126
Pinocchio 80, 281, 443
Pinocchio's Daring Journey 357, 417
Pioneer Hall Dinner Theater 158
Pirates of the Caribbean 12, 25, 132
Pisoni, Larry 351
Pisoni, Peggy 351
Pit Ponies 252
Pithey, Wensley 199
Pixar 385, 405, 496
Plant, William 474
Platt, Howard T. 289
Plausible Impossible, The 275
Playan, Marion J. 38
Playboy 316
Playfair, Wendy 212
Plaza Swan Boats, The 132
Pleasence, Donald 185, 190
Pleshette, Suzanne 21, 24-25, 231, 235, 237
Ploog, Mike 473, 482
Plumb, Edward 204
Pluto and his Friends 387
Pluto's Christmas Tree 177
Pluto's Dream House 191
Pluto's Housewarming 177
Pluto's Kid Brother 45
Poer, John M. 125, 230, 268
Pohl, John 334
Pohlmann, Eric 207
Poindexter 283
Poitevint, Lisa 483
Poky Little Puppy, The 178
Police, Robin 483
Polifroni, Pam 395, 408, 418, 423
Pollock, David 238
Pollyanna 279, 388, 429
Polynesian Village Luau Cove 132
Pomeroy, John 252, 258, 268, 376
Pond, The 177
Pontremoli, David 381
Pooh's Heffelumps Movie 258
Poole, Alan 370

Poole, William R. 35, 90, 96, 185
Poon, Gary 438
Popeye 349-355
Popeye 349-355, 375
Popielinski, Lary Elin 397
Poppe, Herman 172
Porky's 387
Porsche 385
Porter, Bobby 231, 268, 282, 340, 345, 424
Porter, Vern 459
Porteous, Emma 334
Porterfield, Don 396
Portman, Richard R. 418, 424, 446, 459, 467, 482
"Portobello Road" 97, 100, 104
"Portobello Street Dance" 97, 104
Post, Mike 435
Potlatch Forests, Inc. 15
"Pourquoi?" 70
Power, Paul 488
Powerbook 406
Powers, Stefanie 65, 160
Poyner, Stephanie-Stacie 459
Prabucki, George 436
Prador, Irene 390
Prager, Marty 397
Pratt, Judson 54, 82
Pratt, Kelley 431
Praxis Filmworks 397
Prentiss, Ed 82
Presley, Elvis 2, 58
Preston, Heidi 301
Preston, Kerrie 98
Preston, Susan 445
Price, Jeffrey 417
Price, Roger 180, 269, 290, 360
Prickett, Maudie 50
Prieto, David 340
Prima, Louis 262
Prince, William 289
Princess Leia 243, 245
Principality of Monaco, The 262, 380
Prine, Andrew 143
Prine, James (Jim) 247, 345
Prinz, Ronnie 396
Priori, Stefano 475
Private Eyes, The 197, 314
Prize Fighter, The 197, 314
Probert, George 424, 459, 467, 488
Procopio, Ruben 482
Productions Systems, Inc. 301
Project Florida 80
Promises, Promises 95
Proslier, Jean-Marie 263
Protat, Francois 435
Proud Bird from Shanghai, The 132
Proudfoot, Patty 431
Provenghi, Gilberto 350

Province of Alberta Department of Lands and Forests 204
Province of Manitoba Game Branch 204
Provine, Dorothy 31
Provost, Jon 53, 58
Pruiksma, David 482
Pryce, Jonathan 424
PSA 444
Pulford, Don 319
Purdie, Doug 473
Putnam, George 228, 230
Pyle, Denver 185, 283
Pyne, Natasha 199

Quarshie, Hugh 468
Quattromani, Joe 419
Queen Elizabeth National Park of Uganda 204
Quick, David 488
Quillan, Eddie 117, 180
Quilligan, Veronica 275, 279
"Quivira, the City of Gold" 87

R&B EFX 397
Raab, Jane 445
Rabinowitz, Harry 473
Race for Survival 281
Race for Your Life, Charlie Brown 245
Race to Witch Mountain 191
Radio City Music Hall 104
Radmilovich, Joanne 474
Radner, Gilda 355
Rae, Rona 396
Raffa, Nancy 447
Raffill, Joseph 113
Raffill, Stewart 113
Raffler, Ronald 431
Raffles 81-86
Raggedy Ann and Andy 245
Ragheb, Osman 390
Ragwing 158
Raiders of the Lost Ark 324, 358, 375, 406
"Rain, Rain, Rain Came Down, Down, Down, The" 252, 255
Rainbow Bright 444
Rainbow Caverns Mine Train 246, 299
Raine, Jack 87, 97
Ralston, Ken 371
Ramacle, Don 408
Rames, Neva 20, 31
Ramirez, Frank 47
Ramocki-Rosetti, Maria 396, 482
Ramsey 488
Ramsey, Jeff 341
Ramsey, Logan 224
Ramus, Nick 310
Ramsey, Rex 38
Randall, Bill 301

Randall, Chad 294
Randall, Florence Engel 333
Randolph, John 47
Ranger of Brownstone, The 19
Rank Film Laboratories 369, 474
Rankin-Bass 246
Raponi, Isidoro 424, 468
Rapp, Ilana 447
Rassi, Sharleen 96
Rascal 50-53
Rasch, Karen 349
Raskin, Damon Bradley 306
Rathner, Scott 446
Rattray, Eric 198, 369
Ratzdorff, Ron 445
Ravenscroft, Thurl 70, 253
Ray Bradbury's Something Wicked This Way Comes 423-430
Ray, Dell 14, 62
Rayburn, Basil 334
Rayburn, Nick 474
Reagan, Ronald 388
Rechenberg, Otto 365
Rechkemmer, Roy 460
Record, Bill 90
Recton, Susan 424
Red Elk, Lois 143
Red Onion, The 431
Redel, Roger E. 319, 396
Redding, Michael 370
Reddish, Jack N. 300-301
Reddy, Helen 269, 275
Redfield, Marilyn 409
Redgrave, Lynn 105
Redlin, Dwayne 165
Redlin, William 62, 165
Reed, Doc 319
Reed, Forrest 90, 125
Reed, Michael 489
Reed, Oliver 381
Reed, Robert 227
Reed, Stan 20, 39, 65, 90, 97, 125, 133, 396
Reedy, Mike (Michael) 160, 172, 263, 268, 283, 289, 319, 341, 398, 467, 488, 493
Rees, Jerry W. 376, 395, 397
Rees, Melinda 473
Reese, Barbara 438
Reese, Lyza 490
Reese, Ray 21
Reese, Will 438
Refill, Clive 199
Regan, Tony 35, 54, 82, 91, 126, 151, 180
Regula, Frank 65, 81, 90, 96, 121, 125, 169, 185, 192, 218, 223, 227, 230, 268, 318, 418, 424, 446, 459, 467, 482
Reichel, Stephane 349, 350
Reid, Elliott 21

Reimers, Ed 82, 91
Reitherman, Bruce 253
Reitherman, Wolfgang 70, 146, 252, 257-258, 376, 379
Reluctant Astronaut, The 317
Reluctant Dragon, The 203
R.E.M. 4
Renaday, Pete 26, 39, 54, 70, 82, 91, 95, 109, 180, 231, 237, 290, 310, 346, 360, 484
Renard, Ken 224, 269
Renard, Morgan 397
Renoudet, Pete (See Renaday, Pete)
Repola, Arthur 371
Republic of Panama 340
"Rescue Aid Society, The" 258-259
Rescuers, The 159, 177, 245, 258-262, 281, 379, 416
Rescuers Down Under, The 262
Return from Witch Mountain 191, 282-288, 338-339
Return of the Big Cat 158
Return of the Jedi 417
Return of the Pink Panther, The 267
Return of the Shaggy Dog, The 237
Return to Oz 465, 472-481
Reubens, Paul 328, 333
Reynolds, Craig W. 397
Reynolds, Lynn F. 96, 125, 185
Reynolds, Michael J. 437
Reynolds, Norman 472
Reynolds, Ross 289, 397
RH and AHK Associates 397
Rhodewalt, Bruce 54, 82
Rice, James P. 409
Rice, Maureen 447
Rich, Adam 359
Rich, Denis 473
Rich, Lindsay 483
Rich, Richard 252, 258, 376, 481
Richards, Beah 109
Richards, Kim 185, 189-191, 197, 219, 283, 287-288, 339
Richards, Leoda 54
Richards, Kyle 185, 334, 339
Richardson, B. Frank 474
Richardson, Bruce 371
Richardson, George 198
Richardson, John 334
Richardson, Lloyd L. 90, 204
Richardson, Ralph 372
Richardson, Roseline 436
Richmond, Branscombe 169
Richter, Debi 328
Richter, Lori 395
Richwine, Diane 431
Ricotta, Dennis 424
Ridley, Emma 475, 481

Ridley, Laurie 370
Rio, Chuck 437
Ripley, Jay 310
Ritchie, Barbara 370
Ritchie, Clint 224
Ritchie, Joe 199
Ride a Northbound Horse 45
Ride a Wild Pony 212-215
Rodgers, Mary 237
Ringo, the Refugee Raccoon 158
Riha, Bobby 26
Riley, Art 252
Riley, Steve 268
Rinati, Roger 396
Ringold, Francine 409
Rinker, Al 70
Rio-Verde Productions, Ltd. 165
Rippel, Richard 489
Risch, Peter D. 424
Ritter, John 82, 86-87
Ritz Brothers, The 34
Ritz, James 447
River Country 217
Rivers, Nick 370
Roach, Pat 315
Roarke, Adam 283
Robards, Jason 424, 429
Robb, Bruce 350
Robbins, Ayn 258
Robbins, Matthew 369
Robert Abel and Associates 397-398
Robert Lawrence Productions 62
Roberts, Dodie 483
Roberts, Don 389
Roberts, Robyn 483
Roberts, Roy 91, 179
Roberts, Stephen 26
Roberts, Ted 455
Roberts, Tony 91, 95
Roberts, Vincent 301
Robertson, Dennis 306
Robertson, Glynis 473
Robin Hood 210
Robin Hood 80, 105, 131, 146-150, 159, 388
Robinson, Bruce 436
Robinson, Chris 365
Robinson, Edward G. 31
Robinson, Elaine 396
Robinson, Hank 193, 310
Robinson, Lenord 483
Robinson, Randall 341
Robinson, Scott 430
Robinson, Wayne 14
Robles, Walter 192, 289
Robotham, George 31, 345, 424
Robson, Wayne 351
Rocco, Alex 341

Rocha, Ronald 483
Roche, Nicola 475
"Rock-a-Bye Baby" 147
Rock-a-Doodle 358
Rock Around the Mouse 495
Rockett, Norman 289, 305, 310, 340, 345, 359, 445
Rockford Files, The 146, 171
Rockwell International Corporation Trust 437
Rocky Horror Picture Show, The 237
Rode, David 306
Rodgers, Dave 294
Rodgers, Mary 359
Rodgers, Roy 473
Roeg, Waldo 473
Roelofs, Al 90, 96, 109, 121, 138, 172, 184, 227, 318, 395
Roemer, Silvia 70, 147, 252, 258, 376, 483
Roesch, John 398
Rogers, Charles 483
Rogers, Dinah Anne 269
Rogers, Greg 438
Rogers, Monica 369
Rogers, Philip 398
Rogers, Roswell 90, 138
Rogers, Sheila 360
Rolofson, Bobby 306, 310
Rolph, Ian 474
Romano, Patrick 424
Rome, Italy 418
Romero, Cesar 53, 58, 117, 179
Ronald, Paul 350
Ronconi, George 138, 143, 165, 179
Ronconi, Ron 237, 282
Rondell, Ronnie 38
Rook, Heidi 26
Room 222 309
Rooney, Darrell 396, 424
Rooney, Mickey 269, 376
Rorke, Hayden 82, 86
Roscoe, Gene 38
Rose, Jim 113, 341
Rose, Mickey 380
Rose, Tim 474-475
Rosebrook, Jeb 318
Rosebush, Judson 397
Rosemarin, Hilton 436
Rosemond-Watt, Nedra 327, 364, 395
Rosen, Allan K. 436
Rosenbaum, Joel 489
Rosenbaum, R. Robert 125
Rosenthal, Michael 430
"Roses and Rainbows" 359, 363
Ross, Brian 436
Ross, Dana 397
Ross, Herbert 451
Ross, Joe 269
Ross, Joe E. 39, 66, 69

Ross, Len 306
Ross, Phillip 212
Rosseter, Tom 371
Rossi, Alfred 185
Rossi, Alvaro 350
Rossitto, Angelo 424
Roswell, Maggie 327
Rotberg, E. 397
Roth, Marty 65
Rothwell, Robert 117, 295
Rotunnno, Giuseppe 349
Roulette, Bari 360
Rouse, Graham 212
Roush, Curtis 489
Routh, May 445
Rowe, Bill 473
Rowe, Prentiss 301
Rowe, Tom 70
Rowe, Vern 231
Rowland, Bill 165
Rowland, Bob 62
Rowland, Fred 301
Rowland, Oscar 301
Rowland, Terry 62
Roy, Deep 475
Roy, Rob 437
Royal National Parks of Kenya, The 204
Royer, C.W. 301
Roylance, Bron 310
Royle, Jane 370
Rubell, Paul 349
Rubber Duckie and Other Songs from Sesame Street 61
Rubin, Benny 117, 231, 237
Ruggieri, Albamaria 418
Rumble Fish 413
"Rumbly in My Tumbly" 252-254
Rumsey, James A. 350
Run, Cougar, Run 121-125
Runaway on the Rogue River 158
Running Brave 435-441
Runsabove, Billy 437
Rupert, Mike 151
Rural American Organization 459
Rush, Barbara 151
Rush, Cynthia 396
Russell, Bobby 47, 50
Russell, Bing 21, 39, 44, 54, 91, 192
Russell, Brian 15
Russell, Jackie 31, 360
Russell, Kurt 26, 29, 35, 38, 44, 53, 58-59, 82, 107, 117, 131, 139, 151, 155, 179, 184, 376
Russell, Marta 396
Russell, Neil 117
Russell, Wilbur L. "Rusty" 65, 81, 125, 319, 396, 445, 466

Russo, Angelo 455
Russo, Scott 396
Rust, Bob 125
Rutan, Jr., Paul 97
Rutenberg, Mark 350
Rutherford, Todd 364
Rutherford, Laurie 238
Ryan, Christopher 436
Ryan, Fran 87, 91, 192
Ryan, John P. 346
Ryan, Patty 350
Ryan, Tim 446
Ryan's Daughter 406
Ryder, Alfred 185
Ryder Sound Services Inc. 437
Ryman, Herbert 269

Saarahen, Corinne 454
Sabin, Harry 376
Sacino. Andrea 26
Sager, Carole Bayer 359
Saggy Baggy Elephant, The 178
"Sail With Me" 350, 353
Saint, The 189
Sainty, David 474
Saito, Bill 360, 489
Saki, Eileen 447
Salaman, Chloe 372
Salazar, Rita 458
Saliba, Charles 418
Salob, Lorin B. 395
Salome, Tony 328
Salmi, Albert 372
Salten, Felix 230
Salty, the Hijacked Harbor Seal 108
Salvatore, Vladimiro 350
Sam Schatz Disc Co-Coordinator 397
Sam the Eagle 444
Sam the Sham and the Pharaohs 446
Sammy, the Way-Out Seal 59
Sample, Lewis 15
Samuels, David 275
San Francisco, California 95, 370
San Francisco State University 293
San Jose, California 7
Sanchez, Leon 341
Sandeen, Jack 126, 318-319, 327, 340, 345, 359, 364, 395, 408, 418, 423, 445, 458, 466, 489, 493
Sanders, Hal 349
Sanders, Shepherd 185
Sanderson, Carmen 483
Sands, Christopher 327
Sands, Leslie 247
Sandy in Disneyland 158
Sangster, Jimmy 359
Sansom, Ken 161

Santoro, Scott 424, 482, 489
Santos, Bert 341
Sarchielli, Massimo 418
Sardo, Cosmo 82, 180
Sarfoh, Anthony 468
Sargent, Bobby 319
Sargent, John 369
Sariego, Ralph 395
Sarracino, Ernest 82
Sasson, Lilian 447
Saturday Evening Post, The 95, 294
Saturday Night Live 309
Saunders, Anne 455
Saunders, Terence 172, 318
Savage, Brad 192, 197, 219, 283, 287-288
Savage, Paul 74
Savage, Tracie 360
Sax, Michael 398
Sax, Sidney 370
Sayer, Stanley 474
Sayre, Jeffrey 54, 82, 117, 126, 151, 180
Sbarge, Raphael 490
Scaife, Hugh 198, 247
"Scales and Arpeggios" 70-71
Scales, Prunella 247, 252
Scamp 14, 20, 46, 62, 80, 108, 133, 159, 178, 218, 246, 282, 300
Scandalous John 86-90, 95
"Scandalous John Suite" 87
Scanlan, Hean 474
Scanlon, Marianne 454
Scarecrow of Romney Marsh, The (see *Dr. Syn, Alias the Scarecrow*)
"Scarecrow Song, The" 206
Schallert, Williams 53, 121, 179
Schatz, Sam 398, 404
Scheele, John 396, 402, 489
Scheerer, Robert 133
Scheider, Roy 455
Schell, Maximilian 319, 323
Schell, Ronnie 179, 228, 231, 289, 293, 360
Schellenberg, August 437
Schelvis, Gert 357
Schickel, Richard 20
Schiffer, Robert J. 53, 65, 74, 81, 86, 90, 96, 109, 113, 116, 121, 125, 133, 138, 143, 151, 160, 165, 172, 179, 185, 192, 219, 223, 228, 230, 236-237, 262, 268, 282, 289, 294, 305, 310, 318, 327, 340, 345, 359, 364, 380, 395, 408, 418, 423, 445, 458, 466, 488, 493
Schifrin, Lalo 282, 289
Schilz, Mark 418
Schilz, Michael J. 396, 466, 488
Schilz, Ted 81, 86, 113, 143, 395
Schlesinger, Nick 369

Schloss, Hank 122
Schmidt, Albert B. 460
Schmidt, Georgia 328
Schmitz, Larry 38
Schmitz, Jr., Will 460
Schneider, Marlen 436
Schneider, William T. 90, 445
Scifo, Robert 474
Schoen, Claire 430
Scholl, Art 340
Schreck, Virginia 238
Schroeder, Friedel 389
Schulman, Douglas J. 350, 424
Schurmann, Gerard 206
Schultz, Catherine 446
Schwartz, David 301
Schwartz, Howard 359
Schwartz, Jeremy 397
Scifo, Robert 489
Scooby-Doo, Where Are You? 58
Scott, Dave 396
Scott, Deborah 430
Scott, Donovan 351
Scott, Ed 138
Scott, Elliot 333, 369
Scott, Geneve 301
Scott, Tom 283, 341
Scott, Walter 397
Scotti, Vito 70, 113, 134, 160, 341
Scribner, George 482
Scribner, Jim 408, 423
Scribner, Ronnie 365
Scrooge 252
Scrooge McDuck and Money 14, 497
Scruffy 245
SCTV 452
Scully, Sean 207
Seacat, Sandra 459
Seal Island 204
Seaman, Peter 417
Sears 61, 107, 177
Sears, Ted 204
Seaton, Ernest Thompson 62
Sebast, Dick (see Sebast, Richard)
Sebast, Richard 252, 258
Sebern, Brian 376, 482
Secret of Boyne Castle, The 45
Secret of Lost Valley, The 326
Secret of NIMH, The 299, 380, 389
Secret of the Old Glory Mine, The 217
Secret of the Pond, The 177
Secretary of Communications and Transport Ferry Service 340
Secrets of the Pirates Inn, The 45
Seeds, Wesley 371
Seems There Was This Moose 177
Seeta 122

Segal, Michael 276
Segar, E.C. (Elsie) 349, 354
Seiter, Christopher 218, 230, 268, 289, 305, 318
Sekac, Ed 319
Sekely, Jack 327
Selby, Sarah 134
Selfridge, Natasha 483
Selick, Henry 269, 334, 376, 473
Sellers, Peter 267
Semon, Maxine 91, 97
Sendak, Maurice 475
Senechal, Scott 458, 488
Senelly, Anne 446
Senter, Jack 179, 218, 237, 282
Sequoia National Park 46, 159
Serafine, Frank 395
Serafine FX Studios 395
Serengeti National Park of Tanzania, The 204
Server, Eric 295
Sesame Street 132, 403, 487
Seton, Bruce 207
Seton, Ernest Thompson 62
Seven Dwarf Lane 2
Severn, Maid 54
Seybert, Barry 319
Seyferth, Katharina 390
Seymour, Dan 185
Sgt. Bilko 69
Shadow of Fear 299
Shafer, Mavis 483
Shaffer, Diane 351
Shaggy D.A., The 25, 198, 218, 230-237, 294
"Shaggy D.A., The" 231
Shaggy Dog, The 12, 86, 217, 231, 235, 237
Shah, Kiran 371
Shannon, John R. 96-97
Shannon, Leonard 86, 133, 185
Shalit, Gene 53
Shaltz, Mike 74
Shamata, Charles 360
Shanghaied 158
Shapiro, Alan 454
Shaps, Cyril 315
Sharkey, Paddy 467
Sharman, Bruce 472
Sharp, Anthony 199
Sharp, Margery 258
Sharpsteen, Ben 204
Sharrett, Michael 295
Sharrock, Ian 275
Shatz, Leslie 370
Shaughnessy, Mickey 31, 66
Shaw, James Walter 396
Shaw, Kiran 275
Shaw, Melvin (Mel) 258, 376, 482
Shaw, Reta 185
Shaw, Rose Tobias 466

Shaw, Sam 349
Shawver, Cheryl 431
Shay, Dorothy 134
Shay, Mildred 276
Shayne, Robert 82, 91
"She Never Felt Alone" 73
"She Works Hard for the Money" 446
Shea, Christopher 47
Shea, Eric 169
Shearman, Roger 65, 458
Sheckley, Robert 380
Sheehan, Christopher 473
Sheep Dog 45
Sheets, Walter 35, 38, 46, 50, 53, 70, 90, 109, 113, 116, 122, 138, 147, 151, 160, 165, 179, 192, 218, 223, 228, 230, 305, 310, 376
Sheldon, Jack 237-238
Shelley, Carole 70, 147
Shelley, Dave 328
Shelley, Joshua 192
Shelly, Randy L. 237
Shelton, Richard 446
Shelton, Toby 482
Shenberg, Bill 395
Shepard, Bill 445, 458, 466, 488
Shepard, Ernest H. 252, 257
Shepard, Sam 459
Shepard, Sheri 328
Sheppard, A.L. 446
Sheridan, Robert C. 301
Sheridan, Susan 483
Sherman Brothers, The 12, 19, 29-30, 73, 103-104, 108, 131, 257
Sherman, Richard M. 26, 29, 70, 73, 96-98, 103-104, 252
Sherman, Robert B. 26, 70, 96-97, 252
Sherriff, Betty 314, 334
Sherwood, Robert 370
Shields, Brooke 454
Shields, Jim 334
Shimoda, Yuki 346
Shinneman, Ted 125
Shire, David 472-473
Shirley Temple Storybook Theatre 257
Shit 423
Shokee, the Everglades Panther 158
Shook, Roger M. 319, 327, 340, 359, 364, 395, 408, 418, 466
Shor, Dan 398, 404
Short, Robert 446
Shorter, Ken 372
Shoup, Robert 430
Shull, Jennifer 430
Shumow, William 430
Shustak, Martin 436
Shroder, Ricky 346

Shroyer, Sonny 359
Shull, Richard B. 446
Sibley, Brian 210
Sibley, John 252
Siddall, Bryn 247, 370
Siemens, Curtis 460
Sierra, Gregory 169
Sievers, Ille 389
Sigman, Paula 210
Sigmund and the Sea Monsters 129
Sign of Zorro, The 210, 388
Signoretti, Aldo 350
Silly Symphonies 132, 326
Silju, Erik 172
Silva, Henry 31
Silver Fox and Sam Davenport, The 108, 498
Silver, Jesse 396, 424
Silver, Johnny 31, 269
Silver Screen Partners II 465, 472, 481
Silverheels, Jay 47, 143
Silvers, Candace 490
Silvers, Michael 430
Silvers, Phil 65, 69, 179, 184
Silversmith, Boyd 301
Sim, Alastair 247, 252
Simkin, Margery 408
Simmons, David Alan 349
Simmons, Pat 490
Simon, James R. 204
Simon, Mario 237, 263, 269, 341
Simons, Mary 409
Simonds, Walter B. 113
Simpson, Bob 125
Simpson, Moyra 472
Simpson, Rick 423
Sims, Alan 424
Sims, Jeanie 423
Sims, Joan 199, 203
Sinbad and the Eye of the Tiger 245
Sinden, Donald 172
Singer, Larry 349
Singer, Lynn 396
Singer, Stephan 467
Singin' in the Rain 429
Sinutko, Shane 231
Sipes, Carson 365
Siskel, Gene 95
Sisson, Rosemary Anne 212, 247, 275, 333, 481
Sivel, William 380
60 Minutes 245
Skaggs, Ricky 459
Skagway, Alaska 431
Skeaping, Colin 381, 473, 475
Skehan, Peter 371
Sklar, Marty 13
Sky High 184
Sky Trap, The 299

Sky's the Limit, The 177
Slate, Henry 180, 219, 228, 231, 269, 289, 341
Slattery, Richard X. 160, 310
Sleeping Beauty 61, 299
Sloan, Barry 455
Slyfield, C.O. 204
Small & Frye 388, 527
Small One, The 281, 498
Smart, Patsy 199
Smart, Tony 371
Smith! 46-50, 129
Smith, Betty 459
Smith, Bobbie 247, 334, 370
Smith, Charles Martin 219, 223, 341, 430-431, 435, 452
Smith, Dave 61, 197, 210, 257
Smith, Debbie 26
Smith, Elizabeth 169
Smith, Ernie 370
Smith, Frank T. 294, 310
Smith, H.W. Hamilton 474
Smith, Hal 91, 253, 257
Smith, Herb 122, 165
Smith, Howard 408, 466
Smith, Ian 467
Smith, Irby 359
Smith, J. Brennan 328
Smith, Jack 82
Smith, Jack Martin 268
Smith, Karen 238
Smith, Kendall 437
Smith, Kenneth 371
Smith, Leon 455
Smith, Lester 350
Smith, Lynne Bailey 489
Smith, Paul L. 35, 117, 204, 350-351
Smith, Philip 371, 445
Smith, Robert E. 46
Smith, Scott 409
Smith, Sterling 185
Smith, Thomas 371
Smith, Toney 301
Smith, Wendell 438
Smithsonian Institution 204
Smitrovich, Bill 447
Smoke 61
Smoot, Reed 300
Snart, Roy 97
Sneddon, Helen 319
Snel. Otto 198
Snoopy, Come Home 108, 417
Snow Bear 61
Snow White 5
Snow White and the Seven Dwarfs 12, 14, 131, 150, 178, 204, 211, 218, 274, 300, 416, 444
Snow White Live 326

Snow White Village 2
Snowball Express 77, 125-130, 235
Snowdonia National Park 371
Snyder, David L. 488
Snyder, Jack 90
Snyder, William 30, 35, 50, 65, 90
"So Many Ways" 364-365
Soboloff, Arnold 289
Sobul, Jerry 488
Societe Des Bains De Mer De Monte Carlo 380
Soder, Rolf 172
Sodium Screen Vapor Process 104
Soles, P.J. 454
"Solid Citizen" 104
Solomon, Alan 327
Solomon, Charles 11, 19, 45, 245, 357, 388
Solomon, Linda 454
Solon, Ewen 315
"Someone New" 327
"Someone's Waiting for You" 258, 260
Somers, Robert (Bobby) 143, 459
"Something Good's About to Happen" 294, 298
Something Wicked This Way Comes (see *Ray Bradbury's...*)
Sommars, Julie 263, 267
Son of Flubber 58, 164
Song of the South 5, 108, 326
Songs from the Electric Company TV Show 132
Soo, Jack 283, 288
Sorensen, Ann Marie 396
Sorensen, John 334
Sorensen, Paul 144, 185, 231
Sorensen, Rick 290
Sorrentino, Martin 418
Soule, Olan 54, 192, 231
Sound Flash Inc. 455
"Sound Off (Duckworth Chant)" 437
Sounds of Christmas, The 132
South, Leonard J. 262, 305, 364
Southwood, John 198
Space, Arthur 97, 161, 180
Space Mountain 7, 80, 158, 177-178, 246
Space Probe 324
Space Station One 324
Spaceman and King Arthur, The 314, 317
Spaceman in King Arthur's Court, A 317
Spalding, Harry 143, 333
Spangler, Scott Bailey 490
Sparks, Randy 192
Sparks, Rita 350
Spartacus 407
Speake Anthony 371
Spear, David 489
Spector, Maude 198, 206, 247, 275, 314, 334, 418
Speed, Ken 319, 334, 341, 345, 371-372, 381, 488, 493
Speer, John 474

Index   581

Speirs, Jack 14-15, 62, 165
Spell, George 109
Spence, Steve 467
Spencer, Brent 430
Spencer, Dave 483
Spencer, Herbert W. 473
Spetter, R.J. 395
Spielberg, Steven 358, 429, 472
Spier, Carol 435
Spiers, David 370
Spinney, Don 231, 289, 294, 345
Spisak, Neil J. 454
Spiteri, Anthony 419
Spivey, Michael 369
Splash 445-454
Splash, Too 451
Splet, Alan R. 430
Spooner, Kaaren 483
Sport Goofy 416
Sporting Proposition, The 212, 215
Spottiswoode, Roger 466
Springsteen, Pamela 490
Spunbuggy Works 96
"Squeeks" 377
Squire, Anthony 198, 275, 380
St. Amand, Anastasia 466, 489
St. Amand, Tom 371
St. Hilaire, Michael 74, 90, 97, 125
St. John, Stephen 430
St. John, William 218-219
St. Macary, Xavier 263
St. Pierre, Paul 46
Stacy, James 424
Stacy, Michelle 259
Stafford, Jim 376
Stafford, Robert 20, 35, 46, 74, 81, 113, 125, 143, 172, 184, 227
Stagg, Arthur E. 345
Stahl, Ben 20
Stahler, Bob 74, 395
Stallsworth, Larry 409
Stallybrass, Anne 390
Stanchfield, Walt 70, 252, 258, 376, 482
Standard, Karen 459
Stangl, Ron 396, 424
Stanhope, Jr., Paul 74
Stanman, Jeff 409
Stanoch, Mark 87
Stanovich, Marty 459
Stanton, Will 138
"Star Spangled Banner, The" 456
Star Tours 466
Star Trek 387
Star Trek: The Motion Picture 323
Star Trek II: The Wrath of Khan 387
Star Trek III: The Search for Spock 443
Star Wars 6, 176, 190, 217, 243, 245-246, 252, 281, 293, 317, 324, 331, 333, 402, 404, 406, 408, 466
Star Wars Episode I: The Phantom Menace 324
"Starfire" 327, 331
Starjets, The 158
Stark, Betty 483
Starling, Lane 431
Starr, Adam 360
Starr, Ringo 131
Starr, Steve 483
State of Jalisco, Mexico 340
Stateman, Wylie 398
Statue of Liberty National Monument 446
Steadman, John 224, 295
"Steady, Boy, Steady" 21
Stears, John 198
Steck, Harold J. 204
Steele, George 74
Steele, Ray 81, 125
Steele, Tom 39, 289
Steele, Tommy 150
Stein, Howard 371
Stein, Jenny 430
Steinberg, Herbert 397
Steinbrecher, Robert 430
Steiner, Max 437
"Step in the Right Direction, A" 97, 104
Stephan, David (Dave) 396, 483
Stephano, Tony 398
Stephens, Jack 350
Stephens, P.G. 418
Stephenson, John 160, 474
Sterling, Mindy 360
Stern, Steven Hilliard 359
Steve Allen's Music Room 443
Steven, Roxy Novotny 483
Stevens, Alex 446
Stevens, Art 96, 146, 179, 218, 237, 252, 258, 305, 376, 481
Stevens, Fisher 490
Stevens, John M. 125
Stevens, Ken 475
Stevens, Lenore 87
Stevens, Naomi 151
Stevens, Roy 369
Stevenson, Maureen 467
Stevenson, McLean 287, 289, 293
Stevenson, Robert 20, 38, 96, 160, 172, 198-199, 218, 229-230, 235-236
Stewart, Dennis 269
Stewart, Mark 398
Stewart, McLaren 96
Stewart, Paul 74
Still the Beaver 466
Sting, The 138
Stirdivant, Jill 483
Stirdivant, Marc 380, 389

Stockwell, John 490
Stokes, Linda D. 396
Stoll, Russ 482
Stoll, Rusty 376
Stolz, Peter 371
Stone, Noreen 364
Stone, Sharon 454
Stoneham, Charles 474
Stones, Tad 258
Stony Indian Nation, The 62
"Stop! In the Name of Love" 418, 422
Storer, John H. 204
Storey, Raymond G. 466
Storming the Magic Kingdom 416
Story of Robin Hood, The 150
Stoutsenberger, Marvin 301
Strabel, Herbert 389
Strachan, Jr., William T. 455
Stranan, Alois 431
Strange Monster of Strawberry Cover, The 80
Stratton, Chet 82
Stratton, Gil 290
Strauss, Johann 39
Street, James 109
Streets of San Francisco, The 116
Strick, Joseph 430
Streisand, Barbra 363
Striepeke, Dan 380
Stringer, Michael 198, 206
Stromsoe, Fred 38
Strongest Man in the World, The 57-58, 121, 137, 179-184, 230
Strosnider, Lee 185
Strother, Brigitte 483
Stroud, Michael 350
Strumpell, Dale 370
Strutt, Lionel 371, 473
Stuart, Walker 430-431
Stub, the Best Cow Dog in the West 158
Studley, Allan 310
Study, Lomax 161
Sturgess, Ray 206, 275, 314
Submarine Voyage 12
"Substitutiary Locomotion" 97, 101
Suchet, David 418-419
Sudling, Dave 258, 376, 482
Sukara, George 483
Suldo, Valerie 80
Sullivan, Brian 134
Sullivan, Richard T. 424
Sullivan, Rick 483
Sultan and the Rock Star 326
Sultan, Gene 289
Summer, Donna 446
"Summer Sweet" 50
Summerfield, Eleanor 334
Summers, Neil 143

"Summertime Blues" 437
"Sunday Morning Music" 305
Sundby, Emily 26, 35, 38, 46, 50, 53, 65, 74, 81, 86, 90, 96, 109, 113, 116, 125, 133, 138, 143, 151, 160, 169, 172, 179, 185, 192, 218, 223, 228, 230, 237, 262, 268, 282, 289, 294, 305
Sundby, Harry 90
Sundin, Michael 475
Super Goof 14, 20, 46, 62, 80, 108, 133, 159, 178, 218, 246, 282, 300, 326, 358, 389, 417, 444
Superdad 150-155, 230
Superfriends 30
Superman: The Movie 281
Superman II 358
Superman III 417
Superstar Goofy 108, 498
Supertramp 408
Survival of Sam the Pelican, The 217
Suskin, Mitch 446
Sutton, Mark 446
Svendsen, Julius 70, 96, 146, 252
Swain, Grant 430
Swain, James W. 90, 96
Swain, Kathleen 376
Swann, Neil 370
Swanstrom, Daniel 431
Swanton, Harold 50
Swarm, The 142
Swartz, Jerram 294
"Swee'pea's Lullaby" 350, 353
"Sweet Surrender" 165
"Sweet Sweethaven" 350-351
Sweeten, Mike 327, 340-341
Swenson, Karl 75
Swift, David 275, 279
Swiss Family Robinson 12, 45, 86, 108, 178, 357-358
Switched-On Bach 403
Switzerland 453
Swofford, Ken 143
Sword in the Stone 417
Sword in the Stone, The 108, 357, 388, 416
Sword, Robert 424
Sword, Roger 459. 467
Sylvester, Julian 431
Symmetricon 424
Syntauri Corp. 397
Synthavision 403
Synthefex 395
Sztompke, Ewa 431

Taba, Therese 468
Tablian, Vic 418
Tafani, Carlo 418
Taft, Sara 21

Taggart, Hal 54
Tagoe, Eddie 468
Tait, Don 125, 169, 192, 223, 230, 305, 310, 314, 340
Taipei, Taiwan 397
Take Down 300-305, 314, 323, 333, 441
"Take Me Out to the Ball Game" 455
Tale of Two Critters, A 245, 388, 498
Tales of the Apple Dumpling Gang 198, 387
Taliaferro, Al 46
"Talkin' About Charlie" 15
Tallman, Frank 289
Tamakuni, Sarah 275
Tamburro, Charles A. 163, 424
Tampa, Florida 5
Tan, Philip 475
Tansy 475
Tanti, Saviour 418
Tantin, Roland 424, 445, 459, 466, 468
Taplin, Jonathan T. 466, 488
Tartaglia, Luciano 350
Tarzan 116
Tate, Christopher 436
Tate, Louis 483
Tatum, Donn 13, 19, 79-80, 217, 246, 325, 415
Tatum, Shane 109, 138, 151, 192, 224, 231
Tatum, Shelby 138, 151
Tax, Mel 455
Tayback, Vic 219, 231
Taylor, Benedict 334
Taylor, Dub 75, 224, 259
Taylor, Harold 370
Taylor, Herb 113, 121, 125, 133, 138, 143, 147, 151, 160, 165, 169, 172, 179, 184, 192, 204, 218, 223, 227, 230, 237, 252, 258, 262, 268, 282, 289, 294, 305, 310, 318, 327, 340, 345, 359, 364, 376, 380
Taylor, John 416
Taylor, Matthew 390
Taylor, Norm 143
Taylor, Richard 395-397, 403-404, 406
Taylor, Rick 483
Taylor, Robert Lewis 223
Taylor, Vaughn 91
TBS / Video H&A Landaker 397
Teach, Edward 21
Teague, Anthony 82
Tebbs, Susan 247
Technical Magic 327
Technicolor 14, 20, 26, 30, 35, 38, 46, 50, 53, 62, 65, 70, 74, 81, 86, 90, 96, 109, 113, 116, 121, 125, 133, 138, 143, 146, 150, 160, 165, 169, 172, 179, 184, 192, 198, 204, 206, 212, 218, 223, 227, 230, 237, 247, 258, 262, 268, 275, 282, 289, 294, 305, 310, 314, 318, 327, 333, 340, 345, 359, 364, 376, 380, 389, 394, 408, 417, 423, 445, 458, 466, 472, 481, 488
Technovision 318, 349
Tedesco, Tommy 151
Tedrow, Irene 327
Telford, Robert S. 360
Temener, Irving 65
Temple, Barry 481
Temple, Shirley 257
Templer, Jr., Ed 147
"Ten Feet Off the Ground" 26-27
Ten Who Dared 274
Tennant, Andy 327
"Tequila" 437
"Terminus and Hoagy Hunt Elliott" 274
Terran, Tony 455
Terrill, Terry 445
Terrusa, Louis 126, 185, 318
Terry, Bridget 350
Terry-Thomas 147
Tex 387, 408-413
Thatcher, James 345
Theatre Vision International, Inc. 445
Theiss, William Ware 268
Thelen, Jenny 390
"Theme from a Summer Place" 437
"There's Room for Everyone" 269, 271, 274
"These Are the Best of Times" 151, 155
Thibeau, Jack 409
Thin Man, The 198
Thirtle, Robert 475
Thom, Randy 430
Thomas, Barry 109
Thomas, Bill 20, 26, 31, 35, 38, 172, 268, 318, 359
Thomas, Bob 13, 159, 218
Thomas, Bushrod 1, 4, 6
Thomas, Christopher 447
Thomas, Dean 20, 31, 35, 38, 50, 53, 65, 81, 86, 90, 96, 116, 160, 172
Thomas, Frank 70, 146, 252, 257-258, 376, 379
Thomas, Ian 436
Thomas, John 431
Thomas, Joseph 489
Thomas, Lowell 108
"Thomas O'Malley Cat" 70
Thomas, Roy 446
Thomson, Dave 483
Thomson, H.A.R. 198
Thomson, Isis 482
Thompson, Betsy Lynn 327
Thompson, Bill 70, 96
Thompson, Bob 350
Thompson, Carol Gwynn 327
Thompson, Don 159
Thompson, Lynda 424
Thompson, Terry 431

Thompson Street Pictures, A 454
Thompson, Vivian 81
Thordsen, Kelly 21, 66, 117, 139
Thorndike, Russell 206, 210
Thorndyke, Russell (see Thorndike, Russell)
Thorn-EMI Elstree Studios 474
Thorne, David M. 301
Thorne, Lucille 301
Thornton, Randy 98
Thorpe, Dennie 370
Thorpe, Marc 371
Three Lives of Thomasina, The 472
Three on the Run 281
Three Without Fear 80
Three Caballeros, The 34, 197, 245
Thulin, Ron 409
Thum, William 430
Thunderbug 43
Thurman, Lois 74, 96
Tiano, Lou 447
Tiberi, Alfred 350
Tieman, Robert 98
Tiger Town 416, 454-458
Tiger Trouble 45
Tigger Movie, The 30, 258
"Tik-Tak-Polka op. 365" 39
Tilley, Kate 268
Tilly, Meg 409
Tilton, Charlene 238, 243
Tilton, John 301
Timanus, John 38
Times Mirror Foundation 437
Tinne, Alex 87, 341
Tippett, Phil 371
Tipping, Tip 473
Tipton, Brian 488
Toberen, Jacque 349
Tobey, Kenneth 228
Tobias, Jay 446
Tobin, Dan 160
Tobin, Jack 455
Tokar, Norman 35, 50, 65, 125, 192, 197, 218, 275, 289, 294, 299
Tokyo Disneyland 79, 326, 415, 417, 487
Toll, Pamela 50
Tolsky, Susan 139, 360
"Tom Dooley" 437
Tom Sawyer 131
Tom Sawyer Island 131-132
Tom's Chroma Lab 396
Tomes, Lynn 395
Tomiuk, Randy 436
Tomkins, Frank 483
Tomlinson, David 39, 97, 103-105
Tomlinson, Eric 370, 473
"Tomorrow is Another Day" 258, 260
Tomorrowland 12

Tomorrowland Terrace 13
Tomorrow's Champions 113
Toms, Donald 369
Tondreau, Bill 397
Toner, Tom 447
Tonkonogy, Peggy 483
Toomey, Bill 133-134
Topete, Alex 483
Torpin, Don 165
Torrisi, Peitro 351
Totally Minnie 495
Totten, Robert 74, 310
Totter, Audrey 310
"Touch and Go" 87
Touchdown Mickey 158
Touchstone Pictures 288, 380, 415, 445, 451-452, 458, 465-466, 488
Tough Guys 493
Tourjansky, Victor 349
Touyarot, Alex 125
Tovey, Arthur 54, 82, 117, 161, 269, 310
Tower, Jon 445
Towns, Donald 396, 482
Toy Story 405
Toy Story Toons: Small Fry 385
Toyota 409
Track of the African Bongo, The 245
Traeger, Rick 97
Trahant, Mark 436
"Train to Quivara" 87
Trail of Danger 281
Transunto, Gianfranco 350
Travers, P.L. 103
Travolta, John 452
Treasure Island 12, 86, 178, 211, 323
Treasure of Matecumbe 223-227
Treasure of San Bosco Reef, The 19
Treasures of Disney Animation Art 389
Treasury of Stories from Silly Symphonies 359
Tree, Ron 301
Treen, Mary 179
Trelawney, Terre 301
Trenchcoat 417-423, 443
Trent, Jerry 26, 269
Trevino, Antonio 341
Trevis, Martin 473
"Tribes, The" 87
Trieste, Leopoldo 418
Trindale, Margaret 483
Triple I Demo 403, 407
Trolley, Leonard 199
Tron 275, 323, 385, 387, 394-408, 416, 430
Tron Legacy 408
Troubetzkoy, Eugene 397
Trousdale, Gary 483, 489
Troutman, Jim 455
True-Life Adventures 204, 206

True-Life Adventures 14, 65, 133
True-Life Fantasy 65
Trueblood, Maureen 396
Tubes, The 489
Tuchelske, Eric 455
Tuchner, Michael 417
Tucker, Jane 483
Tucker, John 396, 483
Tucker, Mike 467
Tucker, Paul 369
Tucker, Stephen 349
Tufeld, Dick 95
Tundra Summer 132
Tupou, Manu 169
Tupper, Loretta 328
Turk, Daniel 424
Turley, James 364
Turner, Bill 350
Turner, Kathleen 454
Turner, Susan 371, 424
Turner, Timothy 253, 257
Tuttle, Lurlene 35
Twain, Mark 314
Twas the Night Before Christmas 246
Tweten, Roger W. 446
20th Century Fox 12
20,000 Leagues Under the Sea 80, 86, 116, 324
Twinn, Chris 372
Twins of Evil 189
Twister, Bull from the Sky 217
Two Against the Arctic 158
Tyler, Walter 116, 125, 133, 160, 172, 192
Tyner, Charles 269
Tyra, Dan 445
Tyson, Ian 122

UBC 86, 236
Ugly Dachshund, The 25, 235
Uncle Remus 108
Uncle Remus 14, 108
Uncle Scrooge 178, 300
Uncle Scrooge 14, 20, 46, 62, 80, 108, 132, 159, 178, 218, 246, 282, 293, 300, 326, 358, 389, 417, 444, 496
Uncle Scrooge Goes to Disneyland 466
Uncle Scrooge Mini-Comic 218
Underdog 354
Undergrads, The 466
Unger, Bertil 360
Unger, Gustaf 360
Unidentified Flying Oddball 314-318, 333
Unitas, Johnny 228, 230
Universal Amphitheatre 359
Universal Studios 298, 359
University of California, Berkeley 431
"Up, Down, Touch the Ground" 252-253
Upchurch, Bowman 228

Urioste, Frank J. 417
"U.S. Air Force, The" 258
U.S. Department of the Interior 446
U.S. Department of the Interior Bureau of Land Management 143
U.S. Junior Tournament World Tennis Tournament 416
Used Cars 58
Ustinov, Peter 21, 25, 105, 147, 199, 203, 224
Utah 143
Utah Athletic Association 300
Vacationland (see *Disneyland Vacationland*)
Vachon, Paul 473
Vacio, Natividad 86
Valatica, Ralph 455
Valdez, Joe 341
Valencia, California 80
Valentine from Disney, A 416
Valentine, James 396
Valentine, Karen 295, 305, 309
Vallelonga, Nick 447
Valtierra, Gregory 294
Van Citters, Darrell 376
Van Der Veer, Greg 489
Van Der Veer Photo Effects 397, 424
Van Dyke, Dick 19, 31, 34, 429
Van Evera, Jack 62
Van Frey, John 318
Van Hoek, William 301
Van Nuys, Laura Bower 26
Van Patten, Dick 126, 130, 151, 155, 179, 224, 228, 231, 235-238, 243
Van Patten, Jimmy 238, 295, 310
Van Patten, Patricia 341
Van Patten, Vincent 139
Van Sickel, Dale 38, 219
Van Vliet, John 371, 396, 489
Vancouver, British Columbia 431, 480
Vandeman, Steve 340
Vanders, Warren 295
Vandis, Titos 228
Vanishing Prairie, The 204
Vanlint, Derek 369
Varab, Jeffrey J. 376
Varda, the Peregrine Falcon 45
Varela, Migdia 447
Vargas, Don 489
Vargas, Ron 117, 125, 185, 395
Vargo, Mark 371
Vasilovich, Gus 376, 482
Vaughan, Martin 212
Vaughn, Clifford 204
Veiller, Bayard 424
Veilleux, Jim 371
Velasco, Jerry 169
Velin, Robert 262
Vendrell, Michael M. 446

Venegas, William B. 345
Venice, California 403
Venturelli, Gail 489
Verbois, Jack 289
Verity, Erwin L. 14, 62, 122, 204
Verlardi, Valerie 351
Vermont 424
Vermont, Laurie 371
Verne, Jules 176
Vernon, John 341
Vernon, Whit 455
Vertue, Deborah 369
VeSota, Bruno 91
Vessiny, Susan 483
VHS 211, 262
Via Mail Canada, Inc. 437
Vick, Pam 371
Victor, Paul 328
Victor, Ray 341
Victorville, California 349
Victory, Fiona 475
Vidor, John 490
Viewmont High School 300
Vigil, Paul 467
Vigran, Herb 21, 39, 82, 160, 231
Viker, Neil 397, 483, 489
Village of Zermatt, The 380
Vilppu, Glenn V. 376, 482
Vincent 388, 443, 499
Vincent, Jan-Michael 133, 137
Vincent, Larry 193
Vincent, Virginia 91, 224, 365
Vinson, Malcolm 314
Vinton, Will 474
Viola, Jeff 424
Virtue, Tom 409
Vista Vision 407
Visual Concepts Engineering 424
Vitarelli, Arthur J. 20, 38, 50, 53, 65, 74, 90, 96, 116, 125, 133, 160, 172, 179, 192, 218, 228, 230, 262, 289
Vitz, Frank 397
Viva Max! 34
Voland, Herb 306
Volkswagen 43, 95, 121, 164
Volstad, John 328
Von Brockdorff, Margaret 418
Von Weitershausen, Gila 418
Von Wolfgang, Rolph 109
Von Zerneck, Danielle 490
Voormann, Klaus 351
Vote for Pooh in '72 107
Vuilleumier, Pierre 398
VW (see Volkswagen)

Wacker, Stephen 385
Wacky Zoo of Morgan City, The 61

Wadley, Stan 301
Wadsworth, Jack 359, 364, 376, 380, 389, 409, 418, 424, 446, 459, 482
Wagenheim, Charles 193
Wagner, John 74, 86, 269
Wagstaff, Elsie 207
Wahb 62-65
Wahlund, Torsten 172
Wainess, Paul 397, 483
Wait, Robert 489
Waite, Ric 408
Wakefield, Jim 151
Waking Sleeping Beauty 495
Walas, Christopher 371
Walden, Barbara 238
Walker, Card 13, 79, 217, 246, 325, 387, 415, 424
Walker, Charles 446
Walker, Gus 198
Walker, Jack David 179
Walker, Robert 473
Walker, Russ 81
Walker, Toni-Ann 358
Walker, Vivienne 86
Walker, Nancy 133
Wall, Max 199
Wallace, John 350
Wallace, Linda 15
Wallace, Oliver 204
WallaWorks 395, 408
Waller, Garry 371
Waller, Peter 473
Wallin, Dan 319, 349
Walmsley, Jon 26, 29, 252, 257
Walowitz, Marvin 395
Walsh, Bill 20, 25, 38, 86, 96, 133, 160, 178-179, 198. 218
Walsh, David M. 458, 488
Walsh, Frank 370
Walsh, Kay 207, 390
Walsh, Terry 218, 370-371
Walston, Ray 351
Walt Disney (see *Wonderful World of Disney, The*)
Walt Disney – A Golden Anniversary Salute 132
Walt Disney, An American Original 218
Walt Disney and Recollections of the Disney Studios 25
Walt Disney Archives 61, 257
Walt Disney Christmas Parade 246
Walt Disney Comics Digest 20, 46, 62, 80, 108, 133, 159, 178, 218
Walt Disney Company, The 1, 5-8, 210, 435, 441, 443-444, 451-453, 458, 463, 465-466, 472, 480-481, 487, 493, 495-497, 501
Walt Disney Distributing Company, The 80, 246
Walt Disney Feature Animation Research Library 97

Walt Disney Imagineering 495
Walt Disney...One Man's Dream 357
Walt Disney Paint Book Series, The 178
Walt Disney Pictures (see Walt Disney Company, The)
Walt Disney Presents Sport Goofy Olympic Games Special 443
Walt Disney Productions (Studios) 7-8, 11-14, 17, 19-20, 25, 34, 38, 43, 45-46, 49-50, 52, 58-59, 61-62, 69, 73, 77, 79-81, 86, 90, 95, 104-105, 107-108, 116, 121, 125, 129-133, 138, 142, 146, 149-150, 155, 157-159, 164, 171, 176-178-179, 184, 189, 191, 197-198, 203, 210-211, 215, 217-218, 222-223, 227, 229-230, 235-237, 243, 245-246, 257, 261-262, 273-276, 281, 287-288, 293-294, 298-299, 304-305, 309, 314, 317, 323-326, 333, 338-339, 345, 348, 354, 358-359, 363-364, 369, 375, 379-380, 385, 387-389, 394, 397, 403-404, 406-408, 413, 415-416-417, 423, 429-430, 435, 458, 465, 493, 495-497, 501
Walt Disney Showcase 62, 80, 108, 133, 178, 218, 246, 282, 300, 326
Walt Disney Story, The 132
Walt Disney: The Man, The Artist, The Dreamer 357
Walt Disney Treasures 8, 107, 210
Walt Disney World 1-2, 4-7, 13, 19, 44-45, 79, 107, 132, 158, 178, 217, 246, 281, 299, 325, 357-358, 387-388 417, 454
Walt Disney World 80
Walt Disney World Golf Tournament 79, 132, 417
Walt Disney World Happy Easter Parade 465
Walt Disney World National Team Golf Classic 299, 326
Walt Disney World Very Merry Christmas Parade 416, 443
Walt Disney's America 282
Walt Disney's Christmas Classics 282
Walt Disney's Comics and Stories 14, 20, 46, 62, 80, 108, 132, 159, 178, 218, 246, 282, 300, 326, 358, 389, 417, 444, 496
Walt Disney's Fantasia 389
Walt Disney's Fun to Know 133, 159
Walt Disney's Happiest Songs 13
Walt Disney's Magazine 45
Walt Disney's Merriest Songs 20
Walt Disney's Mickey and Donald 416
Walt Disney's Mickey and Donald Presents Sport Goofy 416

Walt Disney's Mickey, Donald and Sport Goofy 443
Walt Disney's Treasury of Children's Classics 282
Walt Disney's Treasury of Classic Tales 14
Walt Disney's Uncle Scrooge McDuck: His Life and Times 359
Walt Disney's World of Fantasy 389
Walt, Mickey and Me 246
Walters, Jimmy 467
Walters, R. Martin 165, 435
Waltons, The 29, 116
"Warbag" 87
Warburton, Cotton 26, 38, 53, 65, 86, 96, 116, 133, 160, 169, 179, 218, 223, 237, 262, 289
Ward, Sophie 475
Wardlow, John 431
Ware, Harlan 150
Waring, Donna 436
Warlock, Dick (Richard) 20, 38, 53, 59, 81-82, 109, 117, 125, 133, 151, 179, 237, 263, 289
Warner Bros. 143, 496
Warner, David 398, 404, 406
Warner, Don 467
Warner, Frank 437
Warner, Richard 247
Warner, Shiela A. 459
Warren, Christopher (Chris) 372, 473
Warren, Lesley Ann 26, 29-30
"Warrior, The" 489
Warschilka, Edward A. 349
Washauer, Gerry Lynn 50
Warshawsky, Ruth 283
Washington, Eddie 436
Washington, Von 455
Wassaba, Paul 467
Watcher in the Wood, A 333
Watcher in the Woods, The 288, 324-325, 333-340
Watergate 107
Waters, Tom 192
Watkin, Lawrence Edward 109
Watkins, David H. 370, 472, 474
Watson, David 474
Watson, Davina 369
Watson, Hilary 473
Watson, Mills 75, 139, 224
Watson, Raymond 415, 443
Watts, Eric 370
Watts, Robert 474
Waugh, Fred 294, 445
Way Down Cellar 19
Way We Were, The 138
"Way We Were, The" 150
Wayland, Len 365
Wayne, David 192
Wayne Fitzgerald Modern Film Effects 418

Wayne, Jesse 38, 117, 263, 268, 446
Wayne, John 168
Wayne, Patrick 165, 168
Weatherly, Lureline 482
Webb, Frank 53
Webb, Jim 458, 488
Webb, Robert M. 20, 38, 65, 86, 96, 310, 364
Webster, Byron 180
Webster, Daimon 397
Webster, Hugh 62, 431
Wechter, David 327
Wechter, Julius 327
WED Enterprises 495
Weddle, Vernon 360
Wedge, Christian 397
Wedgeworth, Ann 490
Weighill, Ian 97
Weinrib, Lennie 97, 180
Weir, Molly 199
Weiss, Jacob 365
Welch, Bill 473
Welch, James 74
Welcome to the "World" 177
Weldon. Mike 395
Welker, Frank 53, 58, 117, 490
Welles, Orson 339
Wells, Danny 180, 228, 231
Wells, Frank 8, 465
Wells, Jack 219
Welsch, Chauncey 455
Welsh, Martin 396
Welsh Office, Ancient Monuments Branch 371
Welsh, Tommy 458
Werden, Robert (Bob) 459, 489
Werner, Byron 396, 489
Wertimer, Ned 180
Wesson, Karl 301
"West o' the Wide Missouri" 26, 28
West, Rebecca 473
Westbury Design and Optical Ltd. 474
Westerfield, James 47
Western Publishing 14, 444
Westheimer, Jody 371
Westlund, R. Chris 327
Westman, Nydia 35
Westmoreland, Peggy 446
Weston, Brad 295
Weston, Robert 206
Wethington, Denise 396
Wetzel, Elizabeth 454
Weyerhaeuser Company 15
Whalen, Fred L. 290
"What a Rather Blustery Day" 252, 254
What a Wonderful Thing is Me! 132
"What, No Mickey Mouse?" 20
What's Up, Doc? 237
Whedon, John 165, 172

Wheeler, Charles F. 81, 138, 143, 237, 262, 289, 345, 381
Wheeler, John 306, 310
Whelchel, Lisa 454
"When I'm Near You" 151
Whipple, Randy 126
Whisper in the Gloom 299
"Whistle-Stop" 147, 149
Whitaker, Billy 147
Whitaker Corporation 437
Whitaker, Dori 147, 253
Whitaker, Johnny 109, 112-113, 126, 129, 131
White, David 126, 130
White, Douglas 431
White, Frank 268
White, Jack Cameron 306
White, Jason 372
White, Jesse 289
White, John 489
White, Julie 301
White, Larry 483
White, Onna 268
White, Sarah 475
White, Sheila 315
White, Ted 398
White Wilderness 204-205
Whitecloud, Jim 295
Whiteman, Gene 371
Whitfield, Eric 349
Whitfield, Leslie A. 349
Whitfield, Richard 349
Whitfield, Ted 349
Whiting, Bob 346
Whitman Comics 14, 358, 389, 444
Whitman, Sr., Jack 97
Whitman, Stuart 122
Whitney, Cyndee 482
Whitney, Jr., John 397
Whitrod, Barry 370, 474
Whittaker, Ian 334, 369-370
Whittaker, David A. 488
Whittington, Brandy 396, 483
Whittle, Will 301
Whiz Kid and the Carnival Caper, The 217
Whiz Kid and the Mystery at Riverton, The 158
Who Framed Roger Rabbit? 495
Wickes, Mary 113, 126, 129
Wieringen, Kevin Van 365
Wiggins, Chris 62
Wiggins, Les 206
Wightmore, Alan 436
Wikipedia 44, 116, 121
Wilcox, Frank 91
Wilcox, Richard 430
Wiley, Bessie K. 371
Wild Country, The 74-77
Wild Geese Calling 45

Wilde, Martin 436
Wilder, Glenn 38, 345, 397, 489
Wildman, Valerie 447
Wildside 443, 527
Wilhite, Thomas L. 325, 395, 415, 474
Wilhoit, Mike 395
Wilhoit, Robert 489
Wilkin, Brad 327
Wilkinson, Barry 369
Wilkinson, Lynn 397
Will Vinton Productions 472
Willard, Robert G. 350, 424
Willat, Carl 474
Williams, Adam 35
Williams, Al 185
Williams, Bert 328
Williams, Bill 87
Williams, Bob 350
Williams, Chuck 147, 252, 258, 268, 376, 482
Williams, Dean 459
Williams, Frank 199
Williams, Grant 301
Williams, Guy 52, 388
Williams, Hal 160
Williams, Jan 25, 164, 176, 218, 230, 263, 289, 345, 380
Williams, John 219, 295
Williams, Larry 455
Williams, Liberty 228
Williams, Nancy M. 455
Williams, Robin 137, 351
Williams, Sam 473
Williams, Wendy 396
Williamson, Freddy 198
Williamson, Nicol 475, 481
Willing, Cas 474
Willis, Allee 359
Willis, Austin 346
Willis, Charles 38
Willock, Dave 82, 117
Willoughby, Jack 90
Wills, Lou 350
Willy Wonka and the Chocolate Factory 80, 394
Wilmar, Hugh A. 204
Wilson, Al 481-482
Wilson, Bert 483
Wilson, Sr., Bob 445
Wilson, Cecil R. 319
Wilson, Christine 435
Wilson, Dick 134
Wilson, Helene 360
Wilson, J.J. 38
Wilson, Jeannie 360
Wilson, Jim 15
Wilson, Karen 370
Wilson, Mak 475
Wilson, Mary 455

Wilson, Robert R. 319, 489
Wilson, Stan 351
Wilson, Terry 144, 185
Wilzbach, Steven 398
Winburn, James 397
Winchell, Paul 70, 253, 257, 377
Wind Cave National Park 204
Windom, William 117, 121
Windsor, Mary 238
Winger, Debra 454
Wingrove, Ian 474
Winnie the Pooh 20, 107, 158, 177, 217-218, 252-258, 282, 497, 501
Winnie the Pooh 14, 246, 282, 300, 326, 358, 389, 417, 444
"Winnie the Pooh" 252-253
Winnie the Pooh and a Day for Eeyore 258, 416, 499
Winnie the Pooh and Friends 387, 416
Winnie the Pooh and the Blustery Day 20, 61, 158, 252, 257, 498
Winnie the Pooh and the Honey Tree 61, 158, 257
Winnie the Pooh and Tigger, Too 158-159, 176-177, 257, 498
Winnie the Pooh Discovers the Seasons 358, 498
Winnie the Pooh for President 218
Winseman, Dana 319
Winslow, Dick 31, 192, 238, 328
Winston, George 459
Winston, Helene 231, 283
Winston, Stan 424
Winter, Vincent 314
Winters, Robin 409
Winters, Shelley 269
Wise, Douglas 301
"With a Flair" 97, 99, 104
Witherick, Albert 275, 314, 380
Witt, Stan 473
Wittliff, William D. 458
Wizard of Oz, The 480
Wizards of Waverly Place, The 104
Wolf, Marc 381
Wolf, Michael 396, 424
Wolfe, Carmen 437
Wolfe, Maurice 435, 437
Wolfington, Iggie 160, 180
Wonderful Adventures of Pinocchio, The 80
"Wonderful Thing About Tiggers, The" 252, 255-256
Wonderful World of Color, The 11-12, 19, 45, 210, 501-505
Wonderful World of Disney, The 17, 29, 34, 38, 45, 50, 58, 61, 65, 69, 74, 77, 80, 86, 104, 107, 113, 116, 121, 125, 132, 138, 143, 146, 150, 155, 164, 168, 171, 177, 184, 191, 198, 211, 215, 217, 223, 227, 230, 237, 243, 245, 275, 281, 294, 309, 314, 326, 344,

349, 357, 364, 387, 416, 454, 458, 493, 497, 501, 505-522
Wonderful World of Disney Digest, The 282
Wonderful World of Disney Magazine, The 45
Wong, Arnie 396
Wong, Arthur 192
Wong, Eddie 489
Woodbury, Al 319, 340
Wood, Andrew 369
Wood, Joyce 275
Wood, Sharon 430
Woodd, Lee 169
Woodington, Thomas 396
Woods, Mary Ellen 454-455
Woods, Raulette 396
Woodside, Bruce 482, 489
Woodson, William 26, 30
Woodward, Morgan 75, 143
Wookey, Karen 86
"Wooly Bully" 446-447
Worden, Hank 97
Wordes, Smitty 26
"Working for Mickey Mouse" 157
"World is a Circle, The" from Lost Horizon 132
World's Greatest Athlete, The 133-138, 150, 198, 358, 364
Worley, David 474
Worley, Jo Ann 231, 236
Worringham, Ken 473
Worth, Rosemary 473
Woxholt, Egil 467
Wright, Diane 53, 263
Wright, Francis 372
Wright, Glenn T. 345
Wright, Jake 247, 275
Wright, John 430
Wright, Norman 62
Wright, Ralph 70, 96, 252, 257
Wright, Richard 224, 295, 340
Wright, Tommy 247, 328, 446
Wrigley, Ben 97, 269
Wunderlich, Jerry 488
Wurzer, Kevin 482
Wuzzles, The 466
Wyatt, Jane 224
Wyenn, Than 447
Wylie, William J. (Bill) 38, 81, 160, 263, 268, 318, 340
Wymark, Patrick 207
Wyn, Michel 262
Wynands Productions Inc. 459
Wynn, Keenan 47, 126, 160, 164, 231, 236

Xeroxography 105

Yahraus, Bill 458
Yankee Doodle Mickey 326
Yarbrough, Janice 454
Yasuda, Kelvin 482
Yates, William Robert 364
Year of the Big Cat, The 158
Year of the Horse, The 35
Yell, Michael 473
Yellow Submarine 19
Yellowstone National Park 204
Yesno, John 62
Yogi Bear 131
Yothers, Bob 283
Yothers, Cory "Bumper" 365
Yothers, Erik 283, 288
Young, Alan 178, 289, 293
Young, Cameron 490
Young, Dennis 185, 224
Young Frankenstein 237
Young, Harry 341
Young Loner, The 19
Young, Peter 268, 376, 481, 483
Young, Phillip 376, 482
Young, Rob 436
Young, Robert Malcolm 184
Young Runaways, The 281
Young, Sean 468
Younger, Jay 74, 185
You're in Love, Charlie Brown 300
"You're Sixteen" 131
Ytuarte, Agustin 340

Zaccaria, Angelo 350
Zampagin, Maurizio 350
Zane, Bertine 360
Zapata, Joy 395
Zar, Cathy 483
Zaremba, John 87, 161
Zavala, Mario 395
Zay, Jean 380
Zegler, Barbara 351
Zegler, Paul 351
Zehetbaur, Rolf 389
Zeigler, Ted 360
Zheutlin, Wendy 430
Zielinski, Kathy 482
Ziff, Stuart 371
Ziker, Dick 294
Zink, Gary 345
Zinnemann, Tim 408
Zinner, Peter 435
"Zip-a-dee-doo-dah" 447
Zoetrope Studios 370
Zoltan 488
Zombo 116
Zorro 14, 20, 46, 107, 197, 210, 314, 501
Zorro and Son 388, 527
Zuckert, Bill 87, 180
Zupkas, Stephan 483

About the Author

When Walt Disney died in 1966, many predicted that it might be the end of Walt Disney Productions, but Walt had a number of ideas and concepts that lasted well into the next decade. He also left behind a well-established group of workers that hoped to continually answer the question, "What would Walt do?" with more magical creations that would dazzle and delight.

With this book, author and historian Mark Arnold explores the major accomplishments of Walt Disney Productions during the years 1966-1985, paying particular attention to their theatrical film output, but also discussing the various new theme park attractions and the TV shows produced during that period.

Things went well until the mid-1970s, when ideas started to run thin and repetition set in, causing shrinking box office success. By the 1980s, threats of corporate takeover were knocking at their door, at which time change had become unavoidable and inevitable if Disney were to survive as an independent company.

Disney had to change their already outdated methods of making movies and running a movie studio geared solely towards family entertainment. As a result, Michael Eisner took over and retooled Disney into the mega-empire that it is today. This is the story after Walt and before Michael…

Mark Arnold is a comic book and animation historian who has written many articles and books, produced comic book art shows, performed DVD commentaries, drawn cartoons and hosted radio podcast interview segments. This is his sixth book and the fourth published by BearManor Media.

www.ingramcontent.com/pod-product-compliance
Lightning Source LLC
Chambersburg PA
CBHW051801230426
43672CB00012B/2591